Essential Law Revision
from Oxford University Press

The perfect pairing for exam success

Concentrate!

For students who are serious about exam success, it's time to Concentrate!

✓ Written by experts
✓ Developed with students
✓ Designed for success

Each guide in the *Concentrate* series shows you what to expect in a law exam, what examiners are looking for and how to achieve extra marks.

'This jam-packed book is a fantastic source, giving a clear, concise and understandable presentation of the law which is essential for revision'

   Stephanie Lawson, Law Student, Northumbria University

'Every law student serious about their grades should use a Concentrate. I would not revise without it'

   Heather Walkden, Law Student, University of Salford

Questions & Answers

Keeping you afloat through your exams.

✓ Typical exam questions
✓ Model answers
✓ Advice on exam technique

Don't just answer the question, nail it. Law examiners share the secret of how to *really* answer typical law questions, giving you what you need to approach exams with confidence.

'The Q&As are a definite must-have for each and every law student!'

   Farah Chaumoo, Law Student, University of Hertfordshire

'What a brilliant revision aid! With summaries, tips, and easy-to-understand sample answers, Q&As really help with exam technique and how to structure answers'

   Kim Sutton, Law Student, Oxford Brookes University

Scan this QR code image with your mobile device to access a range of law revision resources

of DENSO WAVE INCORPORATED

For the full list of revision titles and additional resources visit: www.oxfordtextbooks.co.uk/orc/lawrevision/

✱ Technique ... experts

Interact with your textbook

* **each book in the *DIRECTIONS* series offers free teaching and learning solutions online**

www.oxfordtextbooks.co.uk/orc/directions/

 online resource centre

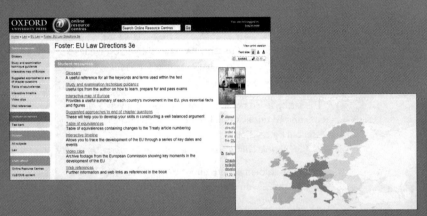

www.oxfordtextbooks.co.uk/orc/foster_directions3e/

Visit the website for access to additional resources.

For Students

* Interactive timeline with key dates in EU legal history

* Interactive map with key information on EU member states

* An audio podcast from the author offering study and examination technique and guidance

* Video clips from the EU archive

* Annotated web links

* Flashcard glossary

* Answers to end-of-chapter questions

* Updates on legislation and case law

* Full tables of equivalence showing both of the changes of numbering made to the EU's governing treaties

For Lecturers

* A test bank of 140 questions with answers and feedback

See the **Guide to the Online Resource Centre** on p. viii for full details.

EU law

DIRECTIONS

3rd edition

NIGEL FOSTER, FRSA

Visiting Professor of European Law, Buckingham Law School, University of Buckingham
Visiting Professor of European Law, the Europa Institut, Universität des Saarlandes, Saarbrücken, Germany

OXFORD
UNIVERSITY PRESS

OXFORD
UNIVERSITY PRESS

Great Clarendon Street, Oxford, OX2 6DP,
United Kingdom

Oxford University Press is a department of the University of Oxford.
It furthers the University's objective of excellence in research, scholarship,
and education by publishing worldwide. Oxford is a registered trade mark of
Oxford University Press in the UK and in certain other countries

British Library Cataloguing in Publication Data
Data available

Library of Congress Cataloging in Publication Data
Data available

ISBN 978-0-19-963980-9

Printed in Italy by
L.E.G.O. S.p.A — Lavis TN

Links to third party websites are provided by Oxford in good faith and
for information only. Oxford disclaims any responsibility for the materials
contained in any third party website referenced in this work.

Dedication

*This book is dedicated to my two elder brothers,
Graham and Michael*

Guide to the book

EU Law Directions is enriched with a range of special features designed to support and reinforce your learning. This brief guide to those features will help you use the book to the full and get the most out of your study.

Learning objectives

In this chapter, you will learn about:

- the transfer of power from the member states to the Union;
- the division of competences between the member states and the Union;
- the principles of proportionality and subsidiarity; and
- the processes by which the binding secondary laws are made.

Learning objectives

Each chapter begins with a bulleted outline of the main concepts and ideas you will encounter. These provide a helpful signpost to what you can expect to learn from the chapter.

Legal bases have been drafted restrictively so that the Commission cannot use the b further legislative intervention.

 See, for example, Article 168(5) TFEU (ex 152 EC), which provides for action to p cooperation in public health matters, but 'excluding any harmonization of the laws ar lations of the member states'. In other words the Union can take action providing it d interfere with the existing laws in the member states.

Further information boxes

Allow you to take your study further by supplying important detail and key insights for you to consider.

Case 11/70 *Internationale Handelgesellschaft* concerned the claim that Community levies were contrary to the German Constitution (Articles 2.1 and 14 *Grundgesetz*) and thus, as far as the national court was concerned, inapplicable. On referral to the Court of Justice, it held that national courts do not possess the power to review Community law. However, in diffusing the question, the Court of Justice held that there had been no breach by Community law of constitutional rights in the case.

Case close-up boxes

Identify and explain key influential cases.

The next and fourth enlargement took place sooner than expected as a result of t changes in eastern Europe and the economic success facilitated by the Single Europea Act (SEA).

Acquis communautaire is the term given to describe the accumulated body of Community law includi Treaties, secondary legislation and judicial developments.

1.4.1.5 The European Economic Area (EEA)

After observing in the late 1980s, the economic benefits of the SEA enjoyed by the mer ber states of the Communities, other European states, most of whom had cooperatio

Definition boxes

Key terms are highlighted when they first appear and are concisely explained in definition boxes. These terms are collected in a glossary which can be found at the back of the book and on the Online Resource Centre that accompanies this book.

---

thinking point
What do the classic freedom of movement of rights provisions require to trigger the rights which the prohibition of discrimination does not?

readily understood because they all relate, more or less, to nationality go to the very foundation of the establishment of the Union; that is, th barriers to the establishment of the internal market. Nationality shou the free movement of goods, persons or capital. Non-discrimination o however, is less readily understandable in this context. On the face of be essentially a socially based discrimination and not economic.

It was, however, originally framed in the EC Treaty as a form of workpla tion. It is helpful and informative to go back to the drafting of the EEC T

Thinking points

Thinking points encourage you to reflect on the implications of legislation and cases and the reasoning behind them.

 ## Summary

The category of general principles is already a wide one and potentially ca expansion. Indeed, in keeping with a system of law in which case law is regarde and can supply legal principles which become general principles to be applied

Chapter summaries

The central points and concepts covered in each chapter are distilled into summaries at the ends of chapters. These reinforce your understanding and can be used for quick revision.

Cross-references

Crucial connections between topics are carefully cross-referenced to provide a fully-integrated understanding of the subject. Links are highlighted to aid quick and accurate navigation through the book.

cross reference
We will come back to the discussion about why the Communities evolved in this way and the difference between the pillars in section 1.5.8 below.

sion by the member states into additional policies and areas of coope
the Lisbon Treaty has now established definitively that the Europe
exactly as that, this was not always the case and whilst the histor
sections following will make this clear, it is nevertheless useful now
ous terms used as you will come across them. Prior to the changes b
TEU, three original Communities (European Coal and Steel Communi
Economic Community (EEC) and European Atomic Energy Comn
existed. The TEU brought these together under one 'so-called' pillar a
Treaty simply as the European Community (EC) Treaty. It also adde

Questions

1 Who is a worker for the purposes of the TFEU?
2 Who is entitled to join a worker in the host state?

End-of-chapter questions

Self-test questions at the end of each chapter help you develop analytical and problem solving skills. The Online Resource Centre that accompanies this book suggests approaches to answering these questions for each chapter. These will help you develop your own successful approach to assessments and examinations.

Further reading

BOOKS

Barnard, C. *The Substantive Law of the EU: the four freedoms*, 3rd edn, OUP, Ox
(chapters 5–8).

Further reading

Selected further reading is included at the end of each chapter to provide a springboard for further study.

Intergovernmental Conference (IGC) A conference of the member states outside the Treaty and Communities set-up, which is established to discuss and agree Treaty change.

Intergovernmentalism The normal way in which international organizations work, whose decisions require unanimity and are rarely enforceable and if so only between the signatory states and not the citizens of those states. The clearest examples are the United Nations or General Agreement on Trade and Tariffs (GATT).

Glossary

A useful reference for all the keywords and terms used within the text.

For more details on this section scan here or visit the Online Resource Centre.

One of the most fundamental elements of an organizational order is th
tence or power between the central body and the constituent parts of t
tion in question. The transfer of powers and thus competences from th
from the EU member states to the Union itself, should in theory be a clear
any exercise of these powers by the institutions of the Union can only
granted by the member states and contained and clearly set out in the Tre
there should be nothing done by the Union institutions that is not expre
Treaties.

QR codes

QR Code images are used throughout the text to enable you to quickly access relevant online material while you are using your book. You can scan the code with your mobile device to launch the relevant webpage from the Online Resource Centre.

If your mobile device does not have a QR Code reader try this website for advice www.mobile-barcodes.com/qr-code-software.

QR Code is a registered trademark of DENSO WAVE INCORPORATED.

Guide to the Online Resource Centre

The Online Resource Centre that accompanies this book provides students and lecturers with ready-to-use teaching and learning resources. They are free of charge and are designed to maximize student learning.

www.oxfordtextbooks.co.uk/orc/foster_directions3e/

For students

Accessible to all, with no registration or password required, enabling you to get the most from your textbook.

Interactive timeline

Allows you to trace the development of the EU through a series of key dates and events, providing a useful source of accurate information for learning and revision.

Interactive map of Europe

Provides a useful summary of each country's involvement in the EU, plus essential facts and figures, which is ideal for students new to the subject and for revision.

Video clips from the EU archives

Fascinating footage is available to view showing the major moments in the development of the EU.

Author podcast: study and examination technique guidance

Useful tips from the author on how to learn, prepare for, and pass exams.

Answers to end-of-chapter questions

Suggested approaches are given for the end-of-chapter questions in the book. These will help you to develop your skills in constructing a well-balanced argument.

Web references

Further information and web links as referenced in the book.

For lecturers

Password protected to ensure only lecturers can access these resources; each registration is personally checked to ensure the security of the site.

Registering is easy: click on 'Lecturer Resources' on the Online Resource Centre, complete a simple registration form which allows you to choose your own username and password, and access will be granted within three working days (subject to verification).

Test bank

A fully customizable resource containing ready-made assessments with which to test your students. Offers versatile testing tailored to the contents of the textbook.

Preface

Dear Reader

At the time of writing, most of the changes introduced into the EU legal order by the Lisbon Treaty are now settling in and, although those were contained within the second edition of this book, adjustments to the text covering those have been made where considered necessary. The expansion of the EU and the possibility of expansion of the EU goes on apace, with Croatia destined to join on 1 July 2013, provided that all twenty-seven present member states of the EU and the Croatians themselves approve. Further, it is not expected to be too long before Iceland also gets the green light to join, if it still wishes to do so. Assimilation progress is also being made with the other Balkan states to prepare them for membership or candidate membership status. So we may well have an EU of over thirty member states in the not-too-distant future.

Progress in widening is not, though, reflected in progress in deepening, at least not for all twenty-seven member states. The eurozone increased in size to seventeen member states, but the severe economic and financial difficulties generated by the worldwide banking crisis is still having severe consequences, which have threatened at times the eurozone membership, with speculation about Greece's continued membership in particular. In an attempt to create financial and economic stability, a new financial Treaty was proposed, but rejected by one member state, the UK. So, for the moment, if the eurozone countries want to go ahead with this, supported, it must be said, by the other nine countries of the EU (minus the UK), they will have to do so by means of international Treaties sitting outside the main Treaties structure. Once again, a single state stands outside the progress of the others, but this is nothing new in the history of the EU, as can be seen from the pages of this book and Chapter 1 in particular.

In contrast to the changes made from the first edition of this book to the second edition, the changes to this edition have been relatively minor. Minor amendments were made to Chapter 2 on the institutions. In Chapter 3, the financing and budget sections have been removed, because it appears this is rarely taught and most probably hardly ever examined in standard undergraduate EU courses. Thus, apart from the usual general updating and amendments to take account of new legislative and case law developments, the only other significant change has been to Chapter 9 and to Article 263 TFEU to reorder that material following a further consideration of the impact of the changes to the Article by the Lisbon Treaty.

As with the previous editions, I would like to thank a few people who have been involved and who have helped me along the way.

First and foremost, massive thanks to my family: my wife, Dawn, and my children, Lynsey and Alexander, for another period of time spent at the computer – although this time, due to a lucky break from the day-to-day job, in a much shorter and more concentrated period.

Next, the staff of Oxford University Press: for their continued excellent assistance and attention to this third edition, Anna Winstanley and Abbey Nelms. Thanks also to the production staff led by Suzy Armitage for their assistance and to Vanessa Plaister and Joy Ruskin-Tompkins at copy-editing and proofreading stages respectively. Thanks also to the reviewers of the book, who made numerous very positive and constructive comments that have helped my decisions in updating and amending this edition. Of course, I did not agree with all of the comments made, but I did think about and reflect on all comments, and many changes were made as a result. Thank you very much.

Finally, twenty-nine years' worth of students, who must number over 10,000 all told, now, I would think. I learn new things and find new ways of expressing some aspect of law with each new cohort of students.

Whilst the presentational features of the book have been highlighted in the guides above, I want to draw particular attention to a new feature for the third edition, the use of QR codes in the margin of the text. These codes replace the web icons of previous editions and provide an instant link (via a mobile device) to additional information and web references on the Online Resource Centre. Whilst these might be regarded as excessive and can take the matter under discussion much further than is necessary, or indeed desirable, for the book or the course that you are on, they do draw attention to a rich source of information for extended essays and provide additional political context to the material in the book. For the most part, these are not only simple references that could have been included in a footnote, but much of this extra information will provide additional background information to complete the picture and give you a better understanding of the context in which the EU rules apply.

Finally, for all readers, I hope that this book serves your purpose and that you find it a useful addition to the material available on EU law. Please let me know either way, and whilst I cannot promise to make any changes you suggest, I will certainly give them some thought. Thanks in advance.

Best regards
Nigel Foster
Cardiff
April 2012

New to this edition

- Fully revised to take account of new legislative and case law developments, in particular relating to free movement of persons and equality law

- Full consideration of the impact of the Lisbon Treaty, including changes to Article 263 TFEU

- Discussion of the UK European Union Act 2011

- Consideration of the latest case law following the *Mangold* case

- New and expanded case summaries added throughout, plus additional and up-to-date further reading advice

Outline contents

Part 1 **Institutional law**   **1**

Chapter 1	**The establishment and development of the European Union**	3
Chapter 2	**The Union institutions**	39
Chapter 3	**Transfer of powers, competences and law-making**	68
Chapter 4	**Sources and forms of EU law**	96
Chapter 5	**Supremacy of EU law**	120

Part 2 **Procedural actions, enforcement and remedies in EU law**   **149**

Chapter 6	**The preliminary ruling (Article 267 TFEU)**	151
Chapter 7	**Treaty enforcement actions against member states**	173
Chapter 8	**Remedies: direct and indirect effects and state liability**	189
Chapter 9	**Direct actions before the European Court of Justice**	219

Part 3 **Substantive law**   **259**

Chapter 10	**Free movement of goods I: tariff and tax barriers**	261
Chapter 11	**Free movement of goods II: non-tariff barriers**	278
Chapter 12	**Free movement of persons I**	306
Chapter 13	**Free movement of persons II: developments and citizenship**	344
Chapter 14	**Discrimination law**	368

Detailed contents

Table of cases	xxvii
Table of legislation	xlvii
Table of treaties and conventions	li

Part I Institutional law

1

Chapter I	**The establishment and development of the European Union**	3
1.1	Why was the Union set up? The motives for European integration	5
	1.1.1 Reaction to the World Wars: the desire for peace	6
	1.1.2 Security against the rising Soviet threat	6
	1.1.3 Political willingness	6
	1.1.4 Economic development	7
	1.1.5 Summary of underlying motives and initial goals	7
1.2	The founding of the European Communities	7
	1.2.1 The Schuman Plan (1950)	7
	1.2.2 The ECSC	8
	1.2.3 The proposed European Defence Community and European Political Community	8
	1.2.4 Progress to the EEC and EURATOM Treaties	8
1.3	The basic objectives and nature of the Communities	9
	1.3.1 Was there an ultimate federal goal for the Union?	9
	1.3.1.1 Intergovernmentalism, supranationalism and federalism	10
	1.3.1.2 Integration in the Communities and EU	10
1.4	Developments following the original Treaties	11
	1.4.1 The widening of the Communities	12
	1.4.1.1 First expansion	12
	1.4.1.2 Second expansion	13
	1.4.1.3 East Germany is assimilated	13
	1.4.1.4 Setting terms for future expansions	13
	1.4.1.5 The European Economic Area (EEA)	14
	1.4.1.6 The 1995 expansion	14
	1.4.1.7 The 2004 expansion	15
	1.4.1.8 The 2007 expansion	15
	1.4.1.9 Future expansion	15
	1.4.1.10 The future of enlargement	16

		1.4.1.11 Accession preconditions	17
1.5	The deepening of the Communities		18
	1.5.1	The primary Treaties	18
	1.5.2	The 1960s and the Luxembourg Accords	18
	1.5.3	Stagnation and 'Eurosclerosis'	19
	1.5.4	The Court of Justice and integration	20
	1.5.5	Revival attempts	20
	1.5.6	The first Intergovernmental Conference (IGC) and the Single European Act	22
		1.5.6.1 Achievements and evaluation of the SEA	22
	1.5.7	Beyond the SEA	23
	1.5.8	The Maastricht Treaty on European Union (TEU)	24
	1.5.9	The Amsterdam Intergovernmental Conference and Treaty	26
	1.5.10	The Nice Intergovernmental Conference and Treaty	27
	1.5.11	The 2001 Laeken Summit	28
	1.5.12	The Constitutional Treaty for Europe	29
	1.5.13	The 2007 Brussels Summit and the Lisbon Treaty	30
	1.5.14	An overview of developments to date and the future	31
1.6	The relationship of the UK with the European Union		32
	1.6.1	The early relationship (to the 1970s)	32
	1.6.2	Two applications rejected	32
	1.6.3	Third application accepted	33
	1.6.4	The timing of the entry	33
	1.6.5	1980 to date	34
1.7	The EU and the world: external relations		35
Summary			36
Questions			37
Further reading			37

Chapter 2	**The Union institutions**		39
2.1	The Commission		40
	2.1.1	Composition of the Commission	41
	2.1.2	Appointment and removal of the Commission	41
	2.1.3	Tasks and duties	43
2.2	The Council (of Ministers) of the European Union		44
	2.2.1	Functions and powers	45
	2.2.2	The presidency of the Council	45
	2.2.3	Role and voting in the legislative procedures	46
	2.2.4	Forms of voting	46
		2.2.4.1 Unanimity	46
		2.2.4.2 Simple majority voting	47
		2.2.4.3 Qualified majority voting	47
		2.2.4.4 How QMV works	48

2.2.5	Council general law-making powers	51
2.2.6	COREPER and the Council Secretariat	51
2.3	The European Council	52
2.3.1	The European Council President	52
2.3.2	The High Representative of the Union for Foreign Affairs and Security Policy	53
2.4	The European Parliament (EP)	53
2.4.1	Membership	53
2.4.2	Elections and political parties	54
2.4.3	Functions and powers	54
2.4.3.1	Legislative powers	54
2.4.3.2	Control of the executive	55
2.4.3.3	Budgetary powers	56
2.4.3.4	Right to litigate	57
2.5	The European Court of Justice (ECJ)	57
2.5.1	Composition and organization	58
2.5.2	Procedure	58
2.5.2.1	The form of judgments	59
2.5.2.2	The reporting of cases	59
2.5.3	Jurisdiction	60
2.5.3.1	Division of jurisdiction	60
2.5.3.2	Direct actions	61
2.5.3.3	Indirect actions	61
2.5.4	Methodology	61
2.5.4.1	Interpretation	61
2.5.4.2	Precedent	62
2.5.5	The General Court (formerly the Court of First Instance, or CFI)	63
2.5.6	Length of proceedings	64
2.5.7	The specialized courts (formerly judicial panels)	64
2.5.8	The European Central Bank (ECB)	65
2.5.9	The Court of Auditors	65
2.6	The Union's advisory bodies	65
2.6.1	The Economic and Social Committee (EESC)	65
2.6.2	The Committee of the Regions (CoR)	65
2.7	Other Union bodies	66
Summary		66
Questions		66
Further reading		67

Chapter 3	**Transfer of powers, competences and law-making**	68
3.1	The transfer of sovereign powers	70
3.2	The division of competences	70
3.2.1	Express policies, powers and legal base	71

	3.2.2	The split between exclusive, concurrent and complementary competences	71
		3.2.2.1 Exclusive competences	72
		3.2.2.2 Concurrent competences	72
		3.2.2.3 Complementary competences	73
3.3		Extension of competences	74
	3.3.1	Express by Treaty amendment	74
	3.3.2	Implied powers	75
		3.3.2.1 Internal implied competences	75
		3.3.2.2 Impact on external competence from internal competences	75
	3.3.3	Residual powers	76
		3.3.3.1 Specific	76
		3.3.3.2 General	77
3.4		Tackling the competence creep	78
	3.4.1	Restrictive drafting	79
	3.4.2	The principle of subsidiarity	79
		3.4.2.1 Challenges for non-compliance with the principle	81
	3.4.3	Proportionality	82
3.5		The participation of the institutions in the legislative processes	83
	3.5.1	The legal base for legislative proposals	83
3.6		Law-making principles and procedures	87
	3.6.1	The law-making procedures	87
		3.6.1.1 The ordinary legislative (formerly co-decision) procedure	88
		3.6.1.2 Special legislative procedures	90
		3.6.1.3 The consent procedure	91
	3.6.2	Why so many changes to the legislative procedures?	91
3.7		The delegation of powers	92
	3.7.1	Implementing acts	94
Summary			94
Questions			95
Further reading			95

Chapter 4   Sources and forms of EU law   96

4.1		The EU legal system	97
	4.1.1	The style of the EU legal system	98
	4.1.2	The classification of the elements of EU law	99
		4.1.2.1 Institutional law	99
		4.1.2.2 Procedural law	100
		4.1.2.3 Substantive law	100
4.2		The sources and forms of Community and Union law	101
	4.2.1	The Treaties	101
		4.2.1.1 The Protocols attached to the Treaties	102
		4.2.1.2 Declarations	103
	4.2.2	Secondary legislation	103

		4.2.2.1	Regulations	104
		4.2.2.2	Directives	104
		4.2.2.3	Decisions	105
		4.2.2.4	Other acts producing binding legal effects	105
		4.2.2.5	Recommendations and opinions	105
		4.2.2.6	Procedural requirements	106
	4.2.3	International agreements and conventions		106
	4.2.4	The Court of Justice's contribution to the sources of law		108
	4.2.5	Human or fundamental rights		109
	4.2.6	Equality and non-discrimination		112
	4.2.7	General principles of procedural law and natural justice		113
		4.2.7.1	The right to judicial review	113
		4.2.7.2	Confidentiality/legal privilege	114
		4.2.7.3	Legal certainty	115
		4.2.7.4	Non-retroactivity	115
		4.2.7.5	Legitimate expectation or vested rights	116
		4.2.7.6	Proportionality	116

Summary — 117
Questions — 118
Further reading — 119

Chapter 5 — Supremacy of EU law — 120

5.1	The supremacy of EU law		121
	5.1.1	The view of the Court of Justice	121
	5.1.2	Supremacy and member state constitutional law	124
	5.1.3	Section summary	126
5.2	EU law in the member states		126
	5.2.1	Theories of incorporation of international law: monism and dualism	127
	5.2.2	EU law in the UK	127
		5.2.2.1 The 'unwritten' constitution	128
		5.2.2.2 The dualist approach to international law	128
		5.2.2.3 The doctrine of parliamentary sovereignty	128
		5.2.2.4 UK entry and the European Communities Act (ECA) 1972	129
		5.2.2.5 The ECA 1972 and parliamentary sovereignty	130
		5.2.2.6 Judicial reception of Community and EU law in the UK	131
		5.2.2.7 The European Union Act 2011	137
5.3	Reception of EU law in other member states		138
	5.3.1	Germany	138
		5.3.1.1 The German Constitution (*Grundgesetz*)	138
		5.3.1.2 The reaction of the German courts	139
	5.3.2	Italy	141
	5.3.3	France	141
		5.3.3.1 The French Courts of Ordinary Jurisdiction	142

		5.3.3.2 French public courts	142
5.3.4	The Netherlands		143
5.3.5	Denmark		144
5.3.6	Sweden		145

Summary	146
Questions	146
Further reading	146

Part 2 Procedural actions, enforcement and remedies in EU law

149

....

| Chapter 6 | **The preliminary ruling (Article 267 TFEU)** | 151 |

6.1 Article 267 TFEU: the preliminary ruling procedure	153
6.1.1	Which bodies can refer?	154
6.1.2	Is the question relevant and admissible?	156
	6.1.2.1 Rejected references: relevance, clarity and basic information	157
	6.1.2.2 No genuine dispute or an abuse of the procedure	158
	6.1.2.3 Acceptances nevertheless	160
6.1.3	The question referred: an overall view	160
6.1.4	A discretion or an obligation to refer?	161
6.1.5	The discretion of lower courts	161
6.1.6	The timing of the reference	162
6.1.7	Courts of last instance	162
6.1.8	Avoiding the obligation to refer: the development of precedent and *acte clair*	164
	6.1.8.1 There is a previous ruling on the point	164
	6.1.8.2 The answer is obvious (*acte clair*)	164
	6.1.8.3 Questions of validity	165
	6.1.8.4 Use of *acte clair* by the national courts	165
6.2 The effect of an Article 267 TFEU ruling	167
6.2.1	The effect on the Court of Justice	167
6.2.2	The effect on the national courts	167
6.3 The evolution of Article 267 TFEU references	168
6.4 Reforms and future	169
6.5 Interim measures within an Article 267 TFEU reference	170

Summary	171
Questions	171
Further reading	172

....

| Chapter 7 | **Treaty enforcement actions against member states** | 173 |

| 7.1 Enforcement actions by the Commission | 174 |
| 7.1.1 | What constitutes a breach | 175 |

7.1.2   Identifying and reporting breaches   175

7.1.3   Defendants in an Article 258 TFEU action   176

7.1.4   The procedure of an Article 258 TFEU action   177

     7.1.4.1   The informal or administrative stage   177

     7.1.4.2   Letters of formal notice   178

     7.1.4.3   The reasoned opinion   178

     7.1.4.4   The judicial stage   179

     7.1.4.5   Defences raised by the member states   180

7.2   Suspensory orders and interim measures   181

7.3   The application and effect of judgments   182

7.3.1   Article 260 TFEU   182

     7.3.1.1   Sanctions under Article 260 TFEU   183

7.4   Actions brought by one member state against another   184

7.4.1   The involvement of the Commission   185

7.4.2   Complaining state may then refer the matter
to the Court of Justice   185

7.5   Alternative actions to secure member states' compliance   186

Summary   187

Questions   187

Further reading   187

Chapter 8   **Remedies: direct and indirect effects and state liability**   189

8.1   Directly applicable and direct effects   190

8.1.1   Definitions and the distinction between directly applicable
and direct effects   190

8.1.2   Directly applicable   191

8.1.3   Direct effects   192

     8.1.3.1   Treaty Articles   192

     8.1.3.2   Regulations   195

     8.1.3.3   Directives   195

     8.1.3.4   Decisions   198

     8.1.3.5   International agreements   198

8.2   Overcoming the lack of horizontal direct effect for Directives   199

8.2.1   Extending the definition of 'the state'   199

8.2.2   Indirect effects   200

8.2.3   'Incidental' horizontal effects   204

8.3   State liability: the principle in *Francovich*   206

8.3.1   The extension of *Francovich*   210

     8.3.1.1   Extension to the private sphere   210

     8.3.1.2   Extension to the national courts   210

8.4   National procedural law and the system of remedies   211

8.4.1   The principle of national procedural autonomy   211

8.4.2   Intervention by the Court of Justice   212

8.4.3   A more balanced approach   213

8.4.4	Section summary	216
Summary		216
Questions		216
Further reading		217

Chapter 9	**Direct actions before the European Court of Justice**	219
9.1	Actions to annul EU acts	220
9.1.1	Admissibility	221
9.1.1.1	The institutions the acts of which are reviewable	221
9.1.1.2	Reviewable acts	222
9.1.1.3	Time limits	224
9.1.2	*Locus standi*: who may apply	224
9.1.2.1	Privileged	224
9.1.2.2	Limited or semi-privileged	225
9.1.3	Non-privileged applicants' *locus standi*	225
9.1.4	Acts addressed to the applicant	226
9.1.5	An act that is of direct and individual concern to the applicant	226
9.1.5.1	Direct concern	227
9.1.5.2	Individual concern	227
9.1.5.3	Other instances in which 'individual' has been recognized	229
9.1.6	Interest groups and party actions	231
9.1.7	The challenge to regulatory acts	232
9.1.8	Merits or grounds for annulment	232
9.1.8.1	Lack of competence or authority	233
9.1.8.2	Infringement of an essential procedural requirement	233
9.1.8.3	Infringement of the Treaty or any rule relating to its application	234
9.1.8.4	Misuse of power by a Community institution	234
9.1.9	The effect of a successful action and annulment	235
9.1.10	A restrictive approach?	235
9.1.11	Alternatives to Article 263 TFEU	237
9.1.11.1	A reference under Article 267 TFEU	237
9.1.11.2	The plea of illegality: Article 277 TFEU (ex 241 EC)	238
9.1.11.3	Action for damages under Articles 268 and 340(2) TFEU	239
9.2	Action for failure to act (Article 265 TFEU, ex Article 232 EC)	239
9.2.1	Admissibility and *locus standi*	239
9.2.1.1	Privileged applicants	239
9.2.1.2	Non-privileged applicants	240
9.2.2	Acts subject to an Article 265 TFEU action	240
9.2.3	Procedural requirements	241
9.2.3.1	The invitation to act	241
9.2.3.2	Definition of position	241
9.2.3.3	The substantive action	242
9.2.3.4	Results of a declaration of a failure to act	242
9.3	Non-contractual liability of the EU	242

	9.3.1	Admissibility	243
		9.3.1.1 *Locus standi*	243
		9.3.1.2 Time limit	243
	9.3.2	The defendant institution and act	243
	9.3.3	An autonomous or independent action	244
	9.3.4	The requirements of liability	244
		9.3.4.1 The standard of liability and fault	245
	9.3.5	Administrative acts	245
	9.3.6	Liability for employees	246
	9.3.7	Liability for legislative acts	246
		9.3.7.1 The rules of law covered	247
		9.3.7.2 The protection of the individual	248
		9.3.7.3 The breach must be sufficiently serious	248
	9.3.8	A new single test for liability?	250
		9.3.8.1 Individual (non-legislative) acts	251
	9.3.9	Liability for lawful acts	251
	9.3.10	The damage	252
	9.3.11	The causal connection	252
	9.3.12	Concurrent liability/choice of court	253
	9.3.13	Section summary	253
9.4	The plea of illegality (Article 277 TFEU, ex 241 EC)		253
	9.4.1	*Locus standi*	254
	9.4.2	Acts that can be reviewed	254
	9.4.3	Grounds of review	255
	9.4.4	Effect of a successful challenge	255
Summary			255
Questions			256
Further reading			256

Part 3 Substantive law 259

Chapter 10	**Free movement of goods I: tariff and tax barriers**		261
10.1	Legislative provisions		262
	10.1.1	The Treaties	262
	10.1.2	Secondary legislation	263
10.2	Progress towards the Treaty goals		263
	10.2.1	A free trade area	264
	10.2.2	A customs union	264
	10.2.3	A common market	264
	10.2.4	An economic union	264
	10.2.5	Which stage has the EU reached?	264
		10.2.5.1 Internal market developments	265
		10.2.5.2 Integration methods	266

10.3 The establishment of the internal market   266

     10.3.1   The common commercial policy (CCP) and common customs tariff (CCT)   266

     10.3.2   The prohibition of customs duties   266

     10.3.3   A charge having equivalent effect (CHEE)   268

         10.3.3.1   The validity of charges for services rendered   269

         10.3.3.2   Where the charge is in fact a tax   271

     10.3.4   The distinction between internal taxation and charges having equivalent effect   271

10.4 The prohibition of discriminatory taxation   273

     10.4.1   Direct and indirect taxation   273

     10.4.2   'Similar' or 'other products'   274

         10.4.2.1   Similar products   275

         10.4.2.2   Other products   275

Summary   276

Questions   277

Further reading   277

Chapter 11   **Free movement of goods II: non-tariff barriers**   278

11.1 Legislation   279

11.2 Quantitative restrictions and measures having equivalent effect   280

     11.2.1   The general scope of the Treaty prohibition   280

         11.2.1.1   What constitutes measures for the purposes of Article 34 TFEU?   281

     11.2.2   The meaning of 'quantitative restrictions'   282

     11.2.3   Measures having equivalent effect (MHEE)   282

     11.2.4   Examples of measures coming within the scope of the prohibition   283

         11.2.4.1   National promotional campaigns   283

         11.2.4.2   Discriminatory national marketing rules   284

         11.2.4.3   Product classification   284

         11.2.4.4   Exports   284

11.3 Article 36 TFEU derogations   285

     11.3.1   General purpose and scope   285

     11.3.2   Public morality   286

     11.3.3   Public policy   286

     11.3.4   Public security   287

     11.3.5   The protection of the health or life of humans or animals   287

     11.3.6   Artistic heritage   289

     11.3.7   The protection of artistic or commercial property   290

     11.3.8   The second sentence of Article 36 TFEU   290

     11.3.9   Decision 3052/95 and Regulation 764/2008   291

11.4 Equally applicable measures (indistinctly applicable measures)   291

     11.4.1   The *Cassis de Dijon* case   292

		11.4.1.1	Examples of acceptable mandatory measures	293
	11.4.2	The application of the rule of reason: the requirements in detail		294
		11.4.2.1	There must be no EU system covering the interest in question	294
		11.4.2.2	The measure must be indistinctly applicable	294
		11.4.2.3	The measure must be neither an arbitrary discrimination nor a disguised restriction on trade	295
		11.4.2.4	The measure must meet the requirements of proportionality	295
	11.4.3	Technical standards and legislative intervention		296
	11.4.4	Summary of *Cassis de Dijon*		296
	11.4.5	Equal burden or dual burden rules		297
11.5	*Keck and Mithouard*: certain selling arrangements			299
	11.5.1	Post-*Keck* case law		300
	11.5.2	Market access or discrimination or both?		301
Summary				303
Questions				304
Further reading				305

Chapter 12	**Free movement of persons I**			306
12.1	The legal framework: primary and secondary legislation			308
	12.1.1	Treaty provisions		308
	12.1.2	The basic right of non-discrimination		310
		12.1.2.1	Indirect discrimination	311
		12.1.2.2	Hindering market access	311
12.2	Who may claim the rights of free movement			312
	12.2.1	Nationality		312
	12.2.2	Union status as a worker or self-employed		313
		12.2.2.1	Part-time work	313
		12.2.2.2	Those seeking work	315
		12.2.2.3	Worker training, education and benefits	316
		12.2.2.4	Self-employed	318
	12.2.3	The scope of establishment and the provision of services		319
12.3	The material rights of free movement			321
	12.3.1	Rights of entry, residence and exit		322
	12.3.2	The rights provided by Regulation 492/2011 (ex Regulation 1612/68) and Directive 2004/38		324
		12.3.2.1	Social and tax advantages under Article 7(2)	325
		12.3.2.2	Family members	326
	12.3.3	Worker's family education and carer rights		329
	12.3.4	Right to remain		330
12.4	Free movement of the self-employed			330
	12.4.1	The intervention of the Court of Justice		331
	12.4.2	Legislative developments		334
		12.4.2.1	Mutual recognition	334

12.4.3	The free movement of lawyers	335
	12.4.3.1 The provision of services by lawyers	335
	12.4.3.2 Establishment by lawyers (Practice under Home Title)	336
12.5	Derogations from the free movement regimes	336
12.5.1	Procedural safeguards	336
12.5.2	Restrictions on the grounds of public policy, security and health	338
12.5.3	Employment in the public service	341
Summary		342
Questions		342
Further reading		343

Chapter 13   Free movement of persons II: developments and citizenship   344

13.1	The wholly internal rule	345
13.2	The treatment of third-country nationals (TCNs)	349
13.2.1	Association and cooperation agreements	349
13.2.2	Workers 'posted' abroad	349
13.2.3	General rights for TCNs	350
13.2.4	Summary of TCN rights	352
13.3	The extension of free movement rights	352
13.3.1	Receiving services	353
	13.3.1.1 Tourist services	353
	13.3.1.2 Educational services	353
	13.3.1.3 Receiving services without movement	354
13.3.2	The general free movement Directives	355
13.3.3	The Maastricht Treaty and European citizenship	356
	13.3.3.1 The definition of 'citizenship'	356
13.3.4	Case law on the citizenship Articles	357
	13.3.4.1 Non-discrimination and residence rights	357
	13.3.4.2 Welfare rights	358
	13.3.4.3 Family and carer rights	361
	13.3.4.4 Citizenship law summary	364
Summary		365
Questions		366
Further reading		366

Chapter 14   Discrimination law   368

14.1	The legislative framework	372
14.1.1	Treaty Articles	372
14.1.2	Secondary legislation	372
14.2	Article 157 TFEU and the scope of the principle of equal pay	374
14.2.1	The meaning of 'pay'	375
	14.2.1.1 The concept of pay and its relationship to pensions	375
14.2.2	The original Equal Pay Directive (Directive 75/117)	379

	14.2.3	The basis of comparison	379
	14.2.4	Part-time work and the development of the concept of indirect discrimination	381
		14.2.4.1 Objective justifications	382
	14.2.5	Work of equal value	383
		14.2.5.1 Job evaluation schemes and the burden of proof	384
	14.2.6	Enforcement and remedies	385
14.3	Equal treatment		385
	14.3.1	The concept of equal treatment/no discrimination on the grounds of sex	386
	14.3.2	The scope of equal treatment	388
	14.3.3	Equality with regard to employment access, working conditions, dismissal and retirement ages	389
	14.3.4	Exempt occupations	391
	14.3.5	The protection of women regarding childbirth and maternity	392
		14.3.5.1 Dismissal during or after pregnancy	393
		14.3.5.2 Pregnancy and illness	396
	14.3.6	The promotion of equal opportunity by removing existing inequalities affecting opportunities	397
	14.3.7	Judicial enforcement and remedies	399
14.4	The Social Security Directive (Directive 79/7)		401
14.5	The Pregnant and Breastfeeding Workers Directive (Directive 92/85)		401
	14.5.1	Scope and application	402
14.6	Article 19 TFEU: the expansion of EU equality law		403
	14.6.1	Secondary legislation issued under Article 19 TFEU	404
		14.6.1.1 The Racial Equality Directive (Directive 2000/43)	404
		14.6.1.2 The Framework Employment Directive (Directive 2000/78)	404
		14.6.1.3 Common characteristics	404
		14.6.1.4 Selective case law from the Article 19 TFEU Directives	405
		14.6.1.5 The Lisbon Treaty and the Union Charter of Fundamental Rights	408
Summary			409
Questions			409
Further reading			410
Glossary			411
Index			413

Table of cases

Alphabetical

A M & S v Commission (175/79) [1982] ECR 1616 . . . 114

Abdoulaye v Renault (C-218/98) [1999] ECR I-5723 . . . 397

Abrahamsson (C-407/98) [2000] ECR I-5539 . . . 398

Adams v Commission (145/83) [1985] ECR 3539 . . . 243, 245–6

Adeneler v ELOG (C-212/04) [2006] ECR I-6057 . . . 203

Admenta v Federfarma, Italy, State Council . . . 141

Adoui and Cornauille v Belgian State (115–16/81) [1982] ECR 1665 . . . 337, 339

AITEC v Commission (T-447–9/93) [1996] ECR II-1631 . . . 231

Akrich (C-109/01) [2003] ECR I-9607 . . . 111, 328, 349, 351–2, 362

AKZO (53/85) [1986] ECR 1965 . . . 114

Albini v Council and Commission (33/80) [1980] ECR 1671; [1981] ECR 2141 . . . 254

Alfa Vita Vassilopoulos (C-158–9/04) [2006] ECR I-8135 . . . 303

Alfons Lütticke GmbH v Hauptzollamt Saarlouis (48/65) [1966] ECR 19 . . . 178, 193, 223, 241

Alliance for Natural Health (C-154–5/04) [2005] ECR I-6451 . . . 82

Allonby (C-256/01) [2004] ECR I-873 . . . 318, 380

Alluè and Coonan v University of Venice (33/88) [1989] ECR 1591 . . . 311, 341

Alpine Investments (C-384/93) [1995] ECR I-1141 . . . 319, 333

Angonese v Cassa di Risparmio di Bolzano SpA (C-281/98) [2000] ECR I-4139 . . . 309, 348, 354–5

Anker et al. (C-47/02) [2003] ECR I-10447 . . . 342

Antonissen (C-292/89) [1991] ECR I-745 . . . 316, 324, 340, 365

Apple and Pear Development Council v Lewis (222/82) [1983] ECR 4083 . . . 281, 284

Arbeiterwohlfahrt der Stadt Berlin v Monika Botel (C-360/90) [1992] ECR I-3589 . . . 375

Arcelor (T-16/04) [2010] nyr . . . 247

Arizona Tobacco, France, Conseil d'État . . . 143

Arsenal FC v Matthew Reed (C-206/01) [2002] ECR I-10273 . . . 168, 171

Atlanta Fruchthandelsgesellschaft (C-465/93) [1995] ECR I-3761 . . . 170

Bacardi-Martini v Newcastle United (C-318/00) [2003] ECR I-905 . . . 159

Badeck (C-158/97) [2000] ECR I-1875 . . . 398

Barber v Guardian Royal Exchange (262/88) [1990] ECR I-1889 . . . 74, 115, 168, 375, 377–9

BASF v Commission (T-79/89) [1992] ECR II-315 . . . 224

Bauhuis v The Netherlands (46/76) [1977] ECR 5 . . . 270

Baumbast (C-413/99) [2002] ECR I-7091 . . . 111, 328–9, 350, 356–8, 362, 364

BBV v Commission (T-138/89) [1992] ECR II-2181 . . . 226

Becker (8/81) [1982] ECR 53 . . . 196–7, 200, 204, 206

Belgium v Humbel (263/86) [1988] ECR 5365 . . . 99, 353

Belgium v Spain (C-388/95) [2000] ECR I-3123 . . . 185, 290

Bergaderm (C-352/98 P) [2000] ECR I-5291 . . . 209, 245, 247–8, 250–1

Bergman v Grows-Farm (Skimmed Milk Powder) (114/76) [1977] ECR 1247 . . . 112

Bethell v Commission (246/81) [1982] ECR 2277 . . . 178

Bettray v Staatssecretaris Van Justitie (344/87) [1989] ECR 1621 . . . 314–15

Bidar (C-209/03) [2005] ECR I-2119 . . . 318, 354, 360

Bilka Kaufhaus v Karin Weber Van Hartz (170/84) [1986] ECR 1607 . . . 376, 378, 382

Blaizot (24/86) [1988] ECR 379 . . . 99, 353

Bleis v Ministry of Education (C-4/91) [1991] ECR I-5627 . . . 341

Bluhme (C-67/97) [1998] ECR I-8033 . . . 297

Bobie v HZA Aachen-Nord (127/75) [1976] ECR 1079 . . . 274

Bock v Commission (Chinese Mushrooms) (62/70) [1971] ECR 897 . . . 227, 229

Boisdet, France, Conseil d'État . . . 142

Bond van Adverteerders and others v The Netherlands State (352/85) [1988] ECR 2085 . . . 338

Bonsignore v Köln (67/74) [1975] ECR 297 . . . 339

Borker (138/80) [1980] ECR 1975 . . . 155

Boyle et al. v EOC (C-411/96) [1998] ECR I-6401 . . . 402

Brasserie du Pêcheur v Federal Republic of Germany (C-46/93) [1996] ECR I-1029 . . . 141, 207, 250

Bresciani (87/75) [1976] ECR 129 . . . 198, 270

Briheche (C-319/03) [2004] ECR I-8807 . . . 397

Brinkmann (C-319/96) [1998] ECR I-5255 . . . 209

Broekmeulen v HRC (246/80) [1981] ECR 2311 . . . 155

Brown v Rentokil (C-394/96) [1998] ECR I-4185 . . . 396

Brown v Secretary of State for Scotland (197/86) [1988] ECR 3205 . . . 317

Brunner et al. v Federal Republic of Germany (Maastricht) 89 BVerfGE 155 (1993) . . . 140, 145

Busch (C-320/01) [2003] ECR I-2041 . . . 395

Cadman (C-17/05) [2006] ECR I-9583 . . . 385

Café Vabre case [1975] 2 CMLR 336 . . . 142

Campus Oil (238/82) [1984] ECR 523 . . . 287

Campus Oil v Ministry for Industry and Energy (72/83) [1984] ECR 2727 . . . 285

Cantina (T-166/98) [2004] ECR II-3991 . . . 248

Carlsen et al. v Prime Minister Rasmussen 6/4/1998, Case I 361/1997 [1999] 3 CMLR 854 . . . 144

Carpenter (C-60/00) [2002] ECR I-6279 . . . 347, 355, 361

Cartesio Oktató és Szolgáltató (C-210/06) [2008] ECR I-9641 . . . 157

Casagrande (9/74) [1974] ECR 773 . . . 329

Castelli v ONPTS (261/83) [1984] ECR 3199 . . . 327

Chatzi (C-149/10) [2010] nyr . . . 113, 370

Chen (C-200/02) [2004] ECR I-9925 . . . 329, 348–9, 363–4

Chevalley v Commission (15/70) [1970] ECR 975 . . . 239–40

Chiron Corporation v Murex Diagnostics Ltd (No. 8) [1995] All ER (EC) 88 . . . 163

CIA Security International SA v Signalson SA and Securitel SPRL (C-194/94) [1996] ECR I-2201 . . . 205

CILFIT (283/81) [1982] ECR 3415 . . . 164

Cinetheque (60–1/84) [1985] ECR 2065 . . . 293, 298

CNTA v Commission (74/74) [1976] ECR 797; [1975] ECR 533 . . . 248, 252–3

Codorniu v Council (Spanish Wine Producers) (C-309/89) [1994] ECR I-1853 . . . 229–30

Coleman (C-303/06) [2008] ECR I-5603 . . . 406–7

Collins v Secretary of State for Work and Pensions (C-138/02) [2004] ECR I-2703 . . . 316, 318, 354–5, 359–61, 366

Comet (45/76) [1976] ECR 2043 . . . 212, 215

Commission v Assidomän (C-310/97 P) [1999] ECR I-5363 . . . 63

Commission v Austria (C-147/93) . . . 354

Commission v Austria (C-150/00) [2004] ECR I-3887 . . . 284

Commission v Belgium (156/77) [1978] ECR 1881 . . . 254–5

Commission v Belgium (Belgian Wood Case) (77/69) [1970] ECR 237 . . . 176, 180

Commission v Belgium (C-344/95) [1997] ECR I-1035 . . . 323

Commission v Belgium (Customs Warehouses) (132/82) [1983] ECR 1649 . . . 269

Commission v Belgium (Public Employees) (149/79) [1980] ECR 3881 . . . 341

Commission v Belgium (University Fees) (293/85) [1988] ECR 305 . . . 181

Commission v Belgium (Walloon Waste) (C-2/90) [1992] ECR I-4431 . . . 297

Commission v Belgium and Luxembourg (90–1/63) [1964] ECR 625 . . . 143, 180

Commission v Council (C-24/94) [1996] ECR I-1469 . . . 222

Commission v Council (ERTA) (22/70) [1971] ECR 263 . . . 69, 75, 105, 222

Commission v Council (Management Committee Procedure) (16/88) [1989] ECR 3457 . . . 93

Commission v Council (Titanium Dioxide Directive) (C-300/89) [1991] ECR I-2867 . . . 86

Commission v Council (Staff Salaries) (81/72) [1973] ECR 575 . . . 116

Commission v Council (Waste Directive) (C-155/91) [1993] ECR I-939 . . . 85

Commission v Denmark (C-192/01) [2003] ECR I-9693 . . . 289

Commission v Denmark (Disposable Beer Cans) (302/86) [1988] ECR 4607 . . . 293

Commission v Edith Cresson (C-432/04) [2006] ECR I-6387 . . . 42

Commission v Federal Republic of Germany (70/72) [1973] ECR 813 . . . 254

Commission v Finland (4, 6, 7–9/98) [2002] ECR I-9627 . . . 76

Commission v France (Advertising of Alcoholic Beverages) (152/78) [1980] ECR 2299 . . . 186

Commission v France (C-1/00) [2001] ECR I-9989 . . . 185

Commission v France (C-64/88) [1991] ECR I-2727 . . . 183

Commission v France (C-304/02) [2005] ECR I-6263 . . . 183

Commission v France (Franking Machines) (21/84) [1985] ECR 1355 . . . 281

Commission v France (Import of Lamb) (232/78) [1979] ECR 2729 . . . 282

Commission v France (Italian Table Wines) (42/82) [1982] ECR 841 . . . 288, 290

Commission v France (Protection of Women) (C-312/86) [1988] ECR 6315 . . . 389, 397

Commission v France (French Merchant Seamen) (167/73) [1974] ECR 359 . . . 175, 180, 309

Commission v France (Reprographic Machines) (C-90/79) [1981] ECR 283 . . . 271, 273

Commission v France (Spanish Strawberries) (C-265/95) [1997] ECR I-6959 . . . 177, 180, 287

Commission v French Republic (C-307/84) [1986] ECR 1725 . . . 341

Commission v Germany (174/84) [1986] ECR 559 . . . 296

Commission v Germany (281, 283–5, 287/85) [1987] ECR 3203 . . . 75

Commission v Germany (Animal Inspection Fees) (18/87) [1988] ECR 5427 . . . 270

Commission v Germany (Beer Purity) (178/84) [1987] ECR 1227 . . . 117, 288, 296

Commission v Germany (C-195/90) [1992] ECR I-3141 . . . 182

Commission v Germany (C-387/99) [2004] ECR I-3751 . . . 284

Commission v Germany (Insurance Services) (205/84) [1986] ECR 3755 . . . 320, 332

Commission v Germany (Lawyers' Services) (427/85) [1988] ECR 1123 . . . 335

Commission v Germany (Sausage Purity Law) (274/87) [1989] ECR 229 . . . 288

Commission v Greece (C-187/96) [1998] ECR I-1095 . . . 325

Commission v Greece (C-240/86) [1988] ECR 1835 . . . 179

Commission v Greece (C-293/89) [1992] ECR I-4577 . . . 289

Commission v Greece (C-387/97) [1988] ECR 4415 . . . 183

Commission v Greece (C-391/92) [1995] All ER (EC) 802 . . . 300

Commission v Greece (Taxation of Motor Cars) (C-132/88) [1990] ECR I-1567 . . . 274

Commission v Ireland (Buy Irish) (249/81) [1983] ECR 4005 . . . 280–1, 283–4

Commission v Ireland (Dundalk Water Supply) (45/87) [1988] ECR 4929 . . . 267

Commission v Ireland (Excise Payments) (55/79) [1980] ECR 481 . . . 274

Commission v Ireland (Irish Fisheries) (61/77 R) [1977] ECR 937; [1977] ECR 1411 . . . 182

Commission v Ireland (Metal Objects/Origin) (113/80) [1981] ECR 1625 . . . 284

Commission v Italian Republic (Customs Posts) (340/87) [1989] ECR 1483 . . . 269

Commission v Italy (101/84) [1985] ECR 2629 . . . 180

Commission v Italy (274/83) [1985] ECR 1077 . . . 178

Commission v Italy (C-129/00) [2003] ECR I-14637 . . . 177

Commission v Italy (C-212/99) [2001] ECR I-4923 . . . 184

Commission v Italy (C-424/98) [2000] ECR I-2001 . . . 355

Commission v Italy (First Art Treasures Case) (7/68) [1968] ECR 423 . . . 183

Commission v Italy (Italian Fruit) (184/85) [1987] ECR 2013 . . . 275

Commission v Italy (Pigmeat Imports) (7/61) [1961] ECR 317 . . . 180, 223, 286

Commission v Italy (Second Art Treasures Case) (48/71) [1972] ECR 529 . . . 182

Commission v Italy (Slaughtered Cows) (39/72) [1973] ECR 101 . . . 179, 191

Commission v Italy (Statistical Levy Case) (24/68) [1969] ECR 193 . . . 268

Commission v Italy (T-95/89) [1995] ECR II-729 . . . 289

Commission v Jego-Quere (C-263/02P) [2004] ECR I-3425 . . . 63, 167, 236

Commission v Luxembourg (Gingerbread) (2 and 3/62) [1962] ECR 425 . . . 268

Commission v Netherlands (Entry Requirements) (C-68/89) [1991] ECR I-2637 . . . 322

Commission v Spain (C-45/93) [1994] ECR I-911 . . . 320

Commission v Spain (C-278/01) [2003] ECR I-14141 . . . 183

Commission v UK (C-508/03) [2006] ECR I-3969 . . . 179

Commission v UK (Equal Treatment for Men and Women) (165/82) [1983] ECR 3431 . . . 391

Commission v UK (Import of Potatoes) (231/78) [1979] ECR 1447 . . . 282

Commission v UK (Imports of UHT Milk) (124/81) [1983] ECR 203 . . . 282

Commission v UK (Nationality of Fishermen) (246/89R) [1991] ECR I-4585 . . . 135, 182, 311

Commission v UK (Pig Producers) (53/77) [1977] ECR 921 . . . 181

Commission v UK (Tachographs) (128/78) [1977] ECR 921 . . . 104, 180, 191

Commission v UK (Wine Excise Duties No. 2) (170/78), unreported . . . 276

Compagnie Continentale Française (169/73) [1975] ECR 117 . . . 252

Conegate v HM Customs and Excise (121/85) [1986] ECR 1007 . . . 286

Conforama (C-312/89) [1991] ECR I-997 . . . 293, 299

Coote v Granada (C-185/97) [1998] ECR I-5199 . . . 400–1

Corbiau v Administration des Contributions (C-24/92) [1993] ECR I-1277 . . . 155

Costa v ENEL (6/64) [1964] ECR 585 . . . 9, 20, 62–3, 122, 124, 126, 130, 141, 146, 157, 163, 207, 210, 212

Courage Ltd v Crehan (C-453/99) [2001] ECR I-6297 . . . 210

Cowan (186/87) [1989] ECR 195 . . . 320, 353

Criminal Proceedings against Karl Prantl (16/83) [1984] ECR 1299 . . . 294

Criminal Proceedings against Luciano Arcaro (C-168/95) 1996] ECR I-4705 . . . 202

Criminal Proceedings against Lyckeskog (C-99/00) [2002] ECR I-4839 . . . 163

Criminal Proceedings against Marchandise (C-332/89) [1991] ECR I-1027 . . . 293, 299

Criminal Proceedings v Bickel and Franz (C-274/96) [1998] ECR I-7637 . . . 357

Cullet v Centre Leclerc Toulouse (231/83) [1985] ECR 305 . . . 287

D and Sweden v Council (125/99 P) [2001] ECR I-4319 . . . 387

Da Costa (28–30/62) [1963] ECR 31 . . . 63, 161, 164, 169

de Coster (C-17/00) [2001] ECR I-9445 . . . 319, 334, 348, 355, 365

De Cuyper (C-406/04) [2006] ECR I-6947 . . . 360

De Geus (13/61) [1962] ECR 45 . . . 161–2

De Groot (C-385/00) [2006] ECR I-11573 . . . 326

Decision 2004/496 of 10 June 2004, France, Constitutional Court . . . 143

Decker (C-120/95) [1998] ECR I-1831 . . . 294

Defrenne v Belgium (No. 1) (80/70) [1971] ECR 445 . . . 375–7

Defrenne v Sabena (No. 2) (43/75) [1976] ECR 455 . . . 115, 168, 193, 371, 374, 377

Defrenne v Sabena (No. 3) (149/77) [1978] ECR 1365 . . . 371

Dekker v VJM Centram (C-177/88) [1990] ECR I-3941 . . . 389

Delhaize v Promalvin (C-47/90) [1992] ECR I-3669 . . . 284

Denkavit v French State (132/78) [1979] ECR 1923 . . . 272–3

Deutsche Telekom v Schröder (C-50/96) [2000] ECR I-743 . . . 371

Deutsche Telekom v Vick (C-324/96) [2000] ECR I-799 . . . 100, 371

Deutscher Apothekerverband (C-322/01) [2003] ECR I-14887 . . . 287

Deutscher Komponistenverband (German Composers Group) v Commission (8/71) [1971] ECR 705 . . . 241

D'Hoop (C-224/98) [2002] ECR I-6191 . . . 359–60, 364

Diatta v Land Berlin (267/83) [1985] ECR 567 . . . 326–7, 329, 350

Dillenkofer (C-178/94) [1996] ECR I-4845 . . . 209

Donatella Calfa (C-348/96) [1999] ECR I-11 . . . 340

Dorsch (C-54/96) [1997] ECR I-4961 . . . 155, 251

Dory (C-186/01) [2003] ECR I-2479 . . . 392, 399

Doughty v Rolls Royce plc [1992] 1 CMLR 1045 . . . 199

Dow Benelux (209–15/78) [1978] ECR 2111 . . . 114

Draehmpaehl v Urania (C-180/95) [1997] ECR I-2195 . . . 400

Duke v GEC Reliance [1988] AC 618; [1988] 2 WLR 359 . . . 132–3, 141, 197, 201

Dumortier Freres v Commission (Gritz and Quellmehl) (64/76) [1982] ECR 1748 . . . 248

Dumortier Frères v Council (Gritz and Quellmehl) (113/76) [1982] ECR 1748 . . . 252

Dynamic Medien (C-244/06) [2008] ECR I-505 . . . 294

Dzodzi v Belgium (C-297/88 and C-197/89) [1990] ECR I-3763 . . . 160

Emmott (C-208/90) [1991] ECR I-4269 . . . 213, 215

Enderby v Frenchay Health Authority (C-127/92) [1993] ECR I-5535 . . . 383, 385

European Parliament see Parliament

Europemballage and Continental Can v Commission (6/72) [1973] ECR 215 . . . 99

Eurotunnel v SeaFrance (C-408/95) [1997] ECR I-6315 . . . 238

Extramet Industrie v Council (C-358/89) [1992]
    ECR I-3813 . . . 231

F (Mr & Mrs) v the Belgian State (7/75) [1975]
    ECR 679 . . . 99
Faccini Dori (C-91/92) [1994] ECR
    I-3325 . . . 202, 204, 207
Factortame (No. 1) (C-213/89) [1990] ECR
    I-2433 . . . 123, 125, 134–5, 161, 170, 213,
    215
Factortame (No. 2) (C-221/89) [1991] ECR
    I-3905 . . . 123, 133–5, 212, 319
Factortame (No. 3) (C-48/93) [1996] ECR
    I-1029 . . . 123, 136, 207, 250
Fantask (C-188/95) [1997] ECR I-6783 . . . 214
Fedechar (8/55) [1954–56] ECR 292 . . . 75
Fediol (70/87) [1989] ECR 1781 . . . 198
FIAMM & FIAMM Technologies et al. v
    Council and Commission (T-69/00) [2005]
    ECR II-5393 . . . 248, 251
Fiorini (Christini v SNCF) (32/75) [1975] ECR
    1085 . . . 325
Firma Feryn (C-54/07) [2008] ECR I-5187 . . . 407
Firma Foto-Frost v Hauptzollamt Lübeck-Ost
    (314/85) [1987] ECR 4199 . . . 165, 237
Foglia v Novello (No. 1) (104/79) [1981] ECR
    745 . . . 158
Foglia v Novello (No. 2) (244/80) [1981] ECR
    3045 . . . 159
Ford of Spain v the Spanish State (170/88)
    [1989] ECR 2305 . . . 270
Förster v IB-Groep (C-158/07) [2008] ECR
    I-8507 . . . 318, 360–1, 366
Foster v British Gas (C-188/89) [1990] ECR
    I-3313 . . . 197, 199–200
Fragd v Administrazione delle Finanze (33/84)
    [1985] ECR 1605 . . . 141
France v Commission (C-325/91) [1993] ECR
    I-3283 . . . 106, 234
France v Commission (C-327/91) [1994] ECR
    I-3641 . . . 233
France v UK (141/78) [1979] ECR 2923 . . . 185
Francovich (22/87) [1989] ECR 143 . . . 179, 206
Francovich et al. v Italy (C-6 and 9/90) [1991]
    ECR I-5357 . . . 62, 99, 123, 179, 206–7,
    209–10, 213
Fratelli Cucchi (77/76) [1977] ECR 987 . . . 272
Frontini v Ministero delle Finanze, in Granital
    v Administrazione delle Finanze [1974] 2
    CMLR 372 . . . 141
Fruit and Vegetable Confederation
    v Commission (17/62) [1962] ECR
    487 . . . 228

Gaal (C-7/94) [1995] ECR I-1031 . . . 329
Gallagher (C-175/94) [1995] ECR
    I-4253 . . . 337

Garage Dehus Sarl v Bouche Distribution
    [1984] 3 CMLR 452 . . . 142
Garcia Avello (C-148/02) [2003] ECR
    I-11613 . . . 348
Garland v BREL (12/81) [1982] ECR
    359 . . . 132, 167, 375
Gebhard v Milan Bar Council (C-55/94) [1995]
    ECR I-4165 . . . 320, 333
Geddo v Ente Nationale Risi (2/73) [1973] ECR
    865 . . . 282
GEMA v Commission (125/78) [1979] ECR
    3173 . . . 242
Germany v Commission (C-280/93) [1994] ECR
    I-4973 . . . 198
Germany v Commission (Wine Tariff Quotas)
    (24/62) [1963] ECR 63 . . . 233
Germany v EEP and Council (C-380/03) [2006]
    ECR I-11573 . . . 77, 86
Germany v EP (C-378/98) [2000] ECR
    I-8419 . . . 233, 235
Germany v EP and Council (Tobacco
    Advertising) (C-376/98) [2000] ECR
    I-8419 . . . 77, 81
Gillespie (C-342/93) [1996] ECR I-475 . . . 402
Giuffrida v Council (105/75) [1976] ECR
    1395 . . . 234
Gourmet International (C-405/98) [2001] ECR
    I-1795 . . . 302
Grad v Finanzamt Traunstein (9/70) [1970] ECR
    825 . . . 191, 195, 198
Grant v South West Trains (C-249/96) [1998]
    ECR I-621 . . . 387
Gravier v City of Liège (293/83) [1985] ECR
    593 . . . 99, 353
Greenpeace v Commission (C-321/95 P) [1998]
    ECR I-1651 . . . 231
Greenpeace v Commission (T-585/93) [1995]
    ECR II-2205 . . . 231
Grimaldi (322/88) [1989] ECR 4407 . . . 105
Groener v Minister for Education (379/87)
    [1989] ECR 3967 . . . 322
Grzelczyk (C-184/99) [2001] ECR
    I-6193 . . . 318, 353–5, 358–9, 364–5
Gül v Regierungspräsident Düsseldorf (131/85)
    [1986] ECR 1573 . . . 329

Habermann-Beltermann v Arbeiterwohlfahrt
    (C-421/92) [1994] ECR I-1657 . . . 393, 402
Haegemann v Belgium (181/73) [1974] ECR
    449 . . . 107
Handels- og Kontorfunktionaerernes Forbund
    i Danmark v Dansk Arbejdsgiverforening
    (109/88) [1989] ECR 3199 . . . 385
Harz v Tradex (79/83) [1984] ECR
    1921 . . . 200–1
Hauer v Land Rheinland-Pfalz (44/79) [1979]
    ECR 3727 . . . 110

Hautala v Council (C-353/99 P) [2001] ECR I-9565 . . . 117

Hedley Lomas (C-5/94) [1996] ECR I-2553 . . . 209

Heimdienst (C-254/98) [2000] ECR I-151 . . . 302, 304

Hertz v Aldi (C-179/88) [1990] ECR I-3979 . . . 396

HNL (83/76) [1978] ECR 1209 . . . 248–9

Hoekstra v BBDA (75/63) [1964] ECR 177 . . . 313, 315

Hoffman v Barmer Ersatzkasse (184/83) [1984] ECR 3047 . . . 393

Holcim v Commission (C-282/05 P) [2007] ECR I-2941 . . . 251

Humblet (6/60) [1960] ECR 559 . . . 62

Hunermund (C-292/92) [1993] ECR I-6787 . . . 300

Hurd v Jones (44/84) [1986] ECR 29 . . . 194

HZA Bremerhafen v Massey-Ferguson (8/73) [1973] ECR 897 . . . 78

Ianelli and Volpi SpA v Meroni (74/76) [1977] ECR 595 . . . 280

ICC (66/80) [1981] ECR 1191 . . . 165, 168, 255

ICI v Commission (Dyestuffs) (Case 48/69) [1972] ECR 619 . . . 60

Institute of the Motor Industry v Customs and Excise Commissioners (C-149/97) [1998] ECR I-7053 . . . 101

International Fruit (21–4/72) [1972] ECR 1219 . . . 107–8, 198

International Fruit Company v Commission (41–4/70) [1971] ECR 411 . . . 230

Internationale Handelsgesellschaft (11/70) [1970] ECR 1125 . . . 111, 117, 124–5, 139

Ioannidis (C-256/04) [2005] ECR I-8275 . . . 360–1, 364, 366

Irish Creamery Milk Suppliers (36 and 76/80) [1981] ECR 735 . . . 162

ITWF & FSU v Viking (C-438/05) [2007] ECR I-10779 . . . 334

Jackson v AG [2005] UKHL 56 . . . 136

Jany (C-268/99) [2001] ECR I-8615 . . . 319–20

Jego-Quere v Commission (T-177/01) [2002] ECR II-2365 . . . 236–7

Jenkins v Kingsgate (96/80) [1981] ECR 911 . . . 382

Jia (C-1/05) [2007] ECR I-1 . . . 328, 351, 363

Jipa (C-33/07) [2008] ECR I-5157 . . . 341

John Walker Ltd v Ministeriet for Skatter og Afgifter (243/84) [1986] ECR 875 . . . 275

Johnston v The Chief Constable RUC (222/84) [1986] ECR 1651 . . . 113, 197, 391

Julia Schnorbus v Land Hessen (C-79/99) [2000] ECR I-10997 . . . 399

Kadi v Council (C-402/05 P and C-415/05) [2008] ECR I-6351 . . . 78

Kalanke (C-450/93) [1995] ECR I-3051 . . . 398

Kampfmeyer (5, 7, 13 and 24/66) [1973] ECR 1599 . . . 248, 252

Katsarou v Greek State (Case No. 3458/1998) (Council of State, 25 September 1998) . . . 165

Kaur v Secretary of State for the Home Department, ex p (C-192/99) [2001] ECR I-1237 . . . 103, 312

KB v NHS Pensions (C-117/01) [2004] ECR I-541 . . . 378, 387

Keck and Mithouard (C-267–8/91) [1993] ECR I-6097 . . . 63, 278, 299–302, 304, 333

Kempf v Minister of Justice (139/85) [1986] ECR 1741 . . . 313–14

Kloppenburg (Bundesfinanzhof 25 April 1985, NJW 1988, 1459) [1988] 3 CMLR 1 . . . 139

Köbler v Republic of Austria (C-224/01) [2003] ECR I-10239 . . . 166–7, 169, 171, 210–11

Kolpak v Deutscher Handballbund (C-438/00) [2003] ECR I-4135 . . . 312

Konsumenten-ombudsmannen v De Agostini (C-34–6/95) [1997] ECR I-3843 . . . 302

Köster (25/70) [1970] ECR 1161 . . . 92

Kowalska v Hamburg (C-33/89) [1990] ECR I-2591 . . . 375

Kreil v Germany (C-285/98) [2000] ECR I-69 . . . 391

Kremzow v Austria (C-299/95) [1997] ECR I-2629 . . . 346

Krohn v Commission (175/84) [1986] ECR 753 . . . 253

KSH v Council and Commission (Royal Scholten Holdings) (103 and 145/77) [1978] ECR 2037 . . . 238, 248–9

KSH v Intervention Board (101/76) [1977] ECR 797 . . . 234, 238

Kühne and Heitz (C-453/00) [2004] ECR I-837 . . . 168

Kuhner (33 and 59/79) [1980] ECR 1677 . . . 114

Kükükdeveci (C-555/07) [2010] nyr . . . 204, 406

Kupferberg (104/81) [1982] ECR 3641 . . . 198

Kziber (C-18/90) [1991] ECR I-199 . . . 198

Lair v Universität Hannover (39/86) [1988] ECR 3161 . . . 99, 317, 354

Land Baden-Württemberg v Tsakouridis (C-145/09) [2010] nyr . . . 340

Land Nordrhein-Westfalen v Uecker and Jacquet (64 and 65/96) [1997] ECR I-3171 . . . 346

Larsson v Dansk Handel & Service (C-400/95) [1997] ECR I-2757 . . . 396

Lassagård, Sweden, Supreme Administrative Court, RÅ 1997, ref. 65 . . . 145

Lawrence v Regent Office Care Ltd (C-320/00) [2002] ECR I-7325 . . . 380

Lawrie-Blum v Land Baden-Württemburg (66/85) [1986] ECR 2121 . . . 314, 341

Lebon (316/85) [1987] ECR 2811 . . . 315

Leclerc Siplec (C-412/93) [1995] ECR I-179 . . . 301

Leclere (C-43/99) [2001] ECR I-4265 . . . 315, 326

Lemmens (C-226/97) [1998] ECR I-3711 . . . 205

Leonesio v Italian Ministry of Agriculture (C-93/71) [1972] ECR 287 . . . 195

Les Verts v European Parliament and Council v European Parliament (294/83) [1986] ECR 1339 . . . 57, 220–2

Leur-Bloem (C-28/95) [1997] ECR I-4161 . . . 160

Levez v Jennings (C-326/96) [1998] ECR I-7835 . . . 214

Levin v Minister of Justice (53/81) [1982] ECR 1035 . . . 313–15

Lisbon Judgment, German Federal Constituional Court, Case 2BvE 2/08 . . . 140

Litster v Forth Dry Dock & Engineering Co. Ltd [1990] 1 AC 546; [1989] 2 WLR 634 . . . 133

Lommers (C-476/99) [2002] ECR I-2891 . . . 399

Luisi and Carbone v Ministero del Tesauro (286/82) [1984] ECR 377 . . . 353

Lütticke (4/69) [1971] ECR 325 . . . 167, 239, 244

Lütticke v Hauptzollamt Saarlouis (57/65) [1966] ECR 205 . . . 273

Luxembourg v European Parliament (230/81) [1983] ECR 255 . . . 221

Macarthy's v Smith (129/79) [1980] ECR 1275 . . . 131, 134, 379–80

McCarthy (C-434/09) [2011] nyr . . . 364

McKenna (C-191/03) [2005] ECR I-7631 . . . 396

Magnavision v General Optical Council (No. 2) [1987] 2 CMLR 262 . . . 163

Mahlberg (C-207/98) [2000] ECR I-549 . . . 394

Manfredi (C-295–8/04) [2006] ECR I-6619 . . . 210

Mangold (C-144/04) [2005] ECR I-9981 . . . 113, 203–4, 405–7, 409

Marks & Spencer plc (C-62/00) [2002] ECR I-6325 . . . 166

Marleasing SA v La Comercial Internacional de Alimentacion SA (C-106/89) [1990] ECR I-4135 . . . 101

Mars (C-470/93) [1995] ECR I-1923 . . . 201, 301–2

Marschall (C-409/95) [1997] ECR I-6363 . . . 398

Marshall II (C-271/91) [1993] ECR I-4367 . . . 182 . . . 213, 399–400

Marshall v Southampton Area Health Authority (152/84) [1986] ECR 723 . . . 197, 376, 390

Martínez Sala v Freistaat Bayern (C-85/96) [1998] ECR I-2691 . . . 358

Mattheus (93/78) [1978] ECR 2203 . . . 157, 162

Mayr (C-506/06) [2008] ECR I-1017 . . . 395

Meade (238/83) [1984] ECR 2631 . . . 349

Meilicke v ADV/OGA (C-83/91) [1992] ECR I-4871 . . . 158

Melgar (C-438/99) [2001] ECR I-6915 . . . 394, 401, 403

Meroni (14/60) [1961] ECR 161 . . . 245

Meroni v High Authority (9/56) [1957–58] ECR 133 . . . 92, 233, 254–5

Metock et al. (C-127/08) [2008] ECR I-6241 . . . 328, 351–2, 363

Meyers (C-116/94) [1995] ECR I-2131 . . . 390

Michel Humblot v Directeur des Services Fiscaux (112/84) [1987] ECR 1367 . . . 274

Minister of Justice v Kramer (3, 4 and 6/76) [1976] ECR 1279 . . . 293

Minister of the Interior v Cohn-Bendit [1980] 1 CMLR 543 . . . 142

Mobistar (C-544/03) [2005] ECR I-7723 . . . 348, 355

Molkerei-Zentrale Westfalen v Haupzollamt Paderborn (28/76) [1968] ECR 143 . . . 273

Morgan and Bucher (C-11–12/06) [2007] ECR I-9161 . . . 360–1

Morgenbesser (C-313/01) [2003] ECR I-13467 . . . 336

Morson and Jhanjan (35 and 36/82) [1982] ECR 3723 . . . 346

Moulins de Pont a Mousson (Maize, Gritz and Quellmehl) (124/76 and 20/77) [1977] ECR 1795 . . . 249

MRAX (C-459/99) [2002] ECR I-6591 . . . 111, 323, 362, 364

M&S (C-309/06) [2008] ECR I-2283 . . . 118

Mulder v Council (C-104/89 and 37/90) [1992] ECR I-3061; [2000] ECR I-203 . . . 250

Munoz v Frumar Ltd (C-253/00) [2002] ECR
I-7289 . . . 195
Murphy v An Bord Telecom Eireann (157/86)
[1988] ECR 673 . . . 380, 383–4
Mutsch (137/84) [1985] ECR 2681 . . . 326

National Panasonic (136/79) [1980] ECR
2033 . . . 114
Navas (C-13/05) [2006] ECR I-6467 . . . 406
Neath v Hugh Steeper (C-152/91) [1993] ECR
I-6935 . . . 378
Netherlands v Bakker Hillegom (C-111/89)
[1990] ECR I-1735 . . . 270
Netherlands v Council (C-58/94) [1996] ECR
I-2169 . . . 117
Netherlands v EP (C-377/98) [2001] ECR
I-7079 . . . 77, 81
Netherlands v Reed (59/85) [1986] ECR
1283 . . . 311, 327
Nicolo, France, Conseil d'État . . . 142
Nimz v Hamburg (C-184/89) [1991] ECR
I-297 . . . 375
Ninni-Orasche (C-413/01) [2003] ECR
I-13187 . . . 314
Noordwijks Cement Accord (8–11/66) [1967]
ECR 75 . . . 105, 222
Nordgetreide v Commission (42/71) [1972]
ECR 105 . . . 240
Nordsee v Nordstern (102/81) [1982] ECR
1095 . . . 155

O'Flynn (C-237/94) [1996] ECR I-2617 . . . 326
Olazabal (C-100/01) [2002] ECR
I-10981 . . . 324, 340, 346
ONE v Deak (94/84) [1985] ECR 1873 . . . 325
Opinion 1/75 [1975] ECR 1355 . . . 72
Opinion 1/94 [1994] ECR I-5267 . . . 69, 76
Opinion 2/94 [1996] ECR I-1788 . . . 78, 112
Outokumpu Oy (C-213/96) [1998] ECR
I-1777 . . . 275

P v S and Cornwall County Council (C-13/94)
[1996] ECR I-2143 . . . 386
Pafitis v TKE (C-441/93) [1996] ECR
I-1347 . . . 204
Palacios de la Villa (C-411/05) [2007] ECR
I-8531 . . . 405
Parliament v Council (Budgetary Procedure)
(34/86) [1986] ECR 2155 . . . 57, 221
Parliament v Council (C-65/93) [1995] ECR
I-643 . . . 91
Parliament v Council (Chernobyl) (C-70/88)
[1991] ECR I-4529 . . . 57, 62, 225
Parliament v Council (Comitology) (302/87)
[1988] ECR 5615 . . . 57, 93, 241
Parliament v Council (Students' Residence)
(C-295/90) [1992] ECR I-4193 . . . 86

Parliament v Council (Transport Policy) (13/83)
[1987] ECR 1513 . . . 242
Pecastaing v Belgian State (98/79) [1981] ECR
691 . . . 337
Peterbroeck Van Campenhout v Belgium
(C-312/93) [1995] ECR I-4599 . . . 161, 214–15
Petrie (T-191/99) [2001] ECR II-3677 . . . 178
Pfeiffer v Rotes Kreuz (C-397–401/01) [2004]
ECR I-8835 . . . 202
Philip Morris Tobacco, France, Conseil
d'État . . . 143
Pickstone v Freemans plc [1989] AC 66; [1988]
3 WLR 265 . . . 133
Pigs Marketing Board (Northern Ireland) v
Redmond (83/78) [1978] ECR 2347 . . . 131,
280
Piraiki-Patraiki v Commission (11/82) [1985]
ECR 207 . . . 227
Plaumann v Commission (25/62) [1963] ECR
123; [1963] ECR 126; [1963] ECR 95 . . . 63,
167, 227–8, 236
Polyelectrolyte Producers Group v Council
and Commission (T-376/04) [2005] ECR
II-3007 . . . 243
Portugal v Council (C-149/96) [1999] ECR
I-8395 . . . 199
Prais v Council (130/75) [1976] ECR
1589 . . . 112
Pretore di Salo v X (14/86) [1987] ECR
2545 . . . 160, 162
Procureur de la Republique v Waterkeyn
(314–316/81) [1982] ECR 4337 . . . 186
Procureur du Roi v Dassonville (8/74) [1974]
ECR 837 . . . 278, 283, 292, 299–300, 304
Public Prosecutor v Kolpinghuis Nijmegan
(80/86) [1977] ECR 815 . . . 115, 201–2
Publico Ministero v Ratti (148/78) [1979] ECR
1629 . . . 196, 203
Pupino (C-105/03) [2005] ECR I-5285 . . . 202

R v Bouchereau (30/77) [1977] ECR
1999 . . . 340
R v Department of Transport, ex p
International Air Transport Association and
European Low Fares Airline Association
(C-344/04) [2006] ECR I-403 . . . 82, 165
R v Henn and Darby (34/79) [1979] ECR
3795 . . . 282, 286
R v HM Treasury, ex p British Telecom PLC
(C-392/93) [1996] ECR I-1631 . . . 208
R v Intervention Board for Agricultural
Produce, ex p Man (181/84) [1985] ECR
2889 . . . 117
R v Kent Kirk (63/83) [1984] ECR 2689 . . . 115
R v London Boroughs' Transport Committee
[1991] 1 WLR 828; [1991] 3 All ER
916 . . . 165

R v Pharmaceutical Society of Great Britain,
ex p Association of Pharmaceutical Importers
(266 and 267/87) [1989] ECR 1295 . . . 280

R v Pieck (159/79) [1980] ECR 2171 . . . 117,
323, 365

R v Saunders (175/78) [1979] ECR
1129 . . . 346

R v Secretary of State for Employment (C-9/91)
[1992] ECR I-4297 . . . 136

R v Secretary of State for Health, ex p
Swedish Match (C-210/03) [2004] ECR
I-11893 . . . 77, 86

R v Secretary of State for Transport, ex p
Factortame and others (No. 1) [1990] 2 AC
85 . . . 130, 133

R v Thompson et al. (7/78) [1979] ECR
2247 . . . 286

Racke v HZA Mainz (98/78) [1979] ECR
69 . . . 116

Raulin v Netherlands Ministry of Education
and Science (C-357/89) [1992] ECR
I-1027 . . . 314, 317

Razzouk and Beydoun v Commission (75 and
117/82) [1984] ECR 1509 . . . 112

Rechberger (C-140/97) [1999] ECR
I-3499 . . . 209

Rewe v Hauptzollamt Kiel (158/80) [1981] ECR
1805 . . . 212

Rewe-Zentral AG v
Bundesmonopolverwaltung für Branntwein
(Cassis de Dijon) (120/78) [1979] ECR
649 . . . 63, 74, 79, 265, 278, 292–3,
295–9, 302–4

Rewe-Zentralfinanz (33/76) [1976] ECR
1989 . . . 211

Rey Soda (23/75) [1975] ECR 1279 . . . 93

Reyners v Belgium (2/74) [1974] ECR
631 . . . 265, 311, 331–2, 335

Reynolds Tobacco Holdings and others
(C-131/03 P) [2006] ECR I-7795 . . . 223

Rheinmühlen-Düsseldorf (146 and 166/73)
[1974] ECR 33; [1974] ECR 139 . . . 161

Richards (C-423/04) [2006] ECR
I-3585 . . . 388

Richez Parise (19, 20, 25 and 30/69) [1970]
ECR 325 . . . 245

Rieser Internationale Transporte GmbH
v Autobahnen- und Schnellstraßen
Finanzierungs AG (C-157/02) [2004] ECR
I-1477 . . . 200

Rinner-Kuhn (171/89) [1989] ECR
2743 . . . 375, 383

Roberts v Cleveland Area Health Authority
[1978] ICR 370; [1977] IRLR 401 . . . 131–2

Roberts v Tate and Lyle (151/84) [1986] ECR
703 . . . 389

Robins (C-278/05) [2007] ECR I-1059 . . . 209

Roquette and Maizena v Council (138–9/79)
[1980] ECR 3393 . . . 65, 91, 225, 230, 234

Rosengren (C-170/04) [2007] ECR
I-4071 . . . 291

Rothley and Others v European Parliament
(C-167/02) [2004] ECR I-3149 . . . 237

Rothmans, France, Conseil d'État . . . 143

Rottmann v Bayern (C-135/08) [2010] ECR
I-1449 . . . 357

Rucksdeschel (117/76 and 16/77) [1977] ECR
1753 . . . 249

Rummler v Dato-Druck (237/85) [1986] ECR
2101 . . . 384

Rush Portuguesa v Office National
d'Immigration (C-113/89) [1990] ECR
I-1417 . . . 195

Rutili v Minister of Interior (36/75) [1975] ECR
1219 . . . 117, 324, 346

Säger v Dennemeyer (C-76/90) [1991] ECR
I-4221 . . . 332

Samenwerkende (C-36/92 P) [1994] ECR
I-1911 . . . 114

Santillo (131/79) [1980] ECR 1585 . . . 191

Sayag v Leduc (9/69) [1969] ECR 329 . . .
246

Schempp (C-403/03) [2005] ECR
I-6421 . . . 348

Schmidberger (C-112/00) [2003] ECR
I-5659 . . . 281, 294

Scholz (C-419/92) [1994] ECR I-505 . . . 347

Schöttle & Söhne v Finanzamt Freuenstadt
(20/76) [1977] ECR 247 . . . 272–3

Schul (C-461/03) [2005] ECR I-10513 . . . 165

Schumacher v Hauptzollamt Frankfurt
(215/87) [1989] ECR 617 . . . 289

Schwarze v EVGF (16/65) [1965] ECR
877 . . . 156

Seymour-Smith and Perez (C-167/97) [1999]
ECR I-623 . . . 375

Sgarlata v Commission (40/64) [1965] ECR
215 . . . 110

Simmenthal (106/77) [1978] ECR 629 . . .
122–5, 141, 157, 207

Simmenthal v Commission (92/78) [1979] ECR
777 . . . 238, 255

Simutenkov (C-265/03) [2005] ECR
I-2579 . . . 107

Sirdar v The Army Board (C-273/97) [1999]
ECR I-7403 . . . 391–2

Slob v Productschap Zuivel (C-236/02) [2004]
ECR I-1861 . . . 156

Sociaal Fonds voor de Diamantarbeiders
(2 and 3/69) [1969] ECR 211 . . . 269

Sofrimport v Commission (C-152/88) [1988]
ECR 2931; [1990] ECR I-2477; [1992] ECR
I-153 . . . 229–30, 250, 252

Solange I, Germany, Federal Constitutional
    Court . . . 139
Solange II, Germany, Federal Constitutional
    Court . . . 139
Sotgui v Deutsche Bundespost (152/73) [1974]
    ECR 153 . . . 341
Spain v UK (C-145/04) [2006] ECR
    I-7917 . . . 185
Spijker Kwasten BV v Commission (231/82)
    [1983] ECR 2559 . . . 229
Star Fruit Company v Commission (247/87)
    [1989] ECR 291 . . . 176–7
Stauder v City of Ulm (26/69) [1969] ECR
    419 . . . 110
Steenhorst-Neerings (C-339/91) [1993] ECR
    I-5475 . . . 213–14
Steff-houlberg Export (C-366/95) [1998] ECR
    I-2661 . . . 117–18
Steinlike und Weinlig v Germany (78/76)
    [1977] ECR 595 . . . 271
Steymann v Staatssecretaris van Justitie
    (196/87) [1988] ECR 6159 . . . 314–15
Stoke City Council v B & Q plc (C-169/91)
    [1992] ECR I-6635 . . . 299
Stork v High Authority (1/58) [1957–58] ECR
    105 . . . 110
Sugar Export (132/77) [1978] ECR
    1061 . . . 253
Sugar Export v Commission (88/76) [1977]
    ECR 709 . . . 116
Surinder Singh (C-370/90) [1992] ECR
    I-4265 . . . 347
Syfait v GlaxoSmithKline (C-53/03) [2005] ECR
    I-4609 . . . 155

Tadao Maruko v Versorgungsanstalt der
    deutschen Bühnen (C-267/06) [2008] ECR
    I-1757 . . . 406–7
Tankstation 't Heustke (C-401 and 402/92)
    [1994] ECR I-2199 . . . 300
Tele Danmark (C-109/00) [2001] ECR
    I-6993 . . . 394
Telemarsicabruzzo SpA (C-320/90) [1993] ECR
    I-393 . . . 158
Ten Oever (C-109/91) [1993] ECR
    I-4879 . . . 378
Test Achats (C-236/09) [2011] nyr . . . 405, 407
Thibault (C-136/95) [1998] ECR I-2011 . . .
    390
Thieffry v Paris Bar Council (71/76) [1977] ECR
    765 . . . 332
Thoburn v Sunderland City Council [2002] 1
    CMLR 50 . . . 129, 136
Timex v Commission (264/82) [1985] ECR
    849 . . . 231
Tommaso Morellato v Unita Sanitaria Locale
    (C-358/95) [1997] ECR I-1431 . . . 289

Töpfer v Commission (106 and 107/63) [1965]
    ECR 405 . . . 115, 230
Töpfer v Commission (112/77) [1978] ECR
    1019 . . . 116, 234
Torfaen BC v B & Q plc and B & Q Ltd v
    Shrewsbury BC (145/88) [1990] 3 CMLR
    535 . . . 294, 298
Traghetti del Mediterraneo SpA v Italy (C-173/03)
    [2006] ECR I-5177 . . . 166, 169, 210
Transocean Marine Paints Association
    v Commission (17/74) [1974] ECR
    1063 . . . 114, 234
Trojani (C-456/02) [2004] ECR I-7573 . . . 315
Tunnel Refineries (166, 124 and 143/77)
    [1979] ECR 3497 . . . 250
TWD Textilwerke (C-188/92) [1994] ECR
    I-833 . . . 159, 238

UK v Commission (Poverty 4) (C-106/96)
    [1998] ECR I-2729 . . . 235
UK v Council (Hormones) (68/86) [1988] ECR
    855 . . . 85
UK v Council (Working Time Directive)
    (C-84/94) [1996] ECR I-5755 . . . 77, 81–2, 85
UNECTEF v Heylens et al. (222/86) [1987] ECR
    4097 . . . 111, 113
Unibet (C-432/05) [2007] ECR I-2271 . . .
    215–16
Unilever Italia SpA v Central Foods SpA
    (C-443/98) [2000] ECR I-7535 . . . 205
Union Royale Belge des Sociétés de Football
    Association v Bosman (C-415/93) [1995]
    ECR I-4921 . . . 107, 302, 312
University of Hamburg v Hauptzollamt
    Hamburg (216/82) [1983] ECR
    2771 . . . 254
UPA v Council of the European Union
    (C-50/00 P) [2002] ECR I-6677 . . . 236

Vaassen (61/65) [1966] ECR 261 . . . 154
Van Binsbergen (33/74) [1974] ECR
    1299 . . . 331–2, 335
Van der Elst (C-43/93) [1994] ECR
    I-3803 . . . 349
Van Duyn v The Home Office (41/74) [1974]
    ECR 1337 . . . 142, 196, 339
Van Gend en Loos (26/62) [1963] ECR 1 . . . 9,
    20, 62–3, 70, 102, 121–2, 143, 152, 154,
    157, 164, 190, 192, 195, 206–7, 210, 265,
    268, 411
Van Landewyck (218/78) [1978] ECR 2111;
    [1980] ECR 3125 . . . 114
Van Schijndel (C-430 and 431/93) [1995] ECR
    I-4705 . . . 214
Vatsouras and Koupatantze v ARGE
    Nürnberg (C-22 and 23/08) [2009] ECR
    I-4585 . . . 360

Verbond (51/76) [1977] ECR 113 . . . 196

Vereinigte Familiapress Zeitungsverlags v Bauer Verlag
(C-368/95) [1997] ECR I-3689 . . . 301

Vinal v Orbat (46/80) [1981] ECR 77 . . . 160

Vlassopoulou (C-340/89) [1991] ECR I-2357 . . . 333

Von Colson (14/83) [1984] ECR 1891 . . . 99, 200–3, 212,
400

Vroege v NCIV Instituut (C-57/93) [1994] ECR
I-4541 . . . 378

Wachauf (5/88) [1989] ECR 2609 . . . 111

Wagner Miret (C-334/92) [1993] ECR I-6911 . . . 201–2

Walrave and Koch (36/74) [1974] ECR 1405 . . . 194, 309

Walter Rau Lebensmittelwerke v De Smedt (Margarine)
(261/81) [1982] ECR 3961 . . . 295

Walter Rau v BALM (133/85) [1987] ECR 2289 . . . 237

Watson v Belman (118/75) [1976] ECR 1185 . . . 323

Webb v EMO Air Cargo (UK) Ltd (C-32/93) [1994] ECR
I-3567 . . . 394

Werhahn v Commission (63–9/72) [1973] ECR 1229 . . . 244

Willame v Commission (110/63) [1965] ECR 649 . . . 252

Wirth (C-109/92) [1993] ECR I-6447 . . . 354

Wöhrmann v Commission (31 and 33/62) [1962] ECR
501 . . . 254

Worringham & Humphries v Lloyds Bank (69/80) [1981]
ECR 767 . . . 376

Wünsche (69/85) [1986] ECR 947 . . . 139, 167

WWF (T-105/95) [1997] ECR II-313 . . . 178

Zambrano v ONEM (C-34/09) [2011] nyr . . . 363–4

Zuckerfabrik Schöppenstedt (5/71) [1971] ECR 975 . . . 83,
208, 243–4, 246–8, 250–1

Zuckerfabrik Süderdithmarschen AG (C-143/88 and 92/89)
[1991] ECR I-415 . . . 170

Zuckerfabrik Watenstedt v Council (6/68) [1968] ECR
409 . . . 228

Numerical

8/55 Fedechar (Federation Charbonniere v High Authority)
[1954–56] ECR 292 . . . 75, 234

9/56 Meroni v High Authority [1957–58] ECR 133 . . . 92,
233, 254–5

1/58 Stork v High Authority [1957–58] ECR 105 . . . 110

6/60 Humblet [1960] ECR 559 . . . 62

14/60 Meroni [1961] ECR 161 . . . 245

7/61 Commission v Italy (Pigmeat Imports) [1961] ECR
317 . . . 180, 223, 286

13/61 De Geus [1962] ECR 45 . . . 161–2

2 and 3/62 Commission v Luxembourg (Gingerbread)
[1962] ECR 425 . . . 268

17/62 Fruit and Vegetable Confederation v Commission
[1962] ECR 487 . . . 228

24/62 Germany v Commission (Wine Tariff Quotas) [1963]
ECR 63 . . . 233

25/62 Plaumann v Commission [1963] ECR 123; [1963]
ECR 126; [1963] ECR 95 . . . 63, 167, 227–8, 236

26/62 Van Gend en Loos [1963] ECR 1 . . . 9, 20, 62–3, 70,
102, 121–2, 143, 152, 154, 157, 164, 190, 192, 195,
206–7, 210, 265, 268, 411

28–30/62 Da Costa [1963] ECR 31 . . . 63, 161, 164, 169

31 and 33/62 Wöhrmann v Commission [1962] ECR
501 . . . 254

75/63 Hoekstra v BBDA [1964] ECR 177 . . . 313, 315

90–1/63 Commission v Belgium and Luxembourg [1964]
ECR 625 . . . 143, 180

106 and 107/63 Töpfer v Commission [1965] ECR
405 . . . 115, 230

110/63 Willame v Commission [1965] ECR 649 . . . 252

6/64 Costa v ENEL [1964] ECR 585 . . . 9, 20, 62–3, 122,
124, 126, 130, 141, 146, 157, 163, 207, 210, 212

40/64 Sgarlata v Commission [1965] ECR 215 . . . 110

16/65 Schwarze v EVGF [1965] ECR 877 . . . 156

48/65 Alfons Lütticke GmbH v Hauptzollamt Saarlouis
[1966] ECR 19 . . . 178, 193, 223, 241

57/65 Lütticke v Hauptzollamt Saarlouis [1966] ECR
205 . . . 273

61/65 Vaassen [1966] ECR 261 . . . 154

8–11/66 Noordwijks Cement Accord [1967] ECR
75 . . . 105, 222

5, 7, 13 and 24/66 Kampfmeyer [1973] ECR 1599 . . . 248,
252–3

6/68 Zuckerfabrik Watenstedt v Council [1968] ECR
409 . . . 228

7/68 Commission v Italy (First Art Treasures Case) [1968]
ECR 423 . . . 183, 267, 289

24/68 Commission v Italy (Statistical Levy Case) [1969] ECR
193 . . . 268

2 and 3/69 Sociaal Fonds voor de Diamantarbeiders [1969]
ECR 211 . . . 269

4/69 Lütticke [1971] ECR 325 . . . 167, 239, 244

9/69 Sayag v Leduc [1969] ECR 329 . . . 246

26/69 Stauder v City of Ulm [1969] ECR 419 . . . 110

19, 20, 25 and 30/69 Richez Parise [1970] ECR 325 . . .
245

48/69 ICI v Commission (Dyestuffs) [1972] ECR 619 . . . 60

77/69 Commission v Belgium (Belgian Wood Case) [1970]
ECR 237 . . . 176, 180

9/70 Grad v Finanzamt Traunstein [1970] ECR 825 . . . 191,
195, 198

11/70 Internationale Handelsgesellschaft [1970] ECR
1125 . . . 111, 117, 124–5, 139

15/70 Chevalley v Commission [1970] ECR 975 . . . 239–40

22/70 Commission v Council (ERTA) [1971] ECR
263 . . . 69, 75, 105, 222

25/70 Köster [1970] ECR 1161 . . . 92

41–4/70 International Fruit Company v Commission [1971]
ECR 411 . . . 230

62/70 Bock v Commission (Chinese Mushrooms) [1971]
ECR 897 . . . 227, 229

80/70 Defrenne v Belgium (No. 1) [1971] ECR
445 . . . 375–7

5/71 Zuckerfabrik Schöppenstedt [1971] ECR 975 . . . 83,
208, 243–4, 246–8, 250–1

8/71 Deutscher Komponistenverband
(German Composers Group) v Commission
[1971] ECR 705 . . . 241

42/71 Nordgetreide v Commission [1972] ECR
105 . . . 240

48/71 Commission v Italy (Second Art
Treasures Case) [1972] ECR 529 . . . 182

93/71 Leonesio v Italian Ministry of
Agriculture [1972] ECR 287 . . . 195

6/72 Europemballage and Continental Can v
Commission [1973] ECR 215 . . . 99

63–9/72 Werhahn v Commission [1973] ECR
1229 . . . 244

21–4/72 International Fruit [1972] ECR
1219 . . . 107–8, 198

39/72 Commission v Italy (Slaughtered Cows)
[1973] ECR 101 . . . 104, 179, 191

70/72 Commission v Federal Republic of
Germany [1973] ECR 813 . . . 254

81/72 Commission v Council (Staff Salaries)
[1973] ECR 575 . . . 116

2/73 Geddo v Ente Nationale Risi [1973] ECR
865 . . . 282

8/73 HZA Bremerhafen v Massey-Ferguson
[1973] ECR 897 . . . 78

152/73 Sotgui v Deutsche Bundespost [1974]
ECR 153 . . . 341

146 and 166/73 Rheinmühlen-Düsseldorf
[1974] ECR 33; [1974] ECR 139 . . . 161

167/73 Commission v France (Re French
Merchant Seamen) [1974] ECR 359 . . . 175,
180, 309

169/73 Compagnie Continentale Française
[1975] ECR 117 . . . 252

181/73 Haegemann v Belgium [1974] ECR
449 . . . 107

2/74 Reyners v Belgium [1974] ECR
631 . . . 265, 311, 331–2, 335

8/74 Procureur du Roi v Dassonville [1974] ECR
837 . . . 278, 283, 292, 299–300, 304

9/74 Casagrande [1974] ECR 773 . . . 329

17/74 Transocean Marine Paints Association v
Commission [1974] ECR 1063 . . . 114, 234

33/74 Van Binsbergen [1974] ECR
1299 . . . 331–2, 335

36/74 Walrave and Koch [1974] ECR
1405 . . . 194, 309

41/74 Van Duyn v The Home Office [1974]
ECR 1337 . . . 142, 196, 339

67/74 Bonsignore v Köln [1975] ECR
297 . . . 339

74/74 CNTA v Commission [1976] ECR 797;
[1975] ECR 533 . . . 248, 252–3

1/75 Opinion [1975] ECR 1355 . . . 72

7/75 Mrs and Mrs F v the Belgian State [1975]
ECR 679 . . . 99

23/75 Rey Soda [1975] ECR 1279 . . . 93

32/75 Fiorini (Christini v SNCF) [1975] ECR
1085 . . . 325

36/75 Rutili v Minister of Interior [1975] ECR
1219 . . . 117, 324, 346

43/75 Defrenne v Sabena (No. 2) [1976] ECR
455 . . . 115, 168, 193, 371, 374, 377

87/75 Bresciani [1976] ECR 129 . . . 198, 270

105/75 Giuffrida v Council [1976] ECR
1395 . . . 234

118/75 Watson v Belman [1976] ECR
1185 . . . 323

127/75 Bobie v HZA Aachen-Nord [1976] ECR
1079 . . . 274

130/75 Prais v Council [1976] ECR
1589 . . . 112

3, 4 and 6/76 Minister of Justice v Kramer
[1976] ECR 1279 . . . 293

20/76 Schöttle & Söhne v Finanzamt
Freuenstadt [1977] ECR 247 . . . 272–3

26/76 Metro-SB-Grossmärkte v Commission
[1976] ECR 1353 . . . 231

28/76 Molkerei-Zentrale Westfalen v
Haupzollamt Paderborn [1968] ECR
143 . . . 273

33/76 Rewe-Zentralfinanz [1976] ECR
1989 . . . 211, 215

45/76 Comet [1976] ECR 2043 . . . 212, 215

46/76 Bauhuis v The Netherlands [1977] ECR
5 . . . 270

51/76 Verbond [1977] ECR 113 . . . 196

64/76 Dumortier Freres v Commission (Gritz
and Quellmehl) [1982] ECR 1748 . . . 248

71/76 Thieffry v Paris Bar Council [1977] ECR
765 . . . 332

74/76 Ianelli and Volpi SpA v Meroni [1977]
ECR 595 . . . 280

77/76 Fratelli Cucchi [1977] ECR 987 . . . 272

78/76 Steinlike und Weinlig v Germany [1977]
ECR 595 . . . 271

83/76 HNL [1978] ECR 1209 . . . 248–9

88/76 Sugar Export v Commission [1977] ECR
709 . . . 116

101/76 KSH v Intervention Board [1977] ECR
797 . . . 234, 238

113/76 Dumortier Frères v Council (Gritz and
Quellmehl) [1982] ECR 1748 . . . 252

114/76 Bergman v Grows-Farm (Skimmed
Milk Powder) [1977] ECR 1247 . . . 112

117/76 and 16/77 Rucksdeschel [1977] ECR
1753 . . . 249

124/76 and 20/77 Moulins de Pont a Mousson
(Maize, Gritz and Quellmehl) [1977] ECR
1795 . . . 249

30/77 R v Bouchereau [1977] ECR
1999 . . . 340

53/77 Commission v UK (Pig Producers) [1977]
ECR 921 . . . 181

61/77 R Commission v Ireland (Irish Fisheries) [1977] ECR 937; [1977] ECR 1411 . . . 182

106/77 Simmenthal [1978] ECR 629 . . . 122–4, 157

112/77 Töpfer v Commission [1978] ECR 1019 . . . 116, 234

132/77 Sugar Export [1978] ECR 1061 . . . 253

166, 124 and 143/77 Tunnel Refineries [1979] ECR 3497 . . . 250

103 and 145/77 KSH v Council and Commission (Royal Scholten Holdings [1978] ECR 2037 . . . 238, 248–9

149/77 Defrenne v Sabena (No. 3) [1978] ECR 1365 . . . 371

156/77 Commission v Belgium [1978] ECR 1881 . . . 254–5

7/78 R v Thompson et al. [1979] ECR 2247 . . . 286

83/78 Pigs Marketing Board (Northern Ireland) v Redmond [1978] ECR 2347 . . . 131, 280

92/78 Simmenthal v Commission [1979] ECR 777 . . . 238, 255

93/78 Mattheus [1978] ECR 2203 . . . 157, 162

98/78 Racke v HZA Mainz [1979] ECR 69 . . . 116

120/78 Rewe-Zentral AG v Bundesmonopolverwaltung für Branntwein (Cassis de Dijon) [1979] ECR 649 . . . 63, 74, 79, 265, 278, 292–3, 295–9, 302–4

125/78 GEMA v Commission [1979] ECR 3173 . . . 242

128/78 Commission v UK (Tachographs) [1977] ECR 921 . . . 104, 180, 191

132/78 Denkavit v French State [1979] ECR 1923 . . . 272–3

141/78 France v UK [1979] ECR 2923 . . . 185

148/78 Publico Ministero v Ratti [1979] ECR 1629 . . . 196, 203

152/78 Commission v France (Advertising of Alcoholic Beverages) [1980] ECR 2299 . . . 186

170/78 Commission v UK (Wine Excise Duties No. 2), unreported . . . 276

175/78 R v Saunders [1979] ECR 1129 . . . 346

209–15/78 Dow Benelux [1978] ECR 2111 . . . 114

218/78 Van Landewyck [1978] ECR 2111; [1980] ECR 3125 . . . 114

231/78 Commission v UK (Import of Potatoes) [1979] ECR 1447 . . . 282

232/78 Commission v France (Import of Lamb) [1979] ECR 2729 . . . 180, 185, 282

34/79 R v Henn and Darby [1979] ECR 3795 . . . 282, 286

44/79 Hauer v Land Rheinland-Pfalz [1979] ECR 3727 . . . 110

55/79 Commission v Ireland (Excise Payments) [1980] ECR 481 . . . 274

33 and 59/79 Kuhner [1980] ECR 1677 . . . 114

90/79 Commission v France (Reprographic Machines) [1981] ECR 283 . . . 271, 273

98/79 Pecastaing v Belgian State [1981] ECR 691 . . . 337

104/79 Foglia v Novello (No. 1) [1981] ECR 745 . . . 158

129/79 Macarthy's v Wendy Smith [1980] ECR 1275 . . . 131, 134, 379–80

131/79 Santillo [1980] ECR 1585 . . . 191

136/79 National Panasonic [1980] ECR 2033 . . . 114

138–9/79 Maizena (Roquette Freres) v Council [1980] ECR 3393 . . . 65, 91, 225, 230, 234

149/79 Commission v Belgium (Public Employees) [1980] ECR 3881 . . . 341

159/79 R v Pieck [1980] ECR 2171 . . . 117, 323, 365

175/79 A M & S v Commission [1982] ECR 1616 . . . 114

33/80 Renato Albini v Council and Commission [1980] ECR 1671; [1981] ECR 2141 . . . 254

36/80 and 76/80 Irish Creamery Milk Suppliers [1981] ECR 735 . . . 162

46/80 Vinal v Orbat [1981] ECR 77 . . . 160

66/80 ICC [1981] ECR 1191 . . . 165, 168, 255

69/80 Worringham & Humphries v Lloyds Bank [1981] ECR 767 . . . 376

96/80 Jenkins v Kingsgate [1981] ECR 911 . . . 382

113/80 Commission v Ireland (Metal Objects/ Origin) [1981] ECR 1625 . . . 284–5, 294–5

138/80 Borker [1980] ECR 1975 . . . 155

158/80 Rewe v Hauptzollamt Kiel [1981] ECR 1805 . . . 212

244/80 Foglia v Novello (No. 2) [1981] ECR 3045 . . . 159

246/80 Broekmeulen v HRC [1981] ECR 2311 . . . 155

8/81 Becker [1982] ECR 53 . . . 196–7, 200, 204, 206

12/81 Garland v BREL [1982] ECR 359 . . . 132, 167, 375

53/81 Levin v Minister of Justice [1982] ECR 1035 . . . 313–15

102/81 Nordsee v Nordstern [1982] ECR 1095 . . . 155

104/81 Kupferberg [1982] ECR 3641 . . . 198

115–16/81 Adoui and Cornauille v Belgian State [1982] ECR 1665 . . . 186, 337, 339

124/81 Commission v UK (Imports of UHT Milk) [1983] ECR 203 . . . 282, 287, 290, 295

230/81 Luxembourg v European Parliament [1983] ECR 255 . . . 221

246/81 Bethell v Commission [1982] ECR 2277 . . . 178, 240

249/81 Commission v Ireland (Buy Irish) [1983] ECR 4005 . . . 280–1, 283–4

261/81 Walter Rau Lebensmittelwerke v De Smedt (Margarine) [1982] ECR 3961 . . . 284, 295, 297

283/81 CILFIT [1982] ECR 3415 . . . 164

11/82 Piraiki-Patraiki v Commission [1985] ECR 207 . . . 227

35 and 36/82 Morson and Jhanjan [1982] ECR 3723 . . . 346

42/82 Commission v France (Italian Table Wines) [1982] ECR 841 . . . 288, 290

75 and 117/82 Razzouk and Beydoun v Commission [1984] ECR 1509 . . . 112

132/82 Commission v Belgium (Customs Warehouses) [1983] ECR 1649 . . . 269

165/82 Commission v UK (Equal Treatment for Men and Women) [1983] ECR 3431 . . . 391

216/82 University of Hamburg v Hauptzollamt Hamburg [1983] ECR 2771 . . . 254

222/82 Apple and Pear Development Council v Lewis [1983] ECR 4083 . . . 281, 284

231/82 Spijker Kwasten BV v Commission [1983] ECR 2559 . . . 229

238/82 Campus Oil [1984] ECR 523 . . . 287

264/82 Timex v Commission [1985] ECR 849 . . . 231

286/82 Luisi and Carbone v Ministero del Tesauro [1984] ECR 377 . . . 353

13/83 Parliament v Council (Transport Policy) [1987] ECR 1513 . . . 57, 239, 241–2

14/83 Von Colson [1984] ECR 1891 . . . 99, 200, 212, 400

16/83 Criminal Proceedings against Karl Prantl [1984] ECR 1299 . . . 294, 296

63/83 R v Kent Kirk [1984] ECR 2689 . . . 111, 115

72/83 Campus Oil v Ministry for Industry and Energy [1984] ECR 2727 . . . 285

79/83 Harz v Tradex [1984] ECR 1921 . . . 200–1

145/83 Adams v Commission [1985] ECR 3539 . . . 243, 245

184/83 Hoffman v Barmer Ersatzkasse [1984] ECR 3047 . . . 393

231/83 Cullet v Centre Leclerc Toulouse [1985] ECR 305 . . . 287

238/83 Mr and Mrs Richard Meade [1984] ECR 2631 . . . 349

261/83 Castelli v ONPTS [1984] ECR 3199 . . . 327

267/83 Diatta v Land Berlin [1985] ECR 567 . . . 326–7, 329, 350

274/83 Commission v Italy [1985] ECR 1077 . . . 178

293/83 Gravier v City of Liège [1985] ECR 593 . . . 99, 353

294/83 Les Verts v European Parliament and Council v European Parliament [1986] ECR 1339 . . . 57, 220–2

60–1/84 Cinetheque [1985] ECR 2065 . . . 293

21/84 Commission v France (Franking Machines) [1985] ECR 1355 . . . 281

33/84 Fragd v Administrazione delle Finanze [1985] ECR 1605 . . . 141

44/84 Hurd v Jones [1986] ECR 29 . . . 194

60–1/84 Cinetheque [1985] ECR 2065 . . . 298

94/84 ONE v Deak [1985] ECR 1873 . . . 325

101/84 Commission v Italy [1985] ECR 2629 . . . 180

112/84 Michel Humblot v Directeur des Services Fiscaux [1987] ECR 1367 . . . 274

137/84 Mutsch [1985] ECR 2681 . . . 326

151/84 Roberts v Tate and Lyle [1986] ECR 703 . . . 389

152/84 Marshall v Southampton Area Health Authority [1986] ECR 723 . . . 197, 376, 390

170/84 Bilka Kaufhaus v Karin Weber Van Hartz [1986] ECR 1607 . . . 376, 378, 382

174/84 Commission v Germany [1986] ECR 559 . . . 296

175/84 Krohn v Commission [1986] ECR 753 . . . 253

178/84 Commission v Germany (Beer Purity) [1987] ECR 1227 . . . 117, 288

181/84 R v Intervention Board for Agricultural Produce, ex p Man [1985] ECR 2889 . . . 117

205/84 Commission v Germany (Insurance Services) [1986] ECR 3755 . . . 320–1, 332

222/84 Johnston v The Chief Constable RUC [1986] ECR 1651 . . . 113, 197, 391

243/84 John Walker Ltd v Ministeriet for Skatter og Afgifter [1986] ECR 875 . . . 275

307/84 Commission v French Republic [1986] ECR 1725 . . . 341

53/85 AKZO [1986] ECR 1965 . . . 114

59/85 Netherlands v Reed [1986] ECR 1283 . . . 311, 327

66/85 Lawrie-Blum v Land Baden-Württemburg [1986] ECR 2121 . . . 314, 341

69/85 Wünsche [1986] ECR 947 . . . 167

121/85 Conegate v HM Customs and Excise [1986] ECR 1007 . . . 286

131/85 Emir Gül v Regierungspräsident Düsseldorf [1986] ECR 1573 . . . 329

133/85 Walter Rau v BALM [1987] ECR 2289 . . . 237

139/85 Kempf v Minister of Justice [1986] ECR 1741 . . . 313–14

184/85 Commission v Italy (Italian Fruit) [1987] ECR 2013 . . . 275

237/85 Rummler v Dato-Druck [1986] ECR 2101 . . . 384

281, 283–5 and 287/85 Commission v Germany [1987] ECR 3203 . . . 75

293/85 Commission v Belgium (University Fees) [1988] ECR 305 . . . 181

314/85 Firma Foto-Frost v Hauptzollamt Lübeck-Ost [1987] ECR 4199 . . . 165, 237

316/85 Marie-Christine Lebon [1987] ECR 2811 . . . 315, 326–7

352/85 Bond van Adverteerders and others v The Netherlands State [1988] ECR 2085 . . . 338

427/85 Commission v Germany (Lawyers' Services) [1988] ECR 1123 . . . 335, 345

14/86 Pretore di Salo v X [1987] ECR 2545 . . . 160, 162

24/86 Blaizot [1988] ECR 379 . . . 99, 353

34/86 European Parliament v Council (Budgetary Procedure) [1986] ECR 2155 . . . 57, 221

39/86 Lair v Universität Hannover [1988] ECR 3161 . . . 99, 317, 354

68/86 UK v Council (Hormones) [1988] ECR 855 . . . 85

80/86 Public Prosecutor v Kolpinghuis Nijmegan [1977] ECR 815 . . . 115, 201–2

157/86 Mary Murphy An Bord Telecom Eireann [1988] ECR 673 . . . 380, 383–4

197/86 Brown v Secretary of State for Scotland [1988] ECR 3205 . . . 317

222/86 UNECTEF v Heylens et al. [1987] ECR 4097 . . . 111, 113

C-240/86 Commission v Greece [1988] ECR 1835 . . . 179

263/86 Belgium v Humbel [1988] ECR 5365 . . . 99, 353

302/86 Commission v Denmark (Disposable Beer Cans) [1988] ECR 4607 . . . 293

C-312/86 Commission v France (Protection of Women) [1988] ECR 6315 . . . 389

18/87 Commission v Germany (Animal Inspection Fees) [1988] ECR 5427 . . . 270

22/87 Francovich [1989] ECR 143 . . . 179, 206

45/87 Commission v Ireland (Dundalk Water Supply) [1988] ECR 4929 . . . 267

70/87 Fediol [1989] ECR 1781 . . . 198

186/87 Cowan [1989] ECR 195 . . . 320, 353

196/87 Steymann v Staatssecretaris van Justitie [1988] ECR 6159 . . . 314–15

215/87 Schumacher v Hauptzollamt Frankfurt [1989] ECR 617 . . . 289

247/87 Star Fruit Company v Commission [1989] ECR 291 . . . 176–7

266 and 267/87 R v Pharmaceutical Society of Great Britain, ex p Association of Pharmaceutical Importers . . . 280, 284

274/87 Commission v Germany (Sausage Purity Law) [1989] ECR 229 . . . 288

302/87 European Parliament v Council (Comitology) [1988] ECR 5615 . . . 57, 93, 241

340/87 Commission v Italian Republic (Customs Posts) [1989] ECR 1483 . . . 269

344/87 Bettray v Staatssecretaris Van Justitie [1989] ECR 1621 . . . 314–15

379/87 Groener v Minister for Education [1989] ECR 3967 . . . 322

5/88 Wachauf [1989] ECR 2609 . . . 111

16/88 Commission v Council (Management Committee Procedure) [1989] ECR 3457 . . . 93

33/88 Alluè and Coonan v University of Venice [1989] ECR 1591 . . . 311, 341

C-64/88 Commission v France [1991] ECR I-2727 . . . 183

C-70/88 Parliament v Council (Chernobyl) [1991] ECR I-4529 . . . 57, 62, 225

109/88 Handels- og Kontorfunktionaerernes Forbund i Danmark v Dansk [1989] ECR 3199 . . . 385

C-132/88 Commission v Greece (Taxation of Motor Cars) [1990] ECR I-1567 . . . 274

C-143/88 and 92/89 Zuckerfabrik Süderdithmarschen AG [1991] ECR I-415 . . . 170

145/88 Torfaen BC v B & Q plc and B & Q Ltd v Shrewsbury BC [1990] 3 CMLR 535 . . . 294, 298

C-152/88 Sofrimport v Commission [1988] ECR 2931; [1990] ECR I-2477; [1992] ECR I-153 . . . 229–30, 250, 252

170/88 Ford of Spain v the Spanish State [1989] ECR 2305 . . . 270

C-177/88 Dekker v VJM Centram [1990] ECR I-3941 . . . 389

C-179/88 Hertz v Aldi [1990] ECR I-3979 . . . 396

262/88 Barber v Guardian Royal Exchange 1990] ECR I-1889 . . . 74, 115, 168, 375, 377–9

C-297/88 and C-197/89 Dzodzi v Belgium [1990] ECR I-3763 . . . 160

322/88 Grimaldi [1989] ECR 4407 . . . 105

C-33/89 Kowalska v Hamburg [1990] ECR I-2591 . . . 375

C-68/89 Commission v Netherlands (Entry Requirements) [1991] ECR I-2637 . . . 322

T-79/89 BASF v Commission [1992] ECR II-315 . . . 224

T-95/89 Commission v Italy [1995] ECR II-729 . . . 289

C-104/89 and 37/90 Mulder v Council [1992] ECR I-3061; [2000] ECR I-203 . . . 250

C-106/89 Marleasing SA v La Comercial Internacional de Alimentacion SA [1990] ECR I-4135 . . . 101, 201

C-111/89 Netherlands v Bakker Hillegom [1990] ECR I-1735 . . . 270

C-113/89 Rush Portuguesa v Office National d'Immigration [1990] ECR I-1417 . . . 195

T-138/89 BBV v Commission [1992] ECR II-2181 . . . 226

C-171/89 Rinner-Kuhn [1989] ECR 2743 . . . 375

C-184/89 Nimz v Hamburg [1991] ECR I-297 . . . 375

C-188/89 Foster v British Gas [1990] ECR I-3313 . . . 197, 199

C-213/89 Factortame (No. 1) [1990] ECR I-2433 . . . 125, 134–5, 161, 170, 213, 215

C-221/89 Factortame (No. 2) [1991] ECR I-3905 . . . 123, 133–5, 212, 319

C-246/89 R Commission v UK (Nationality of Fishermen) [1991] ECR I-4585 . . . 135, 182, 311

C-292/89 Antonissen [1991] ECR I-745 . . . 316, 324, 340, 365

C-293/89 Commission v Greece [1992] ECR I-4577 . . . 289

C-300/89 Commission v Council (Titanium Dioxide Directive) [1991] ECR I-2867 . . . 86

C-309/89 Codorniu v Council (Spanish Wine Producers) [1994] ECR I-1853 . . . 229–30

C-312/89 Conforama [1991] ECR I-997 . . . 293, 299

C-332/89 Criminal Proceedings against Marchandise [1991] ECR I-1027 . . . 293, 299

C-340/89 Vlassopoulou [1991] ECR I-2357 . . . 333

C-357/89 Raulin v Netherlands Ministry of Education and Science [1992] ECR I-1027 . . . 314, 317

C-358/89 Extramet Industrie v Council [1992] ECR I-3813 . . . 231

C-2/90 Commission v Belgium (Walloon Waste) [1992] ECR I-4431 . . . 297

C-6 and 9/90 Francovich et al. v Italy [1991] ECR I-5357 . . . 62, 99, 124, 179, 206–7, 209–10, 213

C-18/90 Kziber [1991] ECR I-199 . . . 198

C-47/90 Delhaize v Promalvin [1992] ECR I-3669 . . . 284

C-76/90 Säger v Dennemeyer [1991] ECR I-4221 . . . 332

C-195/90 Commission v Germany [1992] ECR I-3141 . . . 182

C-208/90 Emmott [1991] ECR I-4269 . . . 213

C-295/90 European Parliament v Council (Students' Residence) [1992] ECR I-4193 . . . 57, 86, 225

C-320/90 Telemarsicabruzzo SpA [1993] ECR I-393 . . . 158

C-360/90 Arbeiterwohlfahrt der Stadt Berlin v Monika Botel [1992] ECR I-3589 . . . 375

C-370/90 Surinder Singh [1992] ECR I-4265 . . . 347

C-4/91 Bleis v Ministry of Education [1991] ECR I-5627 . . . 341

C-9/91 R v Secretary of State for Employment [1992] ECR I-4297 . . . 136

C-83/91 Meilicke v ADV/OGA [1992] ECR I-4871 . . . 158

C-109/91 Ten Oever [1993] ECR I-4879 . . . 378

C-152/91 Neath v Hugh Steeper [1993] ECR I-6935 . . . 378

C-155/91 Commission v Council (Waste Directive) [1993] ECR I-939 . . . 85

C-169/91 Stoke City Council v B & Q plc [1992] ECR I-6635 . . . 299

C-267–8/91 Keck and Mithouard [1993] ECR I-6097 . . . 63, 278, 299–302, 304, 333

C-271/91 Marshall II [1993] ECR I-4367 . . . 213, 399–400

C-325/91 France v Commission [1993] ECR I-3283 . . . 106, 234

C-327/91 France v Commission [1994] ECR I-3641 . . . 233

C-339/91 Steenhorst-Neerings [1993] ECR I-5475 . . . 213

C-24/92 Corbiau v Administration des Contributions [1993] ECR I-1277 . . . 155

C-36/92 P Samenwerkende [1994] ECR I-1911 . . . 114

C-91/92 Faccini Dori [1994] ECR I-3325 . . . 202, 204, 207

C-109/92 Wirth [1993] ECR I-6447 . . . 354

C-127/92 Enderby v Frenchay Health Authority [1993] ECR I-5535 . . . 383, 385

C-188/92 TWD Textilwerke [1994] ECR I-833 . . . 159, 238

C-292/92 Hunermund [1993] ECR I-6787 . . . 300

C-334/92 Wagner Miret [1993] ECR I-6911 . . . 201

C-391/92 Commission v Greece [1995] All ER (EC) 802 . . . 300

C-401 and 402/92 Tankstation 't Heustke [1994] ECR I-2199 . . . 300

C-419/92 Scholz [1994] ECR I-505 . . . 347

C-421/92 Habermann-Beltermann v Arbeiterwohlfahrt [1994] ECR I-1657 . . . 393, 402

C-32/93 Webb v EMO Air Cargo (UK) Ltd [1994] ECR I-3567 . . . 394

C-43/93 Van der Elst [1994] ECR I-3803 . . . 349

C-45/93 Commission v Spain [1994] ECR I-911 . . . 320

C-46/93 Brasserie du Pêcheur v Federal Republic of Germany [1996] ECR I-1029 . . . 141, 207, 250

C-48/93 Factortame (No. 3) v UK [1996] ECR I-1029 . . . 124, 136, 207, 250

C-57/93 Vroege v NCIV Instituut [1994] ECR I-4541 . . . 378

C-65/93 European Parliament v Council [1995] ECR I-643 . . . 91

C-147/93 Commission v Austria . . . 354

C-280/93 Germany v Commission [1994] ECR I-4973 . . . 198

C-312/93 Peterbroeck Van Campenhout v Belgium [1995] ECR I-4599 . . . 161, 214–15

C-342/93 Gillespie [1996] ECR I-475 . . . 402

C-384/93 Alpine Investments [1995] ECR I-1141 . . . 319, 333

C-392/93 R v HM Treasury, ex p British Telecom PLC [1996] ECR I-1631 . . . 208

C-412/93 Leclerc Siplec [1995] ECR I-179 . . . 301

C-415/93 Union Royale Belge des Sociétés de Football Association v Bosman [1995] ECR I-4921 . . . 107, 302, 312

C-430 and 431/93 Van Schijndel [1995] ECR I-4705 . . . 214

C-441/93 Panagis Pafitis v TKE [1996] ECR I-1347 . . . 204

T-447–9/93 AITEC v Commission [1996] ECR II-1631 . . . 231

C-450/93 Kalanke [1995] ECR I-3051 . . . 398

C-465/93 Atlanta Fruchthandelsgesellschaft [1995] ECR I-3761 . . . 170

C-470/93 Mars [1995] ECR I-1923 . . . 301

T-585/93 Greenpeace v Commission [1995] ECR II-2205 . . . 231

1/94 Opinion [1994] ECR I-5267 . . . 69, 76

2/94 Opinion [1996] ECR I-1788 . . . 78, 112

C-5/94 Hedley Lomas [1996] ECR I-2553 . . . 209

C-7/94 Gaal [1995] ECR I-1031 . . . 329

C-13/94 P v S and Cornwall County Council [1996] ECR I-2143 . . . 386

C-24/94 Commission v Council [1996] ECR I-1469 . . . 222

C-55/94 Gebhard v Milan Bar Council [1995] ECR I-4165 . . . 320, 333

C-58/94 Netherlands v Council [1996] ECR I-2169 . . . 117

C-84/94 UK v Council (Working Time Directive) [1996] ECR I-5755 . . . 77, 81–2, 85

C-116/94 Meyers [1995] ECR I-2131 . . . 390

C-175/94 Gallagher [1995] ECR I-4253 . . . 337

C-178/94 Dillenkofer [1996] ECR I-4845 . . . 209

C-194/94 CIA Security International SA v Signalson SA and Securitel SPRL [1996] ECR I-2201 . . . 205

C-237/94 O'Flynn [1996] ECR I-2617 . . . 326

C-28/95 Leur-Bloem [1997] ECR I-4161 . . . 160

C-34–6/95 Konsumenten-ombudsmannen v De Agostini [1997] ECR I-3843 . . . 302

C-57/95 French Republic v Commission [1997] ECR I-1627 . . . 223, 233

C-68/95 T. Port v Bundesanstalt für Landeswirtschaft und Ernährung [1996] ECR I-6065 . . . 240

T-105/95 WWF [1997] ECR II-313 . . . 178

C-120/95 Decker [1998] ECR I-1831 . . . 294

C-136/95 Thibault [1998] ECR I-2011 . . . 390

C-168/95 Criminal Proceedings against Luciano Arcaro [1996] ECR I-4705 . . . 202

C-180/95 Draehmpaehl v Urania [1997] ECR I-2195 . . . 400

C-188/95 Fantask [1997] ECR I-6783 . . . 214

C-265/95 Commission v France (Spanish Strawberries) [1997] ECR I-6959 . . . 175, 177, 180, 281, 287

C-299/95 Kremzow v Austria [1997] ECR I-2629 . . . 346

C-321/95 P Greenpeace v Commission [1998] ECR I-1651 . . . 231

C-344/95 Commission v Belgium [1997] ECR I-1035 . . . 323

C-358/95 Tommaso Morellato v Unita Sanitaria Locale [1997] ECR I-1431 . . . 289

C-366/95 Steff-houlberg Export [1998] ECR I-2661 . . . 117–18

C-368/95 Vereinigte Familiapress Zeitungsverlags v Bauer Verlag [1997] ECR I-3689 . . . 294, 301

C-388/95 Belgium v Spain [2000] ECR I-3123 . . . 185

C-400/95 Larsson v Dansk Handel & Service [1997] ECR I-2757 . . . 396

C-408/95 Eurotunnel v SeaFrance [1997] ECR I-6315 . . . 238

C-409/95 Marschall [1997] ECR I-6363 . . . 398

C-50/96 Deutsche Telekom v Schröder [2000] ECR I-743 . . . 371

C-54/96 Dorsch [1997] ECR I-4961 . . . 155

C-64 and 65/96 Land Nordrhein-Westfalen v Uecker and Jacquet [1997] ECR I-3171 . . . 346

C-85/96 María Martínez Sala v Freistaat Bayern [1998] ECR I-2691 . . . 358

C-106/96 UK v Commission (Poverty 4) [1998] ECR I-2729 . . . 105, 222, 235

C-149/96 Portugal v Council [1999] ECR I-8395 . . . 199

C-187/96 Commission v Greece [1998] ECR I-1095 . . . 325

C-213/96 Outokumpu Oy [1998] ECR I-1777 . . . 275

C-249/96 Grant v South West Trains [1998] ECR I-621 . . . 387

C-274/96 Criminal Proceedings v Bickel and Franz [1998] ECR I-7637 . . . 357

C-319/96 Brinkmann [1998] ECR I-5255 . . . 209

C-324/96 Deutsche Telekom v Vick [2000] ECR I-799 . . . 100, 371

C-326/96 Levez v Jennings [1998] ECR I-7835 . . . 214

C-348/96 Donatella Calfa [1999] ECR I-11 . . . 340

C-394/96 Brown v Rentokil [1998] ECR I-4185 . . . 396

C-411/96 Boyle et al. v EOC [1998] ECR I-6401 . . . 402

C-67/97 Bluhme [1998] ECR I-8033 . . . 297

C-140/97 Rechberger [1999] ECR I-3499 . . . 209

C-149/97 Institute of the Motor Industry v Customs and Excise Commissioners [1998] ECR I-7053 . . . 101

C-158/97 Badeck [2000] ECR I-1875 . . . 398

C-167/97 Seymour-Smith and Perez [1999] ECR I-623 . . . 375, 383

C-185/97 Coote v Granada [1998] ECR I-5199 . . . 400–1

C-226/97 Lemmens [1998] ECR I-3711 . . . 205

C-273/97 Angela Sirdar v The Army Board [1999] ECR I-7403 . . . 391–2

C-310/97 P Commission v Assidomän [1999] ECR I-5363 . . . 63

C-387/97 Commission v Greece [1988] ECR 4415 . . . 183

C-4, 6 and 7–9/98 Commission v Finland [2002] ECR I-9627 . . . 76

T-166/98 Cantina [2004] ECR II-3991 . . . 248

C-207/98 Mahlberg [2000] ECR I-549 . . . 394

C-218/98 Abdoulaye v Renault [1999] ECR I-5723 . . . 397

C-224/98 D'Hoop [2002] ECR I-6191 . . . 359

C-254/98 Heimdienst [2000] ECR I-151 . . . 302

C-281/98 Angonese v Cassa di Risparmio di Bolzano SpA [2000] ECR I-4139 . . . 309, 348, 354–5

C-285/98 Kreil v Germany [2000] ECR I-69 . . . 391

C-352/98 P Bergaderm [2000] ECR I-5291 . . . 209, 245, 247, 250

C-376/98 Germany v Parliament and Council (Tobacco Advertising Ban Directive) [2000] ECR I-8419 . . . 77, 81

C-377/98 Netherlands v European Parliament [2001] ECR I-7079 . . . 77, 81

C-378/98 Germany v European Parliament [2000] ECR I-8419 . . . 233, 235

C-405/98 Gourmet International [2001] ECR I-1795 . . . 302

C-407/98 Abrahamsson [2000] ECR I-5539 . . . 398

C-424/98 Commission v Italy [2000] ECR I-2001 . . . 355

C-443/98 Unilever Italia SpA v Central Foods SpA [2000] ECR I-7535 . . . 205

C-43/99 Leclere [2001] ECR I-4265 . . . 315, 326

C-79/99 Julia Schnorbus v Land Hessen [2000] ECR I-10997 . . . 399

C-125/99 P D and Sweden v Council [2001] ECR I-4319 . . . 387

C-184/99 Grzelczyk [2001] ECR I-6193 . . . 318, 353–5, 358–9, 364–5

T-191/99 Petrie [2001] ECR II-3677 . . . 178

C-192/99 Ex p Manjit Kaur v Secretary of State for the Home Department [2001] ECR I-1237 . . . 103, 312

C-212/99 Commission v Italy [2001] ECR I-4923 . . . 184

C-268/99 Jany [2001] ECR I-8615 . . . 319–20

C-353/99 P Hautala v Council [2001] ECR I-9565 . . . 117

C-387/99 Commission v Germany [2004] ECR I-3751 . . . 284

C-413/99 Baumbast [2002] ECR I-7091 . . . 111, 328–9, 350, 356–7, 362

C-438/99 Melgar [2001] ECR I-6915 . . . 394, 401

C-453/99 Courage Ltd v Crehan [2001] ECR I-6297 . . . 210

C-459/99 MRAX [2002] ECR I-6591 . . . 111, 323, 362

C-476/99 Lommers [2002] ECR I-2891 . . . 399

C-1/00 Commission v France [2001] ECR I-9989 . . . 185

C-17/00 de Coster [2001] ECR I-9445 . . . 319, 334, 348, 355, 365

C-50/00 P UPA v Council of the European Union [2002] ECR I-6677 . . . 236

C-60/00 Carpenter [2002] ECR I-6279 . . . 347, 361

C-62/00 Marks & Spencer plc [2002] ECR I-6325 . . . 166

T-69/00 FIAMM & FIAMM Technologies et al. v Council and Commission [2005] ECR II-5393 . . . 248, 251

C-99/00 Criminal Proceedings against Lyckeskog [2002] ECR I-4839 . . . 177

C-109/00 Tele Danmark [2001] ECR
I-6993 . . . 394
C-112/00 Schmidberger [2003] ECR
I-5659 . . . 281, 294
C-129/00 Commission v Italy [2003] ECR
I-14637 . . . 177
C-150/00 Commission v Austria [2004] ECR
I-3887 . . . 284
C-253/00 Munoz v Frumar Ltd [2002] ECR
I-7289 . . . 195
C-318/00 Bacardi-Martini v Newcastle United
[2003] ECR I-905 . . . 159
C-320/00 Lawrence v Regent Office Care Ltd
[2002] ECR I-7325 . . . 380
C-385/00 De Groot [2006] ECR I-11573 . . . 326
C-438/00 Kolpak v Deutscher Handballbund
[2003] ECR I-4135 . . . 312
C-453/00 Kühne and Heitz [2004] ECR
I-837 . . . 168
C-100/01 Olazabal [2002] ECR
I-10981 . . . 324, 340, 346
C-109/01 Akrich [2003] ECR I-9607 . . . 111,
328, 349, 351, 362
C-117/01 KB v NHS Pensions [2004] ECR
I-541 . . . 378, 387
T-177/01 Jego-Quere v Commission [2002]
ECR II-2365 . . . 236–7
C-186/01 Dory [2003] ECR I-2479 . . . 392
C-192/01 Commission v Denmark [2003] ECR
I-9693 . . . 289
C-206/01 Arsenal FC v Matthew Reed [2002]
ECR I-10273 . . . 168, 171
C-224/01 Gerhard Köbler v Republic of Austria
[2003] ECR I-10239 . . . 166–7, 169, 171,
210–11
C-256/01 Allonby [2004] ECR I-873 . . . 318, 380
C-278/01 Commission v Spain [2003] ECR
I-14141 . . . 183
C-313/01 Morgenbesser [2003] ECR
I-13467 . . . 336
C-320/01 Busch [2003] ECR I-2041 . . . 395
C-322/01 Deutscher Apothekerverband [2003]
ECR I-14887 . . . 287
C-397–401/01 Pfeiffer v Rotes Kreuz [2004]
ECR I-8835 . . . 202
C-413/01 Ninni-Orasche [2003] ECR
I-13187 . . . 314
C-47/02 Anker et al. [2003] ECR
I-10447 . . . 342
C-138/02 Collins v Secretary of State for Work
and Pensions [2004] ECR I-2703 . . . 316,
318, 354–5, 359–61, 366
C-148/02 Garcia Avello [2003] ECR
I-11613 . . . 348
C-157/02 Rieser Internationale
Transporte GmbH v Autobahnen- und
Schnellstraßen . . . 200

C-167/02 Willi Rothley and Others v European
Parliament [2004] ECR I-3149 . . . 237
C-200/02 Chen [2004] ECR I-9925 . . . 329,
348, 363
C-236/02 J. Slob v Productschap Zuivel [2004]
ECR I-1861 . . . 156
C-263/02 P Commission v Jego-Quere [2004]
ECR I-3425 . . . 63, 167, 236
C-304/02 Commission v France [2005] ECR
I-6263 . . . 183
C-456/02 Trojani [2004] ECR I-7573 . . . 315
C-53/03 Syfait v GlaxoSmithKline [2005] ECR
I-4609 . . . 155
C-105/03 Pupino [2005] ECR I-5285 . . . 202
C-131/03 P Reynolds Tobacco Holdings and
others [2006] ECR I-7795 . . . 223
C-173/03 Traghetti del Mediterraneo SpA v
Italy [2006] ECR I-5177 . . . 166, 169, 210
C-191/03 McKenna [2005] ECR I-7631 . . . 396
C-209/03 Bidar [2005] ECR I-2119 . . . 318,
354, 360
C-210/03 R v Secretary of State for Health,
ex p Swedish Match [2004] ECR
I-11893 . . . 77, 86
C-265/03 Simutenkov [2005] ECR
I-2579 . . . 107
C-319/03 Briheche [2004] ECR I-8807 . . . 397
C-380/03 Germany v European Parliament and
Council [2006] ECR I-11573 . . . 77, 86
C-403/03 Schempp [2005] ECR
I-6421 . . . 348
C-461/03 Schul [2005] ECR I-10513 . . . 165
C-508/03 Commission v UK [2006] ECR
I-3969 . . . 179
C-544/03 Mobistar [2005] ECR
I-7723 . . . 348, 355
T-16/04 Arcelor [2010] nyr . . . 247
C-144/04 Mangold [2005] ECR I-9981 . . . 113,
405, 409
C-145/04 Spain v UK [2006] ECR
I-7917 . . . 185
C-154 and 155/04 Alliance for Natural Health
[2005] ECR I-6451 . . . 82
C-158–9/04 Alfa Vita Vassilopoulos [2006]
ECR I-8135 . . . 303
C-170/04 Rosengren [2007] ECR
I-4071 . . . 291
C-212/04 Adeneler v ELOG [2006] ECR
I-6057 . . . 203
C-256/04 Ioannidis [2005] ECR I-8275 . . .
360
C-295–8/04 Manfredi [2006] ECR
I-6619 . . . 210
C-344/04 R v Department of Transport, ex p
International Air Transport Association and
European Low Fares Airline Association
[2006] ECR I-403 . . . 82, 165

T-376/04 Polyelectrolyte Producers Group v
    Council and Commission [2005] ECR
    II-3007 . . . 243
C-406/04 De Cuyper [2006] ECR
    I-6947 . . . 360
C-423/04 Richards [2006] ECR I-3585 . . . 388
C-432/04 Commission v Edith Cresson [2006]
    ECR I-6387 . . . 42
C-1/05 Jia [2007] ECR I-1 . . . 328, 351, 363
C-13/05 Sonia Navas [2006] ECR
    I-6467 . . . 406
C-17/05 Cadman [2006] ECR I-9583 . . . 385
C-278/05 Robins [2007] ECR I-1059 . . . 209
C-282/05 P Holcim v Commission [2007] ECR
    I-2941 . . . 251
C-402/05 P and C-415/05 Kadi v Council
    [2008] ECR I-6351 . . . 78
C-411/05 Palacios de la Villa [2007] ECR
    I-8531 . . . 405
C-432/05 Unibet [2007] ECR I-2271 . . . 215–
    16
C-438/05 ITWF & FSU v Viking [2007] ECR
    I-10779 . . . 334
C-11–12/06 Morgan and Bucher [2007] ECR
    I-9161 . . . 360–1
C-210/06 Cartesio Oktató és Szolgáltató
    [2008] ECR I-9641 . . . 157
C-244/06 Dynamic Medien [2008] ECR
    I-505 . . . 294

C-267/06 Tadao Maruko v Versorgungsanstalt
    der deutschen Bühnen [2008] ECR
    I-1757 . . . 406–7
C-303/06 Coleman [2008] ECR
    I-5603 . . . 406–7
C-309/06 M&S [2008] ECR I-2283 . . . 118
C-506/06 Sabine Mayr [2008] ECR
    I-1017 . . . 395
C-33/07 Jipa [2008] ECR I-5157 . . . 341
C-54/07 Firma Feryn [2008] ECR
    I-5187 . . . 407
C-158/07 Förster v IB-Groep [2008] ECR
    I-8507 . . . 318, 360–1, 366
C-555/07 Kükükdeveci [2010] nyr . . . 204,
    406
C-22 and 23/08 Vatsouras and Koupatantze v
    ARGE Nürnberg [2009] ECR I-4585 . . .
    360
C-127/08 Metock et al. [2008] ECR
    I-6241 . . . 328, 351–2, 363
C-135/08 Rottmann v Bayern [2010] ECR
    I-1449 . . . 357
C-34/09 Zambrano v ONEM [2011]
    nyr . . . 363–4
C-145/09 Land Baden-Württemberg v
    Tsakouridis [2010] nyr . . . 340
C-236/09 Test Achats [2011] nyr . . . 405, 407
C-434/09 McCarthy [2011] nyr . . . 364
C-149/10 Chatzi [2010] nyr . . . 113, 370

Table of legislation

EU Legislation

Regulations

Reg 17 . . . 242
Reg 1612/68 (Freedom of Movement) . . . 310,
  317, 321, 324, 327–9, 347, 350, 358–9,
  361–2
  Arts 1–2 . . . 322
  Arts 1–5 . . . 322
  Art 3(1) . . . 322
  Art 7 . . . 327
  Art 7(1) . . . 325
  Art 7(2) . . . 326, 330, 342, 359
  Art 10 . . . 321, 326–7, 350–1
  Arts 10–11 . . . 325
  Art 11 . . . 321, 328
  Art 12 . . . 329
Reg 1049/2001 . . . 117
Reg 1091/2001 (Freedom of
  Movement) . . . 350
Reg 1/2003 (Rules for the Application of
  Arts 85 and 86 of the Treaty to Maritime
  Transport) . . . 43, 61, 226, 242
  Art 27 . . . 114
  Art 28 . . . 114
Reg 764/2008 (Free Movement) . . . 291
Reg 182/2011 . . . 43, 93
Reg 492/2011 . . . 310, 317, 321, 324
  Arts 1–2 . . . 322
  Arts 1–5 . . . 322
  Art 3(1) . . . 322
  Arts 7–9 . . . 324
  Art 7(1) . . . 325
  Art 7(2) . . . 325–6, 330, 342
  Art 10 . . . 329

Directives

Dir 64/221 (Freedom of Movement) . . . 142,
  196, 321, 337
  Art 1 . . . 353
  Art 8 . . . 337
  Art 9 . . . 337
Dir 68/151 . . . 201
Dir 68/360 (Freedom of Movement) . . .
  321–3, 362

Arts 1–6 . . . 322
Art 3 . . . 362
Art 8 . . . 322
Art 10 . . . 362
Dir 70/50 (Abolition of Equivalent
  Measures) . . . 263, 279, 295, 303
  Preamble . . . 281
  Art 2 . . . 282
  Art 2(3)(f) . . . 295
  Art 3 . . . 283, 292
Dir 70/1251 . . . 321
Dir 73/148 (Freedom of Movement) . . . 321, 351
  Art 8 . . . 362
Dir 75/34 (Freedom of Movement) . . . 321
Dir 75/117 (Equal Pay) . . . 372–4, 379, 384
  Art 1 . . . 379, 384
  Art 2 . . . 384–5
  Art 2(1)(e) . . . 379
  Art 4 . . . 385
  Art 5 . . . 385
  Art 6 . . . 385
Dir 76/207 (Equal Treatment) . . . 51, 78, 132,
  372–3, 385–6, 389–90, 393–6, 400, 403,
  405
  Art 1 . . . 386, 393
  Art 1a . . . 386
  Art 2 . . . 393
  Art 2(1) . . . 389, 394
  Art 2(2) . . . 391
  Art 2(3) . . . 390, 392–3
  Art 2(4) . . . 397–9
  Art 2(6) . . . 386, 391
  Art 2(7) . . . 392
  Art 3 . . . 388, 390, 399
  Art 3(1) . . . 389, 394
  Art 5 . . . 390
  Art 5(1) . . . 389–90, 393–5
  Art 6 . . . 200, 399–400
  Art 7 . . . 400
  Art 8 . . . 401
  Art 8a . . . 401
  Art 8b . . . 401
  Art 9(2) . . . 391
Dir 77/187 . . . 133
Dir 77/249 (Legal Services and
  Establishment) . . . 335
  Art 4(1) . . . 335

Art 4(2) . . . 335
Art 4(4) . . . 335
Art 5 . . . 335–6
Dir 79/7 (Social Security) . . . 372, 377, 390,
    401, 409
    Art 4(1) . . . 388
    Art 5 . . . 389
    Art 7 . . . 74, 376, 389–90
    Art 7a . . . 376
Dir 80/987 (Insolvency Protection) . . . 206
Dir 81/389 . . . 270
Dir 83/189 . . . 205, 296
Dir 83/643 (Inspection of Goods for
    Carriage) . . . 269
    Art 5 . . . 269
Dir 85/384 (Architects) . . . 20, 331
Dir 86/378 (Occupational Pensions) . . . 372,
    378, 401
Dir 86/613 (Self-Employed) . . . 372
Dir 89/48 (Mutual Recognition of
    Diplomas) . . . 106, 335–6
Dir 89/987 (Insolvency Protection) . . . 209
Dir 90/364 (Free Movement) . . . 355–6, 363
Dir 90/365 (Free Movement) . . . 355
Dir 90/366 (Students) . . . 86
Dir 91/156 (Waste) . . . 85
Dir 92/85 (Pregnant and Breastfeeding
    Workers) . . . 373, 393–6, 401–3
    Arts 1–6 . . . 402
    Art 7 . . . 402
    Art 8 . . . 393, 402
    Art 8(1) . . . 402
    Art 9 . . . 401–2
    Art 10 . . . 393–5
    Art 11 . . . 402
    Art 11(2)(a) . . . 403
    Art 11(4) . . . 403
Dir 93/96 (Students) . . . 86, 355
Dir 96/34 (Parental Leave) . . . 373, 393
Dir 96/71 . . . 349
Dir 97/80 (Burden of Proof in Sex
    Discrimination Cases) . . . 373, 385
Dir 97/81 (Part-Time Workers) . . . 373, 383
Dir 98/5 (Lawyers Home Title)
    Art 2 . . . 336
    Art 3 . . . 336
    Art 5 . . . 336
Dir 98/34 (Technical Standards) . . . 205, 263,
    279, 296
Dir 98/43 (Tobacco Advertising) . . . 81
Dir 1999/70 (Fixed-Term Work) . . . 203
Dir 2000/43 (Racial Equality) . . . 113, 380,
    404, 407
    Art 2 . . . 311
    Art 2(1) . . . 404
    Art 2(2)(a) . . . 407

Art 3(1) . . . 404
Art 3(2) . . . 350, 404
Art 4 . . . 404
Art 4(1) . . . 404
Arts 7–12 . . . 405
Art 8(1) . . . 407
Art 13 . . . 404
Art 15 . . . 407
Dir 2000/78 (Framework Employment
    Directive) . . . 113, 203–4, 380, 387,
    404–6
    Art 2 . . . 311
    Art 2(1) . . . 404, 406
    Art 3(1) . . . 406
    Art 3(2) . . . 404
    Art 4 . . . 404
    Art 4(1) . . . 404
    Art 4(2) . . . 404
    Art 5 . . . 404
    Art 6 . . . 203, 404
    Art 6(1) . . . 405
    Art 7 . . . 404–5
    Arts 9–14 . . . 405
    Art 10 . . . 203, 207
Dir 2002/14 (Employee Consultation)
    Preamble, recital 17 . . . 80
    Art 11 . . . 176
Dir 2002/43 . . . 404–5
Dir 2002/73 (Equal Treatment) . . . 401
Dir 2003/86 (Family Reunification) . . . 350
    Art 3 . . . 350
Dir 2004/38 (Free Movement) . . . 105, 307,
    310, 321–2, 324, 327–9, 338–40, 351–3,
    355, 364
    Preamble . . . 356
    Art 2 . . . 326–7
    Arts 2–3 . . . 325
    Art 2(c) . . . 326
    Art 3 . . . 326
    Art 4 . . . 322
    Arts 4–14 . . . 322
    Art 5 . . . 322–3
    Art 6 . . . 323
    Art 7 . . . 356
    Art 7(1()b) . . . 355
    Art 7(3) . . . 316
    Art 7(3)(d) . . . 317
    Art 8 . . . 323
    Art 11 . . . 324
    Art 12 . . . 330, 352
    Art 13 . . . 328, 330, 352
    Art 14 . . . 316, 324, 330, 355–6
    Art 15 . . . 324
    Art 16 . . . 330
    Art 17 . . . 330
    Art 18 . . . 330

Art 22 . . . 324
Art 23 . . . 328
Art 24 . . . 361
Art 25 . . . 324
Art 27 . . . 338, 340–1
Arts 27–29 . . . 357
Arts 27–33 . . . 362
Art 27(2) . . . 338, 340
Art 28 . . . 338, 340
Art 28(2) . . . 339
Art 28(3) . . . 339–40
Art 29 . . . 340–1
Art 30 . . . 337
Art 30(3) . . . 337
Art 31 . . . 337–8
Art 32 . . . 340
Dir 2004/113 (Goods and Services) . . . 113,
    373, 404–5
    Art 5(1) . . . 408
    Art 5(2) . . . 407–8
Dir 2005/36 (Mutual Recognition of
    Diplomas) . . . 335–6
Dir 2006/54 (Equal Treatment) . . . 373,
    379–81, 393, 397, 400–1, 403, 405
    Preamble
    recital 3 . . . 388
    recital 10 . . . 381
    recital 36 . . . 80
    Art 1 . . . 385
    Art 2 . . . 311, 373, 380–1
    Art 2(1)(b) . . . 381
    Art 3 . . . 397
    Art 4 . . . 384–5
    Art 14 . . . 387, 389
    Art 14(1) . . . 386, 388
    Art 14(2) . . . 386, 391, 404
    Art 15 . . . 392
    Art 17 . . . 385, 399
    Art 17(1) . . . 384
    Art 18 . . . 385, 399
    Art 19 . . . 385, 404
    Arts 20–22 . . . 401
    Art 23 . . . 385–6, 388, 399–400
    Art 24 . . . 385
    Art 28(1) . . . 392
    Art 30 . . . 401
Dir 2006/123 (Services) . . . 307, 335, 355
Dir 2010/18 (Parental Leave) . . . 373
Dir 2010/41 (Self-Employed) . . . 373

Decisions

Dec 87/373 (Comitology) . . . 93
Dec 95/3052 . . . 263, 279, 291
Dec 99/468 . . . 93
Dec 2004/752 . . . 64

National Legislation
Belgium
Loi sur le Travail . . . 299

Denmark
Constitution . . . 144
    s 19 . . . 144
    s 20 . . . 144
    s 20(2) . . . 144

France
Code de Travail . . . 299
Constitution
    Art 55 . . . 141–2
    Art 88 . . . 143

Germany
Beer Purity Law . . . 296
Grundgesetz . . . 26, 86, 113, 138–40, 348,
    358, 370, 383, 397
    Art 1 . . . 110
    Art 2.1 . . . 124
    Art 14 . . . 124
    Art 23 . . . 138
    Art 24 . . . 138–9
    Art 25 . . . 138
    Art 101 . . . 139
    Art 101(1) . . . 140
    Arts 101–104 . . . 113
Sausage Purity Law . . . 288
Transformation Act . . . 140

Italy
Constitution . . . 124, 141
    Art 11 . . . 141

Netherlands
Constitution
    Art 93 . . . 143
    Art 94 . . . 143

Sweden
Constitution . . . 145
Law on Alcohol
    Ch 4(2)(1) . . . 291

United Kingdom
Equal Pay Act 1970 . . . 133
    s 6 . . . 131
European Communities Act 1972 . . . 129–32,
    134, 136–7
    s 1 . . . 129
    s 2(1) . . . 129–30, 132, 136–7
    s 2(2) . . . 129

s 2(4) . . . 130–4, 136
s 3 . . . 131
s 3(1) . . . 130
s 3(2) . . . 130
Sch 2 . . . 129–30
European Union Act 2011 . . . 35, 134, 137–8
s 2 . . . 137
s 4 . . . 137
s 4(1) . . . 137
s 4(4) . . . 137
s 5 . . . 137

s 6 . . . 137
s 7 . . . 137
s 8 . . . 137
s 18 . . . 137
Human Rights Act 1998 . . . 128
Merchant Shipping Act 1988 . . . 130, 133, 135
Sex Discrimination Act 1975 . . . 132–3
s 6(4) . . . 132
Transfer of Undertakings (Protection of
Employment) Regulations 1981 . . . 133
Weights and Measures Act 1985 . . . 136

l

Table of treaties and conventions

Note: all references to TEU are to the post-Lisbon TEU.

Accession Treaties . . . 15–16, 18, 31, 53, 101, 139, 194

Charter of Fundamental Rights of the European Union . . . 28–31, 35, 111–12, 236, 340, 408
  Art 20 . . . 113, 370, 408–9
  Arts 20–23 . . . 372
  Art 21 . . . 372, 408–9
  Art 22 . . . 408
  Art 23 . . . 408–9
  Art 47 . . . 215
  Art 51 . . . 409

EC Treaty (former) . . . 8–9, 11, 26, 30–1, 56, 74, 98, 101, 108–9, 113, 128–9, 268, 308, 351, 353, 356, 358, 363, 370, 372–3
  Preamble . . . 98, 262
  Art 2 . . . 62, 71, 98–9, 108–9, 262
  Arts 2–4 . . . 263
  Art 3 . . . 62, 71, 98–9, 108–9, 242, 262, 369
  Art 3(1)(q) . . . 359
  Art 5 . . . 25, 71, 79, 81, 123
  Art 5(2) . . . 82
  Art 6 . . . 135
  Art 7 . . . 40, 80, 123, 225, 232
  Art 8(2) . . . 358
  Art 10 . . . 62, 98–9, 108, 121, 125, 174–5, 194, 215, 262
  Art 11 . . . 27–8
  Art 12 . . . 62, 98–9, 108–9, 112, 121, 175, 194, 212, 262, 310, 315, 317–18, 321, 325, 331, 348, 354, 357–9, 363, 369
  Art 13 . . . 46, 113, 369
  Art 14 . . . 76, 264, 308
  Arts 14–15 . . . 262
  Art 14(2) . . . 263, 412
  Art 17 . . . 24, 318, 345, 348, 357, 359, 363–4
  Art 18 . . . 24, 315, 345, 348, 354, 356–7, 360, 363–4
  Art 18(1) . . . 358
  Art 19 . . . 364

Art 23 . . . 267, 272
Arts 23–25 . . . 262
Art 24 . . . 264
Art 25 . . . 262, 267, 271–2, 289
Arts 26–27 . . . 262
Art 28 . . . 279–84, 286, 288–9, 291–6, 298–303
Arts 28–30 . . . 263, 294
Art 29 . . . 209, 279–80, 284, 290
Art 30 . . . 263, 270, 279, 284, 286–91, 293–6, 298–9, 302
Art 34 . . . 109
Art 34(2) . . . 247–9, 369
Art 34(3) . . . 112
Art 39 . . . 71, 109, 309, 317, 321, 325–6, 357, 360
Arts 39–42 . . . 309
Art 39(2) . . . 109, 112
Art 39(4) . . . 308
Art 40 . . . 71, 88, 321
Art 42 . . . 84
Art 43 . . . 334, 369
Arts 43–48 . . . 309, 319
Art 43(2) . . . 234
Art 45 . . . 342
Art 47 . . . 321
Art 49 . . . 334, 347, 357, 361
Arts 49–55 . . . 309, 319
Art 50 . . . 320, 354, 369
Art 52 . . . 135, 321
Art 53 . . . 321
Art 61 . . . 242
Art 74 . . . 242
Art 75 . . . 242
Art 81 . . . 210, 226
Art 82 . . . 226
Art 83(2)(a) . . . 61
Art 84 . . . 242
Art 86 . . . 94, 369
Art 88(2) . . . 175
Art 90 . . . 263, 267, 271–5, 369
Art 90(1) . . . 273
Art 90(2) . . . 276
Art 93 . . . 51
Art 94 . . . 51, 76–8, 84, 263

Art 95 . . . 51, 76–8, 81, 84, 86, 263, 265
Art 95(9) . . . 175
Art 100 . . . 28
Art 103 . . . 28
Art 106 . . . 28
Art 118a . . . 401
Art 119 . . . 51, 78, 131–2, 371, 374–5, 377, 384, 401
Arts 131–133 . . . 36
Art 133 . . . 44, 107
Art 136 . . . 372
Art 137 . . . 66, 109, 369, 372
Art 141 . . . 51, 109, 112, 369, 372–5, 378–81, 387–8, 397, 399, 401
Art 141(3) . . . 386
Art 141(4) . . . 397
Arts 149–152 . . . 66
Art 149(2) . . . 359
Art 152 . . . 79, 81
Art 157 . . . 66
Art 189 . . . 53, 123
Arts 189–201 . . . 53
Art 190(4) . . . 54
Art 191 . . . 54
Art 192 . . . 28, 43, 55–6
Art 193 . . . 56
Art 197 . . . 56
Art 200 . . . 56
Art 201 . . . 42
Art 202 . . . 43, 45, 92–3
Arts 202–210 . . . 44
Art 205 . . . 46, 48
Art 207 . . . 51
Art 207(2) . . . 51
Art 208 . . . 43
Art 211 . . . 43, 92–3
Arts 211–219 . . . 41
Art 213 . . . 41
Art 214 . . . 41, 45, 55
Art 216 . . . 42
Art 217 . . . 42
Art 219 . . . 44
Art 220 . . . 57, 60, 109
Art 221 . . . 58
Arts 221–223 . . . 58
Art 225 . . . 57, 63–4
Art 225a . . . 64
Art 226 . . . 43, 60, 154, 173, 177, 182, 206, 208, 223, 242
Arts 226–228 . . . 61, 100, 152
Arts 226–243 . . . 60
Art 227 . . . 173–4, 184–5
Art 228 . . . 61, 173–4, 182–3, 242
Art 229 . . . 183
Art 230 . . . 43, 57, 60, 64–5, 81, 83, 100, 105, 109, 152, 159, 167, 219–20, 222–3, 226, 234, 236–40, 243–4, 253–5

Arts 230–232 . . . 61
Art 230(2) . . . 232, 235
Art 231 . . . 223, 235
Art 232 . . . 57, 61, 100, 152, 176, 219, 239–44
Art 233 . . . 235, 242
Art 234 . . . 60–1, 63–4, 100, 139, 142, 152–5, 157–61, 168, 171, 216, 235, 237–8, 253, 255, 337
Art 235 . . . 61, 219, 243–4
Art 236 . . . 61
Art 238 . . . 61
Art 239 . . . 186
Art 241 . . . 61, 100, 219, 238, 253–5
Art 242 . . . 181
Arts 242–243 . . . 173–4
Art 243 . . . 170, 181
Art 244 . . . 108
Arts 246–248 . . . 65
Art 249 . . . 88, 103–5, 107, 121, 190, 195–6, 203, 207, 222–4, 226
Art 251 . . . 45, 55, 84, 88
Art 253 . . . 106, 233
Art 254 . . . 104–6, 197
Arts 257–262 . . . 65
Arts 263–265 . . . 66
Arts 271–273 . . . 44
Art 272 . . . 56
Art 273 . . . 56
Arts 274–276 . . . 44
Art 276 . . . 65
Art 281 . . . 36
Art 287 . . . 246
Art 288 . . . 83, 97, 100, 109, 152, 167, 219, 242–4, 249
Art 288(1) . . . 242
Art 288(2) . . . 61, 208, 243–4
Art 292 . . . 121, 185
Arts 296–298 . . . 175
Art 300 . . . 28, 36, 44, 55, 61, 107, 233
Art 300(6) . . . 60
Arts 302–304 . . . 107
Art 308 . . . 51, 77–8, 144
Art 310 . . . 55, 107
Art 311 . . . 80
Art 372 . . . 45
Title IV . . . 26
European Atomic Energy Community (EURATOM) Treaty . . . 9, 11, 35, 101
European Coal and Steel Community (ECSC) Treaty (former) . . . 8–9, 18, 35, 40, 101
Art 33 . . . 234
European Convention for the Protection of Human Rights and Fundamental Freedoms (ECHR) . . . 51, 55, 78, 110–12, 118, 128, 145, 215, 340, 347, 351, 362, 387, 404
Art 6 . . . 111, 113, 215, 400

Art 7 . . . 111
Art 8 . . . 111, 347, 351, 361–2
Art 13 . . . 111, 113, 215
Protocol 1, Art 1 . . . 110
European Economic Area Treaty (EEA) . . .
14, 60

General Agreement on Tariffs and Trade
(GATT) . . . 7, 44, 76, 107–8, 198–9, 266,
411
General Agreement on Trade in Services
(GATS) . . . 76, 411

Lisbon Treaty . . . 5, 11, 18, 21, 27, 30–2,
36–7, 40–1, 43–7, 49–50, 52–3, 55, 57–8,
63, 65–6, 72–3, 80, 83, 85–7, 90, 92–4,
97, 99, 101–3, 106, 110–11, 121, 129, 140,
144, 169–70, 176, 184, 187, 202, 216,
221–2, 225–6, 232, 235, 267, 304, 312,
352, 356, 369, 374, 408
Declaration No. 1 . . . 111, 409
Declaration No. 7 . . . 48, 50
Declaration No. 17 . . . 121, 126
Declaration No. 18 . . . 72
Declaration No. 24 . . . 72
Declaration No. 38 . . . 58
Declaration No. 41 . . . 78
Declaration No. 42 . . . 72, 78
Protocol 2 . . . 80, 82
    Art 8 . . . 81
Protocol 4 . . . 65
Protocol 6 . . . 53
Protocol 30 . . . 35
Protocol 33 . . . 377–8
Protocol 36 . . . 48, 50
    Art 3(3) . . . 49
Luxembourg Accords . . . 12, 18–19, 47,
265

Maastricht Treaty 1992 . . . 5, 21, 24, 26, 40,
74, 97, 101, 138, 140, 143–4, 174, 356,
373
Art B . . . 25
Merger Treaty of 1965 . . . 8–9, 18, 101

Single European Act 1986 . . . 13–14, 21–3,
34, 47, 54–5, 63, 74, 79, 91, 93, 97–8,
101, 144, 265, 350, 373
Preamble . . . 22–3
Art 2 . . . 52
Statute of the Court of Justice . . . 58
Art 2 . . . 59
Art 20 . . . 59
Art 23a . . . 162
Art 46 . . . 243
Art 50 . . . 63
Art 62a . . . 59

Trade-Related Aspects of Intellectual Property
Rights (TRIPS) Agreement . . . 76, 412
Treaty of Amsterdam 1997 . . . 21, 26–8, 55,
62, 80, 85–7, 97, 101, 103, 113, 144, 193,
225, 371–2, 374, 403
Treaty of Nice 2001 . . . 21, 28–9, 41–2, 49,
86, 97, 101
Treaty on European Union (TEU) . . . 5, 11,
17–18, 21, 24–6, 31, 34, 43, 45, 47, 51–2,
55, 58, 60, 64–6, 78–80, 97–9, 101–2,
106, 109, 112, 140, 144, 174, 183, 200,
203, 207, 225, 232, 240, 263, 266, 356,
369, 377–8, 404
Preamble . . . 98–9
Art 1 . . . 71, 79 80, 101
Art 2 . . . 17, 98, 369, 372
Arts 2–3 . . . 109
Arts 2–4 . . . 99
Art 3 . . . 36, 71, 98, 108, 263, 369, 372
Arts 3–4 . . . 262
Arts 3–6 . . . 62
Art 3(2) . . . 308–9
Art 3(4) . . . 98
Art 4 . . . 52, 71, 108, 194
Art 4(3) . . . 98–9, 121, 123, 125, 174–5,
194, 200, 203, 207, 215
Art 5 . . . 25, 71, 80, 82, 117
Art 5(1) . . . 71, 79
Art 5(2) . . . 71
Art 5(3) . . . 79–80
Art 6 . . . 28, 80, 109
Art 6(1) . . . 102, 111
Art 6(2) . . . 51, 112
Art 6(3) . . . 112
Art 7 . . . 28, 80, 91, 112
Art 8 . . . 18, 36
Art 11 . . . 43
Arts 11–12 . . . 87
Art 13 . . . 40, 46, 52, 65, 80, 113, 225,
240, 369, 372, 387, 403–5
Art 13(2) . . . 232
Art 13(4) . . . 40
Art 14 . . . 53, 55
Art 14(1) . . . 55
Art 14(2) . . . 52–3
Art 15 . . . 52
Art 15(1) . . . 52
Art 15(2) . . . 52
Art 15(3) . . . 52
Art 15(6) . . . 52–3
Art 16 . . . 44, 50
Art 16(1) . . . 45
Art 16(3) . . . 46, 48
Art 16(7) . . . 51
Art 16(8) . . . 45
Art 16(9) . . . 45
Art 17 . . . 41, 43, 174

Art 17(2) . . . 43
Art 17(3) . . . 41–2
Art 17(5) . . . 41, 52
Art 17(6) . . . 42–3, 56
Art 17(7) . . . 41, 45, 55
Art 17(8) . . . 42, 56
Art 18 . . . 52–3
Art 18(1) . . . 41–2
Art 18(4) . . . 41
Art 19 . . . 60, 109
Art 19(1) . . . 57, 216, 237
Art 19(3) . . . 60
Art 20 . . . 17, 27–8
Art 21 . . . 43
Arts 21–46 . . . 36
Arts 23–46 . . . 36
Art 27 . . . 53
Art 27(2) . . . 51
Art 40 . . . 60
Art 46 . . . 137
Art 48 . . . 91, 137
Arts 48–49 . . . 94
Art 49 . . . 17, 55, 91, 112
Art 50 . . . 91
Art 51 . . . 80
Art 267 . . . 64
Art 294 . . . 45
Art 300(3) . . . 91
Art 310 . . . 91
Treaty on the Functioning of the European
    Union (TFEU) . . . 5, 9, 47, 60, 64, 71–2, 79,
    87–8, 91, 94, 97–102, 106–9, 179, 307,
    345
Preamble . . . 97, 99
Art 1 . . . 101
Art 2 . . . 97
Arts 2–13 . . . 99
Art 2(3) . . . 98
Art 3 . . . 72, 97, 263, 265–6
Arts 3–4 . . . 262
Arts 3–6 . . . 71
Art 4 . . . 73
Art 6 . . . 73, 359
Art 8 . . . 108, 369
Arts 8–10 . . . 109
Art 10 . . . 369
Art 18 . . . 62, 99, 108–9, 112, 121, 123,
    175, 194, 212, 262, 310, 317–18, 321,
    325, 327, 331, 348, 353–4, 357–9, 361,
    363, 365, 369, 404
Arts 18–19 . . . 109
Art 19 . . . 46, 91, 113, 369, 372, 387,
    403–5, 407
Art 20 . . . 308, 318, 345, 348, 356–9,
    363–4, 366
Arts 20–21 . . . 24
Art 20(2) . . . 309

Art 21 . . . 308, 345, 348, 354, 356–8,
    360–1, 363–4
Art 22 . . . 364
Art 26 . . . 76, 264, 308–9
Arts 26–27 . . . 262
Art 26(2) . . . 263
Art 28 . . . 272, 304
Arts 28–30 . . . 262, 271
Arts 28–32 . . . 264
Art 29 . . . 266
Art 30 . . . 192, 262, 267, 271–2, 289
Arts 31–32 . . . 262
Art 32 . . . 267
Art 34 . . . 279–86, 288–9, 291–304
Arts 34–36 . . . 263, 281, 294
Art 35 . . . 209, 216, 279–80, 284, 290
Art 36 . . . 263, 270, 279–80, 284–91,
    293–9, 302–4
Art 39(1) . . . 341
Art 39(4) . . . 341
Art 40 . . . 109
Art 40(2) . . . 112, 247–9, 369
Art 45 . . . 71, 109, 309, 312, 317, 321,
    325–7, 341, 346, 357, 360, 369
Arts 45–48 . . . 309
Arts 45–62 . . . 313
Art 45(1) . . . 309
Art 45(2) . . . 112, 309
Art 45(3) . . . 310, 322, 338
Art 45(3)(d) . . . 330
Art 45(4) . . . 308, 310, 341
Art 46 . . . 71, 88, 321
Art 48 . . . 84
Art 49 . . . 310, 312, 319, 321, 331, 333–4,
    369
Arts 49–55 . . . 309, 319
Art 50 . . . 331
Art 51 . . . 342
Art 52 . . . 338
Art 53 . . . 321, 331
Art 56 . . . 215, 310, 312, 319, 321, 331–4,
    347, 350, 353, 357, 361, 369
Arts 56–62 . . . 309, 319
Art 57 . . . 319–20, 353–4
Art 57(1) . . . 319
Art 59 . . . 84, 321, 331
Art 60 . . . 216
Art 62 . . . 338
Art 67 . . . 352
Arts 67–74 . . . 352
Art 67(2) . . . 352
Art 75 . . . 352
Arts 77–79 . . . 352
Arts 77–80 . . . 350
Art 101 . . . 210
Arts 101–102 . . . 226
Art 103(2)(a) . . . 61

Art 106 . . . 94, 369
Art 108(2) . . . 175
Art 110 . . . 193, 263, 267, 271–5, 369
Art 110(1) . . . 273–5
Art 110(2) . . . 273–6
Art 113 . . . 51
Art 114 . . . 51, 76–8, 81, 84, 263, 265
Art 114(9) . . . 175
Art 115 . . . 51, 76, 78, 84, 263
Art 126 . . . 91
Art 134 . . . 66
Art 151 . . . 372
Arts 151–169 . . . 100
Art 153 . . . 66, 109, 369, 372
Art 154 . . . 401
Art 157 . . . 51, 109, 112, 193, 368–9,
    371–9, 381–5, 387–8, 397, 401, 409
Art 157(1) . . . 374
Art 157(2) . . . 374
Art 157(3) . . . 386
Art 157(4) . . . 397–8
Art 165 . . . 359
Arts 165–168 . . . 66
Art 166 . . . 353
Art 168 . . . 81
Art 168(5) . . . 79
Art 173 . . . 66
Art 192 . . . 91
Arts 205–207 . . . 36
Arts 205–222 . . . 36
Art 207 . . . 44, 107
Art 217 . . . 91, 107
Art 218 . . . 36, 44, 55, 61, 91, 107, 233
Art 218(11) . . . 60
Art 220 . . . 107
Art 223 . . . 91
Arts 223–234 . . . 53
Arts 223–287 . . . 40
Art 223(1) . . . 54
Art 224 . . . 54
Art 225 . . . 43, 56
Art 226 . . . 56
Arts 227–228 . . . 56
Art 230 . . . 56
Art 233 . . . 56
Art 234 . . . 56
Art 234(3) . . . 163
Art 234(4) . . . 51
Art 235(1) . . . 52
Art 236 . . . 44–5
Arts 237–243 . . . 44
Art 238 . . . 47, 50
Art 238(3) . . . 50
Art 238(4) . . . 46
Art 240(2) . . . 51, 244
Art 241 . . . 43, 45
Art 244 . . . 52

Arts 244–250 . . . 41
Art 245 . . . 41–2
Art 246 . . . 42
Art 247 . . . 42–3
Art 250 . . . 44
Art 251 . . . 58
Art 252 . . . 58, 91
Arts 253–254 . . . 58
Art 254 . . . 63
Art 255 . . . 58
Art 256 . . . 63–4
Arts 256–279 . . . 60
Art 256(3) . . . 64
Art 257 . . . 57, 64
Art 258 . . . 43, 60, 154, 173–82, 184–7,
    192, 206, 208, 223, 242, 254
Arts 258–260 . . . 61, 100, 152, 187
Art 259 . . . 173–4, 184–5, 187
Art 260 . . . 61, 173–4, 182–4, 187, 208,
    242
Art 261 . . . 183
Art 263 . . . 43, 57–8, 60, 64–5, 81,
    83, 100, 105–6, 109, 152, 159, 167,
    219–28, 232, 234, 236–40, 243–4, 247,
    253–6
Arts 263–265 . . . 61
Art 263(2) . . . 232
Art 263(4) . . . 225
Art 263(6) . . . 224
Art 264 . . . 235
Art 264(2) . . . 235
Art 265 . . . 57, 61, 100, 152, 176, 239–44,
    255
Art 265(1) . . . 239
Art 265(2) . . . 241
Art 265(3) . . . 240
Art 266 . . . 235
Art 266(1) . . . 242
Art 267 . . . 60–1, 63–4, 100, 139–40,
    142, 146, 151, 151–71, 177, 235, 237–9,
    253, 255, 337
Art 267(2) . . . 161
Art 267(3) . . . 161, 163–4
Art 268 . . . 61, 219, 239, 242–4
Art 270 . . . 61
Art 272 . . . 61
Art 273 . . . 186
Art 275 . . . 60
Art 276 . . . 60
Art 277 . . . 61, 100, 219–20, 238–9,
    253–6
Art 278 . . . 181
Arts 278–279 . . . 173–4
Art 279 . . . 170, 181
Art 280 . . . 108
Arts 282–284 . . . 65
Arts 285–287 . . . 65

Art 288 . . . 103–5, 107, 118, 121, 123, 190, 195–6, 203, 207, 222–4, 226–7
Art 289 . . . 45, 55, 87–8, 92, 232
Arts 289–290 . . . 103
Art 290 . . . 55
Art 290 . . . 43, 45, 92, 106, 232
Arts 290–291 . . . 93
Art 290(2) . . . 93
Art 291 . . . 43, 94
Art 294 . . . 55, 84, 88
Art 295 . . . 105
Art 296 . . . 79, 83, 86, 104, 106, 233
Art 297 . . . 103–6, 197
Art 300 . . . 65
Arts 301–304 . . . 65
Arts 305–307 . . . 66
Art 308 . . . 66
Art 314 . . . 45, 56
Arts 314–315 . . . 57
Arts 314–316 . . . 44
Art 315 . . . 56

Arts 317–319 . . . 44
Art 319 . . . 65
Arts 326–334 . . . 27–8
Art 332 . . . 91
Art 339 . . . 246
Art 340 . . . 83, 97, 100, 109, 152, 167, 208, 219–20, 239, 242–4, 249–50, 254–6
Art 340(1) . . . 242
Art 340(2) . . . 61, 239, 243, 247
Art 344 . . . 121, 185
Arts 346–348 . . . 175
Art 352 . . . 51, 72, 77–8, 85, 137, 144, 386
Art 352(2) . . . 78
Art 352(3) . . . 78
Art 352(4) . . . 78
Art 367 . . . 216

World Trade Organization (WTO) Agreements . . . 107, 251

Part 1
Institutional law

The establishment and development of the European Union

Learning objectives

This chapter will first of all provide an overview of why and how the European Union (EU) was established and how it developed. In doing so, it will pay special attention to the two parallel developments in the history of the Communities and the EU known as 'widening' and 'deepening'. After considering these developments, the chapter will then explore the relationship with the UK and how the UK fitted into this development. Finally, it will consider the external relations of the EU. Hence this chapter will enable you to understand:

• why the Union (at first called the Communities) was originally set up;

• how the Communities were first established;

- the perceived aims and goals, and how those aims and goals have changed;
- the expansion and development of the Communities and Union;
- the increase in policies and integration;
- the UK's role in this history;
- the external relations of the EU; and
- where we are today with the EU – developing news.

Introduction

Reasons for considering EU history

As with many things, particularly legal rules, they are easier to understand and rationalize if you are aware of why they were established in the first place. Any study of the law on courses of 'European Union law' and, as it was previously entitled, 'European Community law', must start with a consideration of the history and development of the Union. Without this, it will be much more difficult. Looking at the past helps us to understand why the EU has taken the form it has today, the pressures involved in this process and why certain decisions were taken, along its history. In any subject, merely learning the rules does not help you to understand the purpose for which they were enacted and the reasons that led to them. This is even more the case with the EU. Many of the laws, whilst clearly aimed at specific topics such as ensuring free movement of goods or persons, or requiring the equality of treatment of different groups, or regulating the recognition of a profession in the member states, are a compromise of different perspectives. In the EU, these perspectives come from the different member states, the different cultural understandings, different histories, and different social and economic backgrounds, hence the treaties and laws that have been produced under the Treaties are often achieved only as a compromise. On their own, the individual rules may not make a great deal of sense; with an understanding of the history and development, hopefully, they might make a great deal more sense.

Section 1.4 will consider in more depth two particular aspects of this development: namely, the expansion and further integration of the Communities and Union, which are referred to as 'widening and deepening'.

Explanation of the terms 'European Communities' and 'European Union'

A brief mention needs to be made here in respect of the terms 'European Union' and 'European Community' because their use can be confusing. The term 'European Union' was brought in by the Treaty on European Union (TEU, which is also known and referred to as the Maastricht Treaty – just to make matters more complicated!), and describes the extension by the member states into additional policies and areas of cooperation. Even though the Lisbon Treaty, following its amendment of the EC and EU Treaties, has now established definitively that the European Union be known exactly as that, this was not always the case, and whilst the history and development sections that follow will make this clear, it is nevertheless useful now to outline the previous terms used as you will come across them. Prior to the changes brought about by the TEU, three original Communities existed: the European Coal and Steel Community (ECSC), the European Economic Community (EEC) and the European Atomic Energy Community (EURATOM). The TEU brought these together under one so-called 'pillar' and renamed the EEC Treaty simply as the European Community (EC) Treaty. It also added two further pillars, dealing with Common Foreign and Security Policy (CFSP) and Provisions on Police and Judicial Cooperation in Criminal Matters. Note that the ECSC has now expired and no longer exists. The organization in three pillars was often illustrated in the form of a classical Greek temple.

cross reference
We will come back to the discussion about why the Communities evolved in this way and the difference between the pillars in section 1.5.8.

When the Lisbon Treaty came into force on 1 December 2009, the term 'Community' was replaced by the term 'Union' and it is now correct to refer only to the European Union. Most EU law courses and indeed books did not consider matters previously in the old second and third pillars in any depth, if at all. However, following the Lisbon Treaty, the three-pillar structure was broken up. The CFSP has been kept in the EU Treaty and the freedom, security and justice matters that were in the third pillar are now organized in a Title of the Treaty on the Functioning of the EU. Hence, then, for the most part, the term 'Community' has been replaced by 'Union' in this book, except where the context demands otherwise. It remains to be seen whether EU law courses will be expanded to incorporate freedom, security and justice matters.

1.1

Why was the Union set up? The motives for European integration

This section will go through the various factors that combined to persuade at first two European states, and then six, to start the process of European integration.

For more details on this section scan here or visit the Online Resource Centre.

1.1.1 **Reaction to the World Wars: the desire for peace**

Even a cursory glance at European history will reveal just how long Europeans have been fighting and killing each other. The ultimate in the series of wars was, of course, the Second World War, in which some 55 million souls worldwide, but mostly in Europe, lost their lives. There have been centuries of invasions, occupations and dictatorial rule in most, if not all, of the countries of Europe at some stage. With this firmly in mind, it should come as no surprise that the very strong reaction after the Second World War to this death and destruction was a very important and motivating factor in the moves to create a more peaceful and stable European environment in which countries could develop and prosper without resorting to the obliteration or subjugation of others. It is all too easy, in this period of relative European peace and stability now, to understate this motive. Of course, there are reasons underlying the violence and featuring large is the desire to unify Europe, and, in pursuit of this goal, for one country or ethnic group to impose its culture, often including language or religion or government, on others. Unfortunately, most of these attempts have not been peaceful and, over the ages, these attempts have affected the majority of the citizens of Europe. Generally, the attempts to unite, from the Romans to the Second World War, have led to wholesale loss of life, even attempted genocide and that ghastly modern euphemism for the same, 'ethnic cleansing'. It is therefore this bleak, but simple and understandable, backdrop that led to an increased desire to do something to stop the cycle of wars that caused so much death and destruction. Whilst, over the centuries, there had been ideas and discussions to unite European nations, particularly following the First World War, it was only after the Second World War that these desires and expressions found substantive fruition.

1.1.2 **Security against the rising Soviet threat**

At the time, a further and developing factor that considerably influenced the desire on the part of the European nations to cooperate was the deteriorating relations between the former Allied powers. It was not long after the Americans, British and the Russians had met victoriously in the streets of Berlin in 1945 that the understandings between those countries broke down and they became increasingly suspicious of each other. UK Prime Minister and war premier Winston Churchill described in March 1946 in Fulton, Missouri, the situation of increasing Soviet influence and control over eastern Europe, in a borrowed phrase that was taken up generally, as a kind of 'Iron Curtain' that had descended between western and eastern Europe. The general situation came to be described as the 'Cold War' and lasted in lesser and greater states of tension until the collapse of Communism in Europe in 1989–90. With this increased fear of the possible expansion and domination of Europe by the Soviet Union, combined with the then existing Soviet strict control over the countries of eastern Europe, the tension mounted in the late 1940s and throughout the 1950s. At its worst, in the 1960s, the Cold War threatened the nuclear annihilation of the opposing parties. It thus became increasingly important that the countries of western Europe integrate amongst themselves to form a bulwark against further Soviet expansion. The Cold War was thus a clear and real catalyst for western European integration.

1.1.3 **Political willingness**

The period following the Second World War saw a number of moves towards the integration of European nation states. Political and economic cooperation and development between nations was regarded as crucial to replace the economic competition that was viewed as a major factor in the outbreak of wars between European nation states. Some of these moves were taking place within a worldwide effort for greater political cooperation between nation states, the most notable being the establishment of the United Nations in 1945 and the Council of Europe in 1949.

1.1.4 Economic development

There were also inherently economically motivated steps towards international cooperation that resulted in the establishment of such organizations as the International Monetary Fund (IMF), the General Agreement on Tariffs and Trade (GATT) and, most notably, the Marshall Plan, which funded the establishment of the Organization for European Economic Corporation (OEEC) and later the Organization for Economic Cooperation and Development (OECD), designed initially to finance the post-war reconstruction of Europe.

1.1.5 Summary of underlying motives and initial goals

cross reference

A longer look at the relationship between the UK and the European Union will be taken in section 1.6.

When we come to the three European Communities, which were the forerunners of the European Union that we have today, the ultimate goals are not so distinctly discernible. As remains the case today, even before the foundation of the Communities, there was a conflict of opinion between those who wished to see European integration take the form of a much more involved model, such as a federal model, and those who wished merely to see a purely economic form of integration, such as a free-trade area. The first steps were, predictably, a compromise between the political, economic and social desires of various parties. The scene was set by the address by Winston Churchill at the University of Zurich in September 1946, and his call to build 'a kind of United States of Europe' and in particular the brave (for the time) call for a partnership between France and Germany. However, even within that speech, Churchill and Britain did not envisage a role as a key participant and instead saw Britain as being outside any general European integration, alongside the United States and Russia, observing and assisting the rise of a European state from the ashes of the destruction of the Second World War.

1.2 The founding of the European Communities

This section looks at the mechanics of how the Communities and Union were established.

1.2.1 The Schuman Plan (1950)

For more details on this section scan here or visit the Online Resource Centre.

cross reference

Customs unions are defined in Chapter 10, section 10.2.2.

The climate was certainly ready for a greater form of integration in Europe and the first direct impetus for the Communities came in the form of the plan proposed in May 1950 by the French Foreign Minister, Robert Schuman, in conjunction with the research and plans of Jean Monnet, a French government official. They proposed the linking of the French and German coal and steel industries, which would be taken out of the hands of the nation states and put under the control of a supranational body. This would not only help economic recovery, but would also remove the disastrous competition between the two states. It was aimed to make future war not only unthinkable, but also materially impossible, because it put control over coal and steel production, vital then for the production of armaments and thus the capability of waging war, in the hands of a supranational authority and not the individual states. The plan was deliberately left open for other European countries to join in its discussions. The UK, however, was reluctant to involve itself, even in the negotiations. The plan was readily accepted by Germany under Chancellor Adenauer, and Belgium, the Netherlands and Luxembourg, which form the Benelux nations, had already moved ahead with their customs union and also saw the benefits to be gained from membership and this form of integration. Italy also considered it to be in its economic interest to join and, perhaps more importantly, considered it to be a defence against Communist takeover. Therefore, six nations went ahead to sign the European Coal and Steel Community Treaty in Paris in 1951, which entered into force on 1 January 1952. This first form of integration was thus both politically and economically motivated.

1.2.2 **The ECSC**

The ECSC Treaty was a mix of both intergovernmental and supranational integration, as the institutions set up included both the High Authority (which was later renamed the 'European Commission' by the 1965 Merger Treaty), a supranational body, and the Council of Ministers from the member states, an essentially intergovernmental body. Whilst the Community established did not fulfil all of the wishes of Jean Monnet, who was a federalist, he was appointed the first President of the High Authority. The degree of integration that it achieved was, without any doubt, a very important and indispensable first step from which further integration could follow. Indeed, it was assumed by some, the so-called neofunctionalists, that further integration would be inevitable as successful integration in one area was assumed to spill over into other areas of integration. The ECSC Treaty expired in 2002, but its enduring tasks and commitments were assumed by the EC Treaty.

cross reference

*Intergovern-
mentalism,
supranationalism
and federalism are
defined at section
1.3.1.1.*

1.2.3 **The proposed European Defence Community and European Political Community**

The Schuman Plan, which formed the basis of the ECSC, was not the only proposal for integration being discussed and negotiated at the time. Monnet put forward a proposal (the 'Pleven Plan') for a European Defence Community (EDC) in 1952. In addition, because it was argued to be politically and practically necessary, in support of that a European Political Community (EPC) was also proposed in 1953, to provide overseeing political control and foreign policy for the EDC. The proposals and the negotiations proved to be complex and were drawn out because they were surrounded by other political considerations such as the expansion of Communism in south-east Asia and fears in respect of the rearmament of West Germany. Both of these proposals, with hindsight, were premature and far too ambitious for the time. They faced opposition from outside the ECSC, the UK in particular, and from within the Community, most notably and fundamentally France, which after some prevarication failed to ratify the EDC in the National Assembly. Even today, the prospect of a common European army and political union is very radical; then, it was probably unrealistic.

1.2.4 **Progress to the EEC and EURATOM Treaties**

It might have been thought that the unfortunate failure to agree the EDC would have put paid to any further attempts at European integration and it was without a doubt a blow to the European federalists. However, rather than jeopardize any such attempts, it appeared to strengthen the resolve of some of the original six member states to take matters further. Once again, Jean Monnet was centrally involved. He had resigned as President of the ECSC High Authority in order to promote European integration. Working in particular with the Benelux nations, it was proposed that rather than leave the integration to two industries, the nations should integrate the many more aspects of their economies. Thus, following the Messina Intergovernmental Conference in 1955, the Spaak Report (named after the Belgian

Prime Minister) was prepared to consider the establishment of an Economic Community and, an Atomic Energy Community for energy and the peaceful use of nuclear power. There were also additional external catalysts for further integration, including the Algerian war of independence, the Soviet suppression of the 1956 Hungarian Uprising, and the Suez Canal invasion by France and the UK. This last event served to highlight the real politics at play in the world in the 1950s and the precarious position of individual nation states in Europe, which no longer wielded the influence that they had done prior to the Second World War. All of this assisted in bringing the European Treaty negotiations to a much quicker and more successful conclusion. Thus, in 1957, the Treaties of Rome were agreed by the same six nations establishing the European Economic Community Treaty and the European Atomic Energy Community Treaty. The latter was established to promote the peaceful use of nuclear power and is still in operation.

At first, all three Communities each had their own institutions, but shared a Court of Justice and the parliamentary assembly. The separate institutions were later merged under the Treaty establishing a single Council and a single Commission of the European Communities (the Merger Treaty) in 1965, which entered into force in 1967 and the provisions of which have been incorporated into the present Treaties. Due to the range of subject matters and policies covered, the EEC Treaty was the most important.

The ECSC Treaty, established for fifty years only, expired in 2002 and the EC Treaty (now TFEU) then took over the obligations and responsibilities arising under the ECSC Treaty.

1.3 The basic objectives and nature of the Communities

9

1.3.1 Was there an ultimate federal goal for the Union?

With the initial three Treaties established, what the Communities were intended to do and how they were supposed to function should be considered. The formal aims of the Communities can readily be seen by looking at the preambles to the original Treaties. The stated general aims included the creation of the Common Market, which was to be achieved by abolishing obstacles to the freedom of movement of all of the factors of production: namely, goods, workers, providers of services, and capital. The EEC Treaty also provided for the abolition of customs duties between the member states and the application of a common customs tariff to imports from third countries. There were to be common policies in the spheres of agriculture and transport, and a system ensuring that competition in the Common Market not be distorted by the activities of cartels or market monopolists. A limited start was also made with a social policy and a regional policy. Apart from these formally set-out objectives, there has been a debate older than the Communities themselves as to whether there was a grand plan for the integration of Europe. Even if it was not originally clear that the 'pooling of resources', as then termed, by a transfer of sovereign powers meant that the Communities took over in certain agreed areas, this was made clear not long afterwards by the European Court of Justice in its landmark decisions in *Van Gend en Loos* and *Costa* v *ENEL*.

cross reference
These cases will be fully explored in Chapter 5, section 5.1.1.

At this stage, some terms of integration need to be considered.

1.3.1.1 Intergovernmentalism, supranationalism and federalism

The terms **intergovernmentalism**, **supranationalism** and **federalism** are employed to describe the forms of integration.

. . . .

intergovernmentalism

This is the normal way in which international organizations work, the decisions of which require unanimity and are rarely enforceable, and if so only between the signatory states and not the citizens of those states. The clearest examples are the United Nations or the World Trade Organization (WTO).

supranationalism

This describes the fact that the decision-making takes place at a new and higher level than that of the member states themselves and that such decisions replace or override national rules.

federalism

This is a rather flexible term in that it can refer to a fairly wide band of integration models, but essentially, for the purposes of this discussion, it is used to mean that there will also be a form of political integration whereby the constituent states transfer sovereign powers to the federation, which will control the activities of the members from the centre. There are plenty of examples of states set up on a federal basis in the world, including the United States, Germany, Canada, Australia, Switzerland and Belgium. Certain local issues are still regulated by the constituent states, such as education, culture and land management, but most economic and political power is transferred to the centre, including, most notably, defence and trade.

. . . .

1.3.1.2 Integration in the Communities and EU

A debate continues as to whether the Communities were supposed to integrate only in the specific areas as originally set out in the ECSC and EEC Treaties and arguably confined largely to free trade, or whether something more dynamic was intended. It was originally considered that because there was success in certain policies, this would automatically lead to a spillover from one area to another, thus bringing about increasing integration. This is termed 'functional integration' or 'neo-functionalism'. Others have described this as 'creeping federalism'. In fact, it was considered that, in order for the original policies to work properly, there had to be continuing integration, otherwise the whole project would probably first stagnate and then roll backwards to collapse. Thus sector-by-sector integration and the process of European union was regarded as an inevitable process.

For example, the setting of common trade tariffs and the establishment of the Common Market for the free circulation of goods would require and lead to exchange rates being stabilized to ensure that production factors and costs in the member states were broadly equal. This in turn requires monetary union to be established to ensure that exchange rates do not drift apart, and this requires full economic union to be achieved so that the value of different components of the common currency is not changed by different economic and fiscal policies in different countries. Clearly, then, the fiscal policies must be integrated, and this economic integration would require that political integration would have to follow in order to provide stable and consistent policy control over the economic conditions applying in the Community. The difficulties experienced by Greece and the eurozone from 2010 onwards and the attempts to impose stricter financial and economic rules in 2011–12 highlight this aspect.

According to this view, federalism, in some form, would thus seem to be the probable outcome of this process. Such an outcome, though, is a highly contested one. Only a few persons have argued openly for this degree of integration, although some of the founding fathers of the Community – Monnet, Schuman and Spaak – had expected that sector-by-sector functional integration would lead slowly to ever greater degrees of federalism. It is also arguable that an agenda of federalism has been buried under the euphemisms 'a closer' or 'ever closer' Union, which are terms that have been used in the EEC Treaty (which became the EC Treaty in 1993) and in the TEU, in order to make the progress to the ultimate destination of the Communities and Union more acceptable, although it is unclear, and arguably deliberately so, whether they refer to federalism or something short of that. The TEU, as amended by the Lisbon Treaty, carries on in this vein by using the words 'continue the process of creating an ever closer Union'. The original plans put forward by Monnet for the ECSC may have been much more federal in nature and openly so, particularly as the Community was to be governed by a supranational High Authority only, but it was at the insistence of the member states that the original ECSC Treaty established a Council of Ministers, clearly intergovernmental, and a parliamentary assembly of member state representatives. This mixed model was followed in both the EURATOM and EEC Treaties. Therefore, while the Communities and some of its institutions do operate on the supranational level, it does not signify an inevitable move to federalism.

cross reference

This topic will be considered further in the end-of-chapter Summary after the developments to date have been outlined.

Despite the failure of the EDC and EPC, the ECSC remained successful and was complemented in 1957 by the other two Communities. The EEC proved immediately to be a success under the leadership of the first EEC Commission President, the German Walter Hallstein, and it was far more political in outlook, despite the contrary view of de Gaulle, as to how the Communities should be organized and governed. The success of the EEC seemed to give support to the neofunctionalist view that success in one sector would lead inevitably to success in other sectors and assist the process of European integration. Indeed, the success in the area of the common customs tariff appeared to work as envisaged by the neofunctionalists/federalists, and led to spillover into other areas and in particular to create further pressure for the reform of the Common Agricultural Policy (CAP). This form of functionalism was adopted deliberately by the High Authority and later the EEC Commission as the way in which to achieve further progress with European integration; these bodies put forward a linked package deal of reforms for the Communities. Since then, the Communities and Union have moved on with numerous Treaty revisions, which will be highlighted in the next section.

However, the agreed decision by the member states in June 2007 at the Brussels European Council Summit to abandon the Constitutional Treaty and to replace it by a Reform Treaty far less supranational in nature may be seen as providing a clear and deliberate halt to progress to a federal Europe, although that too can change in time. The Brussels Summit and the Lisbon Treaty are considered in section 1.5.13.

Furthermore, it appears that, as more states join, there may be more resistance to deeper integration.

1.4   Developments following the original Treaties

For more details on this section scan here or visit the Online Resource Centre.

The member states made considerable progress under the original Treaties and the Communities were very successful in achieving the aims set out and promoting economic growth in the member states in contrast with countries such as the UK. The dismantling of customs duties was achieved by the original six member states and the Common Market for the free movement of goods was largely achieved ahead of the target year of 1969, set down in the EEC Treaty. Additionally, Competition Policy and the CAP – successful in terms of guaranteeing production, but the object of criticism ever since because its price-support mechanisms have generated overproduction – are both regarded as successes. However, the Communities did

cross reference
The Luxembourg Accords will be considered under section 1.5.2.

not expand until 1973, nor did it integrate any further until 1986, much of which was to do with the rejection by de Gaulle of the UK applications and the national veto established under the Luxembourg Accords. However, in 1969, a fresh start for the Communities appeared to take place. Whilst in itself it did not lead to massive or immediate change, it did allow for a new agenda for change.

The member states held a summit in The Hague in 1969, to try to get the Communities moving again, which set as its goals the completion, widening and deepening of the Communities. Although the completion of the Common Market, which should have been fully achieved by 1969, took considerably longer and actually had to wait until 1992, the widening and deepening of the Communities were processes always intended to be ongoing. The terms **widening** and **deepening** are those used then and still survive in Community and EU jargon to describe developments in two ways.

. . . .

widening

This term refers primarily to the process of the expansion to include new member states, but can also apply to the extension into new policy areas and in developing new sectors for integration.

deepening

This term refers to the degree of integration that takes place in terms of *how* integration takes place. By this is meant the extent to which integration is intergovernmental or supranational, but deepening can also apply to integration in new policy areas because it would consider the extent to which the Communities have encroached into previously exclusively held areas of the member states' competences.
. . . .

To some extent, the terms are overlapping and the same development, it can be argued, fits into both categories. At a fairly simple level, however, they refer in turn to the quantitative and qualitative changes over the years.

1.4.1 The widening of the Communities

The original founding member states – Belgium, France, West Germany, Italy, Luxembourg and the Netherlands – remained the only six member states from 1952 to 1973.

- 1973 – first expansion of members: Denmark, Ireland and the UK
- 1981 and 1986 – second expansion: Greece, Portugal and Spain
- 1990 – due to the reunification of Germany, East Germany is assimilated
- 1995 – expansion: Austria, Finland and Sweden
- 2004 – expansion: Cyprus, the Czech Republic, Estonia, Hungary, Latvia, Lithuania, Malta, Poland, Slovakia and Slovenia
- 2007 – expansion: Bulgaria and Romania

1.4.1.1 First expansion

The Paris Intergovernmental Conference of 1972 finally paved the way for the first expansion of the member state, which took place in 1973, when the UK, Ireland and Denmark joined. Norway was also to have joined at this time, but a referendum of the Norwegian electorate on the eve of membership resulted in a majority against and Norway failed to become a member – not for the last time!

1.4.1.2 Second expansion

The second expansion actually consists of two smaller expansions spread over five years, when Greece joined in 1981 and, after protracted periods of negotiation, Spain and Portugal entered in 1986. None of these three countries was economically in a strong position in relation to the existing member states, and in view of this all were regarded by some as unfit for membership. Politically, however, their acceptance into the Communities was regarded as crucial to support the recently emerged democracies in all of these countries after varying periods of authoritarian or dictatorial right-wing rule, and further, to act as a counter force to any possible violent reaction to the left and possible establishment of governments sympathetic to Moscow. The Cold War still featured prominently in this period of history; hence entry was facilitated sooner than economic conditions might have permitted.

Note that, in 1982, Greenland withdrew from the EC after a consultative referendum. As part of the Danish realm, Greenland had become a member of the EC when Denmark joined. After being granted home rule, Greenland opted to leave the EC.

1.4.1.3 East Germany is assimilated

A smaller automatic expansion took place in 1990, with the reunification of West and East Germany as the first tangible change to result from the fall of the Communist regimes in the Soviet Union and eastern European countries.

This automatic assimilation of a previously independent country results from the separation of the single-state Germany after the Second World War and the view that East Germany was not a new member state, but that the areas in the former German Democratic Republic simply became part of a larger Federal Republic of Germany and thus automatically a part of the Communities.

1.4.1.4 Setting terms for future expansions

The German mini-expansion awakened the Communities to the possibility of a number of the former eastern European states seeking membership and prompted a longer-term evaluation of the conditions required of aspirant member states. This led to criteria being agreed at the Copenhagen Summit in June 1993, which outlined the requirements for new members. These included the need for stable government and institutions guaranteeing democracy, the rule of law, human rights and the protection of minorities. Economically, applicant states would have to have a functioning market economy and the ability to cope with life in the single market. The applicants would have to accept the *acquis communautaire* in its entirety including the overall political, economic, social and monetary aims of the Union, such as eventual adoption of the euro; no easy task, even for the present member states.

The next and fourth enlargement took place sooner than expected as a result of the changes in eastern Europe and the economic success facilitated by the Single European Act (SEA).

acquis communautaire

The term given to describe the accumulated body of Community and Union law, including treaties, secondary legislation and judicial developments.

1.4.1.5 The European Economic Area (EEA)

After observing in the late 1980s the economic benefits of the SEA enjoyed by the member states of the Communities, other European states, most of which had cooperation or association agreements with the Communities and were members of the European Free Trade Association (EFTA), started to make overtures to the Communities for greater cooperation and some for possible membership. Initially, further expansion was not favoured by the Commission, because it was thought that it would stifle plans for deeper integration of the then existing member states, in particular progress on the single market and possible further progress to monetary union. Additionally, prior to the collapse of Communism in Europe in the late 1980s, some of the EFTA member states were uncertain for various reasons, including their neutrality and post-Second World War constitutional position, about full membership. Therefore a lesser form of integration was proposed by the European Commission in which the participants could benefit from the advantages of the single market and the competition policy, but not be involved in the other economic or political aspects of the Communities, including decision-making. This offer was open to all of the then existing members of the EFTA. However, the negotiations for this new form of cooperation were very drawn out and subject to considerable delays. They were also taking place against the backdrop of the collapse of Communism in eastern Europe.

One of the consequences of this was that the previous objections or difficulties that might be raised by Eastern Bloc countries and the Soviet Union in particular – that full Community membership of militarily neutral countries, such as Austria, Finland and Sweden, would not be compatible with their status as neutral countries – were effectively resolved.

In October 1991, the EFTA member states Austria, Finland, Iceland, Liechtenstein, Norway, Sweden and Switzerland, signed an agreement with the EEC on the creation of the EEA. The agreement reached was that the EFTA members were not represented in the Community institutions and would take no part in the decision-making processes of the Community. They would be subject to all Community law relating to the single market, as defined by the Court of Justice. However, an additional problem was encountered whilst negotiations were being finalized and shortly before the Treaty was to come into force on 1 January 1993. The Swiss electorate rejected membership of the EEA in a referendum in December 1992, which caused considerable political and legal difficulties because Liechtenstein, with which Switzerland has a monetary union, had agreed to join. Less Switzerland, the remaining six EFTA states went on to sign and ratify the agreement, which came into force on 1 July 1993. It was soon clear, however, that, as far as business confidence was concerned, full membership of the EU was the status that attracted investment and not membership of the EEA. Indeed, both the concept and the consequences of the EEA might not, in any case, have been fully understood by outside interests. Hence, almost before the ink had dried on the signatures to the EEA Treaty, Austria, Finland, Norway and Sweden applied for full membership of the EC.

1.4.1.6 The 1995 expansion

In view of the fact that most of the bargaining had already been done for the EEA, entry terms were easily and rapidly decided and the four applications were quickly accepted. On 1 January 1995, therefore, the Union was joined by Austria, Finland and Sweden, bringing the number of member states to fifteen. The Norwegian electorate, however, once again chose to reject membership in a referendum in December 1994 and Norway again failed to join the Communities. The entry of the three former EFTA members meant that the remaining EFTA states, Iceland, Norway and Liechtenstein, were now the only remaining EFTA members of the EEA. Following the economic crisis of 2008–09 and the economic near-collapse of Iceland, it made a membership application and commenced entrance negotiations in July 2010. The other two EEA states do not have membership applications pending. Switzerland remains outside both the EC and the EEA. Its application for full membership, lodged in 1992 was put on hold following the EEA rejection. A special series of bilateral agreements have been negotiated with Switzerland instead, covering many, if not most, of the aspects of the EEA.

1.4.1.7 The 2004 expansion

The expansion that took place on 1 May 2004 was the largest in the history of the EU and ten new states joined in one go, comprising Cyprus, the Czech Republic, Estonia, Hungary, Latvia, Lithuania, Malta, Poland, Slovakia and Slovenia. The overall time taken to resolve terms of entry was surprisingly quick considering the number of states involved and their differing economic and social circumstances. The haste was fuelled by the political events unfolding in the world, in particular by the break-up of the Soviet Union and the bloody fragmentation of former Communist state of Yugoslavia. The ten new countries were thus brought into the fold much more quickly than economic conditions alone would have allowed owing to the political desire to lock these countries into a western liberal democratic club of nations. Hence the eastern expansion took over the agenda and Commission time. The accession agreements with all of the member states were concluded and the entry terms settled for the Treaty of Accession, which was signed in Athens on 16 April 2003. The ten new member states duly joined on 1 May 2004.

1.4.1.8 The 2007 expansion

In September 2006, the EU Commission expressed its view that Bulgaria and Romania were ready for accession, as originally planned in the Accession Treaty concluded in April 2005. Entry into the Union of these two countries took place on 1 January 2007.

1.4.1.9 Future expansion

For more details on this section scan here or visit the Online Resource Centre.

At present, there is one acceding country and five countries that are official candidate states: Croatia is the accending country and Turkey, Iceland, the former Yugoslav Republic of Macedonia, Montenegro and Serbia are the candidate countries.

With regard to Turkey, a candidate country since 1999, the Commission recommended on 6 October 2004 that the EU should open entry negotiations; in December 2004 the Brussels European Council Summit approved this position, and negotiations were started on 3 October 2005. Without doubt, these negotiations will be the most controversial in the history of the Union. The difficulties are the recognition and reunification of Cyprus, the predominantly Muslim population of Turkey, the human rights record of Turkey, and the fact that quite simply, geographically, most of the Turkish land mass lies in Asia and not in Europe. Its economic situation is also regarded as problematic; however, it may be argued that the entry of Turkey is exactly what the EU should come to terms with to create a multi-ethnic, multi-cultural, and multi-religious Union. Negotiations on twelve **Chapters** are taking place and one is completed, but with no fixed timetable for overall completion, which might take many years.

. . . .

Chapter

The name given to each of the various policy areas covered by the Treaties with which Turkey (or another candidate state) must fully conform before it can be accepted for membership. There are about thirty-five Chapters in total to be negotiated and closed.

. . . .

With regard to Croatia, negotiations on the various Chapters commenced on 3 October 2005 and were completed in 2011 for a possible EU entry on 1 July 2013, provided that all twenty-seven existing member states and Croatia ratify the Accession Treaty, which was signed in Brussels on 9 December 2011.

The former Yugoslav Republic of Macedonia made an application to join in March 2004, and was considered as of 17 December 2005 to be a candidate country. Entry negotiations have been recommended by the Commission, but have not yet commenced with Macedonia, although visa liberalization has been put into effect.

Following the economic recession in 2008–09, Iceland, already a member of the EEA, made an application in July 2009 for full membership of the EU. It was envisaged that a fast-track negotiation might take place in view of the existing conformity of Iceland with the EU through EEA membership, although debt repayments to the UK and the Netherlands might interrupt this. In February 2010, the Commission recommended to the European Council that access negotiations should commence and Iceland became an official candidate state. Eleven Chapters have been opened, eight of which have been closed provisionally.

Montenegro applied for membership in 2009 and was granted candidate status in December 2010. Access negotiations have not yet commenced. Serbia was granted candidate status on 1 March 2012.

As to other possible members, there are the remaining Balkan states, presently considered to be potential candidate countries, as well as the possibility in the future for the states of the former Soviet Union that border the EU. Thus the countries of Albania, Bosnia and Herzegovina, and Kosovo have all been formally recognized by the EU as those eligible for future EU membership, but only if they prove themselves to the satisfaction of the EU and existing member states to be fit for membership. They have all now made applications, the latest of which was Serbia in December 2009.

One or two other countries have previously made applications, but have either withdrawn these or put them on hold. Norway has twice concluded entry negotiations only for entry to be rejected by the Norwegian electorate at the eleventh hour. At present, it has no application pending, but the possibility of future membership remains high on the political agenda, with opinion polls showing a majority of Norwegians in favour of full membership.

The rejection by the Swiss of membership of the EEA in 1992 also led to the suspension of its application for full membership. Even though Swiss governments have expressed the view that Switzerland will eventually apply for full membership, that aim was severely dented, at least for a few years, by the categorical rejection by the Swiss electorate of EU membership negotiations in a private initiative referendum in March 2001 when 77 per cent of those voting said 'No'. Therefore there are presently no plans to revive the dormant application by Switzerland, although significant governmental and other elements consider membership of the EU to be necessary and indeed inevitable, if not immediately, then at some stage in the future.

1.4.1.10 The future of enlargement

The fact that the EU is conducting accession negotiations with Turkey invites a final consideration in respect of further widening and enlargement: what is the limit? The answer to this is as much driven by the answer to the question: what is Europe – politically and geographically? Two Mediterranean island states have already pushed the geographical border of the EU further: Cyprus lies closer to the Middle East and is nearer to Asia than Europe and Malta is not much further away from Africa than it is from other parts of Europe. Indeed, there are existing parts of some member states that are clearly beyond any usual definition of Europe. The Canaries (Spain) lie off the west coast of Africa, French Guyana is completely in another continent in South America, the Azores and Madeira (Portugal) are in the Atlantic and the French islands of

Guadeloupe, Martinique and Reunion lie in the Caribbean. Greenland was part of the EU until it was granted home rule from Denmark in 1979 and left the EU in 1982.

In fact, there are not many European states left to apply, depending on the definition of 'Europe': only Norway, Liechtenstein, the smaller states of Andorra, Monaco and perhaps parts of the former Soviet Union, such as the Ukraine, Belarus and Moldova, some of which are deliberately pursuing pro-European policies.

An application by Morocco in 1987 to join was rejected on the geographical ground that Morocco was in Africa and could not be considered as being Europe. There is now also perhaps the more focused question of whether the present citizens of the EU want a bigger Europe. At the time of writing, there appears to be more reticence than support for further expansion.

1.4.1.11 Accession preconditions

Regardless of which state is a candidate, all existing and new member states are required to accept and adopt the entire body of EU law – that is, the *acquis communautaire* – which includes the Treaties, Protocols, Declarations, conventions and agreements with third countries, secondary legislation and the judgments of the ECJ. This requirement was previously noted under Article 2 TEU, but is now to be found indirectly in Article 20 TEU (post-Lisbon). Since the TEU, the criteria for membership has been much more clearly spelled out.

Article 49 TEU

. . . .

Any European State which respects the principles set out in Article 2 and is committed to promoting them may apply to become a member of the Union.

These principles are human dignity, freedom, democracy, equality, the rule of law and respect for human rights. In addition, potential member states will be required to satisfy a number of criteria provided at Copenhagen in 1993 that were established with the membership applications of the newly emergent democracies in eastern Europe in mind. The criteria were essentially a refinement of previous practice. The 1999 Helsinki European Council Summit added a form of 'good neighbour' requirement for entrant states: that disputes with neighbouring countries be resolved before entry. It might have been a good idea, but the most visible case requiring the application of that policy was Cyprus; however, the Greek and Turkish parts of the island were not able to resolve fully their differences prior to the entry of Cyprus to the EU on 1 May 2004. Thus, although the whole island of Cyprus is in the EU, EU law is applied only in the southern Greek half of the island despite the fact that a referendum vote in Cyprus to reunite the island was approved by the Turkish side, but rejected by the Greek Cypriot electorate. Note, though, that Turkish Cypriots are citizens of a member state, the Republic of Cyprus, even though they live in the northern part of Cyprus; therefore their personal rights as EU citizens are not affected.

Potential border disputes existing between Estonia and Latvia and the Russian Federation were also not resolved prior to accession. The Helsinki Summit additionally marked a realization that the Copenhagen criteria could not be strictly applied and that some flexibility had to be exercised. The Laeken European Council Summit in December 2001 also emphasized that membership was dependent on candidate countries ensuring that their judicial institutions were capable of meeting the requirements of EU membership. The applicability of the criteria for deciding whether an eligible candidate can become an admissible one were confirmed at the Copenhagen Summit, which took place in December 2002. In relation to Turkish membership, it emphasized the need to meet the political criteria.

The good neighbour principle has now found Treaty expression in Article 8 TEU.

For more details on this section scan here or visit the Online Resource Centre.

1.5 The deepening of the Communities

This section charts the increasing degree of integration entered into by the member states, from the original Treaties establishing the Communities, to the present position following the entry into force of the Lisbon Treaty in 2009.

1.5.1 The primary Treaties

The first and fundamental movement on the path of integration was, of course, the ECSC Treaty, now expired, which was soon followed by the agreement and ratification of the EEC and EURATOM Treaties by the original six member states. It was clear at the time of negotiation that a transfer of power was involved, particularly in the climate of the time and the clear federalist intentions of the main protagonists of the plan, Schuman and Monnet. The only amendments that were made to the primary Treaties for the first two decades were minor ones brought about, first, by the decision to merge the institutions of the three Communities and then by the Accession Treaties required for the new member states. Prior to the Merger Treaty of 1965, each of the Communities had its own Council and High Authority/Commission; however, the Court of Justice and the Parliamentary Assembly had both been shared by all three Communities from the outset. The merger of the institutions was a practical step to provide common coordination and to avoid the duplication of effort and resources. It was nothing more significant than that. The first Accession Treaties for Denmark, Ireland and the UK dealt specifically with the details of accession of the new member states or merely made the changes to the Treaties considered necessary for it to continue working in the same way as previously, but with adjustments to reflect the increase in member states and the composition of the institutions: for example, to Council voting numbers, and to Commission, European Parliament and Court of Justice memberships. The fundamental constitutional core of the Communities and how they worked remained untouched until 1986.

1.5.2 The 1960s and the Luxembourg Accords

Initially, the Communities were very successful in achieving the aims set out and promoting economic growth in those member states, in contrast with slower economic growth in countries such as the UK. The dismantling of customs duties was achieved by the original six member states before the target date set down in the EEC Treaty. Additionally, Competition Policy was seen to be working and the CAP was clearly successful in terms of guaranteeing production. It was, however, the subject of criticism because its price support mechanisms led over time to the massive overproduction and stockpiling of commodities such as butter, sugar and wine. These cost the Community not only a great deal of money to dispose of, but also political ill-will in the world as Third World agricultural products had no chance of entering the heavily protected EC market.

However, following this initial period of success and achievement, any chance of either further expansion or deeper integration was stifled. The brake on such progress was most effectively applied to the Commission and the Communities in 1965 by de Gaulle, the French President, by a boycott of the institutions that caused lasting damage for decades. In 1965, the Commission proposed that the Communities move to a system of own resources and that the Council should move to majority voting, which was no more than originally envisaged by the Treaty of Rome in 1957. It was further proposed that the Parliamentary Assembly should have some control over the expenditure of the Communities. These proposals were categorically opposed and vetoed by de Gaulle who, when the other member states were not opposed, adopted a policy of non-attendance at the Community institutions by the French representatives, which became known as the 'institutions boycott' or the 'empty chair policy'.

cross reference

Qualified majority voting is also considered in Chapter 2, section 2.2.4.3.

The boycott of the EU institutions by French President de Gaulle was the way in which France objected to an increase in the Communities' own resources and powers.

All progress, indeed everything in the Communities, simply halted. The compromise agreement that broke the deadlock was the infamous Luxembourg Accords, in essence an 'agreement to disagree'. This basically provided that where the member states were not able to agree a proposal and where a vital national interest of any member state was at stake, that member state could finally veto the proposal in Council. There was no definition of a vital interest, and so member states were left to define a vital interest themselves.

> **'Majority Voting Procedure', Extract from the Luxembourg Accords (1966) 3 EEC Bulletin 9**
>
> ....
>
> (I) Where, in the case of decisions which may be taken by majority vote on a proposal of the Commission, very important interests of one or more partners are at stake, the Members of the Council will endeavour, within a reasonable time, to reach solutions which can be adopted by all the Members of the Council while respecting their mutual interests and those of the Community, in accordance with Article 2 of the Treaty.
>
> (II) With regard to the preceding paragraph, the French delegation considers that where very important interests are at stake the discussion must be continued until unanimous agreement is reached.
>
> (III) The six delegations note that there is a divergence of views on what should be done in the event of a failure to reach complete agreement.
>
> (IV) The six delegations nevertheless consider that this divergence does not prevent the Community's work being resumed in accordance with the normal procedure.

1.5.3 **Stagnation and 'Eurosclerosis'**

The whole unfortunate episode surrounding the Luxembourg Accords resulted in stagnation in the decision-making process for many years to come. It led to the long, slow, painful period of the Communities that has become known as the period of 'Eurosclerosis', and which lasted from 1966 until the early to mid-1980s. The basic problem was the near-inability of the member states to reach decisions on Community legislation, and widespread dissatisfaction at the slow pace at which the goals of the EEC were being achieved. Whilst much of the blame can be laid at the door of the French boycott and the Luxembourg Accords, the ability to reach decisions was made much more difficult by the doubling of member states between 1973 and 1986 to twelve.

In 1973, Denmark, Ireland and the UK joined the Communities, followed in 1981 by Greece, and in 1986 by Spain and Portugal.

Trying to obtain the unanimous agreement of first six, then nine, then ten, and then all twelve members proved at times to be simply impossible. Amongst the main concerns were the time taken by the Community institutions to make new laws and the amount of work with which the Council was faced, partly because particular provisions were presented many times as the Commission made amendments to make them acceptable to all member states. A notorious example of this is Directive 85/384, which did nothing more controversial than harmonize the training requirements for architects, but which took the institutions seventeen years to agree and finally enact. Further concerns related to the lack of representative democracy in the decision-making process of the Community and the delays experienced by litigants to the Court of Justice. It was clear to everyone that some change had to be brought about. Whilst it was true that some adjustments had been made in the form of amendments to the original treaties, these were of a limited nature. More significantly, but restricted to a specific process, was the increase in powers of the European Parliament in the budgetary process by the Budgetary Treaties of 1970 and 1975. Otherwise, little further progress had been achieved in this period. However, before looking at the relaunch of the Communities, in the background the European Court of Justice was going about its business of judging cases and, in doing so, laying down some extremely important principles of law.

1.5.4 The Court of Justice and integration

cross reference
This development and these cases will be fully considered in Chapters 5 and 8.

Whilst the Community institutions were busily going nowhere on the path to European integration, the Court of Justice appeared not to be affected by the 'Eurosclerosis' and had, from a very early date, adopted a very supranational tone in its judgments, including the far-reaching decisions on direct effects and supremacy in Case 26/62 *Van Gend en Loos* and Case 6/64 *Costa* v *ENEL*. These judgments contributed greatly not only to building a separate Community legal system, but also to enhancing the supranational status of the new European legal order and constitutionality of the Communities.

1.5.5 Revival attempts

In 1969, following the resignation of de Gaulle and the change in West Germany to a Social Democrat government, a summit of the heads of state and government was arranged in The Hague expressly to relaunch European integration. The 1969 Hague Summit established the system of EPC, but which was deliberately intergovernmental in nature and sat outside the formal Treaty set-up. As such, it can be regarded as another move away from supranationalism and the neofunctionalists' dream of progress on European integration. It was also unfortunate, but the reforms and the relaunching of the Communities envisaged at The Hague were severely disrupted by the world economic situation, which grew steadily worse in the early 1970s. The Middle East wars and ensuing oil crises led to very high inflation and stagnation in the world economies and to the unwinding of the first attempt at some sort of monetary union, the European Monetary Unit (EMU), which bound European currencies into a flexible relationship with each other.

The year 1973 also saw the entry of three new member states, two of which, the UK and Denmark, were even then the least federal-minded member states in the European Communities. There were nevertheless further attempts to revive the flagging fortunes of the Communities. A further summit in Paris in 1974 led to the formalization of the previously informal European Council Summit meetings to provide an overriding political guide to the Communities. This, however, tended to strengthen further the intergovernmental hand of control over the Communities rather than to provoke deeper integration. The Paris Summit also, for the first time, allowed the Commission a role in the summitry, something pressed for by the new Commission President, Roy Jenkins. The Summit also made the decision that the European Parliament should be directly elected as from 1978, although this could not take place until 1979 due to difficulties in the UK in preparing the legislation. Finally, the European Monetary System (EMS) was established in 1978, despite the collapse of the previous attempt (the EMU). The EMS proved to be stable and, with the establishment of the European Currency Unit (ECU), became the precursor to monetary union and the euro (€).

These limited successes, however, did little to counter the generally prevailing malaise that hung over the Communities and institutions. This was not helped by the attitude and activities of certain member states. When de Gaulle disappeared from the international scene in 1979, the new UK Prime Minister, Mrs Thatcher, appeared immediately to take up the baton of intergovernmentalism and the bolstering of purely national interests. Whilst the UK may well have had a case in arguing for a more equitable budget contribution and neither Mrs Thatcher nor indeed anyone else has gone as far as de Gaulle in disrupting the work of the Communities (with the limited exception of David Cameron's veto during the Euro Summit discussions in December 2011), the negotiating style and public pronouncements of Thatcher left much to be desired. These budget wrangles and the sheer lack of progress generally in the Community dragged on seemingly endlessly into the mid-1980s. The stagnation and intergovernmentalism not only thwarted any moves to more integration, but also engendered a period of national protectionism, which itself was threatening to undermine some of the basic goals of the European Communities already achieved. Notably, the Common Market was simply not being completed as envisaged and, if anything, was becoming more fragmented. The situation in the 1980s was that both the stagnation of the Communities and the lack of international competitiveness of Europe in relation to American and Japanese industrial and commercial progress had been clearly recognized. It was abundantly clear and understood that reform, and indeed radical reform, of the Community and institutions was necessary.

cross reference
See section 1.6 for more on the relationship between the UK and the EU.

Numerous reports and studies were conducted by the different Community institutions and additionally many external reports had been commissioned over the years that had all recommended changes. A number of areas in which improvements were required had already been identified by those reports in the lifetime of the Communities. The fact that there were so many of these speaks volumes for their (in)effectiveness in tackling the deep-rooted problems of European stagnation. However, whilst individually, they did not provide a solution, collectively, all of them, especially the latter ones, helped finally to establish and develop the climate for the eventual changes brought about by Treaty change and in particular by the SEA, which led in turn to the TEU (the Maastricht Treaty), the Treaties of Amsterdam and Nice, and lastly the 2009 Lisbon Treaty. In particular, these concerns were taken up by the new Commission President Jacques Delors, who brought a package of reforms to the member states with the measures considered necessary for the completion of the single market. Whilst there remained opposition to any significant institutional changes recommended, especially by the UK, the single market completion was the carrot that brought the Eurosceptic governments on board, particularly the UK and Germany, as the proposals were hailed as a shining example of trade liberalization. Whilst the other member states were undoubtedly also interested in the trade and economic aspects of the reforms proposed, the smaller states in particular had a greater desire to see the institutional reforms recommended. In 1985, a sufficient head of steam had built up for the member states to accept, albeit some reluctantly, that the necessary changes were ones that could effectively be undertaken only by substantively amending the founding Treaties.

1.5.6 **The first Intergovernmental Conference (IGC) and the Single European Act**

. . . .
Intergovernmental Conference
A conference of the member states outside the Treaty and Communities set-up, which is established to discuss and agree Treaty change.
. . . .

An **Intergovernmental Conference** took place in 1985 to discuss the decision-making of the Council of Ministers, the legislative powers of the EP, the executive power of the Commission, the policy areas of the Community and the delays before the Court of Justice.

The SEA was the product of the IGC and came into force in May 1987. The Preamble to the SEA states that it is 'a step towards European Union'. It amended the EEC Treaty in several important respects, perhaps most importantly changing the legislative process affecting some Treaty Articles and generally extending the Community's competence and concern in new policy areas.

The SEA is the first significant amendment of the primary Treaties. It is an important watershed in the historical development of the Communities and is not to be underestimated in its importance, although it was underestimated at the time, not only by external observers and commentators, but also by the heads of state and government who signed up to it. It is sometimes difficult to grasp its importance because it is the first of a series of package-deal changes to the Treaties that not only added new areas of competence, but also simultaneously made various institutional changes and policy amendments.

The SEA proposals that put the primary focus on market liberalization were enthusiastically welcomed by the member states, but were linked to the institutional changes, and it is probably fair to say that the far-reaching political consequences of these were seriously downplayed by the EC Commission. Even its title underplays the significance of the matter: an 'Act' suggests somewhat less than a new Treaty; it suggests secondary legislation rather than primary treaty material. So, in 1985, the draft SEA was put to and debated at the IGC. It was agreed by the ten member states in December 1985 and came into force in July 1987, after signature and ratification by all twelve states.

Portugal and Spain had joined the Communities in January 1986, during this ratification process.

1.5.6.1 Achievements and evaluation of the SEA

Whilst the SEA had its critics and was condemned by some parties, its success lay not in what it actually changed, although there was considerable progress with the internal market; its true success lay in its longer-term influence in reinvigorating integration.

cross reference
See details on the Court of Justice including the CFI (now the General Court) in Chapter 2.

cross reference
All of these matters are further considered in Chapters 2 and 3.

The SEA amended the EEC Treaty in several important respects, and whilst they were not massive changes in themselves, they proved to be a catalyst to further European integration. Apart from the proposals to complete the internal market, perhaps most important was the change of the legislative process affecting ten Treaty Articles and generally the extension of the Community's competence and concern in new policy areas. The SEA also introduced provisions that made it possible to make changes to the judicial structure in the future by supplementing the Court of Justice with a Court of First Instance (CFI), which was regarded as being vital to cope with the significant increases in the number of cases reaching the Court and the increased delay being caused as a result. The SEA also made formal the existence of the European Council of Heads of State and Government, which was originally established as EPC. The SEA reintroduced and extended qualified majority voting (QMV) in the Council, introduced the cooperation procedure in law-making, which provided the European Parliament with more than just a consultative role for the first time, and increased Commission powers.

It is certainly the case that the SEA did not represent a radical shift to supranational or federal integration. In contrast to the original Treaties, the member states were the ones constructing its agenda and not the federalist visionaries of the immediate post-war period. Also, in view of the preceding fifteen to twenty years, which had seen a complete standstill on any such progress, it is not surprising that the changes introduced by the SEA can be regarded as modest and even disappointing. But to view the limited, mainly intergovernmental, changes brought by the SEA as a backward step on the integration road misses the point somewhat. The Preamble to the SEA states that it is 'a step towards European Union' and it therefore represented forward movement at a time of massive political conservatism in Europe; perhaps as important was the fact that, for the first time, the original primary Treaties had been substantively amended. Although this has happened on a number of occasions since then and thus has the appearance of being something easily done, at the time it was, without any doubt, a significant development. The original legal and constitutional base was shown not to be cast in stone and thus set for all time to come; it could be altered – and not just once, but as many times as deemed necessary. For most, if not all, of the states, especially the UK, signing up to and joining the Communities in the first place was a massive and historic commitment. Changing that original deal was not something to be taken lightly and could even be regarded as being as important as the Constitutional Treaty, which failed to gain universal member state approval and was ultimately abandoned. The very substance of the original Treaties was being altered and, in order to amend a treaty, another treaty is needed, so despite its name the SEA is a true amending treaty agreed by the member states. Also, after a twenty-year delay, it did introduce real majority voting in the Council of Ministers, albeit within limited fields for clear and obvious benefits, but it allowed the member states to become comfortable with QMV and thus it prepared the ground for the future use of majority voting in other areas.

cross reference

These aspects were considered earlier in sections 1.4.1.5 and 1.4.1.6.

The success of the SEA and benefit to the Communities was also observed externally at that time as other European states on the outside of the Communities were able to witness the increase in investment from outside Europe into the EC and indeed away from their own countries. They also wished to join in this success and, initially, plans were made to accommodate them in association agreements with the European Communities and, in an extended form of these, with the EEA. It led much more quickly than originally envisaged to the further widening of the Communities.

1.5.7 **Beyond the SEA**

For more details on this section scan here or visit the Online Resource Centre.

It was realized very soon after the signing of the SEA that it was only part of the answer and it was advocated, largely by the Commission, that further institutional changes were required. As a result, even before the deadline of 1992 had passed, plans were being put forward by the Commission President Delors for further Treaty reform, especially on economic and monetary union and social policy. A further IGC was planned and was set up to debate the adoption of common monetary and fiscal policies, which, according to the plan, were deemed necessary to cement in the gains achieved by the largely successful completion of the single market. This further proposal for integration and, again, for the IGC to debate it were both opposed by the UK. However, external political events were moving rapidly in the world. Margaret Thatcher was deposed by her own party as Conservative leader and thus UK Prime Minister. The 'Iron Curtain' was also being dismantled, changing the political situation in Europe radically and leading very quickly to German reunification. The planned IGC for 1991 to discuss and provide for greater economic integration was supplemented by a parallel second IGC to consider political reform and to produce proposals for a new constitutional basis for the Communities. It was also considered necessary that political decision-making should also be integrated further in order to lock in any decisions reached on monetary union; otherwise, it was feared that any gains or decisions reached for monetary and economic union would be lost if the political decisions supporting them could still be taken independently by each member state. This in turn would lead to a drifting apart of the economic conditions in the member states and is a clear example of functionalist integration in action, in that integration in one area demands or inevitably leads to integration in another area in order to maintain the initial integration.

cross reference

Refer to section 1.3.1.1 for explanation and further details.

The parallel IGCs commenced work in December 1990, but, like the EEA negotiations, they were subject to delays as a result of the economic problems in Europe, inflation in Germany due to the cost of unification, and the considerable political social and economic change taking place across Europe.

In 1990, Germany was reunified and the area comprising East Germany joined the Communities.

1.5.8 **The Maastricht Treaty on European Union (TEU)**

The two IGCs of the early 1990s can be regarded effectively as one, particularly because they resulted in proposals for a single amending Treaty. However, the Treaty that was drafted and eventually accepted by the member states considerably complicated the constitutional base of the Communities and Union, not only because it amended the existing Treaties and most notably the EEC Treaty, but also because it added another Treaty to complement and supplement the existing treaties and to remain in force alongside the existing Treaties. It also proved to be a huge compromise, with its opt-outs in some matters for some of the member states, such as the social policy opt-out for the UK.

Chief amongst the main changes introduced by the Treaty were the timetable and convergence criteria to move to a single economy and monetary union, complete with a single currency. It provided more political cooperation, especially in the areas of foreign policy, security, home affairs and justice. The EEC Treaty name was changed to 'European Community (EC)' to represent the changes that had taken place and the huge expansion in the range of topics and policies covered by the Treaty. A new overall term, the 'European Union (EU)', was introduced to describe the extension by the member states into additional policies and areas of cooperation. The Union consists of three pillars comprising the existing Communities (the three original Treaties), a CFSP and Cooperation in the fields of Justice and Home Affairs (CJHA).

cross reference

See the generous interpretation of this by the ECJ in Chapter 13, section 13.3.3, on citizenship.

A large part of the problem facing European governments trying to sell this Treaty at home was that the European public had not been taken on board during the period of negotiation. Whilst European citizenship was introduced to the EC Treaty (Articles 17 and 18 EC, now 20–21 TFEU), it was really given only teeth later by the Court of Justice and the European public had largely been left out of the reform process. There were further improvements for the European Parliament in the law-making process, but the TEU also represented a backward step as far as progress towards deeper integration was concerned. The other two pillars, as first established, were intergovernmental in nature, with decisions having to be taken unanimously by the member states. Very little had been done to increase the democratic credentials of the Communities; the powers of the Council were left largely untouched and indeed were strengthened in respect of the two new pillars.

The TEU also led to new jargon, which was the result of the new complex shape of the Union, the difficulties in getting the Treaty ratified in all member states and reflected the frustrations of some member states not being happy about the more reluctant states.

Hence the terms 'European Architecture' to describe the new three-pillar structure, and 'variable geometry' to describe the way in which combinations of member states might integrate deeper and that certain states could opt out of certain policies. This is also described in the term 'multi-speed Europe'. For example, the UK was able to opt out of the social policy Chapter and economic and monetary union.

cross reference

It is discussed in further detail under the division of 'competences' in Chapter 3, section 3.4.2.

The Treaty did contain an expression of commitment to the rule of law and democracy, but failed to provide for any significant democratic accountability of the EU and the rule of law itself. The European Parliament had no effective voice in the intergovernmental pillars. There was also an attempt to define the relationship between the Union and the member states by the introduction of the term 'subsidiarity', which was written in the new Treaty (Article B) and which was further defined in Article 5 EC (now 5 TEU). However, its true import was vague. It was supposed to delineate the respective powers of the Union and the member states, but instead has merely confused them, and as such is regarded as somewhat reflective of the ambivalence of the member states at the time.

cross reference

These and demo-cratic deficit are considered in detail in Chapter 2, section 2.4.3.1 and Chapter 3, section 3.5.

The TEU was also supposed to redress the serious concerns about the democratic deficit: that the European Parliament is the only directly elected institution, but has less law-making power than the Council. The TEU increased the power of the EU by the introduction of the co-decision procedure to a limited number of Treaty Articles. Whilst this was an important symbolic step, in reality this amounted to no more than a parliamentary veto and did little to establish real demo-cratic decision-making in the Communities. Furthermore, this had the effect of increasing, once again, the range and complexity of law-making procedures in the Community.

cross reference

See, however, the comments on the Amsterdam and Nice Treaty IGC Summits and the 2007 Brussels Treaty Summit in sections 1.5.9, 1.5.10 and 1.5.13.

The TEU was agreed by the member states in February 1992 and was due to come into force on 1 January 1993. However, the process was thrown into confusion on being rejected by a slim Danish majority in a referendum. As a result, further compromises had to be found in order to appease the Danish electorate. The Edinburgh Summit in December 1992 agreed to allow Denmark various Protocols and Declarations to opt out of participation in stage III of economic and monetary union, the single currency and the defence arrangements of Maastricht, whilst not actually changing the Treaty itself. The Treaty finally came into force in November 1993. However, experience of creating this Treaty was clearly an unhappy one and the European lead-ers promised that it would be better handled next time.

cross reference

Noted earlier at section 1.4.1.11.

There was not much time to learn the lessons from Maastricht: the next time was just around the corner. Already in 1992, mindful of the political changes in Europe, further expansion had already been contemplated by the existing member states and the Copenhagen Summit laid down criteria that would have to be met by aspiring member states.

Whilst politically the TEU was supposed to be an attempt to tidy up the constitutional base of the Communities, the end result was far from this. It is criticized for its complex three-pillar construc-tion, which involved a mix of intergovernmental and supranational elements of governance. The TEU also started a trend that was continued thereafter by the attachment to the Treaties of numerous Protocols and Declarations, which help in many cases to define further some provisions of the Treaties themselves and outline the reservations and opt-outs of some member states. Justifiably, this too has been criticized for making the Union and its legal powers too opaque and too splintered. Furthermore, the Union established was only an 'ever closer one' and not the federal union originally mooted, suggesting far greater integration than the reality agreed by the member states; hence the end product was more intergovernmental cooperation.

In 1995, a further expansion took place, with Austria, Finland and Sweden joining the Union.

1.5.9 **The Amsterdam Intergovernmental Conference and Treaty**

As a part of the agreement for the TEU and specified in the EU Treaty, a timetable was planned for the further revision of the Treaties by providing that another IGC be constituted in 1996 with a view to signing another amending Treaty in Amsterdam in 1997. It was given the objectives of proposing changes to reform the institutional structure in preparation for enlargement, to revise social policy and to review the intergovernmental pillars, in particular the CFSP, especially in respect of the rights of the free movement of persons. However, due to the delays in ratifying the Maastricht Treaty, the agenda was increasingly hijacked by new items, foremost being the preparations that would be required for the eastern expansion of the Union. The political landscape for the Union had changed greatly in a very short time. One of the few things upon which sufficient member states were agreed was the opening up of entry negotiations with the new democracies of eastern Europe. Hence the focus of attention soon shifted to further institutional reform for the next, and probably much larger, expansion of the Union. The focus thus became narrowly concentrated on the size of the Commission, the European Parliament, QMV and the rotation of the presidency of the Council of Ministers.

The negotiations were highly problematic. Each member state, it seemed, had its own agenda and was prepared to push it to the limit. The UK government was even seeking to reopen previous Treaties, to curb the powers of the Court of Justice and to reverse some of the decisions not favoured by the UK government. Hence, in this climate, the IGC dragged on into April 1997, when, in the UK, the Labour Party won the May 1997 general election and formed a new government with fewer objections. As a result, final negotiations were soon wrapped up and the Treaty was concluded in Amsterdam in June 1997. It was signed by all member states at a late-night summit in October 1997 and, following a slow, but less troublesome, ratification by all member states, it entered into force on 1 May 1999.

Whilst not as dramatic as those brought about by the TEU, a number of changes were introduced in the Treaty of Amsterdam. Unfortunately, some of these have considerably complicated the structure of the Union and the Treaties.

Following the 1997 landslide Labour victory in the UK, the Protocol and Agreement on Social Policy, previously lying outside of the Treaty structure, was accepted by all fifteen member states and therefore a revised and extended Chapter on social policy could be contained within the EC Treaty in the then Articles 136–45. A new section on employment was introduced, which provided as one of the first examples of a more open method of coordination, that the member states can develop cooperative ventures to combat unemployment. Whilst it retained broadly the division between the supranational EC pillar and the intergovernmental nature of the other two, part of the Justice and Home Affairs (JHA) pillar, concerned with the free movement of persons, was moved within the EC Pillar, with opt-outs for the UK, Ireland and Denmark. It was also agreed that the EU would incorporate the Schengen Agreement on the elimination of all border controls for twelve states, in a new Title IV in the EC Treaty, but not for the UK, Ireland and Denmark, which secured more opt-outs in this area. The Court of Justice and the European Parliament were also given a greater role in the JHA pillar, now renamed the Provision on Police and Judicial Cooperation in Criminal Matters.

The institutional reforms were far more modest. The proposals to extend QMV in Council were severely restricted notably by Germany, amongst others. However, the variety of legislative procedures, which were getting vastly out of hand, were slightly reduced and the European Parliament's powers were modestly increased by the moderately extended use of the

cross reference
Considered in section 1.5.13 and in Chapter 2.

co-decision procedure. The number of Commissioners was capped at twenty, but subsequently amended upwards in line with the number of member states as subsequent IGCs and enlargement reopened this issue along with other institutional matters.

The various changes were consolidated within both the EC and EU Treaties, and unhelpfully these were renumbered as a result, something that has done little to promote the clarity of Union law. Regrettably, the Treaty of Amsterdam added even more Protocols, thus making even more obscure an overall picture of EU and EC law.

The Treaty of Amsterdam, according to some, did very little; others regard it as a necessary consolidation of European political union, although the tangible benefits and progress are hard to discern. Additionally, the Treaty of Amsterdam seemed to throw a spanner in the works of further integration, by the replacement of further supranational integration, with the possibility of allowing some member states to cooperate further, without all member states having to do so. It introduced into the EC Treaty Article 11, and into the TEU a section (Articles 43 *et seq*, now 20 TEU) on 'closer cooperation', which allows any number of member states that so wish to integrate in other areas. This seemed to make the fragmentation of the Communities even more possible and allow for the possibility that the body of Community law known as the *acquis communautaire*, which applies in all member states in the same way, could be undermined as different combinations of member states go their own way with particular policies. Thus far, this has not been taken advantage of, although a revised form of enhanced cooperation was introduced by the Lisbon Treaty (Articles 20 TEU and 326–334 TFEU) and not all member states might participate in the Euro Stability Treaty. (Notably, the UK expects not to take part.)

cross reference
See sections 1.5.14 and 1.6.5.

The Treaty of Amsterdam, as finally agreed, proved to be far from the solution needed for preparing for enlargement, consolidating the political union and establishing a firm basis for European governance. It did little to restore public faith and confidence in the Union. As a result of the fact that Amsterdam failed to resolve the institutional reforms considered essential for the next large enlargement of the EU, there was so much left over that had to be addressed before enlargement could take place that yet another IGC was deemed necessary and was called.

1.5.10 The Nice Intergovernmental Conference and Treaty

The Nice IGC was convened in February 2000 with the more tightly drawn objectives of institutional change ahead of enlargement, to deal with the so-called 'Amsterdam Leftovers'. Whilst the preparatory negotiations were relatively short-lived, the summit in December 2000 proved to be exceedingly difficult. The member states wrangled mainly over the extension of QMV and voting weights in Council, and the conclusions reached were neither conclusive nor satisfactory, despite the various statements of success following the summit. The size of the Commission was also a contentious issue. The QMV discussions were, however, seized on by the member states to defend national positions as rigidly as possible. QMV was extended to twenty-seven more Treaty Articles, but not in as many areas as proposed by the Commission because of the vetoes insisted on by countries, which cumulatively significantly reduced the extension. The discussions were also drawn out because of the arguments over the combinations of country votes to get a qualified majority or a blocking minority, and even qualifications on a majority, were devised defining a minimum number of states and/or a percentage (62 per cent) of population of the EU required. In particular, the three big member states, France, Germany and the UK, were fighting to keep their level of influence against the wishes of many of the smaller states, and whilst agreement was reached at Nice on the voting formula, it was very much an imperfect one and this was soon shown to be the case. The co-decision procedure was extended again for the European Parliament, so that the cooperation procedure became even less important, applicable in only six Articles largely to do with monetary union.

See the Protocol on the Enlargement of the European Union originally attached to the Treaty of Nice. See also ex Articles 100, 103, 106, 192 and 300 EC, the latter as an alternative.

The ultimate maximum size of the Commission was also postponed again, and the temporary agreements reached were put into a Protocol on the Enlargement of the EU, which detracted further from the transparency of the rules governing the Union. The Treaty of Nice was signed by the member states in February 2001, but did not enter into force until 1 February 2003 because of its rejection by a single member state once again, this time Ireland in June 2001. When the Irish government was returned to power with an increased majority, a second referendum was organized, which resulted in a positive endorsement of the Treaty by the Irish electorate (about 63 per cent in favour).

The Nice Treaty was also a Treaty that did not bring about any further radical change to the Union.

One policy that was tightened was the 'closer cooperation' provision introduced by the Treaty of Amsterdam, which was rather open-ended and which enables certain states to proceed to further integration outside of the Treaty (ex Article 11 EC – now 20 TEU and 326–334 TFEU).

Other changes agreed at Nice included amendments to the organization and operation of the European courts whereby more cases can be heard in chambers of judges. It was agreed that a Charter of Fundamental Human Rights should be included within the Union, although the member states did not or could not agree whether it should formally be a part of a treaty or of the Union and it was not legally binding on the member states.

The Nice Treaty also introduced a provision designed to do something about the situation in which there was a clear risk of a serious breach by a member state of one of the respected principles of liberty, democracy, respect for human rights and fundamental freedoms, and the rule of law contained in Article 6 TEU. Article 7 TEU provided that a risk of breach can be determined and recommendations to deal with the situation can be agreed by a four-fifths' majority decision of the member states in Council, including suspension of voting rights of the member state where a persistent breach has been determined. Both of these Articles were carried forward with the same numbers into the amended TEU in 2009.

The Nice Summit also saw the agreement of the member states to move on to the next stage of integration, but it was to be done in a different way, the details of which were to be decided at a later summit of the member states.

1.5.11 The 2001 Laeken Summit

The Laeken Summit in December 2001 was the start of an ultimately unsuccessful attempt to put the EU on a new constitutional footing by Treaty replacement. It formally set up and prepared the agenda for a 'Convention on the Future of Europe', which was headed by a praesidium of twelve members, led by Valéry Giscard d'Estaing, a former French President. It further consisted of representatives of the heads of state and government of the fifteen member states and the thirteen candidate countries, thirty representatives of the national parliaments and twenty-six from the candidate countries, sixteen members of the European Parliament and two members from the Commission.

It laid out in a declaration the goals for making the EU more democratic, transparent and efficient. In particular, attention would be paid to the governance of the Union, institutional preparations for the forthcoming expansion, the division of competences, and democratic participation in the decision-making processes of the Union.

cross reference

This is considered further in Chapter 3, section 3.2, on the division of competences.

There was to be a better definition and understanding of subsidiarity, to determine the status of the Charter of Fundamental Rights, and to simplify the Treaties and numerous Protocols and Declarations (thus finally admitting the complexity of the Treaties as they had accumulated and indeed been added to by the agreements at Nice). Other issues to be addressed included how national parliaments feed their legitimacy into the Union and finally the Convention was charged with establishing a 'Constitutional' Treaty for the EU.

The Convention worked until June 2003, when it wrote up its report and a draft Constitutional Treaty (CT) was finalized and presented to the European Council in Greece on 18 July 2003. This was subsequently considered by the IGC that commenced in October 2003 and the draft CT was presented to the Heads of State and Government Summit in Rome in December 2003.

1.5.12 The Constitutional Treaty for Europe

cross reference

Council voting and in particular QMV are considered in detail in Chapter 2, section 2.2.4.

The main features of the Constitutional Treaty were a new President of the European Council and a Foreign Minister, a smaller Commission, the formal inclusion of the Charter of Human Rights, new simplified legislative tools and more involvement for national Parliaments in law-making. Whilst agreeing on almost everything, the member states failed to agree about the QMV numbers in the Council, with a side argument on the number of Commissioners, and the Rome Summit broke down without agreement on these points.

cross reference

Further explanation of this complication will be provided in Chapter 2, section 2.2.4.4.

Subsequently, ten new member states joined on 1 May 2004, on the basis of the Nice Treaty and this event, combined with the low turnout in the European Parliament elections in early June 2004, refocused the attention of the member states on reaching a compromise on the voting figures. Thus, after some delay, the Constitutional Treaty was signed in October 2004 by all member states and handed over to each of the member states to ratify it by parliamentary approval or referendum or both, according to the constitutional or legal requirements of each state. However, in 2005, during the ratification process, the CT was rejected by the electorates of France and the Netherlands, which resulted in throwing the ratification process into confusion. The member states agreed that there should be a period of reflection, although some states continued the ratification process, taking the total that had ratified to two-thirds.

The EU had also grown to twenty-seven members with the entry of Bulgaria and Romania at the beginning of 2007.

There was a contingency plan in a Declaration (No. 30) attached to the CT, which provided that in the event that one or more countries, up to 20 per cent of the countries, did not ratify the CT, then all member states could meet in the European Council to decide how to go forward and adopt a political solution. Ratification did not go far enough for this Declaration to be invoked before the CT was abandoned.

After being put on ice for two years, the CT was considered at further summit in June 2007, to see if it could be rescued or replaced. The German presidency had the task of either making the CT more palatable or coming up with something in its place that nevertheless addressed the institutional challenges of enlargement. Following another late night of summit discussions, however, it was agreed to abandon the CT entirely and to replace it.

Even though the CT was abandoned, it is worthwhile listing the agreements reached, because most of these matters agreed found expression in the Lisbon Treaty, although slightly altered or in a more complex form. These agreements covered:

- changes to the institutional architecture of the Union and its powers, decision-making procedures and institutions;
- the transfer of power to the EU on fifteen new policy domains;
- the transfer of forty Article bases, ranging from unanimity to qualified majority;
- making the Charter on Fundamental Rights legally binding;
- providing the EU with the status of a legal person to negotiate international agreements for all member countries;
- the establishment of a longer-serving and independent President for the European Council;
- a smaller Commission comprising two-thirds of the number of member states;
- the creation of a common EU Foreign Minister to lead a joint foreign ministry with ambassadors;
- QMV for the election of all high-positioned officials;
- the commencing of a project of a common EU defence;
- an express statement that Union law shall have primacy over the national law;
- procedures for adopting and reviewing the Constitution, some without the need for another IGC; and
- an exit clause for member states.

However, the most controversial change may have been entitling the document a 'Constitution', which was probably a mistake because it was arguably just another Treaty.

1.5.13 The 2007 Brussels Summit and the Lisbon Treaty

For more details on this section scan here or visit the Online Resource Centre.

The member states returned to considering the next move in Brussels in June 2007. It meant that everything was potentially up for renegotiation and some member states in particular wanted to change or amend the things that had previously been agreed at Nice and for the CT. Poland in particular wanted to change the voting arrangements in Council. The German presidency wanted to restrict discussion to more structural aspects of the Union, how to ensure that member states' powers were retained and to remove any symbolism in the Treaty that suggested statehood, such as the flag and anthem. The CT was then officially abandoned and an agreement was reached for a new amending treaty, originally called the 'Reform Treaty', to be signed in Lisbon, which would not replace the existing Treaties, but would amend them. A new IGC was convened in July 2007 to hammer out the details, but many of the features agreed for the CT were incorporated into the 2007 Reform Treaty.

The main changes can be summarized as follows.

(1) The Union was to get its legal personality, the EC Treaty to be renamed as the 'Treaty on the Functioning of the Union' (elegant, eh?) and the term 'Community' to be replaced throughout by 'Union'.

(2) The proposed Union Minister for Foreign Affairs was to be called the 'High Representative of the Union for Foreign Affairs and Security Policy'.

(3) The European Council was to be established as a full institution as envisaged by the CT and a European President was to be established.

(4) The names and types of secondary law 'Regulations, Directives and Decisions' were to be kept, but given new definitions.

(5) The Charter on Fundamental Rights was to become legally binding, but with an opt-out for its internal application in the UK and Poland.

The TEU was to be turned more into an overview Treaty with the EC Treaty being converted into a Treaty dealing with substantive issues; both, however, were to concern the institutions.

Hence, far from consolidating the Treaty, Protocols and Declaration, the European leaders have made the constitutional architecture of the Union even more complicated and fragmented. The Treaty was signed in Lisbon on 13 December 2007 by all twenty-seven member states and subjected to the required ratification process by all twenty-seven member states.

The ratification process of this Treaty was also interrupted by the rejection of the electorate of one state, because in June 2008 the Irish voters for the second time voted against an amending Treaty – this time the Lisbon Treaty. Following a period of consideration and negotiation, in exchange for the agreement by Ireland to hold a second referendum, EU leaders agreed to provide legal guarantees respecting Ireland's taxation policies, its military neutrality and ethical issues. More controversially, they also agreed that each state should maintain one Commissioner each, contrary to the Treaty itself, thus keeping one per member state. Constitutional challenges in other states such as Germany, the Czech Republic and Poland were resolved, and the deliberate delay by the Czech and Polish presidents in completing the constitutional ratification process was overcome. The Treaty was finally ratified by all twenty-seven states in November 2009 and entered into force on 1 December 2009.

cross reference
The meaning of these posts and full institutional changes will be addressed in Chapter 2 and other changes brought about by the Lisbon Treaty will be considered wherever appropriate.

The Union quickly appointed its full-time European Council President and its High Representative of the Union for Foreign Affairs and Security Policy (the Foreign Minister, but referred to as the 'High Representative') in time for the Lisbon Treaty coming into force. It amended the EC and EU Treaties significantly.

1.5.14 An overview of developments to date and the future

Now that the institutional changes needed for the expansion of the Union in 2004 have finally been achieved and the governance of the Union has been put on a new footing by the new Treaty set-up, albeit far less cleanly than originally planned, the Union may be allowed simply to get on with regulating the activities as agreed by its member states. The prior concerns of the Union, which were the further widening and deepening of the Union, are no longer top of the agenda, having been replaced by the continuing economic and financial crisis in the world, and in the eurozone in particular. Whilst five states are currently candidate states, only Iceland has the prospect of entry in a short time frame. Croatia will join on 1 July 2013 if all twenty-seven member states and Croatia ratify the Accession Treaty. The other four candidate states not including Iceland and the prospective candidate states are unlikely to be accepted for many years. The further widening of the Union has already been considered in detail in this chapter, but does represent a serious challenge for the cohesion of the Union, particularly in respect to the attitudes already voiced about possible Turkish and even wider membership. Further deepening, in the form of taking integration even further forward, is also very unlikely in view of the difficulties experienced in bringing the Lisbon Treaty in force. However, as a response to the prolonged economic and financial difficulties among eurozone member states during 2008–12 (Greece in particular), further integration may put in place economic stabilization and a fiscal union. The UK Prime Minister, David Cameron, has declared that the UK will not participate, however, thus forcing the eurozone countries (the Eurogroup of seventeen) and the other nine non-eurozone countries to conclude their own international treaty to put in place the necessary laws, leaving the UK once again isolated in the EU.

1.6 The relationship of the UK with the European Union

This next section may or may not receive attention in all EU law courses. It concerns the rocky relationship between the UK and the European Communities and Union.

1.6.1 The early relationship (to the 1970s)

For more details on this section scan here or visit the Online Resource Centre.

As noted in section 1.1.5, in the late 1940s and early 1950s, the UK was also initially keen to see a united Europe, but without its direct participation. It had at the time a historical legacy that involved quite different economic and social ties, including the Empire and Commonwealth and the Atlantic alliance, both of which featured strongly in the then recently won Second World War. These ties of security and common language are often overlooked, but played no small part in the attitude of Britain to European integration in the immediate post-war years. Britain also regarded its status as being one of remaining a world power, the sovereignty and independence of which might be compromised by membership of such an organization. As well as having the offer to participate in the ECSC negotiations, Britain was also invited to participate in the EEC and EURATOM negotiations. However, she played no significant or indeed useful part and withdrew after minimal participation. Instead, with Austria, Switzerland and other nations, the UK embarked in 1958 on what may have seemed a potentially destructive path of establishing the apparent competitor organization, the European Free Trade Association (EFTA), which involved no supranational or political aims and was intended merely to set up a free-trade area for goods. It was not long, however, before UK governments had a change of heart and policy, which could be regarded as a tacit admission of the error of not becoming involved or joining in the first place.

1.6.2 Two applications rejected

Within months of the entry into force of the EEC Treaty and the establishment of EFTA, the Macmillan Conservative government led the UK application for associate membership and very shortly after that, on 9 August 1961, the UK application for full membership. The reasons for previously not wishing to join had been undermined. Amongst the changes were the demise of the UK's previous world power status, the fact that direct links with most of the world had been weakened by the economic demise of the UK, the Suez climb-down and the continuing conversion of the Empire into a Commonwealth of independent states. Trade patterns were also shifting towards Europe and the Atlantic alliance was less prominent – pointedly so after the disagreement over how to handle the Suez crisis. More than anything, Britain had observed the much faster economic progress made by the six and this provoked its desire for membership. Whether Britain was ever interested in the entire Community package is not clear. Britain had now, however, to bargain from the outside and its applications both for associate and full membership were steadfastly rejected by Charles de Gaulle, the French President. The 1967 application by the Wilson Labour government was similarly vetoed. De Gaulle's opposition to the potentially distorting influence of the UK in the Community was clearly expressed at the time.

1.6.3 **Third application accepted**

In 1970, following the resignation as president and withdrawal from politics of de Gaulle in France, the entry application by the Conservative Prime Minister Edward Heath was successful. Thus the UK joined in 1973, as did Ireland and Denmark, mainly because of their trade dependency with the UK. However, soon afterwards, the UK sought to renegotiate entry terms and held a referendum on membership.

1.6.4 **The timing of the entry**

The timing of the 1973 entry was, in fact, unfortunate. Instead of the UK being able to participate equally in the post-war boom and recovery, the world economy and that of Europe had received a severe setback and Britain, along with the rest of the western world, became the hostage of massive oil price increases. Instead of a period of economic prosperity, the 1970s witnessed high inflation and economic stagnation (sometimes termed 'stagflation'). To aggravate matters still further, the high and arguably inequitable level of the British budget contribution became the focus of attention. It did not take long before disquiet over the terms of entry arose. It seems that Britain paid too high a price to join the club, and that the budget wrangles that both then and in the future were to polarize opinion both in Europe and the UK were inevitable.

The pattern of trade in the UK, which initially favoured imports from Commonwealth non-EEC countries, coupled with having to pay the higher food prices regulated under the EEC CAP, meant that British contributions were extremely high and simply added to the then severe UK domestic economic problems.

To recap for a moment, in the context of the UK entry, the Community was spawned in the aftermath of the Second World War. For membership, the original states exchanged some sovereignty and monetary contribution for security, the stability of democratic nationhood and economic progress. It was argued that Britain did not need the first two, and the third proved illusory in the 1970s and 1980s. Hence when, in 1974, a new government was elected in the UK, a renegotiation of the terms of entry was begun. This culminated in the clear-cut (over 67 per cent in favour) approval of the British public in the then unprecedented 1975 referendum, which not only *post facto* approved membership, but also the renegotiated terms and specifically the revised budget contributions. However, it was only a partial cure for the level of contributions and this dispute was later reopened by UK Prime Minister Margaret Thatcher. Its effect was, however, to cast the UK firmly in the role of the reluctant partner and troublemaker in Europe. Viewed politically, the UK had decided to cast its lot with the EC, aware that some loss of sovereignty was involved and that a potentially high monetary contribution was required. One side of the bargain was not, as with other member states, the security of nationhood or the stamp of approval and stability of the democratic political system that membership gave. The fact that the UK had won the war and had centuries of stability meant that these were so well secured in the UK that the European Communities could never seriously be considered for these advantages, nor to keep the peace, which Britain had secured for itself by victory in the last war, albeit with considerable help. The other side of the bargain was to share in the spoils of European economic progress. Given the changing circumstances, this proved to be a dubious economic gain. No wonder that there was a feeling by some, which still remains, that membership had sold Britain short.

1.6.5 **1980 to date**

In the 1980s, the first part of the decade was occupied with further wrangles over the British budget contribution and the Communities' reluctance to reform, which hindered progress on other matters in the Community and did not engender relaxed relations with Britain's partners in the Community. It was surprising that then Conservative Prime Minister Mrs Thatcher signed the SEA, which saw the first major reform of the original Treaties. The steps contained within it for further integration and some democratization of the Communities were a significant further degree of integration. Indeed, it was regarded later as an error by Mrs Thatcher, who was most probably lured into agreeing to the SEA by the promise of the liberalized trade advantages of the single market.

The budget contributions were settled again in 1984, only to be questioned again in the 1990s and almost annually since. During the negotiations for the second major reform of the Communities, following which the TEU in Maastricht was painfully agreed, Britain demonstrated once again just how out of line it was with its other partners. Part of the agreement reached was that the UK should opt out of the social policy Chapter to which all other member states agreed. The TEU also provided a process and a timetable for moving towards economic and monetary union. The UK negotiated another opt-out in respect of the decision whether to join the final stage, in which a single currency would be established. Exacerbating the poor relationship with the other European partners was the fact that John Major's Conservative government (1992–97) was so clearly and publicly split on the issue of Europe that almost any decision needed was close to impossible to achieve. Hence the idea that any progress could be made by all of the then twelve member states of the Communities was unrealistic.

The change of government in the UK on 1 May 1997 saw an immediate change in the relationship with Europe. In 1997, whilst the delayed negotiations for the TEU were still ongoing, the new Labour government announced its intention to sign up to the social Chapter, carried through soon afterwards, and generally to take a more positive participatory role in Europe. The UK opposition to monetary union seemed to have been removed, at least in principle, although thirteen years on the uncertainty as to when the UK will actually join continues, and in the world and European economic situation now, entry in the short-to-medium-term future appears even less likely. Following the 2010 election and the establishment of a Conservative–Liberal Democrat coalition with different values and support for the EU, a part of the compromise agreement on the EU was an agreement that the UK should not join the euro for at least the term of the present Parliament.

The negotiations for the Amsterdam and Nice Treaties, the Convention and IGC for the Constitution for Europe, the expansion to twenty-five states in 2004 then to twenty-seven in 2007, and the changing political relationships between the leading EU states (notably France, Germany and the UK) have led to a far more complex Union now than previously. Inevitably, in an EU that now has a membership of twenty-seven states, each individual state will have less prominence. France, Germany and the UK remain, however, the largest and most economically powerful three states in the Union, each of them still playing a leading role in EU affairs, both positive and negative. The UK's attitude remains somewhat ambivalent, professing on the one hand to be at the heart of Europe and on the other showing a reluctance to commit as fully as other member states, notably in relation to the euro. Again, in 2007, in the negotiations for the Lisbon Reform Treaty, further opt-outs were secured by the UK Labour government, in particular from the Charter of Fundamental Rights, which, under Protocol 30 attached to the Lisbon Treaty, confirm that the Charter will not apply internally in the UK. This seems on the face of it to contradict the previous step of signing up to the social Chapter in 1997.

 Poland too is subject to Protocol 30.

cross reference
This will be considered further in Chapter 5 on supremacy.

So there is no enthusiasm to make any progress in joining the euro and in efforts to preserve the UK veto in a number of areas, and it seems that the UK is no less a reluctant partner in 2010 than it has been for a number of decades previously, despite having the most pro-European of the major UK parties in the coalition government. In particular, two developments serve to highlight and confirm this renewed lack of enthusiasm for the EU. The first is the enactment of the European Union Act 2011, which introduces measures to ensure that any future transfer of competences or Treaty amendments must be subject to a ministerial statement in the House of Commons as to the impact and whether it requires a further transfer of competences or powers. If that is the case, then either an Act of Parliament would be required to allow the transfer, or if the Treaty proposals were substantial and not, for example, only approving the accession of a new member states, then a referendum would first be required, in which, of course, a majority would have to approve the changes for them to be ratified.

The second development was the stance taken by David Cameron, the UK coalition government Prime Minister, in Brussels December 2011 by refusing to participate in the economic and fiscal Treaty proposals, wielding in effect the UK veto. The long-term political consequences have yet to be felt, but it is clear that the UK is in a far less influential position in the EU than it has been for a long time.

 1.7

The EU and the world: external relations

The EU has diverse roles to play in the world order. Not surprisingly, given the more limited original political scope of the Communities, trade relations with the rest of the world feature most prominently, but not exclusively. However, because these roles and obligations in the areas of external relations have been spread over the various treaties, an overview has been difficult to obtain. Also, the competences to undertake external relations had been granted in different terms under the three original Treaties: for example, the ECSC Treaty expressly granted the legal capacity to make external agreements generally in pursuit of the objectives of the Treaty and the EURATOM (EAEC) Treaty also allowed for general agreements to be concluded, whereas

cross reference

These changes will be considered further in Chapter 2.

cross reference

The types of international agreements are also considered as a source of law in Chapter 4.

the EC Treaty (Article 281) provided that whilst the European Community had been given legal personality, it was provided with powers to conclude specific types of agreement only, such as commercial agreements under the common customs tariff (Articles 131–133 EC, now 205–207 TFEU) or the association agreements. Article 300 EC (now 218 TFEU) provided an express power to conclude international agreements in areas already clearly within the competences of the EU such as the common customs tariff, agriculture and fisheries. However, the Council of Ministers must first give the Commission the go-ahead and the European Parliament must finally assent to the agreement. As a result, there is a confusing array of trade agreements, association agreements and development aid agreements with third countries that have been negotiated by the Commission under a mandate from the Council, but finally concluded by the Council on the basis of a qualified majority. With the entry into force of the Lisbon Treaty, the Union competences in its various relations with the rest of the world have been set out more clearly. There are introduced in Articles 3 and 8 TEU, and provided in greater detail under Articles 21–46 TEU and in a new Part Five of the TFEU, 'External Action by the EU', Articles 205–222, although the policies themselves will not change. They will, however, now be coordinated by the new High Representative of the Union for Foreign Affairs and Security Policy who is appointed by the European Council, but is a Vice President of the Commission, and who will also chair the Foreign Affairs Council.

An extensive chapter on CFSP is now to be found in Articles 23–46 TEU, which also spell out in more detail the roles of the European Council and its relationship with the Council, although in view of the specialized nature of this area, it is unlikely to be covered in most EU law courses. Equally, the details of the various external relations set out in Articles 205–222 TFEU will not be considered in this text.

The three-pillar organization of the EU has now therefore been dismantled, with the Justice and Home Affairs aspects subsumed into the supranational TFEU, but the CFSP remaining intergovernmental, but within the EU Treaty. Until their various roles are fully clarified over time, there will be some overlap in external representation by the European Council President, the High Representative, the Commission, the rotating Council presidency and the still remaining Trade Commissioner.

Summary

The process of further integration has continued with the Lisbon Treaty, which seems for the moment to have settled the argument about whether the EU was moving towards a form of Federal Union or something less than that. At present, the EU enjoys the transfer of considerable powers from the member states, its own institutions and law-making powers, an internal market, a division of powers and competences, the supremacy of EU law, its own catalogue of fundamental rights, its own parliament and also some of the more symbolic external trappings of statehood, such as a currency, a flag, an anthem and a national day, although these aspects have not now been formalized in the Treaties. The EU has a citizenship, but no *demos* – that is, no coherent European population who identify themselves with an embryonic European state. It has been shown in this chapter that the path to European unity is not straight and wide, and is far from certain. It is not planned in advance and any plans that are put in place can easily be hijacked by rapidly evolving European and world political events, such as oil price increases, world economic crises, currency collapses, the collapse of Communism in Europe, the terrorist attacks of 11 September 2001 or rejections of new Treaties by the electorate of a member state.

The European Union of twenty-seven states today, but possibly soon to be thirty-nine states if all of the candidate and potential candidate states join, will play an ever-more-important role in world affairs not just economically, but politically as well, and if for no other reason than because of its economic size. It needs to adapt to do this and, internally also, it still needs to address the issues of governance and democracy, until now not properly dealt with. However, European integration was regarded from the beginning as a process and not an end in itself. The 2007 Lisbon Treaty may nevertheless be regarded as both an example of further deeper integration because it represents a far more comprehensive ordering of the Union and member states, but also as a brake on further unwelcome integration because of its clearer delineation of competences. It makes matters clearer and sets discernible boundaries on the exercise of Union power. It might have been thought also that there would be no appetite for further integration, but the eurozone financial crises have seemingly forced upon the EU the need to integrate more closely economically and fiscally, albeit without the agreement of the UK; thus is it likely that twenty-six states will proceed, without the UK for the time being. Clearly, the integration of European states into the European Union remains an unfolding story and the end is not yet written; quite what the end is will no doubt also continue to be the subject of considerable debate.

thinking point
Which member states have rejected a Treaty?

Questions

For suggested approaches to answering these questions scan here or visit the Online Resource Centre.

37

1   What were the main concerns of the planners of the European Communities after the Second World War? Are these issues relevant to Europe today?

2   What is meant by terms of integration 'intergovernmental', 'supranational', 'functional integration' and 'federalist'?

3   What is the meaning of, and the distinction between, the EU and TFEU?

4   Why do you think the UK joined the European Communities in 1973?

5   How far can the EU keep expanding and integrating?

Further reading

BOOKS

Bache, I. *Europeanization and Multilevel Governance: Cohesion Policy in the European Union and Britain,* illustrated edn, Rowman & Littlefield Publishers, New York, 2008.

Bache, I. and George, S. *Politics in the European Union*, 2nd edn, Oxford University Press, Oxford, 2006 (especially chapters 1–17 and 31).

Bache, I. and Jordan, A. *The Europeanization of British Politics,* Palgrave Macmillan, Basingstoke, 2006.

Blair, A. *The Union since 1945*, 2nd edn, Pearson Longman, Harlow, 2010.

Bulmer, S. and Lequesne, C. *The Member States of the European Union,* Oxford University Press, Oxford, 2005.

Cini, M. and Borragan, N. *European Union Politics*, 3rd edn, Oxford University Press, Oxford, 2009.

Craig, P. *The Lisbon Treaty: Law, Politics and Treaty Reform*, Oxford University Press, Oxford, 2010.

Devuyst, Y. *The European Union Transformed: Community Method and Institutional Evolution from the Schuman Plan to the Constitution for Europe*, revised and updated edn, Peter Lang, Brussels, 2006.

Douglas-Scott, S. *Constitutional Law of the European Union*, Longman, Harlow, 2002 (chapter 1).

Duchene, F. *Jean Monnet: The First Statesman of Interdependence*, W. W. Norton & Co., New York, 1996.

Folsom, H. R. *Principles of European Union,* 2nd edn, Concise Horn Series, Thomson West, St Paul, MN, 2005.

Menon, A. (ed.), *Britain and European Integration: Views from Within*, Blackwell Publishing, Oxford, 2004.

Nicholls, A. 'Britain and the EC: The *European* Historical Background' in S. Bulmer, S. George and A. Scott (eds) *The UK and EC Membership Evaluated*, Pinter Press, London, 1992.

Prechal, S. *Reconciling the Deepening and Widening of the European Union*, Cambridge University Press, Cambridge, 2008.

Rodriguez-Pose, A. *The European Union: Economy, Society and Polity*, Oxford University Press, Oxford, 2002.

Seldon, A. *Blair's Britain: 1997–2007*, Cambridge University Press, Cambridge, 2007.

Szyszczak, E. and Cygan, A. *Understanding EU Law*, 2nd edn, Sweet & Maxwell, London, 2008.

Tatham, A. *Enlargement of the European Union*, Kluwer Law International, London, 2009.

Wall, S. *A Stranger in Europe: Britain and the EU from Thatcher to Blair*, Oxford University Press, New York, 2008.

Ward, I. *A Critical Introduction to European Law*, 3rd edn, Cambridge University Press, Cambridge, 2009 (especially chapters 1, 2 and 7).

ARTICLES

Barratt, G. 'The King is dead, long live the King: the recasting by the Treaty of Lisbon of the provisions of the Constitutional Treaty concerning national parliaments' (2008) 33 EL Rev 66.

Craig, P. 'The Lisbon Treaty: process, architecture and substance' (2008) 33 EL Rev 137.

Craig, P. 'The European Union Act 2011: locks, limits and legality' (2011) 48 CML Rev 1915.

Dougan, M. 'The Treaty of Lisbon 2007: winning minds, not hearts' (2008) 45(3) CML Rev 609.

Eleftheriadis, P. 'The idea of a European Constitution' (2007) 27(1) OJLS 1.

Krisch, N. 'Europe's constitutional monstrosity' (2005) 25(2) OJLS 321.

Majone, G. 'Unity in diversity: European integration and the enlargement process' (2008) 33 EL Rev 457.

Shaw, J. 'Europe's constitutional future' [2005] Public Law 132.

The Union institutions

Learning objectives

This chapter will help you to become familiar with the institutions of the European Union, the work that they do and how they work together. The following topics will be considered:

- the institutional framework;
- the European Commission;
- the Council (of Ministers);
- the European Parliament;
- the European Council and President;
- the European Court of Justice;
- the Court of Auditors;
- the European Central Bank and other Union bodies.

Introduction: the institutional framework

The institutional framework of the Union was originally laid down in the European Coal and Steel Community (ECSC) Treaty, which established a mix of supranational and inter-governmental institutions in a tripartite system consisting of the Council of Ministers, the Commission (then called the High Authority) and the European Parliament (then called the Assembly). These three bodies are the main policymaking and law-making bodies in the Union, but this institutional foundation has been added to and refined considerably since then. There is now an overall policy steering body, the European Council, which has been formalized as a main institution (Article 13 TEU), and additional consultative bodies the European Economic and Social Committee (EESC) and the Committee of the Regions (CoR), which gather the opinions of public interest groups and regional opinions to feed these into the decision-making process. In 1965, a unitary set of four 'official' or principal institutions served the original three Communities. Following the entry into force of the Maastricht Treaty on European Union, they were expanded to five, adding the Court of Auditors and, in 2009 when the Lisbon Treaty entered into force, the European Council and European Central Bank (ECB).

cross reference
See Chapter 1, section 1.2.2, for more on the ECSC Treaty.

Article 13 TEU (ex 7 EC) states that the Union's institutions shall be the European Parliament (EP), the European Council, the Council, the Commission, the Court of Justice, the ECB and the Court of Auditors.

Article 13 TEU requires that each institution shall act within the limits of the powers conferred on it by the Treaty. Article 13(4) provides for two advisory bodies, the European Economic and Social Committee (EESC) and CoR, as a part of a secondary group of bodies completing the institutional structure and which presently include the Committee of Permanent Representatives (COREPER), the European Investment Bank (EIB) and the European System of Central Banks (ESCB). Detailed provisions on the Institutions are contained in Articles 223–287 TFEU.

2.1 The Commission

This section will consider in turn the composition, appointment and removal of the Commission, and its tasks and duties. The Commission fulfils the role of an executive administration for the Union and was given the sole right as the proposer of legislation. This makes the Commission more powerful than a straightforward civil service bureaucracy carrying out the will of an elected government. It is not, however, to be confused with a government itself. It is, however, able to formulate policy within the parameters of the agreed areas contained in the Treaties and to make proposals for legislation to realize this, although the real power of initiative is somewhat compromised by the overall policy formulation and guidance provided by the Council of

For more details
on this section
scan here or
visit the Online
Resource Centre.

Ministers and the European Council. The Commission also has its own powers of decision and is able to exercise powers and enact administrative legislation under powers delegated to it by the Council of Ministers.

2.1.1 **Composition of the Commission**

The composition, tasks and functions of the Commission are determined by Articles 17 TEU and 244–250 TFEU (ex 211–219 EC). It was agreed during the Nice Treaty and 2004 accession negotiation discussions for Bulgaria and Romania that numbers of the Commissioners should be reduced to two-thirds of member states. However, even before the 2008–09 negotiations with Ireland were agreed, a transition period had been established whereby the Commission would consist of twenty-seven members until 2009, extended to 2014 by the Lisbon Treaty. Although Article 17(5) TEU formally provides for a reduction of the number of Commissioners from 2014, the guarantees given to Ireland to encourage it to hold a new referendum in 2009 reinstated the principle of one Commissioner per state. Article 17(5) does, however, empower the European Council, acting unanimously, to alter that number. Croatia will receive one Commissioner if it joins as envisaged in July 2013.

cross reference
See section 2.3
for more on policy
formulation and
guidance.

The Commissioners, although nominated representatives of the member states, are required under Articles 17(3) TEU and 245 TFEU (ex 213 EC) to be completely independent in the performance of their duties and neither take nor seek instructions from any government or any other body. Too often they are regarded as each member state's representatives in Brussels. However, to counterbalance this view, it is suggested that, after a while in Brussels, a member state's Commissioner has a tendency to 'go native' – in other words to take on a much more Union, rather than national, perspective on things.

cross reference
See section 2.1.3
for more on
powers delegated
by the Council of
Ministers.

The Commission is assisted by about 38,000 staff and whilst this sounds a great deal, the Union itself asserts that this is fewer than in most medium-sized city councils in Europe. The Commission, then, is simply not a massive bureaucracy. In the member states, there are hundreds of thousands of civil servants, with some single departments employing far more than the entire European Commission. Part of the reason for the much lower numbers in the European Union (EU) is that most of the work covered or generated by EU legislation is, in fact, carried out by the national agencies, particularly in respect of the Common Agricultural Policy (CAP).

cross reference
QMV is considered
in detail in section
2.2.4.3.

2.1.2 **Appointment and removal of the Commission**

The first part of the process of appointing a new Commission is that the Commission President is considered and then proposed by qualified majority voting (QMV) by the European Council to the European Parliament under Article 17(7) TEU (ex 214 EC). He or she is then subject to approval by the EP by majority vote.

QMV is one of the ways by which the Council votes on legislation.

The Commission President-elect and the member states in Council then jointly propose the other Commissioners, with the exception of the High Representative of the Union for Foreign Affairs and Security Policy, who is selected and appointed independently by the European Council (Article 18(1) TEU), but who is simultaneously a Commission Vice-President (Article 18(4) TEU).

Although the member states chose to reject the term 'Foreign Minister', which was used in the Constitutional Treaty in favour of the more politically acceptable but far more cumbersome and unwieldy term 'High Representative of the Union for Foreign Affairs and Security Policy', it appears that the terms 'HR', or 'High Rep', or 'High Representative' are being used, or that he or she might be informally referred to as the 'Foreign Minister'. The term 'High Representative' will be employed in this volume.

The Commission is then subject to the approval of the EP en bloc. This makes the rejection of a single Commissioner designate technically, although not practically, impossible, as was seen in 2004 by the objection of the EP to the Italian nomination because of the latter's genuinely held, but incongruous, views on homosexuality and the role of women. The Commission President-designate Barroso decided not to submit the Commission for approval for fear of a probable rejection of the entire Commission. Instead, he reshuffled the proposed Commission, without the original Italian nomination, which was then approved by the EP and appointed by the Council.

cross reference

The High Representative is considered briefly in section 2.3.2.

The 'High Representative' is appointed by the European Council by QMV with the agreement of the Commission President. This position is special and unique because the appointee is automatically a Vice-President of the Commission and also presides over the Foreign Affairs Council in conducting the Union's foreign and security policies.

The term of office for all Commissioners is for a renewable period of five years (Article 17(3) TEU). There are seven Vice-Presidents in the second Barroso Commission, whose office will run from 2010 to 2014. The number of Vice-Presidents is no longer specified by the Treaty (Article 17(6) TEU), as was previously the case.

The Commission can be removed by a vote of censure by the EP, but only collectively (Articles 17(8) TEU and 245 TFEU, ex 201 EC) and until the replacement Commission is appointed in its entirety, the old Commission stays in office. It is therefore something of a blunt instrument if the activities of only one Commissioner are objected to, although there is the procedure under Article 247 TFEU (ex 216 EC) for the Court of Justice, on an application of the Council and by a simple majority of the Commission (but not the EP) compulsorily to retire a Commissioner for serious misconduct or where he or she no longer fulfils the conditions required for the performance of his or her duties. However, under a slightly amended procedure now contained in Article 17(6) TEU (ex 217 EC), a member of the Commission shall resign if requested to do so by the President. Article 17 contains a summary of the management powers of the Commission President, first introduced by the Nice Treaty.

Special rules apply to the removal and resignation of the 'High Representative': see Articles 17(6) and (8), and 18(1) TEU and 246 TFEU.

Censure of the entire Commission was threatened in 1999 following a damning report of an independent committee of experts appointed by the EP that exposed serious fraud, cronyism and incompetence on the part of individual Commissioners. Whilst it did not come to a vote of censure, it forced the resignation of the entire Santer Commission on 15 March 1999 as the only way in which to oust the culpable Commissioners. A new Commission was approved by the EP in September 1999 under the presidency of Prodi, who required from the individual Commissioners a promise to resign on demand, thus increasing the power of the President within the Commission. A follow-up case to this episode, Case C-432/04 *Commission v Edith Cresson*, confirmed not only that Commissioner Cresson had breached her duties as a

Commissioner, but also that the Court of Justice had an independent discretionary right to hear such actions, free of any influence of national courts. The Belgium criminal courts had cleared Cresson of any criminal wrongdoing.

In view of the possibilities under Articles 17(6) TEU and 247 TFEU to remove or require the resignation of a single member of the Commission, it would seem less necessary for a vote of censure of the whole Commission to be threatened to tackle the excesses or breaches of individual Commissioners, unless the Council or Commission President would not take action.

thinking point
What improvements could be made to both appointment and removal procedures generally?

2.1.3 Tasks and duties

Article 17 TEU (ex 211 EC) imposes on the Commission the general duty of promoting the general interest of the Union and of taking initiatives to reach that end.
The Commission has a number of main functions within that general duty, as follows.

(1) It must ensure that the provisions of the Treaty and the measures taken by the institutions under them are applied. The Commission is described as the 'guardian' or 'watchdog' of the Communities, because it is given the task of bringing to the European Court of Justice breaches of the Treaty by member states under Article 258 TFEU (ex 226 EC), other institutions under Article 263 TFEU (ex 230 EC), and individuals under various provisions of the Treaty and secondary law, such as Regulation 1/2003 in respect of competition policy.

(2) It formulates and proposes policy initiatives and legislative proposals by way of recommendations or opinions on matters as expressly provided for by the Treaty or as the Commission considers necessary. Here, the Commission is acting as the initiator of legislation. The Commission has the sole right to propose legislation (Article 17(2) TEU), although it may now be requested to submit legislative proposals by either the Council (Article 241 TFEU, ex 208 EC) or the EP (Article 225 TFEU, ex 192 EC). The TEU, as amended by the Lisbon Treaty, now also provides that if at least 1 million citizens of a significant number of member states come together, they may request the Commission to submit a proposal (see Articles 11 and 21 TEU). The chances of this happening must be regarded as very slim.

(3) The Commission has limited powers of independent decision-making by participation in the shaping of measures taken by the Council of Ministers and by the EP. This was outlined previously in Article 211; this Article has now been repealed by the Lisbon Treaty and not directly replaced, although there is no suggestion that the power has been removed, because Article 17 TEU provides that the Commission shall take appropriate initiatives to promote the general interest of the Union.

(4) It has powers under the delegated legislation procedure conferred on it by the Council of Ministers for the implementation of the rules laid down by the latter, thus acting as the executive of the Communities (Article 290 TFEU).

Delegated powers are regulated by Regulation 182/2011, which provides for supervision by a range of committees, known collectively as 'comitology' and which are determined by the Council under Article 291 TFEU (ex 202 EC).

Article 290 provides for the delegation by the Commission of non-legislative acts.

(5) The Commission is also responsible for the external representation of the Union and nego-tiation of international agreements under Articles 207 and 218 TFEU (ex 133 and 300 EC), with the exception of the Common Foreign and Security Policy (CFSP).

(6) The Commission also plays a part in drawing up the Union's annual budget (Articles 314–316 TFEU, ex 271–273 EC) and its implementation (Articles 317–319 TFEU, ex 274–276 EC).

The Commission is regarded as the most federal institution of the EU, owing largely to its inde-pendence from direct national influences. Its decision-making process, under Article 250 TFEU (ex 219 EC), provides that the Commission can decide matters collectively by a majority. All members of the Commission are expected to abide by Commission decisions.

cross reference

This is considered further in Chapter 1, section 1.7, and Chapter 4, section 4.2.3.

Commission activity is most pronounced in the fields of competition policy and in the man-agement of the CAP and Common Customs Policy because of the high degree of day-to-day decision-making necessary. It is also very much involved in representing the Union in interna-tional organizations such as the General Agreement on Tariffs and Trade (GATT) and the World Trade Organization (WTO), and in concluding international agreements on behalf of the Union, such as the association agreements with various countries.

In view of the strengthening of the positions of the EP and European Council following the Lisbon Treaty, the position of the Commission may have been weakened. This will be consid-ered in brief in this chapter, but it may take time for this to be confirmed in reality.

2.2 The Council (of Ministers) of the European Union

For more details on this section scan here or visit the Online Resource Centre.

Unfortunately, the Council of Ministers has undergone a few name changes, presently being called simply 'the Council' in contrast to being previously called 'the Council of Ministers'. Furthermore, unhelpfully, there is also the 'European Council' and it should not be confused with this other body or indeed with the Council of Europe in Strasbourg. This section will con-sider the functions and powers of the Council of Ministers, as well is its role and forms of voting procedures within the legislative procedures and its general law-making powers. Furthermore, although strictly speaking COREPER and the Council Secretariat are not main institutions and should be considered in the section on other EU bodies, they will be considered here because of their direct connection to the work of the Council.

Although there have been various changes to the processes by which Union legislation is enacted that have given more power to the EP, notably more so after the Lisbon Treaty reforms, the Council remains the main legislative organ of the Union. Its tasks, composition and func-tions are outlined in Article 16 TEU and Articles 237–243 TFEU (ex 202–210 EC).

The Council consists of representative ministers of the member states depending on the sub-ject matter under discussion. Thus different configurations of the Council take place, with the foreign ministers attending the General Council, and agriculture or finance ministers, for exam-ple, attending the specialist Councils. There are ten different council configurations following the Lisbon Reforms, which provide now, under Article 236 TFEU, that the European Council shall decide the configuration and presidencies of the Council. The General Affairs Council is attended by the foreign ministers and coordinates the work of the other Council configura-tions, except the Foreign Affairs Council. The Council previously could be constituted by the heads of state and government. However, whilst this is still theoretically possible, the elevation of the European Council, which has the same membership, as a full institution of the Union, renders this unnecessary and unlikely.

cross reference

The European Council is consid-ered under section 2.3.

This explains why Article 214 EC, previously regulating the Council constituted by the heads of state and government, was repealed and replaced when appointing the Commission. The appointment of the Commission is now found in Article 17(7) TEU, placing that right clearly within the prerogative of the European Council.

2.2.1 Functions and powers

Article 16(1) TEU (ex 202 EC) imposes on the Council the general requirement to carry out policymaking and coordinating functions as laid down in the Treaties, as well as jointly with the European Parliament, exercising legislative and budgetary functions. The Treaty gives the Council the power to take decisions and to delegate some decision-making powers to the Commission under Article 290 TFEU.

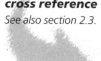

cross reference

The ordinary legislative procedure is considered in Chapter 3, section 3.6.1.1.

Following the Lisbon Treaty reforms, the Council decides on the adoption of legislative proposals predominantly by the co-decision procedure, now referred to as the 'ordinary legislative procedure' (Article 289 TFEU), which provides the EP with a final right of veto, as outlined under Article 294 TEU (ex 251 EC). The Council, with the EP, is also responsible for the adoption of the annual budget (Article 314 TFEU, ex 372 EC). When acting in its legislative capacity, the Council is now required to meet in public (Article 16(8) TEU).

cross reference

See also section 2.3.

The Council is also now able to request that the Commission undertakes studies that the Council considers desirable to attain objectives and to submit proposals on the same. It may do this by simple majority. This compromises the Commission's original sole right of initiative in proposing legislation. The Commission must state reasons if it decides not to submit a proposal (Article 241 TFEU).

2.2.2 The presidency of the Council

The Council of Ministers is chaired by a presidency, which is held by each of the member states in turn for a period of six months only (Articles 16(9) TEU and 236 TFEU).

The newly appointed European President now chairs and coordinates the work of the European Council.

Following the Lisbon Treaty reforms, the Foreign Affairs Council will be chaired by the 'High Respresentative', otherwise the President usually hails from the state holding the rotation governed by Articles 16(9) TEU and 236 TFEU.

Even prior to the Lisbon Treaty reforms, the very short period of Council presidency of six months made it clear that greater continuity between presidencies was required. Hence, a current President and both the previous and succeeding Presidents coordinated to a greater degree to work in conjunction, particularly in the pursuit of international relations. The term *Troika* has therefore been used to describe the eighteen-month rolling Council governance to provide continuity in policy, although it remains the case that each presidency can outline and pursue particular policy objectives that it has identified as its priorities. It remains to be seen whether the formalization of the European Council and the establishment of the European President will disturb this arrangement. The Council no longer represents the EU externally, though, clearly reducing the overall role and impact of this institution.

cross reference
The legal base is outlined in Chapter 3, section 3.5.1.

2.2.3 **Role and voting in the legislative procedures**

Despite the many institutional reforms over the years, the Council still has the leading role in deciding on and enacting secondary legislation, although – and especially following the Lisbon Treaty reforms – it decides now extensively by co-decision with the EP. The actual process used to enact legislation and the degree of participation by the EP and/or other bodies depends on the particular Treaty provision under which legislation is enacted – in other words, the legal base.

cross reference
See Chapter 9, section 9.1, for more on Article 263 TFEU (ex 230 EC) annulment actions.

In broad terms, the political institutional balance has seen a number of changes over the decades, mostly in favour of a power shift from the Council to the EP in the law-making process. However, it is not only the EP that participates with the Council. The Council may have to consult the EESC, and/or the CoR before legislation can be enacted. If it fails to do so, the legislation subsequently enacted may be challenged and annulled. Even when enacting legislation with the EP, there are different processes by which the legislation can be enacted. The Council may consult the EP or co-decide with the EP.

cross reference
The legislative procedures will be explained in Chapter 3, section 3.6.

2.2.4 **Forms of voting**

The Council does not simply vote in one way on all of the decisions that it makes – that is, it does not vote only by a majority or unanimously on everything. In contrast to the previous Treaty provision on voting, the new Article 16(3) TEU is a much more accurate reflection of both law and practice.

Article 16(3) TEU provides that the Council shall act by a qualified majority except where the Treaties provide otherwise.

Previously, Article 205 EC provided that, subject to Treaty exceptions, the Council would vote by a simple majority. In fact, it was even the case from the very beginning that the exceptions were the rule (or the rule was the exception) and voting was mainly either by a qualified majority or by unanimity.

Following the Lisbon Treaty reforms, the rule is reflected in fact and qualified majority voting (QMV) is by far the most common method of voting, although it would be usual practice for the Council President to attempt to gain the consensus of all member states before proceeding to make a decision, and if a consensus view is achieved, the Council may not vote at all. A requirement of unanimity is now much rarer.

2.2.4.1 Unanimity

The meaning of 'unanimity' is clear: all member states must agree, which means that, as from 2007, all twenty-seven member states must agree! This is where a single member state can wield a veto and prevent a particular legislative proposal from being enacted: see, for example, Article 19 TFEU (ex 13 EC) requiring unanimity on the part of the Council to enact measures outlawing different forms of discrimination. The more that voting is done by unanimity, the less potentially and probably will be accomplished; hence a move to more majority voting is crucial. Member states that abstain from voting do not prevent the others from agreeing a measure unanimously, which is then binding on all member states (Article 238(4) TFEU). Unanimity is still used in a considerable number of Treaty Articles, especially following the Lisbon Treaty amendments, which brought within the TFEU areas of law lying previously purely within the intergovernmental EU Treaty, such as Common Foreign and Security Policy (CFSP) and policing.

2.2.4.2 Simple majority voting

Simple majority voting whereby a measure is enacted by an arithmetic majority, such as by fourteen states with thirteen against, is quite rare and is required for only eight Articles of the TFEU, concerned mainly with the setting up of advisory committees and the institutions.

Article 238 TFEU defines this requirement as follows: 'Where it is required to act by a simple majority, the Council shall act by a majority of its component members.'

cross reference

The Luxembourg Accords are considered in Chapter 1, section 1.5.2.

2.2.4.3 Qualified majority voting

In 1965, when the Communities still consisted of only six member states, the Council was due to move from unanimity voting to QMV for certain subject areas of the Treaty. This was objected to by President de Gaulle of France and the ensuing dispute led eventually to a boycott of the institutions by the French members. It was resolved only when a compromise, the 'Luxembourg Accords' or 'Luxembourg Compromise', was reached.

The Luxembourg Accords were essentially an 'agreement to disagree', but provided that where a member state identified a very important national interest, all member states should try to reach a unanimous decision rather than overrule that member. The six member states could not, however, agree on the consequence of a failure to agree. The conclusion, which was certainly that of the French and generally accepted, was that an objecting member state effectively had a veto over the decision.

The legal position of the Accords was always uncertain, but despite the provision in the Treaty for majority and QMV, the Council denied itself this form of voting for many years. Successive enlargements and the difficulties in reaching a consensus every time led the Council to realize that it could no longer make progress using only unanimity. Thus, particularly after the Treaty revisions of the Single European Act (SEA) and TEU, the Council has moved slowly, but significantly, to using QMV in more and more areas (twelve more occasions with the SEA and thirty more with the TEU in 1992) – so much so, that the continued applicability of the Luxembourg Accords has been brought into doubt. The Amsterdam and Nice Treaties extended QMV to another forty-seven instances.

Despite the further considerable move to QMV following the Lisbon Treaty, unanimous voting will be retained for quite a few matters, particularly when measures may be considered necessary to fulfil certain Union aims, but for which express powers have not been foreseen. Unanimity has been retained for the areas of CFSP and defence policy, taxation, social security matters and some budgetary matters, involving about forty Treaty Articles.

QMV has been a very important issue in the Council. To agree that it is to be used more often has often involved much horse-trading. More use of QMV is regarded as necessary because it allows votes to be taken by majorities. The possible alternative, to take decisions by simple majority, is not a real option because it is not politically acceptable for most member states that a simple majority should dictate a policy for the whole Union. This is particularly the case where the majority would consist of smaller states, the population of which represents a clear minority of the overall EU population. Thus the use of QMV enhances both democracy and efficiency in law-making in the EU where otherwise decisions would be extremely difficult to reach in a

Council of twenty-seven possible vetoes. It also encourages debate and consensus, because it is no longer possible for a state or states to fall back on a veto.

2.2.4.4 How QMV works

To reiterate that mentioned earlier in the chapter, new Article 16(3) TEU states that the Council shall act by QMV unless otherwise stated.

Unlike the old Article 205 EC, which provided within the Treaty the numbers of votes that each member state has, the EU and TFEU Treaties no longer contain those figures; these are now contained in Protocol 36 on Transitional Provisions, Title II, as further qualified by Declaration 7 on Articles 16(4) TEU and 238 TFEU, both attached to the Treaties.

Before looking in detail at the now overcomplicated sets of rules for QMV, it is useful to understand the original thinking behind QMV, which will help to explain why layers of supplementary and compensatory rules have been added. The number of votes per state has always been a matter of contention and prior to the reforms adopted at Nice, at the extreme, Germany, with a population of approximately 81 million, had only ten votes, compared with Luxembourg, with a population of about 600,000, which had two votes. This was clearly disproportionate. Additionally, prior to the 2004 enlargement, it was noted that, with a greater number of states, a blocking minority would be harder to achieve as it required more votes and thus more countries. At the same time, however, it was also noted that as the number of states increased, the relative share of influence of the large states decreased, despite their high share of the population. It is worth noting that four countries – Germany, France, the UK and Italy – had just over 57 per cent of the EU-25 population and in the EU of twenty-seven (with Romania and Bulgaria), the big four still have *approximately* 53 per cent of the population. If voting were undertaken by simple majority based directly on population, it would mean that the four large states could always outvote the other twenty-three states combined. This would not be acceptable to the rest of the Union; therefore the QMV voting rules and numbers contain compromises that seek to achieve a balance between facilitating a form of majority decision-making, but nevertheless providing that a sizeable minority of states can block decisions. Hence instead of a simple majority of states or votes being able to secure a result, a predetermined majority of votes has to be achieved from the sum of the blocks of votes of the member states.

Germany, France, Italy, UK	29
Spain, Poland	27
Romania	14
The Netherlands	13
Belgium, Czech Republic, Greece, Hungary, Portugal	12
Austria, Bulgaria, Sweden	10
Denmark, Ireland, Lithuania, Slovakia, Finland	7
Cyprus, Estonia, Latvia, Luxembourg, Slovenia	4
Malta	3
TOTAL	345
Qualified majority	255 (= 73.91 per cent)

The qualified majority with twenty-seven member states is 255 votes (73.91 per cent) from a possible total of 345. Thus a blocking minority of ninety-one votes will prevent a proposal from being passed. If voting on a proposal that has been introduced by the Council rather than the Commission, an additional requirement is imposed that a minimum of two-thirds (that is, eighteen) of the member states must have voted in favour. If Croatia joins as envisaged in 2013, it will have seven votes in Council and the qualified majority will be 260 votes from 352 (that is, 73.86 per cent).

The rationale behind QMV

To go back to basics for a moment first, however, the rationale behind QMV is the idea that the number of Council votes per country should in some way, even if very crudely, represent the populations and thus usually the gross domestic product (GDP) of the countries – or, if you like, their political and economic clout! This is tinged with the fear of domination of Europe by a few large states over the wishes of numerous smaller states. Hence the votes for each country for a qualified majority were deliberately biased for the protection of smaller states and to ensure more of a consensus view. The Treaty of Nice went some way towards addressing the overrepresentation of the smaller states, by giving the larger member states a higher proportion of votes. To some extent, the acceptance of this change by all states is argued to have been regarded as fair compensation for the loss of a second Commissioner by the large states. However, it was not accepted without further condition because this change meant that a smaller combination of larger states could outvote the small states, something with which the smaller member states were not happy. Hence the reform of QMV became a hotly contested issue, with the discussions first concentrating on the number of votes per member state, and then on the additional requirements about the number of states voting and the populations of those states. Further compromises were devised for the Treaty of Nice in that, in addition to the rule that two-thirds vote in favour of Council proposals if requested by a member, a second threshold is added that the qualified majority represent at least 62 per cent of the population of the Union (and now contained in Article 3(3) of Protocol 36, Title II). Even with the Nice reforms, Luxembourg and Malta – the smallest states with populations of about 600,000 and 390,000 respectively, but with four and three votes respectively in Council – have voting power far in excess of their populations by comparison with Germany, which has a population of about 81 million and twenty-nine votes. As soon as the Nice Treaty was agreed, it became clear that Germany and other states were not happy with the voting figures. It was agreed, however, not to reopen the agreement reached at Nice, which had been, almost literally, a nightmare to achieve.

cross reference
See the discussion of the lengthy Nice negotiations in Chapter 1, section 1.5.10.

The next opportunity to address this was not far away: the Rome 2003 European Council summit was set up to discuss and agree the draft Constitutional Treaty, as proposed by the Convention on the Future of Europe. However, it became clear that without changing the actual number of votes, as agreed in Nice, any possibility of addressing the continuing concerns of the imbalance of votes could be done only through further tinkering with the proportions of states required to vote in favour of a proposal and/or the proportion of the population of the EU as a whole required to support a qualified majority vote. This became the argument that led to the very public bust-up and failure to agree in Rome in December 2003. The member states simply could not agree on the further compromises needed to respect the allocation of votes at Nice, which had to take account of the largest states' populations and political clout, and be sensitive to the smaller states' fear of being dominated by a few larger states. It took months of shuttle diplomacy under the Irish presidency in the first part of 2004 to come up with the necessary compromises. In a nutshell, these new reforms will mean that more states will be outvoted more often.

The issue is one that was revisited in the June 2007 summit and finally agreed for the Lisbon Treaty, which retains the hard-fought compromises on voting numbers of previous negotiations, but provides for two transitional periods and adds further to the complication of EU law. QMV is now governed by Article 16 TEU, Article 238 TFEU and Protocol 36 on Transitional Provisions, and added to by a Decision within Declaration No. 7 also attached to the Treaties! This is far from transparent.

It was originally agreed that new rules, lowering the requirements of states or population to 55 per cent for either, would apply, at first from entry into force of the Lisbon Treaty, then postponed until 2017, with an additional period from 2014 to 2017. These new compromises resemble the Ioannina compromise, which was employed in the 1990s to allow a large, but not sufficient, blocking minority under QMV to ask the Council to consider further a matter before it and to try to reach a consensus view rather than adopt it. The reweighing of votes by the Treaty of Nice effectively ended this compromise only for it to be brought back following representations by Poland during the negotiations for the Lisbon Treaty. It now finds expression in Declaration No. 7 attached to the Treaties, whereby member states with a vote that is not sufficient to constitute a blocking minority can ask the Council to continue to discuss an issue to find a satisfactory solution without proceeding on the matter. This is, of course, another example of the political power and numbers games that the member states find so important, but it does mean that EU attempts to make law-making more democratic and efficient are hindered. Instead, the process has become far from transparent and not easy to understand.

The periods that dictate the rules applicable are as follows.

(1) Up to 31 October 2014, the rules will remain as they presently are under the old Article 205 EC – that is, QMV of 255 votes on Commission proposals, otherwise 255 votes representing two-thirds of the member states, unless a member states objects, in which case a second threshold of a minimum of 62 per cent of the EU population must be represented by the majority.

(2) Between 1 November 2014 and 31 March 2017, the rules under new Treaties require that a qualified majority must total at least 55 per cent of Council members, comprising at least fifteen states and 65 per cent population. Where the Council does not act on a proposal from the Commission or from the High Representative, the qualified majority needs to be 72 per cent of the member of the Council. However, the Declaration insists that if states having at least 75 per cent of population or 75 per cent of the number of blocking minority states oppose that, then the above rules do not apply and discussions must continue. The blocking minority must also achieve a threshold of four states to prevent a small minority of large member states from blocking a proposal representing at least 35 per cent population plus one state (Article 238(3) TFEU).

(3) From 1 April 2017, when a single state can no longer ask for a population percentage to be imposed, the requirements to oppose will be reduced to 55 per cent of population or member states that constitute a blocking minority and those states can also ask the Council to continue discussions.

So, in order to try to understand QMV today, one needs to have in mind the Treaties (Articles 16 TEU and 238 TFEU), the Treaty-altering Protocol 36 *and* Declaration No. 7 attached to the Treaties, which modifies the rules again, to see the full picture. This is truly deplorable and something that only politicians could have dreamt up! Of course, most legislative decisions are and will be reached either by consensus or by a clear majority, but the exception-riddled rule on QMV makes it exceedingly difficult to gain a clear and straightforward understanding of the rules.

2.2.5 Council general law-making powers

Apart from specific powers to enact legislation under the particular titles of the Treaty, the form of voting for which is specified in particular Articles throughout the Treaty, the Council also has general powers to enact legislation. Article 113 TFEU (ex 93 EC) empowers the Council of Ministers, acting unanimously, now part of the special legislative procedure, to adopt provisions for the harmonization of legislation concerning turnover taxes, excise duties and other forms of indirect taxes (VAT) whereby harmonization is necessary to ensure the functioning and establishment of the internal market. Article 114 TFEU (ex 95 EC) provides that the Council shall act by a qualified majority on a proposal that has as its object the establishment and functioning of the internal market. Article 115 TFEU (ex 94 EC), as an exception to Article 114, provides for the approximation of laws not catered for by any of the specific parts of the Treaty and requires unanimity by the Council. Further, Article 352 TFEU (ex 308 EC) provides generally that the Council may enact measures to attain the objectives of the Union. These general powers have been used extensively by the Council, particularly for measures not originally sanctioned elsewhere: for example, in 1976, to support the enactment of the Equal Treatment Directive 76/207. The Directive went much further than original Article 119 EC (ex 141 EC, now 157 TFEU) which was concerned narrowly with equal pay matters only. Article 308 EC (now 352 TFEU) was often used to enact environment measures before the Treaty was amended to include a title on environment. However, its proposed use to accede to the European Convention for the Protection of Human Rights and Fundamental Freedoms (ECHR) was prevented by the Court of Justice, which stated in Opinion 1/96 that it could not be used as the basis for acceding to the Convention.

The overuse of the general powers, referred to as the 'competence creep', has been criticized and resisted by the member states. It was addressed both in the Constitutional Treaty and Lisbon Treaty, the latter of which has addressed this by more clearly establishing the division of competences. It also specifically empowers the Union to accede to the ECHR, which is now provided in the amended Article 6(2) TEU.

cross reference
The division of competences is considered in Chapter 3.

2.2.6 COREPER and the Council Secretariat

The Council is not a unitary and permanently constituted body, and in all configurations meets on only about ninety occasions per year. Hence it requires assistance to deal with its workload and to provide preparation for and some continuity between meetings. This help comes in two forms. First, COREPER was established, consisting of representatives of the member states who may be part of the ambassadorial delegation or other civil servants on secondment. It is now formally established within the Treaties, Articles 16(7) and 240(2) TFEU (ex 207 EC). This body was brought in to reduce the workload of the Council, to balance the result of the delegation of decision-making power to the Commission and to sift the Commission proposals. It also oversees and, to a lesser extent, controls the numerous management committees that were set up to supervise the delegation of power to the Commission.

Article 240(2) TFEU (ex 207(2) EC) also provides for a permanent Council Secretariat to undertake much of the more mundane work of the Council, such as the organization of and preparation for meetings, and it also will assist the European Council (Article 234(4) TFEU) and the High Representative in the new External Action Service (Article 27(2) TEU).

2.3 The European Council

Following the entry into force of the Lisbon Treaty, the European Council is now a full Union institution (Articles 13 and 15 TEU). It now comprises the twenty-seven heads of state and government, and in addition the new European President and the President of the European Commission (Article 15(2) TEU), although these last two do not have voting rights (Article 235(1) TFEU). The new High Representative for Foreign Affairs will also participate in its meetings, also without voting rights. The European Council developed from the summit meetings of the heads of state and government of the member states who met from time to time to discuss matters outside the formal scope of the Community Treaties. Amongst other initiatives, it provided impetus for the Community, as then called, to carry on with the process of integration or has acted, or tried to act, in common response to international crises. After this informal start, Article 2 SEA placed the European Council on a legal basis and formalized European political cooperation in the areas of foreign policy consultation and monetary cooperation. These moves were further formalized and brought into the EU framework by Article 4 TEU, which stated that the European Council shall provide the Union with the necessary impetus for its development and shall define the general political guidelines, which are carried into Article 15(1) TEU today. Note, though, that legislative functions are specifically excluded. The European Council therefore enjoys a much broader role than the Council of Ministers, which is restricted to matters included in the Treaties.

The European Council will meet at least twice every six months and member states' ministers may also take part, as may an assistant to the Commission President (Article 15(3) TEU). It meets now in Brussels, where a building is being constructed for it, rather than in each of the member states in turn that hold the Council presidency.

cross reference

The European President is considered further at section 2.3.1.

Previously, decision-making was entirely by consensus; now, in certain areas as provided by the Treaty and as noted in this volume, it also decides by QMV. One of the most notable instances of this – which is also one of the, if not *the*, most notable institutional changes introduced – is the establishment of the new position of the European President. It appoints the High Representative by qualified majority (Article 18 TEU), and decides on both the composition of the EP and its membership by unanimity (Articles 14(2) TEU and 17(5) TEU and 244 TFEU, respectively).

The European Council has been criticized for being a purely intergovernmental organization and for presenting a distinctly intergovernmental attitude at the top of the Union institutional hierarchy. Whilst it has, at times, provided the necessary political will and impetus to achieve very notable goals, such as economic union and the euro, it is feared that trying to achieve the agreement of twenty-seven heads of state or government will prove very demanding. It is, though, regarded as having gained power following Lisbon, not least because of the continuity and leadership provided by the more permanent and independent chair, considered next.

2.3.1 The European Council President

New to the Union, brought forward from the Constitutional Treaty to the Lisbon Treaty, is the creation of a President for the European Council, known already as the 'European President'. The election of this person is by the European Council by qualified majority for a period of two-and-a-half years, renewable once. This was a much-discussed role in terms of the person who might be elected, with Tony Blair, former UK Prime Minister, a favourite candidate. In the end, though, Herman Van Rompuy was elected and stood down as premier of Belgium to comply with requirement of independence (Article 15(6) TEU).

The President is provided with the tasks of chairing the European Council, and driving forward and organizing its work in cooperation with the Commission and General Affairs Council. He or she shall seek to obtain consensus by the European Council and report to the EP after each of the meetings (Article 15(6) TEU). He or she shall also oversee the external representation of the Union, without prejudice to the powers of the High Representative.

2.3.2 The High Representative of the Union for Foreign Affairs and Security Policy

The High Representative is, first of all, chosen from amongst the Commissioners, then elected by the European Council by qualified majority, and then automatically becomes a Commission Vice-President (Article 18 TEU). He or she conducts the CFSP, attends relevant European Council meetings, chairs the Council foreign affairs meetings and leads the Commission in external relations. The present High Representative is assisted by an External Action Service set up for this purpose (Article 27 TEU). The idea of the role is to coordinate the conduct of the EU's external relations, although getting the twenty-seven member states to come to a consensus on particularly sensitive political developments in the world can be understandably difficult. It will be interested to see how this role and office develops.

2.4 The European Parliament (EP)

For more details on this section scan here or visit the Online Resource Centre.

As originally conceived and constituted, the EP was called the 'Assembly', and consisted of members nominated by and largely from the member states' parliaments. It was arguably more aptly named at that time because it was not a true legislative body capable of law-making in its own right and it consists of only one chamber. However, the term 'Parliament' was used by its members from 1962 and with more authority following the direct election of its 518 members for the first time in 1979. The name is now clearly sanctioned by Article 14 TEU (ex 189 EC). The EP is governed by Articles 14 TEU and 223–234 TFEU (ex 189–201 EC), and has enjoyed significant incremental increases in its powers and functions with each amending Treaty. It is still required, by agreement of the member states and now under Protocol 6 attached to the Treaties, to transit between three cities, holding most plenary sessions in Strasbourg and additional sessions in Brussels, but having its supporting Secretariat travelling in from Luxembourg.

The next sections will consider the membership, elections, political groupings, functions and powers of the EP.

2.4.1 Membership

Following the expansions of 2004 and 2007, the number of members of the European Parliament (MEPs) was fixed at 736, a number that, according to the accession Treaty of 2005, shall not be exceeded. However, this number has been extended under the Lisbon Treaty to a maximum of 750 plus the President (Article 14(2) TEU), but the 2009–14 EP was elected under the old agreed numbers before Lisbon came into effect and the additional numbers were not allocated to the member states in time. The additional MEPs were allocated by Decision of the European Council in June 2010; the reduction previously agreed for Germany from ninety-nine to ninety-six was not undertaken so as not to prejudice the currently elected MEPs. Hence the present number stands at 754. If Croatia enters the EU in July 2013 as envisaged, twelve MEPs will be added to the EP.

MEPs are elected to serve the electorate in constituencies and are organized into cross-border political groupings rather than according to member state. Whilst the total number per state should be crudely in proportion to population, the broad political deal reached at Nice was that those member states that had gained in the QMV numbers lost more MEPs, whereas those member states regarded as losing out under QMV either retained the previous numbers of MEPs or lost proportionately fewer MEPs, compared with other member states.

2.4.2 **Elections and political parties**

Article 223(1) TFEU (ex 190(4) EC) requires a common election system to be set up for the EP. Whilst all member states now, including the UK, have used proportional representation (PR) voting systems for the EP elections, this is still not a single common system and although the same four-day period of Thursday into the weekend is used, the actual polling day(s) are different in different member states according to election day traditions: for example, the UK prefers a Thursday, whereas other member states have always used a Saturday or Sunday as polling day. Once elected, MEPs sit in the transnational political groupings, recognized under Article 224 TFEU (ex 191 EC), although there is a strong national element and organization within these, particularly as a result of national political party discipline. There are seven distinct groups and a final group for those members not wishing to be aligned to any of the specific groups.

The European (and UK) membership of the seven groups of MEPs is as follows.

(1) Group of the European People's Party (Christian Democrats) (PPE)	271 (0 in the UK)
(2) Socialist Group in the European Parliament (S&D)	190 (13 in the UK)
(3) Group of the Alliance of Liberals and Democrats for Europe (ALDE)	85 (12 in the UK)
(4) Group of the Greens/European Free Alliance Verts (ALE)	58 (5 in the UK)
(5) European Conservatives and Reformists (ECR)	52 (26 in the UK)
(6) Europe for Freedom and Democracy Group (EFD)	34 (10 in the UK)
(7) Confederal Group of the European United Left–Nordic Green Left (GUE/NGL)	34 (1 in the UK)
(8) Non-attached members (NI)	30 (6 in the UK)
TOTAL	754

2.4.3 **Functions and powers**

Apart from the obvious function of a Parliament, which is that of a discussion and debate forum, the EP has the following powers and functions.

2.4.3.1 Legislative powers

Before the SEA was negotiated, as far as legislative participation was concerned, the EP had advisory and consultative powers only. Original Article 137 EEC provided that the Assembly shall 'exercise the advisory and supervisory which are conferred on it by this Treaty'. The treaty originally specified only seventeen instances in which the EP had to be consulted before legislation could be adopted by the Council. Its participation in the legislative process was increased by the conciliation procedure of 1977 and the introduction of the cooperation procedure by the SEA.

Note that the cooperation procedure was removed entirely by the Lisbon Treaty.

cross reference

This is considered in Chapter 3, section 3.6.1.1.

The present authorization for the EP's law-making role is Article 14(1) TEU (ex 192 EC), which empowers the EP to exercise legislative and budgetary functions jointly with the Council. It was the TEU that gave the Parliament its most extensive role in the legislative process by introducing the co-decision procedure, which has been extended in line with the extension of QMV in the Council of Ministers and has become the most widely used procedure. The Lisbon Treaty extended it very considerably in about forty instances, although not as far as in the draft Constitutional Treaty, which removed unanimity entirely. It is referred to now as the 'ordinary legislative procedure' (see Articles 289 and 294 TFEU) and now accounts for about 90 per cent of law-making.

The recent extension may affect the long-running debate about the EP's legislative role, whether it remains as limited as it was and whether the term 'democratic deficit' can arguably still be used to describe the unsatisfactory degree of democratically legitimized participation in the law-making process in the EU by the EP, the only directly elected Union institution.

cross reference

Considered in Chapter 3, section 3.6.1.3.

Finally, the EP has a power of consent (previously assent), which is a prerequisite for the accession of new member states or the entry of the Union into association agreements, the ECHR and international agreements (Articles 49 TEU and 218 TFEU, replacing the powers contained in ex 300 and 310 EC), and a new power of veto over delegated Acts (Article 290 TFEU). This new power answers the criticism that the EP had been left out of the procedure when decision-making powers are delegated by the Council to the Commission. Quite how it will work is not yet clear.

2.4.3.2 Control of the executive

The EP has, through various Treaty amendments, gained powers of appointment and removal of the Commission, as well as a general role of the scrutiny of the work of the Commission.

Appointment

Starting with appointment, the Treaty of Amsterdam introduced the requirement that the President of the Commission be nominated by the member states; after Lisbon, he or she is now nominated by the European Council by QMV and is then approved by the EP, despite the clear statement in Article 14 TEU that the EP shall elect the President of the Commission. Then, the whole Commission, as selected by the member states in the Council and nominated in conjunction with the President-elect of the Commission, is subject to the approval of the EP (see now Article 17(7) TEU post Lisbon, ex 214 EC). The political strength gained by the EP by such changes was demonstrated in 2004, when the proposed new Commission had to be reconstituted because the EP took objection to the nomination of a particular Commissioner. In order to avoid a likely vote not to appoint the entire Commission, Barroso, the Commission President-designate, instead withdrew his proposed team and resubmitted it a couple of weeks later, having replaced the offending person.

Censure/removal

At least on paper, the most powerful weapon of the EP would seem to be its power to censure the Commission, which means in effect to require it to resign from office. Articles 17(8) TEU and 234 TFEU (ex 201 EC) provide that a two-thirds vote of the majority of the members is needed, but the Commission is required to resign in its entirety. The censure motion cannot be used against individual Commissioners, which is regarded as unfortunate. For example, in 1999, under the Santer Commission, certain Commissioners were accused of financial improprieties and fraud. A censure motion against the entire Commission failed, but following the very critical report of a committee of independent experts set up by the EP and Commission, the entire Commission resigned without a further vote of censure taking place. Whilst the end result was that which was required – that is, that certain Commissioners were removed from office – the result is criticized because the particular Commissioners were able to hide behind the collective resignation and not be singled out. Until new Commissioners are approved, the censured Commissioners remain in office. So far, no motions of censure have been adopted. Whilst not a right of the EP, the Commission President can require an individual member of the Commission to resign (Article 17(6) TEU), and no doubt the EP could bring its political pressure to bear if sufficiently motivated.

Other powers of scrutiny now available to the EP include:

* the ability to set up a committee of inquiry to investigate the alleged contravention or maladministration in the implementation of Union law (see Article 226 TFEU, ex 193 EC);

* the ability to question, orally or in writing, the Commission under Article 230 TFEU (ex 197 EC); and

* the right to discuss the Commission's annual general reports under Article 233 TFEU (ex 200 EC).

The EP is also entitled to request the Commission to submit proposals that the EP considers necessary for the implementation of the EC Treaty (Article 225 TFEU, ex 192 EC), although the Commission is not obliged to do anything about such a submission except inform the EP of its reasons for not submitting a proposal. Finally, under Articles 227–228 TFEU, EU citizens can petition Parliament and complain to the Parliamentary Commissioner (the Ombudsman) to investigate maladministration by the institutions.

2.4.3.3 Budgetary powers

From the 1970s, the EP had been given budgetary powers in the form of the final say over some limited aspects of expenditure. Furthermore, under the Budgetary Treaty of 1975, Parliament was given the power to reject the budget entirely, which it did in 1979 and 1984 (see Article 314 TFEU, ex 272 EC) and had done on a number of occasions since. The 1979 rejection was partly in response to the increase in democratic legitimacy that the Parliament gained as a result of being directly elected in that year for the first time. However, rejection is not so drastic as it sounds because if the budget is rejected, the so-called 'one-twelfth rule' comes into operation, which means that until the new budget is approved, the Commission can spend per month up to one-twelfth of the previous year's head of expenditure (Article 315 TFEU, ex 273 EC). In order to try to avoid future, nevertheless disruptive, budget rejections, from 1988 various inter-institutional agreements have been agreed by the institutions to improve the functions of the budgetary procedure and financial planning. Thus the EP now discharges the Commission's implementation of the budget on an annual basis, although this has become more of a political show event as an opportunity to question and thus hold the Commission to account.

cross reference
For the latest version of the inter-institutional agreements, scan the QR code image at section 2.4 or see the Online Resource Centre.

The Lisbon Treaty provided full parity of the Council and EP in adopting the budget, and removed the distinction between compulsory and non-compulsory expenditure (Articles 314–315 TFEU).

2.4.3.4 Right to litigate

The EP was not originally named as one of the privileged applicants for the purposes of taking actions against the other institutions under Articles 263 and 265 TFEU (ex 230 and 232 EC). The Court of Justice held, however, in the *Transport* case (Case 13/83 *European Parliament* v *Council*) and in *Chernobyl* (Case C-70/88 *European Parliament* v *Council*), that the EP was able to bring an action against the other institutions under Article 232 EC (now 265 TFEU) where the other institutions had a duty to act, but had failed, and whilst originally it was held not to have a general right to challenge legislative acts under Article 263 TFEU (ex 230 EC), in the *Comitology* case (Case 302/87 *European Parliament* v *Council*), the EP was held to have the right to take action to protect its own prerogative powers.

See also in this respect **Case C-295/80 *European Parliament* v *Council* (Students Residence Directive)**.

cross reference
The details of all of these cases are considered in Chapter 9.

Acts of the Parliament that have legally binding consequences can also be challenged under Article 263 TFEU (ex 230 EC) by others: see Case 294/83 *Les Verts* v *European Parliament* and Case 34/86 *Council* v *European Parliament (Budgetary Procedure)*. The TEU amended Articles 230 and 232 EC (now 263 and 265 TFEU) to specify that the acts or omissions of the EP can be challenged, and the Treaty of Nice provided express confirmation that the EP is one of the privileged applicants able itself to challenge acts of the other institutions under Article 263 TFEU (ex 230 EC) without any restriction in its *locus standi*.

2.5 The European Court of Justice (ECJ)

For more details on this section scan here or visit the Online Resource Centre.

The ECJ, once a single-body institution, now comprises the Court of Justice, the General Court (formerly known as the Court of First Instance, or CFI) and specialized courts. These last were first permissible following the Treaty of Nice in 2003, and initially called 'judicial panels' (Articles 19(1) TEU and 257 TFEU, ex 220 and 225 EC). The ECJ is a self-standing independent EU court; it is not in a hierarchical relationship with the national courts as in a system of appeal. Article 19(1) TEU (ex 220 EC) outlines the general function of the Court of Justice, which is to ensure that, in the interpretation and application of the Treaties, the law is observed and to provide remedies sufficient to ensure effective legal protection in the fields covered by Union law. The second general duty was added by the Lisbon Treaty and arguably would seem to allow the Court to expand rights not previously directly sanctioned by the Treaties, although it had no difficulty in the past in finding remedies where needed.

It may thus be possible to make it easier for individuals to challenge Union Acts under Article 263 TFEU, something that previously has proven extremely difficult.

cross reference
The specialized courts are considered in section 2.5.7.

This section will consider the composition and organization of the Court, the main aspects of procedure, its jurisdiction and its methodology. The expansion of the Court to a General Court and the specialized courts will also be included.

2.5.1 Composition and organization

cross reference
Challenging Union acts is an issue that will be covered in Chapter 9, section 9.1.3.

The Court of Justice presently consists of twenty-seven judges, one for each member state (as from 1 January 2007) and eight Advocates General (Article 252 TFEU), nominated and appointed by unanimous agreement by the governments of the member states. The Lisbon Treaty permits the number of Advocates General (AGs) to be increased under the Statute on the Court of Justice without having to wait for a subsequent Treaty amendment. It was agreed at the Intergovernmental Conference (IGC) for the Lisbon Treaty that a Declaration (No. 38) be attached to the Treaties to accommodate an increase of three AGs if requested by the Court of Justice.

The second paragraph of the Declaration provides:

> In that case, the Conference agrees that Poland will, as is already the case for Germany, France, Italy, Spain and the United Kingdom, have a permanent Advocate-General and no longer take part in the rotation system, while the existing rotation system will involve the rotation of five Advocates-General instead of three.

The judges must be chosen from persons whose independence is beyond doubt and who possess the qualifications necessary for appointment to the highest judicial office in their own countries, or from academic lawyers who, in a number of countries, may also be appointed to the highest courts (see Articles 253–254 TFEU, ex 221–223 EC). The Lisbon Treaty also provides that future appointments must take account of the opinion of an advisory panel comprising former members of the Court of Justice (Article 255 TFEU).

The Court can sit as a full court, a Grand Chamber of thirteen judges to hear cases involving either member states or Union institutions, or in chambers of three or five judges and of which there are eight in total, following the 2007 enlargement.

The TEU introduced an amended Article 221 (now 251 TFEU) that reduces the occasions on which the Court may need to sit in plenary session. This now occurs when a member state or a Union institution, as a party to an action, requests plenary jurisdiction.

2.5.2 Procedure

The Court is faced with a large of number of cases, which can arise ad hoc from any of the member states in one of the now twenty-three official languages acceptable to the Court (twenty-four when Croatia joins as envisaged in July 2013), but the Court operates internally in French as its only working language. The procedure of the Court is governed by a Protocol containing the Statute of the Court of Justice and by its Rules of Procedure. Its Rules generally reflect civilian law procedure, with the emphasis on written proceedings rather than oral, as is the case in the UK and other common law systems.

There are essentially four stages to proceedings: written proceedings, followed by investigation and preparatory work on the case; then oral proceedings, including the AG's opinion, which can be omitted in certain circumstances. The final stage is the judgment, which follows deliberation in secret in French. Judgments of the Court of Justice are delivered in a single ruling. Article 2 of the Statute on the Court provides that, before taking up judicial office, each judge shall, in open court, take an oath to preserve the secrecy of the Court's deliberations. Arguments in favour of the single opinion of the Court include: that it supports its authority and that of the EU legal system; that it helps to build up new a common European law and to avoid reliance on the laws of particular states; and also that it provides for more authoritative decision-making for the future. Arguments against include: that it often results in terse and cryptic judgments, with little evidence of reasoning; that it stifles true legal argument; and that it may inhibit judges and the development of law. To some extent these criticisms may be countered by the existence and role of AGs, who are to assist the Court by giving an opinion, in complete independence and impartiality, on the legal issues of a case to be examined in depth and by reviewing critically the jurisprudence of the Court on the subject. Although the opinion of the AG is not binding on the Court, it carries weight and adds to the development of EU law. Thus an opinion of the AG acts like a first-instance decision subject to an automatic and instant appeal. He or she can adopt a public view or the parties' views, but cannot be bound to present any particular view. It is no longer a mandatory requirement that the opinion of the AG be heard before every judgment is given. According to Article 20 of the Statute of the Court of Justice, the Court may decide in a case that raises no new point of law, after hearing the view of the AG, that the case be determined without a submission from the AG. This possibility has been used increasingly, as demonstrated by the statistics of the Court in which it was estimated that about 30 per cent of the cases in 2004, increasing to 52 per cent of the cases in 2009 and 50 per cent in 2010, were decided without an opinion of an AG.

cross reference
See the reports of the ECJ, available via the Online Resource Centre.

Note now that the expedited procedure under Article 62a of the Statute and Article 104 of the Rules of Procedure omits the part of the procedure comprising the chance to reply and rejoinder the original application or defence in a case, and interventions may be refused by the President in order to render a judgment in much less time. These account only for eighteen applications in 2010, though, of which only nine were granted.

2.5.2.1 The form of judgments

The report is drafted first in the language of the case, which is chosen from the twenty-three official languages by the parties or the defending member state. The full report, as required by the Rules of Procedure of the Court, comprises of a brief summary of judgment, followed by the report for the hearing drawn up by the Judge Rapporteur, and containing the facts and procedure, and a summary of the arguments of the parties. The next part of the report contains the opinion of the AG, although this does not form an official part of the report. The final part contains the reasons or grounds for the judgment presented in numbered paragraphs, and the usually very succinct single ruling of the Court.

2.5.2.2 The reporting of cases

There is only one official set of reports of cases emanating from the Court of Justice and the General Court. These are the European Court Reports, cited as 'ECR' and preceded by the year of publication. These are published in all of the official languages. They are divided into Part I, containing the judgments of the ECJ, Part II containing the judgments of the General Court and ECR-SC containing staff cases, which are no longer automatically translated into all of the official languages. Until 2003, all cases were published, but thereafter a selective publication policy was adopted whereby, under Article 20 of the Statute of the Court of Justice, cases can be decided without an AG opinion and not subsequently published in paper form, although they will always be available electronically. Summaries of cases can also be found in the Official Journal and full cases can be found on the Internet.

The principal alternative in which cases are reported very soon after judgment is the Common Market Law Reports, cited as 'CMLR'. These provide reports in English of not only the judgments of the Community and now EU courts, but also of cases from the national courts of member states that have considered or applied important points of Community (EU) law or which have demonstrated the attitude of the nationals courts to such Community (EU) concepts as supremacy or direct effects.

2.5.3 **Jurisdiction**

Article 19 TEU (ex 220 EC) provides that the Court of Justice, including the General Court and the specialized courts, each within their jurisdiction, shall ensure that the law is observed in the interpretation and application of the Treaties. The Court's factual jurisdiction is determined by Articles 19(3) and 256–279 TEU (ex 226–243 EC). The Court's geographic jurisdiction is limited by the Treaties to the area of the member states, but a judgment of the Court can have consequences and effects outside the geographic area.

European Economic Community (EEC)
The original name of the EC before it became the EU!

For example, in **Case 48/69 *ICI* v *Commission (Dyestuffs)***, the ICI head office, then outside the territory of the Community, was fined through subsidiaries based in the **European Economic Community (EEC)**.

cross reference
For references as to where further information on these specialized aspects can be found, scan the QR code image at section 2.5 or visit the Online Resource Centre.

In addition, the Court has jurisdiction under the EEA Treaty to provide interpretations on disputed rules under the EEA Treaty, and under Article 218(11) (ex 300(6) EC) the other institutions and the member states may obtain the opinion of the Court of Justice on the compatibility of proposed international agreements and Treaties with the TEU and TFEU.

Article 275 TFEU excludes the jurisdiction of the ECJ on matters decided under the CFSP, except those relating to compliance monitoring under Articles 40 TEU and 263 TFEU. Article 276 excludes jurisdiction over police and law enforcement agency operations or actions.

2.5.3.1 Division of jurisdiction

cross reference
All of these actions can be found detailed in Chapters 8 and 9.

The Court's jurisdiction can be divided in a number of ways that can be helpful in understanding what the Court of Justice does. One way is to look at the broad types of action available under Union law and adjudicated by the Court of Justice. This division also considers the parties to the actions and three main categories can be established: actions taken against the member states, such as Article 258 TFEU (ex 226 EC); actions concerned with the review of acts of the Union institutions, such as Article 263 TFEU (ex 230 EC); and preliminary rulings under Article 267 TFEU (ex 234 EC).

Certain other aspects of the Court's work, such as interim measures and appeals from the General Court, stand outside such a division and have to be considered separately. One can also consider the way in which the Court is acting, for example as a constitutional court when considering the powers of the institutions and member states or the relations between them. It acts as an administrative court in cases of judicial review of acts of the institutions. It acts as an appeal court in hearing cases from the General Court. It also acts to determine the scale of fines against those offending competition law and also against the member states when they breach Union law obligations. Finally, it acts as a kind of advisory court when providing rulings to national courts in response to preliminary ruling references.

The jurisdiction can also be divided into the following two much more commonly found classifications:

(a) direct judicial control, whereby the Court interprets a rule and applies it to decide the case itself; and

(b) indirect judicial control, whereby the Court interprets and rules on the validity of provisions, not the subject of an action before the Court. (This jurisdiction is mainly concerned with the preliminary rulings on the request of national courts.)

2.5.3.2 Direct actions

cross reference
Considered in section 2.5.7.

Direct actions are also termed the 'contentious jurisdiction' of the Court under which the Court upholds the lawful exercise of the Union legislative and executive powers in actions against the Union institutions under Articles 263–265 TFEU (ex 230–232 EC), concerning the judicial review of legally binding acts. The Court also upholds compliance of the Union obligations by the member states via Articles 258–260 TFEU (ex 226–228 EC) and conformity with Union law by individuals via various Treaty Articles and secondary legislation, for example Article 103(2)(a) TFEU (ex 83(2)(a) EC) and Regulation 1/2003 concerned with competition policy. Articles 268 and 340(2) TFEU (ex 235 and 288(2) EC) confer non-contractual (delictual) jurisdiction and Article 270 TFEU (ex 236 EC) gives the Court of Justice jurisdiction over staff cases, now effectively handed over to a specialized court with limited appeal rights. The Court has a preventative judicial control intended to block the conclusion of an envisaged agreement by the Union with a third state or international organization considered incompatible with the TFEU under Article 218 (ex 300 EC). It can also be called upon to adjudicate in contractual disputes between Union institutions and contractual partners if called to do so under an arbitration clause in the contract (Article 272 TFEU, ex 238 EC). Finally, under Article 277 TFEU (ex 241 EC), the Court of Justice hears indirect challenges to Union legislation in proceedings already taking place before the Court of Justice.

2.5.3.3 Indirect actions

cross reference
Such indirect actions will be considered in further detail in Chapters 6 and 8.

Indirect judicial control is exercised by the preliminary ruling proceeding of Article 267 TFEU (ex 234 EC), whereby references are made from the courts of the member states for judicial rulings by the Court of Justice.

2.5.4 **Methodology**

A consideration of the methodology of the work of the Court is helpful in understanding the very pro-integrationist stance, also referred to as the Court's 'judicial activism', which has often adopted in judgments and how these judgments have helped to build a new European legal order.

2.5.4.1 Interpretation

The European Treaties and some of the secondary legislation are framework measures that often require considerable amplification and interpretation. This has given a wide scope to the Court of Justice to engage in expansive interpretation of the texts. From the beginning, the Court has taken a very proactive role at times in European integration, often to the consternation of some of the member states. Notable judgments are those concerned with what are now fundamental decisions of the Court, including direct effects, supremacy and the liability of the member states. In these respects, the cases of *Van Gend en Loos, Costa v ENEL* and *Factortame* (involving Spanish fishermen and the UK) would be very good examples. The criticisms of the Court's integrationist stance were most strongly voiced during the negotiations for the Treaty of Amsterdam, with a report prepared by the UK government advising a curb on the activity of the Court of Justice. However, this was not taken any further and, in any case, the then Conservative government was voted out of office before the Amsterdam Treaty negotiations were concluded. Indeed, it can be argued that if it were not for the lead given by the Court in certain fundamental questions of then EC law jurisprudence, the Union legal system would not have obtained the coherency or strength that it has today and as a result the Union itself would be less secure. The Court has, as a result, been highly instrumental in European integration and in confirming the constitutional basis of the Union.

thinking point
Should the Court engage in such judicial activism?

The style of interpretation is described as 'teleological', 'far-looking', or 'forward-looking', in that the Court tries to determine, in the light of the aims and objectives of the Treaties and legislation, what was intended and what result would assist those goals. The Court of Justice often refers to the 'spirit' of the Treaty, the Community and now Union project itself, the preamble and to general provisions of the Treaty, notably Articles 2, 3, 10 and 12 EC (now 3–6 TEU and Article 18 TFEU), in order to assist it in reaching a particular conclusion. As such, then, these represent a form of contextual approach, taking many things into account to justify a particular result in a particular judgment.

For example, look at [71]–[75] of the judgment in **Case 26/62 *Van Gend en Loos*** in which virtually all of the above justifications are covered by the ECJ in reaching its conclusions that EC law (as then termed) was capable of giving rise to direct effects, despite there being no express words to that end in the Treaty itself.

cross reference
For a full discussion and reasoning of direct effect, see Chapter 8, section 8.1.3.

The Court often refers to the concept of *effet utile*, or the 'useful effect' of Community (and now Union) law, which would be undermined if a particular provision were not interpreted in a much more expansive way, more in line with the objectives of the Treaty rather than the actual words used.

See, for example, **Cases C-6 and 9/90 *Francovich et al. v Italy***, in which the establishment of liability on the part of member states for a breach of EC law could never have been derived from a literal reading of the Treaty or secondary law.

These Community (and now Union) methods or interpretation are applied in addition to the usual array of methods of interpretation found in the member states' legal systems, including the logical, literal, purposive means of interpretation, although any strict use of such methods has often been rejected by the Court as unsuitable in the Community and now Union context.

See, for example, **Case 6/60 *Humblet*** and **Case C-70/88 *Chernobyl***, in which direct use of the literal and historical intent methods, respectively, were rejected.

2.5.4.2 Precedent

While there is no formal system of precedent, the Court of Justice, just like courts in civil law jurisdictions, tries to maintain consistency in its judgments. Past decisions are often cited in

Court and do therefore carry some persuasive, rather than any formal, authority. In particular, whilst all rulings of the Court of Justice are binding within the case itself, certain decisions are regarded as forming a sort of precedent for the national courts.

> For example, in **Cases 28–30/62 *Da Costa*** it was decided that references need not be made to the Court of Justice where the materially identical question had already been answered by the Court of Justice – in that instance, in the *Van Gend en Loos* case heard shortly before.

Furthermore, leading cases in Community law, such as *Van Gend en Loos* and *Costa* v *ENEL*, have acquired a higher, more authoritative, status than other cases, dealing, for example, with an interpretation of one of the common custom tariff classifications or some other mundane item of Community secondary legislation. This is so much so that this difference in status has now been more formally recognized by the decision no longer to publish all cases in the official series of courts reports, the ECR. Those from the chambers of three are not to be published, nor are rulings from chambers of five in which there has been no opinion of the AG, but this does not include Article 267 TFEU (ex 234 EC) preliminary rulings.

There are instances, however, in which the courts use the terminology of precedent.

> See, for example, **Case C-310/97 P *Commission* v *Assidomän*** in which the Court of Justice mentions *ratio decidendi* at [54], and both identifies previous precedents and distinguishes past cases relied on by one of the parties (at [54]–[62]).

Furthermore, judicial review cases often refer back to the leading Case 25/62 *Plaumann* v *Commission*: in Case C-263/02 P *Commission* v *Jego-Quere*, the *Plaumann* test was virtually held to dictate the result in subsequent cases. Hence, unofficially, the case law developed by the Court of Justice increasingly seems to resemble a true case law system relying on precedents to be taken forward to new cases. It must also be made clear, though, that the Court of Justice will not be constrained by previous case law it if considers that a change in the law is required.

cross reference
These cases are dealt with in detail in Chapter 11.

> For example, see **Case C-267/91 *Keck***, which expressly sought to modify a previous ruling (**Case 120/78 *Cassis de Dijon***).

2.5.5 The General Court (formerly the Court of First Instance, or CFI)

The first measure to attempt to tackle the growing case load and thus to address the long delay in proceedings before the Court of Justice was the setting up of a Court of First Instance in 1986 by the SEA and now governed under Article 256 TFEU (ex 225 EC). The CFI commenced operation on 1 September 1989 and was renamed by the Lisbon Treaty as the General Court. It has presently twenty-seven judges, one from each member state. One of the judges may act as an AG where considered necessary in complex cases (Article 254 TFEU). The Court is divided into chambers of three and five judges, but can sit in Grand Chamber of thirteen judges or a full court. Article 50 of the Statute of the Court of Justice has allowed for a single judge to hear cases in the General Court.

The jurisdiction was initially limited, but has been slowly expanded to any area of jurisdiction including, from 2004, direct actions under Article 263 TFEU (ex 230 EC), but only annulment applications brought by natural and legal persons and the member states, not those brought by the Union institutions. It has also been extended to include Article 267 TFEU (ex 234 EC) preliminary references unless there is a risk to the unity of EU law, in which event the case should be referred to the Court of Justice. However, although the ability to hear preliminary rulings is given by Article 256(3) TFEU, this ability has not yet been designated and remains presently dormant. Article 256 TFEU (ex 225 EC) allows for future changes of jurisdiction of the General Court to be made by amendment of the Protocol containing the Statute on the Court of Justice rather than by Treaty amendment. The General Court also has jurisdiction to hear appeals from the specialized courts (Article 256 TFEU).

cross reference

The specialized courts are considered at section 2.5.7.

Appeals from the General Court may be made on points of law only to the Court of Justice. Three grounds are given:

(a) lack of competence by the Court;

(b) breach of procedure; and

(c) the infringement of a Union provision or rule of law by the Court, or an error in the interpretation or application of law.

2.5.6 Length of proceedings

Despite the low numbers of appeals in the early years and optimism that the bringing into operation of the CFI would significantly reduce the backlog and length of proceedings, the continued increase in the numbers of cases being lodged at the CFI and the large numbers of cases that were transferred to it by the Court of Justice meant that the overall backlog of cases pending judgment before the CFI and the Court of Justice nevertheless increased. After years of increasing case loads and growing backlogs, the expansion of the EU and Court of Justice in 2004, which saw a large influx of new judges, but (at least at first) few new cases from the new member states, combined with the increased jurisdiction of the then CFI, enabled the Court to make inroads into the backlog.

In 1998, there were over 1,000 cases pending before the Court of Justice. In 2005, this was reduced to 740, with only a slight rise to 767 in 2008. With these figures, the length of proceedings, which had increased over the years, also changed for the better, with Article 234 TEU (now 267 TFEU) references, direct actions and appeals all showing annual reductions in the length of proceedings, more so in the period 2009–11, from 25.5 to 16.1 months, 24.7 to 16.7 months, and from 28.7 to 14.3 months, respectively.

2.5.7 The specialized courts (formerly judicial panels)

The Treaty of Nice made changes to the organization of the Community courts and also provided for the establishment of judicial panels (now called 'specialized courts' following Lisbon) attached to the CFI to relieve that Court of some of its case law (Article 257 TFEU, ex 225a EC). Judges are appointed by the Council acting unanimously under Article 257 TFEU. These courts will operate as first-instance courts, with an appeal to the General Court. The first decision under the new power was taken by the Council of Ministers in November 2004 (Decision 2004/752) and an EU Civil Service Tribunal comprising seven judges was established to hear staff cases, with an appeal only on law to the General Court, and exceptional review by the

Court of Justice. Staff cases were an apparently not inconsiderable load on the Court and 117 cases were transferred to the then judicial panel from the then CFI at the end of 2005. The possibility of establishing more tribunals for specialist subjects remains.

2.5.8 The European Central Bank (ECB)

The ECB was set up under the TEU to achieve price stability in the Union and is responsible for monetary policy, regulating eurozone interest rates and the euro (€). Following the entry into force of the Lisbon Treaty, it became a full institution of the EU and is governed by Articles 13 TEU, Articles 282–284 TFEU and Protocol 4 attached to the Treaties. It also cooperates with the national central banks in the European System of Central Banks (Eurosystem, or ESCB).

2.5.9 The Court of Auditors

While the Court of Auditors was made a full institution by the TEU and is regulated under Articles 13 TEU and 285–287 TFEU (ex 246–248 EC), it is not one usually covered in any detail in textbooks and will be mentioned here only briefly. The Court of Auditors was established under the 1975 Budgetary Treaty, and audits the expenditure of the institutions for legality and sound financial management. It produces an annual report, which is forwarded to the EP to debate and to provide the Commission with a discharge if the expenditure is correct (Article 319 TFEU, ex 276 EC). The amended Article 263 TFEU (ex 230 EC) provides that the Court of Auditors can take action to protect its prerogatives in judicial review actions against acts of the main legislative institutions.

2.6

The Union's advisory bodies

The following bodies are not full institutions named in Article 13 TEU, but advisory bodies to assist the main institutions and now established by a new Article 300 TFEU.

For more details on this section scan here or visit the Online Resource Centre.

2.6.1 The Economic and Social Committee (EESC)

The EESC, previously also known under the acronym ECOSOC, was introduced to serve in an advisory role to represent various sectional interests and must be consulted for the adoption of certain legislation as determined by the Treaty – although, once received, its opinion may be ignored by the Council. However, failure to consult would open up the legislation enacted to annulment, by analogy with the Article 263 TFEU (ex 230 EC) action by the EP in Cases 138–139/79 *Roquette and Maizena* v *Council*. Its members are appointed in a personal capacity along national lines by the Council voting by QMV and are drawn from various sections of society to provide a wide-ranging array of views on legislative proposals. They are also able to give opinions on their own initiative without invitation from the Council, Commission or the EP. The committee is governed by Articles 301–304 TFEU (ex 257–262 EC).

2.6.2 The Committee of the Regions (CoR)

A much later Community body, the CoR was established by the TEU and is also an advisory body set up to represent regional and local bodies, and to meet the criticisms that the Union fails to recognize regional interests, particularly those of federal states. Usually, only the central or national bodies of federal states are formally represented in the Union institutional set-up – that is, in the Council of Ministers, which draws its members from the state governments. The Committee must be consulted for the enactment of certain legislation – see, for example, Articles 153, 165–168 and 173 TFEU (ex 137, 149–152 and 157 EC) – and is governed by Articles 305–307 TFEU (ex 263–265 EC). In the UK, membership is drawn from local authorities and the devolved forms of government in Scotland, Wales and Northern Ireland.

2.7 Other Union bodies

Note that there is also a European Investment Bank (EIB), under Article 308 TFEU, to channel funding into European projects, an Economic and Financial Committee (EFC, or ECOFIN) to advise the Council and Commission on internal market coordination matters under Article 134 TFEU, and a Political and Security Committee (PSC, or POLISEC) to advise the Council and the High Representative on international situations under Article 38 TEU. In addition, there is an extensive list of further specialized EU bodies and agencies too numerous to include in this volume.

Summary

The institutional framework of the EU, like the EU itself, is not a static entity, but a changing one. Sometimes, the names of the institutions change; sometimes, new institutions are added to the fold; sometimes, their membership changes; sometimes, the way in which they operate and act also changes. They too are a dynamic part of the EU and its development. Certainly, the powers they enjoy also change: in particular, the changes to functions and power of the only directly elected body, the EP, need to be understood, especially in connection with the discussion about the democratic deficit in the EU. Having a good background to these developments is not only something that is pertinent to this chapter, but it is also relevant to an understanding of other aspects of EU law, which will be considered in the following chapters, such as the numerous inter-institutional disputes that have arisen from the law-making procedures. The Lisbon Treaty too has had a further profound effect on the institutional balance, perhaps more so than anticipated, introducing the European Council as a full institution, creating the European President and High Representative, and increasing significantly QMV in Council and co-decision for the EP. As a result, the EP and European Council are regarded as being much stronger now; the Council consequently and the Commission also much reduced in power and influence. The next few years will see how they all settle into the new institutional order.

Questions

1 Who do the European Commissioners represent?

2 Why was there such a fuss about the number of votes per country and the combination of votes under QMV?

For suggested approaches to answering these questions scan here or visit the Online Resource Centre

3 What role is played by the European Council?

4 Do the changes made by various Treaty amendments to the powers of the European Parliament go far enough to address the Union's alleged 'democratic deficit'?

5 Who or what is the European President and what function is played by the European President?

6 Who or what is the High Representative for Foreign Affairs and Security Policy and what does he or she do?

7 What are the merits or otherwise of: (a) the Court of Justice delivering a single opinion when giving judgment (as opposed to separate and dissenting opinions); (b) the system of Advocates General?

 # Further reading

BOOKS

Burrows, N. and Greaves, R. *The Advocate General and EC Law*, Oxford University Press, Oxford, 2007.

Corbett, R., Jacobs, F. and Shackleton, M. *The European Parliament*, 7th edn, John Harper, London, 2007.

De Búrca, G. and Weiler, J. H. H. *The European Court of Justice*, Oxford University Press, Oxford, 2001.

Devuyst, Y. *The European Union Transformed: Community Method and Institutional Evolution from the Schuman Plan to the Constitution for Europe*, revised and updated edn, Peter Lang, Brussels, 2006.

Douglas-Scott, S. *Constitutional Law of the European Union*, Longman, Harlow, 2002 (chapters 2 and 5).

Earnshaw, D. and Judge, D. *The European Parliament*, 2nd edn, Palgrave, Basingstoke, 2008.

Hayes-Renshaw, F. and Wallace, H. *The Council of Ministers*, 2nd edn, Palgrave, Basingstoke, 2006.

Peterson, J. and Shackleton, M. *The Institutions of the European Union*, 2nd edn, Oxford University Press, Oxford, 2006.

Ward, I. *A Critical Introduction to European Law*, 3rd edn, Cambridge University Press, Cambridge, 2009.

Werts, J. *The European Council*, John Harper, London, 2008.

ARTICLES

Davies, G. 'Subsidiarity: the wrong idea, in the wrong place, at the wrong time' (2006) 43 CML Rev 63.

Transfer of powers, competences and law-making

Learning objectives

In this chapter, you will learn about:

- the transfer of power from the member states to the Union;
- the division of competences between the member states and the Union;
- the principles of proportionality and subsidiarity; and
- the processes by which the binding secondary laws are made.

Introduction

This chapter has as its focus the topic of the transfer and division of competences from the member states to the European Union (EU). The question of whether the EU has the competence for a certain subject area also determines the logic of the supremacy of Union law. However, in order to have competence in the first place, the EU needs to have power transferred to it. Hence the logical way in which to introduce these topics is to outline first the transfer, and then the division and control, of competences between the Union and the member states. In this context, the principles of subsidiarity and proportionality play an increasingly important role as elements of the ways in which the member states are seeking to control the use of transferred powers and competences. Thus the division of competences and the principle of subsidiarity are both political solutions to the very emotive questions about how power is shared between the Union and the member states. Subsidiarity is a way of deciding how to determine where the line between Union and member states' competences should be drawn. The chapter will commence, however, with the start of this process, which is the transfer of powers to the EU. It will then consider the principal reason for the transfer of competences, which is to provide the EU institutions with law-making powers by which the Union is able to carry out its tasks as laid down in the Treaties. A part of law-making is also concerned with using the correct legal base for those laws, itself a topic also allied with competences; hence that will also be considered in this chapter.

cross reference

The supremacy of Union law is considered in Chapter 5.

69

The relationship between transfer, competence and supremacy

thinking point

Why do you think that the very important issue of supremacy was omitted? Do you think that it was done intentionally or merely overlooked?

The original Treaties, and indeed those still applicable, do not provide a clear-cut expression of the relationship between the law of the EU – that is, the law created by the institutions on the one hand, and the national laws or domestic laws of the member states on the other. There was no Treaty Article or rule to say in the event of conflict between laws covering the same subject matter which should take priority. Neither did the original Treaties make any expression as to their own status: were they constitutional rules or just another international treaty between signatory states?

cross reference

If you are confused about the use of the terms EU and EC, look at the explanation in Chapter 1, Introduction.

Whilst the question of supremacy was quickly and clearly settled by the Court of Justice, at least from the Union standpoint, the matter of competence is not so easily dealt with. In order for Union law to be supreme, the Union must possess the competence to act in the first place. If it does not have the competence to act in a certain way or to create certain new laws, then by logic such laws cannot take priority over member states' national law. This interlinked relationship between supremacy and competence can be observed in Case 22/70 *Commission* v *Council (ERTA)* ([30]–[31]) and in Opinion 1/94, in which it was held that if the (then) Community has competence, the member states cannot act contrary to it.

If you think about it, this is another way of saying that, in such circumstances, the EC or EU law is supreme.

First of all in this relationship, however, is the transfer of power from the member states that provides the competences.

3.1 The transfer of sovereign powers

cross reference
For details, refer to Chapter 1.

When the Union was first established, it was in full recognition that, to be able to achieve the goals set for it, the member states had to pool their resources in the new entity – in other words, they needed to transfer some of their sovereign rights to the Union and its institutions for them to be able to carry out their tasks. This was facilitated by the member states providing the competences for the Communities (Union) to make their own laws, a process that was later acknowledged quite clearly by the Court of Justice in the seminal *Van Gend en Loos* case, but with the proviso that the power transfer or transfer of sovereignty was carried out only within limited fields and was not a general transfer of power. A general transfer would include the ability to redefine competences without reference to any other body, the most obvious and important other body in this context being the member states. There was not a general transfer of powers by the member states to the Communities.

Any power that the Communities and Union have been provided is only there by virtue of the transfer by the member states. However, the Communities, as developed into the Union, are not static; they have developed considerably since first being established and the competences have grown hand in hand with the complexity of the Union. Each successive Treaty amendment has transferred further powers to the Union, with a corresponding loss of sovereignty for the member states in those areas as agreed by the member states. The member states, however, remain the bodies that decide whether the competences of the Union should be increased at all. It is to be noted that, so far, the Union has only an incomplete external competence and there is no single Union body that makes law and represents the Union externally, as would the government of a federal state; the creation of the 'High Representative' is, though, a move in this direction. How competence and competences are divided between the member states and the Union and exercised by the institutions of the Union is considered next and involves discussion of another European term: 'subsidiarity'.

3.2 The division of competences

For more details on this section scan here or visit the Online Resource Centre.

One of the most fundamental elements of an organizational order is the division of competence or power between the central body and the constituent parts of the state or organization in question. The transfer of powers and thus competences from the parts to the centre, from the EU member states to the Union itself, should in theory be a clear-cut process whereby any exercise of these powers by the institutions of the Union can only be within the terms granted by the member states and contained and clearly set out in the Treaties. In other words, there should be nothing done by the Union institutions that is not expressly permitted by the Treaties.

The logical consequence of this is that what is attributed to the Union by the member states is necessarily removed from member states' competence. In other words, the member states no longer have competence in the fields transferred.

This principle of **attributed, or conferred, competence** finds expression in both Articles 1 and 5 TEU (ex 5 EC). Article 5(1) provides that 'The limits of Union competences are governed by the principle of conferral' and Article 5(2) amplifies a general statement to the same effect in Article 4 that:

> the Union shall act only within the limits of the competences conferred upon it by the Member States in the Treaties to attain the objectives set out therein. Competences not conferred upon the Union in the Treaties remain with the Member States.

attributed, or conferred, competence

Union law terminology for the competence transferred from member states to the Union.

3.2.1 **Express policies, powers and legal base**

The range of actions to be undertaken by the Union are now set out in Articles 3 TEU and 3–6 TFEU (ex 2 and 3 EC), which list the objectives and activities of the Union, but do not specifically detail any one of them. This is left to specific titles and chapters in the TFEU. Where the Treaty specifies a particular object, it invariably provides a power to achieve that object. This may also be expressed by the concepts of express policies, powers and legal base, all of which are covered in further detail during the course of this chapter. The express policies are those objectives outlined in the Treaties, the power to achieve them and thus simultaneously the legal base for secondary EU law to achieve the objectives will also be provided within a Treaty Article.

For example, Articles 45 and 46 TFEU (ex 39 and 40 EC) set out respectively the objective and power of achieving the free movement of workers in the Union. Article 45 provides the policy, and Article 46 the power and legal base, to enact secondary legislation to achieve the policy aims.

3.2.2 **The split between exclusive, concurrent and complementary competences**

If the division of competences were clearly set out, there would be no particular difficulty, but in 1957 this was not so. However, at that time, the initial Treaties were much more limited in scope, therefore this was less of a concern. The Communities were not, however, intended to be a static one-off creation, but a long-term and evolving one. The initial expectation was that integration in one area was expected to spread to other areas and that powers would be needed to regulate those new areas. In addition, the Community would have to react to events in the world as they unfolded and affected it. Hence, then, it was anticipated that the competences and their division needed to be dynamic and equally evolving, and not static. This meant that the Communities (and now Union) would also have to be reactive and the competences capable of expansion. It is necessary, therefore, to consider what the competences were, how they developed, how the member states considered and reacted to this, and what measures were taken to control the **competence creep** that was observed.

cross reference

These original concerns were discussed in Chapter 1.

cross reference

Competence creep will be explored further in section 3.4.

competence creep

The term given to the slow assumption of competences by the Commission and institutions generally to carry out the policies of the Union. Their power to do so is not expressly granted by the member states, but the Commission and/or Union is seen to take advantage of implied powers.

Competences are divided initially into exclusive and concurrent or shared competences, and until the reforms brought about by the Lisbon Treaty this division was rather vague. Now, it is much clearer and is expressly set out in the Treaties, as will be noted in the next section. Furthermore, a revised Declaration (No. 18) on competences has been attached to the Treaties, which confirms the respective rights of the member states and Union, the latter represented by the Commission in these matters. The clarification of this division is one of the answers to competence creep.

Declaration Nos 24 and 42 are also pertinent here in that they to seek to prevent further competence creep arising from the conferral of legal personality on the EU as a whole and the use of the general law-making power under Article 352 TFEU.

3.2.2.1 Exclusive competences

The Union enjoys exclusive competences in a few areas only, such as commercial policy to third countries (as upheld by the Court of Justice in its Opinion 1/75), and parts of the Common Fishing Policy. These are now set out in Article 3 TFEU and include customs union, competition policy for the internal market, monetary policy for the eurozone, parts of Common Fisheries Policy and commercial policy.

Article 3 TFEU

1. The Union shall have exclusive competence in the following areas:
   (a) customs union;
   (b) the establishing of the competition rules necessary for the functioning of the internal market;
   (c) monetary policy for the Member States whose currency is the euro;
   (d) the conservation of marine biological resources under the common fisheries policy;
   (e) common commercial policy.
2. The Union shall also have exclusive competence for the conclusion of an international agreement when its conclusion is provided for in a legislative act of the Union or is necessary to enable the Union to exercise its internal competence, or in so far as its conclusion may affect common rules or alter their scope.

3.2.2.2 Concurrent competences

In other areas – that is, in most areas – the dividing line is not so clear and competence is concurrent between the member states and the Union.

This is also termed 'shared', or 'non-exclusive', competence.

Following the Lisbon Treaty reforms, the areas covered by shared competences are now set out in Article 4 TFEU.

Article 4 TFEU

· ·

1. The Union shall share competence with the Member States where the Treaties confer on it a competence which does not relate to the areas referred to in Articles 3 and 6.
2. Shared competence between the Union and the Member States applies in the following principal areas:
   (a) internal market;
   (b) social policy, for the aspects defined in this Treaty;
   (c) economic, social and territorial cohesion;
   (d) agriculture and fisheries, excluding the conservation of marine biological resources;
   (e) environment;
   (f) consumer protection;
   (g) transport;
   (h) trans-European networks;
   (i) energy;
   (j) area of freedom, security and justice;
   (k) common safety concerns in public health matters, for the aspects defined in this Treaty.

3.2.2.3 Complementary competences

Areas of law outside those exclusive and concurrent competences remain the competence of the member states, although, following Lisbon, the Union may support or complement member states' activities in these areas as sanctioned by a new Article 6 TFEU.

Article 6 TFEU

· ·

The Union shall have competence to carry out actions to support, coordinate or supplement the actions of the Member States. The areas of such action shall, at European level, be:

   (a) protection and improvement of human health;
   (b) industry;
   (c) culture;
   (d) tourism;
   (e) education, vocational training, youth and sport;
   (f) civil protection;
   (g) administrative cooperation.

It is in the area of shared competences that most difficulties arise, where it can still be unclear whether the Union or the member states have the competence for a particular action. Furthermore, the degree of sharing also alters according to the subject matter: for example, in areas such as the internal market, as soon as the Union acts under its competence, it assumes exclusive power to act and the member states are then deprived of the power to act in conflict. If, however, the Union chooses not to act, the member states retain the power to act.

This assumption of competence is known as 'pre-emption'.

cross reference
The free move-ment of goods will be considered in Chapters 10 and 11.

A good example can be seen from the area of the free movement of goods.

> The Court of Justice held in the leading case of **Case 120/78 *Rewe-Zentral AG v Bundes monopolverwaltung für Branntwein (Cassis de Dijon)*** that only where the Community had not acted could the member states act independently, and even then if concerned with a general area, the member states could act only within prescribed limits.

As a result, it is possible for there to be a genuine grey area between what is within the Union competence and what is still within the member state competence.

This is a matter that has troubled the EU time and again, in particular as it became clear from the progressive judgments of the Court of Justice that the Community (and now Union) had taken over from the member states even in areas to which the member states were either not sure they had agreed, or indeed to which they were of the conviction that they had not agreed, or even where they considered that they had excluded that particular matter from EU competence.

> For example, in **Case C-262/88 *Barber***, private pension scheme payments were held to be pay and therefore within the EC equal pay competence and not therefore a matter of state competence and exclusive regulation. (See Article 7 of Directive 79/7, which reserved state pension matters to member states.) It was considered, however, that state pension policy was a matter still within the exclusive competence of the member states.

As a result, there has been a reaction by some of the member states, which considered that the Commission and Community and Union were extending their competences by stealth and not with the agreement of the member states. The next sections consider how competences could be and were extended, and what measures were developed by the member states to control this.

3.3 Extension of competences

For more details on this section scan here or visit the Online Resource Centre.

In the understanding of traditional international law, the only way in which to add competences to a specific created international organization is if all signatories to the Treaty agree to Treaty amendment. Whilst Treaty amendment has taken place in the EU, it is only one of three ways in which the competences of the Union can be extended, which include express, implied and residual competences.

3.3.1 Express by Treaty amendment

Treaty amendment, the first of these ways, is deliberate and clear-cut. The areas of Union competence have expanded greatly as a result of the member states assigning additional competences to the Union, with successive Treaties adding, for example, a Chapter on environmental policy to the EC Treaty by means of the Single European Act (SEA), or economic and monetary policy by means of the Maastricht Treaty.

The second and third ways are not express and have led to the use of the term 'competence creep' to describe the manner in which the institutions' competences have advanced incrementally. This has been by the use of implied and general powers by the institutions, notably the Commission. This process has been subject to the review of the Court of Justice, highlighting that, as a dynamic and evolving area of Union law, the limits of its development and extension must be judicially controlled, especially where not expressly provided for in the Treaty.

3.3.2 Implied powers

The exercise of implied powers is the second means of extending competences. This was recognized by the Court of Justice in cases dealing with both internal and external powers of the Commission, where, in the absence of express powers in the Treaty, powers are nevertheless required to achieve a Union goal and are thus implied. Furthermore, implied powers to carry out internal competences can also be used to support external powers, although no such external powers are provided in the Treaty.

The Court of Justice confirmed the validity of implied powers in the Union legal order as early as in Case 8/55 *Fedechar* and in subsequent cases.

3.3.2.1 Internal implied competences

In **Cases 281, 283–285, 287/85 *Commission v Germany (Migration Policy)***, a Treaty Article (then Article 118 EEC) provided for cooperation between member states in a social field, but was used by the Commission to enact a decision requiring the member states to supply information. When the decision was challenged, the Court of Justice held that where an Article of the EEC Treaty confers a specific task on the Commission, it must be accepted if that provision is not to be rendered wholly ineffective, and that it confers on the Commission necessarily and per se the powers that are indispensable in order to carry out that task, such as the gathering of information.

3.3.2.2 Impact on external competence from internal competences

Where existing internal powers have been acted upon by the EU, the member states are also prevented from acting externally in those areas in which such action would impact on the internal policy. Under its external trade policy, the Union alone is in the position to carry out the contractual obligations towards third countries.

In **Case 22/70 *Commission v Council (ERTA)***, the then six member states had negotiated independently a road transport agreement, which was then adopted by Resolution of the Council, but subsequently challenged by the Commission because there was a previous Community Act regulating this area. The Court of Justice held that the authority of the Community to conclude international agreements arose not only from express conferment, but was also implied from other Treaty provisions providing express internal competences in the same area. Thus, where the internal competences have been acted upon, the member states are prevented from acting in those areas in which it would impact on the internal policy.

In the particular case, because the member states' negotiations were the continuance of agreements reached originally before the internal policy was formulated, it was held that the member states collectively within the Council were entitled to act.

> See also one of the air transport cases, **Cases 4, 6, 7–9/98 Commission v Finland and others**, in which it was confirmed that where the Community has acted in pursuit of exclusive internal powers that it possesses, any action by the member states in adopting an international agreement affecting the common Community rules is an unlawful intrusion on Community competence.

The most complex agreements are the multilateral trade liberalization agreements carried out by the member states of the organizations of the World Trade Organization (WTO) and formerly the General Agreement on Tariffs and Trade (GATT), which cover so many aspects of external trade that a different view was taken by the Court of Justice of the extent to which the Union could be said to have taken over competence.

Opinion 1/94 was concerned with the competence of the Community or member states acting with the Community to conclude the GATS and Trade-Related Aspects of Intellectual Property Rights (TRIPS) Agreement elements of the WTO talks, but the European Court of Justice (ECJ) held that implied powers operate only between the member states and the Community and not the Commission and the Council; hence whilst there was joint competence in these areas, there was not an exclusive Community competence.

3.3.3 **Residual powers**

The third way by which competences have been expanded is via the residual or general law-making powers, which include both specific and general kinds defined in context in the next sections.

3.3.3.1 Specific

Specific residual powers are those that grant subsidiary law-making powers to complete goals in specific areas, in particular to complete the internal market. Articles 114 and 115 TFEU (ex 95 and 94 EC in reversed order) provide for the approximation of laws affecting the establishment or functioning of the internal market and measures for the completion of the internal market.

cross reference
For details of the voting procedures in Council, see Chapter 2, section 2.2.4.

Article 114 TFEU (ex 95 EC) provides that to achieve the objectives of the internal market, set out in Article 26 TFEU (ex 14 EC), where powers are not otherwise provided by the Treaty, action can be taken by qualified majority voting (QMV). In other words, action can be taken outside of the express and exclusive granting of powers to the Union by a majority and not by the agreement of all of the member states.

Article 115 TFEU (ex 94 EC) is an exception to the powers granted in Article 114 TFEU (ex 95 EC), which is a general power to enact harmonizing legislation. It does, however, contain safety measures so that member states and institutions do not go too far: the Council must act by unanimity and must consult the European Parliament (EP).

> **thinking point**
> *What is consequence of the Union using these powers to enact a harmonizing measure (which is binding)? The states lose competence, and if it happens a lot, states lose a lot of competences. Hence this is important, because any use or misuse of Article 115 TFEU (ex 94 EC) may be seen as part of the competence creep problem.*

It has been held, though, by the Court of Justice that these Articles should not be used where other Articles are more appropriate.

In **Case C-376/98 Germany v European Parliament and Council (Tobacco Advertising I),** Article 95 EC (now 114 TFEU) was held to be inappropriate and thus lacking the competence to enact a measure aimed more at the protection of health, rather at completing the internal market.

However, in **Case C-210/03 R v Secretary of State for Health, ex p Swedish Match,** the ECJ held that if obstacles to trade emerge, the Commission can intervene to harmonize even if the internal market is not the prime motive – that case being concerned with the banning of a type of snuff.

In **Case C-377/98 Netherlands v European Parliament and Council (Biotechnology Directive),** the ECJ held that Article 95 EC (now 114 TFEU) can be used in an area dealing with intellectual property, even though the Directive provided that the member states could restrict patents and thus free movement of goods on the grounds of public morality.

Finally, in the second Tobacco Advertising case, **C-380/03 Germany v European Parliament and Council,** Article 95 EC (now 114 TFEU) could be used to enact a Directive restricting the advertising of tobacco products, where differences in the national laws relating to this advertising would have the effect of creating obstacles to free trade. The Community Directive was thus necessary to harmonize the internal market to allow it to function properly.

Ex Article 94 EC features in Case 84/94 *UK v Council (Working Time Directive)* and ex Article 95 EC features in Case 375/98 *Germany v EP and Council (Tobacco Advertising).* These cases are considered at section 3.4.2.1.

3.3.3.2 General

The general kind of residual power is Article 352 TFEU (ex 308 EC), which provides that, where in furtherance of any of the objectives of the Treaty and where no specific power exists, the Union may act by means of the Council acting unanimously with the consent of the EP. Note that previously it was only necessary to consult the EP.

Article 352 TFEU

. . . .

If action by the Union should prove necessary, within the framework of the policies defined in the Treaties, to attain one of the objectives set out in the Treaties, and the Treaties have not provided the necessary powers, the Council, acting unanimously on a proposal from the Commission and after obtaining the consent of the European Parliament, shall adopt the appropriate measures.

cross reference

The subsidiarity principle is considered in section 3.4.2.

cross reference

For further discussion on Treaty bases, see section 3.5.1.

A new Article 352(2) TFEU requires the Commission to draw such proposals also to the attention of the national parliaments in accordance with the subsidiarity principle.

Article 352(3) TFEU expressly does not permit harmonization of member states' laws or, under Article 352(4) TFEU, apply to the areas of Common Foreign and Security Policy (CFSP); the member states have backed this up in Declaration Nos 41 and 42. Because these are residual powers, they have led to problems regarding just how far they sanction Union activity in the face of member states' activity. However, they have been generously interpreted by the Court of Justice. Article 308 EC (now 352 TFEU) was used as the Treaty base for the original Equal Treatment Directive 76/207 because, at the time, the relevant Treaty base (ex Article 119 EC) extended only as far as equal pay. Article 308 EC (now 352 TFEU) was also used quite extensively to introduce legislation concerned with environmental matters for which there was not, at the time, a Treaty Article base available.

A limit to such use was found when the Court of Justice held in its Opinion 2/94 of 1996 that Article 235 TEU (ex 308 EC, now 352 TFEU) could not be used to accede to the European Convention on Human Rights and Fundamental Freedoms (ECHR) because of the profound constitutional impact it would have on the Community and the member states, which was not envisaged nor indeed sanctioned by the Treaty.

Furthermore, the use of Article 308 EC (now 352 TFEU) would be improper if a specific Treaty base were shown to exist (see Case 8/73 *HZA Bremerhafen* v *Massey-Ferguson*) and which should therefore have been used instead. More recently, in Cases C-402/05 P and C-415/05 *Kadi* v *Council*, a challenge to the use of Article 308 EC (now 352 TEU) was made following a freezing of the assets of persons whom the United Nations (UN) considered to be related to terrorists following the 9/11 attacks. It was argued that this was beyond the competence of the EU, but this argument was not accepted by the ECJ, which linked the economic action of the Council to the Common Market – a link that seems somewhat tenuous. It would seem therefore that even very weak links to the Union and its activities will suffice to justify the use of Article 352 TFEU. Article 352 TFEU can also be used in pursuit of the objectives of the Union now, as opposed previously to only the EC, so its potential scope for use is much wider. This is countered by the requirement that measures taken under this Article will be subject to the same procedure as that required for the monitoring of subsidiarity, requiring consultation of the national parliaments, and that it still restricts the European Parliament's role, but now to consent rather than only consultation. It is also countered by the member states' attachment of Declaration Nos 41 and 42 to the Treaties, which seek to prevent both a general widening of the scope of Union powers beyond those expressly conferred and specifically use in pursuit of CFSP objectives. It remains to be seen whether the ECJ will regard Article 352 TFEU as being so constrained.

3.4 Tackling the competence creep

These increases in the competences of the Union, without express Treaty sanction, have been increasingly criticized and challenged. In general democratic terms, they are suspect because if using either Articles 115 or 352 TFEU (ex 94 or 308 EC), both requiring unanimity on the part of the Council, they require consultation or consent of the EP only and not its greater participation in the ordinary (co-decision) legislative procedure. Even Article 114 TFEU (ex 95 EC), which allows the use of QMV in Council, may be subject to a challenge by one or more aggrieved member states who do not agree with the final Act.

Hence there have been challenges before the Court of Justice to some proposed and completed Community actions for the Council's choice of legal base and more formally by amendments to the Treaties to try to curb this development.

See also now the new requirement in Article 296 TFEU as a further means by which the competence creep may be halted. Article 296 provides that: 'When considering draft legislative acts, the EP and the Council shall refrain from adopting acts not provided for by the relevant legislative procedure in the area in question.'

3.4.1 **Restrictive drafting**

Legal bases have been drafted restrictively so that the Commission cannot use the base for further legislative intervention.

See, for example, Article 168(5) TFEU (ex 152 EC), which provides for action to promote cooperation in public health matters, but 'excluding any harmonization of the laws and regulations of the member states'. In other words, the Union can take action provided that it does not interfere with the existing laws in the member states.

cross reference

These cases concerned with competence are related to or the same cases dealing with where an incorrect legal base has been employed and which are considered in section 3.5.1.

Another method, outside specific Treaty Article amendments to control and review the extension and exercise of competences, is the introduction of the principles of subsidiarity and proportionality. These are designed to address the concerns of the member states about how implied competences were being employed by the Commission, albeit without much clear success thus far.

cross reference

The rule of reason and the principle of mutual recognition are discussed in Chapter 11.

3.4.2 **The principle of subsidiarity**

The principle of subsidiarity requires that decisions be taken at the most appropriate level and, in the EU context, this focuses on whether a decision should be taken at the level of the Union or of the member states. The wish to regulate activities within the Union should not insist on action at the Union level when it is not necessary. While there was arguably always the view that legal measures that were taken centrally by the Union institutions should only be taken where necessary and that, if not suitable, member states were allowed to regulate matters individually, this understanding did not find formal expression in any Treaty provision. There are implied examples of its use, such as the discretion given to the member states to meet the requirements of a Directive or the principles of mutual recognition and the rule of reason established by the Court of Justice in the *Cassis de Dijon* case. Subsidiarity made its first express appearance in the Community legal order among the 1986 SEA Treaty amendments. Essentially, it provided that the Union should take action only where objectives could be better attained at the Union level than at the level of individual member states. It was subsequently introduced generally into the Union legal order by the TEU.

Article 1 of the TEU provides that decisions are to be taken as closely as possible to the citizen; Article 5(1) TEU provides that 'The use of Union competences is governed by the principles of subsidiarity and proportionality' and further provides in Article 5(3) TEU (ex 5 EC) that:

in areas which do not fall within its exclusive competence, the Union shall act, only if and in so far as the objectives of the proposed action cannot be sufficiently achieved by the member states, either at

cross reference
Article 5 TEU and
the principle of
subsidiarity build on
the principle of con-
ferral, are discussed
at section 3.2.

cross reference
Proportionality will
be considered in
section 3.4.3.

central level or at regional and local, but can rather, by reason of the scale or effects of the proposed action, be better achieved at Union level.

The exact meaning of Article 5(3) TEU is, however, far from clear, particularly regarding where the line might be drawn between the competence of the Union and the competences of the member states. Thus the introduction of this concept and proportionality, which has not proved to be the instant fix desired by the member states, let alone a concept that is readily understandable or indeed translatable into a clear-cut process by which it is decided whether Union or member states' action is appropriate and thus lawful within the terms of the concept. It seems to suggest that decision-taking that might be accumulated in the centre – that is, by the institutions – but which is not actually necessary at this level should instead be taken by the member states. Decisions, in short, should be taken closer to the people, which is the formula-tion of the principle contained in the statement made in Article 1 TEU.

In support of Article 5 TEU is Article 13 TEU (ex 7 EC), which requires that each institution acts within the limits of the power conferred on it.

One of the main difficulties with this principle of subsidiarity remains: who decides when to apply it, and whether it has been observed in the decision-making process. If the matter is one within the exclusive competence of the Union, subsidiarity does not apply. The problem is, however, that 'exclusivity' itself is not a clear-cut term. The practice has arisen now that, in order to justify taking the action, the Commission needs to outline why it has competence to take the particular action, and does so in the preamble and recitals to proposed legislation.

See, for example, Directive 2002/14 on employee consultation, recital 17 or recital 36 from Directive 2006/54:

> Since the objectives of this Directive cannot be sufficiently achieved by the Member States and can therefore be better achieved at Community level, the Community may adopt measures in accordance with the principle of subsidiarity as set out in Article 5 of the Treaty. In accordance with the principle of proportionality, as set out in that Article, this Directive does not go beyond what is necessary in order to achieve those objectives.

It may therefore give rise to considerable litigation to determine whether the principle and its requirements have been adhered to correctly. Whilst the principle itself was not disturbed by the Treaty of Amsterdam, it did add a Protocol as an attempt to clarify its meaning, which has been amended and expanded by the Lisbon Treaty and attached to the present Treaties as Protocol No. 2 on the application of the principles of subsidiarity and proportionality.

Protocols have Treaty status, under Article 51 TEU (ex 311 EC).

The Protocol requires the Commission to consult widely before formally proposing legisla-tion and, in an amendment brought in by the Lisbon Treaty, its draft legislative Acts shall be forwarded to the national parliaments at the same time as to the EP and Council, and the Commission must accompany drafts with detailed statements as to how the proposal complies with the principles of subsidiarity and proportionality, and must provide evidential support to demonstrate that Union action is required and the general and financial impact of the proposed legislation.

Articles 6 and 7 TEU further outline the Council members national parliaments' ability to object to the proposal and the procedure involving how those objections are further con-sidered by the Union institutions in the legislative processes, and how the Commission must issue a reasoned opinion if it wishes to maintain the proposal for further consideration in the legislative process. All in all, it is quite a convoluted process, the details of which will go beyond most EU courses and will not therefore be rehearsed here. Previously, paragraph 3 of the earlier Protocol stated that the principle is a dynamic concept that can be expanded or restricted or discontinued where circumstances so require, but this has been removed from the present Protocol and replaced by the process here outlined. Hence, then, it seems that the principle will remain as difficult as ever to tie down. As a last resort – previously impliedly, but now expressly under Article 8 of the Protocol – legislative Acts may be challenged under Article 263 TFEU (ex 230 EC) for infringing the principle. Whilst no new challenges have yet reached the ECJ under the amended Protocol, challenges from before the changes took place have been made.

cross reference
For details of this action, see Chapter 9, section 9.1.8.2.

3.4.2.1 Challenges for non-compliance with the principle

Non-compliance with the subsidiarity principle has been cited as a ground for annulment under an Article 230 EC (now 263 TFEU) judicial review action before the Court of Justice for an infringement of as essential procedural requirement. In its previous form, however, the principle received little judicial guidance. This is no surprise given the obscurity of the principle, which involves the balancing of economic and political priorities with which the Court of Justice is reluctant to interfere. It remains to be seen whether the amended Protocol clarifies this.

In **Cases C-84/94** *UK v Council (Working Time Directive)* and **C-377/98** *Netherlands v European Parliament and Council (Biotechnology Directive)*, arguments raised by the member states in the cases that subsidiarity had not been observed were roundly rejected by the Court of Justice. In the *Working Time Directive* case, the Court of Justice dismissed this part of the action with little discussion, merely to confirm that the Council had a clear power to act on working hours as an issue of the health and safety of workers. In other words, if it had the competence to act, it could not be prevented from acting.

However, in **Case C-376/98** *Germany v Parliament and Council (Tobacco Advertising Ban Directive)*, the harmonizing Directive 98/43 banning most forms of tobacco advertising was enacted under what was then Article 95 EC (now 114 TFEU) as an internal market measure. This was challenged by Germany, which argued that the measure was more closely allied to a public health measure and thus should have been enacted under the then Article 152 EC (now 168 TFEU), which expressly prohibited harmonizing legislation. The Court of Justice held that measures under (the then) Article 95 must have the primary object of improving conditions for the establishment or functioning of the internal market and that other Articles of the Treaty may not be used as a legal basis in order to circumvent the express exclusion of harmonization. It held further that to construe the internal market Article as meaning that it vests in the Union legislature a general power to regulate the internal market would be incompatible with the principle embodied in (the then) Article 5 EC that the powers of the Union are limited to those specifically conferred upon it. The Court of Justice thus held that, as a measure doing little to enhance the internal market, the use of the legal market Treaty base was inappropriate and it therefore annulled the measure entirely.

cross reference
See further details on the legal base in section 3.5.1.

The judgments are not a clear endorsement that subsidiarity is a clearly justiciable issue; more that it is another confirmation that where an incorrect legal base is used or where no powers have in fact been conferred, this provides grounds for the annulment of the measure. The *Tobacco* judgment is regarded as a reply to national courts, in particular the German Constitutional Court, which might have been minded to take Union law into its own hands, by showing that the Court of Justice is prepared to police incursions into the member states' competences by the EU's institutions.

See **Cases C-154/04 and C-155/04 *Alliance for Natural Health*** for another view provided by the Court of Justice that arguments based on a possible breach of subsidiarity will not allow it to interfere with decisions that are the result of the exercise of legislative discretion.

Almost inevitably, the Court of Justice will be invited to come up with a clearer and more workable definition. It is possible that the principle of subsidiarity will also join the ranks of general principles of Union law, although it is one introduced deliberately by the member states rather than created or introduced by the Court of Justice.

3.4.3 **Proportionality**

Proportionality, apart from being a legal principle in its own right and often employed by individuals in challenges to Union action, is also contained in Article 5 TEU (ex 5(2) EC) and is linked to the subsidiarity principle, because both are concerned with the control and exercise of powers by the institutions.

- -

proportionality

Article 5(2) TEU defines proportionality as follows: 'Under the principle of proportionality, the content and form of Union action shall not exceed what is necessary to achieve the objectives of the Treaties.'

- -

Like subsidiarity, it too is subject to Protocol 2 and Union Acts are open to possible challenges if breaching proportionality.

It was, for example, raised in **Case 84/94 *UK v Council (Working Time Directive)*** by the UK under the argument that the restrictions imposed on working time were not minimum requirements, but were excessive – that is, disproportionate. This view was rejected by the ECJ on the grounds that unless there had been a manifest error or misuse of powers, the Council must be allowed to exercise its discretion in law-making involving social policy choices.

The extent to which proportionality can be employed to challenge Union law in an action to annul a harmonization measure dealing with food supplements was shown to be limited.

See **Cases C-154/04 and C-155/04 *Alliance for Natural Health*** for the view provided by the Court of Justice that arguments based on a possible breach of proportionality will not allow it to interfere with decisions that are the result of the exercise of legislative discretion. Legality can be affected only as a result of the legislative act being manifestly inappropriate.

This was confirmed in similar terms in the follow-up case, **Case C-344/04 *R v Department of Transport, ex p International Air Transport Association and European Law Fares Airline Association.*** At [80] of that judgment:

cross reference

This is considered in Chapter 5, section 5.3.1, concerned with Union law reception in Germany.

thinking point

Is the way in which the principle of subsidiarity has been pleaded in the Court more to do with the member states' concerns rather than those of the citizens?

With regard to judicial review of the conditions referred to in the previous paragraph, the Community legislature must be allowed a broad discretion in areas which involve political, economic and social choices on its part, and in which it is called upon to undertake complex assessments.

Consequently, the legality of a measure adopted in those fields can be affected only if the measure is manifestly inappropriate having regard to the objective that the competent institution is seeking to pursue.

thinking point

This is a little like the considerations taken into account by the Court of Justice in deciding locus standi *in Article 263 TFEU (ex 230 EC) actions and in the* Schöppenstedt *formula in Article 340 TFEU (ex 288 EC) actions.*

cross reference
These are both considered in Chapter 9 and proportionality is considered in more detail as one of the general principles in Chapter 4, section 4.2.7.6.

Finally, in the attempt to counter the competence creep, the Lisbon Treaty has introduced a new requirement in Article 296 TFEU that relates to the competence and legal base issues, and states that: 'When considering draft legislative acts, the EP and the Council shall refrain from adopting acts not provided for by the relevant legislative procedure in the area in question.'

3.5 The participation of the institutions in the legislative processes

This section of this chapter deals with how the binding secondary law of the Union is enacted. These forms of law now constitute the vast bulk of Union law and their enactment has unfortunately become rather complex over the years, involving principally three institutions, but, according to the process required, often more of the Union bodies. First, though, an allied issue needs to be addressed in order to provide a complete picture and to explain what determines which particular process should be employed in any given circumstance.

3.5.1 The legal base for legislative proposals

Articles of the Treaties that empower the EU institutions to enact further legislation to carry out the policies of that title or chapter provide the key to the legislative procedure that must be used to enact the laws. In view of the reforms introduced by the Lisbon Treaty, this topic has been considerably simplified, although an awareness of it is still required.

Treaty Articles that set out a policy objective either provide details of the procedure themselves or refer to another Treaty Article, which provides the details of the procedure to be used.

For example, Article 59 TFEU dealing with the liberalization of specific services provides that 'the European Parliament and Council, acting in accordance with the ordinary legislative procedure and after consulting the Economic and Social Committee shall issue directives'.

Alternatively as an example, Article 48 TFEU (ex 42 EC) refers to the ordinary legislative procedure, which is outlined in Article 294 (ex 251 EC, then termed 'co-decision').

cross reference

If in doubt about what qualified majority voting (QMV) means, refer back to Chapter 2, section 2.2.4.3.

The Treaty Article providing the power is known then as the 'legal base', which thus determines the participants in the procedure and the level of their participation. Law-making always involves the Commission and Council plus the EP, and sometimes, as noted in section 3.6.1, the European Economic and Social Committee (EESC) or the Committee of the Regions (CoR). The Treaty base is then fundamental to the relative powers and ability of the other institutions to affect the content of Union law. For example, the use of QMV in the Council of Ministers is extremely important to the Commission, which stands a greater chance of having proposals accepted by a majority rather than by all member states in Council. Minority or marginal views can thus be ignored rather than be taken into account at the draft stages. The legal base is also vital to the level of participation of the EP in the legislative process – that is, whether it is merely consulted, or gives its consent, or whether the co-decision procedure is used, in which case the EP has more power.

For example, measures in support of the single market under Article 114 TFEU (ex 95 EC) require QMV rather than unanimity in the Council.

As indicated, because this makes life easier for the Commission, it has tried to exploit this by introducing as much legislation as possible under Article 114 TFEU (ex 95 EC), whereas the Council has argued that proposals should have as their legal base other Articles requiring unanimity (such as Article 115 TFEU, ex 94 EC, concerned directly with approximating legislation for the Common Market). Looked at from another point of view, a single member state that objects to a particular measure would wish to veto it and would want unanimity voting in Council to have that chance. It would object to the Council deciding to adopt the measure under a legal base requiring QMV if there were even an outside chance of another Treaty Article base being relevant – that is, one requiring unanimity. For the most part, the particular Treaty legal base is clear, in that the subject matter of the proposal is clearly within the subject matter of a specific Treaty Article and therefore base. However, the subject matter may straddle different Treaty subject areas and thus lend itself to more than one Treaty base. Hence there is sufficient ground for differences of opinion as to which is the correct Treaty base to use, and the institutions and member states have often fought over this. In particular, in view of the democratic deficit argument and its long campaign to attain greater involvement in the legislative process, the EP has not refrained from challenging the Council for the use of an allegedly incorrect legal base and regularly brings cases before the Court of Justice.

thinking point

Note that, in order to fully appreciate the importance of these cases in the law-making procedures, you need to read about the procedures themselves. For the moment, though, read through the case examples here and come back to them later, if need be, after reading about the procedures in more detail.

Note that there have been two complete changes of Treaty Article numbers, once when the Amsterdam Treaty came into force and a second now that the Lisbon Treaty is in force, and a number of other less extensive changes and amendments also. This means that cases such as the following, many of which were decided prior to Amsterdam, are now completely adrift from the present Treaty Article numbers, and some of the Articles themselves have been amended quite substantially and some even removed. Rather than use three sets of numbers for these cases in which often the old versions of the Treaty Articles themselves also are needed, only the original Article numbers will be given. The value of the cases is in the issues arising rather than showing what the new numbers are.

An early example, and one likely to be in materials' books, is **Case 68/86 _UK_ v _Council (Hormones)_**, which concerned a Directive banning growth-producing hormones. This first case was based on an earlier Article 43 concerned with measures in support of the Common Agricultural Policy (CAP), which required a qualified majority only. This was objected to by the UK, which argued that it should have been based on an earlier Article 100 – a single-market measure that required unanimity. The question raised was whether this was free movement, as argued by the UK, thus a single-market measure, or really to do with agricultural policy, in which case the Treaty Article under that section would be the most appropriate. The Court of Justice held that the CAP Article was the appropriate one because it lent itself more to the subject matter concerned.

thinking point
One might argue that to transport waste to recycle or to dispose of it is not particularly environmentally friendly.

Similarly, in **Case C-155/91 _Commission_ v _Council (Waste Directive)_**, the Waste Directive 91/156, adopted by the Council under an old Article 130s (an environment measure legal base then requiring unanimity), was challenged by the Commission on the basis that the old Article 100a, which was concerned with the internal market, requiring majority voting only, should have been used as the legal base. On this occasion, the Court disagreed and held that the protection of the environment, as stated in the Directive, was the real reason and not the free movement of waste. Therefore the challenge by the Commission was rejected. The issue was not so much the right to move waste around, but the promotion of the most efficient way of dealing with waste to protect the environment. This was, however, to be achieved by removing any prevention of movement, so that the most efficient operators or disposers of waste could handle it, regardless of where they were situated.

A further case concerned the adoption by the Council in June 1993 of a Directive specifying a minimum working week, albeit with the ability of workers to work longer voluntarily. The UK, which was opposed to this, was unable to veto the proposal, because it was introduced under the Health and Safety of Workers provision under the old Article 118a EEC requiring a qualified majority in the Council. In **Case C-84/94 _UK_ v _Council_**, the UK formally requested the Court of Justice to annul the Directive, arguing that it would have been more appropriate to base the measure on the original Article 235 (the flexibility clause that is now Article 352 TFEU) or the old version of Article 100, either of which would have required unanimity on the part of the Council, thus allowing the UK the chance to veto the measure before its possible enactment. The Court of Justice was, however, satisfied with the choice of Article 118a as a health and safety matter.

In **Case C-295/90 European Parliament v Council (Students' Residence),** Parliament successfully challenged the adoption of Directive 90/366 on the free movement and right to residence of students that the Council adopted under old Article 235, requiring only consultation, rather than under old Article 7 (prohibition of discrimination on the grounds of nationality), which would require the old and now removed cooperation procedure to be used, which provided the greater participation of the EP. The Directive was annulled and has been re-enacted as Directive 93/96. The EP had no objection to the rights provided by the measure itself; merely to the way in which it had been enacted, which denied it its full participation.

A final case here to focus on the issues raised above is **Case C-300/89 Commission v Council (Titanium Dioxide Directive)**. The Council adopted a Directive on the basis of old Article 130s as an environmental measure, which then required unanimity in Council and only consultation of the EP, despite the protests of the EP. The Commission argued that it should have been adopted using old Article 100a as a single-market measure, which then required QMV and the cooperation procedure instead. Whilst the Court acknowledged that both could be valid bases, the use of old Article 130s instead of old Article 100a deprived the EP of its greater role in the legislative process. Even if both were used, as suggested by the Council, it would still have to decide unanimously and be able to overrule any objections of the EP.

What emerges from this case law is that the view of the Court of Justice is essentially that the democratic process in law-making, which now involves the EP, demands that where two legal bases are available requiring differing procedures, the one allowing the EP the greater role must be used so as not to deprive the EP and the Union of its democratic right, unless it can be shown that the matter is primarily more concerned with a particular Treaty base.

cross reference
See section 3.6.1.1 for more on the ordinary legislative procedure.

In view of the simplification of the legislative procedures by the Treaties of Amsterdam, Nice and particularly now the Lisbon Treaty, many more Treaty subject areas have moved under what is now termed the 'ordinary legislative procedure'. Because this is now by far the most prominent procedure, increasingly there is less room for a dispute as to the correct legal base, therefore less scope for argument and less possibility for Court action in the future.

A warning to observe the correct legal base is also now provided in Article 296 TFEU, which provides that: 'When considering draft legislative acts, the EP and the Council shall refrain from adopting acts not provided for by the relevant legislative procedure in the area in question.'

There have been two more recent cases in which the appropriateness of the chosen legal base was challenged.

In **Case C-210/03 R v Secretary of State for Health, ex p Swedish Match,** the Court of Justice held that if obstacles to trade emerge, the Commission can intervene to harmonize even if the internal market is not the prime motive. That case concerned the banning of a type of snuff.

In the second Tobacco Advertising case, **C-380/03 Germany v European Parliament and Council,** Article 95 EC could be used, under the new justifications provided by the Commission for its use, to enact a Directive restricting the advertising of tobacco products, where it was argued that differences in the national laws relating to this advertising would have the effect of creating obstacles to free trade. Thus the Community Directive was held necessary to harmonize the internal market to allow it to function properly.

3.6 Law-making principles and procedures

For more details on this section scan here or visit the Online Resource Centre.

A number of factors have influenced first the establishment of the law-making procedures, and secondly, their expansion and evolution. From relatively straightforward beginnings, these have mushroomed into numerous and complex forms and procedures, but which now have been considerably rationalized by the Lisbon Treaty in 2009. The issues provoking such change include the democratic deficit of the law-making procedure overall, the expansions in the number of member states, voting arrangements in the Council, and the establishment and subsequent removal of the two intergovernmental pillars by the TEU and Lisbon Treaty. Hence there have been numerous Treaty amendments both increasing and complicating the legislative procedures. Whilst the Treaty of Amsterdam made an attempt to rein in the prolixity and complexity of these procedures, it is the Lisbon Treaty that has done most, but unfortunately not to the extent originally proposed by the Constitutional Treaty (CT).

Three institutions are principally involved in law-making. However, it is worth noting that, before law-making even commences, the overall policy is decided by the member states during both Treaty negotiation and amendment, and on an ongoing basis by the European Council in making recommendations and requesting actions by the main institutions, notably the Council, but also the Commission.

3.6.1 The law-making procedures

There are at present essentially three law-making procedures in the EU, plus the delegated legislative power of the Commission. Following the Lisbon Treaty reforms, there has been a radical renaming of these and a clear leading law-making procedure has been established from these three:

- the ordinary legislative procedure;
- special legislative procedures; and
- the consent (formerly known as assent) procedure.

All law-making procedures start with the Commission, which puts policy into effect by means of preparing and proposing legislative instruments, although following the entry into force of the Lisbon Treaty, suggestions and recommendations for legislative acts may also come from the EP, the European Council, the member states, the European Central Bank (ECB), the ECJ, the European Investment Bank (EIB) and EU citizens (Articles 11–12 TEU and 289 TFEU).

> **Article 289 TFEU**
> ....
>
> 1. The ordinary legislative procedure shall consist in the joint adoption by the European Parliament and the Council of a regulation, directive or decision on a proposal from the Commission. This procedure is defined in Article 294.
> 2. In the specific cases provided for by the Treaties, the adoption of a regulation, directive or decision by the European Parliament with the participation of the Council, or by the latter with the participation of the European Parliament, shall constitute a special legislative procedure.
> 3. Legal acts adopted by legislative procedure shall constitute legislative acts.

4. In the specific cases provided for by the Treaties, legislative acts may be adopted on the initiative of a group of Member States or of the European Parliament, on a recommendation from the European Central Bank or at the request of the Court of Justice or the European Investment Bank.

cross reference

The legal base, discussed at section 3.5.1, is the Treaty Article covering the subject matter of the legislation under consideration.

The Council and Parliament, for the most part, then dispose of these legislative proposals – that is, they decide the final shape and enact the legislation. The actual details of each procedure vary according to the way in which the Council votes and the different forms of participation of the EP. Additionally, for some procedures, other institutions are involved, most notably the EESC and the CoR. The institutions and the extent to which they are involved are determined by the Treaty. First, Article 289 TFEU (ex 249 EC) provides details of the procedures available to enact Union legislation. Which particular process is employed depends on the subject matter for which legislation is required and then, in turn, the Treaty Article(s) that govern those matters – that is, legislation is enacted under a particular prescribed procedure.

In addition to the procedures themselves, we need to consider why they have become so convoluted and the consequences of this, although it is not necessary to learn the fine details and points of each and every legislative process. This, apart from being tedious, is not very productive and, like many sets of rules, will simply change over time.

For example, Article 46 TFEU (ex 40 EC), which empowers legislation to be enacted for the free movement of workers, requires that the ordinary legislative procedure be used (detailed in Article 294 TFEU, previously 'co-decision' in Article 251 EC).

3.6.1.1 The ordinary legislative (formerly co-decision) procedure

Article 289 TFEU (ex 249 EC) has been amended over the years to provide that the EP act more extensively with the Council and Commission in the legislative process, notably by the introduction of the co-decision procedure and its renaming as the ordinary legislative procedure, detailed in Article 294 TFEU (ex 251 EC). It provides for the enhanced participation of the EP to the extent that, ultimately, the EP can reject a legislative proposal at a second reading. The EP cannot impose its own will on the content of a legislative proposal, thus parliamentary veto might be an alternative description of the process. Note that, in the procedure, the Council votes mainly by QMV, but at times, according to some Treaty Articles and parts of the procedure itself, it must vote unanimously. The following description takes into account the amendments made to the procedure by the Treaties of Amsterdam and Lisbon, which ironed out some of the initial teething troubles and delays originally experienced in the operation of the procedure. The description has been marked with reference numbers that relate to Diagram 3.1.

The main stages of this procedure are that the Commission proposal (**1**), taking into account the opinions of the national parliaments (**1A**) and other bodies where specified (**1B**), is forwarded simultaneously to the EP for its opinion and the Council for consideration. The EP can, at first reading (**2**), either approve the proposal or amend the proposal by a simple majority or, although not strictly allowed under the procedure detailed in Article 294 TFEU, can reject or substantially amend the proposal, in which case, the proposal is returned to the Commission for an amended proposal (**3**). The Council, at first reading (**4**), can either, within three months, approve those amendments by a qualified majority (**5**), in which case the act can be adopted (**6**), or if there have been no amendments (**7**), it can simply adopt the act by a qualified majority (**8**). This often

Diagram 3.1 *The co-decision procedure*

Source: Reproduced with grateful acknowledgement under the general authorization of the European Commission; see <http://ec.europa.eu/codecision/stepbystep/diagram_en.htm> and <http://europa.eu/geninfo/legal_notices_en.htm>.

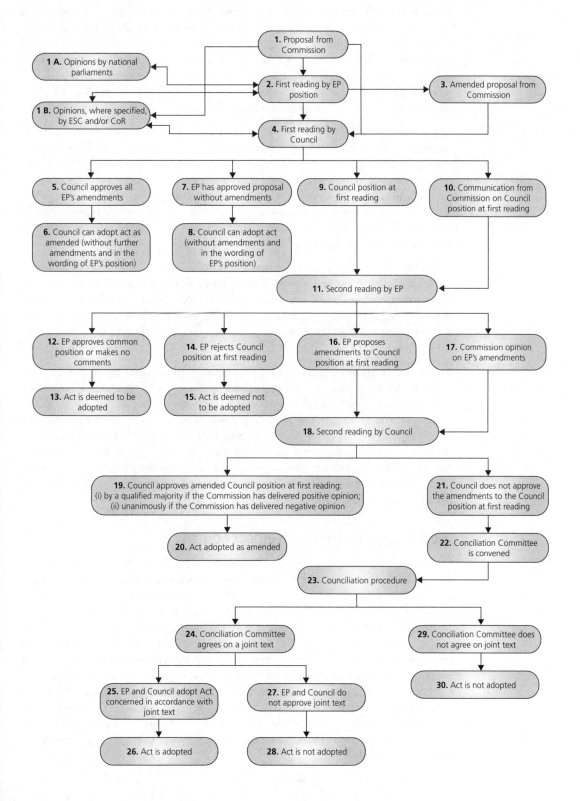

involves considerable exchanges of views between the three institutions to reach an agreement at first reading, but, where successful, disposes with the need to spend time on the rest of the procedure. Instead, the provision can be enacted without further ado. Otherwise, the Council adopts a common position (9) on which the Commission comments (10).

The proposal then goes to the second reading by the EP (11), which can, within three months and with a possible one-month extension, either approve the common position, or for whatever reason do nothing within the time limit (12), in which case the act is deemed to have been adopted (13). If, however, the EP rejects, by an absolute majority, the common position (14), the Act is deemed not to have been accepted (15) – that is, the proposal will not become law and the procedure ends. The EP, however, may propose amendments to the common position (16), which are forwarded to the Commission for comment (17), and the Council for a second reading (18).

At second reading (18), the Council may, within three months plus a one-month extension, approve the EP amendments by a qualified majority or unanimously if the Commission has issued a negative opinion (19), in which case the act is adopted as amended (20). If, on the other hand, the Council does not accept the amended common position (21), the matter is referred, within six weeks, to a conciliation committee to attempt to achieve a compromise also within six weeks, with a possible two-week extension (22 and 23). The committee comprises members of the Council with an equal number of members of the European Parliament (MEPs) and the Commissioner responsible.

If a joint text is approved by the committee (24), the Council, by qualified majority (unless the Treaty base requires unanimity), and the EP, by a simple majority, may adopt the provision together within six weeks (25) and the Act is adopted (26). If, however, there is no approval of the joint text (27), or no agreement by the conciliation committee on a joint text within the time limit in the first place (29), then in both cases the procedure comes to an end and the act is deemed not to have been adopted (28 and 30).

As will be seen, this procedure is not for the faint-hearted, and despite the fact that the powers of the Parliament have been increased clearly and significantly, the EP cannot enforce its own positive view over the Council; if they cannot agree, the EP can defeat the proposal, as it did early in 2010 by rejecting the 'Swift' data-sharing agreement with the United States. The procedure was extended by the Amsterdam, Nice and Lisbon Treaties into many new areas of the Treaty and as the co-decision procedure was made subject to a joint declaration on it use. It is now by far the most frequently employed legislative procedure in the Treaty and, even before taking into account the changes introduced by the Lisbon Treaty, it was employed in about 90 per cent of all secondary law enactment.

3.6.1.2 Special legislative procedures

This second category is really a bundle of procedures that may be referred to in the Treaties variously as 'the' or 'a' special legislative procedure, and essentially groups together a number of procedures that differ in one or more elements from the ordinary legislative procedure. Instead of QMV, the Council may vote by unanimity or the EP may just be consulted or asked for its consent rather than co-decide. Other bodies, such as the EESC, or CoR, or ECB, may also be included in the process. It incorporates the original consultation procedure, which originally featured only in a limited number of Treaty Articles (seventeen) and provided that the Council was required to consult the EP as to its opinion before coming to a decision on Community secondary law. Under this procedure, the Commission proposes legislation that it deems necessary to fulfil a Union aim; the EP is then consulted and it offers its opinion; and the Council decides on the matter, either by QMV, but usually unanimously. However, on receipt of the opinion of the EP, the Council could proceed to ignore it and override any view given by the EP.

See, however, **Cases 138 and 139/79 *Roquette and Maizena* v *Council***, in which the Court annulled a Regulation because the Council had failed to consult or obtain the opinion of the EP before it passed the legislation.

Furthermore, in **Case C-65/93 *European Parliament* v *Council***, it was held that if the Commission proposal has been substantially altered, the EP must be consulted again, and failure to do so will also result in annulment of the measure, which occurred in this case.

It is argued that, without express authority, these considerations will continue to apply to measures adopted under a special legislative procedure that fails to consult the EP when required. Unanimity of Council combined with consulting the EP appears to be the most common form of this procedure.

For examples of special legislative procedure, see Articles 19, 126, 192 and 332 TFEU, which include the unanimity of Council and consultation of the EP alone or with others, Article 252 on the unanimity of Council and consenting of the EP, or Article 223 TFEU under which the EP takes the lead and consults the Commission, plus obtains the consent of the Council.

3.6.1.3 The consent procedure

thinking point
Why does the EU not move to only one law-making process?

The consent (previously referred to as 'assent') procedure was introduced by the SEA and extended under the TEU and Lisbon Treaty, so that the EP's consent is required by the Council in respect of membership and withdrawal applications to the EU, the Union's membership of international agreements and organizations, and for association agreements with third countries (Articles 49 and 50 TEU, and 218 and 217 TFEU, ex 300(3) and 310 EC); in total, in fifteen instances. In the event of disagreement, the EP has effectively a right of veto, but there are no formal mechanisms built in by which a dialogue between the two institutions can be initiated in the event of a disagreement on any aspect or an entire Agreement. In reality, though, any such dispute would have been subject to debate and discussion behind the scenes. Consent may also be employed to confirm serious and persistent breaches by a member state (Article 7 TEU) and in establishing a procedure for the revision of the Treaties (Article 48 TEU). The procedure has not been made subject to time limits.

3.6.2 **Why so many changes to the legislative procedures?**

As was noted at the beginning of this section, the increase of and subsequent changes to the decision-making procedures are the product of a number of developments in the EU: the democratic deficit, the various expansions of member states' voting arrangements in the Council, the movement and expansion of the EU into new policy areas, and as a response to the international regulation of pan-European or even global problems such as the environment or business regulation. One of the unfortunate consequences of the increase in procedures is that it has led to legal disputes between the member states and institutions, and between the institutions themselves, about whether the correct legal procedure and legal base has been used and not, for the most part, concerned with the substance of the final legislative act. Many cases were more concerned with the degree of power wielded by the EP or individual states in the Council. As a result, the procedures have become even further removed from a sensible understanding of the legislative processes by lawyers, yet alone laypersons, and the desire to reform the procedures in addition to the desire to reform the type and number of legal instruments.

Under the original proposal for the abandoned Constitutional Treaty, the co-decision route was to become the only procedure; however, the member states insisted on retaining the consultation procedure, within the new umbrella term of 'specialist legislative procedure', requiring Council unanimity in the areas of tax, some aspects of social and environmental policy, some bases of CFSP and Justice and Home Affairs (JHA) issues.

3.7 The delegation of powers

Prior to the Lisbon Treaty, Articles 202 and 211 EC authorized the delegation of powers to the Commission. Delegation is now regulated by Article 290 TFEU, which specifies that a legislative Act (those enacted under the ordinary and special legislative procedures of Article 289) may delegate to the Commission the power to adopt non-legislative acts of general application.

For more details on this section scan here or visit the Online Resource Centre.

In order for day-to-day decision-making to be effective, in most, if not all, democratic systems of government, some form of executive action is required, either to implement or complete legislative acts, or to be used in respect of detailed, technical issues not requiring the debate or input of the main legislators.

Delegation can be in the form of wide discretionary powers, including legislative, as well as administrative, forms of secondary legislation. Delegation may, however, be subjected to confirmation or limits or rules laid down by the delegating authority, or the delegating authority may retain the right to rescind the act adopted. This latter right is usually subject to a time limit by which the delegating authority must act. In the Union legal order, a system of committees was set up to supervise the exercise of delegated power whereby the Council has retained control over the delegated power. Delegation and the management committees have been considered by the Court of Justice as early as 1958.

In **Case 9/56 *Meroni* v *High Authority***, the Court of Justice stressed the necessity of preserving the balance of powers in the institutional structure of the Communities as envisaged by the Treaties and which would therefore not allow the delegation of discretionary powers involving policy decisions.

In **Case 25/70 *Köster***, the delegation of power to the Commission within the management committee procedure was challenged on the ground that the procedure disturbed the institutional balance of the Community contrary to the Treaty and undermined the independence of the Commission. The Court observed that the management committee could not take decisions itself, but merely provided options for implementation, and therefore the power balance was not disturbed.

Thus, provided that the empowering legislation is adopted by the procedures envisaged by the Treaty, the details can be delegated to the Commission.

The Court of Justice held further in **Case 23/75 *Rey Soda***, that implementing powers under old Article 211 EC must be interpreted widely, especially under the CAP where actions must often be taken on a day-to-day basis and discretion is necessary to cope with changing circumstances.

The SEA amended old Article 202 EC by adding a third indent, which provided that 'The Council may impose certain requirements in respect of the exercise of these powers' and 'The Council may also reserve the right, in specific cases, to exercise directly implementing powers itself'.

Consequent to this, Decision 87/373, known as the Comitology Decision, as amended by Council Decision 99/468 and now replaced by Regulation 182/2011, was adopted to determine principles and rules governing the system of management committees. The Decision provides for three standard committee types: advisory committees; management committees, which have two procedural variants providing greater powers of decision for the Commission; and regulatory committees, which require positive approval of the decisions by the committee. The committees consist of representatives of the member states and a non-voting Commission chair. Amendments were made to the workings of the committees in 2006 and 2008, but it is likely, in view of the new regime set up by Articles 290–291 TFEU, that a new regulatory framework will be drawn up and implemented by the Commission, Council and EP. Article 290(2) TFEU provides that each act that provides for a delegated power to the Commission shall so state and state also the conditions of delegation subject to either revocation by the EP or Council, or if there has been no objection within a set period. The old system will remain in force to oversee the committees required by legislation enacted prior to the Lisbon Treaty, whereas new legislation will be governed by the amended procedures outlined in Regulation 182/2011.

An overview of the changes can be found in Council press release 6378/11, 14 February 2011, available online at <http://www.consilium.europa.eu/uedocs/cms_data/docs/press-data/EN/genaff/119270.pdf>.

In **Case 16/88 *Commission v Council (Management Committee Procedure)*** concerning the Commission's power of implementation under old Article 274 EC, the Council delegated power to conclude certain contracts to the Commission subject to a management committee procedure. The Commission argued that implementation under old Article 274 concerning budgetary procedure was not subject to management committees. The Court held that as the Commission was also legislative in character, it was validly subject to the management committee procedures.

It is argued that, since the formalization of the procedure, too much power has been given to the committees and is consequently lost from the Commission and the EP. The system allows the Council to withdraw delegated powers at any time when decided by the committee. The EP attempted to challenge the committee management structure in the Comitology Decision (Case 302/87 *European Parliament v Council*), particularly because the Council failed to state in which circumstances particular procedures would apply, but the challenge failed due to the inadmissibility, at that time, of the direct challenge by the EP.

3.7.1 Implementing acts

Article 291 now provides separately and expressly for acts that are to be implemented uniformly in the member states, but the control of such powers by the member states. To that end, a Regulation (182/2011) has been enacted setting up a form of Committee structure for these acts also, which, for the purposes of this volume, will suffice.

In other specific circumstances, the Commission has further powers of its own under Article 105 TFEU (ex 85 EC) competition law exemptions and under Article 106 TFEU (ex 86 EC) concerned with state aids.

Summary

The Communities and now Union were established by a transfer of powers by the member states to enable them to act independently of those member states and to create their own laws and legal system. However, the transfer was not a complete transfer of competences, but only a transfer of competences in those areas agreed by the member states. In some areas, exclusive competence was agreed where considered necessary; in others, competence was to be shared. In addition, in order to operate effectively, it was necessary that additional residual and general powers were granted if needed to complete particular aspects without having to have recourse to the member states on each and every occasion. This led to a perceived competence creep by the member states, which considered the Commission to have overstepped the mark. Thus the attention turned to considering the attempts by which this competence creep might be curbed, notably through the principles of proportionality and subsidiarity.

As outlined in this chapter, there are a number of shifting dynamics in the policymaking and law-making procedures of the EU. The most notable remains the balance between the direct democratic legitimacy of the EP in the face of the still legislative superiority of the Council, although clearly under the Lisbon Treaty things have moved further in the direction of the EP. The problem, however, with increasing the input and power of the EP still further or including national parliaments to a greater degree is that it would certainly increase democratic participation, albeit indirectly, although that might jeopardize the present level of efficiency of the law-making process. Whilst it is far from perfect at the moment, it does seem to have achieved a relatively happy medium of getting most things done, albeit sometimes rather slowly. An increase in the power of the EP truly to rival that of the Council or increasing the participation of the national parliaments might have the knock-on effect of creating conflicts between the institutions, which might result in stalling the law-making processes – and if nothing ever gets done, it would hardly be a useful democratic input. In other words, too much participation by the EP or the national parliaments would lead to a slowing down of the legislative processes. So should efficiency be sacrificed for the sake of democracy? The concern presently is whether democracy is being sacrificed for the sake of efficiency.

Under the changes brought about by the Lisbon Treaty, national parliaments have been given a formal say in any future Treaty amendment proposals and new membership applications (Articles 48–49 TEU). The difficulty with this is that the national parliaments may then become a rival for power with the EP and it may also reduce efficiency in the law-making processes if the views of twenty-seven national parliaments have to be obtained before progress can be made.

Questions

For suggested approaches to answering these questions scan here or visit the Online Resource Centre.

1 What role do the principles of subsidiarity, proportionality and attributed competence play in the process of EU law-making? Who should rule on the question of whether these principles are being respected?

2 What is the legal base of a Union law? Why is it important to know this and why have so many disputes arisen as to the proper legal base?

3 Why are there so many law-making procedures?

Further reading

BOOKS

Douglas-Scott, S. *Constitutional Law of the European Union*, Longman, Harlow, 2002 (chapter 3).

Hix, S. *The Political System of the European Union,* 2nd edn, Macmillan, Basingstoke, 2005.

Konstantinides, T. *Division of Powers in European Union Law: The Delimitation of Internal Competences between the EU and the Member States*, Kluwer Law International, London, 2009.

ARTICLES

Davies, G. 'Subsidiarity: the wrong idea, in the wrong place, at the wrong time' (2006) 43 CML Rev 63.

Harbo, T.-I. 'The function of the proportionality principle in EU law' (2010) ELJ 158.

Weatherill, S. 'Better competence monitoring' (2005) 30 EL Rev 23.

Weatherill, S. 'Competence creep and competence control' (2005) 24 YEL 1.

Sources and forms of EU law

Learning objectives

In this chapter, you will learn about:

- the various sources that make up the body of Union law that exists today;
- the different forms of Union law.

Introduction

> Following the entry into force of the Lisbon Treaty, the terms 'European Union law' and 'European Union legal system' are the ones that will now apply to what was previously termed 'Community law' and 'Community legal system'. Both sets of terms, though, are referring to the same things, which is the subject of the rest of this chapter and indeed this book.

4.1 The EU legal system

For more details on this section scan here or visit the Online Resource Centre.

This section will introduce the founding Treaties, which provide the basis of other forms of Union law, but it is to be noted immediately that the European Union (EU) and its Court, the European Court of Justice (ECJ), have also used external sources for some of its laws, notably fundamental rights and general principles, which will be considered in this chapter. Furthermore, the individual style of Union law will be highlighted.

The Treaty on European Union (TEU) and the Treaty on the Functioning of the European Union (TFEU) are, following the entry into force of the Lisbon Treaty, the principal sources of law for the Union and the ones with which we are most concerned. As will be clear from Chapter 1 of this book, the Treaties and Union law are not static bodies of law, but are amended from time to time as the member states agree, as can clearly be seen by the changes introduced by the Single European Act (SEA), the Maastricht Treaty (TEU) and the Treaties of Amsterdam, Nice and Lisbon. In establishing the basic format of the Communities at the time of their founding, legal models were sought on which to build the legal system for the Communities and now Union. At that time, there were no member states from common law jurisdictions and it is therefore to be expected that the initial Community legal system would broadly resemble a civil law system and, in particular, follow legal structures found in the French and German legal systems. For example, much of the procedure of the courts is based on French administrative law, as are actions for damages under the second paragraph of Article 340 TFEU (ex 288 EC). In turn, looking over the longer-term development of Community and now EU law, this has been influenced both by the legal structures and the principles of law in the member states, and in turn Community and now EU law influences the development of law in the member states.

The founding framework Treaties provide broad principles and aims, which reflect the way in which civil law countries approach legislative enactment with codified law. They commence with general abstract principles, such as the Preamble and Articles 2 and 3 TFEU.

Preamble TFEU

DETERMINED to lay the foundations of an ever closer union among the peoples of Europe,

RESOLVED to ensure the economic and social progress of their countries by common action to eliminate the barriers which divide Europe,

AFFIRMING as the essential objective of their efforts the constant improvements of the living and working conditions of their peoples,

RECOGNISING that the removal of existing obstacles calls for concerted action in order to guarantee steady expansion, balanced trade and fair competition,

---

Article 2(3) TFEU

The Member States shall coordinate their economic and employment policies with arrangements as determined by this Treaty . . .

Indeed, this approach has been strengthened by the latest amendments and rearrangement of the Treaties and the material in them. The TEU has been made into a general overview Treaty providing the broad basis for the former EC Treaty, which has become, as it is inelegantly titled, the Treaty on the Functioning of the European Union. This is the Treaty that provides the details of the overall policies set out in the EU Treaty. It too, though, retains its general introduction and Articles.

The TEU also has a general Preamble and Articles 2 and 3 providing a list of objectives including, for example, under Article 3(4), that 'The Union shall establish an economic and monetary Union whose currency is the euro'. It also includes something with which lawyers from civil law countries are quite familiar: a form of good faith clause, included in Article 4(3) TEU (ex 10 EC), which imposes an obligation on the member states both to act positively to achieve the goals of the Treaty and also not to act in any way that would jeopardize those aims.

Article 4(3) TEU

The Member States shall take any appropriate measure, general or particular, to ensure fulfilment of the obligations arising out of the Treaties or resulting from acts of the institutions of the Union. The Member States shall facilitate the achievement of the Union's tasks and refrain from any measure which could jeopardise the attainment of the Union's objectives.

The rest of the TFEU, although putting the broad aims into greater detail, nevertheless provides merely an outline for the areas of law that the member states agreed should be integrated. It provides, for example, the basic legal regime for free movement of goods and workers, competition law and agriculture. Some sections are more detailed than others and whereas free movement of goods has required little secondary legislation, competition law and agriculture have been subject to considerable legislative regulation. Thus, for the most part, the Treaties require completion by detailed Regulations and Directives. The areas agreed by the member states can and have been added to, for example environmental protection and research and technology was added by the SEA, and new policy areas were introduced by the TEU, notably economic and monetary union, public health and consumer protection.

Apart from the secondary legislation needed to put into effect the goals of the various policies, any gaps and ambiguities in the legislation and interpretation of the Treaty and secondary legislation are resolved by the ECJ. As a result, a body of case law has slowly arisen, itself relying on a variety of internal and external sources, such as general principles and fundamental rights.

4.1.1 The style of the EU legal system

Before moving on to consider the individual elements of the Union legal system, it is worthwhile considering how the legal system is intended to work. Similar to the civil law systems, the Union legal system is essentially a deductive system; therefore the result in a particular case is achieved by working from the general to the particular – that is, from the broad framework Treaty rules, which have in the past often included the Preamble, Articles 2, 3, 10 and 12 EC, to the relevant provisions of the specific Chapter or Title of the Treaty.

Then, any secondary legislation on the topic can be considered, and finally, the relevant case law on the interpretation and application of the Treaties or other legislative provisions can be evaluated to help to determine the outcome of a particular case.

As will be demonstrated in the following chapters, the interpretation techniques of the Court of Justice also follow the approach of taking into account the general aims to help to decide in particular cases. The Court will often make reference to the Preamble and general provisions of the Treaty to justify a particular decision and applies law in the scope of the Treaty as a whole, in the light of the basic aims and objectives of the Treaty and not only the specific legislation. Examples from the old Treaties include:

- Article 2 EC is referred to in Case 7/75 *Mrs and Mrs F.* v *Belgian State* concerning social security;

- Article 3 EC in Case 6/72 *Europemballage and Continental Can* v *Commission*; and

- Case 14/83 *Von Colson* was very strongly argued on the basis of Article 10 EC (now 4(3) TEU).

> **Cases C-6 and C-9/90** *Francovich* was also argued strongly on the basis on Article 10 EC to establish, for the first time under Community law, state liability for the failure of the member state to implement a Directive.

Article 18 TFEU (ex 12 EC), the general prohibition of discrimination on the grounds of nationality, is also relevant to all areas of EU law and is used on particular occasions as a general tool of the Court of Justice to reach just results that might not otherwise have been reached by the application of more specific provisions.

> For example, Article 18 TFEU (ex 12 EC) has been used to extend the equality of law requirement in respect of vocational training and fees into more mainstream education, as can be seen in **Cases 24/86 *Blaizot*, 263/86 *Humbel*, 39/86 *Lair*** and ***293/83 Gravier*** amongst others.

4.1.2 The classification of the elements of EU law

EU law can be divided broadly into three main components and it may be that your course makes a similar division that helps to make EU law more accessible. The division is usually along the lines of institutional law, procedural law and substantive law.

4.1.2.1 Institutional law

Institutional law is also called the 'constitutional law' of the EU. It concerns the structure of the Union, the regulation of the main institutions and other bodies of the Union, the sources of EU law and the special principles of EU law, including supremacy and direct effects. Institutional law also concerns the relationship of the institutions among themselves, the relationship of the Union with the member states, and its external relations with other countries and international organizations. The institutions are the bodies responsible for the legislative and budgetary processes and, as their relationship alters in time due to Treaty amendment, disputes arise over the boundaries of the powers and duties of the institutions and their relationships to each other. Such disputes have had to be settled by the ECJ as the institutions seek to protect their powers or legally to extend them: for example, the Court has assisted the European Parliament in gaining increased litigation rights to reflect its democratic power in the Community, now formally recognized by Treaty amendment (Article 263 TFEU, ex 230 EC). Generally, also, the Court of Justice's pronouncements on the status and effects of the provisions of EU law have resulted in the establishment and development of ground-breaking, and now fundamental, leading principles of EU law, including direct effects, supremacy and state liability.

cross reference

Details can be found in Chapter 8.

4.1.2.2 Procedural law

cross reference

Considered in Chapters 6–9.

Procedural law is sometimes referred to as the 'administrative law' of the Union and includes actions for judicial review by the ECJ and the various other actions that can be taken by the institutions, member states, and natural and legal persons under rules provided by the TFEU (see Articles 258–260, 263, 265, 267, 277 and 340 TFEU, ex 226–228, 230, 232, 234, 241 and 288 EC). These actions, then, are mainly concerned with the enforcement of rights against the Union institutions, the member states and individuals. Procedural law covers a range of remedies, and indirect actions involving the national courts and direct actions at the level of the Union.

4.1.2.3 Substantive law

Substantive law comprises the legal rules established to carry out the broad policy areas of law agreed under the Treaties, and can be distinguished from the law relating to the institutions and the procedural law of the Union. The substantive law is largely secondary law and takes effect predominantly in the member states and not at the Union level, despite its primary base in Treaty Articles. The substantive law of the Union has also been described previously as 'economic law' or the 'law of the economy of the Community', and even as 'Community (now Union) private law'. However, this is not a particularly meaningful label because the concept of economic law varies from state to state and between political systems. Additionally, this does not reflect the considerable extension of the EU into new policy areas. The Union is now concerned with far more than the setting up of a regulatory framework for limited aspects of the economies dealing only with free-trade rules. More recently, far more social concerns and policies are being given voice in the EU legal order and Treaties: see, for example, the much-expanded Titles on social policy, education, culture, public health and consumer protection in the TFEU (Articles 151–169) brought about by Treaty amendment and intergovernmental agreements. Further evidence can be found in the statements made by the Court of Justice that the Community places social concerns above economic considerations, for example as in Case C-324/96 *Deutsche Telekom v Vick*.

The substantive law chapters following, however, will deal with three topics only, all of which were within the original policies of the Community, although to a different extent, social provision being at the time very limited. Those included are the free movement of goods, free movement of workers and persons, and sex equality law.

The sources and forms of Community and Union law

For more details on this section scan here or visit the Online Resource Centre.

What should be mentioned at the outset of this particular section of the book is the term *acquis communautaire*. This refers to, or is a way of describing, the whole body of EU law that has been built up over the life of the Communities and now Union, and which comprises all of the sources of law considered in this chapter. It is more likely to be heard in connection with the entry of new member states, which are now required to accept in total the *acquis communautaire*, which is non-negotiable. It was estimated that this amounts now to about 80,000 pages of legal text.

The Commission in 2010 estimated the *acquis* to consist of some 8,400 Regulations and 2,000 Directives.

cross reference
See Chapter 1, section 1.4.1.4.

The Treaties, the Protocols, Declarations, secondary legislation, international agreements and case law and development of legal principles by the Court of Justice all contribute to the *acquis communautaire*.

4.2.1 The Treaties

cross reference
See Chapter 1 for further details.

The Treaties are the primary source of law in the Union, with two main Treaties now of equal standing: the TEU and the TFEU (see Article 1 of both). The EC Treaty (now amended and renamed as the TFEU), the European Coal and Steel Treaty (ECSC), which is no longer in force, and the European Atomic Energy Treaty (EURATOM), which is still in force, were the three original Treaties dating from 1952 and 1957. The original Treaties were amended and supplemented considerably by a number of Treaties, including the 1965 Merger Treaty and the various Acts of Accession providing details for the entry into the Communities and Union of new member states. More fundamentally, they were amended by the SEA, the TEU, the Treaty of Amsterdam, the Treaty of Nice and, finally and most fundamentally, the Lisbon Treaty in 2009.

All of the Treaties of the Union are drawn up in all of the official languages of the Union, which are equally authentic. Any difficulties that arise from the fact that different meanings may, despite all attempts, arise between languages are usually overcome by the Court of Justice applying the teleological interpretation of the spirit of the provision rather than the letter. A comparison of a number of language versions may be necessary in order to discern the true meaning of a particular provision.

See, for example, **Case C-106/89 *Marleasing SA* v *La Comercial Internacional de Alimentacion SA*** and **Case C-149/97 *Institute of the Motor Industry* v *Customs and Excise Commissioners*** in which the different language versions of the Sixth VAT Directive were discussed.

The special nature of these Treaties is encapsulated within the concept of direct applicability, which means that, on the accession of a member state to the Union, all of the provisions of the Treaties automatically become part of the generally binding law of the member state. The provisions are applicable not only to the member states, but also to the citizens of each country. This form of law is also known as 'self-executing law', a term previously recognized in international law. This describes the way in which some provisions of law have legal validity in the member states, in that no further action need be taken by a member state to incorporate or transform the Treaty into the national legal order once it has ratified the Treaty. Some member states, however, such as the UK, may need an introductory Act formally to mark the presence of the Treaty, but even then would not reproduce the text of the Treaty into a national Act. Self-executing law, such as the Treaties, does not rely on the way in which the member state has incorporated it for its validity.

> The early **Case 26/62 *Van Gend en Loos*** is confirmation of the deeper impact of this directly applicable Community law because, in this case, the Court of Justice made it clear that Community law is also the legal concern of individuals and not only of the member states.

The Treaties are framework Treaties in that they lay down broad guidelines for the pursuit of certain agreed aims and objectives. They do not provide extensive details for the implementation of these policies, which is left for the most part to secondary legislation of the Union or, failing that, to the Court of Justice, which will rule on what was intended by the Treaty provision.

The scope of the Treaties has expanded considerably since their establishment and now covers wide areas of the economic and social life of the member states, including economic and monetary policy, culture and tourism, humanitarian aid, judicial and police cooperation, and foreign policy, amongst many others, although not all to the same level of integration and control.

The Lisbon Treaty does not add to these areas of Union influence, with the exception of making the catalogue of human rights binding (Article 6(1) TEU), but not a part of the Treaty, and with opt-outs for the UK and Poland and exemptions from specific aspects of it for Ireland and the Czech Republic.

4.2.1.1 The Protocols attached to the Treaties

The TEU and TFEU do not represent the entirety of primary Union law because, following an unfortunate practice of limited beginnings, each successive intergovernmental conference (IGC) has added what has now amounted to a complex and vast range of Protocols to the Treaties.

Status of the Protocols

Article 51 TEU (ex 311 EC) declares these Protocols to be an integral part of the Treaties, which means that they possess Treaty status, although the value of this status has not yet been questioned before the Court of Justice. What is clear is that, by the addition of so many Protocols, the Treaty constitutional set-up has become increasingly complex. Whilst some steps have been attempted to consolidate them, if anything this has been very limited and half-hearted.

In international law, Protocols would be regarded as a lesser form of international law than Treaties, but no less binding.

One of the aims in drafting the Constitutional Treaty (CT) was that this matter would be looked at and, as with the Treaties themselves, be considerably simplified. However, that simplification amounted only to consolidating the then existing Protocols and Declarations, which would then be attached as a long list of Protocols to the CT. Since the CT was rejected, the Lisbon Treaty has done nothing more than the same, and perhaps worse, by adding more Protocols. In total, there are thirty-seven Protocols now attached to the Treaties.

4.2.1.2 Declarations

In addition to the various Protocols, further attached to each subsequent Treaty is usually a list of Declarations of the member states, sometimes by all member states, but mainly by a few or only one, which makes a unilateral declaration on a particular matter, for example the Declaration by Austria and Luxembourg on credit institutions that was attached to the Amsterdam Treaty. These Declarations need to be noted because, like the Protocols, they may alter our view or perception of the meaning or application of Treaty provisions. However, unlike the Protocols, they enjoy no express Treaty status, and their effect is thus very uncertain in EU law.

The Lisbon Treaty has added more Declarations, so this unfortunate aspect of the EU legislative base has been made worse and not better. There are now sixty-five Declarations attached to the Treaties.

Without making any clear-cut express statement as to the status, the ECJ held in **Case C-192/99 *ex p Manjit Kaur* v *Secretary of State for the Home Department*** that, in order to determine UK nationality, it was necessary to refer to the 1992 Declaration on Nationality attached to the Treaties, thus acknowledging a legal effect of the instrument without, however, expressly declaring it to be binding on the member states.

4.2.2 **Secondary legislation**

For more details on this section scan here or visit the Online Resource Centre.

In the EU, secondary legislation arises entirely subject to the authority, higher rank and procedures provided for in the Treaties. Article 288 TFEU (ex 249 EC) provides the means by which the Union institutions are able to enact secondary legislation, which are also a binding source of law for the member states. The acts of secondary legislation previously and presently consist of Regulations, Directives and Decisions.

The Lisbon Treaty did not change this aspect, but did introduce a distinction in Articles 289–290 and 297 TFEU between legislative and non-legislative acts; thus all forms of secondary legislation can be both legislative acts of the law-makers per se and the non-legislative acts, which are taken to be the delegated administrative or executive acts of the Commission and other Community bodies under the authority of enacted legislative Acts. One might consider that the distinction could have been easy, in providing that the legislative Acts would be the Regulations and Directives, and that Decisions then would be the non-legislative acts, but Articles 288 and 297 TFEU make it clear that legislative and non-legislative acts can be in the form of Regulations, Directives and Decisions. Hence the purpose of this distinction is not clear: possibly, it is simply to confirm that delegated legislation can take the form of a Regulation, a Directive, or a Decision. It appears that it must be left to the ECJ to determine what significance, if any, the distinction has. The choice of which particular act to adopt may be determined by the legal base specifying whether Regulation, Directive or Decision, but where this is not the case, which is more frequent, Article 296 TFEU provides that the institutions shall select it on a case-by-case basis.

All EU secondary legislation is published in the Official Journal (OJ), which, as it suggests, is the official publication of the EU and is published in two main parts with a supplement. The L Series (legislation) contains the binding legislative Acts. The C Series (information and notices) contains a very wide range of documents that are not binding as such, and includes notices, draft legislative acts, press releases, job advertisements and all other non-legally binding publications, with the exception of the public procurement notices, which are published in the S Series (supplement). The OJ is officially authentic only in its printed form and can be found in this format in libraries and official documentation centres.

4.2.2.1 Regulations

Regulations are general provisions of legislation applicable to the entire Union, member states, institutions and individuals, rather than to specific individuals or groups. Regulations are detailed forms of law so that the law in all member states is exactly the same. As far as implementation is concerned, like Treaty provisions, Regulations are directly applicable or self-executing. This is the mode of incorporation of law that is generally or universally binding. Regulations become legally valid in the member states without any need for implementation on the date specified or on the twentieth day after publication in the OJ (see Article 297 TFEU, ex 254 EC).

Implementation of a Regulation is normally prohibited.

For example, in **Case 39/72 Commission v Italy**, it was held that member states cannot subject the Regulation to any implementing measures other than those required by the Act itself.

There may, however, be circumstances in which the member states are required to provide implementing measures to ensure the effectiveness of the regulation.

See **Case 128/78 Commission v UK (Tachographs)** in which administrative rules had to be implemented concerning the enforcement and sanctions for failure to install tachographs in lorry cabs.

4.2.2.2 Directives

Directives are binding on those to whom they are addressed and can be targeted if desired to specific member states, although in practice they are addressed to all member states. Directives set out aims that must be achieved, but leave the choice of the form and method of implementation to the member states. This was done to ease the way in which national law could be harmonized in line with EU law and to give the member states a wider area of discretion to do this. If, for example, a member state considers that the existing national law already conforms with the requirements of a new Directive, then it need not do anything, apart from the requirement now in most, if not all, Directives that the member state inform the Commission of measures taken to implement the Directive.

Regulations

Defined in Article 288 TFEU (ex 249 EC): 'A regulation shall have general application. It shall be binding in its entirety and directly applicable in all member states.'

Directives

Defined in Article 288 TFEU (ex 249 EC): 'A directive shall be binding as to the result to be achieved, upon each member state to which it is addressed, but shall leave to the national authorities the choice of form and methods.'

Directives enter into force either on the date specified or twenty days after publication, which is rare (see Article 297 TEU, ex 254 EC). Member states are given a period in which to implement Directives, which can range from one year to five years or more, depending on the complexity of the subject matter and the urgency for the legislation, but two years is usual. Some Directives, especially if consolidating and adding rules to an existing area of EU law, may contain more than one entry into force date, to take account of the law that should already have been enacted and the new provisions for which the member states is given a further implementation period (see for example, Directive 2004/38 on the free movement of persons).

4.2.2.3 Decisions

Decisions

Defined in Article 288 TFEU (ex 249 EC): 'A decision shall be binding in its entirety upon those to whom it is addressed.'

Decisions are specific binding and enforceable acts of law, which are addressed to member states or to specific individuals, for example in the area of competition law determining the agreements between companies to be either in conformity or in conflict with EU competition law rules.

4.2.2.4 Other acts producing binding legal effects

Article 288 TFEU is not exhaustive of the legally binding acts that can be created by the institutions. The Court of Justice has held that it can review all measures taken by the institutions, whatever their nature and form, which are designed to produce legal effects. Thus such acts need not stem from the specific acts listed in Article 288 TFEU and are often termed *sui generis*, meaning literally 'in a class of its own' or 'unique'.

See **Cases 8–11/66 *Noordwijks Cement Accord***, in which a Commission letter not formally labelled as a Regulation, Directive or Decision could nevertheless be challenged under Article 230 EC (now 263 TFEU), which is the action to challenge the validity of binding acts of Community law. This was accepted by the ECJ because the letter had led to a change in legal status of applicant companies, rendering them subject to competition law liability from which they had previously been immune.

See also **Case 22/70 *Commission v Council (ERTA)***, in which a Decision of the member states outside of the Council of Ministers was nevertheless held to be a reviewable act of the Community.

cross reference
See these cases also in the context of Article 263 actions in Chapter 9, section 9.1.1.1.

In **Case C-106/96 *UK v Commission***, even a press release has been found to have legal effects and was consequently annulled for lacking a legal base.

A new Treaty Article, Article 295 TFEU, now puts on a statutory basis the inter-institutional agreements that have for a long time played a role in establishing the ground rules for the European Parliament, Council and Commission to work together, in particular in areas such as delegated powers or better law-making. These may now be made formally binding under Article 295 TFEU.

4.2.2.5 Recommendations and opinions

Under Article 288 TFEU (ex 249 EC), recommendations and opinions do not have any binding force, but it was established in Case 322/88 *Grimaldi* that, despite this, national courts are required to take recommendations into account when interpreting national law based on

Community law. Recommendations, in particular, often provide a gloss on a Regulation or Directive, or extend its scope of application.

See, for example, Recommendation 89/49, which extended the scope of application of Directive 89/48 to qualifications obtained by EC nationals outside the EC.

4.2.2.6 Procedural requirements

Article 296 TFEU (ex 253 EC) requires that the legal acts of institutions shall state the reasons on which they are based and shall refer to any proposals or opinions that were required to be obtained. In practice, this means that the Treaty base must also be cited. Failure by the institutions to comply with these requirements will give rise to grounds for judicial review and possible annulment of the measure under Article 263 TFEU.

> For example, it was held in **Case C-325/91 *France* v *Commission*** that there was a requirement to state the Treaty base, without which the measure is void.

The Lisbon Treaty has introduced a new requirement in Article 296 TFEU, which relates to the competence and legal base issues. It states that, 'When considering draft legislative acts, the European Parliament and the Council shall refrain from adopting acts not provided for by the relevant legislative procedure in the area in question'. This is another attempt to curb the competence creep and/or use of the incorrect legal base.

cross reference
Competence creep is discussed further in Chapter 3, section 3.2.

Article 297 TFEU (ex 254 EC) provides the rules concerning the publication of legislative and non-legislative acts. Regulations, Directives and Decisions adopted under the ordinary legislative procedure must be signed by the presidents of the European Parliament and the Council, and published in the OJ. They become valid on the specified date, in the absence of which they become valid on the twentieth day following publication.

The Lisbon Treaty clarified the position of legislative and non-legislative acts – in other words, administrative types of act. The shake-up was designed to replace the very many different, less formal, types of act that have been developed over the years or specifically introduced under the TEU. The non-legislative acts – that is, the delegated acts under Article 290 TFEU – must be signed by the President of the institution that adopted them and shall also be published in the OJ.

4.2.3 International agreements and conventions

legal personality
Characteristic of a body establishing that it is capable of entering into formally binding agreements.

Within the Treaties, there are provisions that empower the Council and the Commission to conduct external relations, the agreements of which are binding on both the Union and the member states, and as such then form a further true source of EU law. This is possible because the entire Union, following the entry into force of the Lisbon Treaty, also has **legal personality**.

The Union is usually represented by the European Commission in negotiations, in coordination with the High Representative, who is responsible for negotiating agreements relating to the Common Foreign and Security Policy (CFSP).

The express treaty-making powers of the Union can be found in three principal Treaty Articles. Article 207 TFEU (ex 133 EC) provides that EU commercial and trade policy is conducted by the Commission under the authority of the Council. Under this provision, the EU behaves as a single actor, and the European Commission negotiates trade agreements and represents European interests on behalf of the twenty-seven member states. The Council concludes the agreements and can thus bind the member states to agreements ranging from bilateral trade agreements with individual countries to the multiparty World Trade Organization (WTO) agreements and the General Agreement on Tariffs and Trade (GATT), although, as will be seen, much of the subject matter of the WTO agreements falls outside the express and exclusive competence of the Community.

> Confirmation that particular provisions of the GATT can be binding on the Community was confirmed by the Court of Justice in **Cases 21–24/72 *International Fruit***.

Article 217 TFEU (ex 310 EC) provides for the conclusion of association agreements with non-member states that can be regarded as either a precursor to membership or as agreements in their own right without any view to future membership of the EU. These can be concluded by the Council with the consent of the European Parliament, with either individual third countries or within more extensive multinational agreements to govern, amongst other things, various aspects of the trade relations between them. The most important agreements are the Agreement on the European Economic Area (EEA), the association agreements with candidate member states (at present, Turkey, Iceland, Macedonia and Montenegro, and Serbia, and Croatia, which is envisaged as becoming a new member state on 1 July 2013), the bilateral agreements with Switzerland and the Mediterranean countries, and the preferential treatment agreements that have been concluded with the Mediterranean countries. Furthermore, there are the very comprehensive Yaounde and Lomé Conventions and the Cotonou Agreement (2000) with seventy-eight African, Caribbean and Pacific (ACP) countries, all of which provide binding rules for the EU.

cross reference
Noted in Chapter 1, section 1.4.1.

> For example, in **Case 181/73 *Haegemann v Belgium***, provisions of the association agreement between the Community and Greece were held to be binding on the member states even though such agreements were not envisaged by Article 249 EC (now 288 TFEU). A more recent example is the free movement case **C-265/03 *Simutenkov***, which concerns rights provided under the 1997 EC–Russian Federation partnership agreement and the right of a Russian football player employed by the Spanish Club Deportivo Tenerife. In a similar manner to the ruling in **Case C-415/93 *Bosman***, the number of players that could be fielded from non-EEA countries was restricted in national competitions. The judgment followed the *Bosman* ruling with the interpretation by the ECJ that the partnership agreement contained directly enforceable free movement rights.

cross reference
See Chapter 12, section 12.1.2.2.

Finally and more generally, the Treaty provides under Article 218 TFEU (ex 300 EC) a power for the conclusion of international agreements with non-member states in matters covered by areas of the Treaty not specifically catered for by Articles 207 and 217 TFEU (ex 133 and 310 EC). In furtherance of this, Article 220 TFEU (ex 302–304 EC) requires the Union to maintain appropriate relations with international organizations such as the United Nations (UN), the Council of Europe and the Organisation for Economic Co-Operation and Development (OECD).

cross reference
The direct effects of these agreements will be considered in Chapter 8, section 8.1.3.5. For general information on international agreements, see also Chapter 1, section 1.7.

The Union is to be represented by the Commission and the new High Representative. In many of these areas, however, the EU must act with the member states because the subject matters of the agreements often straddle matters coming both within competence and outside Union competence. However, even agreements and international agreements entered into by the member states alone can bind the Union.

See **Case 214/72 *International Fruit Company***, for example, in which the Court of Justice held that the provisions of the GATT concluded by the member states prior to membership of the then Community or prior to the assumption of responsibility for the agreement by the Community bind the Community.

4.2.4 **The Court of Justice's contribution to the sources of law**

For more details on this section scan here or visit the Online Resource Centre.

When the EC was first established, the Community legal system was to be found only in the Treaties and the limited secondary legislation that existed at the time. However, because the Treaties are largely framework Treaties, they require substantial supplement. Whilst much of this is provided by the secondary legislation, both the secondary legislation and the founding and primary Treaties' Articles may need to be interpreted. There is, then, much scope for judicial creativity on the part of the Court of Justice. Furthermore, as with all legal systems, codified or written law cannot possibly cater for all economic and social developments that can take place, and the judges must at times either adapt existing rules to fit the situation or introduce new rules to settle the matter judiciously. The Court of Justice has previously determined that the EC Treaty (now TFEU) and secondary legislation must be interpreted and applied according to the scheme of the Treaty as a whole and in the light of the broad principles of the Preamble and Articles 2, 3, 10 and 12 EC (now 3 and 4 TEU and 8 and 18 TFEU) to achieve the result required. The case law or jurisprudence has been developed by the ECJ from a wide variety of law sources and is not restricted in origin to the words or phrases from EU legislative provisions. The Court of Justice has developed additional fundamental doctrines and principles of Union law, including direct effects, supremacy and state liability.

cross reference
See also the ECJ methodology section in Chapter 2, section 2.5.4.

In particular, the Court of Justice has drawn inspiration, and even adopted extensively, principles from outside, including general principles, fundamental rights and national procedural rules. These legal principles have become quite clearly an EU source of law and indeed a highly influential one, enjoying a status below Treaty status, but in some instances being directly influential in bringing about Treaty changes well before the formal Treaty amendment of such provisions by the member states. They are often applied to interpret and render unlawful EU secondary legislation, thus may be ranked above Regulations, Directives and Decisions. The decisions of the Court of Justice are binding on the member states not only where the Court decides strictly on the basis of Union treaties or secondary law, but also where it decides on the basis of legal rules that it has applied or used as inspiration that originate from outside the Union or which have been instrumental in developing a new Union rule. To back up this position, Article 280 TFEU (ex 244 EC) provides that judgments shall be enforceable.

cross reference
These developments are considered in Chapter 8.

These general principles and fundamental rights can thus be used both to assist the Court of Justice in the interpretation and application of EU law, and by parties challenging EU law or the actions of EU institutions and additionally the actions of the member states in the application of EU law. There are three principal Treaty Articles that provide justification for the Court of Justice introducing general principles into the EU legal order.

cross reference

See, for example, Articles 230 and 232 EC (now 263 and 265 TFEU) and the extension of judicial review rights to the EP, considered both in Chapter 2, section 2.4.3.4 and Chapter 9.

cross reference

Considered further in section 4.2.6.

cross reference

This will be covered in section 4.2.6 and in Chapter 14.

Article 19 TEU (ex 220 EC) provides that the Court of Justice shall ensure that, in the interpretation and application of the Treaties, the law is observed. It is a general guideline set by the Treaty for the functioning of the Court of Justice. This is taken to mean law from outside the Treaty rather than some duplicated reference back to the Treaty. The Article has thus been employed to justify the introduction of very many different general principles of law, most notably human rights.

Two further Articles of the Treaty, more specifically, mandate the Court to take account of general principles of law. Article 263 TEU (ex 230 EC) refers to the infringement of any rule of law relating to the application of the Treaty as one of the grounds for an action for the challenge to the validity of EU law and Article 340 TEU (ex 288 EC), concerned with damages claims against the Union institutions, allows the settlement of claims on the basis of the general principles of the laws of the member states. Whilst these last two are specific to the claims raised under those Treaty Articles, they do, however, serve to reinforce the Court of Justice's claim that it can rely on general principles as a source of law in the EU legal order. The sources of general principles are the national legal systems, in particular the constitutions of member states and the many rules of natural justice, often found in a majority of the member states. Others have been developed from the Treaty, for example Article 12 EC (now 18 TFEU) involving the prohibition of discrimination on the grounds of nationality, which has been the basis for a general principle of equality and non-discrimination.

These additional sources of law are sometimes classified into broad groupings. Whilst these are far from definitive in terms of establishing clear-cut categories because of the diversity of principles and the degree of overlap, presenting them in this way may, however, aid accessibility. They can therefore be divided into three groups:

- human or fundamental rights;
- equality principles; and
- those relating to general procedural rights.

4.2.5 **Human or fundamental rights**

This section regards 'human' and 'fundamental' rights as synonymous terms. Whilst human or fundamental rights may be considered as a completely separate source of law, it is appropriate to consider them here in this chapter alongside other general sources of law. The Communities and the EU were established as a direct response to the wholesale abuse of rights in the Second World War. Originally, fundamental rights were completely absent from any of the Treaties, although some isolated Articles provided rights that either coincided with general principles or helped in the development of general principles of Community and now Union law.

Previously, most of these Articles were contained solely in the EC Treaty, but now, given the redistribution of the some of the Articles between the TEU and TFEU, both Treaties are now home to general provisions.

Previously, the EC Treaty contained Articles 2 (concerned with social protection, the standard of living and quality of life), 3 and 39 (dealing with the free movement of persons), 12, 34 and 39(2) (concerned with discrimination), 137 (social provision) and 141 (equal pay). Similar Articles with enhanced provision are now to be found in Articles 2–3 and 6 TEU and 8–10, 18–19, 40, 45, 153 and 157 TFEU.

At the start of the Communities, there was no specific and binding set of obligations imposed by the Treaty on the Community institutions to guarantee the individual rights of citizens. This initial apparent lack of commitment to human rights was in turn reflected in the early decisions of the Court of Justice when faced with arguments or pleas raised by litigants based on basic or human rights. Hence the early case law of the Court of Justice presents the view of a Community unsympathetic to the fundamental human rights of individuals.

The following cases were all decided before the Lisbon Treaty came into effect, hence the term 'Community' is retained. In the present context, this should be taken to read 'Union'.

In **Cases 1/58** *Stork* **v** *High Authority* and **40/64** *Sgarlata* **v** *Commission*, arguments based on individual rights were clearly rejected in favour of upholding Community law.

This position can be contrasted with the then six member states' positions regarding human rights. Following the Second World War, western European nations were more than ever ideologically committed to the concept of protecting human rights. The German and Italian Constitutions were rewritten with very strong commitments to basic rights contained within a rights catalogue. By 1955, all of the original members of the EEC, except France, had ratified the European Convention on Human Rights and Fundamental Freedoms (ECHR). The Community and Court were thus morally, if not legally, obliged to observe fundamental human rights. Thus the Court of Justice could not maintain its unsympathetic stance and adopted, from the late 1960s, a new response.

In **Case 26/69** *Stauder* **v** *City of Ulm*, a German citizen protested that his fundamental right of human dignity, protected by Article 1 of the German *Grundgesetz* (its 'Basic Law', or Constitution) was being infringed by having his name on the coupon when claiming reduced-price butter by the Community. The Court of Justice held that the Community legislation did not require his name, but the Community law itself had not prejudiced his fundamental rights, which were 'enshrined in the general principles of Community law and protected by the Court'. This recognition of the right of human dignity in the EU legal order was confirmed by the Court of Justice in the latter **Case C-36/02** *Omega*.

After the French ratification of the ECHR in 1974, the Court of Justice referred also to the ECHR as an example of the member states' commitment to fundamental rights. Further encouragement came from the Joint Declaration by Community Institutions on Fundamental Rights, 5 April 1977, which stressed the importance of national constitutions and the ECHR.

Hence, for the first time, in **Case 44/79** *Hauer* **v** *Land Rheinland-Pfalz*, the Court of Justice considered in some detail a provision (Article 1 of Protocol 1) of the ECHR to help it to decide the case. Although it recognized the right of property in the case, its exercise was subject to overriding Community interests.

Thus, despite recognition of the fundamental rights, previously cases were usually resolved on the basis of either Community law applying or the rights being subject to limitations mainly of the Community interest.

In a number of cases, the Court reaffirmed its statement that fundamental rights form part of the general principles based on the constitutional traditions of member states.

For example, **Case 11/70 *Internationale Handelsgesellschaft*** showed the potential for conflict and ultimate harm to the Community legal order if the Community were to fail to uphold human rights provisions because of a potential clash, in this case, of Community law with the German Constitution. The German Constitution had claimed the exclusive right to decide on cases involving a clash between Community law and the German Constitution. In fact, the Court of Justice had declared that there was no breach by the Community law in question. No self-respecting legal system in Europe could ignore or be seen to be ignoring such ideologically important rights as these and, in the case, the Court of Justice gave a guarantee that members states' constitutions will not be infringed despite the superiority of Community law because of the commitment of the Community to human rights and the fact that they form part of the Community legal order.

cross reference

Non-retroactivity was also confirmed as a principle of Community law in Kolpinghuis Nijmegan, *considered further in section 4.2.7.4 and in Chapter 8.*

In **Case 63/83 *R* v *Kirk***, a fine imposed on a fishing boat captain by a UK court that was based on a national UK statutory order was held to infringe the principle of non-retroactivity, because the order was supposedly validated by later Community legislation. The Court of Justice held that such an action violated the principle of non-retroactivity of criminal law enshrined in Article 7 ECHR and now a principle of Community law.

In **Case 222/86 *UNECTEF* v *Heylens and others***, the Court of Justice was able to refer to Articles 6 and 13 ECHR to support the right to judicial review and the right to be heard in support of a claim for an additional right, the right to free access to employment. In **Case 5/88 *Wachauf***, the Court of Justice extended its support of fundamental rights by holding that the actions of member states in implementing Community measures must also comply with the requirements of human rights provisions.

111

The Court of Justice continues to refer to the ECHR in support of its judgments.

cross reference

Article 8 ECHR is considered further in Chapter 12, sections 12.3.1.and 12.3.2.2.

For example, see recent cases from the area of the free movement of persons **C-413/99 Baumbast**, **C-459/99 MRAX** and **C-109/01 Akrich** all featured Article 8 ECHR, the right to family life.

The elevated status given to the ECHR and to fundamental rights generally by the Court of Justice has been reflected in a greater status within the Treaty base and strengthened further by the Lisbon Treaty. Article 6(1) TEU now provides that the Union recognizes the rights in the EU Charter of Fundamental Rights as having the same legal status as the Treaties, although the Charter itself is not contained within the Treaties, but is referred to in Declaration No. 1 attached to the Treaties.

Declaration No. 1 concerning the Charter of Fundamental Rights of the European Union

The Charter of Fundamental Rights of the European Union, which has legally binding force, confirms the fundamental rights guaranteed by the European Convention for the Protection of Human Rights and Fundamental Freedoms and as they result from the constitutional traditions common to the Member States.

The Charter does not extend the field of application of Union law beyond the powers of the Union or establish any new power or task for the Union, or modify powers and tasks as defined by the Treaties.

Article 6(3) TEU also confirms that the rights contained with both the ECHR and constitutions of the member states shall be recognized as general principles in the EU legal order.

Article 6 TEU further settles years of debate as to whether the EU should or could accede to the ECHR. In 1996, the Court of Justice gave Opinion 2/94 that, under the Treaties at the time, the Union did not have the power to accede. Now that the EU has its own catalogue of rights, in the form of the Fundamental Rights Charter, but still outside the Treaty base, it may be argued that membership is more acceptable, but conversely, with its own catalogue of rights, there may be no further need for either the debate or accession to the ECHR. However, Article 6(2) clearly provides that the Union shall accede to the ECHR and declares in any event that those rights contained in the ECHR shall constitute general principles of the Union's law. This may seem now to be superfluous and even confusing, and prone to conflict in view of the introduction of the EU's own catalogue of rights, however, a further Declaration (No. 2) specifically notes that dialogue between the ECJ and the European Court of Human Rights (ECtHR) should both continue and be reinforced when the EU accedes to the Convention.

thinking point
What would be the difficulties or problems of the EU acceding to the ECHR?

Any applicant states wishing to join the EU are now obligated by Article 49 TEU to have respect for human rights, and any member state that seriously and persistently offends human rights may have its rights under the Treaties suspended by the other member states under Article 7 TEU.

4.2.6 **Equality and non-discrimination**

The prohibition of discrimination is catered for in the Treaties under a number of Articles: Article 18 TFEU (ex 12 EC), on non-discrimination on the grounds of nationality; Article 157 TFEU (ex 141 EC), on non-discrimination between men and women with regard to pay and equal treatment; Article 40(2) TFEU (ex 34(3) EC), on non-discrimination between consumers and producers under the Common Agricultural Policy (CAP); and Article 45(2) TFEU (ex 39(2) EC), on non-discrimination with regard to the free movement of workers. Non-discrimination has also become a general principle recognized by the Court of Justice. It applies in all areas of EU law, especially to the fundamental freedoms.

For example, in **Cases 75 and 117/82 *Razzouk and Beydoun* v *Commission***, the Court held that a Commission decision that discriminated between men and women in relation to a certain pensions payment should be annulled as being contrary to the fundamental right of equal treatment of sexes.

The principle was applied in **Case 114/76 *Bergman* v *Grows-Farm (Skimmed Milk Powder)***, in which the Court of Justice held that a scheme to force animal feed producers to incorporate skimmed milk powder in animal feed discriminated against non-dairy farmers.

It was also applied to religious discrimination in **Case 130/75 *Prais v Council***, although, on the facts involving a Community competition for a post held at a Jewish religious festival, the Council was held not to have breached the general principle of equality. It was nevertheless held by the Court of Justice that, wherever possible, Community employees and citizens should have the general principle of non-discrimination in respect of religious freedom upheld in their favour.

cross reference

Direct effects will be considered in Chapter 8, and the Mangold *case will be considered further both in Chapter 8 and in Chapter 14 on equality law.*

In **Case C-144/04 *Mangold***, the principle of non-discrimination was applied by the Court of Justice as a general principle in the absence of an enforceable specific equality right: although there was such a right in the background, its lack of direct effects prevented its direct employment.

The Union moved further towards the development of a general principle of equality or at least non-discrimination in a range of issues in an amendment made to the EC Treaty by the Treaty of Amsterdam. Article 19 TFEU (ex 13 EC) provides that the Council may take appropriate action to combat discrimination based on sex, racial or ethnic origin, religion or belief, disability, age or sexual orientation, and the Council issued Directives 2000/43, 2000/78 and 2004/113 under this Article.

The existence and value of a general principle of equal treatment has been acknowledged and confirmed by the Court of Justice in a number of cases, including, for example, **Case C-149/10 *Chatzi***, in which the Court held that the principle of equal treatment is one of the general principles of EU law and is now affirmed by Article 20 of the EU Charter of Fundamental Rights. In that case, it was applied to support the right to parental leave on an equal basis.

4.2.7 **General principles of procedural law and natural justice**

For more details on this section scan here or visit the Online Resource Centre.

A number of principles are closely associated with the administrative law principles found in many of the member states, but may also be classified under the rules of natural justice. These can be found in differing forms in the member states' legal systems, for example as common law rules in the UK or as a part of the Constitution in Germany, Articles 101–104 *Grundgesetz* (GG).

Judicial review, confidentiality/legal privilege, legal certainty, non-retroactivity, legitimate expectation and proportionality have been selected here as broad categories of general principles that have been identified and applied by the Court of Justice.

4.2.7.1 The right to judicial review

A general right to have administrative decisions, as opposed to legislative Acts, reviewed by a court exists. The Court of Justice bases its view on the constitutions of the member states, and notably on Article 6 ECHR, dealing with a fair and public hearing, and Article 13 ECHR, dealing with the provision of an effective judicial remedy.

Cases 222/84 *Johnston* v *Chief Constable RUC* and **222/86 *UNECTEF* v *Heylens*** are examples. In the latter case, the Court of Justice had already determined that free access to employment was a fundamental right that should be respected in the Community. It thus becomes essential that there must be a remedy of a judicial nature against any decision of a national authority refusing the benefit of that right. The *UNECTEF* case established that the duty to give reasons was a general principle to be recognized in the Community legal order.

In **Case 17/74 *Transocean Marine Paints Association* v *Commission***, the principle of the right to a fair hearing (under the maxim *audi alterem partem*, meaning literally 'hearing the other side') was introduced by the Advocate General (AG). He argued that, in the absence of being allowed to present its view on the condition imposed in a decision, the Commission's decision would be in breach of a general principle of law, clearly applicable in the UK and other legal systems. This was upheld by the Court.

The Court of Justice held also in **Cases 33 and 59/79 *Kuhner*** that where a person's rights were affected, he or she must be given the opportunity to make his or her views known and the right to be heard must be upheld as a general principle of good administration.

4.2.7.2 Confidentiality/legal privilege

In **Case 175/79 *A M & S* v *Commission***, a company refused to hand over certain documents during a raid by Commission officials under the rules on competition law, on the grounds that, by doing so, the principle of legal privilege would be breached. The Court of Justice held that the principle was recognized in the Community legal order, provided that it was in relation to or preparation for a client's defence, but it must be between a party and an independent lawyer.

Supporting and extending this principle are **Cases 136/79 *National Panasonic*** and **T-30/89 *Hilti***. The *Hilti* case decided that the privilege extends also to the in-house lawyer's reports of the independent lawyer's findings.

In **Case C-36/92 P *Samenwerkende***, a refusal to hand over documents considered to be confidential was held to be unjustified in the light of the existing protections in Community law under which the Commission is required to notify undertakings of the documents that it intends to release to the national authorities and thus give the undertakings the chance to seek judicial review to protect these documents. As such, the refusal to supply would be unjustified.

Case C-550/07 P *AKZO* was appealed on various points to the ECJ, which confirmed the earlier case of Case 175/79 *A M & S* v *Commission*, to the extent that the Court of Justice confirmed that the principle of legal privilege does not extend to in-house lawyers. It held that it made no difference even if the in-house lawyer was a member of the relevant national Bar or Law Society and was subject to the same rules of professional conduct and discipline as an independent lawyer.

The ECJ and the General Court must, however, be the final arbiters of what is privileged. Cases 209/15 *Dow Benelux*, 218/78 *Van Landewyck* and 53/85 *AKZO*, but now backed up by Articles 27 and 28 of Regulation 1/2003, provide that the principle of professional secrecy does not apply to allow a company to protect documents from the Commission, but to ensure that information received by the Commission in an investigation is not disclosed to competitors.

4.2.7.3 Legal certainty

The basic concept underlying legal certainty incorporates a number of ideas concerned with the boundary between legality and illegality or lawfulness and unlawfulness, which should be marked clearly in advance. Additionally, the existence of sanctions or punishment for a breach of a rule or what constitutes overstepping the boundary should also be reasonably ascertainable: not the exact punishment, but at least the type and scope or range of punishment applicable. As such, the principle of proportionality is included in this category. Textbook and writers' considerations of EU law differ in their classification of general principles; therefore proportionality may be classified as a distinct and separate category. The different treatment accorded it is not really important. The point is that it is nevertheless recognized as a general principle by the Court of Justice and is often quoted in cases to defeat the arguments of the member state or the Commission in justifying action or behaviour that has affected the rights of others, mainly individuals in the EU context. Legal certainty thus includes the underlying concepts of legitimate expectations, protection of vested rights, proportionality and non-retroactivity.

Legal certainty was first acknowledged by the Court of Justice in **Case 43/75 _Defrenne_ v _Sabena (No. 2)_** and later confirmed in **Case 262/88 _Barber_ v _Guardian Royal Exchange_** to support the Court's argument that the judgment could not be retroactively effective, although there is an argument to suggest that if a Treaty Article is held to be directly effective, as in the _Sabena_ case, it must have been so from the outset of the Community – that is, from 1957 – and not from the date of judgment of the Court of Justice.

4.2.7.4 Non-retroactivity

cross reference
Barber _is considered at section 4.2.7.3._

The principle of non-retroactivity is seen in its purest form in Case 63/83 _R_ v _Kent Kirk_ and Case 262/88 _Barber_, and is firmly established as a general principle of EU law. Simply put, law should not retroactively impose punishments or be the legal base for punishments, particularly with regard to criminal sanctions, nor should it be the basis for a change in legal status or administrative sanctions.

Case 80/86 _Public Prosecutor_ v _Kolpinghuis Nijmegan_ is also a very good example of the principle being cited by the Court of Justice in defence of the rights of the individual. In this case, the principle was used to protect the company from being prosecuted by the Dutch authorities on the strength of retroactive Community law validating national law where Holland had failed to implement the Directive correctly into national law.

Civil or non-criminal law retroactivity may also occur when a person's actual rights or expected rights are altered, redefined or totally removed.

See, for example, **Cases 106 and 107/63 _Töpfer_ v _Commission_** dealing with the retroactive validation of import licence refusals by the German authorities, which provided Töpfer with the right and _locus standi_ to challenge the decision and have it reviewed by the ECJ.

The principle of non-retroactivity may take on more subtle forms in civil law application to remove the difficulties created by the alteration or withdrawal of rights by EU legal measures. These cases also involve the next principle of legitimate expectations of the individual, which are often argued to have been infringed by the Union measure complained about, particularly where the Commission is trying to regulate a very difficult market in goods. This means that, provided that the legitimate expectations of the parties affected have been respected, then even a measure that is retroactive in effect may be upheld.

In **Case 98/78 *Racke* v *HZA Mainz***, concerned with the regulation of the wine market, then producing massive surpluses and the so-called 'wine lake', regulations with retroactive effect were nevertheless upheld by the ECJ on the basis that the situation was so serious that it demanded such and that the legitimate expectations of the parties had been taken into account.

4.2.7.5 Legitimate expectation or vested rights

The legitimate expectations of affected parties must be observed, especially when they pre-date an EU provision affecting their rights; hence there is some degree of overlap with non-retroactivity.

In **Case 88/76 *Sugar Export* v *Commission***, a Regulation was enacted by the Commission on 30 June 1976, which removed the right of sugar exporters to cancel licences previously granted when refunds payable on sugar exports, to reduce the overproduction of sugar in the Community, dropped in value. The date of entry into force was set as 1 July, but the Regulation was not published until 2 July 1976. Sugar exporters who applied for a cancellation on 1 July 1976 were refused by the Commission. The Court interpreted the Regulation as coming into force on 2 July 1976 and held that whilst there was no intention of retroactivity, the rights vested in the applicant, applicable as on 1 July 1976, must be protected.

The principle was confirmed by the Court of Justice in Case 112/77 *Töpfer* v *Commission* under similar factual circumstances dealing with the sudden removal of the right to cancel an export licence.

In **Case 81/72 *Commission* v *Council (Staff Salaries)***, the principle was employed in different circumstances when the Council adopted a three-year experimental period for a system of staff salary payments, but changed this after only nine months. Despite the view that Council could not bind itself as such – that is, it could not bind itself never to make changes – the Court of Justice held that the employees had a reasonable or legitimate expectation that the Council would abide by its decision.

4.2.7.6 Proportionality

The principle of proportionality embodies the concept that the punishment should fit the crime and not go further, or must be reasonable in the circumstances, and puts the question to the relevant authority of whether the same result could have been achieved by other methods or means less harmful to the party concerned. In the Union context, it means that individuals should not be affected by actions beyond those necessary in the public or Union interest and that any fines or punishment must be in proportion to the seriousness of any breach. It occurs frequently throughout all areas of EU law and especially to the internal market. It was invoked in Cases 11/70 *Internationale Handelsgesellschaft* and 36/75 *Rutili*. Examples from specific areas of law are Cases 159/79 *R v Pieck*, in respect of the free movement of persons, and in 178/84 *Commission v Germany (Beer Purity)*, in relation to the free movement of goods.

A good example is **Case 181/84 *R v Intervention Board for Agricultural Produce, ex p Man***, in which a company was required to give a security deposit to the Intervention Board when seeking a licence to export sugar outside the Community. The applicant was late, but only by four hours, in completing the relevant paperwork. The Board, acting under a Community Regulation, declared the entire deposit of over £1.5 million to be forfeit. The Court held that the automatic forfeit of the entire deposit in the event of any failure was too drastic in view of the function of the system of export licences – that is, it was disproportionate to the aims.

cross reference
See Chapter 3, section 3.4, for further details.

The principle of proportionality has now been given statutory recognition in the Treaties. Article 5 TEU applies to the relations between the Union and the member states in ensuring that any action at the Union level must be in proportion to the aims of the Union and not to go beyond those strict aims.

Article 5 TEU provides that 'the content and form of Union action shall not exceed what is necessary to achieve the objectives of the Treaties'.

Summary

The category of general principles is already a wide one and potentially capable of great expansion. Indeed, in keeping with a system of law in which case law is regarded as important and can supply legal principles that become general principles to be applied in future cases, other new principles – in addition to those considered in this chapter, which are the most frequently raised – can arise. Subsidiarity could also be included here, because it is so connected to the division of competence. Amongst those knocking on the door of more widespread recognition is 'transparency', although the Court of Justice has been equivocal about its status as a possible general principle: see Cases C-58/94 *Netherlands v Council* and C-353/99 P *Hautala v Council*. Its present status in the legal system has now been endorsed by statutory intervention, first in a number of Decisions, but now by Regulation 1049/2001, which provides a right of access to Community and now Union documents. Another example of a potential general principle is 'good faith', which received support as a general principle of EU law.

See **Case 366/95 *Steff-houlberg Export***, concerned with the recovery of exports refunds that had been found to have been unduly paid. The export company was not responsible for the breach of rules and had acted in good faith. Under national law, and also in view of the time elapsed, the refunds should not be recoverable. The Court of Justice held this to be the position under EC law also.

Finally, 'unjustified enrichment' is a principle well established in civil law legal systems and has made its entrance into the EU legal order in a few cases, one of the leading ones being Case C-309/06 *M&S* (although *Steff-houlerg Export* could also be regarded in that category).

In 1973, in **Case C-309/06 *M&S***, chocolate-covered teacakes sold by Marks & Spencer were designated as 'biscuits' by UK tax authorities and therefore value added tax (VAT) was charged on them at the standard rate. However, in the mid-1990s, the tax authorities realized their mistake and redesignated the teacakes as 'cakes'. Cakes are zero-rated for VAT purposes and M&S therefore attempted to recover the VAT previously paid. In their defence, the Commissioners of Customs & Excise argued that any repayment should be capped (at 10 per cent), because the VAT had been passed on to M&S's customers in the price of the teacakes and therefore would result in M&S being unjustly enriched. The House of Lords referred the following questions to the ECJ for preliminary ruling.

(1) Is there a right, derived from principles of Community law, to refund wrongfully paid VAT?

(2) If so, can the right to repayment to wrongfully paid VAT be restricted on the basis of unjust enrichment?

The Court answered the first question in the affirmative – that is, that a right to repayment of wrongfully paid tax derives from the principle of fiscal neutrality. In response to the second question, the Court held that the application of an unjust enrichment defence against a claim was not contrary to Community law, but that the unjust enrichment defence should be regarded as an exception to the right of repayment of wrongfully paid tax and therefore should be interpreted strictly 'following an economic analysis in which all relevant circumstances are taken into account'.

Overall, it can be seen that the EU draws the laws applicable in the EU legal order from a variety of sources, the specific EU sources representing the formal and official sources of Treaties, Protocols, Declarations and EU secondary law mentioned in Article 288 TFEU. The other sources are much more varied and far wider in scope, consisting of a number of forms of international agreements and the vast potential of general principles and fundamental rights that can so easily be added to by new ones. Finally, at some stage, the EU will become a signatory to the ECHR, which will formally add that body of law to the sources of EU law.

Questions

For suggested approaches to answering these questions scan here or visit the Online Resource Centre.

1   Are you able to outline the range of sources of EU law?

2   What forms of EU secondary law exist? Are they all equally binding?

3   How are EU laws transformed into the member states' laws?

4   What is the status of Protocols and Declarations in the EU legal order?

5   What is the justification for the inclusion of general principles in the EU legal order?

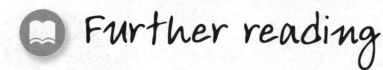# Further reading

BOOKS

Bernitz, U., Nergelius, J. and Cardner, C. *General Principles of EC Law in a Process of Development*, Kluwer Law International, London, 2008.

Birkinshaw, B. *The European Legal Order after Lisbon*, Kluwer Law International, London, 2010.

Douglas-Scott, S. *Constitutional Law of the European Union*, Longman, Harlow, 2002 (chapter 3).

Peers, S. and Ward A. (eds) *The EU Charter of Fundamental Rights: Politics, Law and Policy*, Hart Publishing, Oxford, 2004.

ARTICLES

Arnull, A. 'From Charter to Constitution and beyond: fundamental rights in the new European Union' (2003) Public Law 774.

Jacobs, F. 'Human rights in the EU: the role of the Court of Justice' (2001) 26 EL Rev 331.

Lenaerts, K. 'Fundamental rights in the European Union' (2000) 25 EL Rev 575.

Ortega, L. 'Fundamental rights in the European Constitution' (2005) 11 European Public Law 363.

Schwarze, J. 'Enlargement, the European Constitution, and administrative law' (2004) 53 ICLQ 969.

Van der Berghe, F. 'The EU and issues of human rights protection: some solutions to more acute problems?' (2009) 46 CML Rev 1035.

Supremacy of EU law

Introduction

> This chapter has as its focus the status of European Union (EU) law in the member states, in particular the reasons for the supremacy of EU law. The topic of the transfer and division of competences, which was considered in Chapter 3, provided the starting point for a consideration of supremacy.

5.1 The supremacy of EU law

The supremacy or priority of EU law can be considered from two perspectives: first, from the point of view of the Union; and secondly, the member states, although dealing with this latter aspect in a Union now of twenty-seven, must of necessity be very selective. Therefore, only a sample of the member states will be chosen, concentrating on the older and larger member states. As with the doctrine of direct effects, it is through the decisions and interpretation of the European Court of Justice (ECJ) that the reasons and logic for the supremacy of Community law and now EU law have been developed, and that is the view considered here first.

cross reference

Considered in Chapter 8.

5.1.1 The view of the Court of Justice

For more details on this section scan here or visit the Online Resource Centre.

There is, despite the reforms introduced by the Lisbon Treaty and the inclusion of an express statement in the abandoned Constitutional Treaty (CT), still no express declaration or specific legal base for the supremacy of EU law in the Treaties. It can be argued that some of the Articles of the Treaties impliedly require primacy: for example, Article 4(3) TEU (ex 10 EC), known as the fidelity or good faith clause, which requires member states to comply and not hinder the objectives of the Union; Article 18 TFEU (ex 12 EC) on the general prohibition of discrimination on the grounds of nationality; Article 288 TFEU (ex 249 EC) on the direct applicability of Regulations; and Article 344 TEU (ex 292 EC) on the reservation of EU and not national dispute resolution for matters coming within the scope of the Treaties. In the initial absence of an express statement written into the Treaties, another route was needed to establish this supremacy of EU law over national law.

Note that the Lisbon Treaty sidestepped the direct expression of supremacy that was contained in Article I-6 CT by adding a Declaration (No. 17) that instead supports supremacy by reference to the case law of the ECJ on supremacy, and referring to the Opinion of the Council Legal Service, which confirmed the same conclusion.

cross reference

For further details of the Court, see Chapter 2, section 2.5.

From the outset, the Communities included their own supreme Court of Justice, which is the equivalent of a constitutional court, to adjudicate on disputes between the institutions of the Union and between the member states and the institutions. Without an express statement of priority, the Court of Justice took the lead in providing basic constitutional principles on which the new legal order was based.

> The Court of Justice's view on supremacy is quite straightforward. In the first pronouncement dealing with this, the Court of Justice held, in **Case 26/62 *Van Gend en Loos***, that the member states had limited their sovereignty, albeit within limited fields as agreed in the Treaty, and held that individuals in the Community could uphold rights under Community law in the national courts and in the face of conflicting national law.

The language of the earlier case law will be retained, but where the term 'Community' is used, this is to be read now as also meaning 'Union'.

From its progressive case law, notably Cases 26/62 *Van Gend en Loos*, 6/64 *Costa* v *ENEL* and 106/77 *Simmenthal*, it is clear that Community (EU) law was assumed to be an autonomous legal order that is related to international law and national law, but nevertheless distinct from them and thus subject to its own logic in relation to supremacy over the law of the member states.

Case 26/62 *Van Gend en Loos*, as the leading case in the development of the doctrine of direct effects, substantially prepared the ground for the Court of Justice to build its argument for supremacy of Community law. The case affirmed the Court's jurisdiction in interpreting Community legal provisions, the object of which is to ensure uniform interpretation in the member states. The case established the direct effect of Community law in the national legal orders. The Court of Justice held that:

> the Community constitutes a new legal order of International law for the benefit of which the States have limited their sovereign rights, albeit in limited fields, and the subjects of which comprise not only member states but also their nationals.

cross reference

See also the case coverage of Van Gend en Loos *in Chapter 8, section 8.1.3.1.*

It was not long, though, before this supremacy over national law was stated expressly by the Court of Justice and further elaboration of the new legal order in *Van Gend en Loos* was provided in **Case 6/64 *Flaminio Costa* v *ENEL***. This case primarily concerned the payment of an electricity bill of a very low value (then approximately £1). In 1962, the Italian government passed an Act to nationalize the electricity industry and the newly nationalized industry sent out bills to recover debts previously outstanding. Mr Costa claimed that the action was in conflict with then Article 37 of the EEC Treaty concerned with state monopolies, and he refused to pay his bill. The case, however, also raised the wider issue of whether a national court should refer to the Court of Justice if it considers that Community law may be applicable or, in the view of the Italian government, simply apply the subsequent national law.

In addressing this question, the Court of Justice again stressed the autonomous legal order of Community law:

> By contrast with ordinary international treaties the EEC Treaty has created its own legal system which became an integral part of the legal systems of the member states and which their courts are bound to apply. By creating a Community of unlimited duration, having its own institutions, its own personality, its own legal capacity, and more particularly real powers stemming from a limitation of sovereignty or a transfer of powers from the states to the Community the member states have limited their sovereign rights and have created a body of law to bind their nationals and themselves.

The Court also established that Community law takes priority over all conflicting provisions of national law, whether passed before or after the Community measure in question:

> The integration into the laws of each Member State of provisions which derive from the Community, and more generally, the terms and spirit of the Treaty, make it impossible for

the states, as a corollary, to accord precedence to a unilateral and subsequent measure over a legal system accepted by them on the basis of reciprocity. Such a measure cannot therefore be inconsistent with that legal system.

As additional justifications, the Court of Justice also invoked the use of some of the general provisions of the EEC Treaty: old Article 5 EC (now 4(3) TEU) on the requirement to ensure the attainment of the objectives of the Treaty) and old Article 7 EC (now 18 TFEU) on the prohibition of discrimination, both of which would be breached if subsequent national legislation were to have precedence; and old Article 189 EC (now 288 TFEU), regarding the binding and direct application of Regulations, which would be meaningless if subsequent national legislation could prevail. The Court summed up its position:

It follows . . . that the law stemming from the treaty, an independent source of law, could not because of its special and original nature, be overridden by domestic legal provisions, however framed, without being deprived of its character as Community law and without the legal basis of the Community itself being called into question.

Therefore the conclusion must be that EU law must be supreme over subsequent national law.

Later, in **Case 106/77 Simmenthal**, the Court of Justice ruled that:

A national court which is called upon, within the limits of its jurisdiction, to apply provisions of Community law, is under a duty to give full effect to those provisions, if necessary of its own motion to set aside any conflicting provisions of national legislation, even if adopted subsequently.

The Court of Justice ruled that directly effective provisions of Community law preclude the valid adoption of new legislative measures to the extent that they would be incompatible with Community provisions. Any inconsistent national legislation recognized by national legislatures as having legal effect would deny the effectiveness of the obligations undertaken by the member state and imperil the existence of the Community.

cross reference
Simmenthal *is considered further in section 5.2.1 in respect of constitutional practice.*

123

Therefore the voluntary limitation of sovereignty and the need for an effective and uniform EU law requires supremacy. To give effect to subsequent national law over and above the EU legal system that member states have accepted would be inconsistent.

In **Case 213/89 Factortame (No. 1)**, the Court of Justice, building on the principle laid down in *Simmenthal* that a provision of EC law must be implemented as effectively as possible, held that a national court must suspend national legislation that may be incompatible with EC law until a final determination on its compatibility has been made. Thus national rules that prevented a national court from issuing an interim injunction suspending the application of a national statute during a dispute whilst considering the existence of alleged rights under Community law must be set aside. It was later held, in **Case C-221/89**, that the UK law did in fact breach Community law.

cross reference
Discussed in Chapter 8, section 8.3.

Finally, in this context, it is worth mentioning the consequence of a member state not giving primacy to EU law when it should have done, in that liability on the part of the state will be incurred. This principle was first established by the Court of Justice in Cases C-6 and 9/90 *Francovich* and later confirmed in Case 213/89 *Factortame (No. 3)* and other cases.

So far, the national legislation considered has been so-called 'ordinary' domestic national legislation and the Court of Justice has maintained a consistent position on supremacy. What about provisions of a member state's constitution? It is in this respect that the most serious conflicts between the views of the national judiciaries and the Court of Justice have arisen.

5.1.2 **Supremacy and member state constitutional law**

The Court of Justice's view in respect of national constitutional law differs little from that in respect of 'ordinary' national law.

> **Case 11/70 *Internationale Handelgesellschaft*** concerned the claim that Community levies were contrary to the German Constitution (Articles 2.1 and 14 *Grundgesetz*) and thus, as far as the national court was concerned, inapplicable. On referral to the Court of Justice, it held that national courts do not possess the power to review Community law. However, in diffusing the question, the Court of Justice held that there had been no breach by Community law of constitutional rights in the case.

The important question arising from *Internationale Handelgesellschaft* was whether the Court of Justice was in a position to declare supremacy over national constitutional law and thereby in effect review that law. In doing so, it would effectively deny national courts the right to ignore the distinction or separation of the national and EU law legal systems, but nevertheless do so itself. In other words, national courts could not question the supremacy of Community (now EU) law, but the Court of Justice would be able to determine that national constitutional law was not in conformity with Community (now EU) law, something clearly of great concern to national supreme courts.

This distinction is termed 'the autonomy of jurisdictions'.

The second case arises from a conflict between the Italian Constitution and Community law. In Italy, the constitutional practice existed that the power to disregard or declare invalid a provision of national law was the sole right of the Italian Constitutional Court.

> In **Case 106/77 *Simmenthal***, a lower court was faced with inconsistency between a Community law provision and a national provision. The national court was aware that a reference to the Italian Constitutional Court would have the effect of subrogating Community law to national legal practice, inconsistent with existent Community case law on the matter, as was evident from the earlier Case 6/64 *Costa* v *ENEL*. However, disregarding the national law was contrary to Italian constitutional requirements. The Italian magistrate referred to both courts, but asked the Court of Justice whether subsequent national measures that conflict with the Community must be disregarded without waiting until those measures are set aside by legislative or other constitutional means.
>
> The Court of Justice first declared that the doctrine of direct effects of Community legislation was not dependent on any national constitutional provisions, but a source of

rights in itself. Therefore national courts must give full effect to those rights, including a refusal to apply conflicting national legislation. The Court of Justice also ruled that directly effective provisions of Community law also preclude the valid adoption of new legislative measures to the extent that they would be incompatible with Community provisions. The national court should disregard the inconsistent national law. The Court established that if there was no violation of Community fundamental rights, the Community measures were acceptable and there should be no reference to national constitutions to test their validity.

It held that:

> The law stemming from the treaty, an independent source of law, cannot because of its very nature be overridden by rules of national law, however framed, without being deprived of its character as Community law. Therefore the validity of a Community measure or its effect within a Member State cannot be affected by allegations that it runs counter to either fundamental rights as formulated by the Constitution of that State or the principles of a national constitutional structure.

The Court of Justice has not been so expressly forthright since *Simmenthal*. The conclusion following this case is that any inconsistent national legislation recognized by national legislatures as having legal effect would, in the Court's view, deny the effectiveness of the obligations undertaken by the member states and, in particular, the good faith clause Article 10 EC (now 4(3) TEU), and thus imperil the very foundations of the Community. In its widest interpretation, the judgment holds that 'Inconsistent national measures of any sort which are introduced by member states are effectively invalid from their adoption'.

cross reference
This will be further reviewed from the German perspective in section 5.3.1.

The stance taken by the Court of Justice is in sharp contrast to the initial stance by some of the member states' courts. Indeed, the *Internationale Handelsgesellschaft* case produced a head-on clash between the Court of Justice, the German Federal Constitutional Court and the German Constitution.

Case C-213/89 *Factortame (No. 1)* is a further confirmation that national constitutional practices or rules, in this case no less than the important constitutional doctrine of parliamentary sovereignty in the UK, must not be allowed to stand in the way of a Community law right. It was previously the position in the UK under the doctrine of parliamentary sovereignty that the courts had no power to set aside or not to apply an Act of Parliament. The Court of Justice held that even if the Community law rule were still in dispute, the national procedure should be changed so as not, even potentially, to interfere with the full effectiveness of the Community law right.

cross reference
Considered further in Chapter 8, section 8.4.

This case is also a witness to EU law incursion into national procedure. The Court of Justice is therefore clear that Community and now EU law is supreme over all types of national law. The foregoing cases are only the leading cases on supremacy, those that expressly declare EU law primacy. Many other cases imply EU law supremacy, for example all cases that declare direct effects must also acknowledge supremacy. If EU law were not supreme over national law, especially subsequent law, than direct effects would be denied. Conversely, if direct effects were denied where they fulfil the criteria, supremacy would therefore also be denied because national law would be seen to prevail.

5.1.3 **Section summary**

In summary, the Union view on supremacy is that, because of its unique nature, EU law denies the member states the right to resolve conflicts of law by reference to their own rules or constitutional provisions. EU law obtains its supremacy because of the transfer of state power and sovereignty to the Union in those areas agreed. The member states have provided the Union with legislative powers to enable it to perform its tasks. There would be no point in such a transfer of power if the member states could annul or suspend the effect of EU law by later national law or provisions of the constitutions. If that were allowed to be the case, the existence of the EU legal order and the Union itself would be called into question. A precondition of the existence and functioning of the Union is the uniform and consistent application of EU law in all of the member states. It can achieve such an effect only if it takes precedence over national law.

thinking point

Is it possible to have binding EU law that is not supreme over national law? Equally, is it possible to have EU law supremacy without it being binding in the face of conflicting national law?

The legal and logical consequences of this summary are that any provision of national law that conflicts with EU law must be overruled, regardless of its date of enactment or rank.

The Constitutional Treaty had provided an express statement of supremacy (Article I-6), although without expressly stating that it would be supreme over the member states' constitutions; when that Treaty was abandoned, however, the member states used the opportunity to tone down significantly the clear statement previously made, but without denying this supremacy. Hence supremacy is now dealt with in a Declaration (No. 17), which refers obliquely to the well-settled case law that established the supremacy of EU law, and further by a reference in an annex to the Final Act of the Treaty citing the Opinion of the Council Legal Service on primacy.

Council Legal Service Opinion, Council Document 11197–07 (JUR260) of 22 June 2007

. . . .

It results from the case-law of the ECJ that primacy of EC law is a cornerstone principle of Community law. According to the Court, this principle is inherent to the specific nature of the European Community. At the time of the first judgment of this established case law (*Costa/ENEL*, 15 July 1964, Case 6–6411) there was no mention of primacy in the treaty. It is still the case today. The fact that the principle of primacy will not be included in the future treaty shall not in any way change the existence of the principle and the existing case-law of the ECJ.

The following sections of this chapter will consider how EU law has been received in the member states thus far.

5.2   EU law in the member states

With twenty-seven member states at the time of writing, it would occupy far too much space to look at the reception of EU law in all of them; therefore only a sample of states has been chosen and headlining those is an extended look at the UK. Before this is undertaken, it needs to be considered how international law, as the Treaties and EU law were first thought to be, can be received into the national legal systems.

5.2.1 Theories of incorporation of international law: monism and dualism

The method of incorporation of international law into the member states' legal systems and EU law is determined initially by the particular outlook that a state has in respect of the validity of such law. There are two prevailing theories of the incorporation of external law into national legal systems that are applicable in the context of the initial incorporation of the Treaties into the member state legal systems: **monism** and **dualism**.

cross reference

France is a good example of a monist state and will be considered at section 5.3.3.

monism

Monism basically assumes that international law and national law form part of a single system or hierarchy of law; therefore the acceptance of international law would not require formal incorporation by legislative transformation. After Treaty agreement and assent or ratification, it would be self-executing. In other words, it would be directly applicable within the state. Therefore all that is required by such a state to achieve this is the assent to, or ratification of, an international treaty.

dualism

cross reference

The UK is a very clear example of a dualist state and is considered in section 5.2.2.

Dualism, on the other hand, regards international law and national law as fundamentally different systems of law that exist alongside each other. In order to overcome the barrier existing between the two systems, legislation is required to transform the rules of international law into the national legal system before they can have any binding effect within the state in such circumstances. It is for the member states to determine where the international law is then placed within the national hierarchy of laws.

Dualism does not, however, determine where on the single hierarchy the international law should be placed and this leaves open any difficulties of whether, in individual states, it takes priority over all law or only over municipal/ordinary national law and not over constitutional law.

This is known in EU terminology as 'the acceptance of the *acquis communautaire*'. This term was considered in Chapter 1, section 1.4.1.4.

5.2.2 EU law in the UK

For more details on this section scan here or visit the Online Resource Centre.

The UK was not one of the original and founding member states of the original Communities. It had to overcome a number of difficulties in order to accommodate the duties of member-ship of the European Economic Community (EEC) in 1973. It had to accept all of the previous Community legislation passed, including the Treaties, the Regulations, Directives and the judicial legal developments of this established new legal order.

It had, however, time in which to adjust to this. Being a later entrant state, the UK could see in advance the legal and constitutional problems that would arise as a result of membership and the judicial developments of direct effects and the supremacy, and could take account of them before entry. The particular difficulties faced by the UK legal system in accommodating membership and European Community (EC) law were those relating to the largely unwritten constitution, the dualist approach to international law and the doctrine of parliamentary sovereignty.

These will be considered before looking at how entry was achieved and how Community and now EU law has been received by the UK courts.

5.2.2.1 The 'unwritten' constitution

The UK does not have a single codified constitutional document; instead the UK constitution is made up of a number of written and unwritten elements. Furthermore, there is no concept or form of entrenchment of the constitution itself, nor any parts or elements of it that may be regarded as particularly important. This includes Acts of Parliament, all of which can be removed by simple repeal by the same or any future Parliament. As a consequence, even if a particular political action or legal action is considered so important and envisaged to be required for the long term, if not permanently, it is very difficult, if not impossible, under UK constitutional law to entrench this. Hence, then, it is impossible to alter the UK constitution with any certainty. Thus any transfer of power to the Communities and Union under traditional constitutional thinking could not be regarded as permanent and could always be reversed by a subsequent Act of Parliament.

5.2.2.2 The dualist approach to international law

International treaties are a prerogative of the Crown, as represented by the government in Parliament in the UK, and the courts have no jurisdiction in respect of the validity of such treaties, although they can provide persuasive arguments for the interpretation of national law. In order to apply expressly and be binding in the UK legal order, a provision of an international treaty has to be converted into domestic law by being enacted by the UK Parliament as an Act of national legislation. The Human Rights Act (HRA) 1988, which provided legal validity for the European Convention on Human Rights and Fundamental Freedoms (ECHR) in UK domestic law, is a good example of that. Prior to the HRA 1998, the ECHR had no binding validity in UK domestic law. This particular approach to international law provoked the question of how to convert the original three EC Treaties into national law without transforming every provision into an Act of Parliament, which would have been contrary to the Treaty. Furthermore, it was necessary to ensure that the Treaties or any of their provisions were not simply overruled by the implied repeal of subsequent Acts of Parliament. As it stood, the dualist approach, if followed, would not have recognized the unequivocal supremacy of Community law as set out by the ECJ.

5.2.2.3 The doctrine of parliamentary sovereignty

Formally, UK parliamentary sovereignty means that there are no legal limitations on the UK Parliament and that it has the right to make or unmake any law whatsoever. Further, no person or body is recognized as having a right to override or set aside the legislation of Parliament. The doctrine also implies that, as such, it is impossible to bind future Parliaments. Subsequent Acts can either expressly or impliedly override a prior Act. There is no constitutional role for UK courts, which therefore cannot review the validity of Acts passed by Parliament. The courts must enforce and apply Acts of Parliament equally and without question.

One of the problems in considering this doctrine of parliamentary sovereignty is the nature of the concept itself. It is not a rigid constitutional enactment and is really just a constitutional convention that was built up over centuries and refined by eminent jurists to the position stated by Dicey in the latter half of the nineteenth century. As a convention, it is subject to the erosion of time to reflect the changing circumstances in which it must be employed. Even Dicey conceded that this was not an absolute convention and that there were political, if not legal, limits to it. The fact that there has been considerable comment and publicity about the attack on parliamentary sovereignty as a consequence of Community and Union membership misconceives

cross reference
The cases that we shall consider in section 5.2.2.6 help to demonstrate this.

the status of this particular parliamentary convention. It posed, however, a distinct problem for the UK and, until relatively recently, also for the courts in considering whether, in a situation of conflict, Community law or a national statute should take priority.

5.2.2.4 UK entry and the European Communities Act (ECA) 1972

The ECA 1972 was the Act of Parliament that facilitated UK entry into the Communities. Both entry to the EC and Community law implementation in the UK initially focuses on how the ECA 1972 observes and takes account of such well-established Community law concepts as direct effect and supremacy, and the difficulties noted above in respect of dualism and sovereignty. In contrast to the earlier practice of the incorporation of international treaties, the ECA did not reproduce the whole of the EC Treaties or subsequent secondary legislation as Acts of Parliament. If this were done, the words of any future Act that conflicted with Community law obligations could override the prior Treaty. Instead, the Community Treaties were adopted by a simple assent. Section 1 of the ECA 1972 was intended to future-proof the Act by allowing for subsequent EC and EU Treaties to be regarded in the same way as the original Treaties, including, of course, most recently the Lisbon Treaty and the changes that it has made to the EU and EC Treaties. The Act thus impliedly recognizes the unique new legal system and may be regarded now as a special form of UK legislation, although this is still subject to the argument that it can be repealed.

This is described as *sui generis*, as in not being within a general class, but in a special class of its own.

cross reference
Thoburn *is considered in section 5.2.2.6.*

Some support has been given to this view by the High Court judgment in *Thoburn* v *Sunderland City Council*.

Section 2(1) recognizes the legal validity and direct applicability of Community Treaties and Regulations already in existence in the Community legal order and provides that all such future Community legal provisions shall also be recognized as such. It also recognizes the doctrine of direct effects.

> ### ECA 1972, s. 2(1)
> . . . .
> All such rights powers, liabilities, obligations and restrictions from time to time created or arising under the Treaties, and all such remedies and procedures from time to time provided for by or under the Treaties, as in accordance with the Treaties are without further enactment to be given legal effect or used in the United Kingdom shall be recognized and available in law, and be enforced, allowed and followed accordingly.

It is somewhat convoluted, but the subsection recognizes the doctrine of direct effects and allows for future developments by the Court of Justice. This is termed in the Act as 'enforceable Community right . . . and similar expressions'. Thus those rights or duties that are, as a matter of Community law, directly applicable or effective are to be given legal effect in the UK.

Section 2(2) allows for the implementation of other Community obligations that are not automatically applicable in the UK, via forms of UK secondary legislation such as Orders in Council or statutory instruments. The power that the executive has to make secondary legislation is subject to the limits in Schedule 2 to the Act, in respect of the imposing or creation of taxation, the introduction of retrospective legislation, sub-delegation and the introduction of new criminal offences with more than a two-year period of imprisonment as penalty or a higher value limit of more than level 5 on the fine scale (figures that are subject to revision from time to time as determined by an Order in Council).

Section 2(4) is the subsection that recognizes the supremacy of Community (EU) law and therefore also concerns sovereignty.

> **ECA 1972, s. 2(4)**
> . . . .
>
> Any such provision and any enactment passed or to be passed (that refers to any secondary legislation and act of Parliament which has been passed previously or may be passed in the future) shall be construed and have effect subject to the foregoing provisions of this section.

That is a reference to the entire section and in particular s. 2(1), and means that any future Act of Parliament must be construed in such a way as to give effect to the enforceable Community rights in existence. This is achieved by denying effectiveness to any national legislation passed later that is in conflict and this in turn is controlled by directions to the courts concerned with the application or construction of legislation. The courts are required to interpret any future Act to be consistent with Community (EU) law or, in effect, to be subordinate where inconsistency arises.

> This view was clearly confirmed by the House of Lords in *R v Secretary of State for Transport, ex p Factortame and others (No. 1)* when it held that s. 2(4) of the ECA 1972 should be understood as if:
>
> > a section were incorporated into the Merchant Shipping Act which enacted that the provisions with regard to the registration of British fishing vessels were to be 'without prejudice to the directly enforceable Community rights of national of any member states of the EC'.

cross reference

The latest statutory development of the European Union Act 2011 will be considered in section 5.2.2.7.

Section 3(1) then instructs the courts to refer questions on the interpretation, and hence the supremacy, of Community and now EU law to the Court of Justice if the UK courts cannot solve the problem themselves by reference to previous Court of Justice rulings. This follows the *Costa v ENEL* ruling and is backed up by s. 3(2), which requires the courts judicially to follow decisions of the Court of Justice on any question of Community law. This would include direct effects and supremacy, although it does not expressly say so.

The combination of s. 2(1) and (4) with the control of s. 3(1) and (2) would appear to achieve the essential requirements of the recognition of direct effects and the supremacy of Community and now EU law for past and future UK legislation.

5.2.2.5 The ECA 1972 and parliamentary sovereignty

The view of how the ECA 1972 has affected parliamentary sovereignty is determined by what the Act actually achieves. There are two main viewpoints: either s. 2(4) acts as a rule of construction, or it attempts a form of entrenchment whereby it modifies the doctrine of parliamentary sovereignty. As a rule of construction, it commands the courts to interpret national law to comply with Community and EU law. The earlier decisions on Community law

cross reference

Also considered at the end of the next section.

cross reference

See Factortame *in the next section.*

by courts in England and Wales considered that the rule of construction should apply only where the national legislation is reasonably capable of such construction: see for example, *Macarthy's* v *Smith* and *Roberts* v *Cleveland Area Health Authority*. However, this view is being modified because it is regarded as too restrictive a view of what is achieved by the ECA 1972. The alternative of limited entrenchment means that it allows the courts directly to apply Community and EU law over national law regardless of the actual words. This enables the courts to ignore any implied repeal or unintentional inconsistency of future Acts of Parliament and thus arguably modifies the doctrine of parliamentary sovereignty in that one Parliament has been seen to bind a future one. Express inconsistency and thus repeal remains a problem even under this interpretation. However, how Community and now EU law is received in the member states is often and ultimately dependent on the national judiciary, as well as national parliaments; therefore a consideration of its reception in the courts is vital.

5.2.2.6 Judicial reception of Community and EU law in the UK

Where there is a conflict between an earlier UK law and later EU law, there is no difficulty: the rule of legislative repeal within parliamentary supremacy and the supremacy of EU law will produce the same result.

For example, in **Case 83/78 *Pigs Marketing Board (Northern Ireland)* v *Redmond*** from 1979, the later Common Agricultural Policy (CAP) rule on the organization of the market was held to prevail over earlier national law.

The difficulty arises when there is a conflict between a later UK law and an earlier EU law provision. In such a case, are the words within the ECA 1972 to be taken as a rule of interpretation or as a question of entrenchment that effectively involves the modification of doctrine of parliamentary supremacy by ss. 2(4) and 3?

The most important of the earlier cases is ***Macarthy's* v *Smith*** concerning a clash between the Equal Pay Act 1970, s. 6 and the then Article 119 EC, in which the Court of Appeal clearly held:

It is important now to declare and it must be made plain. The provisions of Article 119 take priority over anything in our English Statute on Equal Pay which is inconsistent with Article 119. That priority is given by our own law, by the ECA 1972 itself. Community law is now part of our law and whenever there is any inconsistency Community law has priority.

However, Lord Denning, in an *obiter* passage, thought that, with regard to an express or intentional repudiation of the Treaty by Parliament or expressly acting inconsistently, the courts would be bound to follow the express and clear intent of Parliament to repudiate the Treaty or a section of it by the subsequent Act. That not being the case, however, Community law takes priority according to the Court of Appeal.

Macarthy's v *Smith* has survived the years, and the subsequent cases of the House of Lords concerned with the relationship between EU and national law have not removed it from our consideration because even though Denning's words are merely *obiter*, they remain the only clear statement by a superior court about what might happen in the event of an express statement by Parliament of the intention to conflict with EU law.

In *Garland v BREL*, the first important statement from the House of Lords, Mrs Garland had complained that the practice of allowing the families of male ex-employees of British Rail Engineering Ltd (BREL) concessionary rail travel facilities after retirement, but not families of female ex-employees, was discriminatory. Under s. 6(4) of the Sex Discrimination Act (SDA) 1975, provisions in relation to retirement were exempted from the rules on sex discrimination and Mrs Garland's claim failed initially.

Previous UK case law, and notably *Roberts v Cleveland Area Health Authority*, had determined that s. 6(4) SDA 1975 be given a wide interpretation so as to discount anything to do with or connected to retirement; therefore discrimination in such circumstance was lawful. Old Article 119 EEC and Directive 76/207, however, made no such exception regarding retirement; therefore UK and Community law were regarded by the House of Lords as inconsistent. The House of Lords asked the Court of Justice to give a ruling on the interpretation of Article 119 to determine if it covered conditions in retirement. The Court of Justice held that it did so. Upon return to the House of Lords, the Law Lords considered themselves bound in view of the Court of Justice ruling and ECA 1972 to interpret the SDA 1975 in such a way as not to be inconsistent with the UK obligations under Community law.

Whilst the House of Lords stated that the case was no occasion to pronounce on any further effects of the ECA 1972, it nevertheless did state *obiter* that UK courts should interpret UK law to be consistent no matter how wide a departure from the prima facie meaning it was. The case therefore very much follows the line that s. 2(4) allows courts to construe subsequent statutes quite widely in order to give consistency to Community and now EU law: clearly, therefore, a rule of construction.

cross reference
For the importance of this, see Chapter 8, section 8.1.3.3.

The case of *Duke v GEC Reliance* is also instructive because it was brought at roughly the same time as the *Marshall* case. The *Marshall* case was one of the leading cases on the direct effect of Directives.

Mrs Duke was required to retire at the age of 60, earlier than men, who could retire at 65. Section 6(4) SDA 1975 applied to the factual discrimination to render the discrimination lawful. The House of Lords considered the *Marshall* ruling in which the Equal Treatment Directive was held to apply to retirement itself and to have direct effects, but because this concerned a private sector employer, the House of Lords rightly concluded that the Directive itself could not be enforced against individuals – that is, that it had no horizontal direct effects. Therefore a head-on clash between the Directive and a UK statute took place, with the Directive being later in time. The post-accession statute was inconsistent with a later Community obligation. It was therefore too late for Parliament to intend to comply with the Directive in the provisions of the national law. Consequently, the House of Lords held that there was no enforceable Community right to which the provisions of the English SDA 1975 would be required to give way under s. 2(4) ECA 1972. Therefore s. 2(4) could not apply to construe a UK statute to enforce Community Directives against individuals. In the view of the House of Lords in the case, it could apply only to directly applicable Community law. The House of Lords held that s. 2(4) refers to s. 2(1), which refers only to directly effective Community law or directly applicable law; therefore it was not appropriate. Mrs Duke was refused relief by the House of Lords and with this judgment was the view that s. 2(4) could be used very widely as a rule of construction. This case was not followed by the House of Lords in later cases.

Pickstone v *Freemans plc* involved a generous interpretation of the UK 1983 Equal Pay (Amendment) Regulations, which amended the Equal Pay Act 1970, to read consistently with Community law obligations. This was largely based on the intention of Parliament in passing the Regulations to ensure that national law complied with the Community Directive, but also in line with Court of Justice rulings. Section 2(4) ECA 1972 was used to justify the Court's interpretation of national law, but only in so far as it was reasonably possible. *Duke* was then distinguished on the basis that the SDA 1975 was not intended to give effect to the later Community law or capable of doing so.

The case of *Litster* v *Forth Dry Dock & Engineering Co. Ltd* concerned the rights of employees on the transfer of the undertaking of a business. A number of employees were claiming unfair dismissal after a ship-repairing company was transferred between owners. The relevant law was the Transfer of Undertakings (Protection of Employment) Regulations 1981, which purported to implement the obligations contained in the EEC Council Directive 77/187, but were considered to be somewhat ambiguous. The Directive could not give rise to direct effects because it involved an attempt to enforce it against a private employer. The House of Lords could not therefore achieve a satisfactory result in keeping with the European Directive and the case law of the Court of Justice by a literal attempt; therefore it concluded that it must use the Community legislation to construe the later UK legislation contrary to its literal meaning and imply additional words to achieve consistency with the purpose of the Directive. Here, s. 2(4) ECA 1972 is clearly being used as a rule of construction and quite a generous one.

The *R* v *Secretary of State for Transport, ex p Factortame Ltd* litigation is a particularly important statement of the view of the House of Lords to the supremacy of Community law. You may find the series of litigation in the *Factortame* cases very confusing, particularly since the case numbers are not always used consistently. To try to clarify the matter, the facts and procedure of the case are as follows.

The UK wanted to protect the British fishing quotas under the European quota system and passed the Merchant Shipping Act in 1988 aimed at stopping the practice of quota-hopping by Spanish-owned vessels registered in the UK by requiring that a minimum percentage of the directors of companies owning fishing vessels registered in the UK be British nationals. The companies and vessel-owners sought an interim injunction against the Crown not to apply a disputed national regulation issued under that Act. This was granted in the main action on merits by the Queen's Bench Divisional Court (QBD), which decided, rather slowly, to refer the substantive issue to the Court of Justice; this case was given the Court of Justice docket number **C-221/89**. This is **Factortame No. 2**. The Crown appealed against the injunction, raising a procedural point and a second line of cases commenced, which was appealed up to the House of Lords, which also made a reference to the Court of Justice, but this time on the procedural matter.

The procedural action was, however, subject to a much faster appeal process, so that it was received earlier by the Court of Justice than the substantive law case and was given the docket number **C-213/89**, hence it is *Factortame* (1). See Figure 5.1 for details of the litigation paths.

The procedural aspect was decided by the Court of Justice, which essentially held that the national court should grant interim relief. On receipt of the ruling, the House of Lords held that if a national rule precludes a national court from granting an interim relief, whilst it was being determined whether there is a conflict between national law and Community law, irreparable harm could be done. Therefore the national court must set aside that rule. If the injunction against the Crown was not granted, the Spanish fishing companies would most probably go out of business whilst waiting for the Court of Justice to decide the substantive issues and for that to be returned to the QBD and decided: a process that actually took two years and seven months. Although the substantive point of Community law in relation to the UK law had not been decided at that stage, the House of Lords nevertheless considered that if Community law rights are to be found to be directly enforceable in favour of the appellants, those rights will prevail over the inconsistent national legislation, even if later. It was held *obiter* that:

This [s. 2(4)] has precisely the same effect as if a section were incorporated into the national statute…which in terms enacted that the provisions…[of an Act]…were to be without prejudice to the directly enforceable Community rights of nationals of any member state of the EEC.

Lord Bridge commented on the view that the earlier Decisions in favour of Community law were an attack on parliamentary sovereignty:

If the supremacy within the European Community of Community law over the National law of member states was not always inherent in the EEC Treaty it was certainly well established in the jurisprudence of the Court of Justice long before the United Kingdom joined the Community. Thus, whatever limitation of its sovereignty Parliament accepted when it enacted the European Communities Act 1972 was entirely voluntary. Under the terms of the ECA 1972 it has always been clear that it was the duty of a United Kingdom court, when delivering final judgment, to override any rule of National law found to be in conflict with any directly enforceable rule of Community law. Thus, there is nothing in any way novel in according supremacy to rules of Community law in those areas to which they apply and to insist that, in the protection of rights under Community law, national courts must not be inhibited by rules of national law from granting interim relief in appropriate cases is no more than a logical recognition of that supremacy.

Factortame No. 2, dealing with the substantive matter, was decided in the High Court as predicted: that Community law had been breached by the UK legislation.

cross reference

The European Union Act 2011 is considered in section 5.2.2.7.

As a result of *Factortame*, the view of s. 2(4) ECA 1972 is that it is a direct rule to give priority rather than a rule of construction that requires there to be national law to construe. It would also seem to suggest that, as far as the Supreme Court is now concerned, entry to the Communities and s. 2(4) ECA 1972 have led to the modification of the doctrine of parliamentary sovereignty and that EU law in the areas agreed by Treaty is supreme over national law. Whether this overrides the dictum in *Macarthy's* v *Smith* is open to question. It remains open for Parliament to expressly repeal the Act or to pass legislation expressly in breach of EU law obligations. Politically, however, this is extremely unlikely, although the recent European Union Act 2011 may yet have a bearing on this debate.

Diagram 5.1

Factortame *litigation*

Substantive law cases

The case commences on 10 March 1989 in the QBD of the High Court (1989) 2 CMLR 353. The substantive law question is raised about the Merchant Shipping Act. The nationality requirement was disputed. QBD refers a question to the ECJ on the substantive questions, but takes its time (this becomes Case C-221/89).

AFTER THE USUAL DELAY of about two years, the ECJ reported.

The ECJ heard the substantive law issue in Case C-221/89 on 25 July 1991 to hold that the discrimination by the UK was contrary to Articles 6 and 52 EC. This is *Factortame II* (1991) ECR I-3905, (1991) 3 CMLR 589.

The QBD hears the returned C-221/89 case on 2 October 1991 and orders that UK law was contrary to EC law. Two years and seven months. Court asks applicants to provide claim for damages suffered.

Aware of the case, the Commission on 16 March 1989 commences an action against the UK for breach of the EC Treaty Articles 6 and 52.

Case C-249/89 *Commission* v *UK*, August 1989. On 10 October 1989, the President of the ECJ granted an interim relief application to suspend the UK measures. This was reported C-249/89R (1989) ECR I-3125. The main case is reported later.

Case 246/89 is heard by the ECJ on 4 October 1991, which Court holds that the discrimination by the UK was contrary to Articles 6 and 52 EC: (1991) ECR I-4585, (1991) 3 CMLR 706.

Procedural issues

High Court QBD: concerned about the delay, Factortame asks for an injunction, which is granted. This starts the fast-tracking procedural court chase as the UK goverment appeals: (1989) 2 CMLR 392.

APPEAL TO THE COURT OF APPEAL
Heard on 22 March1989. Injunction overturned. This is reported in the same issue: (1989) 2 CMLR 392.

APPEAL TO THE HOUSE OF LORDS
Interim relief declined, but the House of Lords decides to ask the ECJ about the grant of interim relief to suspend an Act of Parliament: [1989] 3 CMLR 1, [1990] 2 AC 85 (Case C-213/89).

The ECJ hears the procedural case C-213/89 on 19 June 1990: (1990) ECR I-2433. This is *Factortame I*. ECJ concludes that the UK court must grant interim relief.

RETURN TO THE HOUSE OF LORDS
Heard on 10 July 1990. Parties informed of Decision on principle with speeches to follow. ECJ followed and injunction reinstated: (1990) 3 WLR 856, (1991) 1 AC.

House of Lords, 11 October 1990: (1991) AC 603. Judgment speeches on interim relief.

The series of *Factortame* cases is extremely important for a number of reasons in EU law, in particular from the point of view of supremacy over national law and constitutional doctrine, and should be most carefully studied. The *Factortame* case returned to the High Court (*Factortame No. 3*) on whether damages would be payable, and in arguing ever finer points of law on damages and limitation in *Factortame Nos 4 and 5*, the details of which, thankfully, go beyond those needed for courses on EU law. See the discussion of this in Chapter 8, section 8.3.

Subsequently, the House of Lords confirmed in **Case C-9/91 *R* v *Secretary of State for Employment, ex p EOC*** the conclusion reached in *Factortame* and held that, in judicial review proceedings, UK courts could declare an Act of Parliament to be incompatible with EC law, although this does not extend to being able to annul the UK Act of Parliament nor indeed to command a government to repeal the Act or to compel or command a minister to change the law.

Therefore whilst judicially, in the UK, EU law supremacy appears to be an accepted and settled matter, this does not prevent cases from reaching the courts on this topic.

The most prominent thus far is ***Thoburn* v *Sunderland City Council*** (the ***Metric Martyrs* case**), in which an argument was raised that a later UK Act, the Weights and Measures Act 1985, had impliedly repealed the ECA 1972 and that UK law should then take precedence over EC law. The High Court rejected this view, making the comment that the 1972 Act had acquired a 'constitutional quality' that prevented implied repeal. The case appears to confirm the view that there has been a kind of entrenchment introduced, which does amend our view of parliamentary sovereignty in the UK.

Finally, in ***Jackson* v *AG***, Lord Steyn acknowledged that the supremacy of Parliament remained a general principle of the UK constitution, but that it was a common law principle established by the judges in a different era. This suggests that it is viewed as a doctrine that might need qualification by the courts in future.

In respect of the ECA 1972, in the same case, Lord Hope suggested that even an intentional or express repudiation of EU law might not be followed by the new Supreme Court in the light of his statement that Parliament was careful *not* to say in terms that it could not enact legislation that was in conflict with Community law, which, in practice, has become the effect of s. 2(1) when read with s. 2(4) ECA 1972.

The conclusion for the UK is that it has clearly and unambiguously accepted the supremacy of EU law even over UK Acts of Parliament and over constitutional practice. Whether this is four-square on the basis of the logic of EU law as provided by the Court of Justice and not by reference to the UK, the ECA 1972 remains unclear. The case law points to both conclusions; however, the UK seems to have gone further than some of the other member states. Certainly, the *Factortame* litigation and the conclusion at its end that, in matters of EU law, the UK courts are able not to apply UK Acts of Parliament does introduce a form of constitutional review by the courts, hitherto not the case in the UK, and therefore does impact and undermine the doctrine of parliamentary sovereignty, at least as far as EU law is concerned.

5.2.2.7 The European Union Act 2011

We must now move from the courts and the conclusion that they had, by and large, accepted the supremacy of EU back to the UK Parliament because of the enactment by the 2010 UK coalition government of a new and quite radical Act concerning the relationship between the UK and the EU.

The European Union Act 2011 puts in place a series of conditions on future UK acceptance of new EU powers or indeed even some amendments to existing competences and powers. It may well have been influenced by the types of reservation that will be seen in the courts of some of the other member states featured in subsequent sections, notably Germany and Italy. Whilst not directly pronouncing on supremacy, it will question any open acceptance of new Treaty changes and most other Treaty amendments.

cross reference

See Chapter 3, section 3.5.1, for more on the ordinary revision procedure.

Passerelle provisions

Those Articles that may be changed in terms of voting requirements and specifically from unanimous to qualified majority voting by Article 46 TEU.

cross reference

Proposals under Article 352 TFEU are considered in Chapter 3, section 3.3.3.2.

Section 2 deals with Treaty revisions under the new Article 48 TEU ordinary revision procedure. Such revisions are made subject to a UK procedure, which requires that there be both an Act of Parliament supporting the revision and the positive approval in a national referendum. The same will apply to the simplified revision procedure governed by Article 46 TEU unless an exemption provided under s. 4(4) of the Act applies, such as the accession of new member states, changes that do not apply to the UK (such as those that apply to the eurozone), or the codification of existing laws and practice. There is a further exemption under s. 4(1) if the change is deemed to be not significant for the UK, but that is to be decided by the minister (under s. 5). If the minister determines that the change involves a transfer of power or competence, then a referendum is seemingly inevitable. It is to be noted, though, that s. 4 appears to tie the minister's hand quite considerably: because the reasons for requiring an Act and referendum have been so extensively stated in s. 4 itself, it would appear that very little, if indeed any, change will escape. It depends, of course on just how strictly or not the sections are interpreted, first by the minister, then by the courts, if disputes come before them. Section 6 provides that the same approval regime apply to changes to Treaty voting rules and the procedures for enacting EU secondary legislation under the so-called *Passerelle provisions*.

Section 7 provides that new certain specific decisions of EU cannot be accepted by a minister unless approved by an Act of Parliament. In similar terms, under s. 8, any new EU secondary legislation proposed under Article 352 TFEU cannot be accepted by a minister in Council unless approved of first by an Act of Parliament.

Finally, s. 18 has been termed a 'sovereignty clause', but appears both to restate the provision under the ECA 1972 that EU law should be applicable, but equally states that this is only so because that Act allows it. It ignores, though, the judicial developments and interpretation of the 1972 Act, so at this stage it is difficult to predict how, if it ever is considered by the courts, they will interpret it or whether it will make any change to the existing case law interpretations.

cross reference

The interpretation of the 1972 Act was considered at section 5.2.2.6.

> ### European Union Act 2011, s. 18
>
> Directly applicable or directly effective EU law (that is, the rights, powers, liabilities, obligations, restrictions, remedies and procedures referred to in section 2(1) of the European Communities Act 1972) falls to be recognised and available in law in the United Kingdom only by virtue of that Act or where it is required to be recognised and available in law by virtue of any other Act.

The new Act may well lead to greater scrutiny of proposed changes to EU laws, but at what cost? If the procedures set out in the Act are carried out to the letter and for almost any proposed change, then the UK ministers and Parliament will become very engaged in considering EU matters, which will impact considerably on the use of parliamentary time. Further, if Acts of Parliament and referenda are subsequently necessary, the cost and organization of such will not only involve the expenditure of huge sums of money, but also the whole process in the UK of approving or rejecting proposed EU amendments will be considerably extended. It may well be that there will be a lot of rejections, thus progress on EU matters for the whole Union of twenty-seven member states may be stalled or completely blocked. Presently, however, it is too early to predict how it might work in practice or be received, but, as ever, the passage of time will tell.

5.3 Reception of EU law in other member states

A majority of member states have not experienced any problems so far, although there is always room judicially for this position to change. It would be beyond this particular text to conduct a tour of all of the member states, so only the following states have been selected.

5.3.1 Germany

5.3.1.1 The German Constitution (*Grundgesetz*)

For more details on this section scan here or visit the Online Resource Centre.

In Germany, in contrast with the UK, difficulties were experienced, especially in respect of the relationship between fundamental rights' provision in the German Constitution (*Grundgesetz*, or GG) and in the Community and EU legal order. Traditionally, Germany adopted the dualist approach to the reception of international law whereby some form of transformation or adoption of international law was necessary in order for it to have any direct application in the state. There had to be a process of incorporation by statute and, once incorporated, a law would simply rank as with other *Gesetze* (Acts of the German Parliament). If a later law were in conflict with an earlier law, the later law would prevail. Articles 24 and 25 GG provided for the peaceful cooperation of the German state with international organizations. Article 24 GG allowed for membership of international organizations and a transfer of powers to them, and was used to establish membership of the European Communities. Although article 25 GG declared general rules of public international law to be an integral part of federal law and to take precedence over national law, it was silent as to the effect of international law on German constitutional law. In order to cater specifically for further European integration, particularly into new areas as proposed in the Maastricht Treaty and to take account of the increasing concern about possible infringements of the *Grundgesetz*, a new article 23 GG was added and amendments were made to other key provisions.

Joint approval was also required for the ratification of the EU Treaty and is further required for any future changes affecting the contents of the *Grundgesetz*.

 Article 23 GG provides that sovereign powers can be transferred to the EU provided that the transfer has the approval of both Houses of the German Parliament, the *Bundestag* and *Bundesrat*.

5.3.1.2 The reaction of the German courts

Previously, German courts had been divided as to the effect of Community primary law and secondary law and, at times, had refused to make a reference in cases of doubt or non-acceptance, thus denying the parties to the case the chance to see whether EC law would have affected the outcome of the case. The most important court in Germany is the Federal Constitutional Court (FCC) because of its constitutional position in the German state.

In the ***Internationale Handelsgesellschaft*** (known in Germany as ***Solange I***), the Constitutional Court held that as long as the recognition of human rights in the EEC had not progressed as far as those provided for by the *Grundgesetz*, German courts retained the right to refer questions on the constitutionality of secondary Community law to the FCC, with the possible result that Community law might be ignored if it did not have sufficient regard for basic rights.

This position has been modified with the later rulings by the FCC.

In ***Wünsche Handelsgesellschaft*** (known as ***Solange II***), the FCC accepted that Community recognition and safeguards of fundamental rights through the case law of the Court of Justice were sufficient and of a comparable nature to those provided for by the *Grundgesetz*. Thus it held that as long as EC and now EU law ensures the effective provision of fundamental rights, the FCC will not review EC law in the light of the rights provisions of the Constitution. The Court also stated that it would not be prepared to accept constitutional complaints against Community law from lower courts on this basis. It is argued that a reservation of supremacy is still inherent in the ruling.

The basis for the decision is not, however, the inherent supremacy of EU law, but the fact that article 24 GG allowed a transfer of powers to the Community and the subsequent Accession Act obliges the German courts to accept the supremacy of Community and EU law. The decision by the FCC in *Solange II* also held that the Court of Justice was a statutory court within the meaning of article 101 GG and that individuals have the right to have access to statutory courts. This effectively means that German courts can no longer refuse to make references in the last instance to the Court of Justice.

This happened in the 1985 case of ***Kloppenburg***. The Federal Tax Court had denied the direct effects of Directives and refused a reference to the Court of Justice.

The FCC held in ***Re: VAT Exemption***, the follow-up to the *Kloppenburg* case, and in the separate case of ***Re: Patented Feedstuffs***, that German courts, which are courts of last instance in terms of Article 234 EC (now 267 TFEU), would be in breach of the German Constitution if they were to fail to refer to the Court of Justice when necessary. The earlier judgment of the Federal Tax Court was consequently annulled.

Therefore German courts of last instance are obliged to make a reference where a dispute as to interpretation or application of EU law exists. Applications to the FCC to question the constitutionality of Community legislation have now been declared to be inadmissible because the Court considered that such acts are not acts of German public authorities within the scope of the *Grundgesetz* and cannot thus be complained of to the FCC. Following these cases, there would seem to be no procedural difficulty in getting EU rights at least considered in the proper forum in Germany. Any court that refuses either to follow a previous ruling of the Court of Justice or to make an Article 267 TFEU ruling may be subject to the review of the FCC for a breach of article 101(1) GG.

The German Accession Act to the TEU was passed by the German Parliament in December 1992. However, as a result of considerable criticism that there had been no real debate on the Maastricht Treaty in Germany and that a referendum had not been held to test public opinion on further integration, constitutional complaints were made to the FCC.

> In its judgment in **Brunner and others v Federal Republic of Germany** (known as **Maastricht**), the FCC considered the changes to the Constitution, the constitutionality of the TEU, and generally the relationship between the EC and the German Constitution. Whilst it held that the transfer of powers was compatible with the principles of the *Grundgesetz*, future extensive transfers could not be made without the approval of the German Parliament, and the FCC would reserve to itself a right to review the compatibility of EC law fundamental rights' provisions and the range of rights exercised by the EC with the German Constitution, thus appearing to backtrack on its previous judgments.

After the *Maastricht* judgment, the relationship between the Court of Justice and the FCC remains unclear. Even though the FCC claims that fundamental rights will be protected and upheld by a relationship of cooperation between both courts, it does not clearly explain how this protection will work in practice. It seems that the FCC has accepted the standard of basic rights' protection provided by the Court of Justice, but reserves a right to review EU Acts that could evidently infringe basic rights under the *Grundgesetz* if the Court of Justice does not offer protection. So far, this has been a theoretical proposition.

> A more recent decision of the FCC, **Case 2BvE 2/08 *Lisbon Judgment***, indirectly deals with EU matters, focusing on the constitutional compatibility of German legislation with the Lisbon Treaty. Following the agreement on the Lisbon Treaty on further integration of the EU by the member states, the German *Bundestag* and *Bundesrat* passed the Transformation Act and an accompanying law extending and strengthening the rights of the *Bundestag* and the *Bundesrat* in European matters. This latter law was challenged before the FCC by German members of Parliament (MPs). The Court decided that the Lisbon Treaty and its Transformation Act were compatible with the Constitution, but that the accompanying Act strengthening the rights of the *Bundestag* and *Bundesrat* was not. It held that European integration could not be achieved by means that abolished the member states' discretion to organize or establish economic, cultural and social conditions of life. In this respect, constitutional organs such as the *Bundestag* and *Bundesrat* had a responsibility to integrate. Thus the participation rights of these two organs within negotiations at European level had to be elaborated in a much clearer way than had happened in the challenged statute.

The FCC has made clear that it retains its competence to review any EU acts in order to ensure that they do not exceed the limits of what EU organs have been authorized to do by the member states and has thus, in this latest case, confirmed the line taken already in the *Maastricht* case.

> Turning to the ruling of the highest German court in civil and criminal matters, the German Supreme Court (*Bundesgerichtshof* or BGH) accepted the principle of state liability on

the part of the German state for a legislative breach of Community law in **Case C-46/93 Brasserie du Pêcheur v Federal Republic of Germany**. However, the Court held that the breach, which was the prohibition of the use of additives in brewing beer contrary to EC free movement of goods rules, had not been sufficiently serious to impose liability.

5.3.2 **Italy**

For more details on this section scan here or visit the Online Resource Centre.

In Italy, the position both constitutionally and judicially was and is very similar to that in Germany whereby both had new constitutions set up after the Second World War with strong provision for fundamental rights. Both states allowed a transfer of power to international organizations, but were silent as to its effect on constitutional law.

Article 11 of the Italian Constitution provides for the limitation of national sovereignty in favour of international arrangements to secure peace and justice between nations.

As in Germany, the focus in Italy is on its Constitutional Court. Given that two of the leading EU cases on supremacy, *Costa* v *ENEL* and *Simmenthal*, arose from Italy, it should certainly have been clear to the Italian Constitutional Court what was expected of it. Again, there has been a mixed reaction, also along the lines of the German Constitutional Court.

> Despite the previous less-than-enthusiastic response to Community and EU law, the supremacy of Community law was accepted in the case of **Frontini v Ministero delle Finanze** and the supremacy of the European Court was accepted in the 1984 case **Granital v Administrazione delle Finanze**. *The decision* was based both on the basis of an interpretation of article 11 of the Italian Constitution, allowing for the limitation of sovereignty in favour of international organizations, and by reason of the case law of the Court of Justice.

141

cross reference
Duke *is considered in section 5.4.2.6.*

The case did, however, make the reservation that Italian law should be cast aside only where directly applicable Community law exists – similar, in effect, to the judgment of the House of Lords in the *Duke* case.

> A later decision in **Fragd v Administrazione delle Finanze** suggests that the Italian Constitutional Court is still prepared to review EU law in the light of the fundamental rights provision in the Italian Constitution if EU law was regarded as not respecting these rights. This stance was confirmed in **Admenta v Federfarma** in which the Italian State Council held that fundamental rights, as protected by Italian law, could not be reviewed in the light of EU law and were therefore to be reviewed exclusively in the light of Italian constitutional law.

Thus far, this remains the situation in Italy with the possibility for outright rejection of EU law supremacy.

5.3.3 **France**

The French courts are divided into two hierarchies, each with their own appeal courts and final appeal, and in addition a Constitutional Court (*Conseil Constitutionnel*). They have had, however, significantly different attitudes to EC law, despite the fact that both are subject to article 55 of the French Constitution, which is monist and gives international law a rank above municipal law, but is silent as to the effect on the Constitution. This is the point that has led to discrepancies between hierarchies.

5.3.3.1 The French Courts of Ordinary Jurisdiction

The Courts of Ordinary Jurisdiction have had no hesitation in making Article 234 TEU (now 267 TFEU) references to the Court of Justice, and giving supremacy to Community and thus now EU law on the basis of article 55 of the Constitution. The French Supreme Court of Ordinary Jurisdiction (*Cour de Cassation*) has in fact gone further and found for the supremacy of Community law without direct reference to article 55 of the Constitution, and more on the basis of the inherent supremacy and direct effects of Community law itself.

> See **Café Vabre** in which old Article 95 EEC was held to prevail over a subsequent national statute.

These rulings have been consistently followed by the lower courts and reference to either article 55 of the Constitution or even the decisions is rarely made, for example *Garage Dehus Sarl* v *Bouche Distribution*.

5.3.3.2 French public courts

These courts deal with complaints by citizens against any acts of the state administration. The Supreme Administrative Court, the *Conseil D'État*, has from time to time completely denied the supremacy of Community or now EU law, or the need to make reference to the Court of Justice, relying heavily on the French principle of law *acte clair*.

. . . .
acte clair
Principle that where a provision of law is clear, there is no need to refer to a higher court, but simply to apply it.
. . . .

> The leading case is **Minister of the Interior v Cohn-Bendit**, in which Daniel Cohn-Bendit ('Danny the Red') was deported from France in 1968 and in 1975 requested re-entry, but was refused. He claimed that the refusal was contrary to the Free Movement Directive, Directive 64/221, previously declared directly effective by the Court of Justice in the *Van Duyn* case. The *Conseil D'État* held that individuals could not directly rely on Directives to challenge an administrative act and declined to follow previous Court of Justice rulings or to make a reference itself.

The judgment in the *Cohn-Bendit* case has been followed by the same court and lower courts. Two cases have, though, demonstrated a much more cooperative attitude on the part of the French administrative courts.

> In **Nicolo**, the *Conseil d'État* reviewed the supremacy of international law, including EEC Treaty Articles, and held the latter to take precedence over subsequent national law, largely on the basis of article 55 of the French Constitution. The submissions of the Government Commissioner were instructive in his use and observation of the decisions from the courts of other member states and their acceptance of Community law supremacy.

> Secondly, in **Boisdet**, incompatible national law was declared invalid in the face of a Community Regulation. In doing so, the *Conseil d'État* followed the case law of the Court of Justice.

The cases of **Rothmans, Philip Morris Tobacco** and **Arizona Tobacco** held that not only are EC Directives to be given priority over national law, even where the Directive pre-dated the French statute, but also that an award of damages against the French authorities can be made where damage is suffered as a consequence of non-compliance with EC law, clearly following the lead of the Court of Justice in the *Francovich* case.

Previously receiving no direct mention in the French Constitution, the European Communities and the European Union are now referred to in a new article 88. This was introduced as a result of the *Conseil Constitutionnel* ruling that the move into new policy areas under the Maastricht Treaty would be incompatible with the Constitution. It too, as with article 55, the original validation of Community membership and Community law within the French legal order, still requires **reciprocity**. As a result of the change to article 88 of the Constitution, the French Constitutional Court has declared, in Decision 2004/496 of 10 June 2004, that it will no longer review Community and now EU law in the light of the Constitution, save in relation to express elements, which is taken to mean those protecting fundamental rights.

. . . .

reciprocity

In this context, reciprocity means that in order for any international Treaty and also now the EU Treaties to be upheld and complied with in France, they must be upheld reciprocally by the other party or parties. Failure to comply by another party under the customary international law understanding of this principle would mean that France is itself no longer obliged to comply with the Treaty or the part of it not complied with.

. . . .

cross reference
See also Chapter 7, section 7.1.4.5, on defences to Commission enforcement actions.

Clearly, in a Union of twenty-seven states, this is not very practical; in any event, reciprocity was expressly excluded as a defence to a breach of EU law in Cases 90–91/63 *Commission* v *Belgium and Luxembourg* and C-146/89 *Commission* v *UK (Fishing Limits)*. However, despite the change to the Constitution and the rules more sympathetic to the supremacy of EU law, cases taking a less cooperative position are still being decided by the *Conseil d'État*. In *Compagnie Generale des Eaux*, the Court once again confirmed its earlier position of denying the direct effect of Directives when in conflict with a national administrative act.

143

5.3.4 **The Netherlands**

An original member state, the Netherlands was already part of an economic union (Benelux) with Belgium and Luxembourg, itself conceived and constituted by the governments of those countries in wartime London. At first, in the negotiations leading to the original Treaties, the Netherlands promoted the intergovernmental solution to community governance by the Council of Ministers, a view that gave way to more supranationalism as progress with the Communities was made and as the larger states of the EU exerted more their influence. Supranationalism was regarded as a better buffer against the re-emergence of nationalism.

The Netherlands is a monist country as far as international law is concerned, and the Dutch Constitution specifically recognizes and ranks international law. Article 93 of the Constitution provides that provisions of treaties and of decisions by international institutions may have direct effect in the Dutch legal system, and further that they take precedence over Dutch laws. This is backed up by article 94, which provides that some international rules of law take precedence over all other laws and that national statutory provisions that are incompatible with these rules do not apply. European law under these two articles takes precedence over all national law. As the member state giving rise to the leading case in EU law (*Van Gend en Loos*), one would expect the Netherlands not to have any difficulties with accepting EU law supremacy.

Up to the 1990s, though, the country had a poor record in the transposition of EU Directives; that record improved in that decade when administrative procedures changed.

The Dutch electorate, along with that of France in 2006, voted against the Constitutional Treaty, but there is no serious question that the Netherlands should withdraw from the EU.

5.3.5 **Denmark**

Together with the UK, Norway and Ireland, Denmark applied for membership of the EC in 1961 and 1967, but on each occasion de Gaulle vetoed British membership and Denmark did not wish to enter the Community without the UK largely because of their close trade relationship. As was noted in Chapter 1, entry negotiations were resumed after the summit meeting in The Hague in 1969, and from 1 January 1973 Denmark became a member, together with Ireland and the UK. This was preceded by a binding referendum in which 63.3 per cent voted in favour and 36.7 per cent against membership.

The Danish Constitution, s. 20(2), allows for the delegation of powers to international authorities by statute adopted by a five-sixths parliamentary majority or a simple majority in a popular vote if the former is not reached or not chosen by the Parliament, which has largely been the case in Denmark. Fundamental changes to the EU have been put to the electorate in binding referenda, with the following results:

- in 1986, 56.2 per cent voted for and 43.8 per cent against the Single European Act;

- in 1992, 49.3 per cent voted for and 50.7 per cent against the Maastricht Treaty;

- in 1993, 56.8 per cent voted in favour and 43.2 per cent against the Maastricht Treaty, with the opt-outs agreed in Edinburgh (including defence policy, the third phase of economic and monetary union and a common currency, union citizenship and in the judicial field);

- in 1998, 55.1 per cent voted for and 44.9 per cent against the Amsterdam Treaty; and

- in 2000, 53.1 per cent voted against and 46.9 per cent for Denmark's joining the Single European Currency, the euro, which of course then it did not join.

In contrast, Denmark ratified the Lisbon Treaty, without a prior referendum, by way of consent of the Danish Parliament under article 19 of the Constitution.

Denmark enjoys the dubious reputation, almost equal with the UK, of being the most Eurosceptic EU member state, although two of the 2004 EU entrant states (the Czech Republic and Poland) would clearly rival that honour, largely through the expressed views of their Presidents. However, as with the UK, Denmark also enjoys a positive track record of faithful implementation of EU laws and having very few, if not the fewest, infringement proceedings before the Court of Justice.

Turning briefly to the Danish courts, the Danish Accession Acts were challenged in *Carlsen et al.* v *Prime Minister Rasmussen* **6/4/1998, Case I 361/1997, [1999] 3 CMLR 854**, as providing too much power to the EC institutions and going beyond the transfer of powers authorized by the Danish Constitution, s. 20.

The Danish Supreme Court held that ratification of the TEU did not violate the Danish Constitution and that the transfer of powers under s. 20 was wide enough for the EU to act, including its perceived need to act under the general residual power of Article 308 EC (now 352 TFEU). However, two provisos were laid down: that power to adopt measures contrary to the Constitution cannot be delegated to international organizations; and that the national courts retain the power to review EU law in this light and to hold it inapplicable in the event of conflict.

In 1998, the Danish Constitutional Court considered that Community law might not be applicable in Denmark if the Community or Commission had breached its delegated powers and the issue was not satisfactorily then resolved by the Court of Justice, thus reflecting the reservation in other states such as Germany, Italy and Ireland.

cross reference
See Chapter 1, sections 1.4.1.5 and 1.4.1.6, for more on Sweden's member-ship entry process.

cross reference
Brunner *is considered at section 5.3.1.2.*

cross reference
This issue is, of course, one of the balance between the member states and the EU, also considered in respect of Chapter 3, section 3.4, on competences.

For more details on EU law (initial implementation and reception in the courts) scan here or visit the Online Resource Centre.

145

5.3.6 **Sweden**

Sweden joined the European Union on 1 January 1995, before which it had a free-trade agreement from 1972 and was a founding member state of the European Economic Area (EEA). Its applications in 1961 and 1967 for limited forms of membership were withdrawn consequent to the De Gaulle veto of the UK membership application. Sweden reapplied for membership in 1991. Much of the membership entry work had already been done in connection with the Agreement on the EEA of 1992; hence it was an easier process than might otherwise have been. Sweden is a dualist country and international agreements must be transformed into national law to have binding validity within Sweden, with the exception of the amendments made to the Swedish Constitution to provide for the Swedish Parliament, the *Riksdag*, to transfer decision-making rights to the EU as a whole.

Prior to entry, Sweden held a national referendum, in which a total of 52.3 per cent voted in favour and 46.8 per cent voted against membership in a high turnout of 83 per cent. Whilst not directly allowing for EU membership, the Constitutional provision, the *Regeringsformen*, does regulate aspects of membership such as elections to the European Parliament, approval of EU international agreements and reports to the *Riksdag* on EU matters and most importantly the transfer of powers. Such a transfer of power may not, though, affect the principles of the form of government nor lower the rights protections guaranteed by the Swedish Constitution or the ECHR (Chapter 10 *Regeringsformen*). Both elements were influenced by the German *Brunner* decision. In 2003, Sweden held a second referendum on EU integration, specifically whether to join the European monetary union, although the Swedish government had already decided not to join in prior to that. The vote result was a 'no' (56 per cent voted against and 42 per cent in favour) to Sweden introducing the euro as its currency, and it thus remains outside the eurozone. Note that it did not, though, negotiate an opt out from the euro, but merely decided that it would not join at present. The referendum result thus made it less likely that this would happen in the short-to-medium-term future.

The Swedish jurisprudence acknowledges the supremacy of Community and now EU law over statutes and the Constitution on the basis of a judgment of the Swedish Supreme Administrative Court in 1997, *Lassagård*, RÅ 1997, ref. 65 (there is no Constitutional Court in Sweden). However, as is the case with Germany, Italy and Denmark, with a strong provision for fundamental rights present in the Constitution that international treaties are expected to respect, it is theoretically and constitutionally possible that the Swedish courts may reserve application of EU law that does not respect those rights by reference to Swedish constitutional provisions or to the ECHR.

cross reference

Further details on EU law (initial implementation and reception in the courts) in the member states can be found in the articles listed in the end-of-chapter Further reading.

Summary

The Communities and now Union were established by a transfer of powers by the member states to enable them to act independently of those member states and to create their own laws and legal system, which was, of course, one of the reasons for establishing them in the first place. This chapter has considered the nature of the EU law that stems from this transfer of power, which is the question of supremacy or primacy of EU law, and then its reception in the member states.

A consensus appears to be emerging from the national and constitutional courts that EU law supremacy is accepted only in so far as it does not infringe the individual rights protection of the national constitutions, in which case the constitutional courts will exercise their reserved rights over national constitutions to uphold them over inconsistent EU law. Only a few states appear to be accepting EU law unconditionally, such as Belgium and the UK, which may be because their constitutions are more flexible, at least from the point of view of the judges. Whether it will ever come to a direct rejection of EU law supremacy by a national court is debatable. Perhaps more important is that such a direct rejection is probably avoidable if the Court of Justice is allowed to diffuse any possible conflict before the case reaches a constitutional court, if the question of conflict is first referred to the Court of Justice via the Article 267 TFEU preliminary ruling procedure. In view of the number of constitutional courts that appear to be reserving a power of review, this is something that the member states, the Union and the Court of Justice need to take seriously.

cross reference
This procedure is considered in Chapter 6.

Questions

For suggested approaches to answering these questions scan here or visit the Online Resource Centre.

1   Outline the reasons and logic provided by the ECJ in the *Costa* v *ENEL* and later judgments for the supremacy of EC (now EU) law over national law.

2   Is EU law supreme over any form of conflicting national law in the UK?

3   Would your answer be any different if a UK Act of Parliament were expressly to state that it was aware of a conflict with EU law, but that the Act shall nevertheless apply, or to contain an instruction to the judges that they shall nevertheless apply the UK Act and not set it aside in favour of EU law?

Further reading

BOOKS

Bulmer, S. and Lequesne, C. *The Member States of the European Union*, Oxford University Press, Oxford, 2005.

Claes, M. and de Witte, B. 'Report on the Netherlands' in A.-M. Slaughter, A. Stone Sweet and J. H. H. Weiler (eds) *The European Court and the National Courts: Doctrine and Jurisprudence – Legal Change in its Social Context*, Hart Publishing, Oxford, 1998.

House of Lords European Union Committee, *Strengthening National Parliamentary Scrutiny of the EU: The Constitution's Subsidiarity Early Warning Mechanism*, 14th Report of Session 2004–05, HL Paper 101, HMSO, London, 2005.

Lenaerts, K. and van Nuffel, P. *Constitutional Law of the European Union*, 3rd edn, Sweet & Maxwell, London, 2010.

ARTICLES

Albi, A. and Van Elsuwege, P. 'The EU Constitution, national constitutions and sovereignty: an assessment of a European constitutional order' (2004) 29 EL Rev 741.

Alonso Garcia, R. 'The Spanish Constitution and the European Constitution: the script for a virtual collision and other observations on the principle of primacy' (2005) 6(6) German Law Journal 1001, also available online at <http://www.germanlawjournal.com/index.php?pageID=11&artID=608>.

Beck, G. 'The problem of Kompetenz-Kompetenz: a conflict between right and right in which there is no praetor' (2005) 30 EL Rev 42.

Bursens, P. 'Why Denmark and Belgium have different implementation records: on transposition laggards and leaders in the EU' (2002) 25 Scandinavian Political Studies 173.

Craig, P. 'Sovereignty of the United Kingdom Parliament after *Factortame*' (1991) 9 YEL 221.

Craig, P. 'Constitutions, constitutionalism and the European Union' (2001) 7 ELJ 125.

Craig, P. 'The European Union Act 2011: locks, limits and legality' (2011) 48 CML Rev 1915.

Cygan, A. 'Democracy and accountability in the European Union: the view from the House of Commons' (2003) 66 MLR 384.

Dashwood, A. 'The relationship between the member states and the European Union/ European Community' (2004) 41 CML Rev 355.

Doukas, D. 'The verdict of the German Constitutional Court on the Lisbon Treaty: not guilty but don't do it again' (2009) 34 EL Rev 866.

Enchelmaier, S. 'Supremacy and direct effect of European Community law reconsidered, or the use and abuse of political science for jurisprudence' (2003) 23(2) OJLS 281.

Foster, N. 'The German Constitution and EC membership' [1994] Public Law 392.

Gaja, G. 'New developments in a continuing story: the relationship between EC law and Italian law' (1990) 27 CML Rev 83.

Hoffmeister, F. 'German *Bundesverfassungsgericht*: *Alcan* decision of 17 February 2000 – constitutional review of EC Regulation on bananas, Decision of 7 June 2000' (2001) 38 CML Rev 791.

Hoffmeister, F. 'Constitutional implications of EU membership: a view from the Commission' (2007) 3 CYELP 59.

Knook, A. 'The Court, the Charter and the vertical division of powers in the European Union' (2005) 42 CML Rev 367.

Kostakopoulou, D. 'Floating sovereignty: a pathology or a necessary means of state evolution?' (2002) 22(1) OJLS 135.

Kumm, M. 'The jurisprudence of constitutional conflict: constitutional supremacy in Europe before and after the Constitutional Treaty' (2005) 11 ELJ 262.

Manin, P. 'The *Nicolo* case of the *Conseil d'État*: French constitutional law and the Supreme Administrative Court's acceptance of the primacy of Community law over subsequent national statute law' (1991) 28 CML Rev 499.

Mastenbroek, E. 'Surviving the deadline: the transposition of EU Directives in the Netherlands' (2003) 4 European Union Politics 371.

Mouthan, F. 'Amending the amended Constitution' (1998) 23 EL Rev 592.

Oliver, P. 'The French Constitution and the Treaty of Maastricht' (1994) 43 ICLQ 1.

Posch, A. 'Community law and Austrian constitutional law' (2008) 2(4) International Constitutional Law 272, also available online at <http://www.internationalconstitutionallaw. net/download/0f3dad016fe3c63cc953e543de9f8d3c/Posch.pdf>.

Rosas, A. 'Finland's accession to the European Union: constitutional aspects' (1995) 1 European Public Law 166.

Roseren, P. 'The application of Community law by French courts from 1982 to 1993' (1994) 31 CML Rev 315.

Schmid, C. 'All bark and no bite: notes on the Federal Constitutional Court's "Banana Decision" ' (2001) 7 ELJ 95.

Thomson, R. 'Same effects in different worlds: the transposition of EU Directives' (2009) 16(1) JEPP 1.

Usher, J. L. 'The reception of general principles of Community law in the United Kingdom' [2005] EBLR 489.

Zetterquist, O. 'Sweden and the EU: constitutional aspects', 2010, available online at <http://www.oup.com/uk/orc/bin/9780199581597/01student/sweden/oup_sweden.pdf>.

Part 2

Procedural actions, enforcement and remedies in EU law

6

The preliminary ruling (Article 267 TFEU)

Learning objectives

In this chapter, you will learn:

- about procedural law in the European Union legal order;
- which procedural actions were provided by the Treaty;
- which remedies were developed by the Court of Justice;
- about Article 267 TFEU, the procedure that allowed them to be developed;
- the details of Article 267 TFEU references; and
- the roles and relationship of the European Court of Justice and the national courts under Article 267 TFEU.

Introduction

This chapter and the following three chapters are concerned with the procedural law of the European Union (EU) and how it is enforced, including the remedies available to ensure that EU law is upheld by the member states, by the Union institutions, or by legal and natural persons. The chapters include the actions provided by the Treaties, notably Articles 258–260, 267, 263, 265 and 340 TFEU (ex 226–228, 234, 230, 232 and 288 EC) and the remedies developed by the European Court of Justice (ECJ), notably direct effects, indirect effects and state liability.

This chapter provides a natural link between the last chapter on supremacy and Chapter 8 dealing with direct effects, as it concerns Article 267 TFEU (ex 234 EC), the vehicle that allowed the ECJ to introduce direct effects into the legal order.

cross reference
Both elements of this dual vigilance will be considered in Chapters 7 and 8.

The ECJ and the national courts are both involved in hearing cases in which EU law is pleaded and upheld. This position was made clear following the early intervention by the ECJ. It held that Community law was a matter not only for the member states and to be argued only before the ECJ, but also concerning individuals and giving them rights that they could argue before their own national courts. They did not have to rely on the Commission to enforce and argue Community law under the limited Treaty provisions for this, nor was Community law a matter reserved and to be heard before the ECJ only.

cross reference
Van Gend en Loos will be considered in Chapter 8, section 8.1.3.1, and in other chapters.

The case that establishes this is **Case 26/62 Van Gend en Loos**: it is the leading case in EU law.

This development led to the phrase 'dual vigilance' being coined, which describes the situation whereby, on the one hand, the Commission ensures EU law enforcement procedures against individuals, and, on the other hand, can pursue remedies for breaches of EU law by member states that affect their rights. Clearly, there being many more individuals in the EU than Commission officials, this increases the policing of EU law dramatically.

cross reference
These aspects will be considered in Chapter 8, section 8.4.

Allied to this development is a procedural device that was included in the EEC Treaty in 1957, to facilitate both the even development of the Community and now EU legal system throughout all of the member states, and to provide a link between the ECJ and the national courts faced with EU law from time to time. This is Article 267 TFEU (ex 234 EC), which became the vehicle by which the leading principles and remedies in Community and EU law were developed by the Court of Justice, including direct effects.

Additional means of contesting national laws were developed by the ECJ to provide remedies for individuals in circumstances in which direct effects did not exist. Of these, indirect effects and state liability are the most important. The system of remedies has developed so extensively that it has also made inroads into national procedural law: it had been witnessed how those national rules affect the equal application of EU law rights in the member states. Whilst the Treaty-provided remedies and actions precede the judicial developments of remedies, an understanding of the judicial developments is crucial; therefore it is dealt with before we consider the direct actions before the ECJ, with the exception of the enforcement actions against the member states. The other direct actions include the judicial review of EU acts, the review of a failure to act and the determination of liability of the institutions for damage caused by their acts.

cross reference
Judicial developments are dealt with in Chapter 8; enforcement actions are dealt with in Chapter 7; all of the other direct actions are considered in Chapter 9.

6.1 Article 267 TFEU: the preliminary ruling procedure

Article 267 TFEU (ex 234 EC) is the preliminary ruling or reference procedure, also referred to by the Article number (267 TFEU) by which the courts of the member states can refer questions to the Court of Justice on matters of EU law. A number of details of this procedure need to be considered to gain a true picture of how this works. The procedure provides the link or bridge between the national legal systems and the EU legal system. Under Article 267 TFEU, the courts of the member states may, or sometimes must, seek a ruling from the Court of Justice on the interpretation of all forms of EU law, including international treaties and recommendations, and on the validity of EU secondary legislation.

Article 267 TFEU

. . . .

The Court of Justice of the European Union shall have jurisdiction to give preliminary rulings concerning:

(a) the interpretation of the Treaties;

(b) the validity and interpretation of acts of the institutions, bodies, offices or agencies of the Union;

...

The main task of the Court of Justice is to interpret and rule on the validity of EU law so that a national court can reach a conclusion on a case involving EU law. The national courts' role in the process is to determine the facts of a case, ask a question of the Court of Justice when one arises and later, when the ruling of the ECJ has been sent back to the national court, apply the ruling to the facts of the case. The Court of Justice should not concern itself with the application of the ruling that it has made or advise the national court how to apply the ruling. It is to be noted that, within the national courts, it is the right of the national court to decide whether to refer a question and not an individual right of appeal.

cross reference

Considered in Chapter 9.

Article 267 TFEU has as its purpose the uniform interpretation and application of EU law in all of the member states and contributes to legal certainty by ensuring that EU law means the same thing in each and every member state – even more important now with a Union of twenty-seven member states. It was designed to work with the cooperation of national courts by providing the means whereby national courts would not give their own interpretations to EU law or decide themselves on its validity. The intended relationship was of equality and cooperation, rather than hierarchy or an appeal system; therefore the Court of Justice should provide only a guiding ruling and not direct the national courts. It provides for the sharing of jurisdiction over EU law between the Court of Justice and the national courts.

Article 267 TFEU (ex 177 EEC and 234 EC) was the instrument that allowed the Court of Justice to develop the doctrines of direct effects and supremacy, vital for the development of the system of remedies that have been so helpful to individuals, for example in getting round the restrictions placed on them by the strict *locus standi* requirements of the direct actions, or where the Commission has been slow in ensuring that the member states comply with their obligations under the Treaty-provided enforcement procedure Article 258 TFEU (ex 226 EC). See discussion in Chapter 7, Summary.

Having created such doctrines, the Court receives numerous questions specifically asking whether a particular provision has direct effects.

This section will continue with the issue of which national bodies can make references that will be accepted by the Court of Justice.

6.1.1 Which bodies can refer?

For more details on this section scan here or visit the Online Resource Centre.

The Court of Justice has accepted references from a varied number of bodies that are not courts in the strict sense, but which nevertheless decide legal issues based on EU law, including administrative tribunals, arbitration panels and insurance officers.

For example, it was clear from **Case 26/62 Van Gend en Loos** that not only judicial, but also administrative, tribunals were acceptable.

The determination of what is an acceptable court or tribunal is a question for the Court of Justice and is not dependent on national concepts. Certain criteria have now been established by which it may reasonably be determined whether a particular body may refer to the Court of Justice for guidance under Article 267 TFEU.

Whilst the majority of judicial or quasi-judicial bodies in the member states deciding legal matters pose no problem, it is those partially or entirely outside the state legal system that raise the question of whether they are suitable courts or tribunals for the purposes of Article 267 TFEU. The following cases have helped to define the scope of acceptable bodies.

In **Case 61/65 Vaassen**, a reference was received from the arbitration tribunal of a private mine employees social security fund. The Court of Justice held that because the powers to nominate members and to give approval to both the panel itself and rule changes were in the hands of a government minister and because the panel was a permanent body operating under national law and rules of procedure, it qualified as a court or tribunal in the eyes of Community law.

Case 246/80 *Broekmeulen* v *HRC* concerns a reference made by the Appeal Committee of the Dutch Medical Professions Organization. This was held by the Court of Justice to be acceptable because it was approved and had the assistance and considerable involvement of the Dutch public authorities, its decisions were arrived at after full legal procedure, the decisions affected the right to work under Community law and were final and there was no appeal to Dutch courts.

However, in the next cases, jurisdiction was refused.

In **Case 138/80 *Borker,*** a reference from the Paris Bar Association Council on the right of a French lawyer to appear as of right before German courts was refused on the ground that there was no lawsuit in progress and the Bar Council was not therefore acting as a court or tribunal called upon to give judgment in proceedings intended to lead to a decision of a judicial nature.

In **Case 102/81 *Nordsee* v *Nordstern***, a reference from a privately appointed arbitration body was refused despite the fact that the arbitrator's decision based on law, including Community law, was binding. The Court of Justice held that because there was no involvement of national authorities in the process, there was not a sufficiently close link to national organization of legal remedies and thus the arbitrator could not be regarded as a court or tribunal for Article 234 EC (now 267 TFEU).

Jurisdiction was also refused in **Case C-24/92 *Corbiau* v *Administration des Contributions*** because a reference had been made from the office of the Director of Taxation, a body that acted in both an administrative and judicial capacity and thus lacked sufficient independence to be regarded as a court or tribunal for the purposes of Article 234 EC (now 267 TFEU).

Case C-54/96 *Dorsch* is particularly instructive because the Court of Justice took an opportunity to spell out the criteria to be taken into account in deciding whether the body is an acceptable one, including:

- whether the body is established by law;
- whether it is permanent;
- whether its jurisdiction is compulsory;
- whether its procedure is *inter partes* – that is, between two parties;
- whether it applies rules of law; and
- whether it is independent.

More recently, in **Case C-53/03 *Syfait* v *GlaxoSmithKline***, a reference from a national competition authority was refused because of its close connection to the national executive and supervision by a government minister. The clear independence of the members of the authority was also questioned and the fact that, under Community competition law, the authority could be relieved of its competence to hear particular cases by the EU Commission.

In view of this case law, it would seem that it is not critical to acceptance if the body is private or there is not an appeal from its decision. A strong indicator is the level of involvement by national authorities. Whether all of these criteria will be strictly applied in all cases in the future is uncertain because the lack of an appeal in a case may lead to instances in which the national body itself has to interpret EU law without guidance if the Court of Justice is unwilling to accept jurisdiction, something that must be less than desirable from a EU point of view.

6.1.2 **Is the question relevant and admissible?**

For more details on this section scan here or visit the Online Resource Centre.

This section covers a number of connected issues all relating to whether the question raised by the member state body is one that is either relevant or not, or an admissible question as far as the Court of Justice is concerned. To a degree, the response to some of the questions sent to the Court of Justice by member state courts has varied according to the increase in the case load of the Court of Justice. The content and form of the question must also be decided by the national court and it is possible that this will also be considered by the ECJ.

Article 267 TFEU itself contains little guidance except to provide that if the member state court or tribunal considers that a decision on a question of EU law is necessary to enable it to give judgment, it may request a ruling from the Court of Justice. The relationship or partnership that is supposed to hallmark this procedure requires that, once requested, a ruling be given by the Court of Justice to complete the EU side of the procedure. Unfortunately, this is not always as clear-cut in practice and a question can arise as to who should really decide whether a preliminary ruling is necessary: the parties to the case, the national court or the Court of Justice. According to the letter of the Article 267 TFEU procedure, it is for the national court to decide to refer a question. The drafters of the Treaty did not envisage this system as providing an individual remedy; however, in practice it is often regarded as the initiative of one of the parties to request that a reference be made, but it remains the case that ultimately the national court has the right to decide.

This analysis continues to be the stated view of the Court of Justice as provided in **Case C-236/02 *J. Slob* v *Productschap Zuivel***, in which the Court held:

> It should be stated at the outset that it is for the national court alone to determine the subject matter of the questions which it wishes to refer to the Court. The Court cannot, at the request of one party to the main proceedings, examine questions which have not been submitted to it by the national court.

The initial approach of the Court of Justice is described as 'come one, come all' and it was happy to correct even improperly framed references to accept them.

For example, in **Case 16/65 *Schwarze* v *EVGF***, a court requested a ruling on the interpretation of Community law and the validity of national law in conflict. The Court of Justice concluded that the Court was concerned more with the validity of a Community act and it could therefore answer the question posed.

It has consistently refused to rule on the validity of national laws; however, it has often reformatted such a question in order to give an answer to the underlying reason for the reference, which is whether the EU law conflicts with the national law and which law should take priority.

Turning to further case law, the first of which cases should by now be familiar, according to the Court of Justice in **Case 26/62 _Van Gend en Loos_**, the finding by a national court that it needs to refer is not to be questioned by the Court of Justice.

This position was confirmed in **Case 6/64 _Costa_ v _ENEL_**, in which the Court of Justice held that it is a decision of the national court alone to judge whether a decision on the question is necessary for it to give judgment.

Furthermore, in **Case 106/77 _Simmenthal_**, the Court of Justice has declared that it was unable to review the facts of the case presented to it in the case – that is, it will not go behind the national decision. It also held in this case that, until a reference was withdrawn by the national court referring or if quashed by a national appeal court following an appeal against the order to refer, the Court of Justice would hear the case.

In a slight complication to that position is **Case C-210/06 _Cartesio Oktató és Szolgáltató_**, which concerns an appeal against an order to refer from a court in Hungary. In this case, the Court of Justice held that it would continue to hear the case unless withdrawn by the court making the reference and not the appeal court. The Court acknowledged that the appeal procedure against the order was a matter of national law, but that the Court of Justice itself would not take direct cognizance of that appeal decision.

157

On the face of it, it appears the Court of Justice is taking matters into its own hands; however, the judgment may be argued to be more in line with its previous stated positions, in that the Court of Justice will not go behind national decisions or procedures and will only react to the national court making the reference in the first place. The latter position is probably the correct one.

However, as the number of cases and backlog increased in the 1980s and 1990s, the Court of Justice was seen to be less willing to accept all references and has, from time to time, declined to give a ruling on questions referred to it on the grounds that no real question arises or that such references are an abuse or misuse of Article 234 EC (now 267 TFEU). This is not to say that it has operated a crude quota to cut down references, because the number of cases that were regarded as irrelevant or inadmissible is really minimal.

6.1.2.1 Rejected references: relevance, clarity and basic information

Certain cases have, nevertheless, been rejected by the ECJ, such as those lacking basic information needed for the Court of Justice to decide or in which information is not clearly conveyed to the ECJ.

In **Case 93/78 _Mattheus_**, a disputed contract's continuation was determinable by the entry of Spain, Portugal and Greece to the Community. When a reference was made to help to resolve the disputed contract, the Court of Justice held this to be a matter to be determined by the member states and the potential new states, and refused jurisdiction. The question raised must be one that is justiciable before the courts.

In **Case C-320/90** *Telemarsicabruzzo SpA*, the Court of Justice held that facts and issues must be sufficiently clearly defined. The reference, as with similar cases, was so poorly or inadequately formed or with such information lacking that the Court of Justice was unable to determine either exactly what the questions was or what the dispute was to which an answer would be helpful or how any possible answer would help.

In **Case C-83/91** *Meilicke* v *ADV/OGA*, the Court of Justice held that the questions raised could not be answered by reference to the limited information provided in the file, in which case the Court would be exceeding its jurisdiction in answering what was really a hypothetical question.

There is, in addition, a formal ground for refusing a judgment, following a change to the Rules of Procedure of the Court of Justice (Article 104(3)). The Court of Justice was given the authority to dispose of a case in which the question is manifestly identical to one already answered or can clearly be deduced from existing case law, but only, however, if the Court hears from the Advocate General (AG) first. It may decide also to consult the referring court for the observations of the parties. This was not used a great deal to start with, but use is increasing and the Court issued Guidelines in 1996, replaced in 2011 as the 'Information Note on references from national courts for a preliminary ruling, to the national courts to help them to decide whether a reference should be made. The Court's view is that it is up to the member states' courts to determine if they need a ruling and that the Court of Justice should answer such questions, however formed. References generally, however, should be clear and succinct, but sufficiently complete to give the Court of Justice a clear understanding of the factual and legal context of the main proceedings. National courts should explain why an interpretation is necessary in their view to enable them to give judgment. After another change to the Rules of Procedure, the Court may now, after hearing from the AG, seek clarification from the referring court if the question or issue is unclear (Article 104(5) Rules of Procedure).

6.1.2.2 No genuine dispute or an abuse of the procedure

There are two cases of special importance arising from the same sets of facts and underlying problem.

Case 104/79 *Foglia* v *Novello (No. 1)* concerned a contract for the purchase of wine between a French buyer Novello and the Italian supplier Foglia. Clauses stipulated that the buyer and the carrier (Danzas) should not be responsible for any French import duties that were contrary to Community law. These were, however, charged on the French border and subsequently reimbursed by Foglia. Foglia sought to recover from Mrs Novello, who denied responsibility to pay Foglia on the basis that the duties were illegally charged by the French authorities. The Italian judge made a reference to the Court of Justice asking whether the French tax was compatible with the Treaty. The Court of Justice rejected the reference on the grounds that there was no genuine dispute between the parties and that the action had simply been concocted to challenge French legislation. The Court of Justice considered this to be an abuse of the Article 234 EC (now 267 TFEU) procedure, particularly as there were remedies available to dispute the tax before the French courts. However, not satisfied by this, the Italian judge made a further reference.

In **Case 244/80 *Foglia* v *Novello (No. 2)***, the Italian judge specifically pointed out that the previous case marked a radical change in the attitude of the Court of Justice to a national court's decision to refer. He asked the Court of Justice to give guidelines on the respective powers and functions of the Court of Justice and the referring court. The Court of Justice held that its role was not to give abstract or advisory opinions under Article 234 EC (now 267 TFEU), but to contribute to actual decisions, and that although discretion is given to the national courts, the limits of that discretion are determinable only by reference to Community law.

thinking point

How does this conform with the previous statement that it is up to the national court to decide?

Whilst the *Foglia* case may be regarded as a rarity, it is not alone.

In **Case C-318/00 *Bacardi-Martini* v *Newcastle United***, a French law prohibiting the advertising of alcohol was at the centre of a dispute between Newcastle United and the advertisers whose products had been advertised at the home game of Newcastle and unlawfully broadcast in France. The Court of Justice dismissed the reference after seeking clarification from the English High Court as to why Community law would have a bearing on the case in which the law of another member state law was in question (alcohol advertising in France), but to which case English law was actually applicable. The Court of Justice concluded that it did not have sufficient material to make a ruling.

cross reference
This is considered in Chapter 9, section 9.1.2.

A refusal of jurisdiction on the grounds of it being an abuse of the procedure took place also in **Case C-188/92 *TWD Textilwerke***. A Commission decision addressed to Germany was not challenged within the two-month time limit under Article 230 EC (now 263 TFEU), but instead via the national court. The Court of Justice held this to be an abuse of the procedure for not acting within the time limit provided under the Treaty for a challenge to Community law.

The decision appears to have been reached in contradiction to the perceived promotion of Article 267 TFEU (ex 234 EC) as a vehicle for realizing individual rights in the face of the continued strict application of *locus standi* requirements under Article 263 TFEU (ex 230 EC).

The decision to refer is now assisted by the provision of the Court of Justice Guidelines issued in 1996 and updated in 2009 and 2011.

An order for a reference should include:

- a statement of the facts essential to a full understanding of the legal significance of the main proceedings;
- an exposition of the applicable national law;
- a statement of reasons for the reference; and
- a summary of the main arguments of the parties.

6.1.2.3 Acceptances nevertheless

The decision in *Foglia* v *Novello* has been cited as authority to the Court of Justice in subsequent cases as an argument that the Court of Justice should not hear the case.

> In **Case 46/80 *Vinal* v *Orbat***, which involved Italian law in Italy, the government claimed that the case was not admissible because it was just an excuse to challenge national law under Article 234 EC (now 267 TFEU). The Court of Justice, however, accepted the reference.

The distinction between the two cases was that, in the latter case, it was the national law of the case that was questioned and not the law of another member state.

> In **Case 14/86 *Pretore di Salo* v *X***, there were no actual proceedings between two parties (that is, the case was not *inter partes*), something regarded previously as one of the criteria needed to be classed as a court for the purposes of Article 234 EC (now 267 TFEU). The case involved investigative proceedings only of an Italian magistrate to determine whether a criminal offence might have been committed by a person or persons unknown in the case in which a river had been found seriously polluted. Nevertheless, when a question of a possible breach of Community law was referred to the Court of Justice by the magistrate, it was held to be admissible. The Court of Justice held that it was up to the national court to decide if a reference was necessary to help it.

> In **Cases C-297/88 and C-197/89 *Dzodzi* v *Belgium*** and **C-28/95 *Leur-Bloem***, the Court of Justice has given rulings in what were essentially purely internal matters involving the application of free movement of persons rules to nationals undertaking no cross-border movement, where the national decision was based on Community law. The Court of Justice considered that if it did not do so, Community law might be interpreted differently in the member states applying it in an internal situation; therefore, for the sake of uniformity, the reference was accepted.

6.1.3 **The question referred: an overall view**

Although these cases, and others like them, would appear to be contradictory, the case of *Foglia* v *Novello* must be viewed on its own merits. These were that the Court of Justice did not wish to encourage national courts to challenge the validity of the laws of other member states, especially when there existed the possibility of proceedings in the French courts to challenge the French law and from which an Article 234 EC (now 267 TFEU) reference could be launched if deemed necessary by the French judge. It may be summarized that the Court of Justice may decline to take a case under Article 267 TFEU in a number of situations, including those in which:

- the question referred is hypothetical;
- the question is not relevant to the substance of the dispute;
- the question is not sufficiently clear for any meaningful legal response; and
- the facts are insufficiently clear for the application of the legal rules.

cross reference
Considered in sections 6.1.6 and 6.1.7.

The cooperation between national courts and the Court of Justice still exists, but the Court of Justice no longer simply accepts anything put before it. It has begun to exercise more positive control over its own jurisdiction in a similar manner to superior national courts. This approach is reflected in the case law arising from Article 234(2) and (3) EC (now 267 TFEU).

6.1.4 A discretion or an obligation to refer?

Whether there is a discretion or an obligation to refer a question, once raised, depends first on which sentence of Article 267 TFEU applies. Article 267(2) TFEU states that any court may refer if it considers it necessary to reach a decision in the case, whereas Article 267(3) TFEU states that courts against the decision of which there is no judicial remedy shall bring the matter before the Court of Justice.

> **Article 267(2) and (3) TFEU**
>
> 2 Where such a question is raised before any court or tribunal of a Member State, that court or tribunal may, if it considers that a decision on the question is necessary to enable it to give judgment, request the Court to give a ruling thereon.
>
> 3 Where any such question is raised in a case pending before a court or tribunal of a Member State against whose decisions there is no judicial remedy under national law, that court or tribunal shall bring the matter before the Court.

6.1.5 The discretion of lower courts

161

Courts falling within Article 267(2) TFEU are not obliged to refer, but have a wide discretion to refer at any stage of the proceedings and in any sort of proceedings: see, for example, Cases 13/61 *De Geus* v *Bosch* and 29–30/62 *Da Costa en Schaake*. Part of the reasoning for this rule is that an aggrieved party can appeal to a higher court if a reference is not made.

cross reference
The further effects that the Article 267 TFEU (ex 234 EC) procedure and rulings have had on national procedural law will be considered further in Chapter 8, section 8.4.

In **Cases 146** and **166/73** *Rheinmühlen-Düsseldorf*, the Court of Justice made it quite clear that any national court that considers that a ruling on EU law will help it to decide an issue has the discretion to decide regardless of any national rules of precedent or referral.

This was confirmed by the Court in **Case C-312/93** *Peterbroeck Van Campenhout* **v** *Belgium*, in which the Court of Justice held that a national procedural rule, which prevented a national court from raising a matter of EC law of its own motion concerning the compatibility of a national law with EC law, was itself contrary to Community law and that national courts must set aside rules of national law preventing the Article 234 EC (now 267 TFEU) procedure from being followed.

cross reference
This case was considered in full in Chapter 5, section 5.3.2.6.

Case **C-213/89** *Factortame (No. 1)* also confirms this point that national law rules of any status must not prevent EU law from applying. In the case itself, a constitutional doctrine was involved.

6.1.6 **The timing of the reference**

For more details on this section scan here or visit the Online Resource Centre.

In principle, national courts can refer at any stage of the proceedings and in any sort of proceedings, as has already been noted in Cases 13/61 *De Geus*, 93/78 *Mattheus v Doego* and 14/86 *Pretore di Salo*.

> In **Cases 36/80 and 76/80** *Irish Creamery Milk Suppliers*, the Court of Justice advised that the optimum time would be when facts have been established and any questions involving national law only had been settled.

The Court of Justice has also provided extrajudicial guidelines about when a reference should be made if considered necessary. The 2011 replacement of the 1996 Court of Justice Guidelines, point 19, also recommends that the facts and legal context should be established and both parties' views heard before the reference is sent.

> **Court of Justice Guidelines 2011, point 19**
> . . . .
> It is, however, desirable that a decision to seek a preliminary ruling should be taken when the proceedings have reached a stage at which the national court is able to define the factual and legal context of the question, so that the Court has available to it all the information necessary to check, where appropriate, that European Union law applies to the main proceedings.

Allied to the topic of the timing of the reference are two special procedures, which have been developed by the ECJ to amend the Article 267 procedure in special circumstances. These are the accelerated or expedited procedure and the urgent procedure that are provided for under Article 23a of the Protocol on the Statute of the Court of Justice and detailed further in Article 104a and 104b, respectively, in the Rules of Procedure of the Court of Justice.

Under the accelerated procedure, a national court may request that this procedure be utilized where it is a matter of exceptional urgency and the case will be listed immediately, giving the parties fifteen days to submit observations. The President of the Court will decide on a proposal from the Judge-Rapporteur, after hearing the AG. Up to 2008, none were granted, but in 2008, two were granted, with an average time of 4.5 months from lodging the case to the ruling. In 2009–10, a further five were granted, averaging 2.1 months.

The urgent preliminary ruling procedure relates specifically to the areas of freedom, security and justice (now Title V TFEU) and was introduced to deal quickly with cases involving the detention of persons. In this route, the written procedure can be omitted or undertaken electronically. In 2008, three were heard, and in 2010, six; in both years, there was an average length of proceedings of 2.1 months. Whilst it is useful to know that these procedures exist, it is unlikely that you will need to know the details of the cases.

None of this impinges on the ultimate discretion of national courts provided by Article 267 TFEU to decide when to refer and which criteria are necessary to decide this question.

6.1.7 **Courts of last instance**

In this category, an initial problem exists in deciding which courts are courts of last instance for the purpose of Article 267(3) TFEU. The case law of the Court of Justice advises that the relevant court for Article 234(3) TFEU is the highest court for the case rather than the highest court in the member state.

cross reference

This case was also considered under supremacy in Chapter 5, section 5.1.1.

In **Case 6/64 *Costa* v *ENEL***, there was no right of appeal from the Italian magistrates' court because the sum of money involved was so small. The Court of Justice held that national courts against the decisions of which there is no judicial remedy must refer a question of Community law to the Court of Justice.

In most instances, this is an adequate answer and Article 267(3) TFEU should apply to those proceedings that deny an appeal or judicial review and thus become last instance. However, the situation in member states may not be so easy to determine: for example, in the UK, it was possible and has happened that the Court of Appeal and the House of Lords Appeal Committee (now the UK Supreme Court) can refuse leave to appeal in a case that has been decided by the Court of Appeal. This has the result that the lower of the two courts then becomes the court of last instance and results in a denial of the consideration of EU law to an applicant because the case itself has closed, cannot be reopened and cannot then be referred.

This happened in ***Magnavision* v *General Optical Council (No. 2)***, in which the issue of Community law was raised in the first case under this name, but was neither considered nor referred, nor was an appeal to the House of Lords allowed. The applicant then applied to the High Court stating that the previous refusal meant that the High Court became the court of last instance for the purposes of Article 234. This application was also refused on the grounds that the case had been closed and the High Court refused to refer this question to the Court of Justice, thus denying a consideration of Community law points.

The same situation occurred when the Court of Appeal and the House of Lords refused leave to appeal in ***Chiron Corporation* v *Murex Diagnostics Ltd (No. 8)***, which meant that the Court of Appeal became the last-instance court. Once again, it was too late for a reference to be lodged because the case had been decided and appeals can be lodged and considered only once the case has finished, a point expressly acknowledged by the House of Lords Appeal Committee in the case.

 Note now the reformed court structure in the UK.

The Court of Justice had also recognized this problem in the Swedish case **99/00 *Criminal Proceedings against Lyckeskog***. It suggested that, in such circumstances, the Supreme Court considering the appeal should consider whether a reference might be necessary and thus be sympathetic to the application to seek leave to appeal.

In order both to overcome the unfortunate earlier UK position and to take account of the *Lyckeskog* case, in the UK a change of the appeal procedure was deemed necessary and put into place.

For more details
on this section
scan here or
visit the Online
Resource Centre.

6.1.8 Avoiding the obligation to refer: the development of precedent and *acte clair*

Whilst Article 267(3) TFEU provides the general rule that final courts must refer, over the years the large increase in cases referred to the ECJ led to a closer consideration by the Court of Justice as to the appropriateness of a reference. In two cases, spanning a period of twenty years, the Court of Justice has outlined the circumstances in which it is not necessary to make a reference. This has arguably introduced a form of precedent to the EU legal order and may have brought about changes to the relationship between the national courts and the Court of Justice. The Court of Justice has held that it is no longer necessary to make a reference where the provision in question has already been interpreted by the Court of Justice or the correct application is so obvious as to leave no scope for any reasonable doubt. In the latter case, the view is that no question of EU law arises to be decided; hence there is no need to refer.

6.1.8.1 There is a previous ruling on the point

Cases 28–32/62 *Da Costa* raised the same question as had previously been asked in *Van Gend en Loos*. The Court of Justice referred to its previous judgment in *Van Gend en Loos* as the basis for deciding the issue and advised that such a situation might, if the national court wished, excuse the obligation to refer.

See also, now, the Rules of Procedure of the Court, Article 104(3), which confirms the position stated in *Da Costa*. See also Point 12 of the Article 267 TFEU Guidelines, which makes the same point. For example, in 2008, twenty-two cases were ordered to be removed from the Register.

6.1.8.2 The answer is obvious (*acte clair*)

The judgment by the Court of Justice in Case 283/81 *CILFIT* extended the decision in *Da Costa*.

In **Case 283/81 *CILFIT***, the Italian Supreme Court, from which there was no appeal, asked the Court of Justice directly in what circumstances it need not refer. The Court of Justice replied that, in addition to the reason given in *Da Costa*, a court might not refer if the correct application, but not interpretation, may be so obvious as to leave no scope for any reasonable doubt that the question raised will be solved.

This has introduced into the EU legal system a variation of the French law doctrine of *acte clair* by which a lower court need not refer a case to a higher court if it thinks that the application of law is obvious. In the EU context, this is translated as a national court need not make a reference if it considers the answer to the question on EU law to be obvious. That, however, is not an entirely accurate representation of the judgment in *CILFIT*, which is more restrictive than a straightforward application of *acte clair*. The Court of Justice qualified it by stating that the national court must be convinced that the matter is equally obvious to courts of other member states, that it is sure that language differences will not result in inconsistent decisions in member states and that EU law must be applied in light of the application of it as a whole with regard to the objectives of the EU. These criteria would be extremely difficult to fulfil if properly followed, especially now in a Union of twenty-seven member states. The judgment was, however, arguably provided so as to maintain an appearance of the bridge of equality between EU and national legal systems.

The 1996 Guidelines, as replaced in 2011, in point 12, are clear in describing the court's policy as *acte clair*, although not expressly, and the required restrictive interpretation of it remains.

6.1.8.3 Questions of validity

A question of the validity of secondary EU law must be referred to the Court of Justice.

> In **Case 314/85 *Firma Foto-Frost* v *Hauptzollamt Lübeck-Ost***, the Court of Justice held that national courts could not decide for themselves that Community law provisions were invalid.

If this question were raised and an answer not possible from previous judgments, then national courts were obliged to refer the question to the Court of Justice. If an appeal is still possible under national rules, this could still be done as an alternative.

This point has been written into the Court of Justice Guidelines, points 15–17.

> However, in **Case 66/80 *ICC***, which involved the questioning of a Community provision that had already been declared invalid by the Court of Justice in a previous case, the Court of Justice makes it patently clear that although such a judgment is addressed primarily to the court that requests the original ruling, it can and should be relied on by other national courts before which the matter arises, thus obviating a need to refer the same question again.

> More recently, the point has been confirmed in **Case C-461/03 *Schul*** that only the Court of Justice has the authority to declare Community law to be invalid and further in **Case C-344/04 *IATA*** that a national court is not obliged to refer a question of validity on the argument of one of the parties unless the court itself is sure that a good case for invalidity has been made.

6.1.8.4 Use of *acte clair* by the national courts

To some extent, the fears that *acte clair* will be abused by national courts has been realized in some cases that have come to light.

> In ***R* v *London Boroughs' Transport Committee***, decided in 1992, the House of Lords refused to refer a question to the Court of Justice, claiming that the European Community (EC) law was obvious, which, on the facts, appeared arguable.

> In 1998, a Greek court, the Council of State, itself interpreted EC law (then Article 126(1)) in the case of ***Katsarou* v *Greek State*** against the interests of an applicant seeking mutual

recognition of qualifications. As far as the Greek court was concerned, the EC was regarded as *acte clair*, thus removing any obligation to refer.

In **Case C-62/00 *Marks & Spencer plc***, the Court of Appeal in the UK considered that individuals could rely on the direct effect of sufficiently precise and unconditional Community law provisions only if, and in so far as, the provision had not been properly implemented in national law. If a Directive had been properly implemented, as in the case, but perhaps applied not in the way intended by the Directive, the Directive could not be relied on. However, the Court of Justice held that it would be inconsistent with the legal order of the Community if individuals were able to rely on a Directive that had been incorrectly implemented, but not to be able to rely on it where the national authorities applied the implementing legislation in a way that was incompatible with the Directive.

These cases appear to result in injustice to the litigants affected. This denial of rights may be the price to be paid now for having a more flexible arrangement under Article 267 TFEU.

The attempt to obtain a remedy where a reference was denied has, thus far, not been successful.

In Austria, in **Case C-224/01 *Köbler***, the Austrian Supreme Administrative Court had decided a point of Community law itself relating to the recognition of time spent and experienced gained in another member states. The Austrian court claimed it to be clear after withdrawing a reference to the Court of Justice seeking a ruling on the same point. The applicant in the case then sought damages from the Austrian state for the loss that he had suffered as a result of the decision in the first case, which he claimed to be contrary to Community law. On a reference in the second case, the court of Justice held that the Community law at that point was not clear and that the Austrian court was not entitled to take the view that the matter was clear. However, the Austrian court's infringement for the purposes of the state liability action was not sufficiently serious for the Court of Justice and Köbler lost his claim. However, the ECJ did make it clear that a state could be held liable for an incorrect judgment where the breach was sufficiently serious and stated that the Austrian court, from which there was no appeal, should have made a reference and should have applied it. Generally, the Court of Justice held that courts of last instance must make references in order to prevent rights conferred on the individual by Community and now EU law being infringed.

As such, the judgment may represent a refinement of the *acte clair* principle in the EU legal order by removing its availability to courts of last instance. Confirmation of this is needed, however, from the Court of Justice before this can be stated with certainty.

The final case in this section appears to represent some further movement in favour of aggrieved applicants.

cross reference
The action against a member state for a breach of Community law is also considered under Francovich *state liability in Chapter 8, section 8.3.*

In **Case C-173/03 *Traghetti del Mediterraneo SpA* v *Italy***, it was alleged that a company had been forced into liquidation as a result of the errors in the interpretation of Community law undertaken by the Supreme court in Italy. Furthermore, the chance to correct those errors was denied by that court, which did not make a reference to the ECJ. In a further action by the administrator of the company, the Court of Justice held that it could not rule out that 'manifest errors' by a national court would lead to compensation under the principle of state liability. However, it was up to the national courts to decide in each case.

The consequence of this slight extension of liability is that liability for damage caused by courts is not limited as in *Köbler* to 'intentional fault and serious misconduct' in cases in which that standard would have excluded liability for 'manifest infringement'. In other words, it extends liability to where national courts have manifestly infringed the law in their interpretation, thus causing damage.

6.2 The effect of an Article 267 TFEU ruling

For more details on this section scan here or visit the Online Resource Centre.

cross reference

See Chapter 9, section 9.1.9.

cross reference

For example, see the cases relating to the definition of the term 'worker' in Chapter 12 on free movement of persons.

6.2.1 The effect on the Court of Justice

In strict terms, in the absence of a system of binding precedent in the EU legal order, a ruling by the Court of Justice is binding and effective in that case only and there is no further binding effect on the Court of Justice. However, although it is not restrained by any doctrine of precedent, the Court of Justice tends to follow previous decisions to maintain consistency and will cite previous judgments or parts of a judgment as a basis for a current decision.

In this way, a development and build-up of legal principles as in common law countries does take place. In other circumstances, the Court has been known to overrule previous decisions without much commotion when it feels that the situation warrants it.

> In Article 340 TFEU (ex 288 EC) actions for damages, see **Case 25/62 *Plaumann*** and the later overruling **Case 4/69 *Lütticke***, which decided that an Article 288 EC (now 340 TFEU) action could be mounted as an independent action and not only if preceded by Article 230 EC (now 263 TFEU) action to annul.

> The *Plaumann* case was later confirmed as good precedent in **Cases C-50/00 *UPA*** and **C-263/02 P Commission v Jego-Quere**.

The Court of Justice, however, has appeared to move in the direction of setting up a system that certainly starts to resemble a system of precedent.

6.2.2 The effect on the national courts

An Article 267 ruling is a mandatory judgment and not an advisory opinion. It was held in Case 69/85 *Wünsche* to be fully binding on the national court. A ruling of the Court of Justice is then to be treated in each member state according to how its own system of law regards authoritative judgments. As far as the UK is concerned, national courts are bound under Treaty obligations to apply the ruling received from the Court of Justice to the facts of the case and, where that court is the Supreme Court, the ruling is consequentially binding on all lower courts: see Case 12/81 *Garland* v *BREL*.

The Article 267 TFEU (ex 234 EC) Guidelines, point 31, provide that the Court of Justice wishes to see that its judgment has been applied in the national proceedings and, to that end, must be sent a copy of the national court's final decision.

> From the UK, there is now an informative case in which the national court judge refused to apply the ruling of the Court of Justice because he considered the Court of Justice to have gone beyond its jurisdiction in making findings of fact in a case concerned with trade mark infringement of football merchandise. However, **Case C-206/01 *Arsenal FC* v *Matthew Reed*** was overruled on appeal by the Court of Appeal and the ruling of the Court of Justice was applied conscientiously.

There have been times when the Court of Justice has limited the temporal effect of a judgment, especially when the result of a judgment would have given rise to previously unforeseen extensive and probably harmful economic consequences.

cross reference

Both of these rulings will be considered in further detail in Chapter 14.

> For example, in **Cases 43/75 *Defrenne (No. 2)*** and **C-262/88 *Barber***, the judgments were held not to be retroactive, but only effective from the date of judgment or for claims already commenced, because they would unexpectedly have imposed on employers potentially substantial payouts for numerous backdated claims based on the rulings.

> The Court of Justice held, in **Case 66/80 *ICC***, that although a declaration of invalidity was directly addressed to the referring court only, it was sufficient reason for another court to regard the declaration as generally binding; however, the discretion to refer remains.

> In **Case C-453/00 *Kühne and Heitz***, the Court of Justice stated that the demands of one of the general principles of Community law, namely legal certainty, obliged all state authorities to apply the interpretative rulings of the Court of Justice from preliminary rulings in their activities.

Whilst not expressly stated, clearly included in this are the national courts, which, of course, have so much to do with the application of EU law in their activities.

6.3 The evolution of Article 267 TFEU references

Article 267 TFEU has allowed the Court of Justice to develop a system of remedies because cases referred from the national courts are those predominantly brought to the courts by individuals whose rights have been infringed by the member state authorities. The remedies developed include direct effects, indirect effects and state liability, which can be secured in the member state's courts so that subsequent cases need not be referred to the Court of Justice. The increase in cases and increasing case backlog is argued to have led to a change in attitude on the part of the Court of Justice and it is now less willing to accept all references without question. It has, in a limited number of cases, provided the national courts with the grounds for not making a reference when, under a strict reading of the Treaty, a reference would be required. As a result of the development of this system of remedies and judicial devices to avoid references, a form of precedent (the *Da Costa* case) appears to have been introduced. This means that a Court of Justice ruling now has a far more general importance than only for the parties in a single case and appears to have placed the Court of Justice at the apex of the systems of national courts.

Inevitably, this also appears to have changed the nature of the relationship from a symbiotic or horizontal one more to a vertical or hierarchical one, although some might describe the original understanding of a relationship of equals and cooperation as somewhat illusory. These developments have given rise then to what can be described as a form of conscious, or deliberate, sectoral delegation of responsibility over EU law to the national courts. The national courts then become enforcers of EU law in their own right in cases in which there exists a Court of Justice precedent on which to rely. Hence a more hierarchical relationship than was ever intended by the drafters of the Treaty or the member states has ensued. This view is supported by the change to the Court's Rules of Procedure (Article 104(3)), which allows the Court of Justice to return cases with a reasoned order where a question is identical to a question on which the Court has already ruled, where the answer to such a question may be clearly deduced from existing case law or where the answer to the question is not open to reasonable doubt. It sends a clear signal to the national courts that they too could have reached the same conclusion, thus strengthening further the evolution of the Article 267 TFEU procedure. A part of this evolution is the *acte clair* development, although this has caused some concern, especially when it is abused by member state courts, which results in injustice to individuals who are denied their EU law rights. The *Köbler* and *Traghetti del Mediterraneo* cases appear to narrow the scope for the application of the doctrine to last-instance courts.

6.4 Reforms and future

In the context of the growing numbers of references, many reforms have been considered and changes suggested. Apart from those most recently made (including the foregoing case law changes), which include the expansion of the General Court (formerly the Court of First Instance) jurisdiction to include Article 267 TFEU references and the ability to set up specialized courts (formerly judicial panels), further suggestions for reform include:

(a) limiting the national courts able to make a reference by removing the right of first-instance courts to refer;

(b) only allowing novel or complex cases – that is, those involving new questions of law;

(c) permitting national courts to make suggestions as to the answer;

(d) permitting national courts to decide themselves subject to an appeal to the Court of Justice; and

(e) setting up regional EU courts, again with an appeal to the Court of Justice.

The last two suggestions represent a much more radical shake-up of the system and seem very unlikely in the short-to-medium term, especially in the light of the fact that, during the development of the Lisbon Treaty, there was a clear opportunity to change things radically, which it did not do.

The Lisbon Treaty made a limited amendment to Article 267 worth noting here. A new paragraph is included:

> If such a question is raised in a case pending before a court or tribunal of a member state with regard to a person in custody, the Court of Justice of the European Union shall act with the minimum of delay.

This gives Treaty status to the 2008 supplement to the Court of Justice' Guidelines on preliminary rulings, and the urgent reference procedure.

See section 6.1.6.

6.5 Interim measures within an Article 267 TFEU reference

Interim measures may also be highly relevant to EU law questions that are the subject of a reference to the Court of Justice, particularly as a reference may take on average some seventeen months. In that time, the lack of relief may lead to great damage and in many cases the insolvency of the companies involved.

The clearest and leading case on this is **C-213/89 _Factortame_**, in which the Court of Justice held that, regardless of national rules on whether interim relief should be granted, if rights under Community law were at stake pending a ruling on a reference on the substantive question, then interim relief should be granted.

cross reference
This case is dealt with in Chapter 7.

Cases C-143/88 and 92/89 _Zuckerfabrik Süderdithmarschen AG_ involved the possibility of granting interim relief in a preliminary ruling on the validity of a Community law provision. The Court of Justice took the opportunity to provide guidelines for the national courts along the lines of those developed already by the Court of Justice under its Article 243 EC (now 279 TFEU) jurisdiction in direct actions. It held that relief should be granted only provided that there was sufficient evidence before the Court that serious doubts existed about the validity of the Community law in question, the case was urgent, and relief was necessary to avoid serious and irreparable damage.

cross reference
The effect on national procedural law is considered in further detail in Chapter 8, section 8.5.

Interim relief grant was extended to positive, rather than only suspensory, measures in **Case C-465/93 _Atlanta Fruchthandelsgesellschaft_**, which concerned whether a licence to import bananas be granted whilst awaiting the ruling on whether a Community Act regulating the banana market was valid. The Court of Justice held that national courts could do this provided that they did so in the light of existing Community case law, the Community interest in the matter, and the consequences for the Community regime and the effect on all interested parties.

Hence, then, a common rule has been established that is nevertheless subject to national legal procedure, but only to the extent that the EU law right is not endangered.

Summary

Article 267 TFEU is a simple, but effective, device that fulfils a number of tasks. It provided the link between the Court of Justice and the national courts so that they could each play their own roles and cooperate to ensure the uniform interpretation and application of EU law throughout the Union. For the most part, each has stuck to its own role and the link has worked very well. From time to time, but really very rarely, there has been some overstepping of the mark, such as national courts not doing as they should, as in the *Köbler* or *Arsenal* v *Matthew Reed* cases, or arguably the Court of Justice in *Foglia* v *Novello*. As was stressed a number of times, because Article 267 TFEU (ex 234 EC) provided the ECJ with many references from the national courts, it was able to develop remedies that the Treaties did not and has thus enhanced greatly the shape of the EU legal system.

cross reference
These will be considered in Chapter 8.

Over the years, cases have built up examples of best practice and these have been drawn together in the Court of Justice Guidelines issued in 1996 and revised to 2011.

Finally, the nature of the reference procedure has changed from one clearly between equals to one that now provides a form of precedence, which must mean that the ECJ has taken on something of the role of a higher legal authority. It may also be that when the Union was established, the ECJ was only one amongst seven highest courts; now, it is one amongst twenty-eight and, for that, stands out much more than before. Presently, there are no further plans formally to change radically either Article 267 TFEU or the workings of it, so the slow development that has been observed is likely to continue.

Questions

For suggested approaches to answering these questions scan here or visit the Online Resource Centre.

1   What are the benefits of the Article 267 TFEU preliminary ruling procedure for the development of EU law?

2   Is there a restriction on the bodies that may refer under Article 267 TFEU?

3   In what way, if at all, has the use of Article 267 TFEU led to a system of 'precedence' being developed in the EU legal order?

4   Can you define the circumstances in which the ECJ would refuse to accept a reference under the Article 267 TFEU preliminary ruling procedure?

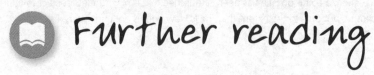

Further reading

BOOKS

Broberg, M. and Fenger, N. *Preliminary References to the European Court of Justice*, Oxford University Press, Oxford, 2010.

Douglas-Scott, S. *Constitutional Law of the European Union*, Longman, Harlow, 2002 (chapter 9).

ARTICLES

Anagnostaras, G. 'Preliminary problems and jurisdiction uncertainties: the admissibility of questions referred by bodies performing quasi-judicial functions' (2005) 30 EL Rev 878.

Biondi, A. 'The ECJ and certain national procedural limitations: not such a tough relationship' (1999) 36 CML Rev 1271.

Bobek, M. 'Learning to talk: preliminary rulings, the courts of the new member states and the Court of Justice' (2008) 45 CML Rev 1611.

Edwards, D. 'The preliminary reference procedure: constraints and remedies', Paper delivered at the CCBE/College of Europe Colloquium *Revising the European Union's Judicial System, Assessing the Possible Solutions, Revising the Preliminary Ruling Mechanism*, Bruges, 19–20 November 1999.

Komarek, J. 'In the court(s) we trust? On the need for hierarchy and differentiation in the preliminary ruling procedure' (2007) 32 EL Rev 467.

Tridimas, G. and Tridimas, T. 'National courts and the European Court of Justice: a public choice analysis of the preliminary reference procedure' (2004) 24 Intl Rev L & Econ 125.

Tridimas, T. 'Knocking on heaven's door: fragmentation and defiance in the preliminary reference procedure' (2003) 40 CML Rev 9.

Treaty enforcement actions against member states

Learning objectives

In this chapter, you will consider the enforcement actions that may be taken against a member state, including:

- Article 258 TFEU (ex 226 EC) actions by the Commission;
- Article 260 TFEU (ex 228 EC) sanctions;
- Article 259 TFEU (ex 227 EC) actions by other member states;
- Articles 278–279 TFEU (ex 242–243 EC) interim measures; and
- alternative actions to direct action.

Introduction

cross reference
Noted in Chapter 6, Introduction.

This chapter considers the actions brought against the member states that are commenced before the Court of Justice and which focus on the actions by the Commission and other member states. As a possible part of such actions, interim measures under Articles 278–279 TFEU (ex 242–243 EC) are also be considered. These direct actions against the member states to ensure compliance with Community and now European Union (EU) law were the first part of the system of dual vigilance enforcement of Community and EU law. They were provided from the outset in the EEC Treaty, but are not regarded as being particularly efficient, although improvements have been made. Breaches of member states' obligation to comply with EU law, which is imposed generally now by Article 4(3) TEU (ex 10 EC), are officially established by the Court of Justice following a procedural action against the state. Article 258 TFEU is the basis for Commission action against member states for failures to fulfil obligations under the Treaties, and in doing so the Commission is acting under its Article 17 TEU duty as the guardian of the Treaties to ensure that the Treaties and other EU measures are complied with.

Article 259 TFEU (ex 227 EC) additionally provides for actions by one member state against another member state. Furthermore, in support of both these actions, Article 260 TFEU (ex 228 EC) imposes an obligation on member states to comply with judgments of the Court of Justice. This was revised by the Maastricht Treaty (TEU) and now provides a system of penalties that can be imposed on member states, which will be considered towards the end of this chapter.

7.1 Enforcement actions by the Commission

For more details on this section scan here or visit the Online Resource Centre.

In contrast to other international organizations, the EU has a much more effective control mechanism under Article 258 TFEU to ensure compliance with its own laws by member states.

Article 258 TFEU

If the Commission considers that a Member State has failed to fulfil an obligation under the Treaties, it shall deliver a reasoned opinion on the matter after giving the State concerned the opportunity to submit its observations. If the State concerned does not comply with the opinion within the period laid down by the Commission, the latter may bring the matter before the Court of Justice of the European Union.

In addition to the action under Article 258 TFEU, there are further actions that the Commission can take against the member state in respect of specific subject matters, including Article 108(2) TFEU (ex 88(2) EC) in respect of infringements of state aids provisions, Article 114(9) TFEU (ex 95(9) EC) in respect of derogations from the internal market and Articles 346–348 TFEU (ex 296–298 EC) in respect of emergency security measures, none of which will be covered in any further detail in this volume.

7.1.1 **What constitutes a breach**

Article 258 is silent as to what constitutes a breach of a duty. The Court of Justice has determined that a breach can be constituted not only by an act of a member state, but also by the failure to act by a member state. A failure to act is most often seen in the form of a member state failing to implement EU legislation, mainly Directives, or failing to remove national legislation that is in conflict or inconsistent with EU legislation. Other breaches are that a member state has implemented the Directive incorrectly – deliberately or inadvertently – or, that the implementation was incomplete or considerably delayed. Apart from the general good faith clause under Article 4(3) TFEU (ex 10 EC) and Article 18 TFEU (ex 12 EC), the duty not to discriminate on grounds of nationality, there are more specific duties under the various Chapters of the Treaty and the very detailed duties imposed by secondary legislation. Thus breaches may arise from the Treaties, secondary legislation, international agreements, decisions of the Court of Justice and general principles. There are numerous examples of breaches by a member state to be found in the chapters of this book.

Failure to remove inconsistent legislation constitutes a breach even if the authorities no longer apply the national legislation and apply the EU rules in preference.

> For example, in **Case 167/73 Commission v France**, provisions of the French Maritime Code restricted the numbers of foreign workers on French vessels, but the French authorities pleaded that the national law was not being applied. The Court of Justice held that this law, even if it is not being applied, might influence the behaviour of people who rely on the law being applied and thus its non-repeal would create uncertainty.

cross reference

This case is also considered under the free movement of goods in Chapter 11, section 11.2.1.1.

> In **Case C-265/95 Commission v France**, France was held to be in breach of Treaty obligation when its enforcement authorities did nothing to prevent criminal damage to imported Spanish strawberries as a part of a protest by French farmers. The Court of Justice held that doing nothing or little to prevent other persons from restricting the movement of goods when action could and should have been taken would constitute a breach of obligation.

7.1.2 **Identifying and reporting breaches**

A possible breach can come to light as a result of the Commission's own investigations or from the failure of the member states to notify how they have implemented EU law as they are now required to do under secondary legislation. See the following example from Directive 2002/14.

Article 11 Transposition

. . . .

(1) Member States shall adopt the laws, regulations and administrative provisions necessary to comply with this Directive not later than 23 March 2005 or shall ensure that management and labour introduce by that date the required provisions by way of agreement, the Member States being obliged to take all necessary steps enabling them to guarantee the results imposed by this Directive at all times. They shall forthwith inform the Commission thereof.

(2) Where Member States adopt these measures, they shall contain a reference to this Directive or shall be accompanied by such reference on the occasion of their official publication. The methods of making such reference shall be laid down by the Member States.

---

cross reference

This will be considered in Chapter 9.

Breaches can be reported by other member states, the European Parliament, or concerned or affected individual citizens or companies. Note that, with regard to these last, they are unable to force the Commission to do anything about a complaint that has been lodged. In 2010, the Commission reported that 35 per cent of cases arose from its own initiative.

cross reference

This case is also discussed in section 7.1.4.1.

> See **Case 247/87 *Star Fruit Company* v *Commission***, in which a company's attempt to use the Article 232 EC (now 265 TFEU) omission to act proceedings to try to require the Commission to take action against France was firmly rejected by the Court of Justice. It held that the Commission was not bound to take action, but had the discretion to do so or not.

The Article 258 TFEU action was not intended to be an individual remedy, so whilst complaints might have been welcomed by the Commission, that right to make a complaint was as far as an individual's interest in the matter formally extended. The Commission is not under an obligation to act on a complaint, nor is it even required to inform the complaining individual of what, if anything, was being done. Although the formal position of an individual in the matter has not changed, the Commission publicizes its progress much more widely than before, usually by issuing notices in the Official Journal (OJ).

It is worth noting that the Lisbon Treaty made no change to this procedure.

7.1.3 **Defendants in an Article 258 TFEU action**

A breach of EU law can arise from any part of a state and is not restricted to purely governmental action or inaction.

> For example, in **Case 77/69 *Commission* v *Belgium (Belgian Wood)***, the government pleaded that it should not be held responsible for the negligence of the Belgian Parliament, which, being out of session, was not able to implement a Community Directive in time. The Court of Justice held that 'Obligations arise whatever the agency of the state whose action or inaction is the cause of the failure to fulfil its obligation even in the case of a constitutionally independent institution'.

Thus the member states are responsible for breaches caused by actions of the legislature, the executive, and local and regional authorities. It could include breaches by the judiciary in a member state for rendering an incorrect decision or for a failure to make an Article 267 TFEU reference to the Court of Justice, although no such action has ever commenced. However, with recent developments to the state liability actions, this is arguably now more possible.

cross reference

See the discussion of this in Chapter 8, section 8.4, and Case C-99/00 Lyckeskög, *in Chapter 6, section 6.1.7, which prompted the Commission to commence an Article 226 EC (now 258 TFEU) action for the Swedish court's failure to refer, although the action was dropped when Swedish practice was amended.*

In **Case C-129/00 *Commission v Italy***, the failure to repeal a law that was interpreted by the Italian courts in such a way as to make a Community law right excessively difficult to realize was held by the Court of Justice to be a breach on the part of the Italian state.

In **C-265/95 *Commission v France (Spanish Strawberries)***, the actions by individuals in disrupting fruit and vegetable imports, against which the French authorities effectively did nothing, rendered the state in breach of Community law.

7.1.4 **The procedure of an Article 258 TFEU action**

Article 258 TFEU requires certain informal and formal stages to be completed before the matter can be brought to the Court of Justice.

7.1.4.1 The informal or administrative stage

The first part of Article 258 TFEU states that, 'If the Commission considers that a Member State has failed to fulfil an obligation under this treaty, it shall deliver a reasoned opinion on the matter'. This means that the Commission must have reached a conclusion that the member state is probably in breach of an obligation before it can commence an action before the Court of Justice. Having formed a view during the pre-procedural investigations and discussions with member state officials in what are described as 'package meetings' that a state has breached its obligations, the Commission will inform the state by letter and give the state the opportunity to answer the allegation or to correct its action or inaction before the formal procedure of Article 258 begins. In view of the discretion that the Commission enjoys, there is no obligation on it to take action. Individuals who complain or who are concerned have been held by the Court of Justice not to be able to force the Commission to take action.

In **Case 247/87 *Star Fruit Company v Commission***, the Court of Justice held that the Commission was not bound to commence the proceedings under Article 258 TFEU, but has a discretion that excludes the right for individuals to require that institution to adopt a specific position. (See also **Cases 48/65 *Lütticke* v *Commission*** and **246/81 *Bethell* v *Commission*.**)

Each year, the Commission prepares a report on the application of Union law, which provides statistics for the number of cases being investigated and numbers for each of the stages of Article 258 actions which will be used to illustrate the following sections. The formal part of the procedure consists of two distinct phases, prior to any court action that may ensue in the judicial stage.

7.1.4.2 Letters of formal notice

Not every suspicion of infringement by the Commission will result in the initial formal letter of notice being sent to the member state.

The 2008 Monitoring Report noted that over 3,400 complaints and infringement procedures were being handled, but that 68 per cent were settled before the formal stage had commenced and that 94 per cent had been settled prior to the Court of Justice giving a ruling.

Whilst, at this stage, the process is informal, it is nevertheless absolutely necessary as a prerequisite for the formal process should the member state fail to take action or correct the alleged breach.

In **Case 274/83 *Commission* v *Italy***, the initial letter was held to be essential for the commencement of proceedings before the Court.

In 1985, the Commission sent out 503 formal letters (1,016 in 1995 and 1,552 in 2003) stating its point of view. Generally, about half of the instances in which a formal notice has been issued are settled at that stage, although this figure varies from year to year. Despite a rise to twenty-five member states in 2006, there was a reduction of formal letters sent out to 1,536, but this was expected to rise. In 2010, with twenty-seven member states, there were 1,168 formal notices.

These letters simply seek a response from the member state and do not automatically lead to the next stage, the reasoned opinion, or the litigation stage.

7.1.4.3 The reasoned opinion

Following the reply from the member state to the formal notice or after the time given by the Commission for an answer, which is usually two months, and during which no reply has been received, the Commission will deliver a reasoned opinion that records the reasons for the failure of the member state. This is delivered to the member state and also provides a further time limit within which the member state is required to bring the alleged infringement to an end. Many of the original complaints are settled informally during this stage. The reasoned opinion is confidential and cannot be obtained by third parties during the course of investigations or where the Commission exercises its discretion and decides not to proceed further against a member state (see, for example, Cases T-105/95 *WWF* and T-191/99 *Petrie*). The Commission often publishes the reasoned opinion, however, along with the rest of the case paperwork after Court of Justice judgments.

The resulting number of reasoned opinions in 1985 was 233 (192 in 1995, 533 in 2003 and 680 in 2006). There were 488 in 2010.

In **Case 39/72 *Commission* v *Italy (Slaughtered Cows)***, the Court of Justice determined that if the state should fail to comply with the reasoned opinion of the Commission within a reasonable time, or as stipulated by the Commission (normally two months), the Commission then has the right, which is still discretionary, to bring the matter before the Court of Justice, specifying its grounds for action.

In terms of the total number of cases each year, about 90 per cent will have been solved by the end of this stage and about 10 per cent only of the original cases will be referred to the Court of Justice. The figures – 107 cases were brought in 1985, 72 in 1995, 215 in 2003 and 189 in 2006 – bear this out. The 2008 Monitoring Report put the percentage at 94 per cent settlement prior to the judicial stage; 2010 saw no break in the trend, with 120 referrals to the Court of Justice, which was about 10 per cent.

7.1.4.4 The judicial stage

The final stage of the procedure is action before the Court of Justice and its judgment, which is merely declaratory. After the judgment, the state is required under Article 228 TFEU to take the necessary measures to comply. Only about 5 per cent of cases reach final judgment.

In 1985, twenty-three cases were removed from the Court's register prior to judgment, the member states having complied with Community obligations, thus judgments rendered by the Court in 1985 were only twenty-six, seventy-two in 1995, eighty-six judgments in 2003 and ninety in 2006. More up-to-date statistics appear on an annual basis in the Court of Justice Annual Report.

The Court of Justice can proceed to judgment even if the member state has complied with the Commission's reasoned opinion, but did so outside the set time limit.

In **Case C-240/86 *Commission* v *Greece***, the Court held that the Commission action remained admissible despite compliance and that the Court of Justice was still entitled to establish the breach.

This is important in that it allows the Commission to establish exactly what the law is or to set a precedent to control other member state behaviour. Equally, the existence of national proceedings, as in Case C-508/03 *Commission* v *UK*, is not a reason to hold the Commission action as inadmissible, as was confirmed by the Court of Justice.

cross reference

This established the individual claim of state liability considered in Chapter 8, section 8.3.

In **Case 22/87 *Commission* v *Italy***, the breach declared by the Court of Justice was the basis for imposing liability on the state in **Cases C-6 and 9/90 *Francovich***.

Presently, there is approximately a seventeen-month delay in the Court hearing enforcement actions, but if the matter is very important, the Court is able to speed up the case. Where such a delay would cause severe difficulties, it is possible for the Commission to request and the Court to order interim measures. Interim measures are considered in section 7.2.

Enforcement actions by the Commission

7.1.4.5 Defences raised by the member states

The member states have raised various defences, often acceptable in international law, but without success in the EU legal order, to justify their non-compliance with obligations. Of the more common are the following.

Force majeure or overriding necessity was raised in **Case 77/69 Commission v Belgium (Belgian Wood)** in which the Belgian government pleaded that the dissolution of Parliament and the separation of powers had forced the failure to implement an EC Directive.

In **Case 101/84 Commission v Italy**, a data-processing centre had been bombed, which might have actually allowed the defence of *force majeure* to be used if it were not for the fact that the delay in implementing it was four-and-a-half years – far too long for the Court.

Community measures being the cause of political or economic difficulties were raised by the UK in **Case 128/78 Commission v UK (Tachographs)** in which the UK pleaded that the cost and interruption to industry of fitting tachographs in lorry cabs would cause extreme difficulties.

In **Case 7/61 Commission v Italy**, Italy claimed that it could take action in the case of an emergency, but this could be done only if expressly sanctioned by the Commission, which, in the case, it was not.

The claim that direct effects had been established by the Court of Justice in another case was not a defence against infringements proceedings for Germany in **Case 29/84 Commission v Germany** on the grounds that there was no need to implement because individuals were already able to enforce the EC law in the national courts.

In **Cases 90–91/63 Commission v Belgium and Luxembourg**, the member states raised reciprocity, arguing that they were justified in not complying because the Council had failed to act, and in **Case 232/78 Commission v France**, France considered itself justified on the basis that other member states had not complied with their obligations.

Likewise, arguments that a conflicting national law is not in fact applied or that the administrative practice is in compliance, as in **Case 167/73 Commission v France**, also fail.

A threat to public order pleaded by France in **Case C-265/95 Commission v France (Spanish Strawberries)** was also rejected.

About the only defence that will work, given the robust dismissal by the Court of Justice of virtually all other defences raised, is that the Commission erred on the facts or in law – that is, that there was no breach. The Commission success rate is about 95 per cent.

7.2 Suspensory orders and interim measures

One of the criticisms of the Article 258 TFEU procedure is the length of time that it takes to secure a judgment. This is about eighteen months at present in terms of the formal judicial stage of proceedings, but which does not take account of the informal stage, which can extend the whole process by years. During this time, a member state's breach can cause considerable economic hardship and damage to individuals affected by it. In order to overcome these, the Court of Justice may order a contested act to be suspended under Article 278 TFEU (ex 242 EC), or in any case before it, the Court may proscribe necessary interim measures under Article 279 TFEU (ex 243 EC), both of which have been ordered occasionally in Article 258 actions.

> ### Article 278 TFEU
> ....
> Actions brought before the Court of Justice shall not have suspensory effect. The Court of Justice may, however, if it considers that circumstances so require, order that application of the contested act be suspended.

> ### Article 279 TFEU
> ....
> The Court of Justice may in any cases before it prescribe any necessary interim measures.

A case for the requested measure must specifically be made; interim measures must be requested prior to final judgment and applied only in urgent circumstances. Interim measures are not in any strict sense a direct sanction, but they can nevertheless have the effect of rectifying the alleged breach until it has been determined by the Court of Justice whether the conflicting national legislation should be removed.

> In **Case 53/77 Commission v UK (Pig Producers)**, the UK was ordered to halt subsidies to pig producers until the Court could decide whether the scheme was compatible with the rules of the Common Market.

> In **Case 293/85 Commission v Belgium (University Fees)**, the Court ordered Belgium, under Article 243 EC, to allow access on equal terms to other non-Belgian Community nationals to vocational training in Belgian universities when non-Belgians were asked to pay enrolment fees.

It also made an interim order in **Case 61/77 R Commission v Ireland (Irish Fisheries)** for Ireland to cease certain fishing measures that the Commission claimed were contrary to Community fishing rules.

In all three cases, the member states complied immediately.

In **Case C-195/90 Commission v Germany**, the Court ordered that a special road tax for lorries be suspended pending the outcome of the Commission Article 226 EC (now 258 TFEU) action against Germany. In response, Germany had requested a security undertaking from the Commission, in case the Commission's application was not upheld, but this was judged not to be justified by the Court of Justice.

In the **Factortame** litigation, **Case 246/89R Commission v UK**, the Commission requested and was granted the suspension of the alleged incompatible UK laws that were causing, and would have caused further, considerable economic damage to the Spanish fishermen in the UK. It was very notable in that case that the UK did not comply with the order without delay.

For more details on this section scan here or visit the Online Resource Centre.

cross reference
These are considered in section 7.3.1.1.

7.3 The application and effect of judgments

Other international tribunals are unable to enforce their judgments against miscreant member states, for example the International Court of Justice (ICJ) at The Hague or the European Court of Human Rights (ECtHR) in Strasbourg. The best that can really be achieved is the issue and discussion of a report on the failure or breach whilst waiting for political pressure to bear on the state concerned. In the EU legal order, the initial judgment of the Court of Justice is only declaratory and carries no specific sanctions. This actually stands in contrast with its greater powers of suspension at the interim stage.

7.3.1 Article 260 TFEU

The member states are nevertheless placed under a further obligation under Article 260 TFEU (ex 228 EC) to comply with the judgment by taking the necessary measures. If they do not do this, a further action may lie against them by the Commission for a further breach, but this time of Article 260. This has taken place a number of times prior to the TEU reforms, but only on nine occasions up to 2010.

The leading instance of this is **Case 48/71 Commission v Italy (Second Art Treasures Case)**. The Commission discerned that because Italy had not complied with the Court's

This unsatisfactory situation without ultimate sanction to encourage compliance can allow
matters to drag on, as, for example, in cases against France for the same infringement that
spanned twenty years. These and other cases prompted the member states to reform Article
228 EC (now 260 TFEU).

7.3.1.1 Sanctions under Article 260 TFEU

The TEU amended Article 228 EC (now 260 TFEU) to enable the Court of Justice to fine
member states for breaches of EU law. The Commission must give the state the opportunity
to submit its observations, but does not need to issue a further reasoned opinion on the
continued failure, as was previously the case prior to the Lisbon changes. The Commission
must state a time limit for compliance, which, if the member state fails to meet it, will allow
the matter to be referred to the Court of Justice, which may ultimately levy the fine. Article 261
TFEU (ex 229 EC) provides that the penalties will be determined by regulations to be adopted
by the Council and a penalty calculation system was established by the Commission whereby
it will state what penalty, if any, it considers appropriate. The basic penalty is fixed at €630
per day multiplied by factors reflecting the gravity and duration of non-compliance and the
financial situation of the member state. This figure will be adjusted for inflation every three
years. The penalty can be levied in the form of a lump sum or periodic payment. Following
Case C-304/02 *Commission v France*, the Court of Justice held that it can be both a lump sum
and a periodic payment fine. The penalty will apply from the date of judgment in the action
and not from the date of original non-compliance, although the Court has discretion to set the
dates. In Cases C-278/01 *Commission v Spain*, C-304/02 *Commission v France* and C-369/07
Commission v Hellenic Republic, the Court set a date after the date of judgment; hence member states have the chance to minimize the penalty. However, following Case C-304/02, the
penalty can penalize a state for the time taken to comply with its obligation. Only nine cases
to 2010 have resulted in fines being imposed.

Commission's suggestions in respect of fines. France was thus fined €57.76 million penalty per six months of continuing breach and a lump-sum fine of €20 million.

Following this case, the Commission has issued new communications on fines.

There has, in fact, been a further case in which a fine was requested, but not imposed by the Court of Justice.

In **Case C-212/99 *Commission* v *Italy***, the Commission's request for a fine was turned down by the Court of Justice because the previous breach had in fact been corrected in a timely manner by Italy and the Court was of the view that a fine would serve no useful purpose.

The Lisbon Treaty adopted the Constitutional Treaty's plan to remove the need for the second reasoned opinion under Article 260 TFEU when seeking a penalty fine in the limited circumstance of when a member state had failed to notify the transposition of a Directive. This appears to mean that the Commission can therefore request the fine in the initial Article 258 action without the need for the declaratory judgment first and the secondary Article 260 action, presumably on the basis that the failure to notify is self-evident. This will certainly speed up the process of judicially establishing the second breach and levying a fine. According to the 2008 Monitoring Report, these cases represent approximately 50 per cent of all enforcement actions.

7.4 Actions brought by one member state against another

Article 259 TFEU (ex 227 EC) is the basis for an action by one member state against another, when one member state considers another to have breached an obligation under EU law.

Article 259 TFEU

. . . .

A Member State which considers that another Member State has failed to fulfil an obligation under the Treaties may bring the matter before the Court of Justice of the European Union.

Before a Member State brings an action against another Member State for an alleged infringement of an obligation under the Treaties, it shall bring the matter before the Commission.

The Commission shall deliver a reasoned opinion after each of the States concerned has been given the opportunity to submit its own case and its observations on the other party's case both orally and in writing.

> If the Commission has not delivered an opinion within three months of the date on which the matter was brought before it, the absence of such opinion shall not prevent the matter from being brought before the Court.

As Article 344 TFEU (ex 292 EC) obligates the member states not to pursue other methods of dispute resolution other than that provided by the Treaty, member states are thus obliged to use Article 259 TFEU to resolve differences under EU law, although this is not always observed to the letter of the law. It must be noted, however, that the use of Article 259 TFEU by the member states has been minimal. The preference is almost exclusively to request the Commission to take action under Article 258 TFEU. The member states have full *locus standi* in relation to Article 259, which means that they do not have to have a specific interest in bringing an action, although the member states in those few cases that have been brought have had a particular interest. The procedure is set out in the following sections.

7.4.1 The involvement of the Commission

Before an action can take place, the member state must bring the matter before the Commission, which will ask both states to submit their observations and will then deliver a reasoned opinion on the matter. The Commission seeks to bring about a solution before Court action is necessary and may even intervene to take over the action, as it did in Case 232/78 *Commission v France*, which commenced as an action by Ireland against France, or as it did in Case 1/00 *Commission v France*, which was commenced by the UK under Article 227 EC (now Article 259 TFEU) and concerned the French measures that continued after the Commission UK beef export ban had been lifted.

7.4.2 Complaining state may then refer the matter to the Court of Justice

If a settlement or solution is not reached at this stage and three months has elapsedm or if the Commission fails to submit an opinion by three months of being informed of the matter, the member state can take the matter before the Court. Judgment has been reached, up to the date of writing, in only five actions. For example:

In **Case 141/78** *France* **v** *UK*, France successfully challenged the UK's unilateral fishery conservation measures.

The second case brought to judgment under Article 227 is **Case C-388/95** *Belgium* **v** *Spain*, in which Belgium, without the support of the Commission, failed in its action to challenge the use of the *Rioja* designation as an impediment to the free movement of goods.

The third case taken to judgment is **Case C-145/04** *Spain* **v** *UK*, which concerned the voting rights of citizens of Gibraltar, and is thus very much tied in with the political dispute between Spain and the UK over the continued British claim to ownership of Gibraltar. Spain had objected to the UK extending the European Parliament voting franchise to Gibraltarians, as required to do under an ECtHR ruling. The ECJ found in favour of the UK.

These rare cases aside, member states usually prefer to ask the Commission to bring actions under Article 258 TFEU because this is a less politically obvious and contentious manner in which to secure compliance of EU law in the interests of the member state concerned. The states can continue with friendly relations whilst the Commission investigates and pursues the action is warranted.

Additionally, under Article 273 TFEU (ex 239 EC), member states may agree to refer any dispute relating to the subject matter of the Treaty to the Court of Justice for adjudication, which appears never to have been employed, presumably because a complaint to the Commission is a better alternative.

7.5 Alternative actions to secure member states' compliance

The alternatives will be considered in more detail in the next chapter, but it is appropriate to mention such actions here because they are equally, if not a great deal more, effective in ensuring compliance with EU law obligations by member states. They include actions where individuals point to the breach of an EU obligation or duty by a member state as a defence against prosecution by that member state, or where they seek to challenge national rules that operate against their interest. The doctrine of direct effects additionally places the policing of EU law in the hands of private individuals, who often have more reason and thus more incentive to bring actions than the Commission officials. Individuals may benefit by their actions, as well as help to bring about compliance by member states, parallel to Article 258 actions.

> In **Case 152/78 Commission v France (Advertising of Alcoholic Beverages)**, it was held that a French ban on advertising foreign spirits was discriminatory and contrary to Community law. France failed to remove its legislation and prosecuted an importer for advertising. Waterkeynm the advertiser, referred to the previous judgment as a defence.

> In the follow-up **cases 314–316/81 Procureur de la Republique v Waterkeyn**, it was held that individuals could rely on such past judgments as a defence to protect their rights.

cross reference
Considered in Chapter 8, section 8.3.

In addition, there are possibilities for individuals to sue a state for loss caused by a breach of EU law, previously established in an Article 226 EC (now 258 TFEU) action against the member states, under the state liability principle established first in the case of *Francovich*. This will also play a strong part in encouraging member states to comply with EU law obligations if they find themselves having to pay out significant damages in an increasing number of cases. More recent case law on state liability shows that it is not necessary for an enforcement action by the Commission to have already demonstrated a breach, although it would always be helpful if that were the case.

Summary

For more details on this section scan here or visit the Online Resource Centre.

cross reference

See the Further reading listed at chapter end for some of this literature.

The biggest criticism of the Articles 258–260 TFEU procedures remains the time taken to reach judgment and it is certainly the case that the entire process is upward of two years; if all of the informal stages are counted, it can be four or more years. However, if due consideration is given to the fact that the vast majority of cases are solved before judgment, then a truer picture is gained on how effective the procedures can be. The other major criticism is the lack of any rights of individual complainants to the Commission. Whilst reform of the Article 258 procedure has been discussed in both academic literature and by the European Ombudsman in favour of making the process more supportive of the individuals who bring complaints, this so far has fallen on deaf ears where the member states are concerned. There was a minor, but possibly significant, amendment to the procedure in the Constitutional Treaty and carried on into the Lisbon Treaty, removing the need for the second Commission action under Article 260 in actions against a member state for the initial breach and also now for failing to notify how Directives had been implemented. This will certainly speed up the enforcement actions that have progressed as far as the second stage involving the possibility of fines against the member state. However imperfect, the procedures nevertheless provide a means whereby, ultimately, member states may find themselves before the ECJ for a breach for which they can be fined. The actions and processes do help to uphold EU law.

Questions

For suggested approaches to answering these questions scan here or visit the Online Resource Centre.

1 What arguments have been raised by the member states in defence of Article 258 TFEU infringement proceedings against them? What success did they meet?

2 What remedies will an individual have, in circumstances in which he or she has called upon the Commission to act under Article 258, and the Commission has declined to do so?

3 Why is Article 259 TFEU so infrequently used?

4 How effective are the actions under Articles 258 and 259?

Further reading

BOOKS

Douglas-Scott, S. *Constitutional Law of the European Union*, Longman, Harlow, 2002 (chapter 12).

Hartley, T. *The Foundations of European Community Law*, 6th edn, Clarendon Press, Oxford, 2007 (chapter 10).

ARTICLES

Harlow, C. and Rawlings, R. 'Accountability and law enforcement: the centralised EU infringement procedure' (2006) 31 EL Rev 447.

Ibáñez, A. J. G. 'Exceptions to Article 226: alternative administrative procedures and the pursuit of member states' (2000) 6 ELJ 148.

Kilbey, I. 'Financial penalties under Art 228(2) EC: excessive complexity?' (2007) 44 CML Rev 743.

Kilbey, I. 'The interpretation of Article 260 TFEU (ex 228 EC)' (2010) 35 EL Rev 370.

Mastroianni, R. 'The enforcement procedure under Article 169 of the EC Treaty and the powers of the European Commission: *quis custodiet custodes*?' (1995) 1 EPL 535.

Prete, L. and Smulders, B. 'The coming of age of infringement proceedings' (2010) 47 CML Rev 9.

Rawlings, R. 'Engaged elites: citizen and institutional attitudes in Commission enforcement' (2000) 6 ELJ 4. This is a very good comprehensive article.

Wenneras, P. 'A new dawn for Commission enforcement under Articles 226 and 228 EC: general and persistent (GAP) infringement, lump sums and penalty payments' (2006) 43 CML Rev 31.

Remedies: direct and indirect effects and state liability

Learning objectives

In this chapter, you will learn about the remedies developed by the European Court of Justice, concentrating on the following issues:

- direct applicability and direct effects;

- direct effects of Treaty Articles, Regulations, Directives, Decisions and international agreements;

- the distinction between vertical and horizontal direct effects;

- the problems resulting from this distinction and solutions to resolve them;

- expanding the concept of the state;

- indirect effects;
- the principle of state liability; and
- the impact on national procedural law.

Introduction

This chapter considers the remedies that have been developed by the European Court of Justice (ECJ). It was relatively early in the life of the Union that the Court of Justice was presented with cases in which individuals were confronted with two sets of laws applicable to their situation – one national and the other European Community (EC) law – but which conflicted in some way. As will be seen in the series of cases that follow in this chapter, the very significant starting point for this development was that the Court of Justice held that Community law concerned not only the member states, but also directly concerned individuals. From this relatively simple concept, the doctrine of direct effects arose. This development was, however, just the starting point for the development of a number of remedies that contribute to the system of dual vigilance, including, most notably, indirect effects and the principle of state liability. In addition, this chapter will consider the concept of direct applicability, found now in Article 288 TFEU (ex 249 EC), to distinguish it from direct effects. This chapter will provide an explanation and review of the development of the doctrine of direct effects through thorough case law. It will include the problems generated by this development in certain circumstances.

cross reference

Dual vigilance is considered briefly in the introduction to Chapter 6.

190

cross reference

Both direct applicability and direct effects are also considered in the next section.

direct effects

Direct effects (in the plural) is the way in which this term was first introduced by the Court of Justice in Case 26/62 *Van Gend en Loos* and, for this reason, is used throughout in this work. 'Directly applicable' is the term found in Article 288 TFEU (ex 249 EC, originally 189 EEC), primarily relating to an individual form of legislation possessing certain characteristics, but direct applicability is also used to describe generally the process whereby international law become directly applicable without separate implementation into domestic law.

 8.1 # Directly applicable and direct effects

8.1.1 Definitions and the distinction between directly applicable and direct effects

These two elements of the European Union (EU) legal system and the distinction between them are fundamental to the study and understanding of EU law. The doctrine of direct effects is a

For more details on this section scan here or visit the Online Resource Centre.

judicial development of the Court of Justice. It is connected and very often confused with direct applicability; however, there are fundamental differences between the two concepts. Direct effects plays a central role in the EU legal order because of its link with the application and enforcement of EU law in the courts of the national legal systems. It is therefore very much related with the supremacy of EU law. Unfortunately, the terminology of the Court of Justice and many of the national courts has not always been consistent. This has without doubt added greatly to the difficulty in understanding these concepts. Very often, the courts do not use the term 'direct effects', but describe a provision of EU law as directly applicable, but in the sense that the provision gives rise to rights enforceable by individuals before the national courts. Thankfully, such confusing use of terms is less frequent these days. Direct effects was sometimes considered to be a sub-concept of directly applicable, such that direct applicability was a prerequisite for direct effects, but that is not the case, as will be demonstrated by the cases that follow.

> The Court of Justice has spoken of Regulations that are directly applicable, but which by their very nature can have direct effects, in **Case 131/79 *Santillo*** , which suggests that this is automatically the case.

> In **Case 9/70 *Grad*** , the Court of Justice stated that the ability of an individual to invoke a decision before a national court leads to the same result as would be achieved by a directly applicable provision of a Regulation, again as if to suggest that the concepts are the same, hence the confusion and the need for clarification. The *Grad* case also involved a Directive, which, combined with the decision, gave rights to individuals. The case, though, is cited generally to support the result that it is not only Regulations because of their direct applicability that can give rise to direct effects and that other forms of EU binding laws, but also Directives and decisions.

8.1.2 **Directly applicable**

'Directly applicable', a term previously recognized in international law, should be used to describe the way in which some provisions of EU law have legal validity in the member states. It is therefore a mode of incorporation of law that is generally or universally binding. In the EU context, it a concept of EU constitutional law that describes the process by which Regulations become directly applicable without separate implementation under domestic law.

'Directly applicable' is specifically mentioned in Article 288 TFEU (ex 249 EC) in relation to Regulations.

The term 'self-executing' is also often used to describe such law, in that the legal provision itself establishes its validity in the host state.

Regulations

A Regulation shall have general application. It shall be binding in its entirety and directly applicable in all member states.

The member states are obliged not to transform Community **Regulations** into national legislation, except where necessary under the Regulation: see Cases 39/72 *Commission* v *Italy (Slaughtered Cows)* and 128/78 *Commission* v *UK (Tachographs)*. In the latter case, the UK, by not putting into place the necessary administrative procedures for the enforcement and monitoring of tachographs, was held to be in breach of the obligations imposed by the Regulation. They become law, usually as specified when published or if not specified, twenty days after publication.

The term applies also in respect of Treaty Articles because these satisfy the criteria of directly applicable law by their automatic validity in the member states following the ratification of the Treaty. The Treaty Articles themselves are not actually transformed into national law and they are generally binding in that they also obligate individuals and not only the member states.

8.1.3 **Direct effects**

'Direct effects' is the term given to judicial enforcement of rights arising from provisions of EU law that can be upheld in favour of individuals in the courts of the member states. Provided that certain criteria are satisfied, an EU law provision will give rise to a right that is enforceable by individuals in the national courts. Whereas directly applicable applies only to Regulations and Treaty Articles, direct effects have been declared by the Court of Justice in a series of cases in respect of Treaty Articles, Regulations, Directives, decisions and provisions of international agreements to which the Union is a signatory.

8.1.3.1 Treaty Articles

The first and leading case in which this doctrine was established is **Case 26/62 *Van Gend en Loos***, which concerned the increase of a customs tariff by the Dutch authorities allegedly contrary to Community law, old EEC Treaty Article 12 (now 30 TFEU), which provided:

member states shall refrain from introducing between themselves any new customs duties on imports or exports or any charges having equivalent effect, and from increasing those which they already apply in their trade with each other.

In the *Van Gend en Loos* case, the defendant customs authority argued that because the Treaty Article was addressed to the member state, it could not be enforced by individuals against the state. In support of this view, the Belgian, German and Dutch governments and even the Advocate General (AG) argued that the correct way in which to enforce the Treaty obligation was by formal action by the Commission under the Treaty (ex Article 169 EEC, now 258 TFEU) or by another member state, but not by individuals. The Court of Justice rejected this view and held that the Community had been endowed with sovereign rights, the exercise of which affects not only member states, but also their citizens, and that Community law was capable of conferring rights on individuals that become part of their legal heritage and enforceable by them before the national courts. It held that the provision (ex Article 12 EEC) was suited by its nature to produce direct effects.

To be capable of direct effects that are enforceable in the national courts, a Treaty provision must satisfy the criteria established by the Court of Justice.

In the words of the Court in **Case 26/62 *Van Gend en Loos***, these were:

The wording of Article 12 contains a clear and unconditional prohibition which is not a positive but a negative obligation. This obligation, moreover, is not qualified by any reservation on the part of states which would make its implementation conditional upon a positive legislative measure enacted under national law. The very nature of this prohibition makes it ideally adapted to produce direct effects in the legal relationship between member states and their subjects.

The implementation of Article 12 does not require any legislative intervention on the part of the states.

These criteria, repeated in many cases since, have been summarized in the following general terms – that the Community (and now EU) law provision in question must:

(a) be clear and precise;

(b) be unconditional (for example, as to time limits);

(c) not require implementing measures to be taken by member states or Community (and now Union) institutions; and

(d) not leave any discretion to member states or Community (and now Union) institutions.

cross reference

This is dual vigilance, previously considered in the Introduction to Chapter 6.

The Court of Justice thus enabled private parties to defend their rights arising in Community (and now EU) law in the face of inconsistent or contrary national law. In doing so, it added to the system of enforcement of EU law by empowering individuals to take action that would have the result of enforcing EU law in situations in which a member state had failed to comply with EU law and in which the Commission had not taken any action. This is regarded as particularly helpful because private individuals have clear reasons of self-interest for bringing actions and, because there are so many of them who may be affected by EU law, the vigilance of EU law is much more widespread and effective.

> **Case 48/65 *Alfons Lütticke GmbH v Hauptzollamt Saarlouis*** is an early demonstration of the difference between Treaty Articles that could give rise to direct effects and those that could not. The case declared that old Article 95 EEC (now 110 TFEU) satisfied the criteria so as to give rise to direct effects, but that Article 97 EEC (now repealed) did not. The Court of Justice ruled that Article 95 had created direct effects, but that since member states had a discretion to decide whether to levy an average rate of tax, Article 97 did not produce direct effects.

> Old Article 95 provided that 'No Member State shall impose, directly or indirectly…any internal taxation of any kind' and old Article 97 provided that 'member states…may, in the case of internal taxation…establish average rates'. (Note that old Article 97 EEC has been repealed by the Treaty of Amsterdam.)

Since these early cases, direct effects have been found to arise from many Treaty Articles, which often obligate not only organs of the state as in a vertical relationship, but also other individuals in a horizontal relationship – in particular, in the EU context, employers (see Diagram 8.1). It was confirmed by the Court of Justice that employers are obligated to comply with the requirements of a Treaty Article and that other individuals may enforce corresponding rights directly against the obligated party who has failed to comply with Community (and now EU) law.

> The first case to confirm horizontal direct effects was **Case 43/75 *Defrenne v Sabena (No. 2)*** in which the rights of an air hostess for equal pay guaranteed under old Article 119 EEC (now 157 TFEU) were upheld against the employing airline Sabena, which was in breach of the obligation.

Diagram 8.1

Vertical and horizontal direct effects

Vertical direct effects

State (or state body)

Individual (natural or legal person)

Horizontal direct effects

Individual Individual

Article 12 EC (now 18 TFEU)

Within the scope of application of the Treaties, and without prejudice to any special provisions contained therein, any discrimination on grounds of nationality shall be prohibited.

Article 12 EC (now 18 TFEU), on the general non-discrimination on the grounds of nationality, which is imposed on the member states was found to be capable of horizontal direct effects in **Case 36/74 *Walrave and Koch***. This is very important because it can be relied on by the Court of Justice and indeed individuals in many circumstances.

However, Article 10 EC (now 4(3) TEU), the good faith clause imposing a general obligation on the member states to act in conformity and not against Community (and now Union) interests, was held in **Case 44/84 *Hurd* v *Jones*** not to give rise to direct effects.

Article 10 EC (now 4(3) TEU)

Member States shall take any appropriate measure, general or particular, to ensure fulfilment of the obligations arising out of the Treaties or resulting from the acts of the institutions of the Union. The Member States shall facilitate the achievement of the Union's tasks and refrain from any measure which could jeopardise the attainment of Union's objectives.

---

cross reference

For example, the Von Colson *case, considered at section 8.3.2, and* Francovich, *considered at section 8.3.*

Nevertheless, Article 10 EC (now 4 TEU) has been highly influential in assisting the Court of Justice to develop other means of enforcing Community and now EU law.

Provisions of the Accession Treaties have also been held to give rise to direct effects.

See, for example, **Case C-113/89 *Rush Portuguesa* v *Office National d'Immigration*,** which provided details of the rights that non-Community workers were entitled to expect whilst working outside their EC country of immigration, in another host member state.

8.1.3.2 Regulations

While Regulations are clearly directly applicable by reason of Article 288 TFEU (ex 249 EC) and can therefore also obligate other individuals, they are not necessarily directly effective. The question of whether they can also give rise to direct effects depends on whether they satisfy the same criteria as for Treaty Articles as laid down in *Van Gend en Loos*.

The leading case for Regulations is **Case C-93/71 *Leonesio* v *Italian Ministry of Agriculture*,** in which Italian farmers were able to enforce a Regulation against the Italian state providing for compensation payments that had been subject to delays by the Italian authorities. The Court of Justice held that the Regulation should not be subject to delays and was immediately enforceable in the national courts.

Given that Regulations are also generally applicable in that they apply to everyone and not only provide rights, but are also capable of imposing obligations on everyone, it should not be a surprise that they are capable of giving rise to direct effects horizontally also.

For example, in **Case C-253/00 *Munoz* v *Frumar Ltd*,** the Court of Justice upheld the right of one individual trader to rely on the rights provided by a Regulation in a civil action against another individual not complying with the Regulation.

8.1.3.3 Directives

Directives have caused particular problems for the Court of Justice. At first, they were thought, as a general rule, not to be precise enough to give rise to direct effects because they were not directly applicable and only obligated the member states to achieve an end result.

Article 288 TFEU provides that a Directive shall be binding, as to the result to be achieved, upon each member state to which it is addressed, but shall leave to the national authorities the choice of form and methods.

Arguably, because they often provide a wide margin of discretion, Directives were considered incapable by their very nature of ever fulfilling the *Van Gend en Loos* criteria.

Case 9/70 *Grad*, however, considered and allowed for the possibility that direct effects could arise from other non-directly applicable forms of Community and now EU law outside Treaty Articles and Regulations.

Case 41/74 Van Duyn v The Home Office confirmed that Directives could give rise to direct effects, provided that they also satisfy the same criteria. The provisions of the Directive would have to contain a clear and precise obligation, which they can and often do. In this case, Article 3 of Directive 64/221 was held to give rise to rights directly enforceable against the state before the national courts by Miss Van Duyn.

A further aspect of Directives that might have caused difficulty was that Directives usually allow the member states time in which to implement them, two years being the most common period provided.

Case 148/78 Publico Ministero v Ratti considered this aspect. It concerned the prosecution of Mr Ratti by the Italian authorities for breaches of national law concerning product labelling. Although Mr Ratti had complied with two Community Product Labelling Directives, the expiry period for implementation of one of the two Directives had not passed. The Court of Justice held that he could rely on the one for which the time period had expired provided that it satisfied the requirements of clarity and precision etc., but not the Directive the implementation period of which had not expired.

Case 51/76 Verbond concerned the situation in which a Directive had been implemented after the time limit had expired, but the implementation was not faithful to the requirements of the Directive. The Court of Justice held that to deny the rights of individuals in such circumstances would be to weaken the effectiveness of Community obligations and that, as a result, individuals helped to ensure that member states kept within the realms of the discretion granted.

cross reference
See later in this section and section 8.2.2 for more on Becker.

The individual nature of the rights contained in the Directive have been stressed in a number of cases, notably **Case 8/81 Becker** as an element in deciding that they can be asserted against the state, although this does not form part of the required criteria. Furthermore, the *Becker* case also highlighted the wider effects of Community and now Union law as a standard by which national law should be judged.

For a considerable time, the question of whether Directives could be held to give rise to horizontal direct effects and thus be enforceable against other individuals received no answer from the Court of Justice. At the time, arguments against horizontal effects were that Directives did not have to be published and this would have offended against legal certainty. Furthermore, Directives are addressed to and obligate member states and not individuals, and therefore the latter should not be obligated by them. It was argued that by making them potentially enforceable against everyone, it would blur the distinction between them and the Regulations because they would resemble directly applicable law, something not intended under the scheme of Article 249 EC (now 288 TFEU). Arguments for horizontal direct effects of Directives are that Community and EU law should be equally actionable against the state and other individuals to ensure uniform consistency throughout the Union and to avoid giving rise to two categories of right. It is also the case that Treaty Articles are addressed to member states, but can nevertheless obligate individuals. Directives, whilst not at first publishable by compulsion, were invariably published and indeed now must be published (see Article 297 TFEU, ex 254 EC).

> **Article 297 TFEU**
> . . . .
> 1. Legislative acts adopted under the ordinary legislative procedure shall be signed by the President of the European Parliament and by the President of the Council....
>
> Legislative acts shall be published in the Official Journal of the European Union.

The Court of Justice came to a conclusion about Directives in **Case 152/84 *Marshall* v *Southampton Area Health Authority***, deciding that Directives could be enforced by individuals only against the state or arms of the state and not against other individuals. The case itself concerned equal treatment of men and women in retirement by the employer, but it involved vertical and not horizontal direct effects because the health authority was held to be a part of the state.

This Court ruling, however, led to a whole host of problems because of the distinction created between the ability to enforce rights against public as opposed to private employers. The result of this decision is that the scope of the concept of what constitutes 'public service' as opposed to a 'private body' became crucial.

cross reference
The Duke *case is considered in greater detail in Chapter 5, section 5.2.2.6.*

This can be seen from the later UK case of **Duke v *Reliance*** in which, on facts similar to those of *Marshall*, Mrs Duke lost her claim for compensation for being forced to retire earlier than men.

197

cross reference
The ways around the unfortunate consequences of the Marshall decision will be explored further in section 8.2.

Two further decisions in **Cases 222/84 *Johnston* v *RUC*** and **C-188/89 *Foster* v *British Gas*** showed that although the concept of public entity was wide enough to include national law enforcement agencies and nationalized industries and included any form of state control or authority, a distinction between public and private sector rights nevertheless remains.

cross reference
Indirect effects are considered in section 8.2.2.

Case 8/81 ***Becker*** confirmed the restriction of the direct effects of Directives as operating on the vertical axis only, but highlighted the further or wider benefits of direct effects for the Community legal order. The Court of Justice in this case stressed that directly effective Community law also operates in a wider sense as a standard by which national law is in effect evaluated by the Court of Justice to see if it meets the standard of EC law, rather than simply providing a narrower individual right only.

cross reference
See Chapter 6 on the Article 267 TFEU (ex 234 EC) reference for further details on this point.

In strict terms, the Court of Justice has no formal right to review the validity of national law; however, the doctrine of direct effects does allow it to declare that there is an incompatibility on the part of the national law with the directly effective standard contained in the EU law. The *Becker* case thus prepares the ground for the establishment of the indirect effects.

8.1.3.4 Decisions

In **Case 9/70 *Grad* v *Finanzamt Traunstein***, the Court held that it would be contrary to the binding nature of Community law if the provisions of a Decision could not be invoked by individuals. They must also satisfy the criteria and can only be enforced against those obligated. In *Grad*, a decision addressed to the German state concerned with the harmonization of tax regimes was held to give rise to effects that could be enforced by an individual affected by it.

8.1.3.5 International agreements

Although there is no statement in the Treaties that international agreements entered into by the Union or by the member states within the Union can give rise to direct effects, the Court of Justice has held that their provisions may also give rise to direct effects provided that they satisfy the criteria previously established. Agreements such as association agreements between the Union and a single state, or even a number of states, are capable of producing direct effects. Indeed, due to the limited nature and scope of the agreements, they lend themselves more readily to producing direct effects than the more complex multilateral agreements, the subject matter of which may well go beyond the jurisdictional scope of the Treaties.

For example, provisions of the EEC–Portugal Association Agreement, parts of the EEC–Morocco Agreement and provisions of the Yaoundé Convention Agreement were held to be directly effective in **Cases 104/81 *Kupferberg*, 87/75 *Bresciani*** and **C-18/90 *Kziber***, respectively.

In contrast, provisions of more complex agreements such as the General Agreement on Tariffs and Trade (GATT), which are mixed agreements involving the competences of both the Community (and now Union) and the member states, have not shown themselves to the Court of Justice to be so amenable to direct effects.

For example, **Case 21–24/72 *International Fruit***, the Court of Justice held that the GATT provisions in question were not directly effective because they were held to be too flexible and too easily subject to change by political negotiation rather than clearly applicable in a strict and reasonably foreseeable way by the courts.

However, in line with the transition of GATT to the World Trade Organization (WTO), the Court of Justice has appeared to soften its stance.

The Court expressed the possibility in **Case C-280/93 *Germany* v *Commission*** that the GATT provisions may have direct effects, but only where the Community intended to implement a particular GATT provision or expressly referred to it in a Community Act.

See also, for example, **Case 70/87 *Fediol***, in which a reference in a Community Regulation to a commercial practice identified in the GATT would allow the Court to interpret the Community Act according to the GATT rule.

It was, however, emphasized by the Court of Justice in **Case C-149/96 *Portugal* v *Council*** that the WTO rules do not give rise to direct effects. The Court of Justice did not wish to tie the hands of the Community by confirming binding rules of law for the Community when those same rules are not considered to be rigidly binding by other parties.

The WTO and GATT regimes are not based on binding and immediately enforceable reciprocal rules, but rules the breach of which lead first to further negotiation.

8.2 Overcoming the lack of horizontal direct effect for Directives

For more details on this section scan here or visit the Online Resource Centre.

8.2.1 Extending the definition of 'the state'

One way in which to avoid the unfortunate results of the *Marshall* ruling, which led to differences in treatment between state and private employees, is to expand the concept of 'public sector' to include more employers and thus more individuals capable of being able to enforce their rights vertically in the national courts through direct effects.

199

In **Case C-188/89 *Foster* v *British Gas***, the House of Lords referred to the Court of Justice the critical question of what was meant by 'state authority'. In *Marshall*, the health authority was clearly regarded as a part of the state. *Foster* involved, at that time, a nationalized, but independently run, organization; it was later privatized. The Court of Justice held that emanations of the state against which direct effects were available were those bodies that provided a public service under the control of the state and which for that purpose were granted special powers.

Direct effects are thus available against such bodies. However, although the case showed that the concept was wide enough to include nationalized industries and includes any form of state control or authority, a distinction nevertheless remains between public, however widely framed, and private employers. So it may be concluded that expanding the scope of what is meant by an 'emanation of the state' will broaden the concept and protect more people, but this still does not reach the heart of the matter. It allows a variation as between public and private employees, and because there are inevitably different situations in each of the member states as regards the public and private sector, there will also be a difference in the rights of individuals between the member states. Thus, because of this distinction, a different result can occur in each member state where national concepts of what is within the control of the state may differ. The difficulties and limits to this approach are demonstrated in a UK case.

In ***Doughty* v *Rolls Royce plc***, the Court of Appeal considered that the, at the time, largely state-owned and nationalized Rolls Royce company was not a public body for the purposes of the claim to direct effects in the case, because it was not providing a public service and was not subject to special powers.

Whilst the result in the *Rolls Royce* case is probably correct, although rather narrow, it can be seen that privatization of once-nationalized companies might also affect the rights of individuals. If decided today, *Foster* v *British Gas* would probably have a different outcome. A further case has shed a little more light on what can be included in the concept of the state.

In **Case C-157/02 *Rieser Internationale Transporte GmbH* v *Autobahnen- und Schnellstraßen Finanzierungs AG***, the Court of Justice held:

> When contracts are concluded with road users, the provisions of a directive capable of having direct effect may be relied upon against a legal person governed by private law where the State has entrusted to that legal person the task of levying tolls for the use of public road networks and where it has direct or indirect control of that legal person.

Therefore private companies undertaking a public duty come within the scope of the *Foster* ruling. There remains, however, no uniformity and indeed no certainty as to the application of EU law between public and private employers within member states and between member states. Certain individuals are thus denied rights that employees in the public sector can enforce in the face of non-compliance by member states. The scope of the concept of public service as opposed to a private body remains a crucial, but sometimes artificial, distinction.

8.2.2 **Indirect effects**

cross reference
Becker *was considered at section 8.1.3.3.*

Case 8/81 *Becker*, and its acknowledgement of a wider concept of direct effects as a standard by which the conformity of national law could in effect be reviewed by the Court of Justice, had already pointed EC (and now EU) law in the direction that was about to be taken in the next development.

Case 14/83 *Von Colson* provided a solution where national law was not in tune with Community law and direct effects could not be considered as an acceptable remedy. The ruling offers an alternative for individuals defeated by the lack of horizontal direct effects. The case concerned Article 6 of the Equal Treatment Directive 76/207 and a claim against a public employer for the lack of adequate compensation when discriminated against.

At the same time, **Case 79/83 *Harz* v *Tradex*** was also heard by the Court of Justice, which involved a similar claim against a private employer. Rather than highlight the unfortunate results of the lack of horizontal direct effects of Directives against the private, but not the public, employer, the Court of Justice concentrated on old Article 5 EEC (now 4(3) TEU), which requires member states to comply with Community obligations.

The Court held that this requirement applies to all authorities of member states, including the courts, which are obliged therefore to interpret national law in such a way as to ensure that the obligations of a Directive are obeyed, regardless of whether the national law was based on any particular Directive.

The effectiveness of this depends on the willingness or ability of the member states' courts to interpret national law, if it exists, to achieve the correct result.

It would, of course, not have been acceptable for *Van Colson* to have succeeded under direct effects against an arm of the state, but *Harz* not to have done so against a private employer; thus an alternative solution was required.

However, the Court of Justice held in **Case 80/86 *Public Prosecutor* v *Kolpinghuis Nijmegen BF*** that the principle of indirect effects could not be applied by a member state to support the retroactive prosecution of a Dutch firm for stocking adulterated mineral water that was in breach of a Community Directive. The implementation period had expired and the Netherlands should have implemented it, but had not; the Court of Justice held, however, that it would not, in such circumstances, give rise to indirect effects.

The decision is consistent with *Marshall* in that Directives cannot impose obligations on individuals. Thus the sympathetic interpretation of Community and now EU law Directives required by *Von Colson* could not be used in breach of the general principles of legal certainty and non-retroactivity. The lack of national law to interpret, however, has caused problems in furthering the principle provided by *Von Colson*. The next case required a further sleight of hand from the Court to achieve a just result that was consistent with its decision in *Marshall*.

Case C-106/89 *Marleasing* concerned Directive 68/151, which had not been implemented in Spain, but which would have determined the outcome of the case. The Spanish courts wanted to know whether the Directive could nevertheless be directly upheld against an individual by another individual. Whilst the Court of Justice reaffirmed that Directives do not give rise to effects between individuals, it also stressed that it was up to the courts to achieve the result required by the Directive by the interpretation of national law, whether the national law post-dated or pre-dated the Directive. The national law relevant, the Spanish Civil Code, pre-dated the Directive, but had to be interpreted in a way clearly not covered by it to conform with the later unimplemented Directive.

cross reference
Also considered in Chapter 5, section 5.2.2.6.

Such retroactive interpretation will cause severe difficulties where there is a clear conflict between the national law and an EU Directive.

This was the case in the UK House of Lords case of ***Duke* v *GEC Reliance*** systems in which the House of Lords refused to interpret pre-existing UK law in the light of the later Equal Treatment Directive, in spite of the decision in *Marshall*.

This difficulty was further highlighted at the Community level before the Court of Justice in **Case C-334/92 *Wagner Miret***, which also involved Spanish legislation pre-dating a Community Directive, but which involved head-on incompatibility. The Court of Justice this time acknowledged the unsuitability of the *Von Colson* sympathetic interpretation for all cases, but nevertheless stressed that national courts should both presume an intention on the part of the state to comply with Community law and try as far as possible to give effect to the Community law in the case at hand.

In **Case C-168/95 *Criminal Proceedings against Luciano Arcaro*,** the Court of Justice acknowledged that the limits of the *Von Colson* principle would be overreached if there were a retroactive interpretation of national law in the light of the Directive that had not been implemented by the member states and which would have imposed criminal liability on an individual, thus confirming the limitation recognized in the *Kolpinghuis* case.

Case C-105/03 *Pupino* is a more recent case confirming much of this earlier case law. The case actually involves a Framework Decision (2001/220) enacted under the Police and Judicial Cooperation pillar of the EU (pre-Lisbon). The Court of Justice held that national courts were obliged to interpret national law in conformity with the Framework Decision on which an individual should be able to invoke them before the national courts, even though it was clear that the Decision, enacted under the third (intergovernmental) pillar, could not have direct effects. The Court of Justice held that the obligation to do so arose from general principles of Community law, in particular legal certainty and non-retroactivity, which would be offended if not respected.

cross reference

If you are unsure about the significance of this, refer to Chapter 1.

The case is also important in that the Court of Justice has applied judicial reasoning and EC law principles to what was an intergovernmental part of the Union, although this latter aspect is no longer important in view of the Treaty reforms introduced by the Lisbon Treaty. The case marked a surprising extension into the intergovernmental pillar of the EU at the time and may be noted as a further example of the Court's judicial activism in the face of failure by the member states in moving things forward, at the time with the Constitutional Treaty and the delay in reforming the Treaty structure of the Union.

More recently, in **Cases C-397–401/01 *Pfeiffer* v *Rotes Kreuz*,** the Court of Justice, in considering how far national courts can go in applying *Von Colson*, confirmed that national courts are bound to interpret national law so far as possible in the light of the Directive to achieve the result sought by a Directive. They should also give full effectiveness to Community law taking into account national law as a whole, as opposed to narrowly looking at a particular national implementing provision.

Despite the opinion of the AG in Case C-91/92 *Faccini Dori* that horizontal direct effects of Directives should be recognized, the Court of Justice declined to follow this advice. It reasoned that whilst there was a case for vertical direct effects to stop states from relying on their own wrongs, recognition of horizontal direct effects would blur the distinction between Regulations and Directives contrary to the Treaty.

Instead, as it did also in Case C-334/93 *Wagner Miret*, the Court of Justice expressed the view that if member states are unable to construe national law to read in conformity, which is a distinct possibility as a result either of the Court being incapable or unwilling to do so, it must be assumed that member states nevertheless intend to comply with its Community law obligations. Thus, if there is a breach, member states must compensate any loss incurred as a result of that breach according to the principles established in *Francovich*.

cross reference

See section 8.3 for more on Francovich.

In other words, the failure to succeed under direct or indirect effects should not unfairly extinguish all remedies available. Individuals have then been provided with a final resort to obtain damages instead.

More recently, though, there have been cases that appear to muddy the waters once more on whether Directives can nevertheless dictate the result of a case between two individuals.

Case C144/04 *Mangold* concerns a German law that made it easier to offer fixed-term contracts to those over the age of 52 in an attempt to make the employment of older persons more attractive, and in this indirect way to help the employment chances and protection of older workers. The law was challenged as contrary to the Directive 2000/78 prohibiting discrimination on the grounds of age, the implementation period of which had at the time, though, not expired. The result of the case, that the German legislation had gone too far and was thus contrary to the prohibition of discrimination on the ground of age, appears to provide for the horizontal direct effects of a Directive and, more surprisingly, even before the period of expiry of the transposition period had taken place. However, note carefully that the Court of Justice held that the principle of law breached by the member state was the prohibition of discrimination which is a general principle of EU law. According to the Court of Justice, this could not be undermined by the unexpired transposition period of a Directive, which provided a more exact setting in which the pre-existing general principle could be applied. The argument in the case was that both a strict application of Article 6 of Directive 2000/78 and the application of the general principle would have had the same result. However, if relying on the Directive only, this would have caused problems because of the non-expiry of the implementation period; therefore, in order to overcome those difficulties, it was better to use the general principle.

In other words, the use of a general principle circumvented the fact that the Directive, according to the past case law (notably the *Ratti* case), was incapable of producing direct effects due to the fact that the obligations contained within it were not yet due. The end result, as far as the Court of Justice is concerned, is that it remains the case that horizontal direct effects of Directives is not recognized.

Case C-212/04 *Adeneler* v *ELOG* provides some clarification of the judgment in *Mangold*. It concerned the Fixed-Term Work Directive (1999/70) to provide greater protection for fixed-term workers. It was due to be implemented by July 2002, but had not been implemented by Greece in respect of Greek employees whose then current fixed-term contracts had ended. New fixed-term contracts, according to the Directive, were only to be allowed if objectively justified. A Greek court wished to know when the obligation under the Directive should be used to interpret national law by national courts. The ECJ held that the general obligation (of the sort established in *Mangold*) arose only following the implementation period, but would apply regardless of whether the Directive was capable of direct effects for any reason.

cross reference
Ratti *and* Von Colson *are noted at sections 8.1.3.3 and 8.2.2.*

Thus far, this case takes things no further than the *Ratti* and *Von Colson* cases.

However, the Court went on to hold in **Case C-212/04 *Adeneler* v *ELOG*** that, in the period between publication of the Directive and the expiry of the implementation period, member states were nevertheless constrained (under Articles 10 and 249 EC, now 4(3) TEU and 288 TFEU) from taking any measures that would compromise attaining the requirements of the Directive.

This means that they should not, prior to the expiry of the implementation, interpret national law in a manner that might compromise the objectives of the Directive when the implementation period has then expired. This would seem almost to mean that, effective the publication date and not the expiry date, the Directive's objectives must be complied with, thus tearing up one of the remaining differences between Regulations and Directives.

The decision in the *Mangold* case was subsequently affirmed by the Court of Justice.

Case C-555/07 *Kükükdeveci* involved a dispute as to a notice period between an employee and a private employer because a German law precluded periods of employment completed while the employee was under the age of 25 from counting towards the notice period. Directive 2000/78 should have been implemented in Germany at the material time, but it had not. The preliminary ruling question was essentially, on what provision of law could Kükükdeveci rely? The Court of Justice held that the general principle of EU law prohibiting discrimination on the grounds of law, as expressed in Directive 2000/78, applies to preclude national law as in the case from discriminating.

Thus, then, the general principle is seen to apply directly between parties, but not the Directive. But is it more controversial to have the general principle give rise to horizontal direct effects or the Directive, bearing in mind that the general principle finds no clear expression anywhere in the Treaties or secondary legislation?

The final category of cases that appear in some way to circumvent the inconsistencies produced by the ruling in *Marshall* is admittedly of less importance and much more limited in scope, and may well be a category that will not attract new case; that being the case, it may well disappear altogether at some stage. For the moment, though, it does warrant brief consideration.

8.2.3 'Incidental' horizontal effects

Although the opinion of the AG in Case C-91/92 *Faccini Dori* that horizontal direct effects of Directives should be recognized by the Court of Justice was rejected, the Court has nevertheless given judgment in a few cases that appear to produce horizontal direct effects. The cases involve Directives that have influenced the outcome of cases involving private parties, but in an incidental rather than a direct way and without imposing a strict obligation on any of the individual parties. The Directives are pleaded not to exert rights directly, but to overcome what would otherwise be the application of incompatible national law in a way detrimental to one of their interests. These cases also support and are supported by the wider view of direct effects put forward in Case 8/81 *Becker*, as a means by which national law is in effect reviewed by the Court of Justice to see if it meets the standard of EC (and now EU) law, rather than providing an individual right to assert an EU law based right against another party. The case law is, at the moment, limited.

In **Case C-441/93** *Panagis Pafitis* **v** *TKE*, shareholders of a bank who were denied a meeting to protest over an increase in capital, as required under EC, but not national, law, were able to question the national law on the basis of the Directive. As a consequence, the new shareholders were prevented from relying on the national law, which was out of line with Community law. Whilst this clearly affected their rights, it was not a case of a direct application of a Directive against them by other individuals.

It was claimed in the leading case in this line, **Case C-194/94 *CIA Security International SA v Signalson SA and Securitel SPRL***, that CIA had breached the national technical standard for alarm systems. CIA pleaded the inapplicability of the national standard because of the failure of the state to notify it to the Commission, as required by Directive 83/189. The Court of Justice accepted this argument, which meant that CIA was assisted by the Directive. This in turn removed the obligation to meet the national standard, which would have been imposed under national law.

The Directive relied on imposed no obligation on the other party; therefore there is no question of horizontal direct effects of a Directive. It is true that the other party, which had alleged that CIA had not met the standard, was affected in that its allegation was legally unfounded and it lost the action as a result. However, the national standard could be rendered lawful only by the state complying with the Directive, thus it remained the state's obligation to ensure that its law was in compliance with Community law; this was not, therefore ,an obligation imposed on an individual. It has been noted that, following this case, the number of notifications of technical standards by the member states increased significantly, thus supporting the free movement of goods regime.

Case C-226/97 *Lemmens* does not follow the trend set by the first cases, for good policy grounds. Lemmens was prosecuted for drink-driving, the evidence having been obtained by the use of a breath analysis machine, the standards for which had not been notified to the Commission as required under Directive 83/189. Lemmens sought to argue the inadmissibility of that evidence for his conviction based on the failure of the state to notify the standard. In line with the *CIA* case that a party need not have to rely on a national standard that has not been notified, he argued that his prosecution should not stand. However, the Court of Justice held that whilst the failure to notify the standard may have hindered the marketing of such machines, it did not render unlawful the use of the product and could not therefore aid the defendant in his claim – that is, it did not affect trade between member states, which was the main purpose of the Directive.

In **Case C-443/98 *Unilever Italia SpA v Central Foods SpA***, the principle established in the earlier cases was extended to contractual relations between two individual parties. The Italian state had adopted a food standard contrary to the Community Standards Directive and Unilever's supply of olive oil, which did not comply with the Italian standard, was rejected by the purchaser, Central Foods. In an action for payment, Unilever questioned the Italian legislation. The Court of Justice held that the Italian law should not apply, that the case was no different in principle from the *CIA* case and did not create horizontal direct effects. No obligation had been placed on an individual; it was merely the case that un-notified national standards could not apply, regardless of the possible consequence on the contractual relations and liability between the two parties.

Trying to rationalize these cases is not easy. The Court of Justice makes it clear that they do not establish the horizontal direct effect of Directives. For the most part, the cases are mainly narrowly restricted to the application of Directive 83/189 and its replacement Directive 98/34, requiring the notification of technical standards, although, as the case law has revealed, this is not the only Directive involved. More to the point is that the Technical Standards Directive essentially involves the relationship between the member states and the Commission, and not, as with most other Directives, the relations between individuals and the state or between individuals.

The following analysis may therefore represent the position reached. Directives are being interpreted to determine the validity of national law in an action that may affect the legal position of a private party to a court action. Any such incidental effect applies only to prevent reliance on national law not conforming with EU law; hence the term or view that the effect as far as the private parties is concerned is incidental. The real or underlying purpose is the Court's willingness to uphold the provisions of the Directive. This translates generally as not allowing the application of non-conforming national law. As such, then, this merely enforces the public law obligations of the state rather than directly interferes with the contractual relations between parties, although, as was seen in some of the cases, those relations are affected by the existence of a Directive. Viewed in terms of estoppel, parties may rely on the Directive as a shield to estop another party from relying on national law that would otherwise harm their interests. They are not using it as a sword to attack the other party. Furthermore, it could be said that both incidental effects and indirect effects are part of the broader view of direct effects in Case 8/81 *Becker* that national law should not be allowed to apply where it does not in comply with EU law.

The cases also serve to highlight the fact that legal difficulties between individuals can be caused by the failure of a member state to comply with an EU law Directive. In such circumstances, in which a failure by a state adversely and directly affects an individual, a judicial remedy has been provided by the Court of Justice that holds the state liable to compensate the individual for any loss sustained. This is considered next.

8.3 State liability: the principle in *Francovich*

'State liability' is the term given to the action first raised and accepted by the Court of Justice in Cases C-6 and 9/90 *Francovich*. This case essentially condoned an action for compensation by an individual against a member state when the member state failed to comply with Community law obligations and which resulted in damage or loss to that individual. The *Francovich* case has both provided an addition, therefore, to Commission actions against member states to enforce EU law and overcome the difficulties generated by the lack of horizontal direct effects of Directives, or indeed the entire absence of direct effects where the EU law provision fails to satisfy the *Van Gend en Loos* criteria. Instead, the state is held liable for its failure that results in damage to an individual.

Cases C-6 and 9/90 *Francovich* concerned a claim by Italian nationals against the state for a guaranteed redundancy payment granted by Directive 80/987, which had not been implemented by Italy, or alternatively for damages incurred as a result of the state failing to implement the Directive in time. Francovich and other workers were made redundant when the company employing them became insolvent. The company itself had made no payments and, as a result of the insolvency, no action was possible against the company. The Court of Justice had held already, following Article 226 EC (now 258 TFEU) proceedings in Case 22/87 *Commission v Italy*, that Italy had breached its obligations by its failure to implement the Directive; however, this could not help Francovich and his co-workers because the purpose of the enforcement action is to establish a breach of Community law by the member states and not to provide an individual remedy.

The Court of Justice held that the Directive was not capable of direct effects because of the discretion granted to the member states as to the result to be achieved. In particular, it was unclear which authority was to be responsible for setting up a compensation agency and, part of the problem for the national court in the first place, there was no national law to interpret in conformity with the Directive, nor any national procedural law to support an action against the state for compensation.

Instead, relying heavily on the fundamental doctrines of direct effects and supremacy, as outlined in the *Van Gend en Loos*, *Costa* v *ENEL*, *Simmenthal* and *Factortame* cases, the Court determined that the duty of the member states to ensure the full application and enforcement under Articles 10 and 249 EC (now 4(3) TEU and 288 TFEU), if breached, would give rise to liability. The Court rejected the defence that the liability of the state was only a matter for the national laws. It held that the protection of individuals would be weakened if they could not claim damages for loss caused by a member state's failure to comply. It considered, therefore, that the principle was inherent in the scheme of the Treaty, that member states should make good any damage caused to individuals that was the consequence of a breach of Community law. The Court held, however, that the claim required the Directive to contain an individual right, which could be determined by the provisions of the Directive itself and that there must be a link between the breach and the damage caused.

thinking point

The ruling has been described by Bebr as the ultimate consequence of Van Gend en Loos. *What do you think that he meant by that?*

The decision in *Francovich* provides individuals with a remedy that stems from the breach by the member state of the general obligations in Articles 4(3) TEU and 288 TFEU (ex 10 and 249 EC) to comply with EU law. Hence this adds a remedy for individuals to fill the gap left where EU law provisions have not been implemented by member states or are held not to be directly effective, or because Directives are effective only on the vertical and not the horizontal axis. Damages are consequently to be assessed in accordance with national procedural rules, subject, however, to overriding EU law principles, which will be considered in the final section of this chapter.

The judgment in *Francovich* adds again to the effective judicial protection by providing individuals with rights against the state and deters the state from breaching EU law. It is, though, an independent action from direct and indirect effects, and provides uniform EU conditions for liability, not dependent on each national set of laws, although the assessment of the quantum of damages is for national procedural law.

Note that the 1994 judgment in **Case C-91/92 *Faccini Dori* v *Recreb Srl*** confirmed the Court's continued opposition to horizontal direct effects. Whilst stressing the need for national courts to interpret national law wherever possible to comply with Directives, the Court pointed out that, in circumstances in which a state had caused damage caused by non-implementation of Community law, the state would be liable to compensate any loss in line with the principle established in the *Francovich* case.

Since those cases, the Court of Justice has had the opportunity to develop the law, starting with joined Cases C-46 and 48/93 *Brasserie du Pêcheur* v *Federal Republic of Germany*; *Factortame* v *UK (No. 3)*.

Factortame concerned the breach of a Treaty Article rather than the failure to comply with a Directive, but this was held by the Court of Justice to be no bar to incurring liability. The result of this case law is that the principle of state liability is applicable to all domestic acts and omissions, legislative, executive and judicial, which are in breach of EU law, directly effective or not,

cross reference

Shöppenstedt *will be considered in Chapter 9, section 9.3.7.*

and in principle by all three arms of state. There was, however, a new focus on the seriousness of the breach. *Factortame (No. 3)* introduced the revised criteria that if the state was facing choices comparable to the institutions when law-making, which essentially involves balancing many interests, the seriousness of breach also must be analogous to that applied to the EU institutions for damage caused unlawfully by legislative acts under Article 288(2) EC (now 340 TFEU).

This is known as the '*Shöppenstedt* formula' after Case 5/71 *Zuckerfabrik Shöppenstedt*.

cross reference

The appropriateness of this standard for member states will be considered further in section 8.4.

In order for liability to arise on the part of the member state, there must have been a sufficiently serious breach of a superior rule of law designed for the protection of individuals. This is the standard applied to damage caused by a legislative Act rather than from administrative action. As such, it is a higher standard because, according to the Court of Justice, the creation of legislative Acts involves choices of economic policy and is thus far more difficult to achieve.

The sufficiently serious requirement was further elaborated by the Court of Justice in *Factortame*. It suggested that this would be satisfied where a member state had manifestly and gravely disregarded the limits of its discretion.

cross reference

This was considered in Chapter 7.

The factors that should be taken into account by the national court assessing this are:

- the clarity and precision of the rule breached;
- the measure of discretion;
- whether the infringement and damage was intentional or involuntary;
- whether the error in law was excusable or inexcusable;
- whether there was any contribution to the problem by the Community institutions; and
- whether any incompatible national law was being maintained.

cross reference

See Chapter 9 for Community Acts and Chapter 2 on voting in Council if you do not understand the significance of how difficult it is to reach agreement.

The cases also confirmed that liability can occur without having to establish a breach by the member state by an Article 226 EC (now 258 TFEU) action by the Commission. However, in cases in which the infringement is not yet clear, this could be problematic. If proven, damages arise from the date of the infringement and not the date of proving the infringement, unlike the Article 260 TFEU penalty. The Article 260 penalty is considered in Chapter 7.

At both the Union and state levels, further case law determined how serious a breach must be to incur liability. At the Union level, it has proved to be extremely difficult to succeed in damages against the Union institutions.

According to the AG in the *Factortame* case, up to 1995, only eight awards had been made in thirty-eight years.

The Court of Justice has taken a similar approach in respect of the member states in **Case C-392/93 *R v HM Treasury, ex p British Telecom plc***. In this case, the UK government successfully argued that its incorrect implementation of a Directive was due to a misunderstanding of what the Directive required. The Court of Justice agreed that the Directive was capable of more than one interpretation and thus no liability arose.

cross reference
See also Chapter 9,
section 9.3.7.

Likewise, in **Case C-319/96 *Brinkmann***, the incorrect application of a tax classification by Denmark, although financially damaging to a company, was not deemed sufficiently serious to incur liability because it was a mistake in the interpretation of the Directive that was also made by other states.

These cases comply with the analysis at the EU level, in that where there is discretion on the part of the member state in deciding exactly what action is necessary to implement the EU law obligation or where there is an excusable error in interpretation, then the standard of fault for liability will be raised, making it more difficult to obtain compensation. In line with this view, where the obligation is much clearer and the breach much more obvious, then liability will be easier to impose.

In addition to *Francovich* and *Factortame*, see, for example, **C-5/94 *Hedley Lomas*** involving a clear breach of Article 29 EC (now 35 TFEU) by the UK for imposing an export ban, **Case C-178/94 *Dillenkofer*** in which the failure to implement the Package Holidays Directive by Germany was in itself a sufficiently serious breach and **Case C-140/97 *Rechberger***, which involved the misinterpretation of the Package Holidays Directive, which simply established liability on the grounds of a straightforward infringement of Community law.

The more recent **Case C-278/05 *Robins*** confirms that the lower the degree of discretion on the part of the member state and the clearer the requirements of the Directive, the higher the chance that the member state would incur liability for a mere breach. Conversely, the more ambiguous or unclear a provision of Community law, the more discretion would be enjoyed by the member state in implementing this and the breach would correspondingly have to be much more serious before the member state incurred liability. In the *Robins* case, the argument hinged on the minimum level of protection required under Directive 89/987 for the protection of employees in the event of insolvency of the employee. It was argued that requirement was imprecise and that this was a view of a number of member states. The Court of Justice accepted this and held that, in view of the discretion to interpret the imprecise duty, the UK was not liable.

cross reference
This will be
considered further
in Chapter 9,
section 9.3, on
damages actions
under Article 340
TFEU (ex 288 EC).

Case C-352/98P *Bergaderm* indicates an approach of the Court of Justice to align the rules on liability for member states and the Community institutions, so that it may be easier in future for individuals to obtain compensation from Union institutions for mere infringements that have not involved a great deal of discretion on the part of the institution.

cross reference
For further details
on the impact on
national procedural
law of EC law rights,
see section 8.4.

In cases in which liability does arise, the determination of the degree of the seriousness of the breach and thus whether and the level of damages to be awarded, if any, remain questions of national procedural law provided that remedies are not excessively difficult to obtain in the national legal systems and that damages, where applicable, are an adequate remedy.

The principle of state liability has been extended in scope or potential scope to the private sector and to national courts.

8.3.1 **The extension of *Francovich***

8.3.1.1 Extension to the private sphere

Case C-453/99 *Courage Ltd* v *Crehan* involved a dispute between two private parties involving a claim that a breach of competition law Article 81 EC (now 101 TFEU) by another private party caused loss to the applicant. Building on the foundation cases of *Van Gend en Loos*, *Costa* v *ENEL* and *Francovich*, the Court of Justice reasoned that the extension of the principle of state liability was required by the new legal order and for the effective protection of rights, which would be undermined if it were not open to any individual to claim damages for loss caused to him by a contract or by conduct liable to restrict or distort competition.

Francovich liability therefore has been extended to determine liability between private parties and not only against member states where one has caused loss to the other by a breach of EU law.

This has since been followed up in **Cases C-295–298/04 *Manfredi*** making it clear that individuals must be able to obtain full compensation as a result of loss caused by a breach of EU competition rules.

8.3.1.2 Extension to the national courts

Whilst previous case law under *Francovich* has indicated that the Court of Justice holds the view that state liability is applicable to all branches of government, there was some reticence that this might apply to the judicial branch given the respect for the independence of the judiciary accorded in western democracies.

The next case introduced the possibility that state liability applies also to breaches of EU law rights by the judiciary, in which case the member state would have to compensate.

cross reference
This case was also considered in Chapter 6, section 6.1.8.4.

In **Case C-224/01 *Gerhard Köbler* v *Republic of Austria***, the Court of Justice held that the State may also, potentially at least, be liable for the breaches of Community (and now EU) law by the national courts of last instance provided that they were manifest and sufficiently serious. It was held, however, in the particular case that the breach complained of was not serious enough, despite the opinion of AG Leger that the error of Community law made by the Austrian Administrative Court was not an excusable error.

The *Köbler* case has now been followed up:

In **Case C-173/03 *Traghetti del Mediterraneo SpA* v *Italy***, it was alleged that a company had been forced into liquidation as a result of the errors in interpretation committed by the Supreme Court in Italy. Furthermore, the chance to correct those errors was denied by that Court, which did not make a reference to the Court of Justice. In a further action by the administrator, the Court of Justice held that it could not rule out that 'manifest errors' by a national court would lead to compensation under the principle of state liability. However, it was held that it was up to the national courts to decide in each case.

The consequence of this slight extension of liability is that liability for damage caused by courts is not limited as in *Köbler* to 'intentional fault and serious misconduct' by a court in situations in which that standard would have excluded liability for 'manifest infringement'. In other words, it extends liability to where national courts have manifestly infringed the law in their interpretation, which has caused damage.

8.4 National procedural law and the system of remedies

The development of individual remedies as established and developed by the Court of Justice has added a second system of vigilance to the existing direct enforcement of EU law by the Union institutions and member states. Inevitably, however, because direct and indirect effects, incidental effect and state liability are individual remedies that are pursued before the national courts, their overall effectiveness is dependent on national rules of procedural law, which are, of course, by their very nature outside the jurisdiction and direct influence of the Union and Court of Justice. These rules can affect and interfere with the realization of EU rights at the national level. Also, in comparison between member states, this situation can be complicated by different rules on standing, or time limits, or burden of proof, or because certain remedies are not simply recognized in some member states. However, because court procedural rules were not within the scope or competence of any of the Treaties, these were originally considered to be entirely within the reserved and exclusive competences of the member states. This idea is given the term 'national procedural autonomy'. However, to counter this, new principles of EU law have been developing to protect individual rights and can be referred to as principles of effective legal protection.

8.4.1 The principle of national procedural autonomy

In the absence of harmonized rules on procedure, rights conferred by EU law must be exercised before national courts in accordance with the traditions laid down by national procedural rules, which, in strict terms, are autonomous from the EU legal system. To what extent, however, should they be respected where they interfere with EU law rights? There are general arguments for and against. For example, if national procedural law were entirely respected, the rule of law and legal certainty of EU law would be undermined, or if respected in each state, differences in remedies would arise between member states, which may distort the uniformity of EU law and the realization of the internal market and other areas of EU competence. On the other hand, some argue that it is better to leave the provision of remedies to those who know their own systems best. The position of the Court of Justice up to the 1980s was one that essentially respected national procedural rules subject, however, to certain guidelines, as developed through its case law.

The idea that the national procedural rules were independent and beyond the influence of EU law is wrapped up within the term 'national procedural autonomy'.

In **Case 33/76 *Rewe-Zentralfinanz***, the Court of Justice held that national courts were entitled to apply national procedural limits provided that national rules are no less favourable for Community law rights as for domestic situations nor make the Community right impossible to realize.

In **Case 45/76 Comet**, the Court of Justice held that it was up to each member state to determine the procedural conditions governing those actions, but that such conditions cannot be less favourable than those relating to similar actions of a domestic nature and should ensure the protection of the rights that citizens have from the direct effect of Community law.

Thus, where an EU law right is involved, national procedural law must not deprive a litigant of their rights under EU law. Both as a consequence of this and in support of it is the general principle of Article 18 TFEU (ex 12 EC) that there be no discrimination of the grounds of nationality, which must not be breached. From the first cases and other early case law stem the principles of practical impossibility and principle of equivalence. The latter holds that EU law rights should be treated in the same way as national rights. It was already seen in relation to cases in respect of supremacy such as Case 6/64 *Costa* v *ENEL* that the Court of Justice will not allow national rules to stand in the way of a reference to the Court of Justice or the supremacy of Community (and now EU) law. Furthermore, it was also seen in the *Simmenthal* and *Factortame (No. 2)* cases, so that it is not only national substantive laws that must give way to EU law, but also any national rules of procedure, including constitutional rules that might get in the way of the effective application of an EU law right, regardless of the origin of these rules.

However, it was clearly stated by the Court of Justice in **Case 158/80 Rewe v Hauptzollamt Kiel** that no new remedies were intended to be created in the national courts to ensure the observance of Community law over and above that already existing in national law. Equally, however, it became clear that, in some cases, further intervention was necessary.

The alternative would be the agreement of the member states to harmonize national procedural rules or to replace them with common Union rules. However, this is neither politically acceptable, because member states do not wish to hand over control of their legal systems to the EU, nor practically possible, due to the very different and nationally idiosyncratic legal systems in existence. It would not be an impossible task, but one that would be exceedingly difficult and time-consuming.

8.4.2 Intervention by the Court of Justice

Whilst the principle of equivalence would ensure the non-discriminatory application of national rules, this does not go far enough to remedy the situation in all cases. National remedies must, however, also provide an effective remedy. Any rule that actually prevents individuals from relying on an EU law right would be incompatible with the principle of effective legal protection.

cross reference

This case is also discussed in section 8.3.2 in relation to indirect effects.

In **Case 14/83 Von Colson**, the compensation offered by the national court for the discrimination suffered was the payment of the rail fare home. This was held not to be a dissuasive and adequate remedy. The remedy, according to the Court, must guarantee real and effective judicial protection and must have a real deterrent effect.

Case **C-213/89** *Factortame* highlighted just how radical the solution had to be to ensure the protection of Community (and now EU) law rights in the national courts, including, in the case, the right to interim relief against the UK Crown, something that was not constitutionally possible previously.

Case **C-208/90** *Emmott* concerned a national three-month time limit in which to bring benefits claims. The time ran from the date on which the claim arose, according to the relevant legislation, in this case the entry-into-force date of a Community Directive. However, it was not clear, due to the faulty transposition of a Community Directive, that the applicant's claim was valid and the claim was rejected in any event as being out of time. The Court of Justice held that whilst reasonable time limits are acceptable in respect of a claim based originally in Community law, time can only run from the date on which the Directive is implemented properly and where the applicant's rights are clear.

In **Case C-271/91** *Marshall II*, the award for compensation suffered by Ms Marshall for discrimination was set at a statutory ceiling, which was much lower than the real loss of earnings suffered. The Court of Justice held that unlawful dismissal based on a Community right should be subject to full compensation including interest, despite the interpretation of the Court of Appeal that, under national law, damages could not include interest.

cross reference
This is discussed in section 8.3.

In a much more interventionist mode, EC law has also required national courts to provide specific and new forms of remedy, most notably in Case C-6/90 *Francovich* and the establishment of the right to damages from the state where liable.

213

Thus national rules are respected to the extent that they do not hinder an EU law right, but where they prevent an EU law right from being realized or applied in some way, then the national procedural law must give way. This period of judicial activism and creativeness on the part of the Court of Justice – particularly the *Emmott* case, which took things surprisingly far – gave way to a less intrusive period as generally the Court was reacting to being criticized for its overt judicial activism.

8.4.3 **A more balanced approach**

A more balanced approach was shown by the Court of Justice in the next case.

In **Case C-339/91 Steenhorst-Neerings**, a Dutch national procedural law concerned the restriction of retroactive claims to benefits to one year. This was held to be acceptable to the Court of Justice.

This apparent step back from *Emmott* means that reasonable time limits are acceptable even though these can vary from state to state. However, *Steenhorst-Neerings* was distinguished from the rule in *Emmott*, which applied after a three-month deadline expired to prevent bringing an action at all. It was held that the state itself had contributed to the failure of the applicant to comply with the strict time limit by advising a wait-and-see attitude to another case concerning the same rule, which had also questioned similar rights to equal treatment in payments. The rule in *Steenhorst-Neerings*, in contrast, permitted a claim, but limited the retrospective payments under it to one year.

In **Case C-188/95 *Fantask***, the Court of Justice gave general grounds for accepting time limits that could result in differences between the member states. It held that national time limits would continue to apply even in situations in which the Directive had not been properly implemented into national law for reasons of legal certainty and to protect the national taxpayer and authorities. The case itself concerned a five-year limitation period for the recovery of debts, which was held to be acceptable – that is, there was to be no Community or now EU rule for the recovery of tax payments.

Two similar cases concerned more closely with procedure were decided differently, although both concerned a variation of a national procedural rule stating that it is up to the parties to introduce legal arguments and not the courts. However, if EU law, which may be relevant, is not introduced, then a party may suffer as a result. In these circumstances, it was argued in the cases that the national court must either introduce the EC law itself or at least make a reference to the Court of Justice, thus infringing the national rule. Questions were referred as to whether indeed the national procedural law must give way.

In **Case C-312/93 *Peterbroeck van Campenhout***, the Court of Justice held that national procedural laws should not prevent references being made.

This was seemingly contradicted by **Cases C-430 and 431/93 *Van Schijndel*** in which a similar procedural rule, which prevented a reference taking place, was upheld as acceptable because the rule was applied in similar domestic circumstances as well and was there to ensure legal certainty and clarity. In other words, the national procedural rules could not be seen to be applied in two different ways according to whether EU or national substantive laws were concerned.

Somewhat unhelpfully in *Van Schijndel*, the Court of Justice held that each rule of procedural law and thus each case has to be judged on its merits, taking into account the rights of defence, legal certainty and the role of the national procedure before determining whether it renders the application of Community law impossible or excessively difficult. This would seem only to provoke further references to the Court of Justice each time a slightly new procedural law is brought into question.

In **Case C-326/96 *Levez v Jennings***, the Court of Justice considered a UK procedural law that limited the period of claim for damages in sex discrimination cases to a period not exceeding two years running backward from the date of commencement of proceedings. The Court of Justice acknowledged that, in the absence of a Community regime on the matter, it was for member states to determine procedural rules governing Community law rights provided that they were equivalent to similar domestic actions and were effective. A limit of two years was not criticized. However, Ms Levez had been misinformed or deliberately misled by the employer as to the higher earnings of a male predecessor and had only learnt the truth on leaving her job. Under such circumstances, the Court of Justice held that, if applied, the rule would serve to deprive an

> employee from effective enforcement of Community law because it would be almost impossible to obtain arrears of remuneration and to enable employers to avoid paying damages by deceit. In such circumstances, the rule would be manifestly incompatible with the principles of EC law.

Following the *Emmott* case, each case requires a clear demonstration that the particular facts of the case will lead to a particular unjust result, but this is not very helpful in general terms to determine whether in future cases the national procedural law will upset EU law rights. The cases previously considered in section 8.3 on *Francovich* state liability are also relevant to this discussion in that they also demonstrate the impact on the national legal systems of remedies developed by the Court of Justice and the extension of those remedies both against other individuals under EU law and the courts of the member states. These EU law remedies were simply not available previously, although some member states may have had national remedies that would have achieved the same result.

The next case considers and summarizes the scope of the EU law remedy.

Case C-432/05 *Unibet* is a case referred to the Court of Justice by the Swedish Supreme Court about the compatibility of a Swedish law on lotteries with Community law. In order to determine this, the national court enquired specifically about the scope of the principle of effective judicial protection and whether Community law required a member state's legal order to provide a self-standing action for a declaration that a provision of its national law conflicted with Community and whether, in waiting for the determination, interim relief must be granted. The Court of Justice held that the principle of effective judicial protection is a general principle of Community law stemming from the constitutional traditions common to the member states, which is also enshrined in Articles 6 and 13 of the European Convention on Human Rights (ECHR) and which has also been affirmed by Article 47 of the EU Charter of Fundamental Rights. It confirmed that Article 10 EC (now 4(3) TEU) required member states to ensure judicial protection of individuals' rights and refer to its earlier case law on this including Cases 33/76 *Rewe*, 45/76 *Comet* and C-312/93 *Peterbroeck*.

---

cross reference

Cases 33/76 Rewe, *45/76* Comet *and C-312/93* Peterbroeck *are considered at section 8.4.1.*

The Court of Justice held in this case, though, that, in the absence of a Community rule, the member states were left to decide according to their own procedural rules. Consequently, the principle of effective judicial protection does not require the national legal order of a member state to provide for a free-standing action for an examination of whether national provisions are compatible with Article 49 EC (now 56 TFEU), provided that other effective legal remedies, which are no less favourable than those governing similar domestic actions, make it possible for such a question of compatibility to be determined as a preliminary issue. Furthermore, the principle of effective judicial protection of an individual's rights under EU law must be interpreted as requiring it to be possible in the legal order of a member state for interim relief to be granted until the competent court has given a ruling on whether national provisions are compatible with EU law, where the grant of such relief is necessary to ensure the full effectiveness of the judgment to be given on the existence of such rights.

This essentially confirms the position previously laid down in Case C-213/89 *Factortame*, which provides that this should be no more difficult to obtain than the application for interim relief in cases concerned with domestic law. The principle of the effective judicial protection thus ensures that, regardless of the existence of national law remedies, EU law rights are subject to protection before the national courts.

8.4.4 Section summary

National procedural autonomy is still the general rule and is still respected under the EU legal order, but the Court of Justice has intruded into the area by developing the demands for effectiveness and equivalence or by providing new remedies in the member states with the aim of ensuring a balance between the objective to protect the national procedural autonomy and at the same time to protect the effectiveness of EU law. Until there is an agreement by all member states to try to harmonize procedural law, a very difficult task at best, the ad hoc case law development that we have witnessed is not likely to change. The only change in this respect, which was introduced by the Constitutional Treaty and retained in the Lisbon Treaty, is quite modest. New Article 19(1) TEU provides as a general statement that member states must provide remedies sufficient to ensure effective legal protection in the fields covered by Union law, which merely reflects, but in far simpler language, the *Unibet* case.

cross reference
See section 8.4.3.

Summary

cross reference
Considered in
Chapters 6, 7 and 9.

The original provision of remedies in the EU legal order were largely those provided by the Treaty and included the direct remedies and the Article 234 EC (now 367 TFEU) preliminary ruling procedure. It can be seen, however, that these provide only half the picture and, more importantly from the perspective of individuals, are the series of remedies that have been introduced and developed by the Court of Justice. Some of these can be regarded as necessary to plug a gap in the first set of remedies – that is, direct effects – developed to supplement and provide an alternative to the Treaty-based remedies and other Court-established remedies, to further develop and plug gaps in the Court-developed remedies – that is, indirect effects, incidental horizontal effects and state liability. It should be clear that a study of the Treaties alone does not provide the complete picture of remedies in the EU legal order and that the remedies in this chapter are equally important, constituting as they do the second half of the system of dual vigilance that has developed, as outlined at the beginning of this chapter and Chapter 6.

Questions

For suggested
approaches to
answering these
questions scan here
or visit the Online
Resource Centre.

1. Are regulations necessarily directly effective? Give reasons for your answer.

2. Has the application of the doctrine of direct effects blurred the distinction between Regulations and Directives? If so, does it matter?

3. Look at Articles 35 and 60 TFEU. Are they capable of direct effects? Explain why or why not, as appropriate.

4. Distinguish between horizontal and vertical direct effects. Do these terms apply to all forms of EU law? If not, why not?

5. How far have the drawbacks that resulted from the denial of horizontal direct effects of Directives been overcome by the Court of Justice's decisions in subsequent case law?

6   What are indirect effects and how are they supposed to assist ind
    legal rights?

7   What difficulties may be faced by national courts in trying to operat
    case law to support your answer.

8   To what extent does the doctrine of 'state liability' first established
    add to the range of individual remedies in EU law?

9   What criteria must be satisfied before a claim under state liability
    is this judged?

10 To what extent is the principle of national procedural autonomy re
    order? To what extent should it be?

DLA PIPER

Articles
to read

Further reading

BOOKS

Prinssen, J. M. and Schrauwen, A. (eds) *Direct Effect: Rethinking a Classic of EC Legal Doctrine*, 2nd edn, Europa Law Publishing, Groningen, 2004.

Ward, A. *Judicial Review and the Rights of Private Parties in EU Law*, 2nd edn, Oxford University Press, Oxford, 2007.

ARTICLES

Anagnostaras, G. 'The quest for an effective remedy and the measure of protection afforded to putative Community law rights' (2007) 32(5) EL Rev 727.

Bebr, G. 'Casenote on *Francovich*' (1992) 29 CML Rev 557.

Brinkhorst, L. 'Case note on the *Grad* and *SACE* decisions' (1971) 8 CML Rev 380.

Broberg, M. '*Acte clair* revisited: adapting the *acte clair* criteria to the demands of the times' (2008) 45 CML Rev 1383.

Craig, P. 'Directives, direct, indirect effect and the construction of national legislation' (1997) 22 EL Rev 519.

Davis, R. 'Liability in damages for breach of Community law: some reflections on the question of who to sue and the concept of "the state" ' (2006) 31 EL Rev 69.

Dougan, M. 'When worlds collide: competing visions of the relationship between direct effect and supremacy' (2007) 44 CML Rev 931.

Drake, S. 'Scope of courage and the principle of "individual liability" for damages: further development of the principle of effective judicial protection by the Court of Justice' (2006) 31 EL Rev 841.

Easson, A. 'The direct effect of EEC Directives' (1979) 28 ICLQ 319.

Eilsmansber, T. 'The relationship between rights and remedies in EC law: in search of the missing link' (2004) 41 CML Rev 1199.

Granger, M.-P. 'National applications of *Francovich* and the construction of a European administrative *ius commune*' (2007) 32(5) EL Rev 157.

Nassimpian, D. '...And we keep on meeting: (de)fragmenting state liability' (2007) 32 EL Rev 819.

Further reading

217

Prechal, S. 'Member state liability and direct effect: what's the difference after all?' (2006) 17 EBL Rev 299.

Prechal, S. and De Vries, S. 'Seamless web of judicial protection in the internal market' (2009) 34(1) EL Rev 5.

Schermers, H. 'No direct effect for Directives' (1997) 3(4) EPL 527.

Steiner, J. 'From direct effects to *Francovich*: shifting means of enforcement of Community law' (1993) 18 EL Rev 3.

Tridimas, T. 'Black, white and shades of grey: horizontality of Directives revisited' (2002) 21 YEL 327.

Vajda, C. 'Liability for breach of Community law: a survey of the ECJ cases post *Factortame*' (2006) 17 EBL Rev 257.

Von Bogdandy, A. 'Pluralism, direct effect, and the ultimate say: on the relationship between international and domestic law' (2008) 6(3–4) ICON 397.

Winter, J. 'Direct applicability and direct effect: two distinct and different concepts in Community law' (1972) 9 CML Rev 425.

Direct actions before the European Court of Justice

Learning objectives

In this chapter, you will focus on the following direct actions against the European Union institutions before the Court of Justice of the European Union:

- the judicial review of acts of the institutions (Article 263 TFEU, ex 230 EC);

- the action against the institutions for a failure to act (Article 263 TFEU, ex 232 EC);

- actions for damages for loss caused as a result of an act of the institutions (Articles 268 and 340 TFEU, ex 235 and 288 EC); and

- the incidental challenge to EU Acts (Article 277 TFEU, ex 241 EC).

Introduction

This chapter concerns actions provided for by the original Treaties, although in some cases in amended versions, which are heard directly before the European Court of Justice (ECJ) or now the General Court. The most important are the Article 263 TFEU action to annul acts of the institutions that have been enacted in error in some way, and Article 340 TFEU, which is an action for damages for loss caused by the actions of the institutions. In both of these actions, individuals have found it very difficult to succeed, even with cases that on their face show great merit; the reasons for this will be explored in the chapter. The chapter also discusses Articles 265 and 277 TFEU, which have not been the subject of many actions before the ECJ and as a result are far less frequently included in European Union (EU) law courses. They have, though, been included for the sake of completeness.

9.1 Actions to annul EU acts

Article 263 TFEU is the action to annul legislative acts of the Union that are defective in some way.

> It was held in **Case 294/83 *Parti Ecologiste Les Verts* v *EP*** that the European Community (EC) is a Community based on the rule of law in as much as neither its member states nor its institutions can avoid a review of the question whether the measures adopted by them are in conformity with the basic constitutional charter, the Treaty.

Thus Article 263 TFEU provides for actions to be brought before the Court of Justice to allow it to review the validity of acts of the Union institutions. The General Court (formerly the Court of First Instance, or CFI) has jurisdiction to hear direct actions brought by natural or legal persons against acts of Union institutions, which are addressed to them or directly concerning them as individuals.

Article 263 TFEU

The Court of Justice shall review the legality of legislative acts, of acts of the Council, of the Commission and of the European Central Bank, other than recommendations and opinions, and of acts of the European Parliament and of the European Council intended to produce legal effects *vis-à-vis* third parties. It shall also review the legality of acts of bodies, offices or agencies of the Union intended to produce legal effects *vis-à-vis* third parties.

If found to be invalid, the Court of Justice has the sole right to declare those acts void. This action helps to ensure that the Union institutions comply with all requirements of EU law when they adopt acts. This section will consider the two main aspects of this action: admissibility and the merits or substance of the action. After these technical elements have been covered, we will also consider the reform and suggestions that have been made for the reform of Article 263 TFEU both generally and to its previous form as Article 230 EC, raised due to its apparent strictness. Finally, alternatives to it will be considered. The sections will include the changes made by the Lisbon Treaty.

9.1.1 **Admissibility**

The issue of the admissibility of Article 263 TFEU has to be addressed first. Failure to satisfy all four requirements of admissibility will result in the case being rejected by the Court of Justice. Admissibility includes the questions of which institutions are subject to review, which acts can be reviewed, the time limit for challenging acts and the applicants who can bring an action. All of these will be considered in turn, but the latter aspect has been the greatest barrier in practice to individual applicants and understandably demands most emphasis in case law and thus also textbooks. One of the problems in getting to grips with this topic in the past has been the wide choice of relevant cases. Many cases are difficult to reconcile with others and an attempt to do so can be frustrating because the decisions of the Court of Justice are very often policy-driven to achieve a just result in cases that merit it and in all other cases to discourage applications by individuals challenging general legislation. Thus it is hard, if not impossible at times, to see clear reasoning and development, although it is hoped that the changes introduced by the Lisbon Treaty will help to rationalize the jurisprudence. However, in view of the vagueness of some of the changes, the changes may also create their own sets of problems, as will discussed in this chapter.

9.1.1.1 The institutions the acts of which are reviewable

Article 173 EEC (now 263 TFEU), as originally constituted, stated that the acts of the Commission and Council were subject to review, but case law extended the power of review additionally to acts of the European Parliament (EP). Over a series of cases, the Court of Justice justified this on the basis that, as the EP's powers grew, it should be responsible for acts that create legally binding effects in respect of third parties and these should therefore be open to review.

> See **Cases 230/81** *Luxembourg* **v** *EP* in respect of the choice of the EP's seat, **294/83** *Parti Ecologiste Les Verts* **v** *EP* in respect of a challenge to the apportionment of election campaign funds and **34/86** *Council* **v** *European Parliament (Budgetary Procedure)* with regard to budgetary decision of the President of the EP.

cross reference
The democratic deficit debate is considered in Chapter 2, section 2.4.3.1.

The development is thus very much allied to the democratic deficit debate. As the EP's role in making law – that is, its rights – increased, so correspondingly should have its duties and obligations, to include the duty to make decisions and legal acts lawfully. Thus there should be a right to challenge decisions of the EP that breach the legal standards required by the Treaties and in general principles of law. This is reflected in the further amendments extending the range of Institutions expressly, which were included in the new Article 263 TFEU by the Lisbon Treaty, which now provides as follows.

> **Article 263 TFEU**
>
> . . . .
>
> The Court of Justice of the European Union shall review the legality of legislative acts, of acts of the Council, of the Commission, of the European Central Bank, other than recommendations and opinions, and of acts of the European Parliament and of the European Council intended to produce legal effects vis-à-vis third parties.

The Court of Justice has held that, to be subject to a challenge, an institution must be empowered under the Treaty to enact binding measures; therefore this does not include for example, the Committee of Permanent Representatives (COREPER; see Case C-24/94 *Commission* v *Council*). The Lisbon Treaty amended this Article to make clear that all Union institutions or combinations of them that enact both legislative acts per se and those that are intended to produce legal effects are bodies the acts of which can be challenged under Article 263 TFEU. The inclusion of the European Council is significant, because this subjects for the first time the political-policy driving force of the EU to legal judicial control and, as such, bolsters the claim of the EU that it too respects the rule of law.

cross reference
See Chapter 2, section 2.2.6, for further details on COREPER.

9.1.1.2 Reviewable acts

Prior to the Lisbon Treaty reforms, the jurisdiction of the Court under Article 230 EC applied to the legally binding acts of the institutions listed in Article 249 EC, which are Regulations, Directives and Decisions, and does not therefore include recommendations or opinions or, strictly applied, anything else. However, the term 'Act' and the definition of what constitutes an act or a decision had been given a very wide interpretation by the ECJ so as to bring many other forms of acts within review that would not, on the face of it, be admissible. The reasoning for such an extension was that because these can create binding legal effects or affect the legal status of third parties, they should be subject to review and, as will be noted following, Article 263 TFEU has been amended to reflect this case law development by expressly including not only legislative acts, but also all acts intended to produce legal effects for third parties. Hence, then, the previous case law, which demonstrated the variety of acts that could then be challenged, but not named in the Treaty Article, now merely serve as examples of what can be challenged, including a letter, the minutes of a Council meeting, a budget decision of the EP, a press release and a Commission Communication.

It was held in **Cases 8–11/66 *Noordwijks Cement Accord*** that the test to apply to a particular act is whether it has binding legal effects or changes the legal position of the applicant. The case involved *a letter*, which changed the immunity from prosecution of certain companies under Competition law.

In **Case 22/70 *Commission* v *Council (ERTA)*** it was held that Article 249 EC (now 288 TFEU) was not exhaustive and special acts such as the *minuted discussions of the Council*, which essentially set down detailed policy decisions and the Community stance for the European Road Transport Agreement, could also be challenged.

Case 294/83 *Parti Ecologiste Les Verts* v *European Parliament* and the EU Treaty extended the list of reviewable acts to those of the EP that give rise to legally binding effects on the position of third parties, in this case concerning *a budget decision of the EP* sharing out of the budget among the party groupings.

In **Case C-106/96 *UK* v *Commission***, the Council had decided not to support 'Poverty 4', a programme to combat poverty and social exclusion, but the Commission decided nevertheless to fund a number of projects amounting to an expenditure of ECU 6 million and issued a *press* *release* to advertise this. If the last case looked a bit like sharp practice, this one looks even more deliberate and helps us to understand why the Commission is criticized in some quarters. The Court of Justice held that the Commission lacked the competence to commit the expenditure and the decision was annulled. However, in view of the fact that much of the expenditure had already taken place, the Court decided, in the interests of legal certainty, to exercise the discretion given to it under Article 231 EC and rule in favour of the payments made or promised.

In **Case C-57/95 *French Republic* v *Commission***, the Court of Justice ruled on a French action to annul a *Commission Communication*, which it was argued imposed new obligations on the member states. It held that the challenged Communication, which was published in the Official Journal (OJ) 'C' Series and was not a legislative Act envisaged by Article 249 EC (now 288 TFEU), was a measure that could be the subject of an annulment action. The content of communication was considered and the Court of Justice thought that the Communication had 'imperative wording' and that its content was the same subject matter as a withdrawn draft Directive that had not found approval in Council. Hence it held that the Communication constituted an act intended to have legal effects on its own, distinct from the Treaty provisions, and an action to annul it could be upheld.

There remain exceptions to this in that there are some acts that create legal effects that cannot be the subject of challenge.

In **Case 7/61 *Commission* v *Italy*** it was held that the reasoned opinion given by the Commission under the Article 226 EC (now 258 TFEU) proceedings did not constitute an act that can be subject of review under Article 230 EC (now 263 TFEU).

Similarly, in **Case 48/65 *Lütticke* v *Commission***, the applicants had requested the Commission to take action against the German Federal Republic regarding a breach of Community law, but the Commission refused. Lütticke applied under Article 230 EC (now 263 TFEU) to annul the decision not to act, but it was held that the refusal to act was not a legally binding act and therefore not reviewable.

In addition, applicants cannot challenge a decision to prosecute.

In **Case C-131/03 P *Reynolds Tobacco Holdings and others***, the Commission took decision to commence legal proceedings against the American company, which it suspected of smuggling cigarettes into the EU. Reynolds challenged that decision, but the CFI and ECJ held that the decision to take legal action was not a reviewable act. The decision had legal effects, but not ones that satisfied the test for Article 230 EC because the decisions did not determine definitively per se the obligations of the parties to the case. That determination can result only from the judgment of the Court. The ECJ confirmed that only acts that were binding on, and capable of affecting the interests of, the applicant by bringing about a distinct change in his legal position could be challenged. In this case, the decision to take legal action would not affect the legal position, while the judgment of the Court would – but, of course, that would be subject to an appeal by the party.

Hence a wide array of measures can be subject to review dependent on the legal effects that they produce or their nature and not only the three formal acts listed in Article 288 TFEU (ex 249 EC).

9.1.1.3 Time limits

Article 263(6) TFEU provides that the applicant has two months from:

- the date of publication of the measure; or
- the date of notification; or
- in the absence of publication or notification, the date on which it came to the notice of the applicant, as the case may be.

These time limits apply regardless of the status of the applicant.

Note that the third ground applies only where the act was not published or notified, which, although clearly not impossible with some of the documents that have been held to be subject to challenge, is certainly rare.

The time limit for challenging a regulation has been determined to run from fifteen days following publication: see Article 81 of the Rules of Procedure of the Court of Justice.

This was to allow time for the dispatch from the Luxembourg Official Publications Office of the Official Journal to the furthest parts of the EU as it was then. Now this seems less necessary with online publication.

In **Case T-79/89** *BASF* **v** *Commission*, the time limits were held by the CFI (now the General Court) not to apply where there are such serious defects in the measure that it is to be regarded as non-existent.

9.1.2 *Locus standi*: who may apply

The question of who may apply relates to what is known as the *locus standi* of applicants.

. . . .

locus standi

Literally meaning 'the place of standing', it relates to the recognition of a legal interest in a matter that produces the right to mount a legal challenge against a legal provision.

. . . .

No standing means no right to challenge, hence this is absolutely crucial to an applicant's chances.

There are now three categories of applicant: privileged, semi-privileged and non-privileged.

9.1.2.1 Privileged

The privileged applicants are named by Article 263 TFEU as the member states, the Council and the Commission, and, following the Treaty of Nice, the EP, all of which have the right to attack any act. Notably, despite its elevation to a full institution by the Lisbon Treaty in Article 13 TEU, the European Council is not included; it may be, as with the EP previously, that the Court of Justice has to step in to provide that right should the European Council seek to bring an action under Article 263 TFEU.

9.1.2.2 Limited or semi-privileged

The semi-privileged applicants comprise a category first established in case law for the EP by the Court of Justice; but following its elevation to a full Union institution, named in Article 7 EC (now 13 TEU), the EP moved out of this category. The Treaty of Amsterdam added to the semi-privileged category the Court of Auditors, which has the right to challenge acts of the institutions, but only for the purpose of protecting its prerogatives. The right was extended to the European Central Bank (ECB) by the Treaty on European Union (TEU). The term 'protection of prerogatives' is one that was essentially developed in case law and means 'where their interests are clearly affected'.

> See, for example, **Case 138/79 *Maizena (Roquette Freres)* v *Council***, as confirmed in **Cases C-70/88 *EP* v *Council* (Chernobyl)** and **C-295/90 *EP* v *Council* (Students Residence Directive)**, in which the challenge by the EP to the legal base used by the Council was successful.

This limited right of challenge is now confirmed in Article 263 TFEU. The original *locus standi* reflected the original much lesser and more limited law-making and participatory role of the EP, and the extensions over time to the EP and now to the Court of Auditors and ECB reflect the fact that the decision-making of those bodies also can have far-reaching consequences. The Lisbon Treaty has added the Committee of the Regions (CoR) to the category of semi-privileged applicants, but oddly in the light of the latter change it does not add the European Economic and Social Committee (EESC) nor even the European Council, which is thus excluded from any privileged applicant status.

All other persons are non-privileged applicants, who must satisfy certain conditions before their right of access to the Court of Justice will be recognized.

9.1.3 **Non-privileged applicants'** *locus standi*

Article 263(4) TFEU provides for circumstances in which non-privileged applicants can bring actions for judicial review.

For more details on this section scan here or visit the Online Resource Centre.

> **Article 263(4) TFEU**
>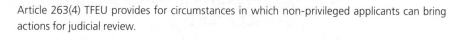
>
> Any natural or legal person may, under the conditions laid down in the first and second paragraphs, institute proceedings against
>
> [i]   an act addressed to that person
>
> [ii] or which is of direct and individual concern to them,
>
> [iii] and against a regulatory act which is of direct concern to them and does not entail implementing measures.

The first thing to note is that all three conditions have been changed in some way by the Lisbon Treaty, as will be explained in the sections following.

The content of this Article represents a distinct change from the former version contained in Article 230 EC, which provided that proceedings could be instituted against a decision addressed to that person or against a decision that, although in the form of a Regulation or a decision addressed to another person, is of direct and individual concern to the former. It remains to be seen through the case law what this means in practice.

9.1.4 **Acts addressed to the applicant**

This first situation has been revised in a rather subtle way, the impact of which will become clear only if and when the Court is asked to rule on it. 'Decisions' in Article 230 EC has been replaced by 'acts' in Article 263 TFEU, which is not defined and thus suggests that, provided that something is addressed to the applicant, whatever its form, it may be subject to review. Hence, where the applicant is directly addressed, he or she will have automatic standing and this is most likely to occur in specific circumstances in which, for example, the applicant has been the subject of a formal decision of the Commission under the competition rules of Articles 101–102 TFEU (ex 81 and 82 EC) and Regulation 1/2003. For the purposes of the addressee mounting a challenge, there is no barrier to admissibility provided that the time limit has been observed.

> In **Case T-138–89** *BBV* v *Commission*, it was held by the CFI that it was not possible to challenge a potential decision (in other words, a decision that might be made, but which had not actually been made at the time of the challenge to the claim that the potential decision would affect the applicant's interest). The applicant cannot be seen to be 'jumping the gun' by challenging a claim that will be heard in court before that claim goes to court.

The next two situations or categories have reformulated significantly the circumstances under which individuals may challenge acts of EU institutions and bodies that have not been addressed to them.

9.1.5 **An act that is of direct and individual concern to the applicant**

This condition reflects previous case law, to which the section will thus refer, that demonstrating 'individual' was and is the most important aspect of the application and thus admissibility.

It replaces the previous formulation in Article 230 EC, which referred to being able to challenge a decision that, although it was in the form of a Regulation, was of direct and individual concern to the applicant. In other words, this concerns any acts addressed to another person. Thus the new Article 263 TFEU no longer specifically mentions 'decision' or 'Regulations', but instead refers more generally and vaguely to 'acts', which is not then defined. At the present time, and without clarification as yet from the Court of Justice, this is assumed to refer to any legislative acts – that is, those defined in Article 288 TFEU (ex 249 EC). This view is formed in view of the previous case law history and the third circumstance for challenge, which refers to 'regulatory acts'. Therefore the focus turns on 'direct and individual concern'. 'Individual' remains the most important aspect, just as it was in the case law developed by the Court in establishing the circumstances in which individuals could challenge regulations, which, by their nature, are not addressed to individuals because they are acts of general application – that is, to everyone. Before looking in particular at 'individual', 'direct concern' will be considered, for which the previous case law remains relevant.

9.1.5.1 Direct concern

With 'direct concern', the general rule is that if a member state is granted discretion to act under the provision, then the provision cannot by its nature give rise to direct concern. Discretion on the part of the member states means that the applicants are only indirectly concerned. This was certainly the initial view taken by the Court of Justice in Cases 25/62 *Plaumann* and 69/69 *Alcan* as examples of how the Court of Justice has interpreted this.

> **Case 62/70 *Bock* v *Commission (Chinese Mushrooms)*** is a good example that involved the authorization for a member state to restrict imports – that is, it had the discretion. An application was made by Bock to import Chinese mushrooms, but was refused by Germany on 11 September and only authorized by the Commission on 15 September. Hence the decision was a retroactive measure in direct response to the application from Bock. In other words, the discretion to act was already waived and Bock was therefore held to be directly concerned.

> This trend was continued in **Case 11/82 *Piraiki-Patraiki* v *Commission***, in which the French authorities applied for, and were authorized to impose, quotas on yarn imports from Greece. In considering an application to review this decision, the Court of Justice held that where interested parties could be identified with certainty or a high degree of probability, direct concern would be satisfied, despite the theoretical discretion on the part of the member state. In other words, the country applied for permission to restrict imports and the Commission had granted it, so whilst in theory the country had the discretion to restrict imports or not, in reality, it had already exercised that discretion and thus had extinguished that discretion.

It may now, following the reform of Article 263 TFEU, be that direct concern will be subject to greater scrutiny because of the extension of the range of acts that can be challenged and that proving individual concern may have become less onerous, considered next.

9.1.5.2 Individual concern

Why is there a requirement of individual concern? The emphasis on 'individual' derives from the previous concerns that led to a general rule about the ability of individual to challenge Regulations, which are general acts, therefore could not be challenged by an individual because true Regulations are directly and generally applicable. They are so-called 'normative' acts, which apply to everyone in the EU – in theory, that is: not everybody, of course, is necessarily interested in the regulation of some of the finer aspects of the Common Agricultural Policy (CAP). In view of Article 288 TFEU, this general rule makes sense. This higher status of regulations demands that they are to be regarded and protected as similar to 'primary law', and that, because of their general applicability, they should not be so easily contested by anyone affected by a Regulation.

cross reference
This issue will be considered in further detail in section 9.1.5.3.

In **Case 17/62** *Fruit and Vegetable Confederation* **v** *Commission*, it was held:

> The essential characteristics of a decision arise from the limitation of the persons to whom it is addressed, whereas a regulation, being essentially of a legislative nature, is applicable, not to a limited number of persons, defined and identifiable, but to categories of persons viewed abstractly and in their entirety.

In **Case 6/68** *Zuckerfabrik Watenstedt* **v** *Council*, the Court held:

> A measure does not lose its character as a normative act because the factual situation to which it applies makes it possible to identify, more or less accurately, the persons affected. A regulation applies to objectively determined situations and produces legal effects with regard to categories of persons defined in a general and abstract manner.

In other words, being able to see clearly whom a regulation specifically affects does not actually deprive it of its general character, which means that we have to find some different or unusual characteristic in order for an applicant to stand out and be able to challenge it.

Previously, there were a number of reasons identified why this general rule should not apply and a lot of the case law considered under these exceptions also helped us to understand the term 'individual concern'. Very often, 'individual' was considered first, as it was in the leading Case 25/62 *Plaumann*. Therefore the reform of Article 263 TFEU makes good sense by simply requiring now an investigation of 'direct and individual', and much of the previous case law and categorization can now be ignored.

Individual concern has been very hard to demonstrate and has often been tested by the Court of Justice first or at the same time as direct concern to decide admissibility, as in the leading and still very much valid judgment of Case 25/62 *Plaumann* v *Commission*. The fact that an applicant no longer has to demonstrate that a Regulation was, in fact, a decision may make life easier for applicants – but it might also be that it makes no difference at all and that the ECJ will continue to be cautious in opening the doors.

The amended Article 263 TFEU now states that an act may be challenged that is of direct and individual concern to the applicant, which thus now tacitly rather than expressly includes a Regulation and indeed acts addressed to other persons. Both are dealt with now in the same breath. Again, these points are ones that hopefully will be clarified at some stage by the General Court or Court of Justice.

First of all, however, the original case law will be considered, starting with *Plaumann*. An applicant must show some factors that distinguish themselves uniquely.

This was the position taken in the leading and still very much valid judgment of **Case 25/62** ***Plaumann* v *Commission***. A decision was addressed to the German government refusing permission to reduce duties on clementines, which was challenged by Plaumann. The test decided for individual concern was: does the decision affect the applicant by virtue of the fact that he is member of the abstractly defined class addressed by the rule, for example because he is a importer of clementines, or does it affect him because of attributes peculiar to him that differentiate him from all other persons? Plaumann was held to be one of a class of importers and not therefore individually concerned. The reasoning is that anyone could become an importer.

Persons other than those to whom a decision is addressed may claim to be individually concerned only if that decision affects them by reason of certain attributes that are peculiar to them or by reason of circumstances in which they are differentiated from all other persons and by virtue of these factors distinguishes them individually, just as in the case of the person addressed. In *Plaumann*, the applicant was affected by the disputed decision as an importer of clementines – that is, by reason of a commercial activity that may at any time be practised by any person – and is not therefore such as to distinguish the applicant in relation to the contested decision as in the case of the addressee.

The next case makes this point all the more clearly and forcefully in view of its facts.

In **Case 231/82 *Spijker Kwasten BV* v *Commission***, an import ban was imposed on Chinese brushes. Spijker Kwasten was the only importer of Chinese brushes in Holland and although SK had previously requested a licence, it was held that the company could not be individually concerned. The reasoning was that the decision restricting imports was valid for the forward period of the next six months; therefore it was possible that others could apply for licences in that period and hence there was no individual concern for SK.

9.1.5.3 Other instances in which 'individual' has been recognized

1. Past events and retroactivity

It is to be noted that there is a great deal of overlap with the next category such that, in future, they might be blended into a single, albeit more complex, category.

In **Case 62/70 *Bock* v *Commission***, the company was individually concerned because applications made by Bock to import Chinese mushrooms were refused by Germany on 11 September, but the required authorization by the Commission was passed only on 15 September. Hence the decision was a retroactive measure in direct response to the application from Bock, which was held to have a vested legal interest and therefore individually concerned.

See also **Case C-152/88 *Sofrimport* v *Commission*** concerning a Regulation restricting the import of Chilean apples, which was adopted whilst some apples were in transit and of which the Commission was specifically notified to take into account when the ban was enacted. Sofrimport was thus part of a closed group of companies with goods in transit when the Regulation was adopted and to which there could be no addition. It was thus individually concerned and the application was held to be admissible.

Case C-309/89 *Codorniu* v *Council (Spanish Wine Producers)* involved a Regulation limiting the use of the 'Cremant' trade mark. Despite the Court of Justice confirming that the Regulation was a legislative measure applying to traders in general, it could still be of individual concern to one of them. Codorniu had distinguished itself by the ownership of a trade mark for the term 'Crement' from the year 1924, which the Community had tried to reserve for French and Luxembourg producers. Codorniu was able to challenge a Regulation that prevented its use of a registered trade mark 'Gran Cremant di Cordorniu', because this fact isolated them from other wine producers that had not registered this term and which were similarly restricted from using the name. Hence it was a Regulation for some or most, but it was a decision for Cordorniu. While the others might take out a trade mark now, they could not back date it to before the Regulation was enacted.

2. Where the identity of the natural or legal persons affected is fixed and ascertainable (the closed group category)

In **Cases 106 and 107/63 *Töpfer* v *Commission***, it was held that, in order to establish individual concern, an applicant must be affected alone or as a member of a fixed and closed class. The closed group enables the identity of the natural or legal persons affected to be fixed and thus ascertainable. Töpfer was so identified because the company had applied for a licence prior to a retroactive Commission decision that empowered the refusal of licences and was therefore identifiable.

In **Cases 41–44/70 *International Fruit Company* v *Commission***, a group of fruit importers were held to be entitled to challenge a Regulation where the identity of the natural of legal persons affected was already known and thus fixed and identifiable. Apple importers had applied in advance for import licences and the decision to issue a limited quantity of licences was made on the basis of applications previously received, therefore finite and known. The Regulation was a response to the individuals; no new persons could be added at the time of challenge or thereafter to the list of applicants.

Other successful cases include **Case C-152/88 *Sofrimport* v *Commission*** concerning a decision taken to restrict the import of Chilean apples whilst some were in transit and of which the Commission was specifically notified to take into account, and **Case C-389/89 *Cordorniu* v *Commission* (*Spanish Wine Producers*)** involving a Regulation limiting the use of the term 'Cremant'. Despite the Court confirming that the Regulation was a legislative measure applying to traders in general, it could still be of individual concern to one of them. Codorniu had distinguished itself by the ownership of a trademark for the term 'Cremant' from the year 1924, which the Community had tried to reserve for French and Luxembourg producers. Codorniu was able to challenge a Regulation that prevented its use of a registered trade mark 'Gran Cremant di Cordorniu', because this fact isolated it from other wine producers, which had not registered this term and were similarly restricted from using the name. Hence it was a Regulation for some or most, but it was a decision for Cordorniu *because of its individual concern*.

3. Where the applicant is named in the regulation

Alternatively, where the applicant is named in the Regulation, as in **Case 139/80 *Maizena* v *Council* (*aka Roquette Frères*)**, the action will be held to be of direct and individual concern. The Court of Justice held that despite being a measure of general application, certain individuals may challenge Regulations as if decisions, especially when one of the Articles of the Regulation specifically referred to the applicant companies. This is very close to the next category.

4. Competition law and anti-dumping cases or where the applicant has taken part in the investigation or issue of the legislation

A number of cases are concerned with alleged breaches of competition law by other companies or the dumping of goods on the EU market. The applicants are those that have made a complaint to the Commission about the activities of another company that appear to breach competition or anti-dumping rules. As a result of an investigation of individual importers, the Commission may take action by issuing a decision seeking to correct the situation or a general Regulation may be issued to catch all imports; thus the complaint has lead to the enactment of a regulation, as in the following examples.

In **Case 264/82 *Timex* v *Commission***, the Timex company had complained about dumping, which led to an anti-dumping Regulation that was nevertheless held to be of direct and individual concern to Timex.

Likewise, the application for review in **Case 26/76 Metro-SB-*Grossmarkte* v *Commission*** was held to be admissible because Metro had a legitimate interest in the decision aimed at another person. Metro had made a complaint under the Competition Law Regulation and had thus played a part that led to the decision.

See also **Case C-358/89 *Extramet Industrie* v *Council***, in which the Court had accepted the special circumstances, which were that the company was the largest importer and end user of calcium from China and the Soviet Union, and the only other supplier was a competitor. The company was also involved in the Commission investigations. A ban on calcium import would have affected it severely.

It would not include those who have merely written to the Commission to complain without further involvement.

9.1.6 Interest groups and party actions

Non-individual applications by their very nature might expect not to have standing. It might be anticipated that, by definition, an application from a group or party cannot be of individual concern. However, trade associations' applications have been recognized in Cases T-447–449/93 *AITEC* v *Commission* on the grounds that associations have standing if they represent the individual interests of some or all of their members or their own interests as an association.

In contrast in **Case T-585/93 *Greenpeace* v *Commission***, the plea that all individuals with an environmental interest, and not only an economic interest, in the consequences of a decision should be able collectively to be represented by a group failed. The CFI rejected this view, which was confirmed on appeal in Case C-321/95 P by the Court of Justice; it held that the decision had affected individuals in an abstract and general fashion only, and that the applicants representing them were thus similarly affected and similarly without standing.

9.1.7 The challenge to regulatory acts

This third condition or circumstance is new to Article 263 TFEU, introduced with the Lisbon Treaty reforms, and provides individual applicants with a right to make an application against a regulatory act that is of direct concern to them and does not entail implementing measures. It is to be stressed that the applicant need show direct concern only, as noted in section 9.1.5.1, but there no definition provided in the Treaties for what is meant by a 'regulatory act'. If the second circumstance does, in fact, refer to a legislative act, then it is to be assumed that this refers to non-legislative acts – hence the easier condition without the need to show individual concern for *locus standi*. Whilst legislative acts are described in new Article 289 TFEU, regulatory acts are not. These are therefore taken to be the delegated non-legislative acts described in new Article 290, which are, essentially, the delegated administrative acts taken by the Commission and, as such, it represents little change (these could include acts that are nevertheless labelled Regulations or Decisions). The condition, though, applies to regulatory acts only not entailing implementing measures, so nothing that allows further executive or otherwise understood to be administrative acts, which would seem to rule out any act delegating powers. It remains unclear, though, whether it means only the administrative acts of the Commission, or non-general legislative acts, such as those used in the anti-dumping cases, or indeed at its very widest interpretation even including Regulations. This would, however, seem to undermine conditions 2 and 3 of Article 263 TFEU. It would, though, probably exclude a challenge to Directives and these do, for the most part, require implementing measures.

cross reference
The anti-dumping cases are considered in section 9.1.5.3.

Hence this is now a description very much in need of the judicial clarification of the Court and it remains unclear as to whether it was intended to make challenges by individuals easier. Equally, at present, we are provided with no definition of what might constitute an implementing measure. Any subsequent formal action to put into effect an EU provision might suffice, thus removing the originating provision from the ability of individuals to challenge. Again, only the Court of Justice can now clarify this, save an unlikely future Treaty amendment.

9.1.8 Merits or grounds for annulment

Once admissibility has been established, the grounds or merits must be proved. These are laid down in Article 263(2) TFEU (ex 230(2) EC) and can often overlap in individual cases.

Article 263(2) TFEU (ex 230(2) EC)

It [the Court of Justice of the European Union] shall for this purpose have jurisdiction in actions brought by a Member State, the European Parliament, the Council or the Commission on grounds of lack of competence, infringement of an essential procedural requirement, infringement of the Treaties or of any rule of law relating to their application, or misuse of powers.

Article 13(2) TEU (ex 7 EC)

Each institution shall act within the limits of the powers conferred on it in the Treaties...

9.1.8.1 Lack of competence or authority

The lack of competence on the part of an institution to adopt a particular measure is really the equivalent of **ultra vires** and concerns the requirement that all measures must have the appropriate legal authority.

Case 9/56 *Meroni* v *High Authority* concerned the successful challenge to decisions taken by the High Authority to which, at the time, no delegated decision-making powers had been granted.

The High Authority was the forerunner of the Commission.

There is a degree of overlap with the fourth category – misuse of power – which will be considered in section 9.1.8.4.

Further examples of a lack of competence or authority include the following.

In **Case C-327/91** *France* v *Commission*, the Commission exceeded its competence when it concluded an international agreement with the United States because Article 300 EC (now 218 TFEU) required it to be concluded by the Council.

Case C-57/95 *French Republic* v *Commission* involves a French action to annul a Commission 'Communication'. The Court of Justice held that the Commission had no such power to adopt an Act imposing new obligations on the member states that were not inherent in the Treaty; thus the Commission lacked competence and the Act was annulled.

The most important and clearest of these cases is probably **Case C-378/98** *Germany* v *EP and Council (Tobacco Advertising)* in which a Directive banning tobacco advertising was introduced under a Treaty Article concerned with the completion of the internal market and which was held not to authorize the enactment of legislation concerned primarily with public health. The Directive was annulled.

9.1.8.2 Infringement of an essential procedural requirement

Specific requirements are laid down by Article 296 TFEU (ex 253 EC) that all Community secondary legislation must give reasons and refer to any proposals and opinions made in respect of the legislation. The Court of Justice has held that insufficient, or vague, or inconsistent, reasoning would constitute a breach of this ground.

It was held in **Case 24/62** *Germany* v *Commission (Wine Tariff Quotas)* that reasons must contain sufficient details of the facts and figures on which they are based.

In **Case 139/80 *Roquette and Maizena* v *Council***, the Council failed to consult the EP as required under old Article 43(2) EC. It had asked for an opinion, but did not wait long enough for the answer before going ahead with the Regulation, which was subsequently annulled.

In **Case C-325/91 *France* v *Commission***, it was held that there was a requirement to state the Treaty base; the failure to observe this led to the annulment of the measure.

Finally, in **Case 17/74 *Transocean Marine Paint Association* v *Commission***, a measure that is not notified will deprive an applicant of the right to protest and of having its views made known or represented to the relevant institution. It was therefore held liable to annulment under Article 230 EC (now 263 TFEU).

9.1.8.3 Infringement of the Treaty or any rule relating to its application

This is the most frequently argued ground because it is capable of embracing all errors of EU law, including breaches of general principles or human rights such as non-discrimination, proportionality, legitimate expectation and the right to a fair hearing. In the following cases, the Court of Justice recognized the general principles pleaded.

cross reference

Further examples of rules that would qualify under this subheading can be found in Chapter 4, sections 4.2.4–4.2.7.6.

Case 101/76 *KSH* v *Intervention Board* considered the principle of equality, **Case 17/74 Transocean** was concerned with the right to be heard and **Case 112/77 *Töpfer*** concerned legitimate expectation and legal certainty.

Case C-325/91 *France* v *Commission* would also be applicable here for infringing a Treaty requirement, which was the requirement to state the Treaty base.

9.1.8.4 Misuse of power by a Community institution

The basis of this ground concerns the use of power for the wrong purpose and was demonstrated very early in the life of the Communities.

In **Case 8/55 *Federation Charbonniere* v *High Authority***, the Court of Justice held in respect of Article 33 ECSC that power exercised must be related to the end result.

See also **Case 105/75 *Giuffrida* v *Council*** concerning the prearranged appointment of a Community official, which was an abuse of the selection system.

cross reference
This last case is considered at section 9.1.7.1.

Case C-378/98 *Germany* v *European Parliament and Council (Tobacco Advertising)* would also fit in here.

This category comes very close to the first one, in that the use of power as the basis of unauthorized action is the equivalent of having no lawful basis for the action undertaken or acting beyond power. The overlap was noted, but not reformed, by the Lisbon Treaty.

9.1.9 **The effect of a successful action and annulment**

Article 264 TFEU (ex 231 EC) provides that if the action is well founded, the Court of Justice shall declare the act concerned to be void. Article 264(2) TFEU (ex 230(2) EC) provides that the Court shall, if it considers this necessary, state which of the parts of an act can be considered as void and which parts not void, and can sever parts where possible. This means that the Court can specify those parts of the measure that will be annulled and those that may remain in force.

cross reference
This case is considered in section 9.1.1.2.

In **Case C-106/96 *UK* v *Commission (Poverty 4)***, the Court of Justice held that the Commission lacked the competence to commit the expenditure and the decision in the guise of an advertisement was annulled. However, in view of the fact that much of the expenditure had already taken place, the Court of Justice decided, in the interests of legal certainty, to exercise the discretion given to it under Article 231 EC (now 264 TFEU) and to rule in favour of the payments made or promised.

Article 266 TFEU (ex 233 EC) provides that where an act has been declared void, the institutions are obliged to take the necessary measures to comply with the judgment of the Court of Justice. The Court may only annul the act referred to it or dismiss the action, but cannot order an institution to pay a sum of money – that is, it cannot fine them.

9.1.10 **A restrictive approach?**

If the changes introduced to this Article by the Lisbon Treaty have made it easier for individuals to mount effective challenges, especially to legislative Acts and specifically to Regulations, this argument may be less valid today. This is, however, yet to be demonstrated.

cross reference
This was considered in Chapter 6, section 6.1.8, on the possible development of a system of precedent.

The reasons for the difficulties in demonstrating *locus standi* have been subject to much debate and policy factors feature large in this discussion. For example, there is a floodgate policy argument whereby *locus standi* requirements have been interpreted particularly restrictively by the Court of Justice to reduce the number of cases coming before it and the General Court. Litigants face lengthening delays to justice; thus keeping the number of cases down will help to reduce delay. Another argument is the suggestion that there is a desire to promote the Court of Justice more as a supreme court of the member states and not one directly accessible as a first-instance court for individuals. In this case, it is argued that the national courts are best placed to defend individuals' interests and that, if required, cases for annulment should be referred by the national courts under Article 267 TFEU (ex 234 EC). To some extent, both of these arguments were answered by the establishment of the CFI primarily to handle these cases, which elevated the Court of Justice into the role of an appeal court in relation to these categories of case. Other arguments revolve around discussions about balancing the interests of the Union and individuals.

The decision-making procedure in the Union is a much more complex procedure and often the result of compromise, which makes legislation more difficult to enact. The inevitable economic choices of the Union are bound to affect individuals and sometimes in an adverse way, but they must be allowed to be made, otherwise the ability of the Union and Commission to operate would be undermined. Individuals' actions should not hinder the institutions' ability to operate. Comparisons with the member states may be made: for example, that such challenges nationally are also subject to equally tight *locus standi* requirements under the constitutional traditions of the member states, which often makes individual challenges to general legislative measures entirely inadmissible and restricts individual challenges to secondary legislation only, and indeed only if they have a proven interest.

By contrast, in those areas in which individuals find it easier to achieve standing, such as competition law, state aids and anti-dumping measures, it may be argued that the often closer involvement of particular individuals makes the difference. The applicants are likely to be the ones involved in the process by informing the Commission of certain situations or can be seen clearly to be affected by the measures complained about. This then sets applicants apart from the many other challenges, arising most frequently against legislative decisions made under the CAP. Furthermore, there are those cases that arise from the application of retroactive legislation where the applicants are seen clearly as belonging to a fixed and identifiable group, and who would suffer an injustice if not allowed standing. In other words, the system works well when it needs to.

Arguments for a more liberalized test were most clearly made by Advocate General (AG) Jacobs in **Case C-50/00 *Union des Pequeños Agricultores (UPA)* v *Council***, influenced by the adoption of an as yet non-binding Charter of Fundamental Rights into the EC legal order under which individuals are entitled to expect an effective judicial remedy. It was argued that the Article 230 EC (now 263 TFEU) restrictive *locus standi* test leads to a possible denial of justice under the current system because the law for individuals is complex and unpredictable. Introducing a less strict test would fit in with a general tendency to extend the scope of judicial protection in response to the growth of powers of the Community; hence the suggestion that an applicant should be regarded as individually concerned where, by reason of his or her particular circumstances, the measure has, or is liable to have, a substantial adverse effect on his or her interests.

The CFI followed AG Jacob's test in **Case T-177/01 *Jego-Quere* v *Commission*** in which it held that, to give rise to standing, the measure must affect the applicant's legal position in a manner that is both definite and immediate, by restricting his or her rights or imposing obligations on him or her.

However, in **Case 50/00 *UPA***, the Court of Justice did not adopt AG Jacob's test nor did it approve the new test provided by the CFI, upholding the status quo for *locus standi* and making clear that the test established in Case 25/62 *Plaumann* remains valid and applicable.

Furthermore, the Court of Justice stated in the appeal **Case C-263/02 P *Commission* v *Jego-Quere*** that any revision to the standing rules was not for the Court, but for the member states in the context of a Treaty amendment. Thus it overturned the CFI decision, which it held had erred in law.

Although the member states have adopted the Constitutional Treaty amendment of old Article 230 EC (now 263 TFEU) whereby the natural or legal person challenge to regulatory acts no longer need show individual concern, it remains to be seen whether the Court of Justice will regard this as reversing its reversal of the former CFI decision in Case T-177/01 *Jego-Quere*.

cross reference

As noted in Chapter 6 and in section 9.1.10.1.

In **Case C-167/02 *Willi Rothley and others* v *European Parliament***, a plea for standing based on the right to judicial protection was dismissed by the Court of Justice, which stated that protection is still available through an Article 234 EC (now 267 TFEU) reference raising a question of the validity of Community law, although there is no guarantee that such a reference will either be made by the national court or accepted by the Court of Justice.

The overall picture remains that of a continuing restrictive *locus standi* for applicants under Article 263 TFEU, although indirect alternatives are available to individuals, albeit with mixed success.

It may be argued that the inclusion of new Article 19(1) TEU, which requires that 'member states shall provide remedies sufficient to ensure effective legal protection in the fields covered by Union law', reinforces the argument that the Court of Justice should not be a court of direct access, but that matters be filtered first by the national courts or alternatively that the General Court or Court of Justice may now interpret more liberally the rights of individuals to challenge Union Acts. Also, the revision of Article 263 TFEU, particularly in allowing a seemingly easier *locus standi* to challenge a regulatory act with no need to show individual concern as opposed to a legislative Act, may allow the Court to condone a more permissive regime. It remains to be seen whether the Court of Justice will regard this as reversing its reversal of the former CFI decision in Case T-177/01 *Jego-Quere*.

Article 263 TFEU, it seems, is destined to remain a difficult action with which to get to grips and will therefore continue to be one that must be studied carefully.

9.1.11 **Alternatives to Article 263 TFEU**

9.1.11.1 A reference under Article 267 TFEU

The first alternative is that a reference from a national court to the Court of Justice for a preliminary ruling on the validity of acts of the institutions is a question that must be referred by all national courts: see Case 314/85 *Firma Foto-Frost* v *Hauptzollamt Lübeck-Ost*. In general terms, actions under Article 267 TFEU avoid the strict time limits of Article 263 TFEU and are instead subject to the national procedural rules and time limits.

For example, in **Case 133/85 *Walter Rau* v *BALM***, a challenge to a Community decision was questioned by a national court because of the possibility that Article 230 (now 263 TFEU) could have been used. The Court of Justice held that if the outcome of the case depended on the validity of the decision, then a reference under Article 234 EC (now 267 TFEU) was permissible without having to decide if Article 230 EC could have been used. Hence the possibility of an Article 263 TFEU action does not preclude an attempt to challenge a Community decision before the national courts.

In **Case 101/76 *KSH***, a challenge to Commission Regulations had failed when raised directly before the Court of Justice, but was successful when made within an Article 234 EC (now 267 TFEU) reference in Cases 103 and 145/77 before the UK courts.

However, Article 267 TFEU cannot be used simply to get round the time limits of Article 263 TFEU.

In **Case C-188/92 *Textilwerke Deggendorf GmbH* v *Germany***, TWD was aware of a decision addressed to Germany that directly concerned TWD; however, it chose to challenge under Article 234 EC (now 267 TFEU) later rather than under Article 230 EC (now 263 TFEU). The Court of Justice held that the time limits in Article 230 EC apply equally to national court proceedings and Article 234 rulings on invalidity, and references will be barred if the applicant would undoubtedly have had standing under Article 230, but failed to take advantage of it within the time limit.

There are further difficulties or requirements facing individuals wishing to raise a question of validity via Article 267 TFEU, as was pointed out by the AG in **Case C-408/95 *Eurotunnel* v *SeaFrance***. There needs to be an element of national law to be able to raise a matter before the national courts.

The use of Article 234 EC (now 267 TFEU) as an alternative has been heavily criticized in **Case 50/00 *UPA*** by AG Jacobs, who argued that justice would be better served if access to the Court of Justice under Article 230 EC were made easier to individuals.

An Article 267 TFEU reference also increases the time involved in obtaining an answer by about two years and may lead to contrived cases being concocted in the national courts in order to challenge Community legislation. Finally, the national court retains the discretion whether or not to refer and may not consider a reference necessary. Hence Article 267 TFEU, as an alternative, is a very uncertain and unpredictable one.

9.1.11.2 The plea of illegality: Article 277 TFEU (ex 241 EC)

If there are other proceedings taking place before the Court of Justice, a party can raise an issue of illegality of a Union act of general application, but only indirectly or incidentally and not as an independent cause of action. Thus Article 277 TFEU is not simply a second chance to get around the strict time or *locus standi* limits of Article 263 TFEU; it is designed to overcome the strict *locus standi* requirements for private parties in cases that would otherwise be unjust.

In reflecting previous case law of the Court of Justice, the new Article 277 TFEU has been amended from the old Article 241 EC to apply not only narrowly to Regulations, but to all acts of general application.

cross reference

Article 277 TFEU is considered in section 9.4.

The Court of Justice held in **Case 92/78 *Simmenthal* v *Commission*** that the action would also cover acts that produce similar effects as, but which were not in the form of, a Regulation on the grounds that individuals should be given the chance to have reviewed implementing decisions that are of direct and individual concern, thus echoing the *locus standi* requirements under old Article 230 EC (now 263 TFEU).

The grounds in the action are expressly those listed in Article 263 TFEU. The effects are a declaration of inapplicability of the general act contested and an annulment of the act due to illegality.

9.1.11.3 Action for damages under Articles 268 and 340(2) TFEU

cross reference

Article 340 TFEU will be considered in further detail in section 9.3.

The action under Article 263 TFEU leads only to the annulment of the act and does not provide compensation for a damaged, but successful, applicant; therefore damages must be pursued under Article 340 TFEU as a follow-on action. However, the Article 340 TFEU action is a separate and autonomous action, and not dependent on an earlier Article 263 or 267 TFEU action: see Case 4/69 *Lütticke* v *Commission*. Therefore the Article 340 TFEU action could be commenced without pursuing an Article 263 TFEU action first. Furthermore, the legality of a measure alleged to have injured the plaintiff may be put in question indirectly under Article 277 TFEU, as noted in the previous section.

Action for failure to act (Article 265 TFEU, ex Article 232 EC)

Article 265 TFEU (ex 232 EC) concerns actions against the EP, the European Council, the Council, the Commission or the ECB, or other bodies, offices or agencies of the Union for a failure to act and constitutes an attempt to compel the institution or institutions concerned to take action. The action is designed to tackle the failure of an institution to act that is in violation of a Treaty duty. This clearly presupposes that there was a duty imposed on the institution to act in the first place. It complements an Article 263 TFEU (ex 230 EC) action to cover inaction and can be pleaded at the same time.

> In **Case 15/70 *Chevalley* v *Commission***, the Court of Justice held that it was not necessary to state which action was the subject of the application.

There are a number of similar features between the two Articles, but they were designed to cover different situations: Article 263 TFEU, illegal action; and Article 265 TFEU, illegal inaction. Both provisions, however, have as their objective the ending of a situation of illegality. Actions are heard at first instance by the General Court (formerly the CFI), with an appeal to the Court of Justice.

9.2.1 Admissibility and *locus standi*

9.2.1.1 Privileged applicants

The Union institutions and member states have, under Article 265(1) TFEU, a privileged right of action that is not subject to restrictions on admissibility – that is, who may bring an action before the Court of Justice to have the infringement of the failure to act established.

> The status of the EP as a privileged applicant was confirmed a long time ago in **Case 13/83 *EP* v *Council (Transport Policy)*** in which it was established that the privileged applicants can request actions requiring general legislative acts as well as decisions, without having to show any special interest.

The ECB was given the right to take action by the TEU in areas falling within its field of competence.

According to Article 265 TFEU, all of the institutions of the Union have the right to commence an action. These are now defined in Article 13 TEU and now include the European Council and the Court of Auditors.

9.2.1.2 Non-privileged applicants

Individuals, on the other hand, have a restricted, albeit more clearly defined, right of *locus standi* under Article 265(3) TFEU and more so than under Article 263 TFEU because there is no equivalent within the Article itself of direct and individual concern; they instead have to be potential addressees.

> **Article 265(3) TFEU**
> . . . .
> Any natural or legal person may, under the conditions laid down in the preceding paragraphs, complain to the Court that an institution, body, office of agency of the Union has failed to address to that person any act other than a recommendation or an opinion.

In **Case 246/81 *Lord Bethell* v *EC Commission***, it was held that to challenge under Article 232 EC (now 265 TFEU), an individual must have been legally entitled to make a claim for action as a potential addressee. The case involved a complaint of a failure to act on price fixing by the airlines, but it was held that any potential act would have been addressed to the airlines and not to Lord Bethell.

This strict view on the *locus standi* requirements has, however, been tempered by the Court of Justice in case law introducing requirements analogous to the direct and individual concern of Article 230 EC (now 263 TFEU).

See, for example, **Case C-68/95 *T Port* v *Bundesanstalt für Landeswirtschaft und Ernährung***, in that a potential act should have concerned an applicant in a direct and individual manner.

9.2.2 Acts subject to an Article 265 TFEU action

In many cases, the Court of Justice has rejected applications by individuals for measures of general legislative content.

Hence, it was held in **Cases 15/70 *Chevalley* v *Commission*** and **42/71 *Nordgetreide* v *Commission*** that applications are therefore restricted to decisions only; also in the *Chevally* case, it further held that a demand for an opinion is not admissible.

Regulations cannot be requested because, by their nature, they are not capable of being addressed to specific individuals only. There must be an obligation under the Treaty to adopt a reviewable act that is enforceable on the part of the institution.

> **Case 13/83** *EP v Council (Transport Policy)* holds, however, that the acts requested need not be spelled out in detail, but must be sufficiently identified.

9.2.3 **Procedural requirements**

9.2.3.1 The invitation to act

There is a preliminary procedural step that must be taken before court action can ensue.

> **Article 265(2) TFEU**
> . . . .
> If, within *two months* of being so called upon, the institution, body, office or agency concerned has not defined its position, the action may be brought within a further period of two months.

The action shall thus be admissible only if the institution concerned has first been called upon to act.

The applicant must request the institution to take a specific action as legally required and advise that failure to do so will result in a court action under Article 265 TFEU. The invitation to act need not follow any precise form to qualify for the purposes of Article 265 TFEU.

Only if the institution fails to define its position within the two-month period can the matter be brought before the Court. The application to the Court of Justice must be made within a further two-month period from the end of the initial two-month period.

> In **Case 302/87** *EP v Council (Comitology)* it was held that if the institution complies with the request to act, the Court of Justice will not allow the action to proceed.

9.2.3.2 Definition of position

This requirement has been seen to defeat most actions because where the institution has explained its refusal to act – that is, has defined its position – further action is inadmissible.

> In **Case 48/65** *Lütticke v Commission*, the applicants had requested the Commission to take action against the German Federal Republic regarding a breach of Community law. The Commission was of the opinion that there had been no breach, so therefore refused to take action, but also notified the applicant of this. The Court of Justice declared the application inadmissible on the grounds that the notification of the refusal was a definition of position.

> In **Case 8/71** *Deutscher Komponistenverband (German Composers Group)* v *Commission*, a complaint that a decision taken by the Commission was wrong did not allow an applicant to proceed under Article 232 EC (now 265 TFEU) on the basis that the right decision was not taken by Commission – that is, that it had failed to act in the right way.

In **Case 125/78 *GEMA* v *Commission***, a competition law complaint was made to the Commission under Regulation 17 (now replaced by Regulation 2003/1) about Radio Luxembourg. When the Commission failed to take any action, GEMA attempted an Article 232 EC (now 265 TFEU) action against the Commission. It was held that the letter from the Commission to GEMA stating its decision not to take action was a sufficient definition of position to defeat GEMA's action.

Until **Case 13/83 *European Parliament* v *Council (Transport Policy)***, a declaration by an institution of its unwillingness to act was regarded by some as constituting a sufficient definition of position for the purposes of the Court of Justice. However, the Court in the *Transport* case stated that in the absence of taking a formal act, the institution called upon to define its position must do more than reply stating its current position, which in effect neither denies or admits the alleged failure nor reveals the attitude of the defendant institution to the demanded measures.

9.2.3.3 The substantive action

The *Transport Policy* case was the first to succeed under this Article.

In **Case 13/83 *European Parliament* v *Council (Transport Policy)***, the EP had complained that the Council had failed in its Treaty obligations under old Articles 3, 61, 74, 75 and 84 EC to introduce a common policy for transport, to lay down a framework for this policy and to act on sixteen specific proposals of the Commission. The Court of Justice held, in response to the first claim, that because the Treaty requirements were so vague, there could not be said to exist sufficiently specific obligations as to amount to a failure to act. This was despite the fact that the obligations should have been completed long ago. The Court held that the obligation of old Article 61 EC could be identified with sufficient precision as to constitute a failure on the part of the Council to lay down a framework. The second claim of failure to act on sixteen proposals of the Commission was successful only in respect of the proposals regarding the freedom to provide services. The other measures were within the greater margin of discretion left to the Council by the Treaty.

9.2.3.4 Results of a declaration of a failure to act

The institution is required under Article 266(1) TFEU (ex 233 EC) to take the necessary measures to comply with the judgment of the Court of Justice within a reasonable time. A continued failure to act would be actionable under Article 265 TFEU. As with Articles 258 and 260 TFEU (ex 226 and 228 EC) actions in respect of the member states, continued intransigence by an institution is insurmountable, but politically unlikely. Article 266 states that it is without prejudice to any action for damages under Article 340 TFEU (ex 288 EC). This is considered next.

9.3 Non-contractual liability of the EU

The contractual liability of the Community is made subject to the jurisdiction of national law pertaining to the contract under Article 340(1) TFEU (ex 288(1) EC), whereas Article 268 TFEU

For more details on this section scan here or visit the Online Resource Centre.

(ex 235 EC) confers jurisdiction over disputes relating to claims for non-contractual liability damages under Article 340(2) TFEU (ex 288(2) EC) to the Court of Justice.

> ### Article 268 TFEU (ex 235 EC)
>
> The Court of Justice shall have jurisdiction in disputes relating to compensation for damage provided for in the second paragraph of Article 340 TFEU [ex 288 EC].

Article 340(2) TFEU requires the Union to make good damage caused by the institutions or servants in the performance of their duties in accordance with the general principles common to the laws of the member states. The term 'non-contractual' is employed to take account of the different legal traditions and to ensure that the Union is responsible for all of its actions outside contractual liability. Non-contractual liability thus covers the civil wrongs caused by the legislative and administrative activities of the Union, whether committed by the institutions or the servants.

9.3.1 Admissibility

As with Article 263 TFEU actions, there are four elements of admissibility to consider: the defendant institution, its action or inaction, a time limit and *locus standi*. Unlike Article 263 TFEU actions, the last aspect of standing is much more easily satisfied and will be considered first this time.

9.3.1.1 *Locus standi*

In contrast to Articles 263 and 265 TFEU (ex 230 and 232 EC), there is not a restrictive *locus standi* imposed on individuals by either Article 268 or 340(2) TFEU. The applicant must be affected and damaged in some tangible and provable way. He or she must be able to demonstrate some degree of loss without necessarily calculating the exact amount. This can be quantified later if the action is found to be admissible and the claim upheld.

cross reference

See the Willame *case under section 9.3.10 as to the types of damages that can be claimed.*

> **Case T-376/04 *Polyelectrolyte Producers Group* v *Council and Commission*** was rejected as inadmissible by the CFI because the allegations of loss made were unsupported by any evidence of loss.

9.3.1.2 Time limit

Established by case law and confirmed in Article 46 of the Statute of the Court of Justice, there is a five-year limitation period on actions, which commences from the occurrence of the event causing the damage (Case 5/71 *Schöppenstedt* v *Council* for legislative-caused loss) or, if not discovered until later, from when the event causing the damage is discovered (Case 145/83 *Adams* v *Commission* for administrative error causing loss).

9.3.2 The defendant institution and act

In an action against the Union, the appropriate institution that should be named as defendant is that the legislative or administrative act of which or the action or inaction of which caused the damage. This can be the Commission, or the Council and EP, or both, which jointly legislate in

cross reference
This is also
considered at
section 9.3.12 on
choice of court and
in relation to Case
175/84 Krohn v
Commission.

many areas of EU law. This was confirmed originally by the Court of Justice in Cases 63–69/72 *Werhahn* v *Commission*. In view of the greater powers of the EP, the EP either alone or in connection with the Council can also be named as a defendant. The ECB is also named in Article 340 as an institution that can be sued. Member states would be only sued where they are responsible for the implementation of Union measures and have exceeded the discretion that they were given. If there is no discretion on their part, the Commission would be the proper defendant.

9.3.3 **An autonomous or independent action**

The action for damages has been held by the Court of Justice to be an autonomous form of action, having its own particular purpose to fulfil within the Treaty system of remedies and subject to conditions on its use dictated by its specific nature.

This is also termed the 'principle of the autonomy of remedies'.

In **Case 4/69 *Lütticke***, damage had been suffered as a result of the Commission failing to act against Germany. The Commission argued that the action under Article 288 EC (now 340 TFEU) was an attempt to circumvent the *locus standi* requirements of a previous unsuccessful Article 232 EC (now 265 TFEU) action. The Court of Justice rejected this argument and declared that the action for damages provided by Articles 235 and 288(2) (now 268 and 340 TFEU) was established by the Treaty as an independent form of action, the object of which was to compensate a party for damage sustained and not to secure the annulment of an illegal measure.

Case 5/71 *Zuckerfabrik Schöppenstedt* v *Council* concerned an action for damages arising from a Regulation. The Council had argued that the action should be ruled inadmissible because to allow it would frustrate the system of judicial remedies provided by the Treaty by allowing a challenge to a Regulation, which is not allowable under Article 230 EC (now 263 TFEU), the reasoning being that such applications would be ruled out as a result of a lack of *locus standi* or as being outside of the short time limit. That argument was firmly rejected by the Court of Justice.

Therefore little difficulty faces applicants in respect of admissibility; the problem lies in proving that an act of the Union caused damage and that there was a sufficiently serious breach of a rule of law.

9.3.4 **The requirements of liability**

Under the Treaty on the Functioning of the European Union, the liability of the Union is to be determined in accordance with the general principles common to the laws of the member states. When the Court of Justice looks to national laws for guidance and general principles, as in other instances of this practice, it is not required to accept the lowest common denominator, but makes a comparative review and selects principles of law appropriate to the situation. Therefore a body of EU law is being built up in this area. From the case law, requirements have been identified to establish liability for the purpose of Article 240(2) TFEU (ex 288(2) EC) that the Union is liable either: (i) for damage caused by one of its institutions; or (ii) for damage caused by its servants in the performance of their duties. There must be a wrongful act or omission on the part of the Union, which has breached a duty, the applicant must have suffered damage, and there must be a causal link between the act or omission and the damage.

9.3.4.1 The standard of liability and fault

Liability can be imposed for not only administrative acts or omissions, but also to legislative acts such as Regulations, Directives or Decisions. Liability can thus be incurred as a result of failures of administration, the negligence of employees of the institutions in the performance of their duties (but not extending to personal faults of employees), and the adoption of unlawful legislative acts. The act or omission of the Union must be shown to be wrongful; however, the degree of wrongfulness or fault varies depending on whether the wrong committed was the result of an administrative act, an act of one the employees or from a legislative act. Note now, however, that, since Case C-352/98 P *Bergaderm*, the Court of Justice has provided the view that a single test should apply to both administrative and legislative acts. This section, though, will chart the development of the law in this area in respect of both types of act as previously developed and return to the new test outlined in section 9.3.7.

9.3.5 **Administrative acts**

While a requirement of fault is not express from the Treaty, case law indicates that it is necessary for the establishment of liability for damage caused by administrative acts.

> In **Case 14/60 *Meroni*,** the Court of Justice ruled that the liability is based on fault in that there must be negligence in the administration or construction of a scheme of regulation for ferrous scrap before there can be liability when the scheme malfunctions. The Court of Justice held that the mere existence of errors in the administration of the scheme is not in itself evidence of a wrongful act or omission, since they might be caused by the fact that the problems tackled by the scheme are difficult to resolve.

> In **Cases 19, 20, 25 and 30/69 *Richez Parise*,** the Commission had supplied wrong information to its staff about pension rights. This information was based on an incorrect interpretation of the rules concerning rights that they could claim on the termination of their service. The Court of Justice held that only in exceptional circumstances would an incorrect interpretation constitute a wrongful act. However, in this case, the Commission was at fault by failing promptly to remedy the error of interpretation as soon as it became obvious that its interpretation was erroneous. Therefore its failure to issue a correction within a reasonable time was of such nature as to render the Commission liable.

There is a notorious case in EU law concerning the liability of the institutions in respect of acts of its servants.

> **Case 145/83 *Stanley Adams* v *Commission*** concerned the liability of the Community for a breach of the duty of care owed to its informants in the sphere of competition law. Adams claimed a breach of confidence of information by releasing documents by which Hoffmann-La Roche could identify Adams as the whistle-blower when it was investigated and fined

under competition law. Article 287 EC (now 339 TFEU) imposed a duty on members of staff of institutions not to disclose information covered by professional secrecy. It was held that the Commission remained under a duty not to reveal its source even when Adams left his employment. Hoffmann-La Roche discovered his identity and the Swiss Public Prosecutor was informed. Adams was tried in his absence and convicted of industrial espionage, which is a criminal offence in Switzerland. The Commission was aware of the risk that Adams would be identified by handing over documents and failed to tell Adams of the threats to prosecute the informant. On return to Switzerland, Adams was arrested and jailed. His wife, who was suffering from depression, committed suicide when informed about a possible twenty-year jail sentence for her husband. The Commission was held liable to make good the damage resulting from the discovery of the applicant's identity, but Adams was held to have been contributorily negligent by not informing the Commission that he could be identified from documents and failing to ask the Commission to keep him informed of progress.

The *Adams* case is an illustration of the rules relating to duty, vicarious liability, causation and contributory negligence.

9.3.6 Liability for employees

The possibility of vicarious liability for employees was raised in an early case.

In **Case 9/69 *Sayag* v *Leduc***, Mr Sayag was employed by the European Atomic Energy Community (EURATOM) and, whilst showing guests of the Community around in his own car, was involved in an accident in which his passengers were injured. It was held that the Commission was not liable because it was not an official act of the Community: 'the Community is only liable for those acts of its servants which, by virtue of an internal and direct relationship, are the necessary extension of the tasks entrusted to the institutions of the Community.'

There was also the possible policy reason that the person's own insurance would, in any event, cover the damage.

The scope of liability is thus limited to activities of institutions or the performance of institutional tasks.

9.3.7 Liability for legislative acts

The principle that there can be liability on the part of the institutions for damage resulting from the adoption of legislative acts was established by the Court of Justice through case law. The legislative acts of the Union are those, in view of their scope and the sheer numbers whom they can affect, that have the potential to cause great damage.

However, in the leading case that confirmed this, **Case 5/71 *Schöppenstedt* v *Council***, the Court of Justice has laid down a strict test to be met to establish liability, which has been repeated often. In the case, the plaintiffs claimed that a Regulation breached the principle of non-discrimination in Article 34(2) EC (now 40(2) TFEU). The Court of Justice held that:

> The Community does not incur liability on account of a legislative measure which involves choices of economic policy unless a sufficiently flagrant violation of a superior rule of law for the protection of the individual has occurred.

> It was held that the prohibition of discrimination was a superior rule of law, but that it had not been breached.

The reasoning for the strict test is very similar to the strict requirements for *locus standi* for Article 263 TFEU in that the high degree of discretion that the institutions need to carry out the economic tasks that they must carry out necessarily affects many persons, hence the imposition of a higher burden when choices of economic policy are involved. The point is that it is not only an administrative decision of the Commission, but a legislative act that has been brought about as the result of reaching the agreement of if not all twenty-seven member states in the Council, at least a significant majority of them. Therefore it is not only unlawful conduct that will attract liability, but also the degree of unlawful conduct required under the formula developed by the Court of Justice. All types of legislative act can be subject to an action under Article 340(2) TFEU.

The formula can be divided into two parts although in some treatments it is divided into three parts, as follows:

(a) a violation or breach of a superior rule of law (which can be linked with the next part);

(b) the rule must exist for the protection of natural or legal persons; and

(c) the violation must have been sufficiently serious.

cross reference

See Chapter 8 for details on Francovich.

Case C-352/98P *Bergaderm* v *Commission* has modified the test laid down in *Schöppenstedt* in that the Court now requires there to be a sufficiently serious breach of a rule of law intended to confer rights on individuals, which is the same for member state liability as developed from the *Francovich* case.

This has been followed up in some CFI cases, such as **Case T-16/04 *Arcelor***, which emphasized, following on from *Bergaderm*, the focus on the degree of discretion rather than the seriousness or arbitrariness of the breach.

Whilst, this development is likely to be followed because it is a logical extension of the arguments about the need for the institutions to have discretion to make the necessary choices of economic policy, there is not as yet a clear line of authority to be sure that the more complex approach in *Schöppenstedt* has been entirely abandoned.

cross reference

All of these are discussed in Chapter 4, sections 4.2.5–4.2.7.

9.3.7.1 The rules of law covered

The rules of law include specific legal rules contained in legislation, fundamental rights and general principles. The principles of proportionality, legal certainty, equality/discrimination and legitimate expectation are often raised.

The rule of law accepted in the *Schöppenstedt* case was a prohibition of discrimination, which is contained in a Treaty Article; hence its acceptance as a superior rule of law.

Article 40(2) TFEU (ex 34(2) EC) provides that the CAP and measures taken under it 'shall exclude any discrimination between producers or consumers within the Union'.

In **Case 64/76 *Dumortier Freres* v *Commission (Gritz and Quellmehl)***, the ending of a subsidy as held to be a breach because it was retained on starch, which was direct competition.

See also **Case 83/76 *HNL*** and **Cases 103 and 145/77 *KSH* v *Council and Commission (Royal Scholten Holdings)***, which are also often cited in respect of the same rule of law.

In **Case T-166/98 *Cantina***, the rule that there should be no unjustified enrichment was breached.

Unjustified enrichment is a principle of quasi-tort.

cross reference
Bergaderm *is considered further in section 9.3.8.*

These rules those that are designed with the individual in mind; hence, in the *Bergaderm* case, the Court of Justice held, in order to reflect this, that there should be a move in future to dealing with the rules of law required and the protection of the individual together and there has also been less emphasis on a rule of law being a superior one.

9.3.7.2 The protection of the individual

The protection of the individual, which scope includes natural and legal persons, has been interpreted to include the protection of classes of person also as with the importers in Cases 5, 7, 13 and 24/66 *Kampfmeyer*, in which a Regulation aimed generally at agricultural markets was held to include individuals within those markets.

Case 74/74 *CNTA* v *Commission* involved the general principle of legitimate expectation. The Commission was held liable to pay compensation for losses incurred as a result of a Regulation that abolished, with immediate effect and without warning, the application of compensatory amounts. This was held to be a serious breach of the principle of legitimate expectation, which was designed to provide individual protection.

See also **Case T-69/00 *Fiamm***, in which individuals were held to be affected indirectly by Community acts, but whose action was held to be admissible, although it was not successful ultimately on a damages issue.

9.3.7.3 The breach must be sufficiently serious

This is required because it is a challenge to an economic policy choice of the Union involving the exercise of wide discretion. Whilst there must be a breach of an important rule of law that is superior to more general rules of law, a mere breach is not sufficient to trigger liability; a sufficiently flagrant or serious breach is required.

> In **Case 83/76** *HNL v Commission*, a Regulation requiring cattle food manufacturers to use more expensive skimmed milk than cheaper soya in their foods (to use up the 'milk lake' of the overproduction of milk) was held to be invalid, and declared null and void, because it offended the principles of proportionality and discrimination (Article 34(2) EC, now 40(2) TFEU).

However, whilst in the Article 288 EC (now 340 TFEU) action, the breach was acknowledged, it was held not to be a sufficiently serious or flagrant breach. Almost inevitably in the regulation of the CAP and particular food products, a legislative decision by the Commission to allow or to restrict the production will affect, often adversely, the economic position of individual farmers. To permit them to succeed in an action for damages each time would completely undermine any attempt to control the market. The Commission and Union would be rendered useless.

> In **Case 83/76** *HNL v Commission*, the Court held:
>
> The legislative authority...cannot always be hindered in making its decisions by the prospect of applications for damages whenever it has occasion to adopt legislative measures in the public interest which may adversely affect the interests of individuals.

Thus liability is incurred only where there has been a manifest and grave disregard of the limits on the exercise of their powers.

> Manifest and grave was itself later interpreted in **Cases 103 and 145/77** *KSH v Council and Commission* as conduct verging on the arbitrary.

> Preliminary rulings in **Cases 117/76 and 16/77** *Rucksdeschel* and **Cases 124/76 and 20/77** *Moulins de Pont a Mousson (Maize, Gritz and Quellmehl)* had held that Regulations providing higher production refunds for maize starch than for maize gritz were incompatible with Article 34(2) EC (now 40(2) TFEU) and thus invalid. New lower refunds had been set for maize gritz and the companies claimed damages. The question was: had the Council of Ministers manifestly and gravely disregarded the limits of power? Thus, in the cases known collectively as the *Maize, Gritz and Quellmehl Cases*, the ECJ held that the Council had manifestly and gravely disregarded the limits of power because:
>
> (1) Article 34(2) (now 40(2) TFEU) was important for the protection of individuals;
> (2) only a small defined and closed group of commercial applicants were affected;
> (3) the damage must be over and above economic risks normal in business;
> (4) the equality of treatment ended without sufficient justification; and
> (5) the Council ignored a Commission proposal.
>
> The *Quellmehl* cases had the same result with regard to a discriminatory treatment by the Commission of maize starch and quellmehl, both products used in the baking industry. In both cases, damages plus interest were awarded.

Another product-specific series of cases dealt with the production of isoglucose, an artificial sweetener that competed with sugar.

Cases 116, 124 and 143/77 *Amylum and Tunnel Refineries (the Isoglucose Cases)* can be typified by **Cases 166, 124 and 143/77 Tunnel Refineries**. The production of isoglucose was heavily penalized by a Regulation later annulled, but the consequence was that the producers had already suffered massive losses, including some producers going out of business. Their claims for losses failed because the breaches were not 'verging on the arbitrary'!

Factors that influence the Court of Justice in its determination of whether the breach is sufficiently serious include the effect of the breach and the manner or nature of the breach. The effect of measure relates to its scope, the number of people affected, the type of damage caused and if that damage was unusual. Other important factors include whether there is a higher Union public interest or, as it is also termed, general economic interest involved. Another consideration is whether a particular group has been disproportionately affected.

Previously, it was considered that only a small defined and closed group of applicants could successfully pursue a claim (see Case 152/88 *Sofrimport*) and that if large numbers were involved, this would defeat a claim.

However, **Cases C-104/89 and 37/90 Mulder v Council** deal with the application of many milk farmers who alleged damage as a result of changes to milk quota regulation. The Court of Justice suggested that a large group of applicants need not be fatal to a claim, although a serious breach still had to be demonstrated and there was no higher public interest of the Community involved.

9.3.8 **A new single test for liability?**

According to the AG in the *Factortame* case, up to 1995, only eight awards had been made against the Community institutions, which seemed to indicate that the *Schöppenstedt* formula, as it had been applied, had been far too strict and needed to be modified.

cross reference
See section 9.3.9 for more on the extension to cover all acts.

In **Case C-352/98 P Bergaderm v Commission**, the Court of Justice took the opportunity to modify or simplify the test laid down in *Schöppenstedt*. The Court of Justice considered the parallel developments in the cases on state liability, including in particular, Cases C-46 and C-48/93 *Brasserie du Pêcheur* and *Factortame*, and adapted the test for liability from those cases.

The modification requires there to be a sufficiently serious breach of a rule of law intended to confer rights on individuals, and considers whether there had been a disregard of the limits of discretion by the institution involved. The slight change in emphasis from superior rules of law for the protection of individuals to those rules conferring rights and the emphasis on discretion brings into line the test for liability under state liability and Article 340 actions. It suggested that where the institutions and member states had manifestly and gravely disregarded the limits of their discretion, then the breach would be sufficiently serious enough to incur liability. It also extended the test for all acts rather than only for legislative acts. Hence, then, as with member states, where there is no discretion, a mere infringement will suffice, but where there is discretion, it will be a matter of the degree by which the institution exceeded that discretion.

cross reference
See the Bergaderm *case also discussed in Chapter 8, section 8.3, on state liability.*

Whilst the new formulation has been followed up in a number of CFI cases and on appeal to the Court of Justice, there is not as yet clear authority to be sure that the more complex approach in *Schöppenstedt* has been abandoned.

9.3.8.1 Individual (non-legislative) acts

The *Schöppenstedt* test was developed specifically to apply to general legislative acts and, because the subsequent *Bergaderm* case was a modification of this, it might have been expected that it would not be appropriate for acts applying or affecting an individual only. However, in *Bergaderm*, the Court of Justice also addressed this point and held that it was not material whether the act alleged to have caused damage was legislative or administrative, but whether the institution had exceeded the limits of its discretion.

> This was confirmed in the later **Case C-282/05 P *Holcim* v *Commission***, in which the Court of Justice held that the requirement to show a sufficiently serious breach should also apply to individual acts.

It would be helpful to see further cases from the Court of Justice supporting this development.

9.3.9 **Liability for lawful acts**

In a further development, the possibility that the Union may be liable, in certain circumstances, for damage caused by lawful acts has been explored.

> For example, the earlier case **C-237/98 P *Dorsch Consult* v *Council*** concerned the banning of trade in Iraq under an EC Regulation complying with a United Nations Resolution and resultant losses. The Court of Justice held that, in order to be held liable, such losses would have to be unusual and special.

> **Case T-69/00 *FIAMM & FIAMM Technologies et al.* v *Council and Commission***, and now the appeal case **C-120/06 P** concern Regulations enacted under the infamous Community Banana Regime, which were incompatible or alleged to be incompatible with the World Trade Organization (WTO) agreements. As a result, the United States took retaliatory measures by increasing customs duties on other products, causing the applicants for damages loss as a result of the impact on their imports to the US. Whilst the disputed Regulations were lawful in the Community regime, internationally they were not. The CFI held that although the conduct was not unlawful, an action for damages could be admissible where the economic operators had borne a disproportionate burden as a result of the counter-measures to the Community regulation of the banana market contrary to WTO rules. The applicants still need to show actual damage, a causal link between the conduct of the Community institution and the damage, and the unusual and special nature of the damage. In the case, it was held that the conduct of the defendant institutions had led to retaliatory measures being adopted, which were the cause of the damage sustained. However, the CFI considered that the extent of damage suffered was neither unusual nor beyond the economic risks that might be expected in the economic sector and the actions failed.

Whilst the case was not successful, it has widened the category of potential acts that can incur liability. On appeal, the Court of Justice confirmed the judgment on the facts of the CFI that no liability accrued in this case, but it was less clear about whether it approved the principle that lawful acts could, given the appropriate facts, give rise to liability. Further case law is thus required on this point.

9.3.10 The damage

Having established the existence of an act or omission attributable to the Union, damage to the applicant must be proved. Damage can be purely economic, as in Cases 5, 7, 13 and 24/66 *Kampfmeyer* involving a cancellation fee and loss of profits, but this must be specified and not speculative, or damage can take the form of moral damage, as in Case 110/63 *Willame* v *Commission*.

> In **Case 74/74 CNTA**, compensation for the losses caused by a sudden change to export refunds contrary to the legitimate expectations of the company was upheld although, in the case itself, currency fluctuations meant that no actual loss was recorded.

It has been held that the damage must be over and above the risk of damage normal in business, in that it exceeds the risks in operation inherent in the sector concerned (see Case 64/76 *Dumortier Frères* v *Council*).

> In **Case C-152/88 Sofrimport v EC Commission**, concerned with Chilean apples in transit, import licences were suspended whilst the cargo was on the high seas. The applicants in *Sofrimport* were successful in obtaining damages because of the complete failure of the Commission to take into account the interests of the applicants when they were required to do so. This amounted to a sufficiently serious breach of legitimate expectation. The damage went beyond the limits of economic risk inherent in business.

9.3.11 The causal connection

Lastly, it must be shown that the act of the Union caused the damage and there must be a sufficiently direct connection between the act and the injury.

> In **Cases 64 and 113/76 Dumortier Frères v Council (Gritz and Quellmehl)**, it was held that there was no need to make good every harmful consequence, especially where remote.

Damage must be a sufficiently direct consequence of the unlawful conduct of the institution concerned.

> In **Case 169/73 Compagnie Continentale Française**, it was held that the causal link was only established if the misleading information given would have caused an error in the mind of a reasonable person.

> In **Case 132/77** *Sugar Export*, it was held that the chain of causation may be broken by an independent act of a third party.

In summary, the damage must be certain, specific, proven and quantifiable, and it may cover imminent foreseeable damage and lost profits: Cases 5, 7, 13 and 24/66 *Kampffmeyer*.

9.3.12 **Concurrent liability/choice of court**

For the most part, the application of EU legislative measures, especially in the agricultural sector, are actually administered and thus dependent on the national intervention agencies that make payments and receive payments. However, if a claim is based on a Union act that was wrongful, the question of whether a national court or the Court of Justice is the appropriate forum arises. Where a claim involves the return of sums unlawfully paid to national authorities, compensation must be sought from the national authorities before the national courts, followed if necessary by a reference under the Article 267 TFEU (ex 234 EC) procedure (see Cases 5, 7, 13 and 24/66 *Kampffmeyer*). It is only really the conduct of the institutions or servants that would require application to the Court of Justice or if the claims are for unliquidated damages – that is, those involving loss of profits suffered as a result of illegal EU action (see Case 74/74 *CNTA* or 175/84 *Krohn* v *Commission*).

9.3.13 **Section summary**

Despite the easier-to-fulfil admissibility factors, it remains the situation that not many cases are successful. As discussed earlier, according to the AG in the *Factortame* case, up to 1995, only eight awards had been made. The same reasoning appears to apply to the merits of this action as apply at the admissibility stage of an Article 263 TFEU (ex 230 EC) action to annul unlawful acts. The difficulty with which Union legislative acts are achieved is not to be easily overcome either by actions to annul or actions for damages. Both of these would undermine the ability of the Union to regulate the markets, and because Union Regulations that seek to regulate particular markets inevitably will affect those individuals operating in that market, they must be protected; hence the view that the strictness is not unreasonable.

9.4 **The plea of illegality (Article 277 TFEU, ex 241 EC)**

This action provides a right to plead the illegality of a Community Regulation in different circumstances from the direct challenge of Article 263 TFEU.

For more details on this section scan here or visit the Online Resource Centre.

> **Article 277 TFEU**
>
> Notwithstanding the expiry of the period laid down in of Article 263, sixth paragraph, any party may, in proceedings in which an act of general application adopted by an institution, body, office or agency of the Union is at issue, plead the grounds specified in Article 263, second paragraph, in order to invoke before the Court of Justice of the European Union the inapplicability of that act.

Article 277 TFEU is not an independent or direct cause of action to the Court of Justice, as confirmed in Case 33/80 *Renato Albini* v *Council and Commission*, which means that an applicant cannot simply commence an action with this Article.

> In **Cases 31 and 33/62 *Wöhrmann* v *Commission***, the Court of Justice held that Article 241 EC (now 277 TFEU) was available only in proceedings already brought before the Court of Justice under some other action and only as an incidental or indirect action.

For example, it may be that, during the course of an Article 263 TFEU challenge to a decision, it comes to light that a Regulation, which was the legal base for the decision, was for some reason unlawful, but was beyond challenge itself due to the time limit or a lack of *locus standi* under Article 263 TFEU, as considered in section 9.1. This would provide the grounds under which Article 277 TFEU might apply. It cannot be used in Article 340 TFEU actions, considered in section 9.3, nor in Article 258 TFEU actions against member states: see Case 70/72 *Commission* v *Federal Republic of Germany*.

9.4.1 *Locus standi*

An Article 277 TFEU action is available to any party, including the member states; however, it is more likely to benefit individuals who, for good reason, are unable to comply with the *locus standi* and time-limit requirements of Article 263 TFEU. However, as noted in the previous section, it is not designed or intended to provide an alternative for those who have simply failed to meet the requirements of Article 263 TFEU.

> In **Case 156/77 *Commission* v *Belgium***, a Community decision was challenged directly before the Court of Justice; however, the Court refused the application because Belgium had allowed its right under Article 230 EC (now 263 TFEU) to expire.

Article 277 TFEU is designed more for those who either have no rights under Article 263 TFEU or were unable to meet the *locus standi* requirements, but who nevertheless are affected by the illegality of a Union act.

> For example, in **Case 216/82 *University of Hamburg* v *Hauptzollamt Hamburg***, the University was able to challenge a decision addressed to the German government indirectly before the national court. The reason was not because it was directly and individually concerned by it, but because the decision was not published; it was therefore unable to challenge it under Article 230 EC (now 263 TFEU).

9.4.2 **Acts that can be reviewed**

Article 277 TFEU refers to acts of general applications only, which, in the EU, essentially means Regulations, which can be challenged only if they form the legal basis of the subject matter of the direct action, as in Case 9/56 *Meroni* v *High Authority*. Article 277 TFEU does not envisage the challenge of decisions or other forms of binding act that are not generally applicable.

However, in **Case 92/78 _Simmenthal_ v _Commission_**, a decision was challenged that was based generally on prior Regulations and Notices. The Regulations could not be challenged directly under Article 230 EC (now 263 TFEU) because of the restrictive _locus standi_ requirements, but could be challenged indirectly via Article 241 EC (now 277 TFEU). The Court held that it was not the form of the act that is important, but the substance. Therefore, according to the Court of Justice, other acts that are normative or general in effect should be regarded as Regulations for the purposes of making a challenge under Article 241 EC (now 277 TFEU).

This is now confirmed by the amended Article 277 TFEU, which refers to any acts of general application and makes it clear that the challenge can apply to acts adopted by any EU institution, body, office or agency.

Addressees, though, of an individual act such as a Decision cannot challenge it indirectly in the Court of Justice because they should have done so directly under Article 263 TFEU within the time limits. To allow otherwise would be to render the time limit meaningless, as confirmed in Case 156/77 _Commission_ v _Belgium_.

9.4.3 **Grounds of review**

The substantive grounds of the action are those listed for Article 263 TFEU.

For example, **Case 92/78 _Simmenthal_** succeeded on its merits that the general measure had been used for purposes other than that for which it was intended – that is, improper purpose.

9.4.4 **Effect of a successful challenge**

The result of such an action is that the Regulation or act is declared inapplicable in that case and not generally void: see Case 9/56 _Meroni_ v _High Authority_. Any acts based on this voidable Regulation will, however, be void and withdrawn. Also, in practice, the Regulation or act will not be applied in subsequent cases, as is the consequence in Article 267 TFEU (ex 234 EC) references: for example, see Case 66/80 _ICC_.

Summary

The direct actions before the ECJ cover a number of grounds of unlawful activity, the most important of which are the action to annul an act of the Union under Article 263 TFEU and the actions for damages under Article 340 TFEU. The aspects of admissibility in Article 263 TFEU and the merits in Article 340 TFEU stand out as those receiving the most attention. Less frequently visited are the actions under Article 265 TFEU for a failure to act and Article 277 TFEU, the incidental plea of illegality. However, the last two should not be entirely ignored because they may be considered as alternative actions if the main actions prove to be fruitless. Certainly, however, we should pay more attention to Articles 263 and 340 TFEU.

Questions

For suggested approaches to answering these questions scan here or visit the Online Resource Centre.

1   Is it true that admissibility is the major hurdle to a successful action under Article 263 TFEU? If so, why?

2   What must an individual show if he or she is to be recognized as having 'individual concern' for the purposes of Article 263 TFEU?

3   Is the test that the ECJ operates in Article 263 TFEU actions too strict?

4   Consider the contrasting approach of the ECJ to Article 340 TFEU and the test for *Francovich* liability. Are the same standards of liability imposed on both the Community institutions and member states?

5   What use is the plea of illegality action under Article 277 TFEU?

 # Further reading

BOOKS

Douglas-Scott, S. *Constitutional Law of the European Union*, Longman, Harlow, 2002 (chapters 11–12).

Gordon, R. *EC Law in Judicial Review*, Oxford University Press, Oxford, 2007.

Hartley, T. *The Foundations of European Community Law*, 7th edn, Clarendon Press, Oxford, 2010 (chapter 10).

Lenaerts, K., Arts, D. and Maselis, M. *Procedural Law of the European Union*, 2nd edn, Thompson, London, 2006.

Ward, A. *Judicial Review and the Rights of Private Parties in EU Law*, 2nd edn, Oxford University Press, Oxford, 2007.

ARTICLES

Albors-Llorens, A. 'The standing of private parties to challenge Community measures: has the European Court missed the boat?' (2003) 62 CLJ 72.

Arnull, A. 'Private applicants and the action for annulment since *Cordorniu*' (2001) 38 CML Rev 7.

Balthasar, S. '*Locus standi* rules for challenges to regulatory acts by private applicants: the new Article 263(4) TFEU' (2010) 35 EL Rev 542.

Cooke, J. '*Locus standi* of private parties under Article 173(4)' (1997) 6 IJEL 4.

Cortes Martin, J. M. '*Ubi ius, ibi remedium*? *Locus standi* of private applicants under Article 230(4) EC at a European constitutional crossroads' (2004) 11 MJECL 233.

Cygan, A. 'Protecting the interests of civil society in Community decision-making: the limits of Article 230 EC' (2003) 52 ICLQ 995.

Enchelmeier, S. 'No one slips through the net? Latest developments, and non-developments, in the European Court of Justice's jurisprudence on Art 230(4) EC' (2005) 24 YEL 173.

Hilson, C. 'The role of discretion in EC law on non-contractual liability' (2005) 42 CML Rev 677.

Sinaniotis, D. 'The plea of illegality in EC law' (2001) 7 EPL 103.

Tridimas, T. 'Liability for breach of Community law: growing up and mellowing down?' (2001) 38 CML Rev 301.

Usher, J. 'Direct and individual concern: an effective remedy or a conventional solution?' (2003) 28 EL Rev 575.

Van Den Broek, N. 'A long hot summer for individual concern' (2003) 30 Legal Issues of Economic Integration 61.

Vogt, M. 'Indirect judicial protection in the EC law: the case of the plea of illegality' (2006) 31 EL Rev 364.

Ward, A. '*Locus standi* under Article 230(4) of the EC Treaty: crafting a coherent test for a "wobbly polity" ' (2003) 22 YEL 45.

Part 3
Substantive law

Free movement of goods I: tariff and tax barriers

Learning objectives

In this chapter, you will learn about:

- the meaning and importance of the Common Market, also known as the internal market;
- the basic definitions relating to economic integration;
- the basic legislative regime for the free movement of goods;
- the prohibitions of tariff and equivalent barriers; and
- the internal tax measures that hinder free movement.

Introduction

For more details on this section scan here or visit the Online Resource Centre.

cross reference
These advantages were dealt with in Chapter 1, section 1.1.

thinking point
Before looking back at that section, are you able to note down other reasons now?

The free movement of goods is a central part of the internal market, and the foundation of the European Community (EC) as originally established and the Union today. It is very much concerned with the economic ideals of the Union to create a single trading bloc in which all factors of production, and particularly goods, flow freely. The free movement of goods is essential to the creation and running of the customs union and the Common Market. Amongst the prime reasons for establishing the European Economic Community (EEC) and the very concept of a common European market was to create a stable trading and producing bloc capable of competing with the American and the then strongly emerging Japanese economy, and as a means of strengthening Europe both economically and politically against the rising threat of the Soviet Union. Today, we would certainly add the Chinese and Indian economies to the list of principal economic competitors.

The advantages of achieving economic integration and a large internal market allow companies to realize growth and to specialize in production. This in turn allows European companies to compete on the world economic stage. This, it is argued, creates a dynamic, competitive market for the benefit of producers, consumers and the member states. The broader underlying advantages are more than merely economic.

However, creating and maintaining the Common Market, or internal market, has proven to be much more difficult than was first envisaged in view of the member states' attempts to protect their own national producers and industries by preventing or restricting imports both by tariff and non-tariff measures.

10.1 Legislative provisions

10.1.1 The Treaties

The Preamble to the former EC Treaty has proved instrumental in the rulings of the Court of Justice in reaching decisions on cases involving the free movement of goods, as have Articles 2 and 3, 10 (the fidelity clause) and 12 (the prohibition of discrimination on grounds of nationality). The relevant Treaty Articles today are Articles 3–4 TEU and 3–4 and 18 TFEU.

There are four main groups of provisions in the TFEU connected with the free movement of goods, which is set out initially in Articles 26–27 TFEU (ex 14–15 EC):

(i) customs duties and charges having equivalent effect (Articles 28–30 TFEU, ex 23–25 EC);

(ii) the Common Customs Tariff (Articles 31–32 TFEU, ex 26–27 EC);

(iii) the use of national taxation systems to discriminate against goods imported from other member states (Article 110 TFEU, ex 90 EC); and

(iv) quantitative restrictions or measures having an equivalent effect on imports and exports (Articles 34–36 TFEU, ex 28–30 EC).

As one of the cornerstones and one of the fundamental freedoms of the EU, the free movement of goods has been stoutly defended by the Court of Justice, interpreting the basic provisions strictly against the member states and being equally strictly in terms of any exceptions pleaded by the member states, as will be seen in the case law considered later in the chapter. The free movement of goods objectives have been set out in a revised briefer form in Article 3 TEU than was the case previously under Articles 2–4 EC.

TEU Article 3

. . . .

…

(3) The Union shall establish an internal market.

(4) The Union shall establish an economic and monetary union whose currency is the euro.

The internal market is now defined in Article 26(2) TFEU (ex 14(2) EC) as 'an area without internal frontiers in which the free movement of goods, persons, services and capital is ensured in accordance with the provisions of the Treaties'.

The aim is to achieve the circulation of goods without customs, duties, charges or other financial or other restrictions, to promote unlimited trade, and to remove from the member states the control over export and import matters. The Union is solely responsible for import and export duties and tariffs by the grant of exclusive competence in this area under Article 3 TFEU.

Articles 114 and 115 TFEU (ex 94 and 95 EC) are also important Treaty Articles designed to help to achieve and maintain the single internal market. Article 114 TFEU specifically provides additional competences for the achievement of the internal market set out in Article 14 by the use of qualified majority voting (QMV) and the co-decision procedure. Article 115 TFEU provides the Council, acting unanimously, with powers to enact Directives to approximate member states' laws that directly affect the establishment or functioning of the common market.

10.1.2 Secondary legislation

There is very little secondary legislation of direct importance in this area of EU law, but Directive 70/50 will be considered in Chapter 11, as will two more recent enactments: Decision 3052/95 and Directive 98/34.

10.2 Progress towards the Treaty goals

Whilst the goals of integration have been outlined, progression towards them is not, of course, achieved overnight, but rather comprises a series of moves. Various stages in economic

For more details on scan here or visit the Online Resource Centre.

integration above that of simple trade between individual sovereign states have been generally recognized, which, in crude terms, are as follows:

10.2.1 A free trade area

The first stage is the establishment of a **free trade area (FTA)**.

free trade area (FTA)

This involves the removal of customs duties between member states; however, the members of a free trade area decide themselves their external policies and any duties payable by third-party countries wishing to export goods into those countries.

Different states may therefore have different external tariffs, so exporters to the FTA may target their imports on the country with lower import duties or tariffs. Any goods entering will compete with internal goods of the FTA; therefore certification of origin and a further import duty may be required, both of which are difficult and expensive to administer.

10.2.2 A customs union

The next stage is a **customs union**, which builds on the above.

customs union

This creates a common external tariff, presenting a common position to the outside world. The same duties are imposed on goods entering the customs union regardless of from where they are imported. Once imported, the goods circulate freely as union goods throughout the union.

10.2.3 A common market

The **common market**, which is also termed an internal or single market, is the next stage.

common market

This adds to the definitions of free trade area and customs union by providing policies and legal regimes for the free movement of the factors of production (goods, persons and capital) and a competition policy.

10.2.4 An economic union

Almost finally comes the **economic union**.

economic union

This involves all of the above, plus the harmonization or unification of economic, monetary and fiscal policies, including the creation of a common currency controlled by a central authority. An economic union is, in fact, a rather rare development with few historical examples.

The final step would then be full political union in a confederation or federal state.

10.2.5 Which stage has the EU reached?

Whilst its goals are clear, just how far has the EU progressed? Note that the EC, as originally established, was never intended to be only a free trade area; it was always intended to go much further. Articles 26 and 28–32 TFEU (ex 14 and 24 EC) make it clear that a customs union should be established, which includes an internal market. The European Union (EU) certainly has a customs union with a common customs tariff, which is exclusively regulated by the Commission (Article 3 TFEU). The degree to which a true common market has been achieved is more doubtful given the considerable case law still arising, which is evidence of the sheer number of obstacles still in the way of the unified market. However, as from 1 January 2011, seventeen countries, which now represent over half of the twenty-seven member states, have gone further and established an economic and monetary union with a European central bank and a single currency, although at the time of writing this 'eurozone' is not without its difficulties.

thinking point
Can you name the states comprising the eurozone?

10.2.5.1 Internal market developments

cross reference
See Chapter 1, section 1.3.1.2, for more on spillover.

The initial means by which the goals of the Community and now Union were to be achieved commenced with an attempt at harmonization. In line with the original views that success or harmonization in one area would lead to 'spillover' to related areas, it was considered that progress would be steady; however, for various reasons, legislative stagnation set in relatively swiftly.

Those various reasons all contributing to slow progress towards the completion of the internal market included:

- the French boycott in the mid-1960s of the Community institutions and subsequent Luxembourg Accords, which led to stagnation in the decision-making process;

- the late 1960s economic downturn;

- the oil crises and world economic recession in the 1970s; and

- the increase in the number of member states, all of which then possessed a veto over legislation that they considered not to be in their national interest.

cross reference
Reyners is considered in Chapter 12, section 12.4.1.

Consider as a classic example, the Architects Harmonization Directive, which took eighteen years to enact. To a certain, but necessary extent, this stagnation was countered by judicial innovation. For example, Case 26/62 *Van Gend en Loos* led to the creation of the doctrine of direct effects. Other leading cases also demonstrated that the Court of Justice was prepared to interpret the Treaty in a purposive approach and not according to the actual words used: see, for example, Case 2/74 *Reyners*. However, in the 1960s and 1970s, the member states remained reluctant to carry the Common Market project forward themselves.

cross reference
This case is considered in full in Chapter 11, section 11.4.1.

From the late 1970s, however, these problems were acknowledged, and when the new Commission President Jacques Delors took office, there was sufficient support from commerce and industry and the member states for a project to be launched, which was called the 'Single Market'. This led to the Commission White Paper *Completing the Internal Market*, which was endorsed by the European Council in 1985. It set out 300 legislative measures needed to 'complete the single market' and the year 1992 was set as target date. This also marked a shift in approach in that whilst national rules would be harmonized where needed, other means of achieving the goals were emerging. These included a shift to new broadly construed technical harmonization and moves towards mutual recognition, spurred on by the Court of Justice judgment in Case 120/78 *Cassis de Dijon*.

cross reference
See Chapter 2, sections 2.2.4.3 and 2.4.3.1, for further details.

The first amending Treaty of the original Treaties, the Single European Act (SEA), provided the institutional and legal reforms necessary to facilitate the meeting of targets set by the '1992 Project'. This was achieved by the introduction of a new Article 95 EC (now 114 TFEU), which provided that single market measures could be enacted in Council by QMV and allowed for the greater participation of the European Parliament in the legislative process.

In addition, other policies were put into place that were regarded as necessary to support the single market following the realization that it could not be achieved in isolation. Therefore an environmental policy was introduced, along with, for example, an economic and social cohesion policy. The single market was given a particular boost by the Treaty on European Union (TEU), which established economic and monetary union, although only for twelve and not for all of the then fifteen member states. The internal market was now regarded as incorporating more than purely economic concerns. It might be argued that this demonstrates a return to functional integration or creeping federalism, in that the desire to move to economic and monetary union led to the establishment at the EU level of other policies that were regarded as vital to economic and monetary union.

cross reference

This was noted in Chapter 1, section 1.3.

10.2.5.2 Integration methods

The integration of what were a number of separate national markets was and is to be achieved by two main integration strategies: namely, **positive integration** and **negative integration**.

positive integration

The modification of existing national laws and institutions either by harmonization or the creation of new laws.

negative integration

The removal of existing impediments to free movement, such as striking down national rules and practices that obstruct or prevent achievement of the internal market.

(10.3) The establishment of the internal market

For more details on this section scan here or visit the Online Resource Centre.

10.3.1 The common commercial policy (CCP) and common customs tariff (CCT)

> The CCP is the overall driving force behind the establishment and maintenance of the CCT.

The Common Market, which is a customs union, provides not only for the elimination of duties regarding goods originating in other member states, but also regarding goods originating in third countries that are in free circulation in the Common Market and on which customs duties have been paid. Under Article 31 TFEU (ex 26 EC), the external duties are fixed by the Council and Commission for the Union for goods imported from outside the Union and a single set of common tariffs is adopted in trade relations with the outside world. The CCT, which is also referred to as the common external tariff (CET), imposes a single tariff for all imports and is set by the Commission. Once a product has been imported into the EU, it is then in free circulation and further tariffs cannot be imposed on the product (Article 29 TFEU, ex 24 EC). This aspect is now within the entire competence of the Union (Article 3 TFEU) and is ever more tied up with world developments on customs duties, most notably the General Agreement on Tariffs and Trade (GATT) and the World Trade Organization (WTO).

cross reference

The general aspects of external relations are considered in Chapter 1, section 1.7.

10.3.2 The prohibition of customs duties

The following sections concern not only customs duties in the strict sense, which are a hindrance to free trade, but also any financial barriers that have an equivalent effect, however named. Necessarily, we must also consider aspects of member states' tax regimes because these may be a disguised way of imposing additional financial burdens on imported products by making them less competitive or even uncompetitive in comparison with domestic

cross reference
This aspect will be considered more fully below in section 10.4.

products. Therefore the Treaty on the Functioning of the European Union (TFEU) also includes a provision (Article 110 TFEU, ex 90 EC) to deal with these. Note that the provisions on goods and tax are mutually exclusive sets of provisions even though often dealing with the same factual situation.

It is worth taking a careful note about the Treaty Article number changes that took place after the Lisbon Treaty. The Article (30 TFEU) now dealing with customs duties and charges was that previously dealing with quantitative restrictions, and it would be very easy when looking at previous case law to get these confused.

Articles 30 and 32 TFEU (ex 23 and 25 EC) are aimed at the abolition of customs duties and charges having equivalent effect and at prohibiting the introduction of any such measures.

> **Article 30 TFEU**
> ....
>
> 1. The Union shall comprise a customs union which shall cover all trade in goods and which shall involve the prohibition between Member States of customs duties on imports and exports and of all charges having equivalent effect, and the adoption of a common customs tariff in their relations with third countries.
>
> . . .

This provision covers 'all trade in goods'.

> 'Goods' was defined by the Court of Justice in **Case 7/68 Commission v Italy (Art Treasures)** as 'products which can be valued in money and which are capable, as such, of forming the subject of commercial transactions'.

> The definition was extended in **Case 45/87 Commission v Ireland (Dundalk Water Supply)** to include the provision of goods within a contract for the provision of services.

thinking point
In which case was this?

Article 32 TFEU provides that 'Customs duties on imports and exports and charges having equivalent effect shall be prohibited between Member States'. Article 32 (ex 12 EEC) also specifically mentions that it applies to customs duties of a fiscal nature and was held to be directly effective in a leading Community law case.

Whilst it is relatively easy to recognize a customs duty, because it is usually designated as such and is a clear duty applied at the border, and because it is so crude and obvious, the imposition of customs duties is no longer something attempted by the member states.

It is less easy to identify 'a charge having an equivalent effect'; thus a considerable body of case law has arisen trying to define this. The total prohibition of customs duties per se means that cases of such an obvious breach rarely arise; hence, then, the concentration on 'charges having equivalent effect', often abbreviated to CHEEs and sometimes CEEs.

In looking at this area of law and the case law, it has now to be borne in mind that a lot of it took place when there were still very visible border posts and customs officials on the border stopping and checking traffic moving through. Now, and especially in the Schengen area, traffic is able to drive straight through, the border posts having been physically removed.

Case 26/62 *Van Gend en Loos* was the leading case referred to which involved a customs duty.

10.3.3 **A charge having equivalent effect (CHEE)**

In **Cases 2 and 3/62 *Commission* v *Luxembourg (Gingerbread)***, the Court of Justice held that:

> a duty, whatever it is called, and whatever its mode of application, may be considered a charge having equivalent effect to a customs duty, provided that it meets the following three criteria: (a) it must be imposed unilaterally at the time of importation or subsequently; (b) it must be imposed specifically upon a product imported from a member state to the exclusion of a similar national product; and (c) it must result in an alteration of price and thus have the same effect as a customs duty on the free movement of products.

In certain circumstances, a charge may be acceptable: if it is a service rendered for the benefit of the importer, if it is specifically required by EU law, or if it is part of a system of internal taxation.

These criteria are all subject to further refinement by the Court of Justice.

In **Case 24/68 *Commission* v *Italy (Statistical Levy)***, a small (10 lira) levy that was imposed on imports and exports for the purpose of financing statistical surveys was held to breach Community law. Whilst there was no discrimination between imports and exports, the Court of Justice stressed that the purpose of using the concepts of customs duties and CHEEs was to avoid the imposition of any pecuniary charge on goods circulating within the Community by virtue of the fact that they cross a frontier. The Court stressed that any charge must be considered in the context of the achievement of one of the fundamental objectives of the EC Treaty.

In modification of its stance in *Commission* v *Luxembourg*, the Court offered a definition of CHEE to include 'any pecuniary charge, however small and whatever its designation and mode of application, which is imposed unilaterally on domestic or foreign goods by virtue of the fact that they cross a frontier'.

Such a charge is a CHEE even if it is not imposed for the benefit of the member state concerned, even if it is not discriminatory or protective in effect, and even if the product on which it is imposed is not in competition with any domestic product.

In **Case 24/68 *Commission* v *Italy (Statistical Levy)***, the levy was found to hamper the interpenetration of goods that the EEC Treaty aimed to secure and thus had an effect equivalent to a customs duty. It was further held that the levy could not be regarded as the consideration for a specific benefit actually conferred, because the advantages of the survey were so general and difficult to assess.

Claims by member states in relation to charges for services rendered, such as for health inspections, and warehousing fees during clearance of customs formalities have been carefully considered by the Court of Justice.

10.3.3.1 The validity of charges for services rendered

In a number of cases, the Court of Justice has developed its rules on when charges can lawfully be made for services rendered.

In **Case 132/82 *Commission v Belgium (Customs Warehouses)***, the Court of Justice considered the questions of whether a CHEE may be permitted when claimed to be consideration for services rendered. The Belgian authorities allowed customs formalities for goods originating in or in free circulation in another member state to be completed either at the frontier or within the country. When the goods were presented for customs clearance at special stores of public warehouses, a fee fixed and levied by the municipal authorities was payable. This fee was payable in consideration of the use by the importers of the premises made available to them to store their goods pending clearance through customs. The state did not receive the money. The only role played by the state was to fix the maximum fee payable. The Court of Justice held that when payment of storage charges is demanded solely in connection with the completion of customs formalities, it cannot be regarded as consideration for services actually rendered to the importer.

In **Cases 2 and 3/69 *Sociaal Fonds voor de Diamantarbeiders***, a levy on imports that was used to go towards a social fund for workers in the diamond industry and not used in any protectionary way over national products was held nevertheless to be a charge regardless of the purpose. The effect of the charge was that imported goods become less competitive.

In **Case 340/87 *Commission v Italian Republic (Customs Posts)***, Italian legislation required importers who presented themselves at Italian customs outside normal Italian opening hours (six hours per day) to pay a fee. Article 5 of Directive 83/643 required customs offices at frontier posts to open for normal business hours of at least ten hours per day, Monday to Friday. Therefore, in order to comply with the Directive, Italian customs officials would have to work four hours' overtime and Italian law sought to impose a charge during that four-hour period. The Italian government maintained that this was a charge for a service rendered that was commensurate to the value of the service. The Court said that it had already held on several occasions that a charge imposed on goods by reason of the fact that they cross a frontier might not be a CHEE to a customs duty provided that it constituted a benefit specifically or individually conferred on the economic operator concerned of an amount proportional to that service. In this case, the Court of Justice held that the charge constituted a breach of the Treaty.

In **Case 170/88** *Ford of Spain* v *Spanish State*, a claim that a charge levied by the Spanish customs for granting customs clearance at the Ford factory was a charge for services rendered and not a CHEE to a customs duty was rejected. The charge was calculated at a rate of 0.165 per cent of the declared value of the goods. The Court of Justice held that even if the contested charge were in fact remuneration for a service rendered to the importer, the amount charged could not be regarded as proportionate to the service. The Spanish government's argument that, in some cases, the charge would be less than the cost of carrying out the inspections only served to confirm this argument. A charge calculated on the basis of the value of the goods could not correspond to the costs incurred by the customs authorities.

The next cases help to outline the circumstances in which charges may be justified and essentially concern a genuine service being rendered.

In **Case 87/75** *Bresciani*, the Court of Justice held that veterinary checks and charges performed as a service are acceptable, but in that particular case they were not, because they were in the public interest at large and not in the interest of each importer.

In **Case 46/76** *Bauhuis* v *The Netherlands*, the Court of Justice held that a fee for health inspections would be acceptable if required by a Community Regulation and covering the actual cost incurred only.

This was followed up in **Case 18/87** *Commission* v *Germany (Animal Inspection Fees)*, in which the Court of Justice held that a charge may escape classification as a CHEE. In this case, fees for inspections carried out under the requirements of Council Directive 81/389 were held to be acceptable. According to the Court of Justice, they satisfied the criteria that:

(i) the fees constituted a payment for a service, not exceeding the cost of the actual inspections in respect of which they are charged;

(ii) the inspections in question were mandatory and uniform for all of the products in question in the Community;

(iii) the inspections were provided for by Community law in the interests of the Community; and

(iv) the inspections promoted the free movement of goods in particular, by neutralizing the obstacles that may result from unilateral inspection measures adopted under Article 30 EC (now 36 TFEU).

The fees in the case were charged by some of the German *Länder* on the importation of live animals from other member states and their purpose was to cover the cost of health inspections carried out under Council Directive 81/389. The charges in this case satisfied the conditions and were justified.

Case C-111/89 *Netherlands* v *Bakker Hillegom* extended the criteria to include the inspection requirements of international conventions.

10.3.3.2 Where the charge is in fact a tax

A second category in which the charge may be justified is if it is an aspect of an internal taxation system. If the charge forms part of a system of internal taxation rules that are applied systematically and under the same criteria to domestic products and imported products alike, it is a non-discriminatory tax and, if questioned, should be considered under Article 110 TFEU (ex 90 EC) and not under Article 30 TFEU (ex 25 EC).

In **Case 90/79 *Commission v France (Reprographic Machines)*,** a levy was charged on all copy machines, both home-manufactured and imports, in order to compensate authors for the breaches of copyright that often occur by the use of such machines. Whilst very few copy machines were manufactured in France, the tax therefore applied mainly to imports and therefore looked like disguised discrimination, but was held to be a genuine non-discriminatory tax. It served a proper purpose.

This situation is sometimes referred to as the 'exotic import rules', whereby a product is available by import only and not manufactured in the importing state, although this case does not exactly fit that rule. However, in order to justify an import tax on such a product, there must be a genuine reason.

The case highlights the often subtle difference between what is a charge and what is a genuine tax, a distinction that will be considered next.

10.3.4 **The distinction between internal taxation and charges having equivalent effect**

If a charge imposed by a member state on imported goods is a measure of internal taxation that is non-discriminatory, then it cannot be a CHEE and cannot be caught by Articles 28–30 TFEU. It is governed by Article 110 TFEU instead, dealing with internal taxation, which opens the door to member states' attempts to justify additional charges imposed on goods as instances of taxation and not charges or duties. Whilst the customs duties and CHEE mentioned in Articles 28–30 TFEU must be abolished, tax measures are allowed because, as a general principle, Article 110 TFEU allows each member state to establish the system of taxation that it considers most suitable. However, Article 110 TFEU prohibits tax from discriminating against imports and was regarded as crucial to complement the free movement of goods to prevent taxation policy from being employed by a state to circumvent the customs rules by the imposition of discriminatory internal taxes. Article 110 TFEU thus represents an early intervention into the member states' tax regimes, which is likely to become more intrusive in future.

Article 30 TFEU specifically prohibits customs charges of a fiscal nature.

The difference between a charge and a tax is crucial. A charge, which is defined by the European Court of Justice (ECJ) as an internal tax to which Article 110 TFEU (EX 90 EC) applies, cannot at the same time be a CHEE to a customs duty and therefore be subject to Articles 28–30 TFEU (ex 23–25 EC).

In **Case 78/96 *Steinlike und Weinlig* v *Germany*,** the Court of Justice held that:

Financial charges within a general system of internal taxation applying systematically to domestic and imported products according to the same criteria are not to be considered charges having equivalent effect.

It may be one thing or the other, but cannot be both. They are mutually exclusive categories. There is now a considerable body of case law of the Court of Justice on the distinction between an internal tax (to which Article 90 EC, now 110 TFEU, might apply) and a CHEE to a customs duty (which might be prohibited by Articles 23 and 25 EC, now 28 and 30 TFEU).

> In **Case 20/76 *Schöttle & Söhne* v *Finanzamt Freuenstadt***, the Court of Justice held that the purpose of old Article 90 EC (now 110 TFEU) is to remove disguised restrictions on the free movement of goods that may result from the tax provisions of a member state. It was held that a German tax on the transportation of goods for more than a certain distance levied, in this case on a lorry-load of gravel, was an indirect tax on the gravel itself. It would discriminate against lorries travelling from greater distances – that is, mainly affecting those from other countries.

cross reference
See section 10.4.2.

However, this type of tax might in the future, if not now, be justified on environmental grounds, as in *Commission* v *Greece*.

> **Case 132/78 *Denkavit* v *French State*** also concerned this distinction. It arose out of a charge on the importation of meat products that was the equivalent of a similar charge imposed on the slaughter of animals in French slaughterhouses. The Court of Justice noted that a charge could escape classification as a CHEE to a customs duty only if it related to a general system of internal dues applied systematically and in accordance with the same criteria to domestic products and imported products alike. In paragraph 8 of its judgment, the Court further emphasized that in order to relate to a system of internal taxation, the charge to which an imported product is subject must be imposed at the same rate on the same product, must be imposed at the same marketing stage and the chargeable event giving rise to the duty must be the same for both products.

It is therefore not sufficient that the objective of the charge imposed on imports is to compensate for similar charges imposed on domestic products at a production or marketing stage prior to that at which the imported products are taxed.

> In **Case 132/78 *Denkavit* v *French State***, the Court held that it was bound to regard the charge in this case as a CHEE because:
>
> * it was charged on imported goods by virtue of the fact that they had crossed a frontier;
> * the tax was imposed at a different stage of production and on the basis of a different 'chargeable event';
> * no account was taken of fiscal charges that had been imposed on the products in the member state of origin; and
> * to find otherwise would render the prohibition on charges having equivalent effect to customs duties empty and meaningless.

> Finally, in **Case 77/76 *Fratelli Cucchi***, the Court of Justice confirmed the mutually exclusive nature of the charges and internal taxation regimes, but stressed that because it is often difficult to tell the difference, both Articles 25 and 90 EC (now 30 and 110 TFEU) should be invoked together before the Court and the Court of Justice asked to determine which should apply.

10.4 The prohibition of discriminatory taxation

Article 110(1) TFEU (ex 90(1) EC) providesthat 'No Member State shall impose, directly or indirectly, on the products of other Member States any internal taxation of any kind in excess of that imposed directly or indirectly on similar domestic products'. This prohibits discrimination in favour of the domestic products.

Article 110(2) TFEU further provides that 'Furthermore, no Member State shall impose on the products of other Member States any internal taxation of such a nature as to afford indirect protection to other products'.

> Article 90 EC (now 110 TFEU) was held to be directly effective and an indispensable foundation of the Common Market in **Case 57/65 *Lütticke v Hauptzollamt Saarlouis***.

> Taxation was defined in **Case 90/79 *Commission v France (Reprographic Machines)*** as a general system of internal dues applied systematically to categories of product in accordance with objective criteria irrespective of the origin of the products.

Internal taxes can never be imposed solely by virtue of the fact that the goods cross a frontier. The reason for their imposition must be that domestic products are subject to taxation and that, for competition reasons, imported goods should be subject to the same tax.

10.4.1 Direct and indirect taxation

Article 110 TFEU seeks to outlaw both directly discriminatory taxation and indirect discrimination in tax regimes. Direct discrimination is where imports and domestic products are deliberately treated differently and is thus automatically unlawful. Direct discrimination cannot be justified. Indirect discrimination, on the face of it, imposes the same rule on both domestic and imported products, but the result is that the import is, in fact, disadvantaged. Indirect discrimination may be objectively justified.

> In **Case 28/76 *Molkerei-Zentrale Westfalen v Haupzollamt Paderborn***, the Court of Justice ruled that the words 'directly or indirectly' were to be construed broadly and embraced all taxation that was actually and specifically imposed on the domestic product at earlier stages of the manufacturing and marketing process. This means that member states cannot escape the conclusion, in line with the earlier-considered *Denkavit* case, by arguing that a tax at an earlier stage on a domestic product is a lawful equivalent of a tax on imports. If it does not conform to the Denkavit criteria, it is unlawful.

It is also capable of including taxes on raw materials and of the assessment of the tax.

> In **Case 20/76 *Schöttle & Söhne v Finanzamt Freuenstadt***, it was held that a German tax on the transportation of goods for more than 50 km and thus more likely to affect imports, levied in this case on a lorry-load of gravel, was an indirect tax on the gravel itself.

In **Case 127/75 *Bobie v HZA Aachen-Nord***, beer production in Germany was taxed at a level according to the quantity produced, with small producers being favoured with a lower tax. Imports were taxed on a mid-range rate not connected with the amount of production. This was held to be indirectly discriminatory against a small Belgian producer.

10.4.2 'Similar' or 'other products'

The criteria for determining whether there is discrimination differ according to whether the case is brought under Article 110(1) TFEU, concerned with similar products, or Article 110(2) TFEU, dealing with other products. The latter serves to cover imported products that may be different, but are nevertheless in competition with the domestic products. In the case of Article 110(1) TFEU, the taxation on the imported product must not be higher than the tax on the similar domestic product, in which case the rule of non-discrimination has been complied with; in the case of Article 110(2) TFEU, the taxation on the imported product must not have a protectionist effect.

To avoid discrimination taking place in breach of Article 110(1) TFEU, not only must the rates of tax on the imported product and the domestic product be the same, but also the basis of the imposition of the tax must not lead to differences between the imported and domestic goods. The rates of tax, the basis of assessment, and the rules for levying and collecting it must all be non-discriminatory. In the case of Article 110(2) TFEU, to be caught by the prohibition on discrimination, it has to be proved that the taxation has a protectionist effect. At the root of this difference is the fact that direct comparisons are possible under Article 110(1) TFEU, whereas under Article 110(2) TFEU they are not.

In **Case 55/79 *Commission v Ireland (Excise Payments)***, under Irish law, producers of beer, wine and spirits enjoyed an extension of four to six weeks of the period for the payment of excise duties, whereas taxes on imported beers, wines and spirits had to be paid immediately on importation or on delivery from the bonded warehouse; hence it was discriminating in application.

So even where the level of taxation is the same, a delay in the collection in favour of domestic goods was held to be discriminatory and a breach of Article 110 TFEU.

In **Case 112/84 *Michel Humblot v Directeur des Services Fiscaux***, the French authorities imposed a higher tax on cars with a higher horsepower rating, none of which were manufactured in France, meaning that the tax applied in practice only to imported cars. The Court of Justice allowed for the possibility that a tax that appears to discriminate against a category of imported goods, because no goods in that category are produced domestically, will not necessarily always be in breach of Article 90 EC (now 110 TFEU). However, it held that because many of the imported cars thus taxed would still be in competition with cars produced in France taxed at the lower rate, the tax was nevertheless in breach of Article 90 EC (now 110 TFEU).

In contrast is **Case C-132/88 *Commission v Greece (Taxation of Motor Cars)*** in which a Greek tax on both new and second-hand cars, whether produced in Greece or imported

For more details on this section scan here or visit the Online Resource Centre.

from outside, rose steeply in respect of cars above 1800 cc capacity. The cars affected were all imported because no cars above 1600cc were produced in Greece. The Court held that this measure would be indirectly discriminatory only if it were shown that the taxation had the effect of discouraging Greeks from purchasing foreign cars. On the face of it, the tax was motivated by other considerations and there was no protective effect.

Even where there may even be benefits for the imported goods, a difference in the way in which a tax is levied may be held to breach Article 110 TFEU.

In **Case C-213/96 *Outokumpu Oy***, a flat rate tax on imported electricity from Sweden was held to infringe Article 90 EC (now 110 TFEU) because the tax rate on domestic electricity was calculated according to the product that was used for its manufacture for environmental reasons. The fact that only in limited circumstances would the rate of imported tax be higher was immaterial to the Court of Justice. The ease of administration in setting up a general system and the fact that it was extremely difficult to determine precisely the method of production of imported electricity were not accepted as grounds justifying the system adopted.

10.4.2.1 Similar products

Article 110(1) TFEU requires that if there is a difference in the way in which similar products are taxed, the levels of tax have to be equalized. First of all, in determining what constitutes 'similar products', whilst obviously including same products, the Commission and Court need to take into account various factors, including the composition, physical characteristics and method of production of the product, as well as to consider whether both producers meet the same consumer needs.

For example, in **Case 243/84 *John Walker Ltd v Ministeriet for Skatter og Afgifter***, the question of 'whether whisky was similar to fruit wine' was posed. Whilst it was clear that both were alcoholic drinks, the Court of Justice held that the two drinks were not similar since they exhibited manifestly different characteristics. The wine was fruit-based and relied on natural fermentation, whereas the Scotch whisky was a cereal-based drink produced by distillation. There were also significant differences in the alcohol volume.

In **Case 184/85 *Commission v Italy (Italian Fruit)*** the similarity between bananas, on the one hand, and peaches and pears, on the other, was considered and, according to the Court of Justice, they were not similar. The Court referred to the **organoleptic** characteristics and the water content, which were different, and which meant that they were suited to different markets.

organoleptic

Essentially meaning 'sensory', organoleptic refers to any sensory properties of a product, involving taste, colour, odour and feel. Organoleptic testing involves inspection through visual examination, feeling and smelling of products.

10.4.2.2 Other products

As far as Article 110(2) TFEU is concerned, for a tax to be caught by the prohibition on discrimination, it has to be proved that the taxation has a protectionist effect to the detriment of imported goods that may be in competition with the other domestic good. The main question focuses on whether the products can be substituted by each other.

Probably the most important case still on Article 110(2) TFEU is **Case 170/78 *Commission v UK (Wine Excise Duties No. 2)***, in which the Court of Justice held that the fact that the UK imposed a higher duty on table wines than on beer was held to give indirect protection to beer (a domestic product) over light table wines (a predominantly imported product) and contravened Article 90(2) EC (now 110(2) TFEU). The UK government had argued that wine and beer could not be regarded as competing beverages, since beer was widely consumed in public houses, whereas wine was generally drunk only on special occasions, and pointed out the difference in the alcoholic volume. The Court took the view that it was necessary not only to examine the present state of the market, but whether the two products were potentially in competition.

Given that the case arose over twenty-five years ago, the argument employed at the time was factual; however, it was a pretty shrewd judgement, because the two products are probably far more in competition with each other now than then.

The Court of Justice decided that such a relationship existed on the basis of volume, price and alcoholic strength, and mentioned the thirst-quenching qualities of both products even when UK beer was then about 3 per cent alcohol and the lightest wines 8–9 per cent.

After such a finding, the member state may abolish discrimination either by lowering the tax on imported goods or by raising the tax on domestic products, or may use a combination of both to remove the discrimination or protection.

 # Summary

The main aspects that were considered in this chapter were not customs duties, which were outlawed very early in the life of the Union and which are now extremely rare. Instead, the emphasis was more on charges having the equivalent effect to customs duties, although these too are much rarer today than in the past. The main focus of attention in the future is likely to be on taxation aspects of this topic, because taxation is still, for the most part, within the competences of the member states unless it is unfairly levied on imports in a discriminatory manner. In that case, the policy or tax provision can be reviewed by the Court of Justice to see if it conforms with the free movement of goods and tax provisions of the Treaty. Such taxation can, however, be justified if for a genuine reason and taxation for environmental reasons is a likely ground for taxation in the future. It must not, however, discriminate against imports.

Questions

For suggested approaches to answering these questions scan here or visit the Online Resource Centre.

1 The four commonly recognized stages in economic integration are free trade area, customs union, common market and then economic union. Define each of these terms, and identify which stage has been reached by the EU.

2 What, according to the ECJ, is a charge having equivalent effect?

3 When is it acceptable to impose a charge on imported goods?

4 Under what circumstances is it possible to impose a tax on imported goods?

Further reading

BOOKS

Barnard, C. *The Substantive Law of the EU: The Four Freedoms*, 3rd edn, Oxford University Press, Oxford, 2010 (chapters 2–4).

Davies, G. *European Union Internal Market Law*, 2nd edn, Cavendish Publishing, London, 2003 (chapters 1–2).

ARTICLES

Banks, K. 'The application of the fundamental freedoms to member state tax measures: guarding against protectionism or second-guessing national policy choices?' (2008) 33 EL Rev 482.

Möstl, M. 'Preconditions and limits of mutual recognition' (2010) 47 CML Rev 405.

Oliver, P. and Enchelmaier, S. 'Free movement of goods: recent developments in the case law' (2007) 44 CMLR 649.

Oliver, P. and Roth, W.-H. 'The internal market and the four freedoms' (2004) 41 CMLR 407.

Weatherill, S. 'Harmonisation: how much, how little' (2005) 55 ICLQ 457.

Weatherill, S. 'Recent developments in the law governing the free movement of goods in the EC's internal market' (2006) 2 ECRL 90.

Free movement of goods II: non-tariff barriers

Learning objectives

In this chapter, you will consider the following aspects of the non-tariff barriers that member states have created and which hinder or prevent the free flow of goods:

- the legislative provisions applicable to non-tariff barriers;
- the definition of quantitative restrictions and measures having equivalent effect;
- case law developments of *Dassonville* and *Cassis de Dijon*;
- the retreat from the *Dassonville* and *Cassis* cases in the case of *Keck*;
- the further explanation of what *Keck* meant in subsequent cases; and
- the further developments in case law since *Keck*.

Introduction

This chapter completes the picture of the free movement of goods commenced in Chapter 10, which concerned the tariff and tax barriers to free movement, and instead concentrates on the non-tariff barriers.

It is worth taking a careful note of the Treaty Article number changes that took place after both the Amsterdam and Lisbon Treaties came into force. The numbers have now swapped around two times and original Article 30 EEC, which provided one of the basic prohibitions in this area, became Article 28 EC and is now Article 34 TFEU. Original Article 36 EEC, which concerned the derogations, became Article 30 EC (the old Article number for the prohibition), but is now once again Article 36 TFEU concerned with the derogations, so be extra careful when reading and referring to case law in this area: it is all too easy to slip up. Hence, then, more frequently than for other chapters, more than one set of both numbers will be provided, hopefully to help to avoid confusion.

This area of law is concerned with the attempts of the member states to prevent or hinder imports and the ways in which the Commission and the European Court of Justice (ECJ) have been tackling this. It also considers where differences in national rules relating to goods are permitted, namely those that are not designed to prevent or hinder the free flow of goods.

11.1 Legislation

The main Treaty Articles applicable are Articles 34 and 36 TFEU (ex 28 and 30 EC), but also be aware of Article 35 TFEU (ex 29 EC) in respect of ensuring the free movement of exports.

> **Article 34 TFEU**
> ....
> Quantitative restrictions on imports and all measures having equivalent effect shall be prohibited between Member States.

> **Article 35 TFEU**
> ....
> Quantitative restrictions on exports, and all measures having equivalent effect, shall be prohibited between Member States.

cross reference
Article 36 TFEU will be considered in section 11.3.

There is very little secondary legislation of direct importance in this area of European Union (EU) law, but Directive 70/50 will be considered in this chapter, as will two more recent enactments: Decision 3052/95 and Directive 98/34.

For more details
on this section
scan here or
visit the Online
Resource Centre.

cross reference

*See Case 8/74
Dassonville as a
good example of
this approach, con-
sidered in further
depth in section
11.2.3.*

cross reference

*This is considered in
section 11.3.*

Quantitative restrictions and measures having equivalent effect

Non-financial barriers to the free movement of goods are contained within the phrase 'quantitative restrictions and measures having equivalent effect'. Restrictions or obstacles to free
movement are caused mainly by different national laws regulating products and trade rather
than the very crude or obvious and clearly prohibited import or export bans. Harmonization
of all products was neither a practical nor a desirable solution. The founding fathers instead
adopted a means of negative integration to tackle the obstacles to free movement caused by
different national laws in each member state. These become the focus of attention in this area
of free movement. Quantitative restrictions are straightforward and usually found in the form
of either a ban or quota. The main concern is about measures that fall short of a quantitative
restriction. It is the extent to which member states can insist that imported products comply
with national standards that can frustrate the attempt to create a genuinely unified single market and which thus requires the closest consideration.

The development of the rules on the free movement of goods reflects the general approach
to the fundamental freedoms in that the Court of Justice has interpreted the principle of free
movement as liberally as it can to promote free movement. The derogations allowed to the
member states, on the other hand, are interpreted restrictively or as narrowly as possible.

11.2.1 The general scope of the Treaty prohibition

Article 34 TFEU lays down a general prohibition on quantitative restrictions and measures having equivalent effect on imports. Article 35 TFEU extends that prohibition to exports.

Article 36 TFEU provides the member states with grounds by which they can escape the prohibitions under Articles 34 and 35 TFEU.

Both Articles 34 and 35 TFEU (ex 28 and 29 EC) have been found to be directly effective, but only
vertically against measures taken by the state: see respectively Cases 74/76 *Ianelli and Volpi SpA* v
Meroni and 83/78 *Pigs Marketing Board* v *Redmond*. However, measures taken by the state have
been interpreted fairly liberally to include measures taken by public, semi-public and even private
bodies in certain circumstances in which there has been a fair degree of state involvement or financing. This then brings the actions of an otherwise private body within Articles 34 and 35 TFEU.

For example, in **Cases 266 and 267/87 *R* v *Pharmaceutical Society of Great Britain,
ex p Association of Pharmaceutical Importers***, the activities of the Association, which
regulated the conduct and set standards for chemists and pharmacists, meant that it could
be included.

In **Case 249/81 *Commission* v *Ireland (Buy Irish)*** a 'buy Irish' campaign was administered by the Irish Goods Council, a registered private company. However, because the Irish
government largely sponsored the campaign to buy Irish products, appointed the management committee and set the broad outlines of the campaign, Article 28 (now 34 TFEU) was
held to be applicable.

In **Case 222/82 *Apple and Pear Development Council* v *Lewis***, a government-sponsored development council was under a duty not to run an advertising campaign to encourage purchase of domestic fruit at the expense of imported products, although it could conduct research into the growing and development of fruit species and disseminate this information.

Without state involvement, the actions of private parties are outside the direct application of Articles 34–36 TFEU, and they would be free to advertise and promote the products of their members.

11.2.1.1 What constitutes measures for the purposes of Article 34 TFEU?

The concept of 'measures' includes not only legally binding acts, but also practices 'capable of influencing the conduct of traders and consumers' (see Case 249/81 *Commission* v *Ireland (Buy Irish)*) and may include state inaction to prevent private individuals' actions that obstruct the free movement of goods.

See **Case C-265/95 *Commission* v *France (French Farmers/Spanish Strawberries)*** in which the state did not take effective action to stop the protests that prevented Spanish produce entering France and which involved the illegal destruction of imported products. France was held to be in breach of Article 28 EC (now 34 TFEU).

cross reference
These cases are also considered in Chapter 7, section 7.1.3.

In contrast is **Case C-112/00 *Schmidberger***. The lack of state action on the part of Austria in not preventing a protest that blocked the Brenner motorway pass in Austria was held to be acceptable and not a breach of Article 28 EC (now 34 TFEU). This case was distinguished on the length of protest, as a single one-off event that was not repeated and as a lawful protest. **Case C-265/95 *Commission* v *France*** concerned repeated illegal sabotages of imported goods that should have been stopped and thus was a breach of Article 28 EC (now 34 TFEU).

281

The term 'measures' has also been interpreted to include administrative practices, if they have a certain degree of consistency and generality.

For example, in **Case 21/84 *Commission* v *France (Franking Machines)***, France had removed a law that had discriminated against imported franking machines, but the French authorities had failed to approve the import of machines from the UK. This administrative failing was held by the ECJ to come within the scope of Article 28 EC (now 34 TFEU).

The Preamble to Directive 70/50 supports this generous view of measures or rules by including non-legally binding **administrative practices**.

. . . .

administrative practices
Any standard regularly followed procedure of a public authority, compared with recommendations, which are instruments issuing from a public authority that, while not legally binding on the addressees thereof, cause them to pursue a certain conduct.

. . . .

11.2.2 **The meaning of 'quantitative restrictions'**

The most obvious examples of quantitative restrictions on imports and exports are complete bans on imports or the subjection of imports or exports to quotas restricting the import or export by either quantity or value. These are clearly in contravention of Article 34 TFEU and are thus prohibited.

> Cases 231/78 *Commission v UK (Import of Potatoes)* and 232/78 *Commission v France (Import of Lamb)* are straightforward examples of total bans, which are prohibited.

> In **Case 2/73 *Geddo v Ente Nationale Risi***, the Court of Justice held that a prohibition on quantitative restrictions covers measures that amount to a total or partial restraint of imports, exports or goods in transit.

> In **Case 34/79 *R v Henn and Darby***, it was held by the Court of Justice to cover measures capable of limiting imports to a finite quantity, including zero, and to include import bans.

A quantitative restriction also includes subjecting the import of goods to the condition of obtaining an import licence.

> In **Case 124/81 *Commission v UK (Imports of UHT Milk)***, the failure to obtain an import licence meant that milk could not be imported even though the requirement was a formality and licences were issued on demand. The Court of Justice held that import licences or other similar procedures, even if a pure formality, are precluded by Article 28 EC (now 34 TFEU).

11.2.3 **Measures having equivalent effect (MHEE)**

The concept of measures having equivalent effect (MHEEs, or often abbreviated as MQRs and MeQRs) has been defined by secondary legislation (Directive 70/50) and by the jurisprudence of the Court of Justice.

The Directive, which was introduced to provide guidelines at the time when the Common Market was being established, continues to provide guidance as to what measures may be considered a breach of the prohibition under what is now Article 34 TFEU (ex 28 EC, ex 30 EEC). It defines measures having an equivalent effect on imports as including distinctly applicable measures – that is, those that apply to imports, but not domestically produced goods – and which (Article 2):

> make imports, or the disposal at any marketing stage, of imported products, subject to a condition, other than a formality, which is required in respect of imported products only, or a condition differing from that required for domestic products and more difficult to satisfy. Equally, it covers, in particular, measures which favour domestic products or grant them a preference, other than an aid, to which conditions may or may not be attached.

Basically, therefore, any measure that makes import or export unnecessarily difficult and thus discriminates between the two, would clearly fall within the definition.

cross reference
We will return to this aspect later in section 11.4.

It also covers, under Article 3, national marketing rules that, on the face of it, are non-discriminatory or 'indistinctly applicable', and:

> which deal in particular, with size, shape, weight, composition, presentation, identification, or putting up and which are equally applicable to domestic and imported products, where the restrictive effect of such measures on the free movement of goods exceeds the effects intrinsic to trade rules.

Further help in understanding this concept comes from the Court of Justice.

The starting point is **Case 8/74 *Procureur du Roi* v *Dassonville*** in which the term 'measures having equivalent effect' was held to include 'all trading rules enacted by a Member State which are capable of hindering, directly or indirectly, actually or potentially, intra-community trade'. The case concerned criminal proceedings in Belgium against a trader who imported Scotch whisky in free circulation in France into Belgium without being in possession of a certificate of origin from the British customs authorities, thus infringing Belgian customs rules. The Court of Justice held that:

> the requirement by a Member State of a certificate of authority, which is less easily obtainable by importers of an authentic product, put into free circulation in a regular manner in another Member State, than by importers of the same product coming directly from the country of origin, constitutes a measure having equivalent effect.

The Court added that, in the absence of a Community system to guarantee a product's origin, a member state may take reasonable measures for the protection of consumers in the area of designation of origin of products without necessarily infringing Article 28 EC (now 34 TFEU).

283

However, this is subject to the further qualification that whether or not such measures were authorized by the derogations provided in Article 36 EEC and TFEU, they could not constitute an arbitrary discrimination or a disguised restriction on trade between member states.

The scope of the prohibition following this definition is extremely wide and means that virtually any measure that hinders imports or exports in any way could be caught.

11.2.4 Examples of measures coming within the scope of the prohibition

11.2.4.1 National promotional campaigns

Measures that do not have a clear visible direct effect on imports may still be caught by the prohibition in Article 34 TFEU.

In **Case 249/81 *Commission* v *Ireland (Buy Irish)***, the Court of Justice held that the activities of a company that was government-controlled, government-financed, and which carried out a government policy of promoting the sale of national products by means of an advertising campaign and promoted the use of a 'home-produced' symbol constituted a measure having equivalent effect. It was held that it was not necessary for the government to have taken any compulsory measures and that simply encouraging the purchase of domestic products through a campaigning body was sufficient to count as a measure having equivalent effect.

The emphasis is therefore on those rules that are capable of having an effect rather than those rules actually having an effect.

In **Case 222/82 *Apple and Pear Development Council v Lewis***, the ruling in the *Buy Irish* case was qualified. The ECJ held that a member state could establish a Development Council for fruit production that was composed of members appointed by the minister responsible and financed only by the growers themselves as long as the activities consisted of compiling statistics, promotion and undertaking of research, and giving technical advice rather than trying to get consumers to purchase only home-produced fruit and not imports.

11.2.4.2 Discriminatory national marketing rules

National marketing rules often impose restrictions on the production, packaging or distribution of goods, which may as a consequence infringe Article 34 TFEU.

For example, in **Case 113/80 *Commission v Ireland (Metal Objects/Origin)***, the requirement to stamp the origin of goods as either Irish or foreign was held to breach the rule.

In **Case 261/81 *Rau v De Smedt***, the Belgian national rule that required margarine to be packed in cubes and in no other form such as tubs or rectangular blocks was held to be in breach of Article 28 EC (now 34 TFEU). It imposed an economic disadvantage on exporters to Belgium.

In **Cases 266 and 267/87 *R v Pharmaceutical Society of Great Britain***, the rule of the Pharmaceutical Society prohibiting dispensing pharmacists from substituting for the product named on a doctor's prescription any other with identical therapeutical effect except under certain exceptional conditions was capable of coming within the operation of Article 28 EC (now 34 TFEU). It was held, however, that it was capable of being justified on the grounds of the protection of public health.

11.2.4.3 Product classification

Cases C-387/99 *Commission v Germany* and **150/00 *Commission v Austria*** concerned the classification of food supplement products as medicines, which resulted in the restriction of imports where the daily doses of particular vitamins was exceeded. This practice was held to breach Article 28 EC (now 34 TFEU) and could not be justified by Article 30 EC (now 36 TFEU) because of the systematic nature of regulation rather than a case-by-case investigation.

11.2.4.4 Exports

In **Case C-47/90 *Delhaize v Promalvin***, a ban on the export of wine in bulk was held to breach Article 29 EC (now 35 TFEU), which states that quantitative restriction on exports, and all measures having equivalent effect, shall be prohibited between member states. There was no evidence to support the contention that bottling was necessary at the source of production, especially where the wine was transported in bulk internally.

11.3 Article 36 TFEU derogations

For more details on this section scan here or visit the Online Resource Centre.

Article 36 TFEU provides exceptions to the general prohibition of Article 34 TFEU.

> **Article 36 TFEU**
> ....
> The provisions of Articles 34 and 35 shall not preclude prohibitions or restrictions on imports, exports or goods in transit justified on grounds of public morality, public policy or public security; the protection of health and life of humans, animals or plants; the protection of national treasures possessing artistic, historic or archaeological value; or the protection of industrial and commercial property. . . .

The application of these exceptions is subject to the limitation, set out in the second sentence of Article 36 TFEU.

> **Article 36 TFEU**
> ....
> . . . Such prohibitions or restrictions shall not, however, constitute a means of arbitrary discrimination or a disguised restriction on trade between Member States.

11.3.1 General purpose and scope

Article 36 TFEU provides the member states with an exhaustive list – in other words, it cannot be added to. Article 36 TFEU allows the member states to restrict the free movement of goods for certain specific reasons only.

> In **Case 72/83 Campus Oil v Ministry for Industry and Energy**, the Court of Justice held that the purpose of Article 36 EC and TFEU was not to reserve certain matters to the exclusive jurisdiction of the member states, but instead to allow national legislation to derogate from the principle of the free movement of goods to the extent to which this is and remains justified in order to achieve the objectives set out in the Article.

> In **Case 113/80 Commission v Ireland (Metal Objects)**, it was held that because the derogations were exceptions to a fundamental principle, namely the free movement of goods, they were to be construed narrowly and could not, for example, be used for economic reasons.

In **Case 7/61** *Commission* **v** *Italian Republic (Pigmeat Imports)* the derogation was claimed by Italy in order to protect its own pig industry, which was suffering economic difficulties. Italy's attempt was rejected by the Court of Justice.

11.3.2 Public morality

The standard of morality varies from member state to member state; hence the Court of Justice has allowed for a margin of discretion on the part of the member states to cater for this within this exception.

Case 34/79 *R* **v** *Henn and Darby* concerned a ban on the importation of pornographic magazines, despite the fact that similar magazines could be lawfully possessed in the UK, but it was noted that the enforcement of the law varied within the UK. The Court concluded that despite the fact that similar pornographic items could be obtained in the UK, there was no lawful trade in them. The Court of Justice therefore ruled that a prohibition that might be stricter than the laws applicable internally, but which was not designed to discriminate in favour of the domestic product, was therefore acceptable under the public morality clause of Article 30 EC (now 36 TFEU). The Court of Justice held that it was up to member states to determine the requirements of public morality in their own state and that they therefore have a margin of discretion in this area.

This means that, provided that the prohibition was not discriminatory in intent, different standards can apply. This was, however, qualified in the next case.

In **Case 121/85** *Conegate* **v** *HM Customs and Excise*, the infamous case concerned with the importation of 'blow-up dolls', it was held that member states did not have complete freedom to exclude such material when similar products could be manufactured lawfully in the UK. The Court held that a member state might not rely on the ground of public morality to prohibit the importation of goods from other member states when its legislation contained no prohibition on the manufacture or marketing of such goods in its own territory. The prohibition was therefore a disguised restriction on trade and a means of arbitrary discrimination, and as such contrary to the second sentence of Article 30 EC (now 36 TFEU).

11.3.3 Public policy

The leading case in this category is **Case 7/78** *R* **v** *Thompson and others*, which concerned the ban on the unlawful importation into the UK of krugerrands and a ban on the export of coins, some of which were no longer legal tender and some of which were. The English coins that were no longer legal tender were held to be goods within the meaning of Article 28 EC (now 34 TFEU). However, it was held that the right to mint and thus to control coinage was a fundamental interest of the state. Therefore a state that prohibits the destruction of coins, even when they are no longer legal tender, and imposes an export ban to prevent their destruction abroad will be justified under Article 30 EC (now 36 TFEU) on grounds of public policy.

Other attempts by member states to invoke this exception have failed: see, for example, those cases dealing with lack of effective action by states to curb illegal protests. It has been claimed that the threat to public order that may be provoked by their action to intervene prevented them from intervening to ensure the free movement of goods.

The Court of Justice therefore did not accept the invocation of Article 30 EC (now 36 TFEU) to justify the lack of action in **Case C-265/95 Commission v France (Spanish Strawberries)**, in which the French authorities did nothing to prevent French farmers from destroying imported Spanish strawberries.

11.3.4 **Public security**

The leading case to deal with security is **Case 238/82 Campus Oil**, which concerned Irish rules requiring importers of petroleum products to purchase a certain proportion of their requirements from an Irish state-owned refinery at prices fixed by the minister. The Court of Justice held that the maintenance of essential oil supplies was covered by the public security exception.

A further attempt to invoke Article 30 EC (now 36 TFEU) was also rejected in **Case 231/83 Cullet v Centre Leclerc Toulouse**, concerned with a law imposing a minimum retail price for fuel. Lower cost imports could not realize their competitive advantage under this law. France argued that, in the absence of the pricing rules, there would be civil disturbances, blockades and violence. The Court of Justice rejected this claim.

cross reference

Proportionality is considered further in section 11.3.8.

Any measures taken by member states are nevertheless subject to the principle of proportionality.

11.3.5 **The protection of the health or life of humans or animals**

This is a frequently argued ground for import restrictions and virtually every sort of good, especially foodstuffs, has been subjected to restrictions on health grounds, most of which have been held by the Court of Justice not to conform with Article 30 EC (now 36 TFEU).

In **Case 322/01 Deutscher Apothekerverband**, the Court of Justice noted that 'the health and life of humans rank foremost among the assets or interests' protected by Article 30 EC and the Court has been extremely vigilant in exposing the disguised restrictions of member states.

For example, in **Case 124/81 Commission v UK (UHT Milk)**, the systematic checking and opening of sealed UHT cartons of milk for health checks, which rendered the contents unusable and thus increased costs to the importer, amounted to import restrictions. The Court of

Justice held that the health of consumers would be adequately protected by the necessary controls being carried out in the country of production to meet all of the reasonable requirements of the country of import.

 This case is a good example of the principle of equivalence.

cross reference
Equivalence is considered further in section 11.4.1.

Similarly, in **Case 42/82 Commission v France (Italian Table Wines)**, systematic checks on three-quarters of each consignment of Italian wine, which was held up at the French border for long periods, sometimes months, was held not to be justified by Article 30 EC (now 36 TFEU). Whilst the Court of Justice acknowledged the right of the member states to carry out checks, it noted that the frequency of analysis of Italian wine was considerably higher than the occasional checks carried out on French wine transported within France. The Court of Justice held that the French authorities had no right to carry out systematic checks and, in the absence of any reasonable suspicion on the basis of specific evidence in a given case, they ought to have confined themselves to random checks.

A number of cases have now been considered by the Court concerned with import bans on the grounds of protecting public health, which have focused on the content of food products and often concerning food additives that were claimed to be hazardous to human health. The Court of Justice has held in these cases that, in the absence of any Community regulation of the manufacture and marketing of products, the member states are free to regulate this matter as long as they do not infringe the Community provisions on the free movement of goods. In the cases that are concerned with an import ban raised on the grounds of protecting the health of the population from harmful additives, the Court of Justice takes into account the following criteria:

• whether the additives were either permitted in another product; or

• whether they were lawfully permitted in another member state; or

• how they are regarded according to the results of international scientific research, in particular the work of the World Health Organization (WHO); and

• the eating habits in the country of importation.

If the additive does not constitute a real danger to public health, a ban would be a breach of Article 34 TFEU (ex 28 EC) and would not be justified under Article 36 TFEU (ex 30 EC). Additionally, bans would be contrary to the principle of proportionality where there was no accessible procedure by which traders were able to request that the use of disputed additives be permitted.

Cases include the ban on the import of beer in **Case 178/84 Commission v Germany (Beer Purity)**, a ban on the import of sausages containing certain non-meat ingredients in **Case 274/87 Commission v Germany (Sausage Purity Law)** and a ban on the import of low-fat cheese in **Case 210/89 Commission v Italy**.

However, a ban would not infringe Article 34 TFEU (ex 28 EC) where the same additives are also prohibited in domestic products and where there is a system to allow the addition of additives to the list of permitted additives: see Cases 95 and 293/89 *Commission* v *Italy and Greece*. In summary of the case law, states must make out on the basis of latest scientific data that a real risk to health exists. However, the Court recognizes 'that such an assessment of the risk could reveal that scientific uncertainty persists as regards the existence or extent of real risks to human health'.

However, in **Case C-192/01 *Commission* v *Denmark***, the Court of Justice stated that, in such circumstances, it must be accepted that a member state may, in accordance with the precautionary principle, take protective measures without having to wait until the existence and gravity of those risks are fully demonstrated.

Finally in this category is **Case C-358/95 *Tommaso Morellato* v *Unita Sanitaria Locale***, which focused on the contents of bread. It was claimed that imported frozen bread contravened national statutory limits by having a moisture content exceeding 34 per cent and an ash content of less than 1.40 per cent, and by containing bran, contrary to national standards for bread. France was unable to demonstrate a threat to public health and it was easy for the Court of Justice to reach the conclusion that the national law constituted a quantitative restriction contrary to Article 28 EC (now 34 TFEU) and was not saved by Article 30 EC (now 36 TFEU).

An area in which the public health proviso in Article 36 TFEU is of great importance is in the importation of pharmaceutical products for which there are often vast price differences between the retail prices in different member states.

Case 215/87 *Schumacher* v *Hauptzollamt Frankfurt* concerned the ban on the import of medicinal products purchased in France for personal use. The medicines in question were available in Germany without prescription, but at four times the price charged in France. The Court of Justice held that national rules or practices that have or are likely to have a restrictive effect on importation of pharmaceutical products are compatible with the Treaty only in so far as they are necessary for the protection of health and human life. In this case, the purchase of the goods in a pharmacy of another member state in effect gives a guarantee equivalent to that resulting from the sale of the product in a pharmacy in the member state into which it is imported. The Court ruled that the rule prohibiting the importation of the goods in this case contravened Article 28 EC (now 34 TFEU) and was not protected by Article 30 EC (now 36 TFEU).

11.3.6 **Artistic heritage**

It was held in **Case 7/68 *Commission* v *Italy (Art Treasures)*** that the ground of artistic heritage does not justify a tax being levied on the export of art treasures, which was therefore held to breach Article 25 EC (now 30 TFEU).

The point of this is that if Italy wants to protect art or to stop it from leaving the country, a complete ban may be justified; simply taxing it was not.

11.3.7 The protection of artistic or commercial property

This derogation protecting intellectual property rights is to be read alongside Article 345 TFEU (ex 295 EC), which provides that the Treaty shall in no way prejudice the rules in member states governing the system of property ownership.

> This derogation was considered in **Case 388/95** *Belgium* **v** *Spain* and the Spanish ban on the export of Rioja wine in bulk, which was held to be a breach of Article 29 EC (now 35 TFEU), but which was justified to maintain its high quality and reputation under the Article 30 EC (now 36 TFEU) derogation for the protection of commercial property.

In view of the vast number of cases on this specialized topic, many of which are also tied up with competition law aspects, it is unlikely that you will go into any further detail on most undergraduate courses on EU law. In view of the reference to competition law in the previous section, the significance of a complementary competition law policy should be stressed because it is vital to the successful running of the internal market. The establishment or foundation of the EU is premised on the desire to promote integration and to create a single unified market. A competition policy within the overall Treaty regime prevents companies from setting up their own rules and obstacles to trade to replace the national rules and obstacles that the EU is trying to abolish. The two go hand in hand: you cannot have one without ensuring you have the other. To have prevented the member states, on the one hand, from restricting the movement of goods only to allow private companies to do it by their agreements and practices would defeat the objectives of the first policy; on the other hand, to prevent companies from artificially dividing the markets, but to allow the member states to do so, would undermine a competition policy. Hence there is a need for both.

11.3.8 The second sentence of Article 36 TFEU

Article 36 TFEU provides that 'Such prohibitions or restrictions shall not, however, constitute a means of arbitrary discrimination or a disguised restriction on trade between Member States'. In addition, any measure taken by the member states to regulate products or markets must be proportionate.

Essentially, this second sentence provides a backstop for the Court of Justice to ensure that any claims raised by the member states under any of the grounds considered in this chapter so far do conform with the overall desire to ensure and promote the free movement of goods within the internal EU market.

> In **Case 42/82** *Commission* **v** *France (Italian Table Wines)*, the systematic checking of every consignment and subjecting inspections to very long delays of weeks, and even months, was held to be disproportionate. It simply went far beyond the alleged purposes of ensuring quality.

> Similarly, in **Case 124/81** *Commission* **v** *UK (UHT Milk)*, the requirement of an import licence was held to be a disguised restriction despite being issued automatically. In other words, it was merely a hurdle that importers had to overcome even though it was easy to obtain a licence, which actually shows that it served no quality control purpose.

> **Case C-170/04 *Rosengren*** involved a Swedish government measure prohibiting the private import of alcohol, unless sanctioned by the authorities and subject to additional import charges. The restriction was held to be contrary to Article 28 EC (now 34 TFEU), but was claimed by Sweden to be justified under the Article 30 EC (now 36 TFEU) health ground, in particular to protect young persons. The ECJ dismissed this because the measure, contained in Chapter 4(2)(1) of the Swedish Law on Alcohol, was unsuitable for attaining the objective of limiting alcohol consumption generally, and not proportionate for attaining the objective of protecting young persons against the harmful effects of such consumption. The state monopoly was not a means of restricting alcohol imports or strength of drinks, but more of preserving the state monopoly to import. The ECJ held therefore that it could not be regarded as being justified under Article 30 EC on grounds of protection of the health and life of humans.

So whilst the Court is acutely aware of the health issues in alcohol abuse and consumption by young people, any measures ostensibly to address those issues must really be designed to do that. The Swedish measures were inadequate in that respect and operated only to ensure the state near-monopoly on alcohol imports.

11.3.9 Decision 3052/95 and Regulation 764/2008

In an attempt to regulate better the introduction by member states of measures that affect the free movement of goods, Decision 3052/95 was adopted, now replaced by Regulation 764/2008. This required the member states to inform the Commission about any measures that may lead to the refusal of the import of goods or require the modification of goods for the market or which withdraws goods from the market. The Commission then informs the other member states to provide them with an opportunity to be able to react or express a view on them. Furthermore, the Commission may decide to seek further details or take action if it concludes that the measures actually breach Article 28 EC (now 34 TFEU). The replacement Regulation 764/2008 is also intended to assist the free movement of goods by providing procedures to assess the impact of proposed technical rules by member states, who must advise the Commission when they propose to enact any such measures.

Further details will not be provided in this text, but links can be found via the Online Resource Centre.

11.4 Equally applicable measures (indistinctly applicable measures)

For more details on this section scan here or visit the Online Resource Centre.

Measures that apply to imports or exports only are called 'distinctly applicable measures'. However, Article 34 TFEU prohibits not only national rules that overtly discriminate against imported products, subject to the possibility of justification under Article 36 TFEU, but may also be used to challenge national rules that, on the face of it, make no distinction between domestic and imported goods. Those measures that apply to both imports and domestic goods are termed 'equally' or 'indistinctly' applicable.

Article 3 of Directive 70/50 provides that measures that are equally applicable to domestic and imported goods will breach Article 34 TFEU only where the restrictive effect on the free movement of goods exceeds the effects necessary for the trade rules – that is, only those measures that are disproportionate to the aim and which thus tend to protect domestic products at the expense of the imports.

> **Directive 70/50, Article 3**
>
> This directive also covers measures governing the marketing of products which deal, in particular, with shape, size, weight, composition, presentation, identification or putting up and which are equally applicable to domestic and imported products, where the restrictive effect of such measures on the free movement of goods exceeds the effects intrinsic to trade rules. This is the case, in particular, where the restrictive effects on the free movement of goods are out of proportion to their purpose; and the same objective can be attained by other means which are less of a hindrance to trade.

The wide definition of measures in **Case 8/74 *Procureur de Roi* v *Dassonville*** made no allowance for some measures introduced by member states that applied to both imports and domestic products and which might be justified on particular acceptable grounds, such as the protection of the environment. The judgment, however, did acknowledge this possibility in the statement that:

> In the absence of a community system guaranteeing for consumers the authenticity of a product's designation of origin, if a Member State takes measures to prevent unfair practices in this connection, it is however subject to the condition that these measures should be reasonable and that the means of proof required should not act as a hindrance to trade between Member States and should, in consequence, be accessible to all Community nationals.

In other words, member states can require importers to satisfy certain rules provided that Article 34 TFEU (ex 28 EC) is not contravened. Thus the case introduced the possibility that the member states could restrict imports for a good reason and marked the foundation of the so-called rule of reason.

This was developed further in a landmark decision in EU law that addressed the difficulties of indistinctly applicable measures, which may be introduced by member states for arguably sound reasons. This is Case 120/78 *Rewe-Zentral AG* v *Bundesmonopolverwaltung für Branntwein*, better known as *Cassis de Dijon*.

11.4.1 The *Cassis de Dijon* case

Case 120/78 *Cassis de Dijon* concerns a prohibition on the marketing in the Federal Republic of Germany of spirits with less than a 25 per cent alcohol content, which included Crème de Cassis de Dijon (a blackcurrant alcoholic liqueur), which contains usually only 15–20 per cent alcohol. The ban applied to all low-alcohol liqueurs regardless of origin and did not distinguish between national and foreign drinks; hence it was indistinctly applicable.

The arguments made by Germany for the ban were that lower-alcohol liqueurs would lead to alcohol tolerance, thus leading to health problems in the future, and that the lower alcohol also provided a price advantage for the imported products that was unfair and which would force down alcohol rates of drinks, and thus quality, contrary to usual manufacturing practice. However, the actual result was effectively a ban, albeit indirect, of the French imports.

The Court of Justice made a number of statements of importance in its judgment. It held that there was no valid reason why, provided that they have been lawfully produced and marketed in one of the member states, alcoholic beverages should not be introduced without restriction into any other member state. As was seen in *Commission v UK (UHT Milk)*, this is a restatement of the principle of mutual equivalence.

The Court of Justice also held that obstacles to the free movement of goods resulting from disparities in the national laws on the marketing of products must be accepted as far as these provisions are necessary to satisfy certain mandatory requirements.

cross reference
See section 11.3.5 for UHT Milk.

cross reference
This is considered further in the following sections.

The judgment was a way of getting around too strict an application of the rule developed in the earlier *Dassonville* case. It means that measures that are equally applicable to imports and domestic products and which hinder trade may be acceptable if they are in pursuit of a reasonable special interest that the member state has the right to protect. However, they are subject to the principle of proportionality and must neither be an arbitrary discrimination nor a disguised restriction on trade. The latter two terms repeat those provided in Article 36 TFEU (ex 30 EC).

The judgment in *Cassis de Dijon* makes it clear that Article 34 TFEU (ex 28 EC) also covers indirect discrimination by the reference to the words 'disparities between national laws' in the sentence 'obstacles to movement within the Community resulting from disparities between national laws relating to the marketing of the products in question'. In other words, where a national rule, although on the face of it applying equally to both imported and domestic products, acts as a hindrance or obstacle, it may also be caught by Article 34 TFEU (ex 28 EC), for example the rule *Cassis de Dijon* itself.

The case is regarded as a very important tool for the Commission in establishing and maintaining the internal market by the creation of a simple rule that goods lawfully manufactured and sold in one member state should be able to move freely throughout the EC. Indeed, the Commission later issued a Practice Note based on its interpretation of what the *Cassis de Dijon* case meant.

11.4.1.1 Examples of acceptable mandatory measures

Examples of the types of mandatory measure – that is, the national rules that may be raised by the member states – suggested by the Court of Justice in *Cassis de Dijon* were 'the effectiveness of fiscal supervision, the protection of public health, the fairness of consumer transactions and the defence of the consumer'. The measures listed are not exhaustive and have been added to by the Court of Justice in subsequent cases. The following list provides a range of the additional measures and interests worthy of protection approved by the Court of Justice.

- environmental grounds, in Case 302/86 *Commission v Denmark (Disposable Beer Cans)*;
- cultural interests, in Cases 60–61/84 *Cinetheque SA v Federation Nationale des Cinemas Francais* (concerning the sale of video recordings);
- conservation of the resources of the sea, in Cases 3, 4 and 6/76 *Minister of Justice v Kramer*;
- the protection of workers, in Cases C-312/89 *Union Department des Syndicats CGT de l'Aisne v Sidef Conforama* and C-332/89 *Criminal Proceedings against Marchandise*;

293

- recognition of socio-cultural characteristics, in Case 145/88 *Torfaen Borough Council* v *B&Q plc*;
- the financial balance of the social security system, in Case C-120/95 *Decker*;
- maintenance of the diversity of the press, in Case C-368/95 *Vereinigte Familiapress*;
- the protection of fundamental rights of freedom of speech and protest, in Case C-112/00 *Schmidberger*; and
- the protection of young persons, in Case C-244/06 *Dynamic Medien*.

11.4.2 **The application of the rule of reason: the requirements in detail**

Once it has been established that the interest comes within the rule of reason, the criteria of the rule of reason must be satisfied as follows.

11.4.2.1 There must be no EU system covering the interest in question

In other words, EU legislation must not have occupied the field and there must be no harmonizing EU legislation.

> In **Case 16/83 *Criminal Proceedings against Karl Prantl***, a German law provided that only certain quality wines from Franken and Baden could be marketed in the bottle known as *Bocksbeutel*. Anyone marketing any other wine in the *Bocksbeutel* committed an offence. The defendant in the main action was charged with selling quantities of Italian red wine in bottles of this type. The German authorities justified the rule under consumer protection and fair trading, and the Court of Justice expressly acknowledged that such mandatory requirements may be justified provided that there was no applicable Community rule.

In fact, wine produced in the Italian Tyrol had been produced in bottles of this type for at least a century, as have Portuguese wines.

At the time of the *Prantl* case, there was in place only a partial system of EU rules governing the types of wine that might be marketed in specific types of bottle. These rules, however, had not yet been concluded to exclude national competences in respect of the shape of the bottle in question in the case at hand. Thus it was held that, until Community rules were implemented, those adopted by the member states could be maintained so long as they did not contravene Articles 28–30 EC (now 34–36 TFEU). The Court held that the rules in question did in fact contravene Article 28 EC and were not saved by Article 30 EC.

11.4.2.2 The measure must be indistinctly applicable

The measure must apply without difference on the face of it to both imports and domestic products; otherwise it cannot be considered under the rule of reason and must fall to be considered under Article 34 TFEU and the derogations allowed under Article 36 TFEU only.

> **Case 113/80 *Commission* v *Ireland (Metal Objects)*** concerns Irish legislation that required souvenirs of Ireland that were not domestically produced to bear the designation 'Foreign'. The Commission considered that the restrictions contravened Article 28 EC (now

34 TFEU) and Article 2(3)(f) of Directive 70/50 because they were measures that had the effect of lowering the value of an imported product by causing a reduction in its value or an increase in its costs. The Irish government argued that the measures were justified on grounds of consumer protection and therefore fell within the scope of the public policy derogation in Article 30 EC (now 36 TFEU).

The Court of Justice held that since Article 30 EC (now 36 TFEU) constitutes a derogation from the basic rule that all obstacles to the free movement of goods between member states are to be eliminated, Article 30 EC (now 36 TFEU) must be construed narrowly. Since neither the protection of consumers nor the fairness of transactions were included amongst the exceptions set out in Article 30 EC (now 36 TFEU), it was held that they cannot be relied on in connection with that Article.

The Court then considered whether the measures might be justified as necessary to meet mandatory requirements; however, the rules were not measures that applied to domestic and imported products without distinction. They applied only to imported products and were therefore discriminatory in nature. Hence, then, the measures were not covered by the decision in *Cassis de Dijon*, which applies only to provisions that regulate both imported products and domestic products. The rules were therefore in breach of Article 28 EC (now 34 TFEU).

11.4.2.3 The measure must be neither an arbitrary discrimination nor a disguised restriction on trade

cross reference
*See also the
Commission v
Germany (Beer
Purity) case con-
sidered in section
11.4.2.4.*

295

In **Case 124/81 *Commission v UK (UHT Milk)***, the requirement of an import licence requiring a second heat treatment and packaging were held to be disguised restrictions. The argument raised by the UK that there was not a Community system in place was not accepted by the Court of Justice, which had noted the very similar regimes applicable to UHT milk in the different member states.

11.4.2.4 The measure must meet the requirements of proportionality

Apart from the *Cassis de Dijon* case itself, there are a number of other cases that serve as good examples of this point.

In **Case 113/80 *Commission v Ireland (Irish Metal Objects)***, the Court took the view that the interests of consumers and fair trading would have been adequately protected if it were left to domestic manufacturers to take appropriate steps, such as affixing, if they so wished, their mark of origin to their own products or packaging. The requirement to stamp 'Foreign' was not reasonable; it was disproportionate.

In **Case 261/81 *Walter Rau Lebensmittelwerke v De Smedt***, Belgian legislation prohibited the marketing of margarine that did not conform to a particular shape. This rule had a clear protective effect and was an obstacle to marketing to importers. The Belgian government argued that the measure was necessary for consumer protection. The Court of Justice ruled that if a member state has a choice between various measures to attain the same objective, it should choose the measure that least restricts the free movement of goods. In this case, consumers might have been protected and informed that the product was margarine by other measures that would have constituted less of an interference with the free movement of goods, such as labelling. Therefore the rules contravened Article 28 (now 34 TFEU).

cross reference
See section 11.4.2.1 for more on Prantl.

In **Case 16/83 Prantl**, the Court of Justice held that the sale of a product may not be prohibited when a labelling requirement will adequately protect the consumer from confusing the particular wine in the wine bottle sold.

The various food additives and constituents cases considered under the Article 30 EC (now 36 TFEU) derogations are also subject to this line of argument that adequate labelling will protect consumers rather than a ban, which would be disproportionate.

cross reference
Relevant cases are considered in section 11.3.5.

See **Case 174/84 Commission v Germany (Beer Purity Law)**, concerning a German law providing that only malted barley, hops, yeast and water may be used in the manufacture of beer, and further that only drinks complying with those provisions could be marketed under the designation 'beer'. A further law prohibited importation of beers containing additives unless the additives were specifically authorized. The Court of Justice held that whilst it was legitimate to seek to enable consumers who attribute special qualities to beer manufactured from particular raw materials to make their choice in an informed way, that end could be achieved by labelling. The prohibition went beyond what was necessary for the protection of German consumers, since such protection could quite easily be ensured by compulsory affixing of labels informing consumers about the nature of the product sold.

11.4.3 Technical standards and legislative intervention

cross reference
See Chapter 8, section 8.2.3, on incidental horizontal effects.

In order to try to regulate the free movement of goods more effectively and more comprehensively, and to avoid some of the difficulties of relying on piecemeal litigation to challenge measures introduced from time to time by the member states, the Commission introduced Directive 83/189, now updated and consolidated by Directive 98/34. These require member states to notify technical standards of products before being adopted so that the Commission could consider whether they created barriers to the free movement of goods. Whilst it was not intended to create rights for individuals and merely intended to provide a channel of communication between the member states and the Commission, the Directives have nevertheless been instrumental in some cases between individuals. These cases have prompted significant use and notifications under the Directive, and have probably helped in preventing some national measures that would have created barriers.

11.4.4 Summary of *Cassis de Dijon*

The rule of reason in the *Cassis de Dijon* case either classifies measures as falling outside the scope of Article 34 TFEU (ex 28 EC) or justifies measures that would otherwise have breached

Article 34 TFEU because the ability given to the member states to rely on mandatory requirements provides, in effect, further derogations to Article 34 TFEU. The case certainly appeared to allow member states to maintain some rules that protected a particular interest, but it was often unclear as to whether the national mandatory requirement fell outside or would breach Article 34 TFEU. As a consequence, in some cases there has been a blurring of the distinction between distinctly and indistinctly applicable measures. Normally, the route taken would be to decide if the measures are distinctly or indistinctly applicable and then decide if they breach Article 34 TFEU: if distinctly applicable, consider whether any of the derogations of Article 36 TFEU apply; if indistinctly applicable, consider whether any of the mandatory requirements or an Article 36 TFEU derogation applies.

> Occasionally, however, as in **Case C-67/97 _Bluhme_** or **C-2/90 _Commission v Belgium (Walloon Waste)_,** the Court of Justice has entertained arguments based on mandatory requirements although the facts related to a situation concerned essentially with a distinctly applicable rule. In both cases, environmental arguments were raised.
>
> In the latter case, a Belgian region prohibited the transfer of waste from other regions of Belgium to Wallonia for storage or tipping or dumping. That the rule was distinctly applicable was effectively ignored by the Court of Justice in both of the cases in the interests of environmental protection.

However, for the most part, the distinction remains. It is, though, necessary to consider the difference between 'equal burden' and 'dual burden' rules, a distinction that was provoked by the development of case law following _Cassis de Dijon_.

Dual burden rules, which add an additional requirement on imports, can be more easily identified and thus regarded as being in breach of Article 34 TFEU. Equal burden rules, on the other hand, which, as might be expected, impose an equal burden on imports and domestic products, were left to be judged by the national courts to decide whether the rule (the mandatory requirement) was one that was worthy of protection.

11.4.5 Equal burden or dual burden rules

An indistinctly applicable rule is one that applies, at least on the face of it, to imported and domestic products alike. The same rule applies and imposes an equal burden on both products. However, this is not the conclusion that should be reached if one takes into account the fact that the importer may have already satisfied a similar rule in the state of export. Therefore the imported product has to comply with two sets of product requirements in order to be marketed lawfully in the state of import: those operated by the state of origin and those by the state of importation. In this situation, the imported product is placed under an additional burden.

cross reference
Noted in section 11.4.2.4.

> For example, in **Case 261/81 _Walter Rau (Margarine)_**, the Belgian authorities required margarine to be packed in cube-shaped containers only, which would have meant that a separate production line would have to be set up for the Belgian market. If other countries adopted similar packaging requirements, maybe round for Luxembourg and so on, further types of packaging and packaging lines would have to be set up, which would not be economically viable for the manufacturer. Hence the conclusion is that it is unfair that two sets of rules must be complied with; therefore the additional or dual burden rule, although applying on the face of it equally, is caught by Article 34 TFEU unless justified by either Article 36 TFEU or the rule of reason mandatory requirements.

Equal burden rules in contrast should not have been considered as even coming within Article 34 TFEU because, by definition, the burden of the rule in question in the state of import falls equally on home and domestic products. The imported product suffers no discrimination or disadvantage. Unfortunately, the Court of Justice appeared to extend the scope of Article 28 EC (now 34 TFEU) to cover equal burden rules that applied fairly to both imported and domestic products in cases in which national measures were neither directly nor indirectly discriminatory and there was no additional burden on the imports.

> For example, **Cases 60–61/84 *Cinetheque*** concerned the prohibition of the hire or sale of film videos in France within the first year of release in order to protect the film industry from production through to the cinemas. The rule applied equally to domestic and imported videos. The Court of Justice held nevertheless that the rule was a measure having equivalent effect because it did restrict the overall import of videos, although it equally restricted sales and rentals of domestically produced videos. These, however, were fewer in number, but it could be justified for a specific reason in the case, 'the protection of artistic works' which was therefore added to the list of mandatory requirements from *Cassis*. Otherwise, it would have breached Article 28 EC (now 34 TFEU).

However, the extension of the scope of Article 28 EC (now 34 TFEU) prohibition to equal burden rules had taken place. The *Cassis* case is both beneficial to the free movement of goods and, at the same time, supports national diversity by allowing regional variations under the mutual equivalence rule. Further, under the rule of reason and the mandatory requirements rule, additional member states' interests and concerns covered by national rules would be recognized. However, if those equal burden rules were also potentially a breach of Article 28 EC (now 34 TFEU), then, as proved to be the case, all sorts of national rules and virtually any nationally imposed regulation of trade practices or commercial freedom that might have restricted in any way the level of imports would be attacked by traders who had been caught infringing the national rules. Traders claimed that their right to import goods and sell them had been infringed. Many of the national laws challenged were concerned with sales and marketing rules and had no impact on the access of imported goods to the national market. Increasingly, however, national laws were questioned, not on the basis that they hindered imports only, but because they affected the volume of trade regardless of origin: see Case 61/84 *Cinetheque*.

> The Sunday trading case law and in particular **Cases 145/88 *Torfaen Borough Council v B&Q plc*** and ***B&Q Ltd v Shrewsbury Borough Council*** serve as good examples of the confusion that can arise. It was assumed that the national laws did affect Community trade and were in breach of Article 28 EC (now 34 TFEU) unless justified. However, as was demonstrated in these cases, the interest worth protecting could vary. A previous ban used to exist in the UK, which prohibited the trading of very many goods on a Sunday. It was not discriminatory, but applied to imported and domestic goods alike. However, traders claimed that it breached Article 28 EC (now 34 TFEU) because, by reducing the volume of sales, it reduced volume of imports and thus it was a measure having equivalent effect. The grounds stated by the member state to justify the law were not contained in Article 30 EC (now 36 TFEU), but arguably within the mandatory requirements of *Cassis*. The case law from the UK had not been particularly helpful, partly as a result of the Court of Justice deciding that national courts must determine for themselves whether the reason for a rule was justified under the rule of reason. The ban on Sunday trading concerned both the idea of 'keeping Sunday special' and the protection of workers, and as a result led to contradictory decisions depending on whether the UK courts took into account the protection of workers, which would appear to justify a ban on Sunday trading, and the attempt to keep Sunday special, which appeared not to justify a ban.

Before a further UK case reached the Court of Justice, **Cases C-312/89 *Conforama*** and **C-332/89 *Criminal Proceedings against Marchandise*** had reached the Court of Justice, which were more instructive from the Community law point of view. In a request for preliminary rulings from French and Belgian courts, the Court of Justice held that national restrictions on the opening of shops on Sundays (the French *Code de Travail* provides for a mandatory day's rest on Sundays, whilst the Belgian *Loi sur le Travail* prohibits the employing of retail shop workers after noon on a Sunday) were not in breach of Community law. It was considered that this area of law was a matter for the regulation of each individual member state. The measures were held not designed to control patterns of trade between member states, nor were they applied so as to discriminate against goods from other member states.

In **Case C-169/91 *Stoke City Council v B&Q plc***, which was another reference concerning Sunday trading from the UK, the Court of Justice held that the UK's restrictions on Sunday trading do not conflict with Community law. It held that such rules reflected 'choices relating to particular national or regional socio-cultural characteristics'.

This means that the member states have the discretion to make such choices. However, this series of cases did raise the question of whether the Court of Justice had gone too far in upholding the sanctity of free movement over national rules by finding that all obstacles to free movement and not merely those concerned with discrimination and protectionism were in breach of Article 28 EC (now 34 TFEU) unless justified under either Article 30 EC (now 36 TFEU) or *Cassis*. In other words, the assumption would be that anything affecting imports whatsoever would breach Article 28 EC (now 34 TFEU) unless it could be justified. Hence, then, the next development.

299

11.5 ***Keck and Mithouard*: certain selling arrangements**

For more details on this section scan here or visit the Online Resource Centre.

Faced with many similar arguments by traders against national rules, when presented with a suitable occasion the Court of Justice was able to redefine its position.

Cases C-267–268/91 *Keck and Mithouard* concerned the French prohibition of goods at a loss, which was argued to be a restriction of sales contrary to Article 30 EEC (now 34 TFEU). The Court of Justice stated that:

In view of the increasing tendency of traders to invoke Article 30 EEC (now 34 TFEU) of the Treaty as a means of challenging any rules whose effect is to limit their commercial freedom even where such rules are not aimed at products from other member states, the Court considers it necessary to re-examine and clarify its case law on this matter.

The Court considered that traders had previously been using EU law to try to challenge laws that were not aimed at restricting imports, but which restricted the sales of all goods, domestic and imported. The Court then stated that it considered that selling or marketing arrangements did not come within the concept outlined in *Dassonville* or Article 30 EEC (now 34 TFEU). The Court of Justice held that:

contrary to what has previously been decided, the application to products from other member states of national provisions restricting or prohibiting certain selling arrangements is not such as to hinder directly or indirectly, actually or potentially, trade between member states within the meaning of the Dassonville judgment provided that those provisions apply to all affected traders operating within the national territory and provided that they affect in the same manner, in law and in fact, the marketing of domestic products and of those from other member states.

Looked at in another way, an impediment to trade is acceptable where the rule in question is merely a selling arrangement that impedes both the trade in domestic and imported products equally. It was an attempt to permit national rules that were introduced for reasons other than those intended to be a restriction on imports. Therefore, provided that national rules do not impede access to markets, but merely regulate them without any form of discrimination, either in law and in fact, they will be acceptable and will not fall within Article 34 TFEU.

thinking point

Consider the Sunday trading rules in the UK, many of which were enacted in Victorian times. At the time of their enactment, could the authorities have had in mind Article 34 TFEU, the internal market or even the EU itself?

However, there are problems with the *Keck* judgment because it did not provide an instant clarification of the law, most notably the questions of 'what are selling arrangements?' and 'how are they to be distinguished from product characteristics?' The scope of this expression and distinction was explored in subsequent cases.

11.5.1 Post-*Keck* case law

Selling arrangements are broadly defined as rules relating to the market circumstances in which the goods are sold. Selling arrangements are usually equal burden rules that, following the *Keck* case, now fall outside of the scope of application of Article 34 TFEU. Selling arrangements are measures dealing with where, when, how and by whom goods may be sold. In contrast are rules relating to the product itself or its characteristics, such as those concerned with the shape, size, weight, composition, presentation, identification or putting up (preparing for sale).

Examples of selling arrangements include, in **Case C-292/92 *Hunermund***, a rule prohibiting pharmacists from advertising para-pharmaceutical products that they sold, which was held by the Court of Justice not to be caught by Article 28 EC (now 34 TFEU).

Similarly, **Cases C-401 and 402/92 *Tankstation 't Heustke*** involving Dutch laws about the opening times of shops at petrol outlets, **Case C-63/94 *Belgapom*** involving Belgian laws prohibiting offering products for sale at a loss of profit and **Case C-391/92 *Commission* v *Greece*** involving the prohibited sale of any processed milk for babies other than in pharmacies were all found to be acceptable and not to breach Article 28 EC (now 34 TFEU). Neither did a rule that required a licence to open a new shop in **Case C-140/92 *DIP***, in view of the public interest and concern for planned commercial development. The rules involved were not concerned with the origin of goods traded.

Therefore it appeared relatively simple to reach conclusions on particular rules that, provided that a rule was classified as a selling arrangement, it should fall outside Article 34 TFEU. However, rules that at first sight may appear to be a selling arrangement, but which do have an impact on the characteristic of the product, would breach Article 34 TFEU if the rule were nevertheless shown to create a requirement physically to alter the product, unless it could be otherwise justified.

For example, in **Case C-470/93 *Mars***, a national law was challenged that prohibited the selling of Mars bars, which had been labelled as providing an extra 10 per cent free of charge. The Court of Justice held that the law actually concerned the product presentation, labelling and packaging, and was thus a physical requirement, which, if upheld, meant that it imposed a dual burden. It was therefore held to be a breach of Article 28 EC (now 34 TFEU).

See also **Case C-368/95 *Vereinigte Familiapress Zeitungsverlags* v *Bauer Verlag***, which considered the difference between a selling arrangement and a physical requirement. An Austrian law prohibiting the offering of free gifts linked to the sale of goods was the basis for an Austrian publisher's action against a German magazine containing a prize crossword puzzle. The Court of Justice repeated its position established since *Keck* that certain national rules would not breach Article 28 EC (now 34 TFEU) unless imposing additional requirements. It held that the Austrian rules would constitute a hindrance to free movement if the content of the magazine had to be altered for the Austrian market. However, maintaining the diversity of the press was the legitimate public interest objective given by the authorities and accepted by the Court of Justice.

Unfortunately, the next twist in the case law was the recognition that some selling arrangements, although equal burden and not relating to physical characteristics, nevertheless had an effect that disadvantaged imports by hindering market access or which seemed to favour domestic products, in particular those in respect of advertising and sales promotion rules – that is, those that had a differential impact on the imported goods. This is then compounded by a few cases that, on the face of it, concern rules relating to the product, such as packaging, but which, on closer examination by the Court, are really selling arrangements and thus to be considered as falling outside of Article 34 TFEU; hence the search for a new test to be able to classify these developments and to provide some form of predictability for the future, which is the subject of the next section.

11.5.2 **Market access or discrimination or both?**

In the post-*Keck* case law, cases have considered in which it is argued that Article 28 EC (now 34 TFEU) has been breached because market access has been hindered in some way or that a selling arrangement, which although equal burden, is nevertheless discriminatory in some way or has a differential impact, and cases in which a product requirement is nevertheless held to be a selling arrangement.

Case C-412/93 *Leclerc Siplec* concerned certain goods that could not be advertised on television, but only in the press – and in particular the local press – in order to maintain a certain level of advertising revenue for local papers and thus ensure the survival of local and independent press. Advocate General (AG) Jacobs argued that the test should be to consider if there was an impediment to market access and that Article 28 EC (now 34 TFEU) should catch measures that directly and substantially impede access to the market.

This was seen previously in relation to the free movement of persons in **Case C-415/93 *Union Royale Belge des Sociétés de Football Association* v *Bosman***, in which it was held that non-discriminatory rules that prevented football player transfers and which prevented market access should be outlawed.

cross reference
The case is considered in Chapter 12, section 12.1.2.2.

This was taken up by the Court of Justice in **Cases C-34–36/95 *Konsumenten-ombudsmannen* v *De Agostini*** in which television advertising directed at children under the age of 12 was prohibited. The measure was considered to be a selling arrangement, which applied without discrimination, thus was equal burden. However, it was held that this would seem to have a greater impact on products from other member states because of the difficulties faced in trying to get access to the market, advertising being the only effective form of promotion. If the national court were to find that the impact of the prohibition was different, it would therefore breach Article 28 EC (now 34 TFEU) unless justified by Article 30 EC (now 36 TFEU) or the mandatory requirements under *Cassis*.

In a subsequent case, **Case C-405/98 *Gourmet International***, a ban on alcohol advertising was challenged under the same argument that it had a greater impact on imported products trying to gain access to the Swedish market. Without advertising, consumers would be familiar only with domestic products. Thus it was held that the measure would be caught by Article 28 EC (now 34 TFEU) if it were to prevent access to the market by products from another state, or to imped access more than domestic products.

Case C-416/00 *Morellato* involved packaging and the requirement that partly baked bread (known as 'bake-off bread') be packaged by the retailer completing the baking. Thus it appeared to be the same as the *Mars* case and thus concerned with product alteration, but it was held to be a selling arrangement because the rule applied only at the final stage of marketing, not physically altering the product prior to distribution.

In **Case C-254/98 *Heimdienst***, a non-discriminatory Austrian law that applied to all operators trading in the national territory (Austrian and other EU operators) required goods sold on the doorstep to come from a locally established premises. It was held to be a selling arrangement, but one that impeded access to the market of the member state of importation for products from other member states more than it impeded access for domestic products. The judgment fits in with the proviso at [16] of the *Keck* judgment because, although non-discriminatory and a selling arrangement, it is the differential manner in which it affects domestic and other member state products that matters; hence the treatment of goods is not equal in fact.

Thus selling arrangements that either in law or in fact discriminate against non-national providers and impede or hinder market access will not escape Article 434 TFEU, but still might be justified.

A further 'bake-off' bread case, **Cases C-158–159/04 *Alfa Vita Vassilopoulos***, concerned the planning requirements to have a full baker's licence and all of the practical needs of a full bakery in order to sell bake-off bread, which is merely thawed and reheated at the sales outlet after otherwise full preparation elsewhere, including transportation whilst frozen from other member states. The requirement, which resembled a selling arrangement in terms of who is permitted to sell a product, according to the Court of Justice affected part of the production of a product and was therefore, on the face of it, in breach of Article 28 EC (now 34 TFEU). It made marketing more difficult and costly, thus was a barrier to imports.

Thus cases involving situations that, although classified as certain selling arrangements, have a different burden on imported goods, albeit that some domestic goods might also be affected, breach Article 34 TFEU and, to be saved, must be justified. The differential treatment in the *Alfa Vita* case was not justified under public health grounds.

The test, as so far developed, looks at the differential manner in which a national rule affects domestic and other member state's products. Selling arrangements that either in law or in fact discriminate against non-national providers and thus impede or hinder market access will not escape Article 34 TFEU. They might, however, still be justified under either Article 36 TFEU or the rule in *Cassis de Dijon*. This test of differential impact – that is, affecting imports more than domestic products – focuses both on market access and the fact that the effective result is discriminatory. This area of law is still in need of clarification.

Summary

Non-tariff barriers have proved to be more difficult to eradicate than the tariff barriers considered in Chapter 10 because of the huge variety of national rules that can apply and the fact that not all national rules regulating trade law should be considered as coming within Article 34 TFEU. Hence the difficulty has been determining where to draw the line and deciding which rules offend Article 34 TFEU and which do not. We start with a perfectly sound rule (Article 34 TFEU), which seeks to ensure that there are no restrictions on the free movement of goods (see Diagram 11.1). To this, we add a further statutory rule (Article 36 TFEU), which provides exceptions to the first rule because it is recognized that there are genuine circumstances in which restrictions and different treatment are justified. So far, so good…

Then there are statutory guidelines (Directive 70/50) and case law, which help to determine how the rule applies and the circumstances that breach the rule or come within the exceptions. Additionally, there is a focus on the concepts of distinctly applicable measures, which can only be justified by Article 36 TFEU, which is easy to see, and indistinctly applicable measures. The indistinctly applicable measures may also come within and thus breach Article 34 TFEU unless justified by Article 36 TFEU or a further set of justifications introduced by *Cassis* and subsequent cases (the mandatory requirements). Thus certain national rules or laws could escape the prohibition of Article 34 TFEU, but strict criteria were laid down so that member states would not be able to exploit this new possibility (the second sentence requirement of Article 36 TFEU and proportionality), which apply to both the Article 36 TFEU derogations and any national rule claimed to come with the *Cassis de Dijon* rules of reason.

It is worth noting that Article 36 TFEU applies to both direct and indirect discrimination, but has an exhaustive list of exceptions, whereas *Cassis de Dijon* applies to indirect discrimination only, but has potentially a much wider range of exceptions.

Diagram 11.1

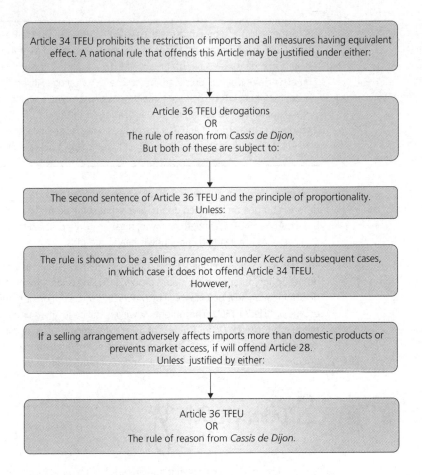

Article 34 TFEU prohibits the restriction of imports and all measures having equivalent effect. A national rule that offends this Article may be justified under either:

Article 36 TFEU derogations
OR
The rule of reason from *Cassis de Dijon*,
But both of these are subject to:

The second sentence of Article 36 TFEU and the principle of proportionality.
Unless:

The rule is shown to be a selling arrangement under *Keck* and subsequent cases, in which case it does not offend Article 34 TFEU.
However,

If a selling arrangement adversely affects imports more than domestic products or prevents market access, if will offend Article 28.
Unless justified by either:

Article 36 TFEU
OR
The rule of reason from *Cassis de Dijon*.

Then, because it started to happen that every single national rule that applied to goods might be considered to come within the ambit of the *Cassis de Dijon* case, there is another important case (*Keck*). This seeks to lay down another rule or gloss on the original rules to say that certain types of law applicable to the marketing of goods (selling arrangements) should not even be considered as coming within the original rule (that is, if you can remember it… Article 34 TFEU!) and there is further case law now to provide further clarifications of what was meant in *Keck*. Indistinctly applicable selling arrangements are thus presumed outside of Article 28 unless they introduce discrimination or prevent market access by adversely affecting imports more than domestic products (see *Heimdienst* or *Alfa Vita*), but these can be justified by Article 36 TFEU or *Cassis* (*Familiapress*).

The 2007 Lisbon Treaty made no significant changes to this area of law.

Questions

1   What is a measure having equivalent effect (MHEE)? (If stuck, see Article 34 TFEU.)

2   What was the very wide definition of an MHEE in the *Dassonville* case?

For suggested approaches to answering these questions scan here or visit the Online Resource Centre.

3 What are distinctly applicable and indistinctly applicable measures?

4 In what circumstances can a member state lawfully restrict or prohibit the free movement of goods from another member state?

5 What are selling or marketing arrangements?

6 Distinguish between equal burden and dual burden measures.

Further reading

BOOKS

Barnard, C. *The Substantive Law of the EU: The Four Freedoms*, 3rd edn, Oxford University Press, Oxford, 2010 (chapters 5–8).

Davies, G. *European Union Internal Market Law*, 2nd edn, Cavendish Publishing, London, 2003 (chapter 3).

ARTICLES

Connor, T. 'Accentuating the positive: the "selling arrangement", the first decade, and beyond' (2005) 54 ICLQ 127.

Davies, G. 'Can selling arrangements be harmonised?' (2005) 30 EL Rev 371.

Greaves, R. 'Advertising restrictions and the free movement of goods and services' (1998) 23 EL Rev 305.

Kaczorowska, A. 'Gourmet can have his *Keck* and eat it!' (2004) 10(4) ELJ 479.

Möstl, M. 'Preconditions and limits of mutual recognition' (2010) 47 CML Rev 405.

Oliver, P. 'Some further reflections on the scope of Articles 28–30 (ex 30–36) EC' (1999) 36 CML Rev 783.

Oliver, P. and Enchelmaier, S. 'Free movement of goods: recent developments in the case law' (2007) 44 CMLR 649.

Reich, N. 'Europe's economic constitution, or a new look at *Keck*' (1999) 19 OJLS 337.

Shuibhne, N. 'The free movement of goods and Article 28: an evolving framework' (2002) 27 EL Rev 408.

Snell, J. 'The notion of market access: a concept or slogan?' (2010) 47 CML Rev 437.

Weatherill, S. 'After *Keck*, some thoughts on how to clarify the clarification' (1996) 33 CML Rev 885.

Weatherill, S. 'Recent developments in the law governing the free movement of goods in the EC's internal market' (2006) 2 ECRL 90.

Wenneras, P. and Boe Moen, K. 'Selling arrangements, keeping *Keck*' (2010) 35 EL Rev 387.

Wilsher, D. 'Does *Keck* discrimination make any sense? An assessment of the non-discrimination principle within the European Single Market' (2008) 33 EL Rev 3.

Free movement of persons I

Learning objectives

In this chapter, you will:

- learn about the history and development of the free movement rights of workers and the self-employed;

- explore the concept of who may be considered an EU worker;

- consider the basic rights that economically active EU nationals enjoy;

- learn how the rights were extensively developed for both workers and members of the family;

- consider the rights of free movement of the self-employed;

- be made aware of the derogations allowed the member states; and

- consider the exception for employment in the public service.

Introduction

Before European citizenship was introduced as a European Union (EU) law concept and became an important source of rights itself, EU law was concerned originally with the free movement of economically active persons only, providing the direct freedom of movement for workers and self-employed persons – the latter establishing themselves or providing services in a host member state. Free movement of persons is now a much wider concept and includes the rights provided by European citizenship (which is the subject of Chapter 13). The Court of Justice has, however, expanded the range of persons who could take advantage of the Treaty provisions and additionally secondary EU legislation has been enacted that has provided rights for non-economically active members of a worker's family.

In this chapter, the free movement of workers, establishment and services will be dealt with together. The reasons for this are that, increasingly, case law – and in particular the new case law – applies without distinction across all of these categories and new secondary legislation, the Services Directive (2006/123), as far as services and establishment are concerned, has brought much of the secondary legislation in line for all three. It therefore seems of less merit to try to maintain an increasingly irrelevant distinction.

cross reference
*Directive 2006/123
is considered at sec-
tion 12.4.2.1.*

As ever, in considering a legal regime, the basics for each of these categories must be considered. These are now the Treaty on European Union (TEU) and Treaty on the Functioning of the European Union (TFEU) provisions, followed by any pertinent secondary legislation and the extensive case law of the Court of Justice. A particular feature of this area of law is the extensive rights that apply to the family members of EU citizens. Integrated into these aspects are the provisions of Directive 2004/38, which has both consolidated the previous secondary legislation and case law and has introduced amended and new rules relating to those taking advantage of free movement rights.

The original Treaty Articles on free movement of persons have altered little since 1957, but their scope and our understanding of them have developed considerably since then. It is not only the original personal scope of the legislation that has been expanded by both additional statutory law and judicial interpretation, but also the consequences for the Union and national legal regimes, which are much greater than those that may have been anticipated by the member states. Free movement of persons is now a much wider concept, and has become inextricably linked with the concept of European citizenship and other wider issues of free movement, including third-country nationals (TCNs). Therefore, in view of this substantial expansion of the law of the free movement of persons, Chapter 13 of the book will consider those persons who are able to move and reside in other member states under the general rights of movement provided by the Treaty and secondary legislation – notably now through the citizen provisions Articles 20 and 21 TFEU.

However, before looking at any of these particular provisions, it is useful to try to discover the original reasons and intentions behind the Treaty provision for the free movement of persons. Was the right of free movement, as originally conceived, provided in order to complete the freedom of the factors of production, along with the goods and capital for economic or capitalist development? In other words, without providing for the free movement of persons, the development of economic activities, the balanced expansion and accelerated raising of the standard of living referred to originally in the Preamble to the EC Treaty would not be possible. Capital (that is, employers operating productive facilities) needed to take advantage of freely movable labour without border restrictions. Hence the argument that the rights were provided merely or deliberately to help to create the Common Market in the same way as for the free movement of goods. By ensuring the free movement of workers across the member countries of the Common Market, capital can easily import labour when required, which in turn ensures that economic conditions in all member states of the market are broadly similar and thus that competition is not distorted by labour shortages and higher labour costs in some parts of the market. The free movement of persons was originally contained in the economic part of the EC Treaty concerned with free movement. This provided a basic definition of the internal market, which is now outlined in Article 26 TFEU (ex 14 EC), and it was not originally located as a part of the social policy section of the Treaty. Whilst the rights were originally restricted to those engaged in an economic activity in another member state and as a form of support for the Common Market and economic progress in the Community, as developed they have undoubtedly become a clear part of the social policy of the EU. In support of the view that social concerns now dominate, the Court of Justice has adopted a very liberal approach to the interpretation of the free movement of workers provisions, both the Treaty principles and the further extensions of these principles in the secondary legislation, such as the widely construed concept of 'worker'. In contrast, the exceptions to the rights granted to the member states are interpreted strictly: see, for example, the case law on Article 45(4) TFEU (ex 39(4) EC), the public service proviso.

cross reference
The definition of 'worker' is considered in section 12.2.2.

cross reference
The public service proviso is considered at section 12.5.2.

(12.1) The legal framework: primary and secondary legislation

12.1.1 Treaty provisions

Article 3(2) TEU provides as follows.

Article 3(2) TEU

. . . .

The Union shall offer its citizens an area of freedom, security and justice without internal frontiers in which the free movement of persons is ensured . . .

Article 20(2) TFEU, which is concerned with citizenship and will be considered further in Chapter 13, further provides as follows.

Article 20(2) TFEU

. . . .

Citizens of the Union . . . shall have, inter alia:

(a) the right to move and reside freely within the territory of the Member States,

. . .

Article 26 TFEU provides, in paragraph 2, as follows.

Article 26 TFEU, paragraph 2

. . . .

The internal market shall comprise an area without internal frontiers in which the free movement of goods, persons, services and capital is ensured in accordance with the provisions of the Treaties.

The following Treaty Articles outline the basic requirements to facilitate the free movement of the economically active: Articles 45–48 TFEU (ex 39–42 EC) for workers; Articles 49–55 TFEU (ex 43–48 EC) for those wishing to establish; and Articles 56–62 TFEU (ex 49–55 EC) for those wishing to provide services.

For workers, Article 45(1) and (2) TFEU provides as follows.

Article 45 TFEU

. . . .

1. Freedom of movement for workers shall be secured within the Union.

2. Such freedom of movement shall entail the abolition of any discrimination based on nationality between workers of the Member States as regards employment, remuneration and other conditions of work and employment.

. . .

Article 39 EC (now 45 TFEU) was held to be vertically directly effective in **Case 167/73 Commission v France (French Merchant Seamen)** and later horizontal direct effects were implied in **Case 36/74 Walrave and Koch**, which was concerned with a private body, but one established under public law. They were definitively established in **Case C-281/98 Angonese v Cassa di Risparmio di Bolzano SpA**, which involved an action by an individual against a bank.

cross reference
Directive 2004/38 is considered in section 12.3 and throughout the chapter.

Article 45(3) TFEU provides the basic rights for workers, but subjects those rights to the limitations on grounds of public policy, public security or public health, amplified in Directive 2004/38. The rights as listed are as follows.

> **Article 45(3) TFEU**
>
> . . .
>
> (a) to accept offers of employment actually made;
> (b) to move freely within the territory of member states for this purpose;
> (c) to stay in the member state for the purpose of employment in accordance with the provisions governing the employment of nationals of that state laid down by law, regulation of administrative action; and
> (d) to remain in the territory of a member state after having been employed in that state.

Article 45(4) TFEU provides as follows.

> **Article 45(4) TFEU**
>
> The provisions of this Article shall not apply to employment in the public service.

For establishment, Article 49 TFEU provides as follows.

cross reference
Article 49 TFEU is considered in section 12.6.2.

> **Article 49 TFEU**
>
> Freedom of establishment shall include the right to take up and pursue activities as self-employed persons and to set up and manage undertakings, in particular companies or firms.

Finally, for the provision of services, Article 56 TFEU provides as follows.

> **Article 56 TFEU**
>
> Restrictions on freedom to provide services within the Union shall be prohibited in respect of nationals of Member States who are established in a Member State other than that of the person for whom the services are intended.

For more details on section 12.1.2 scan here or visit the Online Resource Centre.

With regard to secondary legislation, Directive 2004/38 and the new consolidating Regulation 492/2011, which has repealed and replaced Regulation 1612/68, comprehensively cater for the rights of workers and their families in the EU.

12.1.2 **The basic right of non-discrimination**

The most basic or fundamental right in free movement is that there shall be no discrimination on the grounds of nationality. Article 18 TFEU (ex 12 EC), which prohibits discrimination on the grounds of nationality, has been highly influential in the development of this area. It has been employed by the Court of Justice to outlaw various discriminatory rules and practices by member states and organizations that were not a clear and direct breach of the provisions on workers, establishment or services, but which nevertheless discriminated against non-nationals. It has been applied, inter alia, for workers in Case 59/85 *Netherlands* v *Reed*, for services in Case 2/74 *Reyners* v *Belgium* and for establishment in Case 246/89 *Commission* v *UK (Nationality of Fishermen)*.

cross reference

All of these cases are considered in this chapter.

12.1.2.1 Indirect discrimination

The Court of Justice has often stressed that the concept of discrimination not only covers direct discrimination in which different rules apply to nationals and non-nationals, but also covers covert or indirect discrimination that leads to the prejudicial treatment of non-nationals – rules that seem to apply fairly to both, but which have an indirect discriminatory effect on non-nationals. The measure may, however, be objectively justified on other grounds. Furthermore, the prohibition of national rules has also been expanded to catch rules that hinder market access.

> Indirect discrimination was demonstrated in **Case 33/88 *Alluè and Coonan* v *University of Venice***. The applicants, after five years of employment as foreign language lecturers, were informed that they could not be retained under a 1980 Italian decree that limited the duration of employment of foreign language lecturers. Not all of the foreign language lecturers were non-national: some 25 per cent were nationals; therefore there was no dissimilar treatment – that is, no overt discrimination. Although the rule applied regardless of the nationality, it nevertheless mainly affected the nationals of other member states who made up 75 per cent of such language teachers. It was held by the Court of Justice to be discriminatory where such limitations did not exist in respect of other workers.

cross reference

For a more detailed discussion of objective justification, see Chapter 11, section 11.4.1, on the free movement of goods.

311

The rules may also be objectively justified if there is a legitimate aim compatible with the Treaty, if the measure is justified by pressing reasons of public interest and if the measure is proportionate.

There are now statutory definitions of **indirect discrimination** in EU secondary legislation dealing with other forms of discrimination. See Directive 2000/43, 2000/78 or 2006/54, all Article 2, for similar definitions to the following.

. . . .

indirect discrimination
Arises if an apparently neutral provision, criterion or practice would put persons of one (sex or age or nationality, etc.) at a particular disadvantage compared with persons of the other sex etc., unless that provision, criterion or practice is objectively justified by a legitimate aim, and the means of achieving that aim are appropriate and necessary.

. . . .

cross reference

Services and establishment are considered in sections 12.2.3 and 12.4.1, respectively.

12.1.2.2 Hindering market access

In the same way as will be seen for services and establishment, there has been an attack on national rules that, although applying without discrimination to both home professionals and those establishing in the host country, are regarded as inappropriate because they are seen to hinder access in taking up opportunities, thus restricting movement.

> **Case 415/93 *Bosman*** concerns football transfer fee rules that certainly restricted transfers, but which applied to both national and cross-border transfers; hence there was no discrimination and nationality was not a factor. The Court of Justice held that they were nevertheless an obstacle to movement.

> The *Bosman* ruling was applied in **Case C-438/00 *Kolpak* v *Deutscher Handballbund*** to a similarly restrictive German handball rule that limited the number of foreign players to two in each squad. The rule was held to be contrary to free movement by the Court of Justice and not justified on sporting grounds. It clearly limited the chances of non-Germans to enter the market.

Thus, for persons, the prohibition of harmful rules goes beyond discrimination to cover rules that impede market access.

12.2 Who may claim the rights of free movement

For more details on this section scan here or visit the Online Resource Centre.

cross reference
The material scope is considered in section 12.3.

This section determines who may benefit from the rules provided. The personal scope and the material scope of the rights have to be determined. In terms of the personal scope, two basic definitions have to be established: first, nationality; and secondly, whether the person concerned is a worker or self-employed by establishing or providing services, or is otherwise entitled to enter and remain in the member state. The material scope of the rights has been determined largely by secondary legislation and concerns the actual rights provided.

12.2.1 Nationality

For workers and the self-employed, the right to move freely and obtain other benefits, especially those rights that can be taken up by members of the worker's family, is initially dependent on being defined a national of one of the member states. Article 45 TFEU secures freedom for workers of the member states. 'Establishment' under Article 49 TFEU and 'services' under Article 56 TFEU refer to the right of nationals of the member states either to establish or provide services in the host member states. Because establishment also includes legal persons predominantly in the form of companies, companies that are registered in one of the member states are also included within the personal scope of the rights.

The actual determination of member state nationality is a matter for each of the member states, as expressly stated in Declaration No. 2 on nationality, which was attached to the original TEU before its removal by the Lisbon Treaty. It provided that nationality of a member state shall be settled solely by reference to the national law of the member state concerned.

> This position was upheld in **Case C-192/99 *Manjit Kaur*** involving the attempt by a Kenyan national to obtain British residence rather than only the limited British overseas citizen status. The Court of Justice confirmed that it is for each member state to lay down the conditions for the acquisition and loss of nationality.

cross reference
See section
12.3.2.2.

It is not, however, necessary for the members of a worker's family to be member state nationals to obtain benefits, as will be seen in the secondary legislation and case law considered later in the chapter.

12.2.2 **Union status as a worker or self-employed**

thinking point
Who do you think
is a worker for the
purposes of EU free
movement of work-
ers law?

The second part of the personal scope of the law is that in order for a person to benefit person-ally or for his or her family to benefit from rights arising under Articles 45–62 TFEU and laws made hereunder, the person needs to be classified as a worker or self-employed person. The definition of these concepts, as indicated in the heading, is a matter for EU law and not for each of the national legal systems to determine. Turning first to the term 'worker', there is no definition of the term in the Treaties, but the Court of Justice has held from its early days that the term must have an EU meaning and cannot be the subject of differing interpretations by the courts of the member states.

In **Case 75/63 _Hoekstra_ v _BBDA_**, the Court of Justice declared the reason for this view:

> If the definition of this term were a matter for the competence of the national courts, it would be possible for every member state to modify the term worker and so to eliminate at will the protection afforded by the EEC Treaty to certain categories of person.

> In the case itself, the Court of Justice gave this limited definition: 'A worker is any employed person, irrespective of whether he is wage-earning or salaried, blue collar or white collar, an executive or unskilled labourer.'

The Court of Justice has, in subsequent cases, gone on to develop the definition to include part-time workers, those seeking work under certain circumstances, those undertaking a period or course of study and those who were effectively self-employed, but nevertheless included by the European Court of Justice (ECJ).

12.2.2.1 Part-time work

Case 53/81 **_Levin_ v _Minister of Justice_** concerned the value of work that a person needs to do before he or she can be classed as a worker. The woman plaintiff was a British citizen working in the Netherlands as a chambermaid for twenty hours a week and whose earnings were below the subsistence level in the Netherlands. The Dutch government argued that because she was a part-time worker earning below the government-set subsistence level, she was not a 'favoured EEC citizen' and could not benefit from the provisions of EEC law guaran-teeing freedom of movement of workers. The Court of Justice held that these considerations were irrelevant to her status as a worker, and declared that, whether she was a full-time or part-time worker, she was entitled to the status of worker provided that the work was genuine and effective, and not so infinitesimal as to be disregarded. The Court of Justice ruled that work will only be disregarded if it is so minimal that it does not constitute economic activity at all. The essential defining characteristic of work is that it is activity of an economic nature.

In **Case 139/85 _Kempf_ v _Minister of Justice_**, a German national worked as a part-time flute teacher for only twelve lessons a week. His limited income was topped up to the Dutch minimum income level with supplementary benefit under the Unemployment Benefit Act.

He too was refused a residence permit on the grounds that he was not a 'favoured EEC citizen'. The Court of Justice ruled that if a person is in effective and genuine part-time employment, then he (or she) may not be excluded from the sphere of application of the rules on freedom of movement of workers merely because the remuneration he derives from it is below the minimum level of subsistence set by national law. The Dutch court had found that the work was genuine and effective.

In this regard, it is irrelevant whether the supplementary means of subsistence are derived from property, from the income of another member of the family (as in *Levin*) or from public funds of the member state of residence (as in *Kempf*).

The Court of Justice has held, in **Case C-357/89 *Raulin* v *Netherlands Ministry of Education and Science***, that, in considering whether work is genuine and effective, the national court should take account of all of the occupational activities of the person only in the host state and the duration of those activities. The case concerned a French national who worked for sixty hours in total as a waitress in the Netherlands, but who, whilst doing so, was granted the status of worker.

In deciding that the national courts make the final decision on the status of the person concerned according to the facts, this appears to present the member states with the discretion to define who is a worker, although the national courts are obliged to follow EU law in this respect and in particular the criteria as developed by the ECJ in its case law.

See the similar case of **Case C-413/01 *Ninni-Orasche***, which involved a person who was engaged in only two-and-a-half months' work in three years, but who would nevertheless qualify according to the ECJ to be classified as a worker, but who would not necessarily to be able to take advantages of long-term rights as an EU worker. Again, however, it was up to the national authorities ultimately to decide.

In **Case 66/85 *Lawrie-Blum* v *Land Baden-Württemburg***, the Court of Justice considered the compatibility of German rules restricting access to a preparatory service stage that was necessary to become a teacher. It laid down three essential characteristics to establish an employment relationship: the provision of some sort of service, for and under the direction of another person (that is, not self-employed) and in return for remuneration.

The above ruling was applied in **Case 196/87 *Steymann* v *Staatssecretaris van Justitie***, whereby work in Bagwhan religious community's commercial activities, for which remuneration was paid in the form of pocket money and the meeting of material needs, was considered sufficient to be classified as a Community worker.

Some limits to the definition appear to have been found in **Case 344/87 *Bettray* v *Staatssecretaris van Justitie***. The Court of Justice held that a national of a member state employed in another member state under a social employment scheme involving therapeutic work as part of drug rehabilitation merely as a means of retraining or reintegration cannot be regarded as a worker for the purposes of Community law. The activities could not be carried out as real and genuine economic activities.

Here, the position was artificially created with government money and not therefore genuine. Although carried out under supervision and remunerated, the Court of Justice (in contrast to its position in *Levin*) looked at the purpose of the scheme and found that Bettray was not a worker.

However, this decision might not hold good any longer in view of a subsequent decision.

In **Case C-456/02 *Trojani***, Trojani had secured accommodation in a Salvation Army hostel, where, in return for board and lodging and some pocket money, he undertook various jobs for about thirty hours a week as part of a personal socio-occupational reintegration programme. He applied for social assistance, which was refused. The Court of Justice held that he had a direct right of residence under Article 18 EC, and where such EU citizens are in possession of a residence permit, they are thus entitled, according to Article 12 EC, to social assistance on the same basis as nationals. Whilst no real decision was taken on his actual status, which was left to the national court to decide, the ECJ advised that the national court should have regard to factors such as whether the services performed could be regarded as a part of the normal labour market.

This case straddles both the previous *Steymann* and *Bettray* cases in terms of fact, but is one of those cases that has been caught up by the developments in European citizenship. As a result, it can be argued that the definition of worker is of lesser importance now in that if the person involved is nevertheless entitled to receive the rights or benefits claimed, his or her status becomes irrelevant.

The term 'worker' is, however, wider than only referring to those in employment and, in certain circumstances, also applies to those who are seeking work and to those who, having lost one job involuntarily, are capable of taking another.

12.2.2.2 Those seeking work

cross reference
The Leclere *case is considered in section 12.3.2.1.*

In **Case 75/63 *Hoekstra* v *BBDA***, it was established, and confirmed in the later **Case C-43/99 *Leclere and Deaconescu***, that certain rights were retained by a former worker who was in employment in the host state, but who lost his or her job, notably the right to retain the status of worker for a certain period of time and benefits derived therefrom.

Two cases follow that have considered these matters.

In **Case 316/85 *Marie-Christine Lebon***, the Court of Justice held that those in search of work are not entitled to receive workers' benefits (in this case, a social security support payment). Miss Lebon no longer lived with her parents, who were ex-workers; therefore she did not qualify for benefits as a dependant of a worker. She then asked if she qualified for workers' benefits if she was looking or intended to look for work. The Court of Justice held that the benefits provided by legislation on free movement were only for those in actual employment and not for those who migrate in search or work and not find it. She could temporarily be classified as a worker, but not for the purposes of benefits.

Case **C-292/89** *Antonissen* clarifies how long the temporary status entitles a person to remain to look for work. The UK wished to deport Antonissen, who had been convicted of possession and intent to supply cocaine, and asked the Court of Justice whether it could do so. UK legislation gave EC citizens six months in which to find employment. Antonissen was in the country for over three years without work before his imprisonment. The Court of Justice held that statements recorded in minutes regarding the acceptable time for the pursuit of work before deportation would not be allowable, have no legal significance and cannot be used to interpret the relevant legislative provisions. A member state may deport an EC migrant worker subject to an appeal if he or she has not found employment after a period of six months. However, the six months' time period is to be taken as a guideline only. Where there is evidence that indicates that he or she is continuing to seek employment and that there are genuine chances of being engaged, the Court of Justice suggested that it would probably not be appropriate to deport. It would, however, be up to the national court to decide on the facts.

Therefore after the expiry of a reasonable period, depending on the circumstances, persons may no longer be afforded the status and benefits of worker under Community law and may lawfully be deported by the member state.

Case **C-138/02** *Collins* has subsequently confirmed that those seeking work who do not have a sufficiently close connection to the host state may not claim benefits.

cross reference
Collins is noted briefly in section 12.2.2.3 and in Chapter 13, section 13.3.4.2, on citizenship.

Article 7(3) of Directive 2004/38 makes it clear that workers and also the self-employed may retain their status and right to remain in the following circumstances:

(a) he or she is temporarily unable to work as the result of an illness or accident;

(b) he or she is in duly recorded involuntary unemployment after having been employed for more than one year and has registered as a jobseeker with the relevant employment office;

thinking point
When does a person cease to be a worker for the purposes of EU free movement of persons law?

(c) he or she is in duly recorded involuntary unemployment after completing a fixed-term employment contract of less than a year or after having become involuntarily unemployed during the first twelve months and has registered as a jobseeker with the relevant employment office (in which case, the status of worker shall be retained for no less than six months); or

(d) he or she embarks on vocational training (but unless he or she is involuntarily unemployed, the retention of the status of worker shall require the training to be related to the previous employment).

cross reference
These issues will be taken up in Chapter 13, section 13.3.4.2.

Directive 2004/38, Article 14, further provides that residence may be retained provided that the persons concerned do not become an unreasonable burden on the social assistance of the host state. EU citizens not possessing a sufficiently close link to the host state will be ineligible for benefits according to the Court in Case C-138/02 *Collins*.

12.2.2.3 Worker training, education and benefits

A further extension to the scope of the concept of worker took place in favour of those no longer in employment who were employed previously, but who subsequently became engaged in some form of study. This category was rather limited, but its boundaries may now have been considerably extended by the respect now shown by the Court of Justice to the concept of citizenship. The new cases are very often crossover cases in that they deal with both a consideration of a specific aspect such as whether the person is a worker, or work seeker or entitled student, but now wrapped in the context of citizenship.

cross reference

Citizenship is considered in Chapter 13, section 13.3.4.

> The leading original case is **Case 39/86 *Lair* v *Universität Hannover***, in which a French national employed in West Germany was refused a grant by the university for a maintenance award and training fees because she had not worked in the country continuously for at least five years. Therefore, whilst at university, she was not a worker and did not retain the status of worker. It was stated in the case that the period at university would lead to a vocational qualification and that the time at university represented a break in employment only. The Court of Justice held that since there was no fixed legislative definition of worker, there was nothing to say that the definition must always depend on a continuing employment relationship. Certain rights have been guaranteed to workers after employment has finished, for example the right to stay and social security rights. This could also apply to university training provided that there was a link or continuity between the previous work and university, in which case the university support could be considered one of the social rights coming within Regulation 1612/68 (now Regulation 492/2011). The status of worker was therefore retained if a link existed between the previous occupation and the studies in question.

> In contrast, in **Case 197/86 *Brown* v *Secretary of State for Scotland***, the Scottish education department refused Brown a grant for university. He had worked for eight months in the UK prior to and as a precursor to university and gained the status of worker. The Court of Justice held that, whilst university training is to be regarded as mainly vocational, it was only covered by Article 12 EC (now 18 TFEU) generally outlawing discrimination. This covers tuition fees, but not the maintenance grant; therefore a person who entered employment for eight months and who did so as a precursor or prerequisite to attend university did not retain the status of worker for the purposes of claiming a grant.

> In the light of the citizenship cases considered in Chapter 13, section 13.3.4, the *Brown* case may not be decided in the same way today or at best be subject to the integration requirements considered in this section.

> Returning to **Case C-357/89 *Raulin***, the Court of Justice held that the sixty hours' work had enabled Raulin to claim the protection of Article 39 EC (now 45 TFEU), despite its very temporary nature. However, a migrant worker who then left that employment to begin a course of full-time study unconnected with the previous occupational activities did not retain the status as a worker, a finding upheld by the Dutch court. Raulin, however, did have a right of residence in the host state for the duration of the course of study, regardless of whether or not the host state had issued a residence permit.

Thus definitions of what constitutes vocational training and the link to work are crucial for the determination of the status of a worker and the consequent benefits and rights, as is the number of weeks or hours worked. This case law is now essentially confirmed by Directive 2004, Article 7(3)(d), which provides that the status of worker is retained if the EU citizen embarks on vocational training that is related to the previous employment.

However, in **Case C-184/99 _Grzelczyk_**, a French national who studied and worked on a part-time basis to help to support himself for three years in Belgium applied at the beginning of his fourth and final year of study to the Centre Public d'Aide Sociale [Public Social Welfare Centre] (CPAS) for payment of the minimex, a non-contributory minimum subsistence allowance. The CPAS granted Mr Grzelczyk the minimex, but then later denied this on the basis that he was not Belgian; hence clear discrimination on the grounds of nationality. This case did not consider whether he enjoyed the status as a worker. The Court of Justice emphasized that the new citizenship provisions and new competences in education, albeit limited, allowed it to hold that Articles 12 and 17 EC (now 18 and 20 TFEU) preclude discrimination as regards the grant of a non-contributory social benefit to Union citizens where they are lawfully resident.

Note, however, that no status of worker was attributed in this case, nor indeed even a link to previous employment; however, even if a person is confirmed as a jobseeker, social assistance may be denied.

In **Case C-138/02 _Collins_**, the Court of Justice held that, once citizenship had been established, then even work seekers could claim certain benefits, in contrast to _Lebon_, but that some benefits could be restricted on objective grounds, such as the habitual residence requirement for a jobseeker's allowance, which depended on the existence of a genuine pre-existing link between the work seeker and the state.

In other words, a person such as Collins, who nevertheless enjoyed EU citizenship, could not just arrive in the UK and demand a jobseeker's allowance alongside nationals. A residence qualification period can be demanded.

A further case now appears not only to confirm Collins, but also to roll back slightly the previous generous interpretation of individuals' rights.

cross reference
See also the discussion in Chapter 13, section 13.3.4.2.

Case C-158/07 _Förster_ v _IB-Groep_ concerns Ms Förster, a German national in the Netherlands who, from 2000, worked from time to time there and qualified for a study maintenance grant, but which was withdrawn when the responsible authority (IB-Groep) discovered in 2003 that she was no longer working. Her challenge to the decision failed because she was not sufficiently integrated in the Netherlands and because she had not satisfied the requirement of five years' residence in the Netherlands. On reference to the Court of Justice, the Court it upheld its previous decision in Case C-209/03 _Bidar_ that member states were entitled to require a certain degree of integration and, in this case, a five-year period was justified and proportionate. The work–study relationship did not play a role in the Court's decision.

12.2.2.4 Self-employed

In **Case C-256/01 _Allonby_**, the definition of the term 'worker' was effectively extended to cover self-employed persons. The case concerned the re-employment of former college lecturers in the same establishment, but under a self-employed scheme paid by a private independent company. In considering the new relationship, the Court of Justice held that:

> The formal classification of a self-employed person under national law does not change the fact that a person must be classified as a worker within the meaning of that article if his independence is merely notional.

This case is thus very important for the rights of the person concerned.

12.2.3 The scope of establishment and the provision of services

The self-employed are granted rights under the Treaty to move to another member state to establish either permanently or on a long-term basis (Articles 49–55 TFEU, ex 43–48 EC) or to provide services temporarily (Articles 56–62 TFEU, ex 49–55 EC). The definitions for the personal scope of establishment and for the provision of services are much more straightforward than for workers. The primary Treaty Articles have laid down the basic concepts.

Article 49 TFEU deals with rights of freedom of establishment as the right to enter another member state and stay on a long-term or permanent basis, to take up and pursue activities as a self-employed person, and to set up and manage undertakings. This includes legal, as well as natural, persons.

> A basic definition was given in **Case C-221/89 *Factortame*** as 'the actual pursuit of an economic activity through a fixed establishment in another member state for an indefinite period'.

> In **Case C-268/99 *Jany***, the Court of Justice characterized self-employment as a relationship outside a relationship of subordination as would be the case with workers, and in which the remuneration earned was paid directly and in full to the self-employed person.

'Services' under Article 56 TFEU envisages a temporary state of affairs, and appearance, if at all, in the host state would only be for a limited period to provide specific services. There would be no permanent personal or professional presence in the host state or a necessity to reside. The concept of services is defined by Article 57(1) TFEU as those 'provided for remuneration, in so far as they are not governed by provisions relating to freedom of movement of goods, capital and persons'. In particular, Article 57 TFEU specifically includes activities of industrial and commercial characters, and those of craftsmen and the professions. The provision of services is potentially a much wider category and can be associated with the areas of banking, finance, insurance and legal services, and now, with modern technology, telephone, broadcasting and Internet services will become big services areas, notably without the need to move from the host state to provide services in other member states.

> See, for example, **Case C-384/93 *Alpine Investments*** concerned with cross-frontier telephone sales calling or, in **Case C-17/00 *de Coster***, the satellite transmission of television services.

The scope of the term 'services' has been held by the Court of Justice to include the recipients of services.

Case 186/87 *Cowan*, for example, involved a claim for criminal injury compensation by an EU citizen in France, **Case C-45/93 *Commission v Spain*,** the right of EU nationals to visit museums without charge on the same basis as nationals, and **Case C-268/99 *Jany et al.*** found that receipt of services includes prostitution.

Originally, establishment and the provision of services were regarded as if not absolutely distinguishable, certainly clearly distinct concepts with no overlap. At times, the distinction between services and establishment can be difficult to ascertain.

In **Case 205/84 *Commission v Germany (Insurance Services)*,** the provision of insurance included the setting up of offices on a long-term basis and staffing those offices with nationals of the host state. This was considered by the Court of Justice as establishment even though the legal entity (owner/principal) remained in the home state.

This ruling is very important as the application of home rules may be stricter for establishment because the Treaty provision appears to be based on achieving complete equality of treatment.

Article 57 TFEU

. . . the person providing a service may, in order to do so, temporarily pursue his activity in the State where the service is provided, under the same conditions as are imposed by that State on its own nationals.

The provision of services under Article 57 TFEU (ex 50 EC), on the other hand, whilst allowing for the same conditions to be imposed by the host state, has developed on the basis that not all home rules have been found by the Court of Justice to be suitable or acceptable to those providing services. The distinction therefore between 'establishment' and 'services' is important. The Court of Justice has now advised that the provision of services may even justify the setting up of an infrastructure in the host state.

In **Case C-55/94 *Gebhard v Milan Bar Council*,** the Court of Justice characterized 'establishment' as the right of a community national to participate on a stable and continuous basis in the economic life of a member state other than his or her own, and 'services' by the temporary, precarious and discontinuous nature of the services. The Court held:

The temporary nature of the activities in question has to be determined in the light, not only of the duration of the provision of the service, but also of its regularity, periodicity or continuity. The fact that the provision of services is temporary does not mean that the provider of services within the meaning of the Treaty may not equip himself with some form of infrastructure in the host member state (including an office, chambers or consulting rooms) in so far as such infrastructure is necessary for the purposes of performing the services in question.

In this case, the setting up of chambers in Italy by a German lawyer on a long-term basis, although still practising in Stuttgart, Germany was nevertheless held to be establishment.

cross reference
See section 12.2.2.2.

The case was then in line with Case 205/84 *Commission v Germany*.

As with workers, the status of self-employed is retained even if the activity ceases: see Article 7(3) of Directive 2004/38.

12.3 The material rights of free movement

For more details on this section scan here or visit the Online Resource Centre.

Apart from the basic rights being provided by the main Treaty Articles 45, 49 and 56 TFEU, the material rights of free movement have largely been provided in secondary law. Each of the free movement sections has its own Treaty base to empower the enactment of secondary legislation in pursuit of the Treaty objectives. Consequently, for workers under Article 40 EC (now 46 TFEU) and the self-employed under Articles 53 (now repealed), 47 and 52 EC (now 53 and 59 TFEU), the Commission was empowered to propose Directives to obtain the general objectives set out in the Treaty. The legislative function is now carried out by the European Parliament and Council on Commission proposals. To a large extent, the rights provided deal with relatively mundane things, such as paperwork in support of exit and entry rights, and only infrequently result in important new case law. Furthermore, the Court of Justice has been able to derive very extensive rights from the EU primary legislation, and in particular Article 12 EC (now 18 TFEU). In 2004, the secondary law underwent radical transformation and therefore the focus of attention will turn to the new provisions. The rights for workers, outlined in Article 39 EC (now 45 TFEU) of the Treaty were amplified and supplemented most importantly by three measures. Directive 64/221, Regulation 1612/68 and Directive 68/360 (now replaced or amended by Directive 2004/38 and Regulation 492/2011) were enacted, first, to facilitate the original rights provided and, secondly, to provide genuinely new rights, particularly when it came to members of the member state national's family.

Regulation 1612/68, as repealed and replaced by Regulation 492/2011, provides for equality of access to employment for all community nationals, equality of treatment in employment rights and housing rights, and the right for his or her children to be educated on the same terms as the children of nationals of the member state concerned.

Articles 10 and 11 of Regulation 1612/68 had already been repealed and replaced by Directive 2004/38, which provided rights for a worker to be joined by his or her family. The rest of the Regulation remains in force.

For the self-employed, legislative intervention was employed to facilitate entry and procedural rights in a similar manner to workers and also to initiate a programme of harmonization of the various professions on a one-by-one basis by means of one or more Directives for each profession. These are too numerous for a book of this nature; thus only the general Directives will be considered.

For the self-employed, Directives 73/148 and 75/34 are the equivalents of Directives 68/360 and 1251/70, and they too have been repealed and replaced by Directive 2004/38.

Directive 2004/38 is now the main and most important provision of secondary legislation for the free movement of Union citizens. It has replaced most of the previous secondary legislation and covers both workers and the self-employed. It generally revises the law and has incorporated much of the previous case law of the Court of Justice. The Directive clarifies who should be regarded as a member of the family or person otherwise provided with rights derived from an economically active EU citizen. It also establishes permanent rights of residence for citizens after a certain period and restricts the member states' right to refuse entry on the grounds of public policy. Whilst the right of permanent residence appears new, in reality it merely reflects the previously established right to remain for many union citizens and families who have chosen to live in another member state.

12.3.1 Rights of entry, residence and exit

The rights to enter, move freely and to seek and take up employment are governed by a combination of Article 45(3) TFEU, Articles 1–5 of Regulation 492/2011 (ex Articles 1–5 of Regulation 1612/68) and Articles 4–14 of Directive 2004/38.

Note that much of the case law is based on the repealed Directive 68/360, Articles 1–6 and 8, but it is helpful to be aware of this because you will come across references to the old Directives in the cases and literature.

Articles 1 and 2 of Regulation 492/2011 (ex Articles 1 and 2 of Regulation 1612/68) provide the right to take up employment in the host state under the same conditions as nationals without discrimination.

Article 3(1) of Regulation 492/2011 (ex Article 3(1) of Regulation 1612/68) permits member states to impose a requirement of linguistic ability on non-nationals according to the nature of the post to be filled.

This is illustrated and interpreted by **Case 379/87 *Groener v Minister for Education***, in which the Court of Justice upheld an Irish requirement that teachers in Ireland should be proficient in the Irish language as part of a public policy to maintain and promote the Irish language and culture. Any requirement, however, must be proportionate.

Directive 2004/38 provides the rules to regulate the conditions by which workers can leave one member state and enter the territory of another. It prescribes the entry formalities that it is permissible for member states to impose, in particular the rules regarding the issue and withdrawal of residence permits. Cases arising under the previous Directive sought to remove the unnecessary restrictions on free movement.

Article 4 provides that exit states are obliged to allow nationals and their families with valid passports to leave with an exit visa or other formality. The exit state is obliged to issue a passport or identity (ID) card.

Article 5 provides that entrance states cannot demand an entry visa or equivalent documents from EC nationals. They can, however, require a passport or valid ID card and visas from non-Union members of the family.

In **Case C-68/89 *Commission v Netherlands (Entry Requirements)***, the Court of Justice held generally in respect of Directive 68/360 that the requirements under the Directive for documentation do not give the member state the right to further questioning regarding the purpose and duration of stay, once the correct papers have been shown.

Whilst this is reasonable in theory, in practice it is not so likely in today's more security conscious climate.

In **Case C-344/95 *Commission* v *Belgium***, a delay in issuing documents, the limited duration of residence permits and payments demanded in excess of that comparable for national ID cards were all measures held by the Court of Justice to breach former Directive 68/360.

Article 6 of Directive 2004/38 permits the right to enter, travel and reside in a host member state for a period of up to three months by an EU citizen and his or her family. It is not restricted to the economically active, but extends to any EU citizen without any conditions other than the requirement to hold valid ID and/or visa documentation, the latter covered by Articles 5 and 6. The financial self-sufficiency requirements that were contained in the previous general free movement Directives are not repeated for the initial period of residence of up to three months. However, the right to reside for a period of more than three months under Article 7 is made conditional on being engaged in a gainful activity, being self-employed, or a recipient of education or being self-sufficient with comprehensive sickness insurance cover. As well as residence permits for family members, a registration certificate can be demanded, which must be granted to any worker who produces a passport and certificate of proof of employment. Members of the worker's family must also be afforded a registration certificate on production of a passport and relationship or proof of dependence.

In **Case C-459/99 *MRAX***, the Court of Justice considered that it was disproportionate and therefore prohibitive to send back a TCN married to a national of a member state who was not in possession of a valid visa where he or she was able to prove his or her identity and conjugal ties. In particular, if there was no evidence to establish that he or she represented a risk to the requirements of public policy, public security or public health, then expulsion would be excessive.

Article 8 of Directive 2004/38 reflects previous case law by providing that the failure to comply with the registration requirement may render the person concerned liable to proportionate and non-discriminatory administrative sanctions only.

For example, in **Case 159/79 *R* v *Pieck***, Mr Pieck, a Dutch national, re-entered the UK after his original six-month entry permit had expired and he had failed to renew it. The authorities sought to deport him. The Court of Justice held that a failure to obtain a permit could result only in penalties for minor offences.

In **Case 118/75 *Watson* v *Belman***, Miss Watson, a UK national, was acting as an au pair whilst staying in Italy with Mr Belman. Both had failed to report this to the national authorities as required, and faced imprisonment and fines under national law. In addition, Miss Watson was to be deported. The Italian magistrate asked the Court of Justice if the punishments were compatible with EC law. The Court of Justice held that the use of internal rules – that is, the requirement to report – was acceptable, but that the penalty must be in proportion to the offence/damage caused – that is, it should be only a small fine; therefore, any decision to deport would be contrary to the Treaty.

In line with previous case law, Article 25 of the Directive provides that the registration certificate and residence permit are not preconditions for residence, but merely evidence of the entitlement to enter and reside – that is, not the right itself, but merely the proof of it. Administrative rules requiring registration are acceptable, as is an appropriate sanction for their breach, but not deportation, which would be regarded as disproportionate.

Articles 22 and 11 of Directive 2004/38 provide normally that the right to residence and permits must be valid for the whole territory of the member state and valid for at least five years with automatic renewal. Article 22 states, however, that 'Member States may impose territorial restrictions on the right of residence and the right of permanent residence only where the same restrictions apply to their own nationals'.

It was confirmed in **Case 36/75 *Rutili* v *Minister of Interior*** that an administrative prohibition restricting movement to parts of France could only be for the entire territory of the member state and must be justified.

As held in **Case C-100/01 *Olazbal***, however, when it comes to criminal measures being taken to restrict movement, a partial restriction of movement would be acceptable. However, the action would have to be justified and the seriousness of the crime would otherwise have led to a complete banishment and nationals too would have to be subject to similar punitive measures.

Article 15 of Directive 2004/38 states that the expiry of the documentation does not constitute grounds for expulsion.

cross reference
The case law on citizenship is considered in Chapter 13, section 13.4.4.

Temporary involuntary unemployment does not remove the employed or self-employed status (Directive 2004/38, Article 14). Whilst the period is not specified, previous case law (Case C-292/89 *Antonissen*) suggests that six months would be the limit, after which the favoured status would then be lost. Whether the host member state would then be entitled to deport the citizen concerned is doubtful in view of the case law on citizenship, unless there were serious grounds for deportation other than involuntary unemployment.

12.3.2 The rights provided by Regulation 492/2011 (ex Regulation 1612/68) and Directive 2004/38

Of all of the earlier legislation, Regulation 1612/68, now repealed and replaced by Regulation 492/2011, has certainly proved to be the most supportive of free movement, in particular in the way in which Article 7 of the Regulation has been interpreted by the Court of Justice. The Regulation details access to employment and rights for workers, and more importantly, as far as an extension of the rights is concerned, introduces the rights of free movement for members of the workers' family. Whilst economically active persons received confirmation that their rights extended to matters such as tax and social advantages, vocational training, trade union membership and housing rights and benefits under Articles 7–9 of Regulation 402/2011, the most significant provisions introduced by the first expansion of the rights related to the members of the family of the EU worker or self-employed person moving. This was made even more significant by the fact that these additional rights of free movement and to take up employment or to take up education or vocational training applied also to non-EU member state family members, termed TCNs. In respect of the extension of the rights to family members, Articles 10 and 11 of Regulation 1612/68 have been repealed, replaced and extended by Articles 2 and 3 of Directive 2004/38.

Article 7(1) of Regulation 492/2011 (ex Article 7(1) of Regulation 1612/68), reflecting Article 18 TFEU (ex 12 EC), prohibits discrimination against workers on grounds of nationality and specifically mentions terms and conditions of employment, dismissal and, where relevant, reinstatement.

It has been decided that, when a worker commences a job in another country the same as that previously undertaken in the home state, this previous service may count for advantages in the host state. The Court of Justice held that to ignore this is to discriminate contrary to Article 7(1).

In **Case C-187/96 *Commission* v *Greece***, the Court of Justice held that a Greek administrative regulation and practice that did not take into account periods of employment in the public service of other member states when determining seniority increments and salary grading breached Article 39 EC (now 45 TFEU) and Article 7(1) of Regulation 1612/68 (now Article 7(1) of Regulation 492/2011) – that is, that service elsewhere counts.

12.3.2.1 Social and tax advantages under Article 7(2)

Article 7(2) has proved to be a provision with extremely wide scope. It refers specifically to equality in social and tax advantages, which also apply to the family of the worker.

Regulation 492/2011, Article 7(2)

He shall enjoy the same social and tax advantages as national workers.

Family is open to wide interpretation, as are the benefits under Article 7(2).

In **Case 32/75 *Fiorini aka Christini* v *SNCF***, a reduced fare entitlement was claimed by the widow of an Italian SNCF worker. Widows of French workers were allowed such a family entitlement, but it was denied to the Italian. The SNCF claimed that since it was not express in the contract of employment, it was not available to foreign workers. The Court of Justice was asked if this was the kind of social advantage envisaged by Article 7 and it held that Article 7 applies to all advantages, not only those limited to a contract of employment. It therefore applies to the family of an EC worker in the same way as for nationals.

In **Case 94/84 *ONE* v *Deak***, an unemployed Hungarian national living with his mother, an Italian national working in Belgium, was refused special unemployment benefits for non-nationals on the basis that no agreement for such benefits existed between Belgium and Hungary. The Court of Justice held that special unemployment benefits were a social advantage within the meaning of Article 7 and that Deak, regardless of nationality, could derive rights as the descendant of a worker; otherwise a worker might be hindered from moving if the descendants were discriminated against, thus causing financial difficulty.

In **Case 137/84 *Mutsch***, a Luxembourg national living in a German-speaking commune in Belgium was denied the use of German before a court, a right granted to the Belgian German minority. The Court of Justice held that right to be a social advantage under Article 7(2) despite there being no link to a contract of employment.

Article 7(2) has even been interpreted to include a grant to cover funeral expenses in **Case C-237/94 *O'Flynn***, in which nationals were provided with the same assistance.

Some limit to Article 7(2) seems, however, to have been found.

Case C-43/99 *Leclere* involved a Belgian national who was working in Luxembourg, but who was injured in an accident. He was granted an invalidity allowance by the Luxembourg authorities, but was later refused child benefit because he was no longer a worker. Whilst the invalidity benefit was regarded as linked to his former work, the child allowance was not held to be connected, therefore could lawfully be refused.

In **Case C-385/00 *De Groot***, Article 7(2) applied to provide that there should be no discrimination in tax matters, and that any discrimination in the way in which personal and family circumstances are taken into account that results in less favourable treatment of the frontier worker amounts to an obstacle to the free movement guaranteed by Article 39 EC (now 45 TFEU). This judgment is despite – but in full recognition of – the fact that member states are ostensibly still in full competence of deciding their own tax regimes.

It is, of course, debatable whether the presence of this provision and the social advantages do in fact figure highly in a worker's original decision to move to another member state to take up or find work, bearing in mind the facts of these cases – that is, that the dependants have mostly followed on afterwards. The Court of Justice, however, has not considered the relevance of this and has upheld that very wide benefit regardless. As noted already, the ECJ held in Case 316/85 *Lebon* that equal treatment with regard to social and tax advantages laid down by Article 7(2) of Regulation 1612/68 operates only for the benefit of workers and does not apply to nationals of member states who move in search of employment.

12.3.2.2 Family members

Article 10 of Regulation 1612/68 (now repealed), which features in the older case law and needs thus to be noted, has been replaced and extended by Directive 2004/38, which provides that the rights enjoyed by the Union national under the Directive also apply to family members, which are defined generously in Article 2 as spouses, registered partners, descendants and ascendants. Article 2 has provided that the partners will also be considered to be family members provided that the partners have contracted a registered partnership in the home states and if the host state treats registered partnerships as equivalent to marriage. This brings the secondary EU law in line with the case law of the Court of Justice in the *Reed* and *Diatta* cases considered in this section. Article 2(c) considerably widens the definition of 'the family' in providing that members of the family include the direct descendants and ascendants of the spouse and partner also. Article 3 further provides rights of entry and residence for any other family members not within the definitions in Article 2 who, in the country from which they have come, are dependants or members of the household of the Union citizen having the primary right of residence, or where there are serious health or humanitarian grounds for doing so.

Members of the family can be any nationality and include those under the age of 21 and adult children over 21 who are dependent on the worker. 'Dependency' was defined in Case 316/85 *Lebon* as a factual situation of support provided by the worker.

> By way of example, in **Case 261/83 *Castelli* v *ONPTS*,** the Italian mother of a retired Italian worker in Belgium claimed an old-age pension. Mrs Castelli had never worked herself in Belgium, therefore her claim was based on her status as a member of her son's family. The Belgian authorities refused to pay on the grounds that she was not Belgian and they did not have a reciprocal agreement with Italy. The Court of Justice held that Mrs Castelli was entitled to install herself with her son under Article 10 of Regulation 1612/68. She was also entitled to remain after her son's retirement and had a right to the pension under Article 7.

In a judgment concerned with both Articles 7 and 10 of the Regulation, but which has now been partly overtaken by the new Directive 2004/38, the Court of Justice was required to consider whether the term 'spouse' included cohabitees.

> In **Case 59/85 *Netherlands* v *Reed*,** Miss Reed applied for a residence permit in the Netherlands, claiming that her right to remain was based on her cohabitation with a UK national working in the Netherlands. The Dutch government refused to recognize this. The Court of Justice was aware that provisions of national laws regarding cohabitees' legal rights could be quite varied. It was unable to overcome the clear intention of Article 10, which referred to a relationship based on marriage. The Court referred instead to the social advantages guaranteed under Article 7 of the Regulation as being capable of including the companionship of a cohabitee, which could contribute to integration in the host country. The Court of Justice held that where such relationships amongst nationals are accorded legal advantages under national law, these could not be denied to nationals of other member states without being discriminatory and thus breaching Articles 7 and 48 EEC (now 18 and 45 TFEU).

This is a somewhat convoluted decision, but it does provide justice to free movement in the case. The cohabitee does not have rights in his or her own right, but the companionship of a cohabitee is merely regarded as one of the advantages to which workers are entitled. Hence, then, the case merely supports the well-established right in EU law not to be discriminated against on the grounds of nationality. Of course, in some countries, cohabitees are not afforded the same rights as married couples. The reasoning of the Court has been carried over into Article 2 of the Directive 2004/38 in respect of same-sex partner rights. Where national law supports this, EU law will demand that other Union nationals are equally treated; where national law does not support such rights, EU law cannot impose them on member states. The UK does, of course, now formally recognize same-sex partnerships. The *Reed* case remains important for its wide interpretation of Article 7(2).

The rights of a spouse have been held not to be dependent on residence with the entitled worker.

> In **Case 267/83 *Diatta* v *Land Berlin*,** Mrs Diatta, a Senegalese citizen, was married to a Frenchman living and working in Berlin. She obtained work in Berlin, shortly after which the couple separated to live apart. Upon application to extend her residence permit, the German authorities refused on the ground that she was no longer a member of the family

for the purposes of Regulation 1612/68. The Court of Justice ruled that the rights under Regulation 1612/68 were not dependent on the requirements as to how or where members of the family lived. Therefore a permanent common family dwelling cannot be implied as a condition of the rights granted under Regulation 1612/68.

cross reference
The case will be outlined more fully in section 12.3.3.

In **Case C-413/99 Baumbast**, the Court of Justice confirmed that divorce will bring to an end the spousal relationship for the purposes of free movement rights. This means that the right to remain in the host state would also be brought to an end unless saved by any other reason, which was the circumstance in the case.

cross reference
Article 13 of Directive 2004/38 is also considered in section 12.3.4.

However, under Article 13 of Directive 2004/38, in certain circumstances divorce will not affect the right to remain in the host state. These include where the spouse is a national of another member state or, if not, where the marriage or relationship has lasted at least three years including one year in the host state, or, reflecting the *Baumbast* case, where the person is a carer of the Union citizen's children.

cross reference
See also a consideration of this case in Chapter 13, section 13.3.4.1.

In reviewing a case that had the appearance of a marriage of convenience, the Court of Justice has held in **Case C-109/01 Akrich** that Article 10 of the Regulation, and now by analogy the new Directive, applies to TCNs only if they are lawfully resident in one member state before they can move to another one. It is also not applicable where a marriage of convenience has been arranged to circumvent a member state's immigration laws.

There have been cases subsequent to the *Akrich* case on related family issues.

The first of these, **Case C-01/05 Jia**, held that Community law does not require member states to make the grant of a residence permit to TCNs who are members of the family of a Community national subject to the condition that those family members have previously been residing lawfully in another member state.

cross reference
The case will be considered further in Chapter 13, section 13.3.4.3.

The second case, **Case C-127/08 Metock et al.**, confirms *Jia*, but this time was based on Directive 2004/38 and expressly reverses part of the judgment in *Akrich* by making clear that the Directive is not conditional on a requirement that a TCN must have been lawfully resident in another member state to stay in a member state as a spouse or member of the family of an EU citizen. The case considered numerous Articles of Directive 2004/38 and related to four TCNs who had been refused asylum in Ireland, then married EU citizens lawfully resident in Ireland. The facts of the case stated that there were not marriages of convenience.

Article 23 of Directive 2004/38 entitles the family members of an entitled Union citizen to take up any activity as an employed person to include any activity or profession, provided that the appropriate qualifications and formalities are observed.

This was previously encapsulated in Article 11 of Regulation 1612/68.

For example, in **Case 131/85** *Emir Gül* v *Regierungspräsident Düsseldorf*, the Court of Justice held that this right includes the right of such concerned persons to access to employment also under the same conditions as nationals of the host state.

This was also affirmed in the case of *Diatta* v *Land Berlin* in favour of Mrs Diatta.

12.3.3 **Worker's family education and carer rights**

Article 10 of Regulation 492/2011 (ex Article 12 of Regulation 1612/68) provides that the children of a member state host worker shall be admitted to general educational, apprenticeship and vocational training courses under the same conditions as nationals.

Case 9/74 *Casagrande* had already extended the right under Article 12 of Regulation 1612/68 to include not only access to educational facilities, but also equality of measures intended to facilitate educational attendance.

In **Case C-7/94** *Gaal*, the Court of Justice extended the right under Article 12 of Regulation 1612/68 to an independent and over-21-year-old child of a migrant worker who had been employed in another member state. Gaal was the Belgian son of an EC worker in Germany who had since died. Gaal was attending university and applied for a grant to undertake an eight-month period of study in the UK. This was refused on grounds that he was over the age of 21 and was not dependent. He was therefore denied, as no longer being applicable, his rights as a descendant of an EC worker. The Court of Justice held that he still fell within the personal scope of Article 12 of the Regulation as the definition of a 'child' was not subject to the same definition as in Articles 10 and 11. Article 12 extends to all forms of education including university education and must include older children no longer dependent on their parents. The case was, however, decided on the basis that the child must have lived at some time with a parent who was an EC worker and thus derived his rights in this manner.

Two cases heard together have extended the Court's view of the effect of Articles 12 of Regulation 1612/68 (now Article 10 of Regulation 492/2011) to provide rights for carers of Union citizen children who are receiving education.

In **Case C-413/99** *Baumbast*; *R v Home Secretary*, the non-EU national mothers would otherwise have been deported if the Court had not held that the children had the right to be cared for even where the original basis of their right to stay in the UK had disappeared. In the cases, the original rights disappeared: one through divorce and the other because there was no longer a Community national working in the UK or indeed any member state.

It is probable that such a convoluted decision is no longer necessary under rights provided by the Directive 2004/38, considered in the next section.

The protection of carers was taken even further in **Case C-200/02** *Chen*. This involved a child born in Northern Ireland to two Chinese nationals. The baby daughter became a

cross reference

This case will also be considered in further detail in Chapter 13, section 13.3.4.3.

Community national as a result of Irish law conferring Irish nationality on anyone born on the island of Ireland. The family had not even moved from one member state to another; however, in view of the fact that the baby was an EU national with a right to remain, but was below school age and thus unable to care for herself, the Chinese nationals gained a right to remain in the UK to care for her.

12.3.4 **Right to remain**

Article 45(3)(d) TFEU provides the right to remain after retirement or incapacity and applies also to members of the family even if a worker dies, and to whom Article 7(2) of Regulation 492/2011 (ex Article 7(2) of Regulation 1612/68) continues to apply. In support of this, Article 12 of Directive 2004/38 provides that the Union citizen's death or departure from the host member state shall not affect the right of residence of his or her family members who are nationals of a member state and also to non-member state family members who were living with the Union citizen for at least one year before his or her death. In line with previous case law, any children retain the right to attend educational establishments also. Article 13 of Directive 2004/38 provides that divorce, annulment of marriage or termination of the partnership or relationship shall not affect the right of residence of a Union citizen's family members who are nationals of a member state and also those who are not nationals of a member state. The latter category is subject to the requirement that the marriage or partnership has lasted at least three years, one being in the host state or where the spouse or partner has custody of family children or is warranted by particularly difficult circumstances. The rights to remain under Articles 12 and 13 are further dependent on the persons considered not being a burden on the host state (Article 14 of Directive 2004/38).

Article 16 of Directive 2004/38 provides that Union citizens who have resided legally for a continuous period of five years in the host member state shall have the right of permanent residence there and that continuity of residence shall not be affected by temporary absences not exceeding a total of six months a year or by longer absences not exceeding twelve months at a time for important reasons such as compulsory military service, serious illness, pregnancy and childbirth, study or vocational training or a work assignment in another member state or a third country. Paragraph 1 shall apply also to family members who are not nationals of a member state and have resided with the Union citizen in the host member state for five years. Furthermore, Article 17 provides that this period may be reduced in cases of the death or injury of the union national. In respect of family members who are not nationals of a member state, Article 18 provides that they shall acquire the right of permanent residence after residing legally for a continuous period of five years in the host member state.

12.4 **Free movement of the self-employed**

Putting into effect the basic Treaty rights providing for free movement of the self-employed proved to be slower and much more difficult than the simple Treaty expression of the rights

For more details on this section scan here or visit the Online Resource Centre.

would suggest. The national rules, including rules, regulations and conditions of the various professional organizations and bodies, were very often the biggest impediments to the free movements and it was first considered by the Commission that these could be removed only by harmonization. Both main Treaty Articles (Articles 52 and 59 EEC, now 49 and 56 TFEU) envisaged that the basic freedoms provided would be fleshed out by the enactment of secondary legislation issued under Articles 54 and 63 EEC (now 50, 53 and 59 TFEU). The attempts by the Commission to harmonize the various professions proved to be very arduous and time-consuming, and it was not until the intervention of the Court of Justice in leading cases that much more rapid and expansive progress took place.

The initial approach of the Commission therefore was the harmonization of rules by the adoption of a programme of Directives to abolish the restrictions on free movement, and the mutual recognition of qualifications in all sorts of trades and professions on an occupation-by-occupation basis. This, however, was achieved only painfully slowly by the enactment of some forty sectoral Directives, for example it took eighteen years for the Architects' Directive 85/384 to be agreed upon and finally enacted. This approach also encouraged the view throughout the EU that the only way in which these rights could be promoted and relied on was if Directives were enacted to establish them and not directly from the Treaty. Thus little progress was made and even prior to the issue of some Directives considered essential in the process case law had developed the law considerably.

12.4.1 **The intervention of the Court of Justice**

Whilst the Commission was attempting to realize the free movement of establishment and services and the harmonization of the various nationals' rules governing the professions by negotiation with all of the interested national bodies, cases were starting to reach the Court of Justice concerned with self-employed persons who were facing severe restrictions in trying to practise their professions in another country. Two leading cases in particular had a considerable impact on the thinking and approach of the Commission in trying to achieve free movement in these areas. They had highlighted the slow progress and denial of the most basic rights of free movement. The cases, in which Articles 52 and 59 EEC (now 49 and 56 TFEU) were held to create direct effects by the Court of Justice, were decided in favour of the applicants. It was previously assumed that completing secondary legislation was necessary before the rights of free movement could be fully realized; however, the Court of Justice decided the cases on the basis of the Treaty Articles themselves and on the basis of the general prohibition of discrimination, Article 12 EC (now 18 TFEU).

Concerned with establishment, **Case 2/74 Reyners v Belgian State** involved the attempt by a suitably qualified Dutchman to gain an access to the Belgian Bar, but who was refused on the grounds of nationality. The Dutch government argued that Article 52 EEC (then) was not directly effective because it was incomplete without the issue of Directives required by Article 52 EEC. The Court of Justice held that the prohibition of discrimination under Article 52 EEC (now 49 TFEU) was directly effective and declared that nationality could be no barrier to appropriately qualified lawyers entering a country to practise. The Directives were simply to facilitate free movement and not to establish it, which had already been done by the Treaty by the end of the initial transition period of the Communities (1969).

In **Case 33/74 Van Binsbergen**, it was not nationality that was the problem, but a residence requirement. The case concerned a professionally qualified Dutchman, resident in

Belgium, who was refused audience rights before the Dutch courts. The Court of Justice held that Article 59 EEC (now 56 TFEU) was directly effective and was not conditional on the issue of a subsequent Directive in respect of the specific professions, nor on a residence requirement in the Netherlands.

These decisions meant that the Court of Justice had opened the way for the basic Treaty rights to establish and provide services in a host state to be enjoyed without discrimination or the imposition of unnecessary requirements and on the basis of the direct effects of the Treaty Articles themselves. It was not necessary to wait for the enactment of Directives for each and every profession. Other cases soon followed that fleshed out even further the rights available under the Treaty. As with workers, free movement cases tackled the various ways in which national or professionals' rules restricted free movement either by direct or indirect discrimination and rules that were non-discriminatory, but which nevertheless prevented access.

The next case backs up the *Reyners* and *Van Binsbergen* cases.

In **Case 71/76 *Thieffry* v *Paris Bar Council***, the applicant was refused access to the Paris Bar despite having obtained a Belgian diploma in law, recognized by the University of Paris as the equivalent of a French diploma, and having sat and passed the French Certificate for the Profession of Advocate. The Court of Justice held that the relevant national authorities should apply any laws or practices that allow for the securing of freedom of establishment in accordance with the EEC policy, although no Directives may have been enacted in that particular area. Therefore, where the competent authorities have recognized a foreign diploma as equivalent to a domestic qualification, recognition of that diploma may not be refused in an individual case solely because it is not a diploma of the host state.

Moving beyond clear-cut discrimination, in **Case 205/84 *Commission* v *Germany (Insurance Services)***, Germany had required the providers of insurance to be resident on German soil. The Court of Justice held that member states were under a duty not only to eliminate all discrimination based on nationality, but also all restrictions based on the free provision of services on the grounds that the provider is established in another member state. It also emphasized that all those national rules that apply to the providers of services permanently established in a member state will not necessarily automatically apply to those 'activities of a temporary character which are carried out by enterprises established in other member states'. It was held that the residence requirement was not justified.

The Court of Justice has moved further in the development of a rule that prevents the restriction of services from other member states, but may still persist to limit activities of the home providers of services. The following cases also follow similar developments in moving away from prohibiting not only discriminatory rules, but also any that restrict or hinder the movement of the self-employed, unless they can be justified.

In **Case C-76/90 *Säger* v *Dennemeyer***, Dennemeyer wished to provide patent services in Germany, something requiring a licence, the issue of which was restricted. His right to obtain a licence was challenged by a German patent agent. D claimed breach of Article 59 EEC (now 56 TFEU). The rule was non-discriminatory in that it applied to all patent agents regardless of residence. The Court of Justice held that not only discriminatory rules are prohibited, but any rules that are liable to prohibit or otherwise impede persons providing a service that they already lawfully do in the state of their establishment. Laws applying to the temporary provision of services must be justified by an imperative reason relating to the public interest, the public interest must not already be protected by the rules of the state of establishment and the same result must not be able to be obtained by less restrictive means.

In view of the limited activities undertaken by the patent agents, the ECJ was of the view that the national measures went too far.

In **Case C-55/94** *Gebhard*, a German lawyer who had set up a second chamber in Milan was prevented from using the title *Avvocato*. No secondary law was held to apply to the situation. The issue was whether the Italian rules could be imposed on him. In principle and according to the general Treaty provision Article 52 EEC (now 49 TFEU), he was required to comply with national rules, but the Court of Justice held that national measures that hinder or make less attractive the exercise of fundamental freedoms must fulfil four conditions. They must be:

- non-discriminatory in application;
- justified by imperative reason relating to the public interest;
- suitable to secure the objective sought; and
- proportionate.

In **Case 340/89** *Vlassopoulou*, a Greek lawyer who had worked in Germany and gained some partial qualifications and experience in German law had her request for admission to the German Bar rejected on the grounds that she did not have the necessary German qualifications. On reference to the Court of Justice, if was held that national authorities must take into account qualifications and experience that fall short of full qualification and undertake a comparison of the qualifications to see if they are the equivalent of the national requirements, and not dismiss them out of hand.

It is left to the national courts to determine whether qualifications are equivalent and here lies the danger is that some courts will and some will not.

The consequence of these decisions is that 'establishment' is now very close to 'services'. Perhaps this is a fair result to achieve: that it does not matter where or how you practise, either on a temporary or permanent basis, provided that qualifications are roughly equivalent. Rules that seek to prevent this must satisfy the criteria or be struck out, at least as far as non-national EU citizens, and eventually this might also lead to internal pressure in member states so that the rules are abolished in respect of nationals also; otherwise, they are seen to be discriminated against in comparison with host EU free movers. Hence, as with goods, as with workers, the prohibited rules applying to the self-employed also include indirect discrimination and thus market access, but similarly such rules may be objectively justified.

cross reference

See the discussion of reverse discrimination in Chapter 13, section 13.1.

In **Case C-384/93** *Alpine Investments*, a Dutch law that prevented financial services providers from making cold-calling telephone calls either within or outside the Netherlands was challenged as breaching Article 59 EEC (now 56 TFEU). The Court of Justice held that the rule was not to be equated with the selling arrangements rule established in cases *Keck and Mithouard* for goods and thus outside the scope of EC law, but held instead that because the rule affects access to other markets and thus is capable of hindering intra-Community trade in services, it will breach the Treaty. Such measures can be objectively justified by imperative reasons of public interest that are necessary and proportionate. In the case itself, it was decided that the Dutch government's arguments of consumer protection and safe-guarding the reputation of Dutch financial markets satisfied those criteria; therefore the prohibition did not offend Article 59 EEC (now 56 TFEU).

In **Case C-438/05** *ITWF & FSU* v *Viking*, the right to establish was balanced with the rights of workers to strike. The Viking line wanted to re-register a Finnish ship under the Estonian flag to employ lower-paid Estonians, to reduce costs and to increase competitiveness with other lines plying the same route, but was prevented from doing so by the threat of strike action and a general boycott of Viking line ships by the unions ITWF and FSU. Viking's claim that this was a breach of Article 43 EC (now 49 TFEU) was recognized by the ECJ between the two private parties, but the right to strike was a fundamental right and a public interest right that could be a justified breach of Article 43 EC (now 49 TFEU) provided that action was necessary to safeguard jobs and that any action was proportionate. It is for the national courts to undertake the final balancing of those rights according to the facts.

This case also makes it clear that Article 43 EC (now 49 TFEU) can also be relied on horizontally against non-state organizations.

In a similar case, **C-341/05** *Laval*, concerned with the provision of cross-border services, a Swedish union and workers attempted to force a Latvian company undertaking work in Sweden, but employing lower-paid temporary workers, to observe the Swedish collec-tive bargaining terms and conditions. The Court held that, provided that the conditions observed by the company were lawful, which they were, the attempt to force higher stand-ards represented a breach of Article 49 EC (now 56 TFEU).

Case C-17/00 *de Coster*, concerned strictly with a domestic tax regime, was eligible to be considered under EU law, in the view of the Court of Justice, because the taxation applied to the installation of satellite television dishes, which received broadcasts from other member states, but there was no equivalent tax on apparatus receiving domestic broadcasts only.

The interpretation of the rights of the freedoms to establish or provide services has thus been as extensive fundamentally upheld by the Court of Justice as for the freedom of workers.

12.4.2 **Legislative developments**

Even as a result of the early case law, the Commission realized that the previous harmoniza-tion approach that had been attempted was not the best solution with which to realize free movement and commenced work on a new approach to achieving free movement that was applicable to many professions across the board.

12.4.2.1 Mutual recognition

A change of tactic was undertaken by the Commission to overcome the problems of tackling one profession at a time, which involved the enactment of mutual recognition Directives to apply to many professions. The new approach was prompted by the slow progress on specific professions. Following the *Reyners* and *Van Binsbergen* cases, the Commission decided that it was not necessary to issue Directives for each individual trade and profession. The Directives that had already been worked on and ones in the pipeline were not rendered redundant and were, in cases before the Court of Justice, held to be amplifications or guidelines to the requirements of the Treaty Articles, although work on a number were abandoned. The first general Directive was the Mutual Recognition of Diplomas Directive 89/48, applied to numerous professionals, excepting those subject to specific Community Directives, who have completed a period, a minimum of three years, of post-secondary education and professional training, and who are regulated under national law or subject to the requirement of a diploma or other similar professional qualifications equivalent to a diploma. It applied to professionally qualified persons as opposed to those who have completed only the university or college element of instruction and included workers, not only the self-employed. It has now been replaced by Directive 2005/36, which has incorporated both the general and specific professions Directives. No further details will be provided in this introductory text on EU law. Likewise, the Provision of Services Directive 2006/123 needs only to be noted. This was designed to consolidate further the freedoms to provide services and to establish in the new, much-liberalized markets of the member states, but seems rather to have maintained and possibly increased the distinction between them. Unfortunately, this new Directive is ridden with exceptions and will overlap with existing Directives; thus, in view of its comprehensiveness and complexity, it is unlikely to be covered in any detail in general and introductory courses on EU law and no further details will be provided here.

12.4.3 **The free movement of lawyers**

Whilst not dealing with any other professions, as an exception in a book on EU law, it is appropriate to consider briefly the legislative provisions affecting the legal professions. It was considered necessary, against the trend of moving away from sectoral Directives, to issue a Directive to realize the freedom to provide services and establishment for lawyers.

12.4.3.1 The provision of services by lawyers

Directive 77/249 is limited to the recognition of practising lawyers from member states, who must be accepted based on understanding that the training of lawyers in other member states is similarly strict as that in the host state. Article 4(1) dispenses with residence and registration requirements for 'the representation of a client in legal proceedings'. Article 4(2) provides that lawyers providing services in judicial proceedings are required to observe both those sets of rules of professional conduct of the home and host states. Article 4(4) states that, where justifiable, the same rules apply to those providing services as nationals. Article 5 provides that:

> for the pursuit of activities relating to the representation of a client in legal proceedings, a member state may require lawyers . . . to work in conjunction with a lawyer who practises before the judicial authority in question and who would, where necessary, be answerable to that authority . . .

The requirements of Directive 77/249 have been specifically considered by the Court of Justice.

In **Case 427/85 Commission v Germany (Lawyers' Services)**, the Court of Justice held that local rules were acceptable, but could not go beyond the strict requirements of Community law as to become a hindrance to free movement and the requirement to have local lawyers alongside at all times, and also before courts where there was no compulsory representation and the requirement to live locally when only providing services was far too restrictive and therefore a breach of the Treaty. The rule that lawyers could operate only in strictly defined areas was not justified by Article 5 of the Directive and could not be applied to activities of a temporary nature carried out by lawyers established in another member state, although they may still apply to national lawyers.

This case is an example of reverse discrimination, whereby the rule cannot be applied to Union lawyers from other member states, but can still be applied to national lawyers. Germany has now repealed that rule.

12.4.3.2 Establishment by lawyers (Practice under Home Title)

The Lawyers Home Title Directive 98/5 provides, under Article 2, that any lawyer shall be entitled to practise in any other member state under his home country professional title as an independent or salaried lawyer on a permanent basis. Lawyers need only register with the competent authority in the host state on the basis of their registration in the home member state (Article 3).

cross reference
For further details of the rights provided by this, see the Online Resource Centre.

Article 5 provides that the host lawyer may give advice on the law of his or her home member state, on EU law, on international law, and on the law of the host member state. He or she must comply with the rules of procedure applicable in the national courts.

This so-called 'third approach' provides an easier way of acquiring the professional title of the host member state and, in effect, circumvents the necessity under the Mutual Recognition Directive 89/48 and its replacement Directive 2005/36 to undertake the aptitude test to establish in another member state. The reason given for providing this is that it was primarily directed at experienced professionals, for whom an aptitude test would constitute an obstacle on account of the time that has elapsed since they obtained their qualifications, but it is hard to see how it would not be used by lawyers of any length of service.

In **Case C-313/01 *Morgenbesser***, the Court of Justice ruled that the refusal to enrol paid trainee lawyers because their prior academic legal qualifications were obtained in other member states was unjustified. Hence the Court of Justice held that national authorities are obliged to compare the applicant's professional knowledge, as certified by his or her qualifications or acquired through professional experience either in the member state of origin or in the host member state, with the professional knowledge required by national law. If the comparison reveals that these correspond only partially, the host member state is entitled to require the person concerned to show that he or she has acquired the knowledge that is lacking.

12.5 Derogations from the free movement regimes

12.5.1 Procedural safeguards

Before considering the substantive grounds that member states may invoke in order either to refuse entry in the first place or to justify deportation, it makes sense first to consider any

For more details on section 12.5 scan here or visit the Online Resource Centre.

procedural rights that persons may have who are faced with such decisions. If immediate deportation can be prevented, then there is more time in which to consider the substantive grounds given. Article 31 of Directive 2004/38 provides a number of procedural rights that further support free movement by providing for non-discriminatory rights of appeal, rights to remain to hear the appeal result, rights to be given reasons for deportation and rights to the judicial review of decisions.

There is a right to remain in the member state pending a decision either to grant or refuse a residence permit, other than in emergency situations. Article 30 of Directive 2004/38 provides that the grounds for deportation must be precisely and comprehensively stated. The concerned person has a right to be informed of the grounds of refusal or deportation unless security is at stake.

These rights were developed previously in case law, notably in **Cases 115–116/81 *Adoui and Cornauille v Belgian State***, in which two French ladies euphemistically described by the Court of Justice as 'waitresses' had their residence permits withdrawn by the Belgian authorities on the grounds that their personal conduct justified the invocation of the public policy proviso. The conduct was described by the court as 'Displaying themselves in windows in scant dress and being able to be alone with clients'. Basically, Belgium was trying to clamp down on the number of French prostitutes settling in Belgium. A reference was made to the Court of Justice, which held that the public policy proviso does not allow expulsion where similar conduct by nationals does not incur penalty or repressive measures. However, it does not require illegality to be invoked. It was noted that Belgian prostitutes were tolerated and not prosecuted. The Court of Justice held also that the reasons for expulsion must be sufficiently detailed to allow a migrant to defend his or her interests and be drafted in such a way and language as to enable the person to comprehend the content or effect.

thinking point
Avoid February! Why?

Article 30(3) provides the right to be notified of any decision to expel or the refusal of a permit and should also state the minimum period given to leave the country, which cannot be less than one month in any circumstance. Article 31 provides that there should also be a system for appeal against decisions on their merits as well as legality.

Previously, **Case C-175/94 *Gallagher*** considered the body hearing the appeal. Gallagher, who had been convicted of the possession of rifles for unlawful purposes in Ireland, had been deported from the UK. In questioning this decision, he was interviewed in Ireland, before the case was heard by the Home Secretary. He challenged these bodies as not being independent. The Court of Justice held, however, that it was a matter for the national courts to decide whether the body hearing an appeal was independent, but that the Directive did not specify how it should be appointed. It should, however, be genuinely independent.

In **Case 98/79 *Pecastaing v Belgian State***, a French prostitute was asked by the Belgian authorities to leave on grounds of personal conduct. She claimed under Articles 8 and 9 of Directive 64/221 that she should be able to stay in the country whilst the decision was being reviewed, which could be up to three years during the course of an Article 234 EC (now 267 TFEU) reference. The Court of Justice held that, even under Article 234 EC (now 267 TFEU), the right of appeal is not to be diluted and only in cases of emergency should automatic expulsion take place; however, the urgency could finally be determined only by the member states.

Articles 8 and 9 of the now repealed Directive did not expressly grant rights to remain in the host state pending hearing as long as the person can obtain a fair hearing and full facilities even whilst out of the country: see now Article 31 of Directive 2004/38.

12.5.2 Restrictions on the grounds of public policy, security and health

Member states are able to restrict entry and deport EU nationals on the grounds set out under Article 45(3) TFEU, which are public policy, security and health. Under Directive 2004/38, these apply expressly now to workers and the self-employed.

Articles 52 and 62 TFEU subject establishment and provision of services to the same derogations as workers.

> These grounds have been held to be exhaustive in **Case 352/85 *Bond van Adverteerders and others* v *The Netherlands State*** in which economic grounds were pleaded in support of a decision not to allow broadcasts by non-national organizations, but rejected by the Court of Justice.

Article 27 of Directive 2004/38 has consolidated both the previous statutory law and the case law of the Court of Justice, setting out what the member states could or could not do under the derogations.

Directive 2004/38, Article 27(2)

Measures taken on grounds of public policy or public security shall comply with the principle of proportionality and shall be based exclusively on the personal conduct of the individual concerned.

Previous criminal convictions shall not in themselves constitute grounds for taking such measures.

The personal conduct of the individual concerned must represent a genuine, present and sufficiently serious threat affecting one of the fundamental interests of society. Justifications that are isolated from the particulars of the case or that rely on considerations of general prevention shall not be accepted.

Personal conduct may not be considered a sufficiently serious threat unless the member state concerned takes serious enforcement measures against the same conduct on the part of its own nationals.

Directive 2004/38, Article 28

Before taking an expulsion decision on grounds of public policy or public security, the host Member State shall take account of considerations such as how long the individual concerned has resided on its territory, his/her age, state of health, family and economic situation, social and cultural integration into the host Member State and the extent of his/her links with the country of origin.

Under Article 28(2), removal decisions cannot be taken against Union citizens or family members, irrespective of nationality, who have the right of permanent residence within its territory or against family members who are minors. Article 28(3) increases the seriousness of the grounds needed for deportation for EU citizens who have resided for more than ten years in the host state and for minors. In these cases, the decision to deport must be based on 'imperative' grounds of public security. Furthermore, any deportation orders that are taken must be subject to review for possible lifting under Article 32 at least three years after being made.

Most of the case law thus far relating to this part of the Directive relates to the previous legislation.

'Personal conduct' was defined in **Case 67/74 *Bonsignore* v *Köln***, in which an Italian national faced deportation as a general preventative measure after conviction for fatally shooting his brother in a firearms accident. The Court of Justice held that measures adopted on grounds of public policy and for the maintenance of public security against the nationals of member states of the Community cannot be justified on grounds extraneous to the individual case, and that only the personal conduct of those affected by the measures is to be regarded as determinative.

As a departure from the rules concerning the free movement of persons constitute exceptions that must be strictly construed, the concept of 'personal conduct' expresses the requirement that a deportation order may be made only for breaches of the peace and public security that might be committed by the individual affected.

In the earlier judgment in **Case 41/74 *Van Duyn* v *The Home Office***, the Court of Justice held that restrictions on the grounds of public policy must be interpreted very strictly and be subject to judicial review. In this case, a Dutch woman obtained a position as secretary with the Church of Scientology in the UK, but was refused entry by the Home Office on the grounds that public policy declared the Church to be socially harmful. Miss Van Duyn claimed that the refusal was not made on the basis of personal conduct, but the conduct of the group. The Court of Justice held that personal conduct must be an act or omission to act on the part of the person concerned and must be voluntary. It need not, however, be illegal or criminal to offend public policy. However, the Court then further held that present association reflecting participation in the activities and identification with the aims of a group may be considered a voluntary act and could therefore come within the definition of conduct, which hands back some of the discretion to the member states to determine whether an individuals' association in a group constitutes personal conduct.

This part of the judgment is now rather suspect in the light of later case law and Directive 2004/38.

In **Cases 115–116/81 *Adoui and Cornaille***, French prostitutes facing expulsion from Belgium on public policy grounds could not be denied residence on the basis of their personal conduct when similar conduct on the part of nationals did not attract similar repressive measures to combat such behaviour.

Concerning previous criminal convictions, **Case 30/77 *R v Bouchereau*** involved a Frenchman who had been convicted in the UK on a number of occasions for drugs possession. The UK magistrate asked the Court of Justice whether he could be deported to stop him committing acts in the future. The Court of Justice held that it was not possible to look at past records to decide future conduct unless it constituted a present threat. Public policy measures could be relied on only where conduct and criminal convictions were a genuine and sufficiently serious threat affecting one of the fundamental interests of society.

cross reference
Considered above in section 12.2.2.2 concerned with work seekers.

See also the case of *Antonisson* whereby the lack of employment and the lack of any serious chance of obtaining one would justify expulsion.

In **Case C-348/96 *Donatella Calfa***, a Greek rule of automatic life expulsion from Greek territory was applied following conviction of certain offences. As an exemption, the Court of Justice held that it must be interpreted restrictively and that, where a person has been convicted, expulsion could be based only on personal conduct outside of the conviction itself; in any event, a life ban was disproportionate. Indeed, it would now not conform with the requirement in Directive 2004/38 for a review of the expulsion after a minimum of three years (Article 32).

The public security proviso was specifically considered in **Case C-100/01 *Otieza Olazabal***, which involved the French imprisonment and ban on residence for activities undertaken for ETA, the Basque separatist movement. This was challenged, but upheld by the Court of Justice as coming within the public security proviso.

Articles 27 and 28 have now been considered themselves by the Court of Justice in **Case C-145/09 *Land Baden-Württemberg v Tsakouridis*** in which Article 28(3) was considered requiring imperative grounds for deportation. The case involved the criminal activity of dealing in narcotics with an organized crime gang. The Court of Justice held that, as a deliberate raising of strictness, the measures taken under Article 28(3) had to be exceptional. Whilst the Court concluded that organized drug trafficking could be such an exceptional circumstance, the member states nevertheless still had to consider the personal conduct of the individual, as still required by Article 27(2) of Directive 2004/38, and that any decision must be proportionate having regard to the time spent and degree of integration in the host state, especially where the person had spent most – even all – of his childhood in the host state. The national court must also consider the sentence passed on conviction and have account of fundamental rights in both the EU Charter of Fundamental Rights and the European Convention on Human Rights and Fundamental Freedoms (ECHR).

A national court thus has quite a balancing act to come to a decision on whether authorities can lawfully, under EU law, deport an EU citizen of more than ten years' residence in a host state.

Public health measures are given further definition in Article 29 of the Directive and, rather than listing particular diseases as was the previous practice, the Directive now provides as follows.

Directive 2004/38, Article 29

· ·

The only diseases justifying measures restricting freedom of movement shall be the diseases with epidemic potential as defined by the relevant instruments of the World Health Organization and other infectious diseases or contagious parasitic diseases if they are the subject of protection provisions applying to nationals of the host Member State.

A case that has considered Article 27 is **Case C-33/07 Jipa**, dealing with expulsion, in which it was held that, in deciding on the matter, member states could not simply rely on a previous expulsion or information from the home states, but that both could be considered in the context of the overall decision provided that personal conduct was also considered and judged to be a threat to society.

The case is therefore in line with previous judgments on personal conduct.

12.5.3 **Employment in the public service**

Article 45(4) TFEU exempts employment in the public service from the provisions of Article 45 TFEU. The initial difficulty was that there is no Treaty definition of 'public service', which can vary considerably from state to state, and thus its understanding in different member states could vary considerably and could be claimed by the member states to apply to a vast range of workers employed by the state. Hence the Court of Justice has constantly stressed the need for a strict interpretation of this Article. It has been held to apply to entry and not to conditions of employment.

341

In **Case 152/73 Sotgui v Deutsche Bundespost**, Mr Sotgui, an Italian national, was employed by the German Post Office, but was not paid the same travel allowance as German nationals. This was held to be discrimination contrary to Article 39(1) and was not excused by Article 39(4).

In **Case 149/79 Commission v Belgium (Public Employees)**, the Court of Justice held that public service derogation applies only to typical public service posts that exercise powers conferred by public law and which are there to safeguard the interests of state, regardless of the actual status in each of the member states.

The Court of Justice has, on this basis, excluded from the scope of Article 45(4) TFEU:

- nurses, in Case 307/84 *Commission* v *French Republic*;
- trainee secondary school teachers, in Case 66/85 *Lawrie-Blum* v *Land Baden-Würtemberg*;
- secondary school teachers, in Case C-4/91 *Bleis* v *Ministry of Education*; and
- foreign language lecturers, in Case 33/88 *Alluè and Coonan* v *Università degli Studi di Venezia*.

In order to try to clarify the posts that the member states claim to come within Article 45(4) TFEU, the Commission has issued a notice (OJ 1988 C72/2), confirmed by a 2002 Commission Communication (COM (2002) 694 final), of those sector positions that it thinks would rarely be covered by the public service proviso. These include public health care, teaching in state educational establishments, non-military public research and public administration of commercial activities. This has been confirmed in its later Communication of December 2002.

Occasionally, restrictions are accepted by the Court of Justice, as in **Case C-47/02 Anker et al.**, in which restricting the appointment of ships' masters to Germans was held to be acceptable in view of the public duties that had to be undertaken by the masters of ships. These included the maintenance of safety and exercise of police powers. However, the Court advised that such duties should not be a minor part of the activity of a Master and should be exercised regularly.

There is the equivalent of the public service exception for establishment in Article 51 TFEU (ex 45 EC), but only on the more tightly defined ground of 'positions concerned with the exercise of official authority'. The Court held, in the case of *Reyners*, that the derogation was more concerned with the exercise of the prerogative power of the state rather than the preventing particular occupations from exercising rights under EU law.

Summary

The EU law provision for the free movement of persons has changed considerably from its inception. Whilst the Treaty Articles themselves have hardly changed since 1957, the scope of the rights available now to individuals has expanded considerably due to both secondary legislation and judicial interpretation.

The rights were not, in the end, employed in a way that helped to promote the economies of the EC and later Union and its member states by the mass migration of workers from one member state to another. Instead, the rights were assumed by individuals alone and consequently on a small scale. The secondary legislation and continued liberal interpretation of it by the ECJ opened up free movement for persons in the EU and their families, and it is argued that because families were granted derived rights from the workers to work and obtain various social benefits, these aspects helped further to remove the disincentives in moving to a new country in order to engage in an economic activity.

Since then, more general rights of free movement have been introduced into the EU legal regime not dependent on an economic activity and these will be the subject matter of Chapter 13.

Questions

For suggested approaches to answering these questions scan here or visit the Online Resource Centre.

1 Who is a worker for the purposes of the TFEU?

2 Who is entitled to join a worker in the host state?

3 Give four case law examples of how the ECJ has interpreted social and tax advantages from Article 7(2) of Regulation 1612/68 (now Article 7(2) of Regulation 492/2011).

4 To what extent does the public service proviso allow member states to exclude all entry to public service employment in its territory?

5 For what reasons may a member state refuse entry to, or lawfully deport, an EU worker?

 # Further reading

BOOKS

Barnard, C. *The Substantive Law of the EU: The Four Freedoms,* 3rd edn, Oxford University Press, Oxford, 2010 (chapters 11–14 and 16).

Van der Mei, A. P. *Free Movement of Persons within the European Community: Cross-Border Access to Public Benefits*, Hart Publishing, Oxford, 2003.

Weiss, F. and Wooldridge, F. *Free Movement of Persons within the European Community*, 2nd edn, Kluwer Law International, The Hague, 2007.

White, R. *Workers, Establishment and Services in the European Union*, Oxford University Press, Oxford, 2005.

ARTICLES

Acierno, S. 'The *Carpenter* judgment: fundamental rights and the limits of the Community legal order' (2003) 28 EL Rev 398.

Barnard, C. 'Unravelling the Services Directive' (2008) 41 CML Rev 323.

Barrett, G. 'Family matters: European Community law and third-country family members' (2003) 40 CML Rev 369.

Costello, C. '*Metock*: Free movement and "normal family life" in the Union' (2009) 46 CML Rev 587.

Dautricourt, C. and Thomas, S. 'Reverse discrimination and free movement of persons under Community law: all for Ulysses, nothing for Penelope?' (2009) 34 EL Rev 433.

Davies, G. 'The high-water point of free movement of persons: ending benefit tourism and rescuing welfare' (2004) 26 J Soc Wel & Fam L 211.

Foster, N. 'Family and welfare rights in Europe: the impact of recent European Court of Justice Decisions in the area of the free movement of persons' (2003) 25 J Soc Wel & Fam L 291.

Hatzopoulos, V. and Do, T. 'The case law of the ECJ concerning the free provision of services 2000–2005' (2006) 43 CML Rev 923.

Iliopoulou, A. and Toner, H. 'A new approach to discrimination against free movers? *D'Hoop v Office National de l'Emploi*' (2003) EL Rev 389.

Spaventa, E. 'From *Gebhard* to *Carpenter*: towards a (non-)economic European Constitution' (2004) 41 CML Rev 743.

Tryfonidou, A. 'Family reunification rights of (migrant) Union citizens: towards a more liberal approach' (2009) 15 ELJ 634.

Tryfonidou, A. 'In search of the aim of the EC Free Movement of Persons provisions: has the Court of Justice missed the point?' (2009) 46 CML Rev 1591.

Free movement of persons II: developments and citizenship

Learning objectives

In this chapter, you will consider a number of developments in EU law relating to the free movement of persons that are not dependent on the movement of an economically active EU person, including:

- the concept and meaning of the 'wholly internal' rule;
- the treatment of independent third-country nationals;
- the extension of free movement rights to general rights of free movement; and
- the rights provided as a result of European citizenship.

Introduction

For more details on this section scan here or visit the Online Resource Centre.

This chapter will consider a number of topics associated with the free movement of persons that do not fall within the original understanding of that freedom. It will commence with a brief consideration of two matters allied to the free movement of persons: the wholly internal rule, which concerns situations not covered by European Union (EU) law, and the treatment of those third-country nationals not coming within the EU law provisions relating to the family members of workers or the self-employed – that is, those who entered an EU country in their own right, although, as will be seen from the case law, because of changing factual circumstances, some of these are then to be considered under the category of family members.

 Third-country nationals are designated TCNs in the literature.

The chapter will conclude with a consideration of those persons who are now able to move and reside in other member states under the general rights of movement provided by the Treaty and secondary legislation, notably now through the citizen provisions in Articles 20 and 21 TFEU (ex 17 and 18 EC). These persons do not need now to be economically active to move to move to another member state, which was the original understanding under the Treaty. European citizenship has supported a whole range of rights through its development by the Court of Justice and the case law on this topic is rapidly becoming expansive

13.1 The wholly internal rule

EU law will not apply when a situation is regarded as being wholly within the internal legal competence of a member state. Thus there is no reason why EU law rights are triggered. It has been observed that EU law sometimes has the effect of producing reverse discrimination against nationals of member states when compared to EU nationals who have moved to a host member state and can benefit from EU law: for example, where strict professional rules continue to apply to nationals established and providing services, but which are held by the Court of Justice not to be suitable or appropriate to apply to EU professionals providing services temporarily in the host state.

> In **Case 427/85 Commission v Germany (Lawyers)**, concerning the restriction on areas of practice for lawyers in Germany, the consequence of the judgment was that whilst EU lawyers could be restricted in some circumstances because they were only providing services in Germany and not establishing either permanently or on a long-term basis, they could not be geographically restricted. In contrast, the German lawyers could still be restricted in the geographical areas in which they could practise because this was an entirely internal matter of the application of national rules to German nationals.

Note, though, that the internal German rules on this have now been changed.

cross reference

See the discussions in Chapter 12, section 12.4.3.1.

In **Case 175/78 *R* v *Saunders***, a criminal sanction imposed a mobility restriction on Saunders that was applicable within the UK only. This was claimed by Saunders to be contrary to Article 48 EEC (now 45 TFEU). The Court of Justice held that there was no factor connecting the situation with Community law because there was no movement to or from another member state. Hence the provisions on free movement of workers cannot be applied to situations that are wholly internal to a member state.

The *Saunders* case can be compared with another to demonstrate the difference when EU law now applies.

In **Case 36/75 *Rutili* v *France***, a restriction by France on the Italian national Rutili entering certain departments of France was regarded as contrary to both the Treaty and Community secondary legislation. The Court of Justice held that Article 48(3) EEC (now 45 TFEU) derogations may be imposed only in respect of the whole of the national territory.

There is, however, **Case C–299/95 *Kremzow* v *Austria***, concerning a national imprisoned in his own state, in which the European Court of Justice (ECJ) ruled that whilst the deprivation of liberty might prevent the person from exercising the Community right to freedom of movement, the purely hypothetical possibility did not involve a sufficient connection with Community law.

Further, in **Case C-100/01 *Olazbal***, dealing with the restriction of movement of a Spanish national who had connections with ETA, the Basque separatist organization, to specific regions in France, the ECJ held that when criminal measures are taken to restrict movement, they are acceptable if the action was justified owing to the seriousness of the crime, which would otherwise lead to a complete banishment. Furthermore, in similar circumstances, nationals would also be subject to similar punitive measures.

Two further cases illustrate how the wholly internal rule appears to give rise to unfair and arbitrary results, and thus reverse discrimination, because nationals or those lawfully resident in the member state in question are denied rights on which EU nationals from other member states and their family members from outside the EU are able to rely.

In **Cases 35 and 36/82 *Morson and Jhanjan***, the applicants, both Surinamese nationals, claimed the right to stay in the Netherlands with their Dutch national son and daughter working there. It was held by the Court of Justice that there was no application of Community law to the wholly internal situation in which national workers had not worked in any other member state. There was no movement from one member state to another; therefore Community law did not apply and movement from a third country did not qualify.

This was confirmed in **Cases 64 and 65/96 *Land Nordrhein-Westfalen* v *Uecker and Jacquet*** concerning two TCNs trying to rely on Community law as spouses of German nationals living in Germany. The case was deemed to be wholly internal and thus not within the scope of application of European Community (EC) law.

If both cases had concerned, for example, Spanish nationals moving to either the Netherlands or Germany, they would be allowed to take TCN spouses or relatives with them. Of late, however, there appears to be some softening of the wholly internal rule. Some cases look wholly internal, but because there was some prior movement involved, EU law rights can be triggered against the home state. The amount of movement or degree of economic activity deemed necessary to take a situation out of being wholly internal to one in which EU law applies appears to be decreasing, as exemplified by the following cases.

In **Case C-370/90 *Surinder Singh***, an Indian spouse of a British national was able to use EC law to derive a right of residence in the UK on the basis that the spouse had previously exercised the right of free movement by providing services in another member state, but who then re-established herself in the UK.

In **Case 419/92 *Scholz***, it was held that a frontier worker who continues to live in his or her home state whilst employed in another state, but who crosses the border to work, triggers Community rights that can be claimed within the home state.

In **Case C-60/00 *Carpenter***, a Philippine national claimed a right of residence in the UK with her British spouse on the grounds that he provided services from time to time in other member states. The case is similar to *Singh* in as much as the fact that services had been provided in another member state before returning to the UK, except that Mrs Carpenter had not left UK soil whilst services were being provided by her husband both from the UK and travelling to other member states. The argument put forward by the applicants was that if Mrs Carpenter had also gone to another member state, both would have had rights of residence and the right to work in the other host EU states. However, she chose to remain in the UK to look after the children and thus to assist her husband in providing services in other member states.

The Court of Justice referred to Regulation 1612/68, which, strictly speaking, does not apply to the provision of services, but provides rules protecting of the family life of national workers of the member states in order to eliminate obstacles to the exercise of the fundamental freedoms guaranteed by the Treaty. The Court held:

> It is clear that the separation of Mr and Mrs Carpenter would be detrimental to their family life and, therefore, to the conditions under which Mr Carpenter exercises a fundamental freedom. That freedom could not be fully effective if Mr Carpenter were to be deterred from exercising it by obstacles raised in his country of origin to the entry and residence of his spouse.

The Court of Justice noted that the marriage appeared genuine, that there were no official complaints against Mrs Carpenter and that she looked after the children while Mr Carpenter was providing services. The Court held that Article 49 EC (now 56 TFEU), read in the light of the fundamental right to respect for family life (Article 8 ECHR), is to be interpreted as preventing a member state from refusing the TCN spouse of a provider of services established in that member state who provides services to recipients established in other member states a right to reside in its territory.

In **Case C-281/98** *Angonese*, an Italian citizen applied for a job in Italy, but was refused entry to the selection process becuase he did not have the appropriate local authority certificate of bilingualism, despite being accepted by the local court as perfectly bilingual and possessing certificates of language study from the University of Vienna where he had studied. The Italian government and defendant bank argued that the matter was wholly internal and had no connection with Community law. Whilst there was movement in this case in that Mr Angonese had studied in Austria, the only economic activity was the receiving of educational services. The Court of Justice held that the previous movement for the purposes of study had triggered Community law rights.

A further case in this category is **Case C-403/03** *Schempp*. Divorce maintenance was being made in another member state, which meant that the German tax regime that would normally apply was denied in this case and a tax exemption on the payments was lost. It was argued by Germany and other governments that this was a wholly internal situation that had involved no movement on the part of Mr Schempp. The ECJ held, however, that the exercise of the right of free movement by the former spouse of Mr Schempp had an effect on his right to deduct tax in Germany and was therefore not a wholly internal situation with no connection to Community law. The difference in treatment offended Article 12 EC (now 18 TFEU), although the Court stressed that, in view of the different tax regimes, Community law does not guarantee neutrality of treatment if a person takes advantages of the free movement rights under Article 18 EC (now 21 TFEU).

Case C-148/02 *Garcia Avello* looks very much wholly internal, with no movement taking place that was directly connected with the facts of the case. It involved dual nationality children of a Spanish father living in Belgium, who wished to register the children's names according to Spanish custom and practice and not Belgian. The Court of Justice, relying on Articles 17 and 12 EC (now 20 and 18 TFEU), held that the children's future rights to move back to Spain might be prejudiced by Belgium, contrary to the Treaty.

In **Case C-17/00** *de Coster*, concerned in strict terms with a domestic tax regime, was eligible to be considered under EU law, in the view of the Court of Justice, because the taxation applied only to the installation of satellite dishes that could receive television broadcasts from other member states, but was not applied to the installation of receiving equipment capable of receiving domestic broadcasts. The signals could easily come from another member state, which introduced the cross-border element.

In similar vein, **Case C-544/03** *Mobistar* was concerned with mobile phone masts, and also triggered the application and consideration of EU law because mobile phone signals can equally satisfy the cross-border service element.

Finally, in this context, is **Case C-200/02** *Chen*, which involved no movement from one member state to another, but, because of the particular legal rules in Ireland, nevertheless triggered the application of EU law. Ireland, at the time of the case, granted nationality to

cross reference

This case will be considered further in section 13.3.4.3.

anyone born on the geographic island of Ireland, regardless of origin and nationality of parents, so when a daughter of Chinese parents was born in Northern Ireland, she became Irish and thus an EU citizen, from whom rights for the parent derived.

cross reference

Akrich is considered further in section 13.2.3.

Thus a factual circumstance, which on the face of it appears to be wholly internal, may nevertheless be subject to EU law, provided that there has been some previous movement into another member state or that services have or can be received, physical or metaphysical, or that payments made in another member state or that other facts intervene to establish some cross-border element, such as a change in legal status. This last would include the *Chen* case and the marriage of TCNs cases such as Case C-109/01 *Akrich*.

13.2 The treatment of third-country nationals (TCNs)

For more details on this section scan here or visit the Online Resource Centre.

Nationals from third countries lawfully or unlawfully resident in a member state were not previously subject to EU law unless specifically catered for, for example as family members of EU persons taking advantage of the free movement of persons rules. Independent TCNs were originally entirely a matter for national law regulation despite the fact that there are millions of TCNs lawfully or unlawfully resident in the EU. Estimates put the figure at approximately 18.5 million TCNs lawfully resident in the twenty-seven EU states. Whilst it might have been the case in the past that the treatment of TCNs was regarded as being below the standards of treatment to be expected from the EC, more recently the Court of Justice, the Commission and the member states in the Council of Ministers have been addressing the rights of TCNs. Much attention has been directed to the immigration policies and the Schengen Agreement regarding the entry and visa regulation of TCNs, whereas less attention has been paid to the rights, including rights of free movement, of those already in the EU.

Previously, the Court of Justice has held, for example in Case 238/83 *Mr and Mrs Richard Meade*, that the Treaty Articles on free movement of workers apply solely to EU nationals and not therefore to TCNs.

13.2.1 Association and cooperation agreements

The first of the exceptions to the absence of EU regulation is where TCNs have been provided with rights under the various association and cooperation agreements with countries such as Turkey, Algeria and Morocco.

13.2.2 Workers 'posted' abroad

Secondly, TCNs may form part of the workforce of a company established in the EU that sends workers abroad to complete a contract in another member state and covered by Directive 96/71.

In **Case C-43/93 *Van der Elst***, the Court of Justice confirmed that TCNs also have the right of free movement within the context of the right of free movement of companies that are established within the EU. This right is subject to the condition that the non-EU nationals are part of the legal labour force of the company established in the home member state and where the employer provides services in another member state.

In 2010, the Commission proposed a new Posted Workers Directive to take into account case developments, but it has not yet been adopted.

13.2.3 General rights for TCNs

For more details on this section scan here or visit the Online Resource Centre.

There has also now been legislative intervention in this area and further proposals have also been made. Regulation 1091/2001 was enacted, which provides limited rights of free movement for those TCNs in the EU on a long-stay visa. TCNs may also be helped by Directive 2000/43, which prohibits discrimination based on race; however, Article 3(2) of the Directive states that it is without prejudice to the provisions and conditions relating to the entry and residence of TCNs and to any treatment that arises from the legal status of TCNs. So whilst it may prevent unequal treatment in the country of residence, it is unlikely to provide a right of free movement.

Specifically, addressing the situation of divided families with TCN family members, the institutions have enacted Directive 2003/86, which provides that lawfully resident TCNs in member states may apply to have their family join them from a third country provided that they are self-sufficient and have been in the member state for a year or more. Furthermore, Article 3 of the Directive requires that the resident TCNS must have a reasonable prospect of remaining longer. The definition of family has been restrictively drawn and member states retain much discretion in deciding whether to grant an application. The Directive does not apply to the UK, Ireland and Denmark, which have opted out of the governing section of the Treaty (Articles 77–80 TFEU).

cross reference
Further details can, however, be found on the Online Resource Centre.

Article 59 EEC (now 56 TFEU) was amended by the Single European Act (SEA), and now provides that the European Parliament and the Council, acting in accordance with the ordinary legislative procedure, may extend the provisions of the Chapter to TCNs who provide services and who are established within the Union. However, the further legislative interventions and proposals in this area are beyond most courses on EU law and will not be rehearsed here.

Case law has also had an impact in this area of law, although, as will be seen, some cases concerning TCNs are accommodated within the existing EU free movement regime after consideration of the facts by the Court of Justice. The first case, concerned with the rights of TCNs, actually contains two sets of factual circumstances, but is referred to under one name.

Case C-413/99 *Baumbast* also concerns 'R', an American woman who had neither personal nor derived rights to remain in the EU. Nevertheless, it was held by the Court of Justice that she had a right of residence under Community law and was able to resist an attempt to deport her. R moved to the UK with her French husband, who had obtained work in the UK. Later, the couple divorced and, in line with the jurisprudence of the *Diatta* and *Reed* cases, R lost her own legal right to remain in the host state as no longer coming within Article 10 of Regulation 1612/68 as a spouse. R and her children nevertheless remained in the UK. Whilst the children were granted indefinite leave to remain, she was not. The UK authorities wanted to deport her and, by necessity, her children. However, the children remained the children of an EU national, but who was no longer working in the UK. The Court of Justice held that Regulation 1612/68 must be interpreted as entitling the parent who is the primary carer of those children, irrespective of nationality, to reside with them in order to facilitate the exercise of that right, notwithstanding the fact that the parents have meanwhile divorced. The fact that only one parent is a citizen of the Union who ceased to be a migrant worker in the

cross reference

Considered in Chapter 12, section 12.3.2.2.

host member state and whose children are not themselves citizens of the Union is irrelevant in this regard. According to the Court of Justice, to refuse to grant permission to remain to a parent who is the primary carer of the child exercising his (or her) right to pursue his (or her) studies in the host member state infringes that right (at [73] of the judgment).

Hence, then, there is an implied right within Article 12 of the Regulation that the child of a migrant worker can not only pursue his or her education in the host member state, but also that the child has the right to be accompanied by the person who is his or her primary carer. Furthermore, that person is able to reside with him or her in that member state during his or her studies.

Case C-109/01 *Akrich* involves a Moroccan, who, after both lawful and unlawful attempts to enter and remain in the UK, married a UK national and moved to Ireland for a short period expressly in order to take advantage of EC law rights. The Secretary of State considered that Mr and Mrs Akrich's move to Ireland was no more than a temporary absence deliberately designed to manufacture a right of residence for Mr Akrich on his return to the UK and thereby to evade the provisions of the UK's national legislation. Therefore the view was formed that Mrs Akrich had not been genuinely exercising rights under the EC Treaty as a worker in another member state. The Court of Justice was asked, amongst other questions, whether an engineered situation to evade national immigration laws was an abuse of Community law rights and, if so, whether the UK authorities could lawfully refuse entry. The Court of Justice held that the motive for going to Ireland is not relevant to the status of a worker, nor the decision to return to the home state. The Court of Justice did, however, acknowledge that there would be an abuse if the facilities afforded by Community law in favour of migrant workers and their spouses were invoked in the context of marriages of convenience entered into in order to circumvent the provisions relating to entry and residence of nationals of non-member states. If genuinely married, however, Article 8 of the European Convention on Human Rights (ECHR) should be taken into regard in considering the unlawful residence status of the TCN.

The Court of Justice held that Article 10 of Regulation 1612/68 applies to TCNs only if they are lawfully resident in a member state before they move to another one to take advantage of the rights provided by the regulation. It is not applicable where a marriage of convenience has been arranged to circumvent a member state's laws.

Therefore, if the marriage is genuine, despite a lack of lawful residence, member states should pay regard to Article 8 ECHR. This judgment does not provide a full answer and the main question that is left to the member state is whether or not the marriage was genuine.

In **Case C-1/05** *Jia*, in which the scope of the *Akrich* judgment was raised, the ECJ held that neither the *Akrich* judgment nor Community law in general permitted member states to restrict the entry of a TCN relative of the spouse of a Community citizen to only where the TCN relative had first been resident in another EU country. In other words, the TCN could move directly to join her relative in the EU direct from the third country. The Court also held, though, that the proof of dependency for such moves, required previously under Directive 73/148, but now catered for by Directive 2004/38, required real proof of factual dependency from any appropriate means, but not only an undertaking from a member of the family.

A further group of claims in Case C-127/08 *Metock* confirm the *Jia* judgment and were based on Directive 2004/38.

> **Case C-127/08 *Metock et al.*** considered numerous Articles of Directive 2004/38 where four TCNs who had been refused asylum in Ireland then married EU citizens lawfully resident in Ireland. In the judgment, the Court of Justice expressly reverses part of the judgment in *Akrich* by making clear that the Directive is not conditional on a requirement that a TCN must have been lawfully resident in another member state to stay in a member state as a spouse or member of the family of an EU citizen. The Court held that rights provided for spouses to accompany EU citizens apply irrespective of where the marriage took place and how the TCN entered the host member state. The facts of the case stated that there were not marriages of convenience, although, under Article 35 of the Directive, member states can take action to penalize those who do abuse rights or engage in fraud.

The member states are somewhat concerned as to the further consequences of this judgment.

13.2.4 **Summary of TCN rights**

The statutory and case law developments represent some slight improvement in the position of lawfully resident TCNs in the EU. The EU legislature and the Court of Justice are having to be very careful in trying to provide rules for TCNs who have a reasonable claim to reside and exercise rights of free movement, but without opening the door too widely so that unlawful residents gain a right to remain and obtain benefits against the wishes of the member state. These are matters that are highly politically charged in the present day. Another way of regulating TCNs and simultaneously prompting further recognition of their rights in the EU is by the policies pursued by the Schengen Agreement, which is not considered in this text.

Where TCNs are members of the family of a Union citizen who has exercised his or her rights under Community law, then Articles 12 and 13 of Directive 2004/38 now provide the most secure rights with, after five years, the right of permanent resident, even in the event of the death of the Union citizen or divorce from the Union citizen.

The Lisbon Treaty has provided a better basis for the rights of TCNs and, under Article 67(2) TFEU, aims to frame a common policy on asylum, immigration and external border controls that is fair towards TCNs. The provisions from both the EU and EC Treaties have been regrouped in Articles 67–74 TFEU. In order to achieve the broad objectives of Article 67, Article 75 provides for the ordinary legislative procedure to be used, which involves the co-decision procedure, a very positive move away from intergovernmentalism to supranationalism in this more controversial area of Union activity. The individual areas of border controls, asylum and immigration are then set out respectively in Articles 77–79, the further details of which go beyond the necessary remit of this work.

13.3 The extension of free movement rights

Freedom of movement now exists for persons other than workers and the self-employed as this concept has been widened to include those receiving services, as opposed to providing services, and also because rights of free movement are no longer necessarily anchored to

For more details
on section 13.3
scan here or
visit the Online
Resource Centre.

an active economic activity. This was initially addressed by three general Directives, then by the introduction of a citizenship section into the EC Treaty and now additionally by Directive 2004/38, which has replaced the three general rights of movement Directives. In the following two subsections, those receiving services and those having a right to move that is not based on an economic activity are considered.

13.3.1 **Receiving services**

The concept of services has been expanded to those who do not actively pursue an economic activity, but instead passively receive services of an economic activity. Whilst there is nothing to confirm this category within the Treaty, it was expressly mentioned in Article 1 of Directive 64/221 (now repealed), but strangely has not been mentioned in its replacement, Directive 2004/38. Services can be received either by movement to another member state or by receiving services from another state in the home state. Initially, cases that confirmed this arose from the areas of educational provision and tourist travel.

13.3.1.1 Tourist services

In **Case 286/82 *Luisi and Carbone* v *Ministero del Tesauro***, two Italian nationals were prosecuted under Italian currency regulations for taking money out to pay for tourist and medical provisions abroad. These were held by the Court of Justice to be payments for services and thus to come under the provisions of the EEC Treaty, payments also being a fundamental freedom of the Community, and the case was covered by Articles 59, 60 and 7 EEC (now 56, 57 and 18 TFEU).

Case 186/87 *Cowan* confirms that tourists travelling and receiving services bring themselves within the protection of EC law not to be discriminated against even in areas, as in the case itself, such as participation in the French criminal injuries compensation scheme.

13.3.1.2 Educational services

In **Case 293/83 *Gravier* v *City of Liège***, a decision to charge foreign students a fee for vocational training courses, but not nationals, was claimed to be contrary to Community law Articles 6, 59 and 128 EEC (now 18, 56 and 166 TFEU). This was upheld.

cross reference
*Grzelczyk is con-
sidered in section
13.3.2.*

It was confirmed in two subsequent cases, **Cases 24/86 *Blaizot* v *University of Liège*** and **263/86 *Belgium* v *Humbel***, that university study was, for the most part, vocational training in EC law terms and that Community nationals have a right to equal access to receive that under equal conditions as nationals even where fees were financed by the host state.

Note, though, that the judgments did not extend to establishing a right to scholarships and grants, although the *Grzelczyk* case may have altered the view on this.

In **Case C-281/98 *Angonese***, it was the activity of receiving educational services that triggered other citizenship rights including under Article 12 EC (now 18 TFEU), the right not to be discriminated against on the grounds of nationality.

Case C-109/92 *Wirth* involved a question from a German court regarding whether courses available in an institute of higher education had to be classified as services under Article 50 EC (now 57 TFEU). A German national was attempting to obtain a grant from German authorities to study in the Netherlands. The Court of Justice held that courses given in a university or institute of higher education that is financed essentially out of public funds do not constitute services within the meaning of Article 50 EC. However, it noted that many courses were financed by the students themselves paying fees, with the aims that the course generates profit; they could, in these circumstances, be regarded as coming within the concept of services.

In many countries, university fees have become the norm.

In **Case C-147/93 *Commission v Austria***, Austria was held to account for imposing more demanding entry conditions of university entry on other EU nationals in comparison with Austrian students that served to restrict access. The Court of Justice stressed the EU desire to promote the mobility of students and their right to receive education. The measure was not justified by the argument that, by not imposing stricter requirements, it would lead to a flood of non-Austrian students swamping the universities and resources because Austria had offered no evidence on this. The ECJ held that access to education under the same conditions was the very essence of the free movement of students.

The conclusions from this case law are that access to institutions and tuition fees are subject to EU law; the earlier judgments did not, however, extend to establishing a right to grants or other social assistance whilst studying. More recent case law, including the citizenship cases and in particular *Grzelczyk* and *Bidar*, seem to indicate that this is no longer the case.

In **Case C-209/03 *Bidar***, a French person residing in the UK decided to undertake study and applied for a student loan, which was refused on the grounds that Bidar was not 'settled' in the UK for the purposes of obtaining a student loan. The Court of Justice held that despite the previous case law, including the *Brown* and *Lair* cases, which excluded student maintenance grants from the scope of the Treaty, the introduction of the citizenship Article and a Chapter on education and training meant that student assistance can now be counted as falling within the scope of the Treaty. As such, then, as in the previous cases, Articles 12 and 18 EC (now 18 and 21 TFEU) in combination provided Bidar with the right to equal treatment in loans. However, in building on the *Collins* case, a member state could require a certain amount of integration before awarding a loan, but national laws that completely excluded the possibility of students from other member states of obtaining the status of a settled person would be incompatible with Article 12 EC (now 18 TFEU).

cross reference
Collins *is considered in section 13.3.4.2. See also Case C-403/03* Schempp *in section 13.1.*

13.3.1.3 Receiving services without movement

It is further suggested that the receipt of services can also be 'metaphysical', such as receiving services over the telephone or, more probable these days, over the Internet. Such argument does, of course, raise the question, not yet decided by the Court of Justice and certainly not express in any legislative provision, of whether receiving services in such a manner is within the concept of engaging in an economic activity. If the simple receipt of services, irrespective of the manner of delivery of these services, triggers the application of EU law, then it could be argued that potentially any receipt of services will do, regardless of how minimal, such as telephoning another country to obtain advice or other services or downloading advice packages from a computer server in another member state. The *de Coster* and *Mobistar* cases lend some support to this view that receiving metaphysical services will trigger EU law rights.

cross reference
de Coster *and*
Mobistar *are*
considered in
section 13.1.

In view of the ease by which EU law rights may be triggered for persons otherwise not entitled to those more extensive rights, the Advocates General (AGs) in the *Carpenter*, *Angonese* and *Collins* cases had suggested a new test to determine whether EU law is triggered, which relates specifically to the connection to the state of the person concerned. In other words, an economically determined level of activity could be set below which EU rights would not be triggered for the reason that the services received were marginal. The extent to which the Court of Justice took up this new test will be considered later in the chapter.

cross reference
See section 13.3.4.

The receipt of services will be governed also by the New Services Directive 2006/123, but which will not be considered further here.

13.3.2 **The general free movement Directives**

cross reference
See section 13.3.3.

The three general free movement Directives (Directives 90/364, 90/365 and 93/96) have now been repealed and replaced by Directive 2004/38 and are mentioned here only in respect of the case law generated by them. Indeed, the Directives were soon overtaken by the introduction of the citizenship rights and other developments in EC law. The Directives allowed for free movement not linked to an economic activity in the same way now as provided by the new Directive 2004/38. In place of an economic activity, proof of self-sufficiency is instead required (Article 71(b) of Directive 2004/38).

> The Court of Justice has confirmed, in **Case C-424/98 Commission v Italy**, that member states may ask for evidence of self-sufficiency, but cannot dictate what that evidence should consist of.

'Unreasonable' was the qualifying word used in the Preamble to the Directives rather than simply 'burden', which appeared in the Article itself. In other words, a reasonable burden on the state, particularly if temporary in nature, would be acceptable, which is a quite different matter and category.

cross reference
The Grzelczyk *case*
is considered in
further detail in
section 13.3.4.2.

> The Court of Justice held, in **Case C-184/99 Grzelczyk**, that it may be possible to make a claim on the social funds of a member state provided that the burden on the state is not unreasonable.

Not being an unreasonable burden is now contained in Article 14 of Directive 2004/38 in terms of retaining the right of residence.

The decision leaves open who should define reasonableness in similar circumstances. Is it a matter for the Court of Justice or the member states? Presumably, in line with the Court of Justice's comments in *Grzelczyk*, this would be within the member states courts' discretion.

> The Court of Justice has also considered Directive 90/364 in **Case C-413/99 *Baumbast***. It held, in view of the facts, that Baumbast and family were not a burden on UK social security. They had German insurance cover, albeit not for emergency treatment; therefore the requirement for all-risks insurance did not have to include emergency insurance, which the Court noted was provided as a matter of course in the UK.

The new Directive does not use 'unreasonable' in Article 7, but, as did the previous Directives, does include it in the Preamble and in Article 14 in respect of retaining an existing right of residence; thus the same ECJ qualification should apply.

13.3.3 **The Maastricht Treaty and European citizenship**

The Treaty on European Union (TEU) signed at Maastricht introduced a small section on European citizenship to the EC Treaty. It is now to be found in Article 20 TFEU.

> **Article 20 TFEU**
> ....
> Citizenship of the Union is hereby established. Every person holding the nationality of a member state shall be a citizen of the Union. Citizenship of the Union shall complement and not replace national citizenship.

Furthermore, Article 21 TFEU (ex 18 EC) provides as follows.

> **Article 21 TFEU**
> ....
> Every citizen of the Union shall have the right to move and reside freely within the territory of the Member States, subject to the limitations and conditions laid down in the Treaties and by the measures adopted to give them effect.

The rights provided by the Treaty under citizenship, as those under the earlier general free movement Directives, remove the economic activity requirement of the original free movement of persons regime. However, its true importance was not immediately obvious and has only become clearer as a result of Court of Justice judgments. It must also be noted that the right of residence under Article 21 TFEU (ex 18 EC) is still subject to the limitations and conditions laid down in the Treaty and by the measures adopted to give it effect – in other words, by limitations already in existence – and those that might be contained in future implementing measures.

cross reference

The general free movement Directives were considered in section 13.3.2.

13.3.3.1 The definition of 'citizenship'

The first matter to be considered is a definition of 'EU citizenship'. Article 21 TFEU provides this definition as based and dependent on the nationality of the member states. There can be no Union definition of European citizenship and the concept can be determined only as the collective definition of citizenship from all of the member states, as was made clear by the member states in a Declaration (No. 2) that was attached to the original TEU, but removed by the Lisbon Treaty. If a person is a national of a member state, then Articles 20 and 21 TFEU apply.

> Case C-135/08 *Rottmann v Bayern* considered whether the false/illegal acquisition of nationality nevertheless brought the person within the material scope of EU citizenship. Mr Rottmann, an Austrian had failed to reveal pending criminal proceedings when he applied and was granted German citizenship (which meant the loss of his Austrian citizenship). The revocation of the German citizenship would lead to him being stateless. The Court of Justice, not following the AG, held that EU did apply to him. The Court considered it had not interfered with the right of the member states to decide nationality themselves, but the consequence of withdrawing nationality by a state had the consequence that a once-enjoyed right, EU citizenship, was also lost.

cross reference
This is also considered in Chapter 12, section 12.2.1.

The Court rather fudged the decision, though, by concluding that, ultimately, it was up to the national court to decide whether the decision to withdraw citizenship was proportionate in view of both national law and the loss of EU citizenship, even if the citizenship was acquired by a lack of disclosure, but also in view of whether his original nationality could be recovered. Thus it remains thus uncertain whether under those circumstances whether and how EU citizenship can then be lost.

The scope and restrictions of citizenship rights need then to be determined. Article 21 TFEU is subject to restrictions on the grounds of public policy, security and health, which are stated in Article 45 TFEU (ex 39 EC) and now clarified in Articles 27–29 of Directive 2004/38.

13.3.4 Case law on the citizenship Articles

The earliest case law in which Articles 17 and 18 EC (now 20 and 21 TFEU) were raised are not considered in this volume because they simply acknowledge the Articles and do not help us to understand their true importance. The first significant cases establish that citizenship provides a right of continued residence and a link to other rights, notably the right not to be discriminated against on the grounds of nationality contained in Article 12 EC (now 18 TFEU). Subsequent case law demonstrates that further rights can be realized in a number of areas (as are considered in the following sections) in which the protection from discrimination now under Article 18 TFEU is the key factor in the citizenship cases.

13.3.4.1 Non-discrimination and residence rights

> In **Case C-274/96 *Criminal Proceedings v Bickel and Franz***, Article 18 EC (now 21 TFEU) was upheld as a right that could be pleaded in support of other rights, in this case to support the view that the refusal to allow Germans the use of German in the Italian South Tirol courts would be contrary to Article 12 EC. German-speaking Italian citizens of Austrian extract in South Tirol were allowed to use German. Two German nationals, Bickel and Franz, had lawfully entered Italy under Article 49 EC (now 56 TFEU), but were not allowed to conduct their case in German in court proceedings.

> In **Case C-413/99 *Baumbast***, Mr Baumbast, a German national, was self-employed in the UK, where he resided with his Colombian wife and two children, who were being educated in the UK. He was subsequently employed by a German company and worked outside the EU. His family remained in the UK. Their residence permits were not renewed, however, and Mrs Baumbast and the children faced deportation. The case was referred to the Court of

Justice, which emphasized the right of children of EU nationals under Regulation 1612/68 to continue their education even if the worker, from whom their rights derived, was no longer working. The Court of Justice further held that the text of the Treaty does not permit the conclusion that citizens of the Union who have lawfully established themselves in another member state as an employed person are deprived, where that activity comes to an end, of the rights that are conferred on them by virtue of that citizenship.

In the most important statement of the judgment, the Court of Justice held that this right to stay under Article 18(1) EC (now 20 TFEU) is conferred directly on every citizen of the Union by a clear and precise provision of the EC Treaty. Purely as a national of a member state, and consequently a citizen of the Union, Mr Baumbast therefore had the right to rely on Article 18(1) EC. The Court held (at [94]):

> The answer to the first part of the third question must therefore be that a citizen of the European Union who no longer enjoys a right of residence as a migrant worker in the host member state can, as a citizen of the Union, enjoy a right of residence by direct application of Article 18(1) EC.

Subsequent Court of Justice judgments also show how the Court of Justice has upheld and extended the no discrimination rule into welfare and family rights.

13.3.4.2 Welfare rights

The citizenship cases appear to go further than intended by the EU legislation by establishing welfare benefits rights of EU citizens who were not supposed to be a burden on the host member state. They do, however, show the Union to be concerned with the welfare rights of EU citizens over national concerns about the possible drain on national resources.

In **Case C-85/96 *María Martínez Sala* v *Freistaat Bayern***, Sala, a Spanish national who had worked in Germany for many years, lost her job, but remained in Germany with social assistance from 1989. Her residence permit had expired, but the German authorities supplied her with certificates stating that she had applied for an extension to her permit. The authorities refused her a child allowance because she did not have a valid residence permit, which she claimed was contrary to Article 12 EC (now 18 TFEU) because German nationals were not subject to the same condition. Her status as a worker was not determined, but the Court of Justice held that, in any event, she was lawfully resident in Germany. Sala thus came within the personal scope of Treaty citizenship and that (old) Article 8(2) EC (now 21 TFEU) citizenship triggered other rights, including, most importantly, Article 12 EC, the right not to be discriminated against according to nationality. This, in consequence, included the right to receive, on equal terms, social welfare benefits, including the non-contributory child allowance, the subject matter of the case.

Note that there was no discussion in the case as to whether the past employment could have been used as the trigger or possible justification to support the claim for welfare rights.

In **Case C-184/99 *Grzelczyk***, a French national, who studied and worked on a part-time basis to help support himself for three years in Belgium, applied at the beginning of his fourth and final year of study to the *Centre Public d'Action Sociale* [the Public Social Welfare Centre] (CPAS), for payment of the minimex, a non-contributory minimum subsistence allowance. The CPAS granted Mr Grzelczyk the minimex, but then later denied this on the basis that he was not Belgian; hence clear discrimination on the grounds of nationality. The Court did not determine the possible status as a worker, but nevertheless held that the citizenship rights enable Union citizens to be treated equally. The Court of Justice emphasized the new citizenship provisions and new competences, albeit limited, in education (Articles 3(1)(q) and 149(2) EC, now 6 and 165 TFEU). Those, it reasoned, allowed it to rule that Articles 12 and 17 EC (now 18 and 20 TFEU) preclude discrimination as regards the grant of a non-contributory social benefit to Union citizens where they are lawfully resident, even though not economically active.

In **Case C-224/98 *D'Hoop***, a Belgian national had studied in France. She was refused a tide-over allowance between study and work granted to nationals by the Belgian authorities because she had studied in another member state. The Court of Justice had held that the tide-over allowance was a social advantage under Article 7(2) of Regulation 1612/68, but to take advantage of it the person must either have participated in the employment market or obtained a derived right in some way. She was not a worker and her parents had remained in Belgium; therefore she had no rights in her own right nor derived rights from the parents. The Court of Justice referred to the new contribution to education by the EC in encouraging mobility of students and teachers (Articles 3(1)(q) and 149(2) EC, now 6 and 165 TFEU)) and, citing *Grzelczyk* at [31], held that it would be incompatible with the right of freedom of movement if a citizen who had taken advantage of free movement then suffered discrimination with regard to a social benefit right as a consequence.

The Court held that such inequality of treatment is contrary to the principles that underpin the status of citizen of the Union – that is, the guarantee of the same treatment in law in the exercise of the citizen's freedom to move. The condition at issue could be justified only if it were based on objective considerations independent of the nationality of the persons concerned and were proportionate to the legitimate aim of the national provisions [35]–[36]). The Belgian authorities offered none; hence the limiting of places of education that qualify for the tide-over allowance, according to the Court of Justice, went beyond what is necessary to attain the objective pursued.

In the *Collins* case, the claim to welfare rights appears to have been made subject to a close connection test.

In **Case C-138/02 *Collins* v *Secretary of State for Work and Pensions***, Collins entered the UK in 1998 on an Irish passport to seek work. He claimed an income-based jobseeker's allowance on the strength of ten months' part-time work that he had undertaken as an American citizen from 1980 to 1981. The UK authorities refused the benefit on the grounds that he was not habitually resident in the UK. Collins claimed that this was discrimination because nationals were advantaged by automatically satisfying the time period required, whereas other Community nationals would have to fulfil this extra requirement. The Court of Justice held that it was permissible for member states first to require that there be a genuine link between the work seeker and the state for the purposes of claiming a jobseeker's allowance. There was indirect discrimination in that nationals could far more easily establish this link, but it was objectively justified as the jobseeker's allowance was designed to reduce national unemployment for those living long-term in the UK.

The link requirement was confirmed in the next case, which, however, also confirms that, where appropriate, welfare rights can be claimed by EU citizens.

In **Case C-256/04 *Ioannidis***, a Greek national had spent three years in Belgium obtaining a graduate diploma, followed by a training course in France, and, on his return to Belgium to look for work, claimed a tide-over allowance (as in the *D'Hoop* case). This was refused on the grounds that he had not completed secondary education in Belgium or pursued education of the same level in another member state and was not the dependent child of a migrant worker residing in Belgium. The ECJ held that Ioannidis fell within the scope of Article 39 EC (now 45 TFEU) whilst seeking work and that, according to the citizenship provisions of the Treaty, under certain conditions, financial assistance cannot be denied to Union citizens. In line with the *Collins* case, the Court of Justice acknowledged that a link with the employment market could be required, but the fact that Ioannidis had completed a diploma in Belgium had already provided such a link.

In **Case C-406/04 *De Cuyper***, a Belgian national claimed unemployment benefit, but moved to France whilst continuing to claim. Once that information was revealed to the authorities, his claim was denied on the grounds that he was not in residence. The ECJ held that the requirement to reside in Belgium whilst claiming was contrary to Article 18 EC (now 21 TFEU), but that Article 18 EC (now 21 TFEU) breaches can be objectively justified. In this case, the public interest of being able to verify and monitor the right to benefit, which would be very difficult or impossible to do if the claimant were not in the country, was held to be proportionate.

In **Cases C-11–12/06 *Morgan and Bucher***, two students moved to study abroad, but claimed the benefits to do so from their home state, which demanded that they study in the home state for at least one year. This would add a considerable disincentive by adding a year or at best complicating studies, but was insisted on by the home state to establish a clear link to the state for the purposes of receiving the benefit. The ECJ approved a need to demonstrate a sufficient level of integration with the home state in line with its previous case law. However, it held that, in the cases before it, that need was satisfied because both persons were raised and schooled in the home state. Consequently, the home state could not demand that they study there first for one year.

The *Förster* case now appears not only to confirm *Collins*, but also to roll back slightly the previous generous interpretation of an individual's rights.

Case C-158/07 *Förster* v *IB-Groep* concerns Ms Förster, a German national in the Netherlands, who, from 2000, worked from time to time there and qualified for a study maintenance grant, but which was withdrawn when the responsible authority (IB-Groep) discovered in 2003 that she was no longer working. Her challenge to the decision failed on the grounds she was not sufficiently integrated in the Netherlands and that she had not satisfied the requirement of five years' residence in Holland. On reference to the Court of Justice, it upheld its previous decision in Case C-209/03 *Bidar* that member states were entitled to require a certain degree of integration and, in this case, a five-year period was justified and proportionate.

In **Cases C-22 and 23/08 *Vatsouras and Koupatantze* v *ARGE Nürnberg***, the Court of Justice was asked to consider the rights to social welfare in some circumstances under

Articles 18 and 21 TFEU and the ability of member states under Article 24 of Directive 2004/38 to deny social welfare to EU migrants jobseekers and their families. The Court held, in view of the Treaty Articles and previous case law, that, provided that the EU citizens can establish a genuine link with the host state, then a jobseeker's allowance should be available and was not to be regarded as a social assistance purely, which could be excluded under the Directive. The link must nevertheless be established.

Thus, as far as welfare rights' entitlement is concerned, the economic status of the person – that is, whether a worker or self-employed or even a previous worker or self-employed – is no longer an important factor. Provided that there is movement in some way, even back to the home state or lawful residence in the host state, EU citizens will be entitled to be treated without discrimination compared to nationals. This is the situation now in cases concerning a variety of claims, the only limitation appearing to be the requirement in some cases, according to circumstances, of a close link between the person seeking benefit and the host states or a period of residence requirement, as in the *Collins, Ioannidis, Morgan and Bucher* and *Förster* cases.

The next cases are concerned, for the most part, with non-EU citizens, but who are family members of an EU citizen. There is a degree of overlap with the cases considered in relation to TCNs and welfare rights, because members of the family are also those claiming additional rights.

13.3.4.3 Family and carer rights

cross reference
Also considered in section 13.1.

These cases, in which a greater respect for family life has emerged, are also a product of the move from regarding free movement rights in the EU legal order as wholly dependent on the pursuit of an economic activity to recognizing rights that are based on citizenship combined with fundamental freedoms and residence.

In **Case C-60/00** *Carpenter*, the Court of Justice was more concerned with family rights than arguments about what was the legal basis of the lawful residence of TCN members of the family. The Court of Justice referred to Article 49 EC (now 56 TFEU) and Regulation 1612/68, which, read strictly, did not apply to the provision of services. These provisions, according to the Court of Justice, provide rules protecting the family life of nationals of the member states in order to eliminate obstacles to the exercise of the fundamental freedoms guaranteed by the Treaty. The Court held (at [39]):

It is clear that the separation of Mr and Mrs Carpenter would be detrimental to their family life and, therefore, to the conditions under which Mr Carpenter exercises a fundamental freedom. That freedom could not be fully effective if Mr Carpenter were to be deterred from exercising it by obstacles raised in his country of origin to the entry and residence of his spouse.

The Court of Justice considered that the rights of residence could be subject to objective restrictions, but which must comply with fundamental rights and (at [42]–[43]) that:

The decision to deport Mrs Carpenter constitutes an interference with the exercise by Mr Carpenter of his right to respect for his family life within the meaning of Article 8 of the Convention for the Protection of Human Rights and Fundamental Freedoms and does not strike a fair balance between the competing interests, that is, on the one hand, the right of Mr Carpenter to respect for his family life, and, on the other hand, the maintenance of public order and public safety.

cross reference

Considered also in section 13.2.3.

In **Case C-413/99 Baumbast and R v Home Office**, the UK authorities wanted to deport the American national, R. However, because her children had a right to remain and to pursue, under the best possible conditions, their education in the host member state, the Court of Justice reasoned that this necessarily implies that those children have the right to be accompanied by the person who is their primary carer. Accordingly, that person is able to reside with the children in that member state during their studies. To refuse to grant permission to remain to a parent who is the primary carer of the child exercising his or her right to pursue his or her studies in the host member state infringes that right.

The Court of Justice held that Regulation 1612/68, interpreted in the light of Article 8 ECHR, entitled the parent who is the primary carer of those children, irrespective of nationality, to reside with them in order to facilitate the exercise of that right, notwithstanding the fact that the parents have meanwhile divorced. The ECJ considered that the fact that only one parent is a citizen of the Union and that parent has ceased to be a migrant worker in the host member state and that the children are not themselves citizens of the Union were irrelevant in this regard.

This derived right stems this time not directly from the worker, but from the children of the worker, who are themselves recipients of derived rights. This could be termed 'indirect derived rights'.

A further case that provides express support for family life is **Case C-459/99 *MRAX***, which involves the challenge by an interest group to the Belgian authorities' application of Community law in respect of the visa requirements for TCN family members. Certainly, according to Article 3 of Directive 68/360 (now repealed), member states were entitled to demand a visa from the TCN family members. The Court of Justice reasoned (at [53]) that it is apparent, in particular from the Council Regulations and Directives on freedom of movement for employed and self-employed persons within the Community, that the Community legislature has recognized the importance of ensuring protection for the family life of nationals of the member states in order to eliminate obstacles to the exercise of the fundamental freedoms guaranteed by the Treaty. In this light, the Court of Justice considered (at [61]) that it is, in any event, disproportionate and therefore prohibitive to send back a TCN married to a national of a member state not in possession of a valid visa where he or she is able to prove his or her identity and the conjugal ties, and there is no evidence to establish that he or she represents a risk to the requirements of public policy, public security or public health within the meaning of Article 10 of Directive 68/360 and Article 8 of Directive 73/148.

 These aspects are now covered by Articles 27–33 of Directive 2004/38.

Hence, then, the right to a family life protected by Article 8 ECHR has been instrumental in achieving far-reaching judgments on the rights of family members of Union citizens and clearly beyond any strict interpretation of EU law rights.

Case C-109/01 *Akrich* also concerns Article 8 ECHR, which, if the marriage in the case were determined to be genuine, would be taken into account when considering the importance of the unlawful residence of the TCN seeking to stay in the UK, although the Court of Justice attached no actual weight to the consideration that must be given.

cross reference
Jia and Metock *are considered in section 13.2.*

The cases of *Jia* and *Metock*, also concerned with TCNs and marriage, have reinforced the weight given to family life, which, unless an abuse of fraud is present, entitles TCN family members to lawfully remain with their EU spouses in a host or home member state.

Finally in this section is a case that took the protection of EU law for the family to remarkable lengths.

In **Case C-200/02 *Chen***, the EU citizen concerned was Catherine, the newborn daughter of a Chinese national, Mrs Chen, who was visiting the UK with her husband and who went to Belfast to give birth to Catherine. Under Irish law, any person born in any part of the island of Ireland can acquire Irish nationality and Catherine was subsequently issued with an Irish passport. It was noted as a matter of record by the ECJ that this factual situation was deliberately engineered in order for the child to get EU citizenship and so that the parents could subsequently acquire a right to reside in the UK. The parents were financially self-sufficient with full private medical insurance, but their application for UK long-term residence permits had been rejected. The UK and Ireland had contended that no Community law rights should arise because there had been no movement and Catherine was not exercising any Community law rights. It was already clear that the conferring of nationality was a matter for the member states. In other words, the conferring of Irish nationality and thus EU citizenship was beyond challenge in the UK. The ECJ concluded that Article 18 EC (now 21 TFEU) and Directive 90/364 confer a right to reside for an indefinite period on a young minor who is a national of a member state, and who is covered by appropriate sickness insurance and is in the care of a parent who is a TCN having sufficient resources for that minor not to become a burden on the public finances of the host member state in that state. In such circumstances, those same provisions allow a parent who is that minor's primary carer to reside with the child in the host member state.

---

cross reference
See Chapter 12, section 12.2.1, for more on Declaration No. 2.

The judgment is quite ironic because the member states expressly reserved the definition of nationality to themselves in Declaration No. 2 previously attached to the EC Treaty. Hence, once national rules had been complied with, other member states could not question the rights under EU law that arose as a consequence. The case escaped the fate of being determined as wholly internal, even though no movement out of an EU state had taken place. The particular legal circumstances of this case are no longer in place in that Ireland has withdrawn its generous nationality provision.

However, in **Case C-34/09 *Zambrano* v *ONEM***, Zambrano and his wife, Colombian nationals seeking asylum in Belgium, had two children in Belgium who acquired Belgian nationality; their own applications for Belgium residence had, though, been rejected. In the national court reviewing that decision, they asked whether Articles 12, 17 and 18 EC (now 18, 20 and 21 TFEU) confer rights of residence in the state in which the EU citizen was born. Despite interventions by member states that the situation was wholly internal and thus beyond the scope of EU law, the ECJ held that Article 20 TFEU did indeed prevent a member state from denying residence to the parents (and carers) of an EU citizen by reason of the fact that the EU citizen dependant would otherwise be denied full exercise of his or her rights, including most importantly the right to reside in the EU and thus to exercise all of his or her rights under EU law.

Thus the Court (and the AG before it) upheld the sanctity of EU citizenship once acquired, in the face of member state objections.

More palatable to the member states would be the ruling in **Case-434/09** *McCarthy*, which followed shortly after the *Zambrano* ruling. An EU citizen born and living exclusively in the UK with British and Irish nationality was denied residence based on EU law. She had hoped to obtain that residence so that her Jamaican husband could also obtain residence under the Treaty and Directive 2004/38. The ECJ this time rejected those claims as not being based on the exercise of any movement by a national of the state in which the rights were claimed. The Court did distinguish the case from *Zambrano* on the ground that there was no fear that she would have to leave the state or residence.

The cases, *Zambrano* in particular, appear to reduce even further the concept of 'wholly internal'.

13.3.4.4 Citizenship law summary

In summary, the citizenship law, as developed through the cases by the Court of Justice, would appear to be as follows. Article 21 TFEU (ex 18 EC) has been declared to be directly effective and it can be activated in favour of EU citizens by:

- exhausted free movement rights – that is, those once enjoyed by a member state national and which gained him or her lawful entrance and residence in the host state when exercised, but which no longer are or can be relied upon because of changed circumstances (as in the *Baumbast*, *Sala* and *Grzelczyk* cases);

- the movement to another member state to receive services, which movement then triggers the general rights of citizenship even when the EU citizen returns to his or her home state (as in the *D'Hoop* and *Ioannidis* cases); and

- acquisition of nationality of one of the member states (*Chen*), each of which has its own rules for this.

Citizenship rights obtained then further serve to protect the family of the EU citizens in circumstances that previously might have led to the expulsion of a member of the family (as in the *Chen*, *MRAX* and *Baumbast and R* cases).

Whilst the right of residence under Article 21 TFEU (ex 18 EC) continues, according to the Court of Justice, to be subject to the restrictions inherent in the Treaty and Directive 2004/38, Articles 20 and 21 TFEU (ex 17 and 18 EC) appear, according to the Court of Justice, to ensure that, provided that union citizens are lawfully resident in a host state, this will trigger citizenship rights, the most important of which are not the political rights contained in Article 22 TFEU (ex 19 EC), but the general right to be treated without discrimination compared to nationals. However, a clear definition of what constitutes 'lawful residence' is thus far missing in EU law, with the judgments of the Court of Justice in *Sala* and *Grzelczyk* suggesting that, provided that an EU citizen had a lawful right to enter the host state in the first place and has not done anything to endanger his or her residence subsequently, the right to remain continues.

In *Grzelczyk*, the Court of Justice held that its judgment does not, however, prevent a member state from taking the view that a student who has recourse to social assistance no longer fulfils the conditions of his or her right of residence or from taking measures, within the limits imposed by EU law, either to withdraw his or her residence permit or not to renew it.

Nevertheless, in no situation may such measures have the automatic consequence that a student who is a national of another member state requiring recourse to the host member state's social assistance system is required to leave as a matter of fact. This would seem to suggest that if a member state does decide to withdraw the status of lawful residence, the member state would be entitled to deport the student. Such a decision is subject to proportionality and the review of the Court of Justice.

> For a review of the right of member states to determine whether EU citizens can or cannot remain in the UK, see the previous case law of **Cases 159/79 *R* v *Pieck*** and **C-292/89 *Antonissen***, in which, respectively, the Court of Justice held that deportation of Pieck would be disproportionate and thus contrary to EC law, whereas Antonissen could be deported.

Hence it would seem that previous case law provides us with a workable model of how we decide lawful residence. A deportation that could be condoned by the Court of Justice would remove lawful residence and with it, of course, any entitlement to rights in the host state.

Summary

This chapter considered the extension of free movement rights, which affected three main areas: wholly internal situations; the position of TCNs; and the extension of free movement rights into European citizenship.

Whilst any true wholly internal situation would exclude the validity of the application of EU law, the case law on this and on the receipt of services mean that even a fairly low level of activity, or even potential activity, as in the *de Coster* case, can turn a wholly internal matter into a EU matter.

We have seen through the case law that TCNs may derive rights from their EU family members, including children. Even where the children are non-EU nationals, but who nevertheless have rights of their own to stay in the host state, as in the case of *R*, EU nationals and TCN family members can derive further rights from those children to stay in the host state. With regard to the rights of free-standing TCNs, lawfully resident in the member states, EU law developments in free movement and citizenship appear to add even more pressure for legal reform to bring their rights into line.

Where citizenship rights are established through lawful residence, Article 18 TFEU applies, and if an EU citizen is lawfully resident in another member state, there is no requirement to be economically active to be entitled to equal treatment, including, for example, equal treatment in non-contributory welfare benefits on the same basis as nationals. It is even possible to be a burden on the state, albeit a reasonable one only, as in *Grzelczyk*.

It would seem that EU citizens who do not move at any time to another member state to receive or provide services are the only ones unable to obtain these welfare and family rights unless provided for under national law.

It is clear that the legal regime regulating the free movement of persons has come a long way from the near-empty and little-used original Treaty provision for it. It is ironic, then, that, at the present stage of the evolution of free movement rights, the concern is whether those rights have now actually gone too far and encroached too much on areas of the member states' own national laws more than is universally acceptable. For example, does EU citizenship and the right not to be discriminated against apply to rule out all discrimination against host EU citizens in comparison with nationals in all areas of law? Does an unemployed tourist on holiday receive services? If so, do these activate Article 20 TFEU citizenship rights? Again, if so, does this then trigger the general right of equal treatment – that is, the right to obtain benefits on the same basis as nationals if, for the sake of argument, he or she runs short of money whilst on holiday? These dangers of an over-expansive interpretation of EU law may now mean that EU citizens who have established lawful residence in a host state will have equal rights to the full spectrum of contributory and non-contributory social benefits, and that, as such, the spectre of 'benefit tourism' has effectively been raised whereby EU nationals and their TCN family members can roam the member states in search of the 'good life'. Recent case law, however, has suggested that there is a limit to this that the member states can control by requiring a close connection to the state or a period of residence requirement, as in the *Collins*, *Ioannidis* and *Förster* cases.

 These issues are considered in some of the articles noted in the end-of-chapter Further reading list.

However, as is often the case with the very dynamic system of law that we have with EU law, the burning questions with which we are left will only be answered by either the Court of Justice in future cases or by the intervention of the member states.

Questions

1 What is meant by 'reverse discrimination'?

2 What is the 'wholly internal rule'?

3 Is European citizenship to be equated with European nationality?

4 It seems, following the case law on citizenship, that it is no longer necessary actively to engage in an economic activity to trigger valuable EU law rights. What will now trigger those rights?

For suggested approaches to answering these questions scan here or visit the Online Resource Centre.

Further reading

BOOKS

Barnard, C. *The Substantive Law of the EU: The Four Freedoms*, 3rd edn, Oxford University Press, Oxford, 2010 (chapters 15 and 17).

Shaw, J. *The Transformation of Citizenship in the European Union*, Cambridge University Press, Cambridge, 2007.

ARTICLES

Cousins, M. 'Citizenship, residence and social security' (2007) 32 EL Rev 386.

Dougan, M. 'The constitutional dimension to the case law on Union citizenship' (2006) 31 EL Rev 613.

Foster, N. 'Family and welfare rights in Europe: the impact of recent European Court of Justice decisions in the area of the free movement of persons' (2003) 25 J Soc Wel & Fam L 291.

Hailbronner, J. 'Union citizenship and access to social benefits' (2005) 42 CML Rev 1245.

Hofstoetter, B. 'A cascade of rights, or who shall care for little Catherine? Some reflections on the *Chen* case' (2005) 30 EL Rev 548.

Jacobs, F. 'Citizenship of the European Union: a legal analysis' (2007) 13 ELJ 1591.

Jacqueson, C. 'Union citizenship and the Court of Justice: something new under the sun? Towards social citizenship' (2002) 27 EL Rev 260.

Kocharov, A. 'What intra-Community mobility for third-country workers?' (2008) 33(6) EL Rev 913.

Kostakopoulou, D. 'European Union citizenship: writing the future' (2007) 13(5) ELJ 623.

Kunoy, B. 'A union of national citizens: the origins of the Court's lack of avantgardisme in the *Chen* case' (2006) 43(1) CML Rev 179.

Mather, J. 'The Court of Justice and the Union citizen' (2005) 11 ELJ 722.

Newdick, C. 'Citizenship, free movement and health care: cementing individual rights by corroding social solidarity' (2006) 43 CML Rev 1645.

Peers, S. 'Implementing equality? The Directive on long-term resident third-country nationals' (2004) 29 EL Rev 437.

Reich, N. 'The constitutional relevance of citizenship and free movement in an enlarged Union' (2005) 11 ELJ 675.

Reich, N. and Harbacevica, S. 'Citizenship and family on trial: a fairly optimistic overview of recent court practice with regard to free movement of persons' (2003) 40 CML Rev 615.

Shuibhne, N. 'Free movement of persons and the wholly internal rule: time to move on?' (2003) 39 CML Rev 731.

Tryfonidou, A. 'In search of the aim of the EC free movement of persons provisions: has the Court of Justice missed the point? (2009) 46 CML Rev 1591.

Further reading

367

Discrimination law

Learning objectives

In this chapter, you will learn about:

- why the discrimination provisions were originally included in the EC Treaty;

- the main legislative provisions on discrimination law and, in particular, sex discrimination law;

- the basic scope of the main Treaty provision, Article 157 TFEU;

- the meaning of 'equal pay for equal work' and 'work of equal value';

- the concepts of indirect discrimination and how comparison is made;

- equal treatment, especially relating to pregnancy and childbirth; and

- principal aspects of other discrimination law.

Introduction

For more details
on this section
scan here or
visit the Online
Resource Centre.

Although discrimination law in the European Union (EU) legal order has broadened out into other areas outside of its base in discrimination on the grounds of nationality and sex, this chapter focuses mainly on sex discrimination law, which is the subject of study in many law schools, rather than a wider study of general equality or non-discrimination law. This chapter will, however, also include an overview of other forms of laws to combat discrimination as a result of the expansion of what can be termed 'EU equality law' or 'equal treatment law' in the EU legal order, for example race, age, or sexual orientation. In particular, Article 19 TFEU and the legislation enacted thereunder will be considered.

There are a number of examples of express prohibitions of discrimination on different grounds within the Treaty, but there is not, as such, an express general principle of non-discrimination or equality in the Treaty. The specific prohibitions do, however, support the emergence of a general principle in the EU legal order that is additionally supported by the judgments of the Court of Justice and academic commentary. The Treaty Articles that seek either to prohibit discrimination or promote equality on the grounds are:

- Articles 2 and 3 TEU on equality between men and women;
- Article 8 TFEU (ex 3 EC);
- new Article 10 TFEU;
- Article 18 TFEU (ex 12 EC) on nationality;
- Article 19 TFEU (ex 13 EC) on the general power to prohibit discrimination across a range of issues;
- Article 40(2) TFEU (ex 34(2) EC) concerned with equality between producers and between consumers in the Common Agricultural Policy (CAP);
- Articles 45, 49 and 56 TFEU (ex 39, 43, and 50 EC) providing for equal treatment of workers and the self-employed;
- Article 106 TFEU (ex 86 EC) on public undertakings;
- Article 110 TFEU (ex 90 EC) on taxation;
- Article 153 TFEU (ex 137 EC) on the promotion of equality of men and women in the work environment; and
- Article 157 TFEU (ex 141 EC) on equal pay and now the promotion of equality between the sexes.

Without going into details, all of these Articles support the development of a general principle of equality by the establishment of a legal culture that does not tolerate the different treatment of like or the same treatment of unequals across a range of subject matters. Added to these now, since the Lisbon Treaty, is the Charter on Fundamental Rights, which hasprovided a section (Articles 20–23) prohibiting discrimination an any ground and which will be considered at the end of this chapter. Hence the existence and value of a general principle of equal treatment has been acknowledged and confirmed by the Court of Justice in a number of cases: recently, for example, in Case C-149/10 *Chatzi*, in which the Court held that the principle of equal treatment is one of the general principles of EU law and is now affirmed by Article 20 of the EU Charter of Fundamental Rights (in that case, to support the right to parental leave on an equal basis).

Apart from discrimination in the area of free movement of persons, which was considered in Chapters 12 and 13, this final chapter of the text will consider sex or gender discrimination in depth only, but provide an overview of the new developing areas of discrimination law at its end. Before looking in depth at sex discrimination provisions, the reasons for its inclusion will be discussed.

Reasons for the original inclusion of sex discrimination in the Treaty

The inclusion of prohibitions of discrimination in other Articles of the Treaties can be quite readily understood because they all relate, more or less, to nationality and therefore go to the very foundation of the establishment of the Union – that is, the removal of national barriers to the establishment of the internal market. Nationality should not play a role in the free movement of goods, persons or capital. Non-discrimination on the grounds of sex, however, is less readily understandable in this context. On the face of it, it would appear to be essentially a socially based discrimination and not economic.

thinking point
What do the classic freedom of movement of rights provisions require to trigger the rights that the prohibition of discrimination does not?

It was, however, originally framed in the EC Treaty as a form of workplace-based discrimination. It is helpful and informative to go back to the drafting of the EEC Treaty to see why what has clearly become a social law right was included in the EU in the first place. Additionally, and viewed in the context of the initial, more limited aims of the original Communities to eliminate discrimination based on nationality, there is an odd feature to sex discrimination law.

The right not to be discriminated against on the grounds of sex does not require a cross-state border or Union context. There needs to be no movement between member states, unlike the fundamental freedoms, goods, persons and capital, which do. EU sex discrimination law is applicable in wholly internal situations. Given the original more economic nature of the Community, the European Community (EC) then would seem an unlikely source of women's equality rights. Fundamentally, the EC was a vehicle to promote economic integration and development of the member states, rather than to provide equality between the sexes. However, it is now generally accepted that the immediate reason for including

Article 119 in the EEC Treaty (now 157 TFEU) was not for reasons of social justice, but out of economic considerations – that is, the creation of level playing fields for industry in terms of the application of national social laws. The Article was alleged to have been included at the request of the French, whose law provided for equality of pay between male and female workers. It was feared that French industry would be at a disadvantage if equal pay were not enforced in the other member states, in particular Germany, the post-war workforce of which relied far more heavily on women workers. Regardless of the exact underlying motive, its inclusion would appear to be based on economic arguments the aim which was to ensure that similar economic conditions apply in all of the member states. There appears to be no social justification for its inclusion, but we do have the chance to see a Court of Justice view on the matter.

In **Case 43/75 *Defrenne* v *Sabena (No. 2)***, the Court of Justice declared that Article 119 EEC also forms part of the social objectives of the Community, which is not merely an economic Union, but is at the same time intended, by common action, to ensure social progress and to seek the constant improvement of the living and working conditions of their peoples, as is emphasized by the Preamble to the Treaty. It held that this double aim, which is at once economic and social, shows that the principle of equal pay forms part of the foundations of the Community.

Hence, it was regarded in 1976 as one part of a double aim and was even promoted in subsequent judgments.

In **Case 149/77 *Defrenne* v *Sabena (No. 3)***, a couple of years later, the Court of Justice declared the elimination of discrimination based on sex as part of the fundamental rights within Community law.

More recently, the Court of Justice has confirmed in **Cases C-324 and 325/96 *Deutsche Telekom* v *Vick*** and **C-50/96 *Deutsche Telekom* v *Schröder*** that the social aims of Article 119 EEC (now 141 TFEU) prevail over the economic aims.

It must be concluded that the economic aim pursued by Article 119 EC, namely the elimination of distortions of competition between undertakings established in different member states, is secondary to the social aim pursued by the same provision, which constitutes the expression of a fundamental human right.

Article 119 EC (now 157 TFEU) was the sole original provision for the EC to concern itself with sex discrimination. In contrast, there now exists a considerable body of EU law on the subject, in the form of Treaty additions introduced notably by the Treaty of Amsterdam, a growing body of EU Directives and the very many progressive decisions of the Court of Justice.

14.1 **The legislative framework**

For more details on this section scan here or visit the Online Resource Centre.

14.1.1 Treaty Articles

Article 157 TFEU (ex 119 EEC and 141 EC) on equal pay for equal work originally provided the only specific mention of equal treatment of the sexes in the EC Treaty, but, following amendments by the Treaty of Amsterdam, Treaty references to the promotion of equality are more extensive. In addition to the main Treaty Article, Article 157 TFEU (ex 141 EC), the Treaty of Amsterdam introduced as one of the goals now outlined in Article 2 TEU, 'equality between men and women', and Article 3 TEU states the aim 'to promote . . . equality, between men and women'.

Equality between men and women in the working environment was also included in the 1989 Community Social Charter, which was brought into Article 136 EC (now 151 TFEU). The amended Article 137 EC (now 153 TFEU) provides that, inter alia, the Union shall complement and support the activities of the member states in the field of equality between men and women with regard to labour market opportunities and treatment at work.

Article 157 TFEU was expanded beyond its simple original provision to ensure that men and women should receive equal pay for equal work. The Treaty of Amsterdam amended and added two sentences to locate within a Treaty base the principles of equal pay for work of equal value and action to promote equality, but which falls short of out-and-out positive discrimination.

 These rights were previously contained in Directives only, which meant that they could not give rise to direct effects against other individuals.

cross reference
For a full consideration of the direct effect of Directives, see Chapter 8, section 8.1.3.3.

cross reference
Article 19 will be considered briefly at section 14.6.

Finally, as far as the Treaties are concerned, a new enabling power has been provided in Article 19 TFEU (ex 13 EC), which provides:

> the Council, acting unanimously in accordance with a special legislative procedure and after obtaining the consent of the European Parliament, may take appropriate action to combat discrimination based on sex, racial or ethnic origin, religion or belief, disability, age or sexual orientation.

Added to the Treaty Articles now must be included the section in the EU Charter of Fundamental Rights, Articles 20–23, which prohibits discrimination on any grounds in Article 21. It is starting to be referred to by the Court of Justice and will no doubt feature much more in case law in the future.

cross reference
These Charter Articles are considered in section 14.6.1.4.

14.1.2 Secondary legislation

The first secondary legislative interventions in this area were enacted following the publication of a social action programme in 1974 by the Commission. Three Directives concerned with equality between men and women were adopted:

- the Equal Pay Directive 75/117;
- the Equal Treatment Directive 76/207; and
- the Social Security Directive 79/7.

 A second social action programme was commenced in 1982, which led to the enactment of Directive 86/378 on equal treatment in occupational pensions and Directive 86/613

on equal treatment of the self-employed and protection of self-employed women during pregnancy and motherhood (and now replaced by Directive 2010/41).

Following the amendment of the EC Treaty by the Single European Act (SEA) in 1986, another action programme was launched in 1989 and resulted in the enactment of the Pregnancy and Maternity Directive 92/85.

The new initiatives introduced by the Maastricht Treaty led to the enactment of further Directives, including the Parental Leave Directive 96/34, repealed and replaced now by Directive 2010/18, the Burden of Proof in Sex Discrimination Cases Directive 97/80 and the Part-time Workers Directive 97/81.

While the last Directive is not directly aimed at addressing sex discrimination, it will have this effect becuase it aims to reduce the inequality between full-time workers and part-time workers, the majority of whom are women and thus likely to be indirectly discriminated against.

cross reference
An aspect considered in this chapter at section 14.2.4.

The more recent secondary legislation includes Directive 2004/113 on equality in the access to and the supply of goods and services, Directive 2010/41 on equal treatment between self-employed men and women, and Directive 2010/18 on parental leave.

Article 157 TFEU and the early legislation in particular have been subject to very liberal interpretation by the Court of Justice far beyond a literal reading of the provisions, due in large part, no doubt, to the fact that, for the first twenty years of the Communities' life, there was only Article 119 EEC (now 157 TFEU) to provide for equal treatment and that was confined to equal pay. During the subsequent ten years, this was supplemented by only the first three Directives dealing with equal treatment. The Court of Justice had to be inventive in order to make any progress. Whilst greater effort is being shown now by the EU institutions and the member states by the setting up of various fora in which to promote equality, in the beginning action was more likely to be taken by individuals, sometimes with the support of the national equality agencies, such as the Equal Opportunities Commission (EOC) in the UK, rather than the Commission in enforcement actions.

cross reference
See, for example, the Defrenne, Garland *and* Marshall *cases, considered in this chapter.*

This chapter will concentrate on the core aspects of sex equality law in the EU, notably Article 157 TFEU (ex 141 EC), Directive 75/117 and the case law generated by the Equal Treatment Directive 76/207, both of which have now been replaced by the new consolidating Directive on Equal Treatment between Men and Women, Directive 2006/54, which came into force on 15 August 2008. They will still be referred to in this chapter, with the either the new or old Directive Article numbers in parentheses, according to the context, and particularly because the case law, for the moment, derives largely from those old Directives.

The consolidating Directive carries an extended concept of discrimination. Article 2 of Directive 2006/54 provides as follows.

Directive 2006/54, Article 2

. . . discrimination includes:

(a) harassment and sexual harassment, as well as any less favourable treatment based on a person's rejection of or submission to such conduct;

(b) instruction to discriminate against persons on grounds of sex;

(c) any less favourable treatment of a woman related to pregnancy or maternity leave within the meaning of Directive 92/85/EEC.

For more details on this section scan here or visit the Online Resource Centre.

14.2 Article 157 TFEU and the scope of the principle of equal pay

Article 157 TFEU (ex 141 EC and 119 EEC) originally provided for equal pay for equal work only, but was amended by the Treaty of Amsterdam to refer to 'equal pay for work of equal value' by the Lisbon Treaty, a concept that was first introduced by Directive 75/117.

Article 157(1) TFEU
....

Each member state shall ensure that the principle of equal pay for male and female workers for equal work or work of equal value is applied.

Secondly, it attempts to define what equal pay actually means. Article 157(2) TFEU narrowly defines 'pay' as 'the ordinary basic or minimum wage or salary or any other consideration, whether in cash or in kind, which the worker receives either directly or indirectly, in respect of his employment, from his employer'.

Article 157(2) TFEU defines equal pay without discrimination to mean the following.

Article 157(2) TFEU
....

. . .

(a) that pay for the same work at piece rates shall be calculated on the basis of the same unit of measurement; and

(b) that pay for the same work at time rates shall be the same for the same job.

Payment by piece rates is not so common now and basically means that a person is paid per each unit or piece of a product that is made. It was previously common in factory work for producing many component parts or in home-working, such as the assembling of biro parts. The more assembled or made, the more that is paid.

It took a long time, however, before the principle of equal pay was properly realized. Much of the delay was due to a deliberate postponing of the application of the principle by the member states and it was only action by individuals that allowed the Court of Justice to step in and provide for the application of the principle.

Case 43/75 *Defrenne v Sabena (No. 2)* is the first significant case under Article 119 EC (now 157 TFEU) and concerns an applicant who was previously unsuccessful in challenging a discriminatory national pension system that was held to be outside Community law competence. However, she commenced a second action to challenge unequal pay. Gabrielle Defrenne was paid at a substantially lower rate than her male colleagues for the same work and claimed compensation for the damage suffered from February 1963 until February 1966. The case was sympathetically received by the Court of Justice and Gabrielle Defrenne was successful. The Court of Justice held that the principle of equal pay was sufficiently clear and precise to have direct effects. However, in response to the fears expressed by employers and the interventions of some member states about the costs to industry if the judgment were backdated to 1957 (that is, all of the back pay that would have to be paid), the Court of Justice declared the ruling to be prospective only, from the date of the original litigation commenced by Defrenne and any cases in the pipeline.

This prospective-only ruling is a type of ruling that is rare, but repeated again in equality law in the *Barber* case.

cross reference

Considered in section 14.2.1.1.

With *Defrenne* having opened the gate, many more cases were referred to the Court of Justice, which was then able to refine the definition of pay and thus the scope of Article 119 EC (now 157 TFEU).

14.2.1 The meaning of 'pay'

Although previously, Case 80/70 *Defrenne* v *Belgium (No. 1)* seemed to rule out a wider definition of 'pay' to exclude pension benefits in retirement, the term 'pay' has been progressively defined.

In **Case 12/81 *Garland* v *British Rail Engineering***, Article 119 EEC was held to include concessionary rail travel facilities for the family of an ex-employee. The Court of Justice held that the travel facilities in question were granted in kind by the employer to the retired male employee or his dependants directly or indirectly in relation to his employment, and could be regarded as an extension of travel facilities granted during employment.

375

Pay, as interpreted by the Court of Justice, also includes:

* rules by which seniority/loyalty payments are achieved in favour of full-time employees in Case C-184/89 *Nimz* v *Hamburg*;

* sick pay, even though part of a statutory scheme, in Case 171/88 *Ingrid Rinner-Kuhn* v *FWW Spezial-Gebaudereiningung*;

* a severance grant in Case C-33/89 *Kowalska* v *Hamburg*; and

* compensation for lost wages for attendance on training course for works council members in Case C-360/90 *Arbeiterwohlfahrt der Stadt Berlin* v *Monika Botel*.

Unfair dismissal compensation and redundancy pay have also been confirmed to come within Article 141 EC (now 157 TFEU) in Case C-167/97 *Seymour-Smith and Perez*.

Hence 'pay' is given a very wide meaning and any payments and benefits that arise from the employment relationship may be held to be pay under Article 157 TFEU. One particular problem was the status of pensions because of the link that exists with retirement and the fact that the EC secondary legislation at the time appeared to preserve this whole area within the competence of the member states and not the Union.

14.2.1.1 The concept of pay and its relationship to pensions

This topic has particular complications not only because the concept of pay is being stretched, but also because it straddles the very grey area of the boundary between the jurisdiction of the member states and that of the EU and Court of Justice. In particular, Article 7 of Directive 79/7 provides as follows.

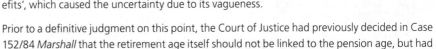

Directive 79/7, Article 7

This Directive shall be without prejudice to the right of Member States to exclude from its scope:

(a) the determination of pensionable age for the purposes of granting old-age and retirement pensions and the possible consequences thereof for other benefits;

(b) . . .

It was the meaning of the latter part of the Article, 'the possible consequences for other benefits', which caused the uncertainty due to its vagueness.

cross reference
Defrenne (No. 1) *is considered in section 14.2.1.*

Prior to a definitive judgment on this point, the Court of Justice had previously decided in Case 152/84 *Marshall* that the retirement age itself should not be linked to the pension age, but had to be equal for men and women for it to comply with Community law. Hence a clear distinction was drawn between retirement and pensions. In *Defrenne (No. 1)* it was held that contributions into a statutory pension or social security scheme were not to be considered as coming within the concept of pay under Article 119 EEC (now 157 TFEU). As a result, it was widely assumed that this ruling was good for all forms of pension schemes.

The reasons for the allowance in EU law for a difference in pension ages are starting to become lost in time. Essentially, the difference stems from the fact that many states provided that women retired earlier and obtained their state pensions at an earlier age.

However, many pension arrangements are now the result of private and contractual negotiation. How are these regarded by the Court of Justice?

In **Case 69/80 *Worringham and Humphries* v *Lloyds Bank***, the defendant bank operated an arrangement whereby male workers under the age of 25 were paid 5 per cent more than their female counterparts to enhance a pension. The total enhanced payment package, however, formed the basis of calculation of other social advantages and welfare benefits. The bank argued that the enhancement was linked to pensions; therefore it could lawfully discriminate. The Court of Justice ruled that such a contribution, which determined other benefits linked to salary paid by the employer, is pay within the meaning of Article 119 EEC (now 157 TFEU), even if the contributions are deducted at source and paid on behalf of the employee – that is, the employee never sees them directly.

This could include anything supplied by the employer to or on behalf of the employee on a pro rata basis such as annual bonuses. Thus, in this case, the pension itself was not considered to be pay, but not all of the linked consequences could be excluded automatically under Article 7a of Directive 79/7.

Case 170/84 *Bilka Kaufhaus* v *Karin Weber Van Hartz* concerned different access rules to a pensions scheme for full-time and part-time workers, the part-timers being mainly female. It was held that where supplements were made by the employer to the basic state pension under a contractual agreement and where the amount was linked to pay (that is, as a proportion or percentage), it was pay for the purposes of Article 119 EEC. Furthermore, if access to this scheme was discriminatory, as it was proved to be in the case, it also breached Article 119 EEC (now Article 157 TFEU).

The next case was, like *Defrenne (No. 2)*, highly significant in the EU legal order because of the impact that it had on employers.

In **Case C-262/88** *Barber* v *Guardian Royal Exchange (GRE) Assurance Group*, Barber was made redundant by GRE at the age of 52. There was an agreed contracted-out – that is, private – pensions scheme. His redundancy package included a statutory redundancy payment, and an ex gratia payment (a top-up), but entitlement to his occupational pension was deferred until the agreed pension age under the scheme of 62 for men and 57 for women. There was an agreement in the redundancy package that, if within ten years of the state pension ages, the pension could be obtained earlier: a redundant woman aged 52 would be entitled to immediate access to her pension because she was within ten years of the statutory pension age, whereas Barber and other male employees were not (because they were ten or more years adrift). It was this discrepancy between the two sexes' treatment that was the basis for the claim of unlawful discrimination.

The defence claimed that there was a link to the pension age and the case therefore fell under the Directive 79/7 exemption, in which case it was lawful discrimination. The UK government, intervening, claimed that the scheme, which replaced the state scheme, should be regarded as coming within social security and not Article 119 EEC (now 157 TFEU). The Court of Justice concluded that the statutory redundancy pay and the benefits from his contracted-out occupational pension scheme – that is, the pension itself – were 'pay' within Article 119 EC. The deciding factor is whether the rules and thus payment of the specific scheme are a part of the employment contract even by the voluntary inclusion of the employer. Only if entirely to do with the compulsory state pension does a case now fall outside Article 157 TFEU. The Court of Justice emphasized (at [25]) the importance of the fact that the occupational scheme was funded without any contribution being made by the public authorities.

The *Barber* decision gave rise to severe concern. It was not expected that pensions should be pay; indeed *Defrenne (No. 1)* suggested that they were not. It would mean that there would be unlawful discrimination not previously thought to be the case, for which huge amounts of compensation, not previously contemplated, would be payable. This would not have been taken account of in the actuarial calculations and the pensions schemes would have had severe difficulties in making payments not previously foreseen. Hence the Court of Justice declared Article 119 EC to be directly effective for pensions from date of judgment only – that is, 17 May 1990 – and for any cases in the pipeline. In other words, like the second *Defrenne* judgment on the direct effects of Article 119 EEC before it, the judgment was prospective only, applying from the date of judgment on and not validating any backdated claims for equal treatment, which would have cost the industry severely. Indeed, the member states were so concerned about the judgment and possible future interpretations of it that they attached a specific Protocol (No. 2) to the Treaty on European Union (TEU), which has now been replaced by a Protocol (No. 33) attached to the Treaties by the Lisbon Treaty:

> **Protocol Concerning Article 157 of the Treaty on the Functioning of the European Union**
>
> ....
>
> THE HIGH CONTRACTING PARTIES,
>
> HAVE AGREED UPON the following provision, which shall be annexed to the Treaty on European Union and to the Treaty on the functioning of the European Union:
>
> For the purposes of Article 157 of the Treaty on the Functioning of the European Union, benefits under occupational social security schemes shall not be considered as remuneration if and in so far as they are attributable to periods of employment prior to 17 May 1990, except in the case of workers or those claiming under them who have before that date initiated legal proceedings or introduced an equivalent claim under the applicable national law.

This means that the judgment applies to benefits payable for service after 1990. This prospective-only judgment, like the *Defrenne (No. 2)* judgment, was to overcome the economic effect on employers in the case of a retroactive application of the ruling. Thus the period of earnings before the *Barber* judgment does not give rise to a claim.

The Protocol clarified the judgment and was expressly accepted by the Court of Justice in Case C-109/91 *Ten Oever*, which also extended the *Barber* ruling to pension benefits payable to the pension holder's survivors; it was further confirmed by the Court of Justice as coming within Article 141 EC in Case C-117/01 *KB* v *NHS Pensions*.

The *Barber* case, however, prompted many more cases seeking to establish its exact meaning and consequences, only one or two of which are considered here.

 It also led to the extensive amendment of Directive 86/378 on occupational social security schemes, but which is not considered further in this text.

> In **Case C-152/91 *Neath* v *Hugh Steeper***, it was held that inequality in employees' contributions arising from actuarial factors such as life expectancy, which differed according to sex, would not be caught by Article 141 EC (now 157 TFEU). The case involved a conversion of a periodic payment to a lump sum payment. In this case, the male applicant received less and claimed that this was unlawful discrimination; however, according to the Court of Justice, the difference in treatment was objectively justified as a result of the actuarial factors.

Whilst benefits and lump sum payments must be regarded as pay, this is not the case for the contributions that determine the size of the fund, because factors other than a simple difference in sex are involved. The funding system to provide the amount of pension to be available does not come under Article 157 TFEU (ex 141 EC). The amount needed for a pension is determined by actuaries. They base their figures on the fact that women live longer after retirement, and in the past and at the time of the case they had a right to a pension at an earlier age; thus they needed more capital to be paid into the scheme to supply this. If they work for the same length of time, they must pay more. This becomes clear when converted to a lump sum: women will receive more.

cross reference
Considered at section 14.2.4.1.

It has subsequently been established that the time limit in *Barber* and Protocol No. 33 do not apply to discrimination in relation to the right to join – that is, access to an occupational pension scheme – which is governed by the judgment in *Bilka Kaufhaus* and confirmed in Case C-57/93 *Vroege* v *NCIV Instituut*.

There are still many cases arising from this very complex relationship between pay and pensions. It is complicated because there remains a lawful discrimination on the part of member states as to when females and males receive state pensions. Any difference that relates to the amount paid in or out to achieve a pension is in law entirely acceptable unless, according to *Barber*, the payments have become part of the contractual relationship by the intervention of an agreement between the employer and employee. It is then pay, it comes within Article 157 TFEU and the employer cannot lawfully discriminate.

14.2.2 The original Equal Pay Directive (Directive 75/117)

The Equal Pay Directive added little to that interpreted for old Article 119 EEC, but did extend the principle of equal pay to 'work to which equal value is attributed' and extended the equality requirement to 'all aspects and conditions of remuneration' (Article 1), which Article 119 EEC at the time did not. This is now contained in the new Article 157 TFEU.

> **Article 157 TFEU**
>
> Each Member State shall ensure that the principle of equal pay for male and female workers for equal work or work of equal value is applied.

thinking point
What difference does including equal value in Article 157 TFEU make? Hint: Think about the employment relationship covering most sex equality issues.

By including equal value in the Treaty Article, it makes the situation much easier for claimants who work for a private employer – that is, the vast majority of workers. It was with these concerns in mind that many of the cases that were originally raised in respect of Directive 75/117 alone or in combination with Article 141 EC (ex 119 EEC) were decided upon by the Court of Justice with reference to Article 141 EC (ex 119 EEC) only. If the Court of Justice were not able to bring the case circumstances within the scope of Article 141 EC, there would have been severe difficulties for many of the applicants because of the absence of horizontal direct effects in Directives. A more concise equal pay principle is now to be found in Article 4 of Directive 2006/54, although, of course, the case law still relates to the previous Directive and Treaty Article. The definition of pay in Article 157 TFEU is also contained in Article 2(1) e of Directive 2006/54.

14.2.3 The basis of comparison

In most situations in which there is direct discrimination, it is usually clear and obvious that there is discrimination, for example it is easy to compare a man and woman who are doing the same job in the same workplace for the same employer, but are being paid differently. There are, however, complications where the comparison is not so obvious, where the times of work differ, or the job differs slightly, or the workplace differs. It then becomes important that there is a valid comparator.

In **Case 129/79 *Macarthy's* v *Wendy Smith***, Smith was employed from March 1976 at a salary of £50 per week, and complained of discrimination because her predecessor, a man, had received a salary of £60 per week. The Court of Justice held that although the work actually performed by employees of different sex must be within the same establishment, the employees need not be employed at the same time. However, the Court of Justice was careful to point out that:

> It cannot be ruled out that the difference in pay between two workers occupying the same post but at different periods in time may be explained by the operation of factors which are unconnected with any discrimination on grounds of sex.

This is a question of fact for the national courts to decide. The Court of Justice had therefore expressly left open the possibility of a genuine material factor defence. Hence the scope of the concept of equal pay for equal work (same work) could not be restricted by a requirement by member states that the person whose work was being compared be contemporaneously employed.

Comparison can also be made with members of the other sex who do work of a lesser value to ensure that a woman doing work of higher value cannot be paid less than the male comparator.

> This was held in **Case 157/86 *Mary Murphy An Bord Telecom Éireann***, which was decided by the ECJ on the basis of old Article 119 EEC, even though it was an equal value claim, and Article 119 EEC only covered equal pay claims on the basis that it would be even more of an infringement to pay the higher value work less than the lower value work. The Court of Justice had also expressed the view in the *Macarthy's* case that it would not entertain a hypothetical comparator.

There is now a statutory definition of direct discrimination in the Equality Directives (Directives 2000/43 and 2000/78) and also now Directive 2006/54, which defines this concept.

> **Directive 2006/54, Article 2**
> ....
> Direct discrimination: Where one person is treated less favourably on grounds of sex than another is, has been or would be treated in a comparable situation.

Comparison, or the lack of it, has become a crucial factor in cases that have arisen from the compulsory competitive tendering schemes that were imposed on local authorities in the UK, requiring them to contract out jobs to outside private companies in order to achieve cost savings. In these schemes, some members of staff (predominantly women) were removed from direct employment by the local authority and then re-employed by an independent employer. They were then returned to the same job, but on less money than their (mainly) male counterparts doing the same job or work previously evaluated to be of equal value.

> For example, in **Case C-320/00 *Lawrence v Regent Office Care Ltd***, dinner ladies who were previously employed directly by the local authority had their contracts taken over by a private company. They continued to work in the same job, but were paid less in comparison with male colleagues who were retained by the local authority, but who had been rated to be doing work of equal value. The Court of Justice held that whilst Article 141 EC was not restricted to employees working for the same employer in the same place, Article 141 EC could not apply where there was no a single overall authority responsible for deciding pay.

> Similarly, in **Case C-256/01 *Allonby***, teachers who were mainly female had been made redundant by a college, but taken on by an agency in a self-employed capacity and returned

to work in the same college. However, they were paid less than an alleged male comparator employed by the college. The Court of Justice held that because there was not a single source that led to the unequal pay, the work and the pay of those workers could not therefore be compared on the basis of Article 141 EC.

With the Court of Justice having held twice now that an indirect comparison is not possible, the conclusion is that there can be no factual, yet alone illegal, discrimination, because there is no single employer responsible to make the pay adjustment if inequality were found to be unlawful. These cases would appear to open up a very big loophole that permits unequal pay for women by condoning the hiving off of employment contracts according to sex, thus either directly or indirectly discriminating against women. However, with the new Directive definition, it is now arguable that 'would be' in the text opens the door for a hypothetical comparator test to be used by the Court of Justice in view of the unfortunate consequences of those earlier cases.

Legislative intervention to correct this has not happened and despite the fact that recital 10 of Directive 2006/54 states that 'The Court of Justice has established that, in certain circumstances, the principle of equal pay is not limited to situations in which men and women work for the same employer'; however, those words did not appear in the body of the Directive. Thus it appears that suitable cases will need to come along for the ECJ to make its own correction, perhaps encouraged by recital 10?

These cases have also involved an issue that occurs a great deal in discrimination law, that of indirect discrimination, which will be considered next.

14.2.4 Part-time work and the development of the concept of indirect discrimination

It is in the area of part-time work that the concept of indirect discrimination has been most thoroughly explored by the Court of Justice. Direct discrimination on the grounds of sex can arguably never be justified: either it is discriminatory and thus contrary to EU law, or it is not. Indirect discrimination, however, can be justified, but it is more difficult to determine. It covers cases in which a class of persons is mainly or entirely constituted of one sex (usually women), and a difference is drawn between that class and another class, which can consist of members of both sexes. In either class, no direct discrimination takes place – that is, both genders are treated the same – but, in comparison with the other class, a rule or measure operates in a discriminatory manner against the predominant sex, which can be either women or men. Whether the discrimination is actually unlawful is often dependent on the motives behind it and whether it can be justified objectively by those motives.

There is a statutory definition of 'indirect discrimination' contained in Directive 2006/54.

Directive 2006/54, Article 2(1)(b)

'indirect discrimination': where an apparently neutral provision, criterion or practice would put persons of one sex at a particular disadvantage compared with persons of the other sex, unless that provision, criterion or practice is objectively justified by a legitimate aim, and the means of achieving that aim are appropriate and necessary.

Even with the statutory definition, it is still useful to see how this was developed by the Court of Justice in a number of cases concerning pay differences between full-time and part-time workers. These are also usually combined with objective justifications as elements of the cases.

In **Case 96/80** *Jenkins* v *Kingsgate*, the employer paid full-time workers 10 per cent more per hour than part-time workers, in order, it was claimed, to discourage absenteeism and to achieve a more efficient use of their machinery. All but one of the part-time workers were women. The Court of Justice held that a difference in rates of remuneration between full-time and part-time employees did not offend against Article 119 EEC (now 157 TFEU), provided that the difference was attributable to factors that were objectively justified and did not relate directly or indirectly to discrimination based on sex. If it is established that a considerably smaller percentage of women than men perform the number of hours necessary to be a full-timer, the inequality will contravene Article 119 EEC. In particular, in the light of the difficulties encountered by women in arranging to work the minimum number of hours per week, the pay policy of the undertaking cannot be explained by factors other than the discrimination based on sex.

In other words, it is more likely that women will find it harder to work full-time and may have to seek part-time work because of commitments to family and home, but this does not make it lawful to discriminate against them.

14.2.4.1 Objective justifications

The existence or not of an objective justification is crucial, but, as observers of the cases, we do not, for the most part, see this, because this is usually a matter of factual consideration for the national court. For example, the justification given by an employer may be that the company needs to encourage the recruitment of full-time employees, in which case the national court could require evidence that demonstrates the relative number of full-time and part-time vacancies and applications for those posts, to see whether the facts bear out the claim made by the company. Where there is no plausible explanation to account for the difference in pay, it is likely to be discrimination contrary to Article 157 TFEU.

In **Case 170/84** *Bilka Kaufhaus* v *Karin Weber Van Harz*, a store gave all full-time employees a non-contributory pension on retirement, whereas part-timers qualified only if they had been employed permanently for at least fifteen years. The undertaking claimed that the store needed to pay more and offer further benefits to full-timers to attract them in sufficient numbers. The Court of Justice ruled that Article 119 EEC (now 157 TFEU) is infringed where a company excludes part-time workers from its occupational pension scheme and where that exclusion affects a far greater number of women than men, unless the undertaking shows that the exclusion is based on objectively justified factors unconnected with discrimination based on sex.

The Court of Justice went on to consider the question whether the undertaking could justify that disadvantage on the ground that its objective is to employ as few part-time workers as possible. It held that, in order to show that the discrimination was objectively justified, the employer must show that the measures giving rise to the difference in treatment:

- correspond to a genuine need of the enterprise;
- are suitable for attaining the objective pursued by the enterprise; and
- are strictly necessary for that purpose – that is, proportionate.

A further requirement laid down by the Court of Justice was that it was for the company to show that the discrimination was not based on sex rather than the complainant having to prove discrimination. This was part of a move by the Court of Justice to shift the burden of proof to the company, which it advanced over a number of cases. In the particular case, the German court applying the ruling held that the difference was not objectively justified

> In **Case 171/92 *Rinner-Kuhn***, the Court of Justice suggested that an objective factor that was based on a social policy might be acceptable, but not the reason for a difference in pay in the case based on the assumption that part-time workers were not integrated into the business in the same way as full-time workers, even where based on national law.

> In **Case C-167/97 *Seymour Smith and Perez***, for example, the Court of Justice held that national courts should look at both the numbers of men and women who can and cannot satisfy a particular requirement, such as full-time work, to determine whether there is a disproportionate effect on one sex, in which case discrimination will be assumed unless justified.

The next section considers equal value claims, but is also instructive in terms of the investigation that the national court should undertake to assess the grounds for the indirect discrimination.

The case law on part-time work has essentially been put into statutory form by Directive 97/81.

14.2.5 **Work of equal value**

Work of equal value claims cause further difficulties because it is not often clear that two jobs are of the same value and an appraisal has to be done, either by the national court or using a formal job evaluation scheme.

> **Case C-127/92 *Enderby* v *Frenchay Health Authority*** involved an equal value claim and the comparison of lower-paid speech therapists, comprising mainly women, with higher-paid pharmacists and clinical psychologists, comprising mainly men. The Court of Justice held that is was for the national court to determine, if necessary by applying the principle of proportionality, whether and to what extent the shortage of candidates for a job and the need to attract them by paying higher pay constituted an objectively justified ground for the difference in pay between jobs of equal value. The Court of Justice held that it was up to the national court to decide whether the available statistics are representative enough to provide significant enough evidence to judge the justifications given. The difficulty with indirect discrimination is that there is often higher demand for lower-paid, but flexible, jobs, especially where this demand is created by women seeking such jobs. This can be argued by the employer to constitute evidence that it needs to pay at a premium less flexible and thus less attractive jobs, occupied mainly by men.

> In **Case 157/86 *Mary Murphy* v *An Bord Telecom Éireann***, an employee claimed equal pay for her work, which was considered to be of even higher value than her comparator. The Court of Justice held that Article 119 EEC (now 157 TFEU) must be interpreted as covering

> the case in which a worker who relies on that provision to obtain equal pay is engaged in work of higher value than that of the person with whom a comparison is to be made.

The conclusion that has to be drawn from the case was that Article 119 EEC (now 157 TFEU) could also be applied to equal value claims, although not expressly stated in the Article at the time. Under the amended Article 157 TFEU, it is expressly covered.

The Court of Justice reasoned in the *Murphy* case that whilst it was true that Article 119 EEC (now Article 157 TFEU) applies only in the case of equal work, nevertheless if that principle forbids workers of one sex engaged in work of equal value to be paid a lower wage than the other sex, it prohibits much more strongly such a difference in pay where the lower-paid category of workers is engaged in work of higher value.

Interestingly, in this case, the defendant was a public body and, if it had so wished, the Court of Justice could have resolved the case under Directive 75/117, because it would have involved vertical direct effects. It chose instead to widen the scope of Article 119 EC, which, in the long run, would assist more potential litigants than the Directive.

14.2.5.1 Job evaluation schemes and the burden of proof

In order to back up the principle of equal pay for work of equal value, Article 1 of Directive 75/117, now reproduced in Article 4 of Directive 2006/54, provided that 'where a job classification system is used for determining pay, it must be based on the same criteria for both men and women and so drawn up as to exclude any discrimination on grounds of sex'.

Furthermore, Article 17(1) of Directive 2006/54 (replacing Article 2 of Directive 75/117) requires member states to provide the legal means by which all employees who consider themselves discriminated against are able to pursue a claim.

> **Directive 2006/54, Article 17(1)**
> ....
> Member States shall ensure that, after possible recourse to other competent authorities including where they deem it appropriate conciliation procedures, judicial procedures for the enforcement of obligations under this Directive are available to all persons who consider themselves wronged by failure to apply the principle of equal treatment to them, even after the relationship in which the discrimination is alleged to have occurred has ended.

In a number of cases, the Court of Justice has ruled that any job evaluation schemes used must not be based on criteria that valued one sex only and had to be transparent, so that a claimant could see how particular wages were achieved.

> For example, in **Case 237/85 *Rummler* v *Dato-Druck***, a job evaluation scheme that was based on muscular effort, fatigue, and physical hardship was held by the Court of Justice not to be in breach of Article 1 of Directive 75/117 as long as the following condition was met: it must, in so far as the nature of the tasks carried out in the undertaking permits, take into account criteria for which workers of each sex show particular aptitude. The Court

of Justice said that criteria based exclusively on the values of one sex contain a 'risk of discrimination'.

Additionally (as was noted in the *Bilka* and *Enderby* cases), the Court of Justice shifted the burden of proof so that the employer had to prove that there was no discrimination, direct or indirect, rather than the employee having to show that there was discrimination – something that would be much harder for the employee.

See, for example, **Case 109/88 *Handels- og Kontorfunktionaerernes Forbund i Danmark* v *Dansk Arbejdsgiverforening (Danfoss)***, which involved a pay structure so complex that it was impossible for a woman to identify the reasons that led to a difference in pay between her and a man doing the same job.

The results of this case law were consolidated into the Burden of Proof Directive (Directive 97/80), which has now been replaced by Article 19 of Directive 2006/54.

Danfoss also made it clear that a length-of-service criterion for higher pay was acceptable with special justification.

This was clearly confirmed in **Case C-17/05 *Cadman***, in which a significant difference in pay between men and women existed based on length of service. It would be only in the case of doubt that the burden would fall on the employer to justify the difference.

14.2.6 **Enforcement and remedies**

The remedies and enforcement procedures have been consolidated in Directive 2006/54 for all of the Directives that it has replaced. Member states are required, under Articles 17 and 18 of Directive 2006/54 (ex Article 2 of Directive 75/117), to ensure that judicial or conciliation procedures are available with adequate compensation measures. Article 23 of Directive 2006/54 (ex Article 4 of Directive 75/117) requires member states to take the necessary measures to ensure that any provisions in collective agreements, wage agreements, or in individual contracts that breach the principles of the Directive are to be null and void or to be removed. Article 24 of Directive 2006/54 (ex Article 5 of Directive 75/117) requires the member states to take measures to protect employees against dismissal as a result of a complaint made by them of discrimination to an employer or where the employee takes legal proceedings aimed to enforce the principles provided by the Directive. The member states were required, under Article 6 of Directive 75/117, to take the necessary measures to ensure that the principle of equal pay is applied and to see that effective means are available to take care that the principle is observed. This requirement has not been carried over verbatim and has been consolidated with the overall requirement to ensure equal treatment in Articles 1 and 4 of the new Directive 2006/54.

Equal treatment

14.3

The original Equal Treatment Directive 76/207 went well beyond the original scope of Article 119 EEC (now 157 TFEU), which was concerned only with pay; therefore the Directive had to be

For more details on section 14.3 scan here or visit the Online Resource Centre.

enacted under the general legislative power of Article 235 EEC (now 352 TFEU). It extended the prohibition of discrimination on the grounds of sex into many facets of the employment relationship including, inter alia, access, appointment, dismissal, retirement, training and working conditions. It has now been repealed and replaced by Directive 2006/54, which was enacted under the amended Article 141(3) EC (now 157(3) TFEU) allowing for direct intervention under a dedicated Treaty legal base.

Article 14(1) of Directive 2006/54 (ex Article 1 of Directive 76/207) refers to equal treatment for men and women, which is required to be applied to working conditions, access to employment, including promotion, and to vocational training. A previous Article 1a of Directive 76/207 (now Article 23 of Directive 2006/54) sets out what is known as 'gender mainstreaming'. It requires member states actively to take into account the objective of equality between men and women when formulating and implementing laws, regulations, administrative provisions, policies and activities in the areas referred to in all of the new Directives.

14.3.1 The concept of equal treatment/no discrimination on the grounds of sex

cross reference
See section 14.1.2.

The concept of equal treatment, which was defined in Directive 76/207 as no discrimination on the grounds of sex directly or indirectly by reference, in particular, to marital or family status, has not been carried over into Directive 2006/54, which has adopted the extended definitions of discrimination and harassment noted earlier in the chapter. The now single exception to the principle of equal treatment is that relating to particular occupational activities previously contained in Article 2(6) and now to be found in Article 14(2) of Directive 2006/54, which will be considered after the cases that previously helped to determine the extent of discrimination covered by the earlier Directive.

The concepts of equal treatment and non-discrimination are largely treated as being synonymous, but any distinction that there is took on greater significance because of the much greater subject matter coverage of the earlier Directive 76/207. Does equal treatment mean more than non-discrimination? Case law has considered the scope of the protection provided for by these provisions in so far as what is meant by the right to equality within the framework agreed by the member states and interpreted by the Court of Justice.

For example, in **Case C-13/94 *P* v *S* and Cornwall County Council**, a male-to-female transsexual was dismissed from employment in an educational establishment after informing the employers about the forthcoming gender reassignment. The Court of Justice moved away from a simple interpretation of no discrimination on the grounds of sex simply to mean a comparison of how each gender is treated, and held that the dismissal was unlawful discrimination on the grounds of sex because it was 'based, essentially if not exclusively on the sex of the person concerned'.

thinking point
Which comparator: a female-to-male transsexual? All other workers, male or female? The male-to-female transsexual with herself?

One of the difficulties in sex discrimination law is that the need to find a comparator is not always convenient or helpful in determining whether discrimination has been suffered (this is also a difficulty in relation to the pregnancy cases). The pregnancy cases are considered in section 14.3.5.1. In the *P* v *S* case, if this is discrimination based on sex, as the Court of Justice held, with whom can a comparison be made? There is no direct comparator as such, such as a female-to-male transsexual.

The Court of Justice held that where a person is dismissed on the ground that he or she intends to undergo, or has undergone, gender reassignment, he or she is treated unfavourably by comparison with persons of the sex to which he or she was deemed to belong before undergoing gender reassignment. Therefore the Directive appeared to remove any discrimination where sex, in a wider sense, was concerned and not limited only to a difference in treatment between genders! The question that was raised after this case was whether the concept of no discrimination on the grounds of sex had been transformed into no discrimination on the grounds of sexuality, or even no sexual-orientation discrimination. However, in the next case, the limits of EC equality law at that time were found.

In **Case C-249/96 *Grant v South West Trains***, SW trains regulations specifically excluded benefits from same-sex partnerships. Whereas opposite-sex partners were included even when they were not married, provided that a stable relationship was established, same-sex partners were excluded. The Court of Justice held that this was not discrimination based on sex because the rule would apply also using a direct comparison, to male same-sex relationships. This was discrimination based on sexual orientation. The Court of Justice discussed a number of points in connection with this and found that, in some member states, such a relationship would, but only for a limited range of rights, be treated the same as an opposite-sex relationship and, in other states, such relationships were not recognized in any particular way. The Court of Justice referred to the then new Article 13 EC (now 19 TFEU) by which the member states in Council were empowered to take action to outlaw sexual orientation discrimination, but stated that the state of law in the EC at that time did not equate same-sex relationships with opposite-sex ones; therefore the discrimination in respect of sexual orientation, although present, was not contrary to Article 141 EC (now 157 TFEU) or the Directive (now also within Article 14 of Directive 2006/54).

The Court of Justice confirmed this stance in **Case 125/99P *D and Sweden v Council***.

In both cases, the Court of Justice decided to leave the response to this form of discrimination to the legislative intervention of the member states, which have now responded, with Directive 2000/78 providing a framework for combating discrimination on grounds of sexual orientation.

However, **Case C-117/01 *KB v NHS Pensions***, although decided on the basis of Article 141 EC and not the Directive, is worthy of a brief note here because of the much more sympathetic judgment given by the Court of Justice in a case involving transsexual rights under the existing Community legislation at the time of the case. The case concerned the inability to nominate a transsexual partner as a pension beneficiary because national legislation required the partner to be an opposite-sex spouse. National legislation would not allow the original sex of a partner to be altered to enable him or her to marry and thus satisfy the pension law requirement. The Court of Justice held that national legislation must be regarded as being, in principle, incompatible with the requirements of Article 141 EC on the grounds that it had already been found to be in breach of the European Convention on Human Rights and Fundamental Freedoms (ECHR), and prevented a couple such as KB and R from fulfilling the marriage requirement, necessary for one of them to be able to benefit from part of the pay of the other. However, the Court of Justice was not specific as to how exactly Article 141 EC might be offended, apart from the fact that Article 141 EC would regard the benefit as pay. The Court of Justice acknowledged, however, that it was up to the member state to determine the conditions under which legal recognition is given to the change of gender of a person in R's situation and it would be up to the national court to decide whether KB can rely on Article 141 EC (now 157 TFEU).

Equal treatment in this case, then, has been given a very wide scope to include the right to have a change in sex officially testified. Quite where a comparison fits in is difficult to see. Now that same-sex civil partnerships have been given statutory recognition in the UK and other countries in the EU, this would no longer be a problem.

> Finally in **Case C-423/04** *Richards*, it was held that the correct comparator for a male-to-female transgendered person when determining pensionable ages was a female who had not undergone gender reassignment. Article 4(1) of Directive 79/7 was held not to permit a distinction in national law as to how a pension was determined.

Directive 2006/54 adds a little light to this area.

> ### Directive 2006/54, Recital 3
>
> The Court of Justice has held that the scope of the principle of equal treatment for men and women cannot be confined to the prohibition of discrimination based on the fact that a person is of one or other sex. In view of its purpose and the nature of the rights which it seeks to safeguard, it also applies to discrimination arising from the gender reassignment of a person.

This is not, however, addressed in the body of the Directive.

14.3.2 **The scope of equal treatment**

The scope of the prohibition of discrimination within Directive 2006/54 is spelled out in detail in Article 14(1) (ex amended Article 3 of Directive 76/207), which had consolidated much of the previous case law in the process. It provides that the application of the principle of equal treatment means that there shall be no direct or indirect discrimination in the public or private sectors, including public bodies, in relation to:

(a) conditions for access to employment, to self-employment or to occupation, including selection criteria and recruitment conditions, whatever the branch of activity and at all levels of the professional hierarchy, including promotion;

(b) access to all types and to all levels of vocational guidance, vocational training, advanced vocational training, and retraining, including practical work experience;

(c) employment and working conditions, including dismissals, as well as pay as provided for in Article 157 TFEU (ex 141 EC);

(d) membership of, and involvement in, an organization of workers or employers, or any organization the members of which carry on a particular profession, including the benefits provided for by such organizations.

Now, Article 23 of 2006/54 requires member states to take the necessary measures to ensure that:

(a) any laws, regulations and administrative provisions contrary to the principle of equal treatment are abolished;

(b) provisions contrary to the principle of equal treatment in individual or collective contracts or agreements, internal rules of undertakings or rules governing the independent occupations and professions, and workers' and employers' organizations, or any other arrangements, shall be, or may be, declared null and void, or be amended.

The scope of application can be avoided for specific reasons given in the Directive only, considered next.

14.3.3 Equality with regard to employment access, working conditions, dismissal and retirement ages

Article 14 of Directive 2006/54 provides that there shall be no direct or indirect discrimination relating to all aspects of employment, and notably access to jobs and conditions of employment. Situations that were previously considered under the previous Directive – notably Article 5, which required equality of treatment in working conditions and conditions governing dismissal – are now covered also by Directive 2006/54.

Most cases have concerned retirement and pensions. In **Case C-177/88 *Dekker* v *VJM Centram***, VJM (a social training centre) refused to employ Mrs Dekker because she was pregnant and this would mean that insurance law, which did not recognize pregnancy as a reason for paying insurance money, would not reimburse the employers during her maternity leave. As a social institution, it argued that it could not afford to hire a replacement for her. The Court of Justice held that the employer had directly discriminated in contravention of Articles 2(1) and 3(1) of Directive 76/207 by its refusal to employ even though national rules forced this situation. Furthermore, it was pointed out by the Court of Justice that direct discrimination removed the need to compare the treatment with a man.

In **Case C-312/86 *Commission* v *France (Protection of Women)***, French legislation allowed certain privileges for women, including extended maternity leave, reduction in working hours of women aged 59, bringing forward retirement age, time off for sick children, an extra day's holiday each year per child, a day off on the first day of a school term, and others. The Court of Justice considered that these special provisions only for women discriminated against men contrary to the Directive. They were not justified by Article 2(3) (now Article 14 of Directive 2006/54), which protects women during pregnancy and maternity, because the reasons given for the protection applied equally to male and female workers.

Turning to dismissal and retirement, we know from the section on equal pay above that member states can, under Article 7 of Directive 7/79, exclude the determination of pensionable age for the purposes of granting old-age and retirement pensions and the possible consequences thereof for other benefits. It was thought and argued that this meant that any difference to do with either pensions entitlements or pensionable ages were excluded, and thus that retirement and dismissal ages were also excluded.

In **Case 151/84 *Roberts* v *Tate and Lyle***, Mrs Roberts was aged 53 and a redundancy scheme allowed access to a redundancy for both men and women at the age of 55. Roberts claimed unlawful discrimination because men could gain access ten years before their pensionable age, but women only five. The Court of Justice held that access to a redundancy scheme was concerned with dismissal and therefore covered by Article 5 and not excluded by Article 7 of Directive 79/7. Access was not linked to the state security system. The Court of Justice held that Article 5(1) of Directive 76/207 must be interpreted as meaning that a contractual provision that lays down a single age (55) for the dismissal of men and women under a mass redundancy involving the grant of an early retirement pension, where the normal retirement age is different for men and women, does not constitute discrimination on grounds of sex contrary to Community law.

In the leading case concerned with retirement, **Case 152/84 *Marshall***, the compulsory earlier retirement of women was considered. National legislation allowed employers to retire women earlier than men. The Court of Justice held, however, that retirement also came within the scope of working conditions, including dismissal, and was thus covered by the Directive. When the Court of Justice came to consider whether the retirement age was linked to pensions, it decided relatively easily that the enforced earlier retirement for women than men did not fall within the justification of Article 7 of Directive 79/7 and was therefore direct discrimination.

 Directive 76/207 was held by the Court of Justice to be directly effective, but only vertically; therefore other means of enforcement must be pursued if a private employer is involved.

Case C-136/95 *Thibault* is notable for the clear statement from the Court of Justice about how Community (now EU) law on equal treatment should be regarded and thus applied. Pay rises and promotion were assessed on the basis of the previous six months' work presence, which was argued clearly to discriminate against women on maternity absence, who lost the chance to be assessed for pay increases or promotion. The Court of Justice held that this amounted to unlawful discrimination contrary to Articles 2(3) and 5(1) of Directive 76/207 (as they were then).

These provisions, in the view of the Court of Justice, required substantive and not only formal equality – that is, real rights, not only those on paper!

Finally in this section, **Case C-116/94 *Meyers*** is worth noting because it extended the scope of the Directive to the social security benefit, family credit, something that quite reasona-bly might be considered to come under the Social Security Directive 79/7 and not Directive 76/207. The credit was designed to supplement low-paid workers in an attempt to persuade them to remain in work, thus satisfying the Court of Justice that it could be construed under the terms of access to employment and working conditions, covered by Articles 3 and 5 (then of Directive 76/207), because it would both encourage employees to take up job offers and also to be considered to be a condition of work. Working conditions thus applies to all aspects of the working relationship and not just those contained within the contract of employment.

Having regarded the widening scope of the principle of equal treatment, we now need to consider the derogations or exemptions that are provided under the Directive to exclude cer-tain circumstances or situations from being subject to the principle of equal treatment. The first provision seeks to take out of the application of the principle of equal treatment circum-stances in which factors other than sex allow discriminatory treatment. The second provision was designed to take account of the unique circumstance of pregnancy and the third to allow for the possibility of promoting equality for women.

14.3.4 **Exempt occupations**

Article 14(2) of Directive 2006/54 replaced Article 2(6) of Directive 76/207, which provides the member states with the ability to exempt certain occupations from the application of the equal treatment principle where a characteristic not related to sex itself is a factor. The characteristic must constitute a genuine and determining occupational requirement in order not to constitute unlawful discrimination on the grounds of sex. Previously, cases showed that the member states were perhaps permitted a greater degree of discretion than more recently.

> For example, in **Case 165/82 *Commission v UK (Equal Treatment for Men and Women)***, the restriction of access of males to midwifery was held to be acceptable, but, in such cases, member states are required to assess the restrictions periodically in order to decide, in the light of social developments, whether there is justification for maintaining the exclusions concerned. They must notify the Commission of the results of this assessment under Article 9(2) of Directive 76/207.

Indeed, it is now the case that male midwives are common in the UK and other countries.

In the same case, a blanket exemption from the provisions of the Directive that applied to all companies with less than six workers was held by the Court of Justice not to be sanctioned by the exemption and thus contrary to the Directive.

> In **Case 222/84 *Johnston v Chief Constable of the RUC***, the RUC did not renew the contracts of a number of female police officers and justified this under Article 2(2) of Directive 76/207 because of a policy decision that women could not carry firearms. The Court of Justice held that the exception might apply to certain activities carried out by police officers, but not to police activities in general. The member states might therefore restrict such specific activities and the training for that activity to men, provided that the situation was reviewed regularly to ensure that the restrictions remained justified and that the restrictions complied with the principle of proportionality. The Court of Justice suggested that women could do other duties not involving use of firearms, rather than be dismissed outright.

Recent case law concerning employment in the armed forces, however, questions the restriction permitted in *Johnston*.

> In **Case C-273/97 *Angela Sirdar v The Army Board***, the Court of Justice said that although EC law can also apply to employment in the Army, in that case the exclusion of a woman as a cook in the Royal Marines was acceptable because of the Marines' requirements of interoperability and front-line duties – that is, the unit's cook was expected to undertake all duties and also be involved in front-line duties; therefore sex was a determining factor and the UK could rely on the exemption. Sirdar, who was previously a cook for a commando regiment not having these same requirements, could not be a cook for the Marines.

> In **C-285/98 *Kreil v Germany***, a case resembling *Johnston*, but dealing with the Army rather than the police force, the Court of Justice did not accept a general exclusion from

military posts that meant that all armed units could remain exclusively male. The Court of Justice held that the national authorities contravened the principle of proportionality in taking the general position that the composition of all armed units in the *Bundeswehr* had to remain exclusively male. By rejecting the application by Ms Kreil to the weapons electronics maintenance service of the Federal German Army out of hand, the German authorities had unlawfully discriminated against her.

The armed forces are thus categorically included, but with discretion preserved for the member states to discriminate for particular circumstances, as in *Sirdar*.

cross reference
See, however, the Schnorbus *case in section 14.3.6.*

Finally in this trio of Army cases is **Case C-186/01 *Dory***, in which the compulsory military service for males only in Germany was challenged. The Court of Justice held that, while 'the Equal Treatment Directive applies to equality in the access to posts, it does not govern the member states choices of military organization for the defence of their territory or of their essential interests'. Germany's choice of compulsory male-only military service, enshrined in its Constitution, was immune from Community law scrutiny. The negative consequences for males as a result of their time spent in military service, such as a delay in comparison to females in arriving at the job market, can therefore be remedied only by the national authorities and courts.

14.3.5 **The protection of women regarding childbirth and maternity**

Article 28(1) of Directive 2006/54 (replacing Article 2(3) and (7) of Directive 76/207) provides as follows.

Directive 2006/54, Article 28(1)

This Directive shall be without prejudice to provisions concerning the protection of women, particularly as regards pregnancy and maternity.

This is another derogation from the principle of equal treatment. It means that a different legal regime can apply, but this time specifically to protect women. However, these provisions should not be used to disguise discrimination. Article 15 of Directive 2006/54 (ex Article 2(7) of Directive 76/207) provides as follows.

Directive 2006/54, Article 15

A woman on maternity leave shall be entitled, after the end of her period of maternity leave, to return to her job or to an equivalent post on terms and conditions which are no less favourable to her and to benefit from any improvement in working conditions to which she would be entitled during her absence.

Directive 2006/54 repeats the prohibition that 'Less favourable treatment of a woman related to pregnancy or maternity leave within the meaning of Directive 92/85/EEC shall constitute discrimination within the meaning of this directive'. Thus another piece of EU secondary legislation needs to be introduced at this time and read alongside of Directive 2006/54.

Directive 92/85 concerns the protection of pregnant and breastfeeding workers. Its title comes across as somewhat inelegant, but it also helps to determine the rights to which women are entitled when pregnant and on maternity leave. Article 10 of the Directive, in combination with Article 8, designates a period of special protection, from the beginning of pregnancy to the end of maternity leave (which must be a fourteen-week minimum continuous period of leave), in which women are protected from dismissal for any reason connected to pregnancy. After the period has expired, the special protection is lost.

Note that, even during the period of special protection, they can be dismissed where the reason is not connected to pregnancy, such as for theft.

In this particular area of law, the need to make a comparison is removed because of the special circumstances of pregnancy. Case law had, however, already expanded and clarified the then existing EC law ahead of Directive 92/85 coming into force.

> In a case that predates the Parental Leave Directive, **Case 184/83 *Hoffman* v *Barmer Ersatzkasse***, a father claimed that the refusal to grant six months' paternity leave following the birth of his child while the mother went back to work was discrimination contrary to Articles 1, 2 and 5(1) of the Equal Treatment Directive (Directive 76/207). The Court of Justice held that the Directive was not designed to settle questions concerned with the organization of the family, nor to alter the division of responsibility between parents, and that parental leave may therefore be reserved to the mother by the member states by virtue of Article 2(3).

The case makes it clear that Article 2(3) was an exception to the general principle of equal treatment established by the Directive exclusively in favour of women.

Note, now, that the protection against dismissal during a period of parental leave is extended to workers of both sexes by the Parental Leave Directive (Directive 96/34), but because this is not usually the subject of study in most EU courses, it is not considered further here.

14.3.5.1 Dismissal during or after pregnancy

A series of cases has demonstrated how protective the EU legal regime of pregnant women is. The first case deals with a national law designed to protect pregnant women, albeit by excluding them from a certain type of work.

> In **Case C-421/92 *Habermann-Beltermann* v *Arbeiterwohlfahrt***, HB was employed on a permanent nights contract and was dismissed when discovered to be pregnant, under a national law prohibiting the night-time work of pregnant women. The employer argued that the prohibition of night work was allowed by the Directive (then Directive 76/207) and

to that extent the Court of Justice agreed, but not to justify dismissal. The Court of Justice held that neither national legislation nor employment contract rules could render void an employment contract by reason of the fact that the female worker was found to be pregnant. Dismissal was clearly disproportionate and the employer should, for example, find other work for her.

In **Case C-32/93 *Webb* v *EMO Air Cargo (UK) Ltd***, a woman who was employed on an indefinite contract to replace her predecessor, who was on pregnancy and maternity leave, was dismissed when it was discovered that, as a replacement, she was also pregnant. The Court of Justice held that to be direct discrimination contrary to Articles 2(1) and 5(1) of Directive 76/207. This case arose before Directive 92/85 came into force and could be applied, and was therefore decided exclusively on Directive 76/207.

It is clear that dismissal because a woman is pregnant is a clear and direct breach of the EU law.

The clear and forthright position taken by the Court of Justice in *Webb* was confirmed in **Case C-207/98 *Mahlberg*** in respect of the appointment of full-time permanent employees.

In the next cases, temporary employment contracts were considered by the Court of Justice to determine if they too are included within the scope of the Directive.

In **Case C-438/99 *Melgar***, a woman was employed on a series of back-to-back fixed-term contracts. Her fourth one expired, allegedly according to the employee, without being renewed or extended, as it had been in the past. Prior to that occurring, her employer learned of her pregnancy. However, the employer *had* offered a fifth contract, but Melgar had refused to sign it on the basis that her last contract had not expired and she had been dismissed unfairly. The national court did not determine whether the case concerned a dismissal from an indefinite employment contract or a failure to employ on a new contract. The Court of Justice held that the failure to renew a fixed-term contract was not strictly a case of dismissal discrimination contrary to Article 10 of Directive 92/85. However, it considered that the non-renewal could be regarded as a refusal to employ based on pregnancy, and thus directly discriminatory and contrary to Articles 2(1) and 3(1) of Directive 76/207.

The facts in the case, however, do not seem to support the view that there was a refusal to appoint, with the employer having offered a contract.

In a case with clearer facts concerning a fixed-term contract, **Case C-109/00 *Tele Danmark***, a post was advertised as a six months' temporary contract. Training for the post, however, required two months before the person appointed could undertake full duties usefully. Ms Brandt-Nielsen was appointed as from 1 July 1995, but, in mid-August, she informed her employer that she was pregnant and due to give birth in early November. Under Danish law, she was entitled to paid maternity leave as from 11 September 1995 – that is, after two weeks' post-training work. She had not previously informed the employer that she was pregnant and was dismissed with effect from 30 September 1995. She claimed unlawful dismissal. The Court of Justice held that it was direct discrimination contrary to both Articles 5(1) of Directive 76/207 and 10 of Directive 92/85. The fact that employment was fixed-term was irrelevant, because the inability to work was due to pregnancy. The duration of employment was also not a factor that would influence the result. The Court of Justice held: 'Had the Community legislature wished to exclude fixed-term contracts, which represent a substantial proportion of the employment relationships, from the scope of those directives, it would have done so expressly.'

Not much later, **Case C-320/01 *Busch*** involved a woman who was on parental leave after the birth of her first child, but who became pregnant a second time. Whilst pregnant, she sought to return early to work, before the full amount of paid parental leave for the first pregnancy had expired. Her employer had a vacancy and she was permitted to return to work. She was seven months' pregnant when she did. She had not mentioned her pregnancy to her employer, nor had her employer asked whether she was pregnant. On 9 April 2001, she started work; on 10 April 2001, she informed her employer that she was seven months pregnant and was entitled to paid maternity commencing 23 May 2001 (that is, after six weeks of work). The employer rescinded the permission to return to work (not actually dismissal) on grounds of misrepresentation and mistake as to an essential characteristic. The reason given subsequently for returning to work early by Ms Busch was that the maternity leave allowance was higher than the parental leave allowance. The Court of Justice held that an employee is not under an obligation to inform her employee in seeking to return to work that, because of certain legislative prohibitions, she is not able to carry out all of her duties. Furthermore, the Court of Justice held that an employer is not entitled to withdraw consent given to return to work because it was in error as to the employee being pregnant.

These last two cases may seem to be acting increasingly harshly on the employers. However, it is clear that the Court of Justice is taking a firm position on the law as it presents itself. The Court is providing substantive support for women in achieving equal treatment in circumstances in which it is impossible to compare how a man might have been treated and in which the Union has provided a special protective legal regime because of this. These laws may not have universal support from employers, but the point is that, as a society, we have decided to correct an iniquitous situation: that pregnancy is an acceptable ground for dismissal or non-appointment.

To counter the cynical preparation of a notice of dismissal prepared to be delivered after the period of protection expired, the Court of Justice held this to be included in the prohibition under Article 10 of Directive 92/85 in Case C-460/06 *Paquay*.

Dismissal and pregnancy by in vitro fertilization (IVF) treatment has also come under the judicial spotlight.

In **Case C-506/06 *Sabine Mayr***, there had been a dismissal of a woman who was undergoing IVF treatment. Whilst her ova had been fertilized, they had not been re-implanted, and the national court asked whether this was to be regarded within the protected period of pregnancy under Directive 92/85. The Court of Justice held that, at this stage of the treatment, it did not. However, if the woman had been dismissed as a consequence of undergoing the treatment, this would amount to direct discrimination contrary to Directive 76/207. It was left to the national court in this case to determine the exact reasons for the dismissal.

14.3.5.2 Pregnancy and illness

Cases that involve illness resulting from pregnancy are particularly difficult ones to resolve and have caused the Court of Justice to make hard decisions on both sides of the line.

> In **Case C-179/88 *Hertz* v *Aldi***, Mrs Hertz was dismissed because of repeated absence due to illness that originated from her prior pregnancy. The Court of Justice held that although pregnancy-related discrimination was a form of direct discrimination, Directive 76/207 did not apply to dismissals due to illness absence that took place outside the maternity leave time granted. In such circumstances, it was necessary to look at national legislation to consider whether there was any direct or indirect discrimination in the grounds of dismissal.

In this and similar cases, when the period of special protection has expired, it becomes possible again to make a comparison with men to see how they are treated if absent through illness over a long time.

The approach taken in *Hertz* was confirmed in Case C-400/95 *Larsson* v *Dansk Handel & Service* after entry into force of Directive 92/85. The Directives do not, therefore, prevent dismissals for absences due to illness attributable to pregnancy even if it is the case that the illness arose during pregnancy and continued during and after the period of maternity leave. Dismissal is prohibited and unlawful only during the period of protected maternity leave. The dismissal after the leave period is not specifically catered for by EU law. Whether such dismissal is unlawful reverts to comparing it with the dismissal of a man for illness. A woman dismissed for taking too much time off due to illness arising from pregnancy should therefore be compared with a man suffering from any illness. Therefore pregnancy played its role as the source of the illness outside of the protected period and it is the normal comparison that determines the legal position, something that is argued represents formal equality only and not substantive equality.

> This is confirmed by the ECJ in **Case C-191/03 *McKenna***, in which the Court held that pregnancy-originated illness outside of the protected period and absence by men under ordinary sick pay schemes were rightfully to be regarded as comparable.

> **Case C-394/96 *Brown* v *Rentokil*** also concerned a dismissal that resulted from time off taken due to an illness originating during pregnancy, but before maternity leave had commenced. The Court of Justice made it clear that the period or protection incorporated the entire pregnancy and maternity leave.

The result in the *Hertz* and *Larsson* cases was corrected by the Court of Justice to the extent that any off time taken during pregnancy and maternity leave cannot now be taken into account in calculating the entire off time taken for the purpose of dismissal – that is, time can only start to accrue for this purpose after the period of protection has ended. A woman would therefore be best advised to take her maternity leave as late as possible to maximize the period of protection.

14.3.6 The promotion of equal opportunity by removing existing inequalities affecting opportunities

The statutory attempt to promote equal opportunity is often described as 'positive discrimination', although this is not an accurate description for what is allowed under the Union legal regime, as will be observed from the judgments of the Court of Justice. Both the Treaty and Directive 2006/54 contain provision for some sort of action by the member states to try to promote equality. Directive 76/207, which was first on the scene, originally provided for this in Article 2(4). Article 3 of Directive 2006/54 has replaced old Article 2(4) and provides that 'member states may maintain or adopt measures within the meaning of Article 141(4) [EC (now 157 TFEU)] with a view to ensuring full equality in practice between men and women in working life'. Hence, the Directive Article now essentially backs up the Treaty provision, but refers specifically to women, whereas the Treaty Article mentions both men and women.

> ### Article 157 TFEU (ex 141 EC)
>
> With a view to ensuring full equality in practice between men and women in working life, the principle of equal treatment shall not prevent any Member State from maintaining or adopting measures providing for specific advantages in order to make it easier for the underrepresented sex to pursue a vocational activity or to prevent or compensate for disadvantages in professional careers.

> The Court of Justice, in **Case C-319/03 Briheche**, concluded that Article 141(4) EC (now 157 TFEU) and Article 2(4) of Directive 76/207 needed to be looked at separately, suggesting that their scope differed. Hence the Directive Article now essentially backs up the Treaty provision of Article 157(4) TFEU.

Whilst the measures concerned mostly contemplate women, this is not exclusively the position, as can be observed in the case law. The extent to which the authorities of the member states can provide legislation, or indeed private employers able to discriminate positively in favour of women by, for example, shortlisting or interviewing only female candidates or. if dismissals are required, dismissing males only, is a difficult question. Article 3 of Directive 2006/54 would seem to allow more positive action than was previously the case by the use of the term 'equality in practice' – that is, not only on paper! Cases that arose under the old Directive Article and the Treaty amendment include the following.

cross reference
Considered in section 14.3.3.

> In **Case 312/86 Commission v France (Protection of Women)**, it can be seen that not all measures adopted by a member state to assist women will be considered to be fair by the Court of Justice.

> In contrast, in **Case C-218/98 Abdoulaye v Renault**, additional or guaranteed payments for females on maternity leave over and above those paid to males on paternity leave was recognized by the Court of Justice as acceptable due to the occupational disadvantages suffered by women during absence and was held not to be discriminatory.

There is a series of cases concerned with appointment procedures that have been adapted to introduce an element of rebalancing in favour of the under-represented sex.

In **Case C-450/93** *Kalanke*, the Court of Justice ruled that a national rule, which provided that where equally qualified men and women were candidates for a position with fewer women women are automatically to be given priority, constituted direct discrimination on the grounds of sex contrary to the Directive. According to the Court of Justice, the rule had gone beyond promotion and had overstepped the exception provided for in Article 2(4) of Directive 76/207.

This decision was not taken kindly in some quarters, because it seemed to undermine any possibility of providing affirmative action to improve the equality position of women; however, there was soon a refinement of the position both in the subtlety of approach by the member state authorities and the interpretation by the Court of Justice.

Case C-409/95 *Marschall* involved an application for a teaching post by a qualified man being rejected by the local authority according to a law that provided that women should be given priority in the event of equal suitability. However, in contrast to *Kalanke*, a 'saving clause' provided that if a particular male candidate has grounds that tilt the balance in his favour, women are not to be given priority. Thus the Court of Justice was able to conclude that the provision was one that could fall within the scope of Article 2(4) of Directive 76/207 and did not offend the prohibition of discrimination. There were, however, two safety mechanisms that should be set up: the first, to avoid discrimination against men, and the second to stop the pendulum from swinging back against women. The Court of Justice considered such priority clauses to be acceptable provided that the candidates are objectively assessed to determine whether there are any factors tilting the balance in favour of a male candidate, but that such criteria employed do not themselves discriminate against women.

This is a somewhat convoluted judgment, but probably gets there in the end.

Case C-158/97 *Badeck* confirms the decision in *Marschall* that such laws are not in breach of EC law provided that the priority for women was not automatic and unconditional.

The amended Article 157(4) TFEU backs up the ability of the Court of Justice to pursue the more liberal approach adopted in *Marschall*, although the first case reaching it under the amended Treaty Article did not give the Court an opportunity to be expansive.

In **Case C-407/98** *Abrahamsson*, a woman was appointed to a university chair in preference to a man on the basis of a positive discrimination regulation and despite a clear five-to-three vote in favour of the man, based on his qualifications and his overall higher ranking even after the positive discrimination factor had been taken into account. The university contended that the difference was not so great as to breach the objectivity requirement imposed by Community law in the light of the recent case law of the Court of Justice. The Court of Justice held that EC law, primary or secondary, does not support appointments based on automatic preference for the under-represented sex irrespective of whether the qualifications are better or worse and where no objective assessment of each candidate has taken place.

It seems that only where women have equivalent or imperceptibly near qualifications, will EU law permit any affirmative action to be exercised.

A case involving female-only access to childcare facilities, save in emergency, was considered under Article 2(4) of Directive 76/207.

> In **Case C-476/99 Lommers**, a government ministry restricted access to subsidized childcare to women to address the lack of affordable facilities that caused many women to give up their jobs. Whilst this was held by the Court of Justice to be acceptable under Article 2(4) of Directive 76/207, it could be so only provided that the emergency rule that permitted single fathers to seek places was applied on the same conditions as for female workers.

It seems that there must always be a saving clause in the background to prevent positive being too positive and thus unlawfully discriminatory.

cross reference
Dory *is considered in section 14.4.4.*

> Finally in this area is **Case C-79/99 Julia Schnorbus v Land Hessen**, in which a national decision addressed an imbalance that had disadvantaged men. The result is one way of addressing the Army case conclusions reached by the Court of Justice in *Dory*.
>
> In Germany, military or civilian service is compulsory, but for males only. According to which service is performed, this can take between nine and eighteen months, and means that men wishing to go to university enter later and all men enter the job market later. The *Land Hessen* provided rules in respect of entry to the second stage of German legal training that gave priority to men by deferring acceptance of applications by females by up to twelve months in comparison with males who applied at the same time. It argued, when challenged by a female applicant, that the rule was designed to counterbalance the disadvantage suffered by men. It was accepted by the Court of Justice under Article 141 EC as being a proportionate response to the situation.

The measures found to be acceptable by the Court of Justice represent only modest steps in providing substantive and not only formal equality for men and women. However, as with all areas of EU law, it is an area that will certainly not stand still for long, and therefore it is always wise in EU law to be looking out for new cases and the impact that they have on the development of EU law.

14.3.7 Judicial enforcement and remedies

Article 23 of Directive 2006/54 (ex Article 3 of Directive 76/209) requires member states to take the necessary measures to ensure that any provisions in collective agreements, wage agreements, or in individual contracts that breach the principles of the Directive are to be null and void or to be removed.

Member states are required under Articles 17 and 18 of Directive 2006/54 (ex Article 6 of Directive 76/209) to ensure that judicial or conciliation procedures are available with adequate compensation measures even after the employment relationship has ended. It also provides that individuals can pursue claims for real and effective compensation without a fixed upper limit, which was the situation established previously by the ECJ in Case C-271/91 *Marshall II*, that damages means full compensation not restrictively limited by national statutory rules.

Case 14/83 *Von Colson and Kamann* concerned the reimbursement of travel expenses as damages for discrimination. The Court of Justice ruled that full implementation of the Directive entails that sanctions must be such as to guarantee real and effective judicial protection and must therefore have a real deterrent effect on the employer. Where a member state chooses to penalize the breach of the prohibition of discrimination by the award of compensation, that compensation must be adequate in relation to the damage sustained and amount to more than purely nominal compensation.

cross reference

Considered in Chapter 8, section 8.2.2.

The Court of Justice held in the case that Article 6 of Directive 76/207 was not horizontally directly effective; hence the development of the principle of indirect effect from this case.

In Case C-271/91 *Marshall II*, it was held that 'damages' means full compensation not restrictively limited by national statutory rules.

Another notable case is **C-180/95 *Draehmpaehl* v *Urania***. A job was advertised to females only, contrary to both Community and German law. In the consequent claim, damages were limited to a maximum of three months' salary, but dependent on proving fault on the part of the employer. If more than one plaintiff sued, the aggregate compensation payable was limited to six months' salary. The Court of Justice held that liability to compensate cannot be made dependent on fault; compensation itself must guarantee real and effective judicial protection, have a real deterrent effect on the employer and be adequate in relation to the damage suffered. Limits such as three months' salary are acceptable where the employer can prove that, notwithstanding the discrimination, a better-qualified person was appointed and the complainant would not have been appointed in any event. However, an aggregate award ceiling regardless of the number discriminated against is not acceptable under Directive 76/207 because it might have the effect of dissuading applicants so harmed from asserting their rights.

These decisions are now reflected statutorily in Directive 2006/54.

In a mixed equal pay and treatment case, **C-185/97 *Coote* v *Granada***, Ms Coote settled a sex discrimination claim with Granada outside of court and the employment relationship was terminated by mutual consent. She found it difficult to obtain another job due to Granada's refusal to supply an employment agency with a reference. It was claimed that this was contrary to Article 6 of Directive 76/207, under which member states should take measures to achieve the aims of the Directive and must ensure that the rights can be enforced by the individual before the national courts. The Court of Justice held that this right of recourse to the courts is a general principle of Community law reflected in the member states' constitutions and Article 6 ECHR. The Court of Justice held that Article 6 of Directive 76/207 also covers measures that an employer might take as a reaction against legal proceedings of a former employee outside of dismissal, because if employees were to find it difficult to obtain other jobs, it might deter them from taking action when they considered that they had been discriminated against on the grounds of sex.

This extends the scope of EU protection beyond the protection against dismissal.

Article 23 of Directive 2006/54 (ex Article 7 of 76/207) requires member states to take the necessary measures to protect employees against dismissal by the employer as a reaction to a complaint within the undertaking or to any legal proceedings aimed at enforcing compliance with the principle of equal treatment. This had been extended by Directive 2002/73 to protect employees' representatives who act in cases involving complaints against the employer.

Article 30 of Directive 2006/54 (ex Article 8 of Directive 76/207) requires the member states to ensure that provisions of implementing laws are brought to the attention of employees by all appropriate means and Articles 20–22 of Directive 2006/54 (ex Articles 8a and 8b of Directive 76/207) have been introduced for member states to set up bodies to promote equality and to engage in research and discussion to bring forward proposals for agreements and action to achieve equality.

thinking point
But this case involves a private employer and a Directive, so are there any difficulties with this? If so, how did Ms Coote succeed?

14.4 The Social Security Directive (Directive 79/7)

cross reference
Article 7 and pensions were discussed in section 14.2.1.1.

As the third instalment of the first wave of secondary legislative additions to Article 119 EC (now 157 TFEU), Directive 79/7 was enacted to apply the principle of equal treatment to the field of social security and other elements of social protection. The scope of the Directive is limited to statutory schemes, whereas private schemes and the increasing number of contracted-out schemes were catered for later by Directive 86/378 (now repealed and replaced by Directive 20006/54), but Directive 79/7 has not been replaced by Directive 2006/54. Because most courses do not deal with this in any further detail than already dealt with here in respect of Article 7 and pensions, no further treatment will be given.

401

14.5 The Pregnant and Breastfeeding Workers Directive (Directive 92/85)

The Pregnant and Breastfeeding Workers Directive (Directive 92/85) was enacted as a measure for the protection of workers under Article 118a EC (now 154 TFEU) rather than a measure of equal treatment under Article 141 EC (now 157 TFEU), which now allows general measures of equal treatment to be adopted rather than only pay, as was the case prior to amendment. Directive 92/85 is essentially, then, a health and safety measure to protect pregnant and breastfeeding workers, including part-time workers, in the workplace. Article 10 of the Directive has already been considered in relation to the special period of protection in relation to dismissal for pregnant women from the beginning of pregnancy to the end of maternity leave. However, what constitutes a dismissal and what constitutes a refusal to take on an employee is not necessarily a clear-cut point, as was observed in Case C-438/99 *Melgar*. This is because the practice of employment on back-to-back or fixed-term contracts, which is commonplace in industry and commerce, confuses the issue. Thus, whilst strictly concerning health and safety issues, the Directive is nevertheless important in providing a level of protection for women in a situation that is not comparable with men. Without such protection, women might otherwise suffer further inequality. For example, if paid time off to attend antenatal clinics was not required by Article 9, not only might the time taken off not be paid, but it also might be counted towards the amount of time absent from work for the purposes of dismissal.

14.5.1 **Scope and application**

Articles 1–6 of Directive 92/85 outline the purpose of the Directive, the definitions of those workers who are covered, the guidelines on the assessments that employers should make to identify tasks that carry a risk for pregnant and breastfeeding workers, and the actions that employers must take to eliminate the workers' exposure to the risks identified. In particular, Article 7 of the Directive provides that protected workers cannot be obliged to work nights.

> However, as was observed in **Case C-421/92 _Habermann-Beltermann_**, where national legislation actually prohibits night work by pregnant workers, this does not permit dismissal as the employer's reaction to a night worker employee's pregnancy.

Article 8 provides for a minimum fourteen-week maternity leave, Article 9 for paid time off to attend antenatal examinations and Article 10 for protection from dismissal from the beginning of pregnancy to the end of maternity leave. Article 11 provides that employment rights during the maternity leave must be secured, including payments and allowances at least the equivalent of those payable to workers on sick leave.

> Article 11 was considered in **Case C-342/93 _Gillespie_**, which held that the level of pay must be such that it is not inadequate and thus undermines the protection intended, and must take into account any pay increases awarded to other workers during the maternity absence.

> In **Case C-411/96 _Boyle et al._ v _EOC_**, Articles 8 and 11 were considered in some detail. The EOC, set up to promote and defend equal rights, was accused of unlawful discrimination. Boyle and five colleagues raised a number of questions about the maternity scheme run by the EOC, which reflected the UK civil service maternity scheme and was thus applicable to many thousands more workers.
>
> It is in this light that the case should be seen. It had been agreed in the industrial tribunal and accepted by the Court of Justice that, for the purposes of direct effects of the Directives, the EOC was an emanation of the state.
>
> The Court of Justice decided the various questions raised as follows. A clause that required the repayment of additional maternity payments, which were made over and above the statutory minimum if a woman did not return to work following maternity leave when she had undertaken to return, was not contrary to the Directive. Although, in comparison, there was no similar clause applying to those receiving higher-rate sick leave payments, this was not discrimination against women according to the Court of Justice, because maternity leave under Directive 92/85 was a special provision not to be compared with that of a man or woman on sick leave. Higher-rate sick leave pay would apply to both women and men.
>
> In answer to a question about the commencement of maternity leave, the Directive specified only the minimum number of weeks to be granted and left it to member states to lay down provision as to when it should commence.
>
> A clause that prohibited women from taking sick leave during the minimum period of fourteen weeks' maternity leave unless she elected to return to work and thus to terminate her maternity leave was held to be contrary to Article 8(1) of the Directive.

However, a similar clause in respect of supplementary maternity leave was found to be compatible with Directives 76/207 and 92/85 because EC law does not apply to supplementary maternity leave paid out by the employer. A woman can be restricted to taking either maternity leave or sick leave.

Article 11(2)(a) of Directive 92/85 requires maternity leave rights in the fourteen-week minimum period to be at least the same as minimum statutory rights when on sick leave. A clause that limited the period during which annual leave accrues to that fourteen-week period and not to any additional leave granted by the employer over and above the statutory fourteen-week period was held to be compatible with EC law. Outside of that period, no annual leave would accrue. There was no discrimination, direct or indirect, according to the Court of Justice, because all employees on unpaid leave accrued no annual leave entitlement. A right to obtain supplementary leave over and above the protection provided by the Directive, and which was available to women only, could not constitute less favourable treatment.

In contrast, in answer to the fifth question, a clause that restricted the accrual of pension rights to the fourteen-week period and denied it during the supplementary period of unpaid leave was held to be contrary to Directive 92/85. Although, under Article 11(4), entitlement to benefits could be made subject to the workers satisfying national legislation, this was not possible where the pension scheme was wholly occupational and governed by the employment contract. Therefore the accrual of pension rights was not dependent on receiving pay during the supplementary period.

cross reference
Considered in section 14.4.5.1.

The case was a part-success for the individual applicants, but, more importantly, the offending clauses could no longer be enforced either by the EOC or other employers with the same clauses (that is, most of the UK civil service).

403

Otherwise, Directive 92/85 has not featured in case law to any significant extent, so whilst it was originally assumed following its enactment that all cases concerned with dismissal during pregnancy or maternity would come under its provisions, the *Melgar* case shows that we still need to have an eye on Directive 2006/54 in similar circumstances.

14.6 Article 19 TFEU: the expansion of EU equality law

For more details on this section scan here or visit the Online Resource Centre.

The introduction of Article 13 EC (now 19 TFEU) by the Treaty of Amsterdam provided the Treaty with a new legal base for the enactment of legislation to tackle discrimination across a range of issues. However, it is to be noted that the Article does not actually prohibit anything in its own right, but empowers the Council to take action to combat discrimination based on sex, racial or ethnic origin, religion or belief, disability, age or sexual orientation.

Directives were issued with little delay under this Treaty Article and before a further ten member states came on board, which would have made it even more difficult to reach the unanimity required for measures under the Article. It can be said, however, in contrast with the debate about the reasons for the inclusion of the original Article 119 EEC in the first place, that there is no suggestion that Article 13 EC was included on economic grounds; instead, it is a clear representation of the social concerns of the EU and to be welcomed for this reason. Legislation to combat discrimination was enacted under Article 13 EC.

14.6.1 Secondary legislation issued under Article 19 TFEU

Two Directives were enacted in 2000 that, between them and the 2006 recast Equal Treatment Directive, encompass many of the matters identified in Article 13 EC where action was deemed necessary to combat discrimination. Directive 2004/113 on equal treatment in the access to and supply of goods and services is also briefly considered following.

14.6.1.1 The Racial Equality Directive (Directive 2000/43)

This was the first Directive to be adopted under the new Article 13 EC (now 19 TFEU) and seeks to apply the principle of equal treatment to persons regardless of racial or ethnic origin in matters of employment, social protection, education and access to public goods and services, including housing (Article 3(1)). An exception is provided that is similar to Article 14(2) of Directive 2006/54, whereby differential treatment can be justified where a certain characteristic is a genuine and determining occupational requirement (Article 4(1)). The Directive requires the member states to establish a body to promote equal treatment on grounds of race and ethnicity and to combat discrimination in these areas (Article 13).

14.6.1.2 The Framework Employment Directive (Directive 2000/78)

This Directive, known as the 'Horizontal Framework Directive' because it applies across all sectors of employment, deals with all of the other forms of discrimination identified by Article 19 TFEU (ex 13 EC), with the exception of the matters covered by the Racial Equality Directive and Directives on equality between men and women. As part of the justification for the Directive, it makes reference to the ECHR, as cited in Article 6 TEU. It provides that there should be no discrimination direct or indirect on the grounds of religion or belief, disability, age, or sexual orientation. As with forms of indirect discrimination under previous Directives, indirect discrimination can be objectively justified provided that it is proportionate (Article 4). An exception exists that is also similar to Article 14(2) of Directive 2006/54 whereby different treatment can be justified by a certain characteristic that is a genuine and determining occupational requirement (Article 4(1)). There is also a special exemption for access to employment in religious organizations (Article 4(2)), and there are further exceptions in respect of disability (Article 5) where measures to accommodate disabled persons would cause employers a disproportionate burden, along with numerous exceptions in respect of age (Article 6). There is no requirement under this Directive to establish a body to promote equality for the matters covered by this Directive, in contrast to the Equal Treatment and Racial Equality Directives.

14.6.1.3 Common characteristics

Both Directives share the definitions of equal treatment as being no direct or indirect discrimination (Article 2(1)), thus effectively removing any need for a prolonged debate as to whether these concepts are synonymous, similar, overlapping, or different. They both then define, as does the amended recast Equal Treatment Directive, direct and indirect discrimination, as well as 'harassment'.

Neither of the Directives encroach on the existing prohibition on the ground of nationality (Article 18 TFEU) and do not apply in favour of third-country nationals (TCNs) (Articles 3(2) in both Directives). Both contain the objective justification defence as first statutorily defined in Article 19 of Directive 2006/54. Both also contain a provision to allow for positive action in support of achieving equality of treatment (Article 4 of Directive 2002/43 and Article 7 of Directive

2002/78). Remedies and enforcement considerations have been provided that are similar to those provided for in Directive 76/207, as amended, replaced by Directive 2006/54 (Articles 7–12 in Directive 2002/43 and Articles 9–14 in Directive 2002/78).

Whilst there is quite a bit of overlap and common ground between the Directives, there are also differences, the details of which at this stage in their lives would be too great to consider in this volume. The Directives have already generated considerable academic comment, some of which is cited in end-of-chapter 'Further reading' list.

cross reference

Test Achets *is considered in section 14.6.1.4.*

In 2004, Directive 2004/113 was enacted under Article 13 EC (now 19 TFEU) to implement the principle of equality between men and women in the access to and supply of goods and services. It applies to the provision of all public and private sector supply of goods and service outside the sphere of private and family life transactions, and, apart from a notable derogation in the Directive dealing with insurance leading to case law and in particular a 2011 judgment in Case C-236/09 *Test Achets*, it has not provoked much attention in academic and university studies of EU law. Further details are not therefore included within this text.

cross reference

See Chapter 2, section 2.2.4.1.

In 2008, a new Directive was proposed that aimed to combat discrimination based on religion or belief, disability, age, or sexual orientation, and to put into effect the principle of equal treatment, but outside the field of employment. Its scope is social protection, including social security and health care, social advantages, education, and access to and supply of goods and services that are available to the public, including housing, but only professional or commercial activities are covered. Following wide consultation, with reported opposition from some countries to the inclusion of sexual orientation, the proposal was made and approved by the European Parliament in 2009, but awaits further progress and the unlikely unanimous support of the Council.

14.6.1.4 Selective case law from the Article 19 TFEU Directives

Whilst largely outside the main remit of undergraduate EU courses on discrimination law, a few sample cases arising from the new Directives will be considered here.

cross reference

See Chapter 8, section 8.2.2, for more on this case.

Case C-144/04 *Mangold* v *Helm* concerns age discrimination that resulted from a scheme seeking to ease the employment of older workers. It was held that a change of German law to assist older workers in finding work went beyond the objectively justified exceptions permitted in Article 6 (1) of Directive 2000/78, despite the fact that the time allowed for its implementation had not expired. Mangold became subject to the change, which allowed workers over the age of 52, previously 58, to be employed on fixed-term contracts without accruing compensation rights on termination, as opposed to permanent contracts, which would allow such rights. The justification for the ruling was that non-discrimination on the grounds of age was part of the general principle of non-discrimination in Community law and thus applicable in its own right, but with reference to the norms contained in the Directive for assistance. The Court was of the view that the German law was too general and did not permit the taking into account of personal circumstances or the actual conditions of the labour market.

In a second case concerned with age discrimination, **Case C-411/05 *Palacios de la Villa***, a general scheme of compulsory retirement at the age of 65 under national law, but reflected within a collective agreement, was questioned as to whether this amounted to age discrimination prohibited by Directive 2000/78. The age was determined by the eligibility to the national pension. It was held by the Court of Justice to be justified, but the measure had to be objectively and reasonably justified in the context of a national law, with legitimate aims in regulating employment policy and the labour market, and proportionate. In view of the need for the state to regulate the labour market, the fact that the agreement to arrange for retirement at this age was part of a collective agreement and that it was set at the age by which a pension was payable were justified considerations satisfying those requirements.

The decision in the *Mangold* case was subsequently affirmed by the Court of Justice in **Case C-555/07** *Kükükdeveci*, which involved a dispute as to a notice period between an employee and a private employer because a German law precluded periods of employment completed before the employee reached the age of 25 from counting towards the notice period. Directive 2000/78 should have been implemented in Germany at the material time, but it had not. The preliminary ruling question was essentially: on what provision of law could Kükükdeveci rely? The Court of Justice held that the general principle of EU law prohibiting discrimination on the grounds of law, as expressed in Directive 2000/78, applies to preclude national law, as in the case, from discriminating.

Thus, then, the general principle is seen to apply directly between parties, but not the Directive.

But is it more controversial to have the general principle give rise to horizontal direct effects or the Directive, bearing in mind that the general principle finds no clear expression anywhere in the Treaties or secondary legislation?

The scope of the term 'disability' within Articles 2(1) and 3(1) of Directive 2000/78 was considered in **Case C-13/05** *Sonia Navas*, in which the Spanish referring court enquired whether it extended to cover dismissal due to sickness. The Court of Justice held that whilst dismissal due to disability was prohibited where a person was not competent, capable and available to perform essential functions due to a disability, this did not extend to dismissal solely on the grounds of sickness.

In **Case C-267/06** *Tadao Maruko* v *Versorgungsanstalt der deutschen Bühnen*, a same-sex partnership survivor's claim for a pension benefit was denied on the grounds that the compulsory occupational pensions scheme did not provide for persons who were not married. Because this was held to be pay, according to the Court of Justice, it came within the Framework Directive 2000/78 and could be considered discrimination based on sexual orientation. Whilst the Directive did not provide a direct answer to the problem, it was noted that this was within a same-sex registered partnership, which, in Germany, was increasingly being equated with marital partnerships. Thus it was left to the national court to decide if the particular right to pension entitlement was also to be equated with spousal rights. If so, it would be direct discrimination prohibited under the Directive.

A further case involves a disability discrimination claim under Directive 2000/78.

Case C-303/06 *Coleman* concerns the claim that the carer of a disabled person suffered indirect discrimination by her employer, which was upheld by the Court of Justice, stating that the Directive was not limited to applying only to those suffering direct discrimination, but also, as in this case, to the primary carer of a disabled person, who sought, but was not granted, flexible working arrangements to care for the disabled person.

The above cases include three mildly generous interpretations (*Mangold*, *Maruko* and *Coleman*) and two mildly conservative judgments (*Palacios* and *Navas*), but these cases merely scratch the surface of the issues and cases that could, and probably will in the future, arise under these Directives. Whether many standard undergraduate courses will be able to deal with these in depth, or indeed at all, is uncertain, but equally unlikely. Undoubtedly, the jurisprudence of EU equality will be richly enhanced.

One of the few cases drawing attention so far under the Race Directive 2000/43 is **Case C-54/07 *Firma Feryn***, which involves an action in Belgium against a firm's owner, who expressed the view that persons of certain races would not employed by them. Within the reference going to the Court of Justice was whether the Directive covers this statement rather than discriminatory action, although this was the opinion of the Advocate General. The Court of Justice held that the fact that an employer states publicly that it will not recruit employees of a certain ethnic or racial origin constitutes direct discrimination in respect of recruitment within the meaning of Article 2(2)(a) of Directive 2000/43 for the reason that such statements were likely to dissuade certain candidates from submitting their applications and, accordingly, to hinder their access to the labour market. It further held that the public statements by which an employer lets it be known that, under its recruitment policy, it will not recruit any employees of a certain ethnic or racial origin are sufficient for a presumption of the existence of a recruitment policy that is directly discriminatory within the meaning of Article 8(1) of Directive 2000/43. It is then for that employer to prove that there was no breach of the principle of equal treatment, which it can do by showing that the undertaking's actual recruitment practice does not correspond to those statements. It is thus for the national court to verify that the facts alleged are established and to assess the sufficiency of the evidence submitted in support of the employer's contentions that it has not breached the principle of equal treatment. It was also held that Article 15 requires that rules on sanctions must be effective, proportionate and dissuasive, even where there is no identifiable victim.

On 1 March 2011, the Court of Justice delivered its judgment in **Case C236/09 *Test Achets***, which concerned the application of Directive 2004/113 (equal treatment between men and women in access to and the supply of goods and services) and in particular of Articles of the Directive dealing with insurance contracts.

The case was brought against a Belgian law that implemented the derogation permitted under Article 5(2) of the Directive allowing for sex to be used as one of the criteria in the determination of insurance premiums. The Directive, whilst clear about the fundamental nature of the equality between men and women as outlined in various Articles of the Treaties and Directive, was conscious of the widespread use in insurance and financial services of sex as an actuarial factor to determine risk and thus premiums or payouts. Hence the Directive permitted an exception from the general requirement of unisex premiums and benefits, if supported by reliable and transparent data. The derogation could last up to five years after the transposition date, namely 21 December 2007 plus five years, but after that date the Directive required a re-examination of the relevant data.

The Court of Justice noted the wealth of general provisions aimed at the elimination of discrimination between men and women, including very specifically Articles 21 and 23 of the EU Charter of Fundamental Rights, but also noted that legislative attempts to achieve that must be undertaken with account for the economic and social conditions and therefore allow, for limited transitional periods, derogations where appropriate; hence the derogation in Article 5(2) of the Directive. However, the Directive failed to specify a temporal or date limit and thus there was a risk, in the view of the Court, that the derogation would be employed without limit by the member states contrary to the general rule requiring unisex premiums in Article 5(1).

The result was a simple statement making it clear that the derogation expires on the 21 December 2012.

In the light of the high visibility of this ruling, which affected car insurance, pensions and life insurance, it attracted much comment.

14.6.1.5 The Lisbon Treaty and the Union Charter of Fundamental Rights

Gender equality and equality generally were issues that were discussed during the drafting of the Constitutional Treaty, which was abandoned and replaced by the Lisbon Treaty, but which dealt with these rights in a radically different way. It is worth noting that, with regard to their inclusion in the Constitutional Treaty, the burning question was not whether they should feature in the Treaty at all, but where they should be placed. The Constitutional Treaty contained in its Preamble the equality of persons as one of the European values, which was then repeated in Article I-2. The Lisbon Treaty attached the Union Charter to the Treaties by way of a Declaration, but with opt-outs for Poland and the UK applying internally in those two countries, and a political deal to do the same for the Czech Republic agreed prior to its ratification of the Lisbon Treaty.

cross reference
See Chapter 1.

The Union Charter includes a third title dealing with equality rights in Articles 20–23.

Article 20 Equality before the law

Everyone is equal before the law.

Article 21 Non-discrimination

1. Any discrimination based on any ground such as sex, race, colour, ethnic or social origin, genetic features, language, religion or belief, political or any other opinion, membership of a national minority, property, birth, disability, age or sexual orientation shall be prohibited.

2. Within the scope of application of the Constitution and without prejudice to any of its specific provisions, any discrimination on grounds of nationality shall be prohibited.

Article 22 Cultural, religious and linguistic diversity

The Union shall respect cultural, religious and linguistic diversity.

Article 23 Equality between men and women

....

Equality between men and women must be ensured in all areas, including employment, work and pay. The principle of equality shall not prevent the maintenance or adoption of measures providing for specific advantages in favour of the under-represented sex.

As set out, the rights provided would appear not to disturb the existing provision of equality law in the EU, with the possible exceptions of Article 20, which could be argued to apply to TCNs, not presently covered by the EU equality regime, and Article 21, which provides that any discrimination based on any ground shall be prohibited. It will be interesting to see how that is interpreted by the Court of Justice in the EU context. Article 51 of the Charter defines the scope of the application of the Charter as not extending to the member states when not implementing EU law and that the Charter does not extend the field of application of EU law nor modify its powers and tasks, a proviso that is repeated in Declaration No. 1 attached to the Treaties. Time and case law will determine just exactly how it will be employed in the EU legal system.

Summary

Equality law provision in the EU has developed, from limited beginnings, a number of genuine and comprehensive legal instruments for the combating of discrimination in a range of areas. Furthermore, a general principle of equality is emerging more and more visibly through the judgments of the Court of Justice. We also have as yet to see how the new rights in the new Directives will be received by the courts of the member states. The Court of Justice will no doubt have opportunities to expand on the general principle endorsed, for example, in C-144/04 *Mangold*.

Questions

1   Why was a sex equality provision (Article 119 EEC, now 157 TFEU) included in the Treaties?

2   How, if at all, is 'pay' defined?

3   Why were pensions considered as pay when they were meant to be excluded under Directive 79/7?

4   With whom can an applicant be compared in an equal pay claim?

5   What is 'indirect discrimination'?

6   When can a difference in pay be justified?

7   When is it lawful to dismiss a woman who is pregnant or who has given birth?

8   What does 'positive discrimination' mean in the EU context?

For suggested approaches to answering these questions scan here or visit the Online Resource Centre.

Further reading

BOOKS

Ellis, E. *EU Anti-Discrimination Law*, Oxford University Press, Oxford, 2005.

Shaw, J. (ed.) *Social Law and Policy in an Evolving European Union*, Hart Publishing, Oxford, 2000.

Tridimas, T. *The General Principles of EC Law*, 2nd edn, Oxford University Press, Oxford, 2006 (chapter 2).

ARTICLES

Ahtela, K. 'The revised provisions on sex discrimination in the European Law: a critical assessment' (2005) 11 ELJ 58.

Anagnostaras, G. 'Sex equality and compulsory military service: the limits of national sovereignty over matters of army organisation' (2003) 28 EL Rev 713.

Bell, M. and Waddington, L. 'Reflecting on inequalities in European equality law' (2003) 28(3) EL Rev 349.

Besson, S. 'Never shall the twain meet? Gender discrimination under EU and ECHR law' (2008) HRLR 647.

Burrows, N. and Robinson, M. 'An assessment of the recast of Community equality laws' (2006) 13 ELJ 18.

Burrows, N. and Robinson, M. 'Positive action for women in employment: time to align with Europe?' (2006) J L & Soc 24.

Howard, E. 'The European Year of Equal Opportunities for All 2007: is the EU moving away from a formal ideal of equality?' (2008) 14 ELJ 168.

Masselot, A. 'The state of gender equality law in the European Union' (2007) 13 ELJ 152.

Prechal, S. 'Equality of treatment, non-discrimination and social policy: achievements in three themes' (2004) 41 CML Rev 533.

Trybus, M. 'Sisters in arms: European Community law and sex equality in the armed forces' (2003) 9 ELJ 631.

Glossary

Acquis communautaire The accumulated body of Community law including Treaties, secondary legislation and judicial developments.

Acte clair A French principle of law which states that where a provision of law is clear, there is no need to refer to a higher court, but simply to apply it.

CCP The Common Commercial Policy which is the overall driving force behind the establishment and maintenance of the CCT (Common Customs Tariff).

Common Market Free movement of the factors of production (goods, persons and capital).

'Competence creep' The term given to the slow assumption of competences by the Commission to carry out the policies of the Community and Union. Its power to do so is not expressly granted by the member states, but the Commission uses implied powers.

Customs union Creates a common external tariff, presenting a common position to the outside world. The same duties are imposed on goods entering the customs union regardless of from where they are imported. Once imported, the goods circulate freely as Union goods throughout the Union.

Decisions Article 249 defines a Decision as a specific and binding act which is addressed to member states or specific individuals.

'Deepening' This is the term given as to the extent to which integration is intergovernmental or supranational. However, deepening can also apply to integration in new policy areas because it considers the extent to which the Communities have encroached into previously exclusively held areas of the member states' competences.

Direct effects First introduced by the ECJ in Case 26/62 *Van Gend en Loos*. The term refers to judicial enforcement of rights arising from provisions of Community law which can be upheld in favour of individuals in the courts of the member states.

Directly applicable Used to describe the process whereby international law and EU Regulations in particular become directly applicable without separate implementation into domestic law.

Direct discrimination Where one person is treated less favourably on grounds of sex than another is, has been or would be treated in a comparable situation.

Directives Set out aims which must be achieved, but the choice of the form or method of implementation is left to the member states. Each member state must inform the Commission of implementation measures.

Dualism Regards international law and national law as fundamentally different systems which exist alongside each other. In order to overcome the barrier existing between the two systems, legislation is required to transform the rules of international law into the national legal system before they can have any binding effect within the state in such circumstances. It is for the member states to determine where the international law is then placed within the national hierarchy of laws.

Federalism Refers to a form of political integration whereby the constituent states would transfer sovereign powers to the union, which would control the activities of the members from the centre. Certain local issues are still regulated by the constituent states such as education, culture and land management but most economic and political power is transferred to the centre including, most notably, defence and trade.

Free Trade Area (FTA) Involves the removal of customs duties between member states; however, the members of a free trade area decide their external policies and any duties payable by third-party countries wishing to export goods into those countries.

GATS General Agreement on Trade in Services.

GATT General Agreement on Tariffs and Trade.

Indirect discrimination Where an apparently neutral provision, criterion or practice would put persons of one sex at a particular disadvantage compared with persons of the other sex, unless that provision, criterion or practice is objectively justified by a legitimate aim, and the means of achieving that aim are appropriate and necessary.

Intergovernmental Conference (IGC) A conference of the member states outside the Treaty and Union set-up, which is established to discuss and agree Treaty change.

Intergovernmentalism The normal way in which international organizations work, whose decisions require unanimity and are rarely enforceable and if so only between the signatory states and not the citizens of those states. The clearest examples are the United Nations or General Agreement on Trade and Tariffs (GATT).

Internal market Defined in Article 14(2) EC as 'an area without internal frontiers in which the free movement of goods, persons, services and capital is ensured in accordance with the provisions of the Treaty.

Legal personality Establishes that as a legal person the EU is capable of entering into formally binding agreements.

Monism The belief that international law and national law form part of a single system or hierarchy of law, therefore the acceptance of international law would not require formal incorporation by legislative transformation. After Treaty agreement and assent or ratification, it would be self-executing and directly applicable within the state.

Negative integration The removal of existing impediments to free movement such as striking down national rules and practices which obstruct or prevent achievement of the internal market.

'Own resources' The Union can rely on certain incomes which have been designated Union income. These include agricultural levies, duties received under the Common Customs Tariff, and a percentage on the revenues from Value Added Tax (VAT) as agreed by the member states and currently set at 1.6 per cent of the rate used for VAT assessment. This system became self-sufficient as from 1 January 1980.

Proportionality Any action by the Union should not go beyond what is necessary to achieve the Treaty objectives.

Regulations General provisions of legislation and detailed forms of law to ensure that the laws in question are the same in all member states.

They become legally valid in the member states, without the need for implementation, on the date specified therein as on the twentieth day after publication in the Official Journal.

Sexual harassment Where any form of unwanted verbal, non-verbal or physical conduct of a sexual nature occurs, with the purpose or effect of violating the dignity of a person, in particular when creating an intimidating, hostile, degrading, humiliating or offensive environment.

Sui generis Not being within a general class, but a special class, of its own.

Supranationalism Where decision-making takes place at a new and higher level than that of the member states themselves and such decisions replace or override national rules.

TRIPS Trade-Related aspects of Intellectual Property Rights.

'Widening' Primarily referring to the process of the expansion of the Union to include new member states, but can also apply to the extension of the Union into new policy areas and in developing new sectors for integration.

WTO World Trade Organization.

Index

Introductory Note

References such as "178–9" indicate (not necessarily continuous) discussion of a topic across a range of pages. Wherever possible in the case of topics with many references, these have either been divided into sub-topics or only the most significant discussions of the topic are listed. Because the entire work is about 'EU law' and 'commercial law' the use of these terms (and certain others which occur constantly throughout the book) as an entry point has been restricted. Information will be found under the corresponding detailed topics.

A

abuses 109, 157–9, 234, 351, 363
accession 15, 17–18, 35, 101, 112
    see also expansion
    preconditions 17
Accession Treaties 15–16, 18, 31, 194
ACP 107
acquis communautaire 13, 17, 27, 101, 127, 411
acte clair 142, 164–6, 411
    development 169
actions
    for damages 97, 167, 219, 253, 255
    direct 61, 64, 153–4, 170, 173–4, 219–20, 254–6
    enforcement 153, 173–80, 182, 184, 186–7, 206, 373
    indirect 61, 100, 254
    procedural 133, 151, 174
acts
    administrative 142, 232, 245
    binding 61, 105, 222, 281
    of general application 92, 227, 238, 254–5
    judicial review of 60, 219–56
    legal 87, 106, 221
    non-legislative 43, 92, 103, 106, 232
    normative 227–8
    regulatory 225–6, 232, 237
    reviewable 105, 222–3, 240
    validity of 128, 220, 237
Acts of Parliament 128–9, 131, 138
actuarial factors 378, 407
additives 141, 288–9, 296
administrative acts 142–3, 232, 245
administrative provisions 176, 386, 388
administrative rules 104, 324
admissibility 226, 228, 232, 255–6
    direct actions for non-contractual liability 243
    direct actions to annul EU acts 221–4
    failure to act actions 239–40
    non-contractual liability 243
advertising 77, 81, 86, 159, 186, 233, 301–2
    campaigns 281, 283
advisory bodies 40, 65

Advocates General 58–9, 67, 114, 158, 192, 236, 355
African, Caribbean and Pacific (ACP) countries 107
age 132, 203–4, 302, 329–30, 376–8, 389–90, 403–6
    discrimination 405
    pensionable 376–7, 388–9
agencies 66, 153, 176, 220, 239–41, 253, 380
agreements 14, 17–18, 26–31, 34, 36–7, 90–1, 105–8
    association 14, 23, 36, 44, 55, 107, 198
    collective 385, 399, 405–6
    cooperation 349
    international 30, 36, 44, 55, 75–6, 106–8, 145
    and direct effects 198–9
Albania 16
alcohol 159, 276, 291–2, 302
Alliance of Liberals and Democrats for Europe (ALDE) 54
Amsterdam Intergovernmental Conference and Treaty 26–7
annulment 65, 81, 91, 232, 234–5, 239, 244 *see also* direct actions, to annul Union acts
anti-dumping 231, 236
appeals 59–61, 64, 133, 153–7, 163–6, 168–9, 337
applicability, direct 101, 121, 129, 189–91
application 15–17, 163–4, 203–7, 226–7, 229–32, 253–5, 345–8
    correct 164
    direct 123, 138, 204, 281, 358
        see also direct applicability
    incorrect 209
    mode of 268
    strict 159, 203
appointment
    Commission 41–3, 55
    judges 58
architects 20, 265, 331
armed forces 391–2
art treasures 182–3, 267, 289
artistic heritage 289
artistic or commercial property 290

assent 36, 55, 87, 91, 127, 129, 412
association agreements 14, 23, 36, 44, 55, 107, 198
asylum 328, 352, 363
attributed competence 71, 95
Austria 14, 25, 166, 302, 348, 354, 357
autonomy of remedies 244

B

backlogs 64, 157, 168
bake-off bread 302–3
balance, institutional 46, 66, 92
bananas 170, 251, 275
banks 40, 65, 204, 265, 309, 376
basis of comparison 379–81
beer 117, 141, 274, 276, 288, 296
Belgium 8, 192, 269, 284, 326–7, 337, 359–60
    reception of EU law 143, 146
binding acts 61, 105, 222, 281
Blair, Tony 52
blocking minority 27, 48–50
Bosnia and Herzegovina 16
boycotts 19, 47, 334
bread 289
    bake-off 302–3
breastfeeding workers 393, 401–2
Britain 23–7, 31–5, 54, 179–82, 346–7, 350–1, 362–5
    applications 12, 32, 145
    courts 111, 128, 130, 132, 135–6, 238, 298
    doctrine of parliamentary sovereignty 128–9
    dualist approach 128
    entry and European Communities Act 1972 129–31
    European Union Act 2011 137–8
    judicial reception of Community and EU law 131–6
    reception of EU law 127–38
    relationship with EU 32–5
        to 1970s 32
        1980 to date 34–5
        accepted application 33
broadcasting 159, 319, 334, 338, 348

Brussels Summits 11, 15, 30–1
budget 44–5, 56–7, 222
    contributions 21, 33–4
budgetary procedure 56–7, 93, 221
budgetary processes 20, 100
Bulgaria 12, 15, 29, 41, 48
burden of proof 211, 373, 383–5
butter 18, 110

C

Cameron, David 21, 32, 35
candidate countries 15–17, 28, 31, 37, 107
CAP 11, 18, 33, 41, 44, 85, 112
capital 9, 204, 263–4, 308–9, 319,
    370, 411–12
carers
    primary 350–1, 362–3, 407
    rights 329–30, 361–4
case law 63–4, 134, 156–7, 297–9,
    323–4, 350, 360–1
Cassis de Dijon case 63, 74, 79, 278,
    292–3, 295–9, 302–4
CCP 72, 266, 411
CCT 9, 11, 36, 113, 262, 265–7, 411–12
censure, vote of 42–3, 56
certainty, legal 113, 115, 154, 201–2,
    214, 223, 234–5
CET 264, 266, 411
CFI 22, 57, 63–5, 220, 223–4, 235–6,
    251–2 see also General Court
CFSP 5, 24, 36, 44, 46–7, 60, 92
chargeable events 272
charges 192, 262–3, 267–72, 276–7,
    301, 320, 353
    having equivalent effect (CHEEs)
        267–72, 276
    and taxes 271–2
    validity of charges for services
        rendered 269–70
    pecuniary 268
    for services rendered 269
Charter of Fundamental Rights 28–31,
    35, 111–12, 236, 369, 409
CHEEs 267–72, 276
childbirth 330, 368, 392–6
children 302, 321, 329–30, 347–8,
    350–1, 357–8, 362–3 see also
    family members
choice of court 253
circulation, free 10, 266, 269, 283
citizenship 36, 309, 316–18, 324, 344,
    356–66
    case law 357–64
    definition 356–7
    rights 354–5, 357, 359, 364–6
    summary of law 364–5
clarity 27, 157, 196, 208, 214
closed groups 229–30, 249–50
co-decision procedure 25, 27, 45–6, 55,
    84, 88–90, 92
cohabitees 327
Cold War 6, 13
collective agreements 385, 399, 405–6

comitology 43, 57, 93, 241
commercial policy 72, 266, 411
Commission 40–5, 84–94, 173–87,
    220–4, 226–36, 238–55,
    279–91
    appointment and removal 41–3
    and Art 258 TFEU 174
    composition 41
    decisions 44, 112, 159, 230
    and defendants in Art 258 TFEU
        action 176–7
    enforcement by 174–81
    identification and reporting of
        breaches 175–6
    members 27, 29, 31, 41–3, 53, 56, 90
    officials 114, 152, 186
    President 11, 21, 23, 41–3, 52, 56
    and procedure of Art 258 TFEU
        action 177–81
    proposals 88, 91, 249
    Santer 42, 56
    smaller 29–30
    tasks and duties 43–4
Commissioners 27, 29, 31, 41–3, 53,
    56, 90
Committee of Permanent
    Representatives 40, 44, 51, 222
Committee of the Regions (CoR) 40, 46,
    65, 84, 88–90, 225
Common Agricultural Policy (CAP) 11,
    18, 33, 41, 44, 85, 112
Common Commercial Policy (CCP) 72,
    266, 411
Common Customs Tariff (CCT) 9, 11, 36,
    113, 262, 265–7, 411–12
Common External Tariff (CET) 264, 266,
    411
Common Fisheries Policy 72
Common Foreign and Security Policy
    (CFSP) 5, 24, 36, 44, 46–7,
    60, 92
common market 9–12, 21, 60, 78, 181,
    261–6, 308
Commonwealth 32–3
Community, term 5
Community competence 36, 71, 74, 76,
    79, 108
Community Directives 103–6, 195–7,
    321–32, 335–41, 372–4,
    376–81, 383–409
    and direct effects 132, 139, 143, 195–7
    overcoming lack of horizontal direct
        effect 199–206
    general 321, 353
    sectoral 331, 335
    unimplemented 201
Community institutions 18–21, 39–66,
    82–5, 103–6, 219–22, 239–47,
    250–3 see also Commission;
    Committee of the Regions;
    Council (of Ministers) of the
    European Union; Court of
    Auditors; European Central
    Bank; European Council;
    Economic and Social Committee

Community interest 110, 170
Community law see also Introductory
    Note
    applicable 102, 132, 141
    direct effect 125, 129–30, 132–3,
        142–3, 152–4, 166, 189–207
    effective 132, 197
    effective provisions of 123, 125
    general principles of 97–8, 108–10,
        112–15, 117–18, 201–4,
        243–4, 406
    reception
        Belgium 143, 146
        Denmark 144–5
        France 141–3
        Germany 138–41
        Italy 141
        Netherlands 143–4
        Sweden 145
        UK 127–38
    supremacy of 121–2, 128, 133, 141–2
companies 114–15, 133, 206, 209–10,
    229–31, 349–50, 382–3
comparators 379–80, 383, 386, 388
    hypothetical 380–1
comparison, basis of 379–81
compensation 166, 197, 206–7, 209–10,
    212–13, 252–3, 400
    full 210, 213, 399–400
competence creep 51, 71–2, 75–6,
    78–9, 81, 83, 94
competences 35–7, 68–84, 94, 106,
    156, 232–3, 411
    attributed 71
    concurrent 72–3
    division of 29, 51, 68–71, 73, 117, 121
    exclusive 72, 74, 79–80, 94, 107, 211,
        263
    extension of 74–8
    implied 75, 79
    internal 72, 75
    lack of competence 64, 232–3
    principle of conferral 71
    shared 72–3
    transfer of 35, 69, 94
    Union 36, 71, 74, 76, 79, 108
competition 9, 222, 231, 268, 274–6,
    308, 371
    law/rules 61, 98, 210, 231, 242,
        245–6, 290
    policy 11, 14, 18, 43–4, 61, 72, 290
competitiveness 21, 334
complaints 142, 176, 178, 186–7, 231,
    240–1, 401
    constitutional 139–40
compliance 61, 174, 179–80, 183, 186,
    205
composition 18, 275, 283, 292, 300,
    392
    Commission 41
    Council 44
    Court of Justice 58
    European Parliament 52
compromises 4, 7, 24–5, 29, 45, 47–50,
    203–4

compulsory expenditure 57
compulsory military service 330, 392
concerted action 97
Conciliation Committees 89–90
conciliation procedures 55, 384–5, 399
concurrent competences 72–3
concurrent liability 253
confidentiality 113–14
conflicting national law 121, 126, 146,
    180
consensus 46–50, 52–3, 146
consent 55, 77–8, 84, 87, 90–1, 107,
    395
conservation 72–3, 185, 293
consistency 62, 132–3, 167, 196, 281
constitutional basis 23–5, 62
constitutional complaints 139–40
constitutional courts 60, 121, 125, 139,
    141, 145–6
constitutional law 99, 124, 127–8, 141,
    191
    national 124, 138, 141
constitutional practice 124–5, 136
constitutional traditions 110–11, 215,
    236
Constitutional Treaty, abandoned 11, 23,
    29–30, 42, 51–2, 87, 408
constitutionality 20, 139–40
constitutions 30, 35, 109–13, 124–8,
    139–46, 392, 408
consultation procedure 90, 92
consumer protection 73, 98, 100, 283,
    294–5, 334
continuity 45, 51–2, 317, 320, 330
contracts 61, 93, 210, 267, 325–6, 380,
    394
    of employment 316, 325–6, 377, 381,
        390, 394, 403
    fixed-term 203, 394–5, 401, 405
    indefinite 394
    individual 385, 399
contractual liability 242–3
convenience, marriages of 328, 351–2
cooperation agreements 349
cooperation procedure 22, 27, 55, 86
CoR 40, 46, 65, 84, 88–90, 225
COREPER (Committee of Permanent
    Representatives) 40, 44, 51,
    222
correct application 164
Council (of Ministers) of the European
    Union 39–53, 75–94, 105–7,
    220–5, 228–36, 241–4, 246–52
    configurations 44
    COREPER (Committee of Permanent
        Representatives) 40, 44, 51, 222
    Council Secretariat 44, 51
    Foreign Affairs 36, 42, 44–5
    forms of voting 46
    functions and powers 45
    general law-making powers 51
    presidency 29–30, 36, 45–6, 52
    qualified majority voting (QMV) 22–3,
        26–7, 29–30, 41–2, 46–50,
        65–6, 84

role and voting in legislative
        process 46
    simple majority voting 47
    unanimity 10, 30, 46–7, 51–2, 76,
        84–5, 90–2
Council of Europe 6, 44, 107
Court of Auditors 39–40, 65, 225, 240
Court of First Instance (CFI) 22, 57,
        63–5, 220, 223–4, 235–6,
        251–2 see also General Court
Court of Justice 107–17, 151–71, 174–
        86, 190–216, 219–48, 311–29,
        345–61 see also European
        Court of Justice
    and integration 20
courts, specialized 64–5
creeping federalism 10, 266
criminal convictions 338, 340
Croatia 15–16, 31, 41, 49, 53, 58, 107
culture 6, 10, 73, 100, 102, 322, 411
currency 36–7, 72, 98, 145, 263
    common 10, 144, 264
    single 24–5, 34, 265
customs duties 9, 192, 262, 264,
        266–72, 276, 411
    dismantling of 9, 11, 18, 267
customs formalities 269
customs tariff, common 9, 11, 36, 262,
        265–7, 411–12
customs union 7, 72, 262, 264, 266–7,
        411
Cyprus 12, 15–17, 48
Czech Republic 12, 15, 31, 48, 102,
        144, 408

D

damages 135–6, 143, 166–7, 206–9,
        213–14, 242–6, 399–400
de Gaulle, President 11–12, 19–21, 33,
        144–5
decision-making powers 45, 51, 55, 233
Decisions 105, 198
Declarations 29, 50, 58, 103, 111–12,
        121, 168
deepening 3–4, 12, 18–32, 411
    Amsterdam Intergovernmental
        Conference and Treaty 26–7
    Brussels Summit and Lisbon
        Treaty 30–1
    Constitutional Treaty 29–30
    Court of Justice and integration 20
    first IGC 22–3
    Laeken Summit 28–9
    Luxembourg Accords 18–19
    Maastricht Treaty on European
        Union 24–5
    Nice Intergovernmental Conference
        and Treaty 27–8
    primary Treaties 18
    revival attempts 20–1
    Single European Act 22–4
    stagnation and 'Eurosclerosis' 19–20
defendant institutions 242–3, 251

deficit, democratic 25, 55, 66–7, 84, 87,
        91, 221
definition of position 241–2
delegated acts 55, 106, 232
delegated powers 43, 87, 92–3, 105, 145
delegation of powers 51, 92–3, 144
democracy 13, 17, 25, 28, 37, 47, 94
democratic deficit 25, 55, 66–7, 84, 87,
        91, 221
democratic legitimacy 56, 94
Denmark 12–13, 17, 20, 25–6, 33, 48,
        209
    reception of EU law 144–5
dependants 315, 326–7, 375
deportation 316, 323–4, 336–7,
        339–40, 350, 361–2, 365
derogations 279–80, 285–6, 290,
        294–7, 336–9, 341–2, 407–8
    Art 36 TFEU 285, 287, 289, 297,
        303–4
descendants 325–6, 329 see also family
        members
deterrent effect 212, 400
development of Union 3–4, 8, 12–15,
        17–32, 411
diplomas 332, 335, 360
direct actions 61, 64, 100, 153–4, 170,
        173–4
    against EU institutions 60, 219–56
    to annul EU acts 220–39
        and actions for damages 239
        acts addressed to applicant 226
        admissibility 221–4
        alternatives 237–9
        challenge to regulatory acts 232
        direct and individual concern
            226–31
        effect of successful action and
            annulment 235
        grounds for annulment 232–5
        and illegality pleas 238–9
        interest groups and party
            actions 231
        locus standi 224–32
        and non-privileged applicants
            225–6
        and preliminary ruling
            references 237–8
        restrictive approach 235–7
    for failure to act 239–42
        acts subject to action 240–1
        admissibility and locus standi
            239–40
        definition of position 241–2
        invitation to act 241
        procedural requirements 241–2
        substantive action 242
    non-contractual liability 242–53
        administrative acts 245–6
        admissibility 243
        autonomous or independent
            action 244
        causal connection 252–3
        concurrent liability/choice of
            court 253

direct actions (*cont.*)
    damage 252
    for employees 246
    for lawful acts 251–2
    for legislative acts 246–50
    liability requirements 244–5
    locus standi 243
    new single test 250–1
    protection of individual 248
    rules of law covered 247–8
    sufficiently serious breach 248–50
    time limits 243–4
    plea of illegality 238–9, 253–5
    acts open to review 254–5
    effect of successful challenge 255
    grounds of review 255
    locus standi 254
direct and individual concern 225–6,
    228, 230–1, 238, 240
direct applicability 101, 121, 129,
    189–91
direct application 123, 138, 204, 281,
    358
direct concern 225, 227–8, 232
direct discrimination 273, 311, 379–81,
    389–90, 394–6, 398, 406–7
direct effects 125, 129–30, 132–3,
    142–3, 152–4, 166, 189–207
    and Decisions 198
    and definition of 'state' 199–200
    definitions 190–1
    and direct applicability 190–9
    and Directives 132, 139, 143, 195–7
    overcoming lack of horizontal direct
        effect 199–206
    doctrine of 121–2, 125, 129, 186, 190,
        197, 207
    horizontal 132, 189, 193–4, 196–7,
        199–207, 216, 309
    and international agreements (and
        conventions) 198–9
    and Regulations 195
    and Treaty Articles 192–5
    vertical 194, 202, 216, 384
Directives 103–6, 195–7, 321–32,
        335–41, 372–4, 376–81,
        383–409
    and direct effects 132, 139, 143, 195–7
    overcoming lack of horizontal direct
        effect 199–206
    general 321, 353
    sectoral 331, 335
    unimplemented 201
disability 113, 372, 403–8
discretion 159, 161, 176–8, 193, 207–9,
        227, 250–1
    lower courts 161
    to refer 161, 168
discretionary powers 92
discrimination 273–6, 298–302,
        309–12, 369–70, 378–88,
        402–6, 408–9
    age 405
    Art 19 TFEU 46, 113, 369,
        403–5, 407

Art 157 TFEU 112, 368–9, 372–85,
        388, 397
    direct 273, 311, 379–81, 389–90,
        394–6, 398, 406–7
    equal pay 371, 374–85
    equal treatment 112–13, 365–6,
        368–70, 372–3, 385–401,
        404–5, 407
    expansion of EU equality law 372,
        403–9
    Framework Employment Directive 404
    indirect 273, 303, 311, 332–3, 381,
        383, 404
    positive 372, 397–8, 409
    Pregnant and Breastfeeding Workers
        Directive 401–3
    prohibition of 203, 247–8, 331,
        369–70, 388, 398, 400
    racial 350, 369, 404, 407–8
    Racial Equality Directive 404
    secondary legislation 372–3, 404–9
    sex 132, 370–1, 381, 386–7, 391, 398
    sexual orientation 387
    Social Security Directive 372, 390, 401
    Treaty Articles 372
discriminatory taxation 273–6
disguised restrictions 272, 283, 285–7,
        290, 293, 295
dismissals 325, 385–6, 389, 393–7,
        400, 406
    during or after pregnancy 401–3
diversity 294, 301
    linguistic 408
    national 298
division of competences 29, 51, 68–71,
        73, 121
division of jurisdiction 60–1
domestic goods 274, 291, 298, 303
domestic law 69, 123, 128, 190–1, 215,
        411
domestic products 271–4, 276, 282–3,
        286, 291–5, 297–8, 300–4
    similar 273–4
domestic tax regime 334, 348
dual burden rules 297–9, 301, 305
dual vigilance 152, 174, 190, 216
dualism 127–9, 138, 411
dumping 231–2, 236, 297

E

East Germany 12–13, 24
Eastern Europe 6, 13–14, 17, 26
ECB 39–40, 65, 87–8, 90, 220–1, 225,
        239–40
ECJ 57–65, 76–8, 114–16, 135, 151–3,
        219–20, 362–4 *see also* Court
        of Justice
    actions brought by one member state
        against another 184–6
    Advocates General 58–9, 67, 114,
        158, 192, 236, 355
    application and effect of
        judgments 182–4

backlogs 64, 157, 168
    composition and organization 58
    Court of First Instance 22, 57, 63–5,
        220, 223–4, 235–6, 251–2
    direct actions 61, 64, 100, 153–4,
        170, 173–4
        against EU institutions 219–56
    division of jurisdiction 60–1
    form of judgments 59
    General Court 57–61, 63–4, 220, 226,
        231, 235, 243
    indirect actions 61, 100, 254
    and integration 20
    interpretation 61–2
    jurisdiction 60–1
    length of proceedings 64
    methodology 61
    and national procedural
        autonomy 211–16
    precedent 62–3
    preliminary rulings 60–1, 63–4, 118,
        146, 151–66, 168, 170–1
    President 59, 135, 162
    procedure 58–60
    remedies 189–217
    reporting of cases 59–60
    Rules of Procedure 58–9, 158, 162,
        164, 169, 224
    and self-employed persons 318–19,
        331–4
    specialized courts 57–8, 60–1, 64–5,
        169
    Statute 58–9, 63, 162, 243
    and supremacy 121–4
economic activity 308, 313, 315, 342,
        347–8, 353, 355–6
Economic and Social Committee 40, 46,
        65, 84, 88, 90, 225
economic conditions 10, 13, 15, 24,
        308, 371
economic development 7
economic integration 10, 23, 261–2,
        276, 370
economic law 100
economic policy 208, 247–8
economic risks 249, 251–2
economic union 10, 24, 52, 143, 264,
        276, 371
ECSC (European Coal and Steel
        Community) 5, 8–11, 18, 35,
        40, 101, 234
ECU (European Currency Unit) 21, 222
EDC (European Defence Community) 8, 11
education 10, 73, 318, 322–3, 354,
        358–9, 404–5
educational establishments 330, 342,
        386
educational services 348, 353–4
EEA (European Economic Area) 14–16,
        23–4, 60, 107, 145
EESC (EESC) 40, 46, 65, 84, 88, 90, 225
effective judicial/legal protection 57,
        207, 211–12, 215–16, 237, 400
effectiveness 21, 104, 123, 125, 130,
        201–2, 215–16

EFTA (European Free Trade Association) 14, 32
EIB (European Investment Bank) 40, 66, 87–8
elections 26, 29–30, 34, 52–4, 145, 221
electorates 12, 14, 16, 29, 31, 37, 53
employees 204, 245–6, 378–80, 383–5, 394–5, 400–1, 406–7
  full-time 375, 382, 394
  liability for 246
  private 199
employers 214–15, 374–83, 385–6, 388–90, 393–5, 400–4, 406–7
  private 132–3, 197, 199–201, 204, 379, 390, 406
  public 200
employment 203–4, 309–11, 315–17, 321–6, 374–5, 388–91, 404–6
employment contracts 316, 325–6, 377, 381, 390, 394, 403
employment relationships 314, 317, 375, 386, 395, 399–400
employment rights 321, 402
EMS (European Monetary System) 21
EMU (European Monetary Unit) 20–1
enforcement 100, 104, 191, 197, 207, 286, 385
  actions against member states 153, 173–87, 206, 373
  actions brought by one member state against another 184–6
    Commission involvement 185
    referral to Court of Justice 185–6
  alternative actions to secure member states' compliance 186
  application and effect of judgments 182–4
  Art 258 action 174–81
    defences by member states 180–1
    defendants 176–7
    identification and reporting of breaches 175–6
    informal or administrative stage 177–8
    judicial stage 179
    letters of formal notice 178
    procedure 177–81
    reasoned opinions 174, 177–9
  by Commission 174–81
  equal pay 384–5
  equal treatment 399–401
  suspensory orders and interim measures 181–2
  Treaties 153, 173–87, 206, 373
enlargement 13–18, 26–9, 47–8, 58
enrichment, unjustified 118, 248
entrenchment 128, 130–1, 136
entry
  negotiations 15–16, 26, 144 see also accession
  rights of 322–4, 326
environment 51, 73, 85, 91, 292
EOC 373, 402–3
EPC 8, 11, 20, 22
equal burden rules 297–302, 305

Equal Opportunities Commission (EOC) 373, 402–3
equal pay 371, 374–85
  basis of comparison 379–81
  enforcement and remedies 384–5
  meaning of 'pay' 375–9
  original Directive 379
  part-time work and indirect discrimination 381–3
  and pensions 375–9
  scope of principle 374–85
  work of equal value 368, 372, 374, 379–80, 383–5
equal treatment 112–13, 365–6, 368–70, 372–3, 385–401, 404–5, 407
  no discrimination on grounds of sex 386–8
  equality with regard to employment access, working conditions, dismissal and retirement ages 389–90
  exempt occupations 391–2
  judicial enforcement and remedies 399–401
  promotion of equal opportunity by removing existing inequalities affecting opportunities 397–9
  protection of women regarding childbirth and maternity 392–6
  scope 388–9
equal value, work of 368, 372, 374, 379–80, 383–5
equal work 368, 372, 374, 379–80, 384
equality 112–13, 369–73, 386, 389–90, 401, 404–5, 407–9
  general principle 109, 112–13, 369, 409
equally applicable (indistinctly applicable) measures 283, 291–9
equivalence 212, 216, 288, 293
ESCB 40, 65
establishment 6–10, 20–2, 51–2, 266–7, 310–12, 318–20, 331–3
  lawyers 336
  scope 319–21
Estonia 12, 15, 17, 48, 334
EU (European Union) see also Introductory Note
  definition 5
  establishment and development 3–37
  law see also Introductory Note
    applicable 102, 132, 141
    direct effect 125, 129–30, 132–3, 142–3, 152–4, 166, 189–207
    effective 132, 197
    effective provisions of 123, 125
    general principles of 97–8, 108–10, 112–15, 117–18, 201–4, 243–4, 406
  reception
    Belgium 143, 146
    Denmark 144–5
    France 141–3
    Germany 138–41
    Italy 141

    Netherlands 143–4
    Sweden 145
    UK 127–38
  EU law see also Introductory Note
    sources and forms 96–118
    supremacy 36, 120–3, 125–6, 128, 131, 136, 141–3
EURATOM 5, 9, 11, 35, 101, 246
European Central Bank (ECB) 39–40, 65, 87–8, 90, 220–1, 225, 239–40
European citizenship 36, 309, 316–18, 324, 344, 356–66
  case law 357–64
  definition 356–7
  rights 354–5, 357, 359, 364–6
  summary of law 364–5
European Coal and Steel Community (ECSC) 5, 8–11, 18, 35, 40, 101, 234
European Commission 40–5, 84–94, 173–87, 220–4, 226–36, 238–55, 279–91
  appointment and removal 41–3
  and Art 258 TFEU 174
  composition 41
  decisions 44, 112, 159, 230
  and defendants in Art 258 TFEU action 176–7
  enforcement by 174–81
  identification and reporting of breaches 175–6
  members 27, 29, 31, 41–3, 53, 56, 90
  officials 114, 152, 186
  President 11, 21, 23, 41–3, 52, 56
  and procedure of Art 258 TFEU action 177–81
  proposals 88, 91, 249
  Santer 42, 56
  smaller 29–30
  tasks and duties 43–4
European Communities
  basic objectives and nature 9–11
  definition 5
  founding 7–9
European Council 29–31, 36, 40–2, 44–5, 51–3, 220–2, 225
  High Representative of the Union for Foreign Affairs and Security Policy 30–1, 36, 41–2, 45, 50–3, 66–7, 107–8
  President 31, 36, 45, 52–3, 66–7
European Court of Human Rights 112, 182
European Court of Justice 57–65, 76–8, 114–16, 135, 151–3, 219–20, 362–4 see also Court of Justice
  actions brought by one member state against another 184–6
  Advocates General 58–9, 67, 114, 158, 192, 236, 355
  application and effect of judgments 182–4
  backlogs 64, 157, 168
  composition and organization 58

European Court of Justice (*cont.*)
Court of First Instance (CFI) 22, 57, 63–5, 220, 223–4, 235–6, 251–2 *see also* General Court
direct actions 61, 64, 100, 153–4, 170, 173–4
against EU institutions 219–56
division of jurisdiction 60–1
form of judgments 59
General Court 57–61, 63–4, 220, 226, 231, 235, 243
indirect actions 61, 100, 254
and integration 20
interpretation 61–2
jurisdiction 60–1
length of proceedings 64
methodology 61
and national procedural autonomy 211–16
precedent 62–3
preliminary rulings 60–1, 63–4, 118, 146, 151–66, 168, 170–1
effect on Court of Justice 167
President 59, 135, 162
procedure 58–60
remedies 189–217
reporting of cases 59–60
Rules of Procedure 58–9, 158, 162, 164, 169, 224
and self-employed persons 318–19, 331–4
specialized courts 57–8, 60–1, 64–5, 169
Statute 58–9, 63, 162, 243
and supremacy 121–4
European Currency Unit (ECU) 21, 222
European Defence Community (EDC) 8, 11
European Economic and Social Committee (EESC) 40, 46, 65, 84, 88, 90, 225
European Economic Area (EEA) 14–16, 23–4, 60, 107, 145
European Free Trade Association (EFTA) 14, 32
European integration 4–5, 7–12, 18, 20–4, 27–8, 36–7, 140
Communities and EU 10–11
and Court of Justice 20
degree of 8, 10, 12, 34, 318, 340, 360
and desire for peace 6
economic 10, 23, 261–2, 276, 370
and economic development 7
functional 10, 24, 37, 266
initial goals 7
motives for 5–7
negative 266, 280, 412
political willingness 6
positive 266
and Soviet threat 6
European Investment Bank (EIB) 40, 66, 87–8
European Monetary System (EMS) 21
European Monetary Unit (EMU) 20–1
European Ombudsman 187

European Parliament 39–46, 52–7, 76–80, 86–91, 93–4, 220–2, 224–5 *see also* Parliamentary Assembly
and appointment of Commission 55
budgetary powers 56–7
and censure/removal of Commission 56
control of executive 55–6
elections and political parties 54
functions and powers 54–7
legislative powers 54–5
membership 53–4
President 53, 106, 197, 221
right to litigate 57
European Political Community (EPC) 8, 11, 20, 22
European President 31, 36, 45, 52–3, 66–7
European System of Central Banks (ESCB) 40, 65
Eurosclerosis 19–20
eurozone 10, 31–2, 37, 72, 137, 145, 265
exclusive competences 72, 74, 79–80, 94, 107, 211, 263
exempt occupations 391–2
existing national law 104, 266
exit, rights of 321–4
expansion 4, 8, 12–15, 17–18, 25–6, 29, 31 *see also* accession
1995 14–15
2004 15
2007 15–16
East Germany 13
European Economic Area 14
first 12–13
second 13
terms for future 13
expectations, legitimate 113, 115–16, 234, 247–8, 252
expenditure 19, 56–7, 65, 138, 223, 235
compulsory 57
non-compulsory 57
export bans 209, 280, 286
exports 117, 192, 263, 267–8, 279–80, 282–6, 290–1
expulsion 323–4, 337, 339–41, 364
extension of competences 74–8
external relations 3–4, 35–6, 53, 100, 106

F

failure to act, direct actions for 239–42
family education rights 329–30
family life 111, 347, 361–3
family members 307, 325–6, 328, 330, 339, 345–6, 361–2
non-member state/TCN 330, 350, 362–3, 365–6
fault 209, 245, 400
intentional 167, 211

Federal Republic of Germany 48–9, 137–41, 332–3, 345, 347–8, 358, 391–2
Constitution 111, 113, 124–5, 138–40
courts 139–40, 155, 354, 383
East 12–13, 24
Parliament 138, 140
reception of EU law 138–41
federal union 25, 36
federalism 10–11, 411
creeping 10, 266
fees 99, 181, 269–70, 317, 353–4
fidelity clause 262
fines 61, 117, 184, 187, 323
Finland 12, 14, 25, 48, 76
fiscal policies 10, 23
fixed-term contracts 203, 394–5, 401, 405
flexibility clause 85
Foreign Affairs Council 36, 42, 44–5
foreign policy 8, 24, 102 *see also* High Representative of the Union for Foreign Affairs and Security Policy
founding Treaties 21, 97
Framework Employment Directive 404
framework Treaties 102, 108
France 158–9, 175–7, 180, 183–6, 281–3, 287–90, 346
Constitution 141–3
courts 141–2, 158, 160
President 11–12, 19–21, 28, 33, 47, 144–5
reception of EU law 141–3
Francovich case 62, 99, 124, 143, 179, 206–7, 209–10
free circulation 10, 266, 269, 283
free trade area (FTA) 7, 32, 264, 411
freedom of movement
of goods 4, 11, 74, 77, 98, 261–305, 308–9
Art 36 TFEU derogations 285–91
charges having equivalent effect (CHEEs) 267–72, 276
common market 264
customs union 264
economic union 264
equally applicable (indistinctly applicable) measures 283, 291–9
establishment of internal market 266–72
free trade area 264
integration methods 266
internal market developments 265–6
Keck and Mithouard 299–303
legislative provisions 262–3
measures having equivalent effect (MHEEs) 279–83, 285, 304
non-tariff barriers 278–304
progress towards Treaty goals 263–9
prohibition of discriminatory taxation 273–6
quantitative restrictions 263, 267, 278–84, 289

and secondary legislation 263
stage reached 264–5
tariff and tax barriers 261–77
and Treaties 262–3
of lawyers 335–6
of persons 26, 85–6, 160, 263–4,
279–80, 301–2, 306–66
basic right of non-discrimination
310–12
citizenship 36, 309, 316–18, 324,
344, 356–66
case law 357–64
definition 356–7
rights 354–5, 357, 359, 364–6
summary of law 364–5
derogations from free movement
regimes 336–42
employment in the public
service 341–3
procedural safeguards 336–8
public policy, security, and
health 338–41
educational services 348, 353–4
extension of rights 344, 352–65
family members 326–9
general free movement
Directives 355–6
indirect discrimination 311
and jobseekers 315–16
legal framework—primary and
secondary legislation 308–12
and Maastricht Treaty 356–7
market access 311
material rights 321–30
and nationality 312–13
and part-time work 313–15
personal and material scope of
rights 312–21
receipt of services 353–5
without movement 354–5
Regulation 492/2011 (ex
Regulation 1612/68) and
Directive 2004/38 324–9
right to remain 330
rights of entry, residence and exit
322–4
scope of establishment and
provision of services 319–21
self-employed 318–19, 330–6 see
also self-employed persons
social and tax advantages 325–6
TCNs (third-country nationals) 323,
328, 344–6, 349–52, 361–3,
365, 404
tourist services 353
Treaty provisions 308–10
Union status 313–19
wholly internal rule 345–9, 364, 366
worker training, education, and
benefits 316–18
worker's family education and carer
rights 329–30
of workers 71, 88, 100, 112,
307–8, 346, 349 see also free
movement, of persons

frontier workers 326, 347
full-time employees 375, 382, 394
functional integration 10, 24, 37, 266
functions 5, 9, 41, 44–5, 53–4, 56, 66–7
fundamental freedoms 28, 78, 110–12,
340, 347, 361–2, 387 see also
human rights
fundamental rights 28–31, 35–6, 108–13,
138–41, 340, 361, 370–2

G

gender discrimination 132, 370–1, 381,
386–7, 391, 398
General Agreement on Tariffs and Trade
(GATT) 7, 44, 76, 107–8, 198–9,
266, 411
general application 92, 104, 192, 227,
230, 238, 253–5
General Court 57–61, 63–4, 220, 226,
231, 235, 243
general Directives 321, 335, 353
general legislative acts 232, 239, 251
general principles of Union law 97–8,
108–10, 112–15, 117–18, 201–4,
243–4, 406
Germany 48–9, 137–41, 332–3, 345,
347–8, 358, 391–2
Constitution 111, 113, 124–5,
138–40
courts 139–40, 155, 354, 383
East 12–13, 24
Parliament 138, 140
reception of EU law 138–41
good faith 98, 117, 121, 125, 175, 194
goods
domestic 271–4, 276, 282–3, 286,
291–5, 297–8, 300–4
free movement of 4, 11, 74, 77, 98,
261–305, 308–9
Greece 12–13, 20, 107, 157, 179, 183,
274–5
courts 165–6, 203
Greenland 13, 17
grounds for annulment 232–5
groups, closed 229–30, 249–50

H

habitual residence 318
harassment 373, 386, 404
sexual 373, 412
harmonization 51, 79, 81, 198, 264–6,
280, 331
health 73, 77, 81, 85–6, 287–9, 338–9,
401
inspections 269–70
public 98, 100, 233, 284, 288–9,
293, 362
High Authority 8, 11, 40, 92, 110,
233–4, 254–5
President 8
High Court 129, 134–6, 159, 163

High Representative of the Union for
Foreign Affairs and Security
Policy 30–1, 36, 41–2, 45,
50–3, 66–7, 107–8
home member state 336, 350, 363
home rules 320
horizontal direct effects 132, 189,
193–4, 196–7, 216, 309, 379
and Directives 199–206
incidental 204–6, 216
host states 314–17, 319–20, 328–30,
335–6, 338–42, 350–3, 361–6
House of Lords 118, 130–6, 141, 163,
165, 199, 201
housing rights 321, 324
human health 73, 77, 81, 85–6, 287–9,
338–9, 401
inspections 269–70
public 98, 100, 233, 284, 288–9,
293, 362
human rights 28–31, 35–6, 108–13,
138–41, 340, 361, 370–2
Hungary 9, 12, 15, 48, 157, 325
hypothetical comparators 380–1

I

Iceland 14–16, 31, 107
IGCs (Intergovernmental
Conferences) 22–4, 26–7,
29–30, 35, 58, 102, 411
illegality pleas 238, 253–6
and direct actions to annul EU
acts 238–9
illness 316, 396
IMF (International Monetary Fund) 7
immigration 195, 349, 351–2 see also
free movement, of persons
implementation 43–4, 56, 92–3, 104,
190–3, 196, 411–12
periods 105, 196, 201, 203–4
implementing measures 104, 193, 225,
232, 356
implementing powers 93
implied competences 75, 79
implied powers 72, 75–6, 411
import bans 229, 282, 288
import licences 115, 230, 252, 282,
290, 295
import restrictions 287
importers 186, 228–31, 268–70, 283,
287, 290, 295
imports/imported goods/products
266–9, 271–4, 279–85, 288–9,
291–5, 297–300, 302–4 see
also free movement, of goods
inaction 176–7, 239, 243
incidental horizontal effects 204–6,
216
inconsistent national legislation 123,
125, 134
incorporation of law 104, 127, 191
incorrect application 209
indefinite contracts 394

independence 9, 32, 44, 52, 58–9, 155, 319
indirect actions 61, 100, 254
indirect discrimination 273, 303, 311, 332–3, 381, 383, 404
indirect effects 152–3, 189–90, 196–8, 200–4, 206–8, 210–12, 216–17
indirect taxation 51, 272–3
indistinctly applicable measures 283, 291–9
individual concern 225–6, 228, 230–1, 238, 240, 256
individual contracts 385, 399
individuals 152–4, 177–8, 190–204, 206–7, 226–32, 235–8, 247–50
  private 186, 193, 281
  protection of 207–8, 248–50
inequality 359, 373, 378, 381–2, 397, 401
informants 245–6
infringement(s) 64, 81, 109, 178, 183–4, 208–9, 232–4
injunctions 123, 133–5
injustice 166, 169, 236
insolvency 170, 206, 209
inspections 269–70, 275, 290
institutional balance 46, 66, 92
institutional change 21–3, 27, 31, 52
institutional framework 39–40, 66
institutional law 99–100
institutional reforms 21, 26–7, 46
institutions 18–21, 39–66, 82–5, 103–6, 219–22, 239–47, 250–3 see also Commission; Committee of the Regions; Council (of Ministers) of the European Union; Court of Auditors; European Central Bank; European Council; Economic and Social Committee
  advisory bodies 40, 65
  main 40, 44, 65, 87, 99
  participation in legislative processes 83–6
  sundry Union bodies 66
insurance 246, 319–20, 332, 356, 363, 389, 407–8
integration 4–5, 7–12, 18, 20–4, 27–8, 36–7, 140
  Communities and EU 10–11
  and Court of Justice 20
  degree of 8, 10, 12, 34, 318, 340, 360
  and desire for peace 6
  economic 10, 23, 261–2, 276, 370
  and economic development 7
  functional 10, 24, 37, 266
  initial goals 7
  motives for 5–7
  negative 266, 280, 412
  political willingness 6
  positive 266
  and Soviet threat 6
intellectual property 76–7, 290, 412
intentional fault 167, 211
interest groups 40, 231, 362
Intergovernmental Conferences (IGCs) 22–4, 26–7, 29–30, 35, 58, 102, 411

intergovernmentalism 10, 21, 352, 411
interim measures 60, 170–1, 173–4, 179, 181
interim relief 134–5, 170, 213, 215
internal competences 72, 75
internal frontiers 263, 309, 412
internal market 22, 51, 72–3, 76–7, 81, 85–6, 308–9 see also common market; single market
  developments 265–6
  establishment 266–72
internal policy 75–6
internal situations 160, 346, 348, 365, 370
internal taxation 193, 261, 268, 271–3
international agreements (and conventions) 30, 36, 44, 55, 75–6, 106–8, 145
  and direct effects 198–9
international law 102, 122, 127–8, 138, 143, 190–1, 411–12
International Monetary Fund (IMF) 7
international organizations 10, 44, 61, 74, 100, 138, 141
invitation to act 241
Ireland 26, 283–5, 294–5, 328, 337, 348–52, 363
Italy 12, 48, 177–80, 182–4, 206, 267–8, 288–9
  courts 124, 141, 158–9, 164, 166, 210
  reception of EU law 141
IVF treatment 395

J

JHA (Justice and Home Affairs) 24, 26, 36, 92
job evaluation schemes 383–4
jobseekers 315–18, 359, 361
judicial activism 61, 202, 213
judicial panels 57, 64–5, 169 see also specialized courts
judicial protection 215, 236–7, 400
  effective 57, 207, 211–12, 215–16, 237, 400
judicial review 60–1, 65, 81, 83, 100, 106, 113–14 see also direct actions, against EU institutions
jurisdiction 60–1, 64, 123, 153–6, 158–9, 168–70, 242–3
  Court of Justice 60–1, 122
jurisprudence 63–4, 134, 156–7, 297–9, 323–4, 350, 360–1
justice, natural 109, 113
Justice and Home Affairs (JHA) 24, 26, 36, 92

K

Keck and Mithouard cases 63, 278, 299–304, 333
Kosovo 16

L

labelling 196, 296, 301
labour market 315, 405–7 see also employment
lack of competence 64, 232–3
Laeken Summit 28
languages, official 58–9, 101
Latvia 12, 15, 17, 48, 334
law-making powers 22, 36, 44, 51, 54, 69, 76
law-making principles 87, 89, 91
law-making procedures 25, 66, 84, 87–92, 94–5
  ordinary 45, 55, 84, 86–8, 90, 106, 197
  special 51, 87, 90–2, 372
  specialist 92
law-making processes 22, 24, 55, 80–1, 83–6, 88, 94
  participation of institutions 83–6
lawful acts, liability for 251–2
lawful discrimination 377, 379
lawful residence 351, 361, 364–6
lawfulness 65, 82–3, 115, 220–1, 239, 337
lawyers 92, 98, 331, 335–6, 345
  establishment 336
  free movement of 335–6
  independent 114
  provision of services by 335–6
legal acts 87, 106, 221
legal base 71, 78–9, 81, 83–6, 90–1, 104–6, 234
legal certainty 113, 115, 154, 201–2, 214, 223, 234–5
legal effects 103, 105, 123, 125, 129, 220–4, 228 see also direct effects
legal order 79, 108–14, 118, 128–9, 166–7, 215–17, 369
  new 20, 61, 121–2, 210
legal personality, conferral of 72
legal persons 30, 64, 100, 194, 200, 230, 247–8
legal privilege 113–14
legal protection, effective 57, 207, 211–12, 215–16, 237, 400
legal systems 62, 97–9, 108, 122–4, 127, 152–4, 211–12
  classification of elements of EU law 99–100
  national 97, 102, 109, 122, 127, 143, 215
  style of EU system 98–9
legality 65, 82–3, 115, 220–1, 239, 337
legislative acts 79–81, 86–8, 103–4, 197, 208, 220–3, 245–7
  general 232, 239, 251
  liability for 246–50
legislative powers 22, 36, 44, 51, 54, 69, 76
legislative procedures 25, 66, 84, 87–92, 94–5
  ordinary 45, 55, 84, 86–8, 90, 106, 197

special 51, 87, 90–2, 372
specialist 92
legislative processes 22, 24, 55, 80–1, 83–6, 88, 94
participation of institutions 83–6
legitimacy 29, 56, 94
legitimate expectations 113, 115–16, 234, 247–8, 252
less favourable treatment 326, 373, 393, 403
letters of formal notice 178
liability 62, 129, 137, 167, 207–11, 244–7, 249–52
for administrative acts 245–6
concurrent 253
contractual 242–3
for employees 246
for lawful acts 251–2
for legislative acts 246–50
non-contractual 242–53
requirements of 244–5
standard of 245
state 99–100, 152–3, 166, 186, 189–90, 206–12, 216–17
vicarious 246
licences 116–17, 170, 229–30, 282, 290, 300, 332
Liechtenstein 14, 17
linguistic diversity 408
Lisbon Treaty 30–2, 43–7, 52–3, 57–8, 85–7, 101–3, 221–2
Lithuania 12, 15, 48
local authorities 66, 380, 398
locus standi 57, 83, 115, 235–7, 243–4, 247, 254
direct actions for failure to act 239–40
direct actions for non-contractual liability 243
direct actions to annul EU acts 224–32
non-privileged applicants 225–6, 240
plea of illegality 254
privileged applicants 224, 239–40
semi-privileged applicants 225
lower courts 124, 139, 142, 164, 167
discretion 161
lump sums 183–4, 378
Luxembourg 7, 12, 48–9, 53, 143, 268, 326
Luxembourg Accords 12, 18–19, 47, 265

M

Maastricht Treaty 5, 21, 24–6, 40, 74, 143–4, 373
Macedonia 16, 107
majority voting 19, 23, 46–7, 85, 137
qualified 22–3, 26–7, 29–30, 41–2, 46–50, 65–6, 84
simple 47
maladministration 56
Malta 12, 15–16, 48–9
management committees 51, 92–3, 280
manifest errors 82, 166, 210
marine biological resources 72–3

market access 301–4, 311–12, 333
marketing 205, 286, 292–5, 299–300, 302–5
national rules 283–4
stages 272, 282
markets 131, 248–9, 253, 275–6, 290–1, 302, 308
marriages 326–8, 330, 347, 349, 351–2, 362–3
of convenience 328, 351–2
material rights of free movement 321–30
maternity 373, 389, 392–7, 401–3
measures having equivalent effect (MHEEs) 279–83, 285, 304
MEPs (Members of the European Parliament) 28, 53–4, 90
Merger Treaty 8–9, 18, 101
migrant workers 317, 329, 350–1, 358, 360, 362 see also free movement, of persons; free movement, of workers
military service 330, 392
milk 249–50, 282, 287, 290, 293, 295, 300
minority, blocking 27, 48–50
misuse of powers 82, 232, 234–5
mobile phone signals 348
monetary policy 65, 72, 74, 102
monetary union 14, 20–1, 23–5, 34, 98, 144–5, 265–6
monism 127, 143, 412
Monnet, Jean 7–8, 10–11, 18
Montenegro 16, 107
morality, public 77, 285–6
Morocco 17, 198, 349
multi-speed Europe 25
mutual recognition 79, 265, 331, 334–6

N

national authorities 113–14, 155–6, 166, 253, 314, 332–3, 392
national constitutional law 124, 138, 141
national courts 121–5, 151–4, 156–71, 207–15, 237–8, 313–16, 382–3
see also preliminary ruling references
extension of state liability to 210–11
national law 121–8, 130–4, 160–2, 196–7, 200–7, 212–15, 387–8
applicable 159, 378
conflicting 121, 126, 146, 180
existing 104, 266
inconsistent 123, 125, 134
subsequent 122–3, 142
validity of 156, 197, 206
national legal orders/systems 97, 102, 109, 122, 127, 143, 215
national parliaments 28–9, 78, 80, 88–9, 94, 123, 125
national procedural autonomy 211–16
national procedural law 108, 153, 161, 190, 207, 209, 237
and system of remedies 211–16

national promotional campaigns 283–4
national workers 325, 346–7
nationality 194, 309–12, 330–2, 349–50, 356–9, 362–4, 369–70
and free movement of persons 312–13
nationalized industries 122, 197, 199
nationals 310–12, 320–2, 324–7, 329–30, 340–1, 345–7, 359
Chinese 329–30
family life of 361–2
of member states 292, 310, 313, 320–1, 345–6, 353–4, 358–9
non-EU 323, 328, 344–6, 349–52, 361–3, 365, 404
association and cooperation agreements 349
family members 330, 350, 362–3, 365–6
general rights 350–2
workers 'posted' abroad 349–50
natural justice 109, 113
natural persons 152
negative integration 266, 280, 412
negligence 176, 245–6
negotiations 7–8, 13–16, 18, 24, 26, 34–5, 140
neofunctionalism 8, 10–11, 20
Netherlands 143–4, 270, 313–14, 318, 327, 332–3, 360
courts 155, 314, 317, 332
reception of EU law 143–4
new legal order 20, 61, 121–2, 210
Nice Intergovernmental Conference and Treaty 27–8
non-compliance 81, 143, 180, 183, 200
non-compulsory expenditure 57
non-contractual liability 242–53
non-discrimination 112–13, 194, 271, 302, 332–3, 369–70, 405 see also discrimination
non-legislative acts 43, 92, 103, 106, 232
non-member state family members 330, 350, 362–3, 365–6
non-member states 9, 17, 36, 72, 107, 266–7, 351
non-privileged applicants 225–6, 240
non-retroactivity 111, 113, 115–16, 201–2
non-tariff barriers 278–304
Art 36 TFEU derogations 285–91
equally applicable (indistinctly applicable) measures 283, 291–9
Keck and Mithouard cases 63, 278, 299–304, 333
measures having equivalent effect (MHEEs) 279–83, 285, 304
quantitative restrictions 263, 267, 278–84, 289
normative acts 227–8
Northern Ireland 131, 329, 349
Norway 12–14, 16–17, 144
notifications 205, 224, 229–30, 241, 296
nuclear power 9 see also EURATOM

O

objective justifications 382–3
obligation to refer 161–6
occupational pensions 372, 377–8, 382, 406
OECD (Organisation for Economic Co-operation and Development) 7, 107
official authority 342
official languages 58–9, 101
Ombudsman 56
   European 187
one-twelfth rule 56
opt-outs 24–6, 34–5, 102, 144, 408
ordinary legislative procedure 45, 55, 84, 86–8, 90, 106, 197
Organisation for Economic Co-operation and Development (OECD) 7, 107

P

packaging 284, 295, 297, 301–2
panels, judicial 57, 64–5, 169 *see also* specialized courts
parental leave 113, 370, 373, 393, 395
parents 315, 329, 349–51, 359, 362–3, 393
Parliament 39–46, 52–7, 76–80, 86–91, 93–4, 220–2, 224–5 *see also* Parliamentary Assembly
   and appointment of Commission 55
   budgetary powers 56–7
   and censure/removal of Commission 56
   control of executive 55–6
   elections and political parties 54
   functions and powers 54–7
   legislative powers 54–5
   membership 53–4
   President 53, 106, 197, 221
   right to litigate 57
Parliamentary Assembly 9, 11, 18–19
Parliamentary Commissioner 56, 187
parliamentary sovereignty 125, 128, 130–1, 134, 136
parliaments, national 28–9, 78, 80, 88–9, 94, 123, 125
part-time work 313–15, 359, 381–3
part-time workers 313, 373, 376, 382–3, 401
party actions 231
passports 322–3, 359
'pay', meaning of 375–9
payments 205–6, 253, 269–70, 318, 323, 348–9, 353
   periodic 183, 378
penalties 130, 174, 183–4, 323, 337
pensions 327, 359, 375–9, 382, 388–90, 406, 408–9
   accrual of rights 403
   and equal pay 375–9
   occupational 372, 377–8, 382, 406
   pensionable age 376–7, 388–9

periodic payments 183, 378
Permanent Representatives (COREPER) 40, 44, 51, 222
permanent residence 322, 324, 330, 339
permits, residence 314–15, 317, 324, 327–8, 337, 358, 364
personal conduct 337–41
personal scope 307, 312–13, 319, 329
pillars 5, 24–6, 87, 202
plea of illegality 238, 253–6
   and direct actions to annul EU acts 238–9
Poland 12, 15, 30–1, 35, 48, 58, 102
police 5, 26, 60, 82, 102, 342, 391
political cooperation 6, 20, 22, 24, 52
political groupings 53–4
Portugal 12–13, 16, 20, 22, 48, 157, 199
positive discrimination 372, 397–8, 409
positive integration 266
posted workers 349–50
poverty 222, 235
powers
   budgetary 56–7
   Council 45, 51
   decision-making 45, 51, 55, 233
   delegated 43, 92–3, 105, 145
   delegation of 51, 92–3, 144
   discretionary 92
   European Parliament 54–7
   general 51, 75–6, 81, 94, 369
   implementing 93
   implied 72, 75–6, 411
   law-making 22, 36, 44, 51, 54, 69, 76
   misuse of 82, 232, 234–5
   residual 76–8, 144
   sovereign 9–10, 70, 138
   special 199–200
   transfer of 18, 30, 68–70, 94, 122, 137–41, 144–6
precedence 123, 126, 136, 138, 142–3, 171
precedent 62–3, 161, 164, 167, 169, 179, 236 *see also* case law
pregnancy 330, 368, 373, 389–90, 392–6
   dismissal during or after 401–3
   and illness 396
   Pregnant and Breastfeeding Workers Directive 401–3
preliminary ruling references 60–1, 63–4, 118, 146, 151–66, 168, 170–1
   abuse of procedure 158–9
   acceptance in spite of defects 160
   and *acte clair* 164–5
      use by national courts 165–7
   basic information lacking 157
   courts of last instance 162–3
   and direct actions to annul EU acts 237–8
   discretion or obligation to refer 161
      avoidance of obligation 164–7
   effect on Court of Justice 167
   effect on national courts 167–8
   evolution 168–9
   no genuine dispute 158–9

interim measures 170–1
lower courts 161
and previous rulings 164
procedure 153–67
question referred 160–1
referring bodies 154–6
reforms and future 169–70
rejected references 157–8
relevant and admissible questions 156–60
timing 162
and validity 165
presidency, Council (of Ministers) of the European Union 29–30, 36, 45–6, 52
President
   Commission 11, 21, 23, 41–3, 52, 56
   Council 29–30, 36, 45–6, 52
   European Council 31, 36, 45, 52–3, 66–7
   European Parliament 53, 106, 197, 221
   France 11–12, 19–21, 28, 33, 47, 144–5
   High Authority 8
price-support mechanisms 11, 18
primacy 30, 121, 124–6, 146 *see also* supremacy of EU law
primary Treaties 18, 22–3
private employees 199
private employers 132–3, 197, 199–201, 204, 379, 390, 406
private individuals 186, 193, 281
private parties 204, 206, 210, 238, 281, 334
privileged applicants 57, 224–5, 239–40
procedural actions 133, 151, 174
procedural autonomy, national 211–16
procedural law 99–100, 151–2, 211, 214, 216
   general principles 113–18
   national 108, 153, 161, 190, 207, 209, 237
procedural requirements 81, 232–3, 241
   failure to act actions 241–2
   secondary legislation 106
procedural rights 109, 321, 337
product classification 284
professional knowledge 336
professional titles 336
professions 4, 319, 321, 328, 331–2, 334–5, 388
promotional campaigns, national 283–4
proof, burden of 211, 373, 383–5
proportionality 79–80, 82, 115–17, 333–4, 359–60, 391–2, 406–7
Protocols 25–9, 31, 35, 48–50, 80–2, 101–3, 377–8
provision of services 267, 310, 319–20, 332, 338, 347, 361
   lawyers 335–6
public employers 200
public health 98, 100, 233, 284, 288–9, 293, 362
public interest 249–50, 270, 301, 311, 333–4, 360

public morality 77, 285–6
public policy 285–6, 295, 310, 322–3,
   337–40, 357, 362
public security 285, 287, 310, 323,
   338–40, 362
public service 197, 199–200, 306, 308,
   310, 325, 341–3

Q

qualifications 58, 106, 136, 166, 333,
   336, 398–9
qualified majority voting (QMV) 22–3,
   26–7, 29–30, 41–2, 46–50,
   65–6, 84
   mechanism 48–9
   rationale 49–50
quantitative restrictions 263, 267,
   278–84, 289
   Art 36 TFEU derogations 285–91
      artistic heritage 289
      Decision 3052/95 and
         Regulation 764/2008 291
      general purpose and scope 285–6
      protection of artistic or commercial
         property 290
      protection of the health or life of
         humans or animals 287–9
      public morality 286
      public policy 286–7
      public security 287
      second sentence of Art 36 290–1
   Cassis de Dijon case 63, 74, 79, 278,
      292–3, 295–9, 302–4
   definition 282
   dual burden rules 297–9, 301, 305
   equal burden rules 297–302, 305
   equally applicable (indistinctly
      applicable) measures 283,
      291–9
   exports 284–5
   general scope of Treaty
      prohibition 280–1
   Keck and Mithouard cases 63, 278,
      299–304, 333
   legislation 279
   measures concept 281
   measures having equivalent effect
      (MHEEs) 279–83, 285, 304
   national marketing rules 284
   national promotional campaigns
      283–4
   product classification 284
   rule of reason requirements 294–6
   selling arrangements 299–304, 333
   technical standards and legislative
      intervention 296
quotas 133, 157, 227, 280, 282

R

racial discrimination 350, 369, 404,
   407–8

Racial Equality Directive 404
ratification 8, 14, 18, 22, 26, 29, 31
   process 22, 29, 31
reason, rule of 79, 292, 294–8, 304
reasoned opinions 81, 174, 177–9,
   183–5, 223
   second 184
receipt of services 320, 354–5, 365
reception of EU law
   Belgium 143, 146
   Denmark 144–5
   France 141–3
   Germany 138–41
   Italy 141
   Netherlands 143–4
   Sweden 145
   UK 127–38
reciprocity 123, 143, 180
recognition, mutual 79, 265, 331, 334
recommendations 28, 87–8, 105–6,
   153, 220–2, 240, 281
redundancy 206, 375, 377, 389
referenda 12–14, 16–17, 25, 28–9, 33,
   137, 144–5
Reform Treaty 30–2, 43–7, 52–3, 57–8,
   85–7, 101–3, 221–2
reforms 11, 20–1, 34, 48–9, 92, 169,
   220
   institutional 21, 26–7, 46
   legal 265, 365
   preliminary ruling references 169–70
registered partnerships 326, 406
registration certificates 323–4
registration requirements 323, 335
Regulations 103–6, 191–2, 195–6,
   226–31, 247–51, 321–2, 324–31
   anti-dumping 231
   and direct effects 195
regulatory acts 225–6, 237
   challenges to 232
rejected references 157–8
reliance 59, 197, 206
relief, interim 134–5, 170, 213, 215
remain, right to 330
remedies 189–217
   autonomy of 244
   direct applicability 101, 121, 129,
      189–91
   direct effects 125, 129–30, 132–3,
      142–3, 152–4, 166, 189–207
   equal pay 384–5
   equal treatment 399–401
   and national procedural law 211–16
   state liability, Francovich
      principle 206–11
removal of Commission 41–3
repeal 128, 131, 134, 136, 177
residence 314–18, 322–4, 330, 350–1,
   355–8, 360–1, 363–4
   habitual 318
   lawful 351, 361, 364–6
   permanent 322, 324, 330, 339
   permits 314–15, 317, 324, 327–8, 337,
      358, 364
   requirements 318, 331–2, 361, 366

rights 347, 351, 357–8
   unlawful 351, 362
residual powers 76–8, 144
restrictions 284–5, 290–1, 293–5,
   299–300, 331–2, 345–6, 391
   disguised 272, 283, 285–7, 290, 293,
      295
   quantitative 263, 267, 278–84, 289
restrictive drafting 79
retirement 132, 197, 330, 375–6,
   382, 389–90, 405–6 see also
   pensions
retroactivity 115–16, 229 see also non-
   retroactivity
review 60–1, 65, 81, 83, 100, 106,
   113–14, 219–56
reviewable acts 105, 222–3, 240
right to remain 330
rights of entry 321–4, 326
rights of exit 321–4
rights of residence 347, 351, 357–8
Romania 12, 15, 29, 41, 48
rule of reason 79, 292, 294–8, 304

S

same-sex partnerships 327, 387–8, 406
Santer Commission 42, 56
Schengen 26, 268, 349, 352
Schuman Plan 7–8
second reasoned opinions 184
Second World War 6–7, 9, 13, 32–3, 37,
   109–10, 141
secondary legislation 98–9, 101–6, 108,
   129–30, 175–6, 307–13, 345–6
   Decisions 105
   Directives 104–5 see also Directives
      discrimination 372–3, 404–9
   and free movement of goods 263
   procedural requirements 106
   recommendations and opinions
      105–6
   Regulations 104 see also Regulations
   sundry acts producing binding legal
      effects 105
sectoral Directives 331, 335
security 5–6, 24, 32–4, 36, 73, 287,
   337–8
   policy 5, 24, 30–1, 36, 41–2, 44, 53
   public 285, 287, 310, 323, 338–9,
      362
self-employed persons 307, 310, 313,
   318–19, 324, 330–6, 362
   and Court of Justice 318–19, 331–4
   free movement of lawyers 335–6
   legislative developments 334–5
   and mutual recognition 334–5
self-executing law 102 see also direct
   applicability
selling arrangements 299–304, 333
semi-privileged applicants 225
Serbia 16
servants (of Community/
   institutions) 243, 245–6, 253

services 267–70, 309–12, 319–20,
        331–6, 347, 352–5, 404–5
    educational 348, 353–4
    provision of 267, 310, 319–20, 332,
        335, 338, 347
    receipt of 320, 354–5, 365
    tourist 353
sex discrimination 132, 370–1, 381,
        386–7, 391, 398
sexual harassment 373, 412
sexual orientation 113, 369, 372,
        387, 403–6, 408 see also
        discrimination
shared competences 72–3
similar domestic products 273–4
simple majority voting 47
Single European Act 13–14, 21–3, 34,
        47, 54–5, 97–8, 373
    movement beyond 23–4
single market 13–14, 21, 23, 34, 84–6,
        264–6, 280 see also common
        market; internal market
Slovakia 12, 15, 48
Slovenia 12, 15, 48
social and tax advantages, free
        movement of persons 325–6
social assistance 315–16, 318, 354, 358,
        361, 364
social benefits 318, 342, 359, 366
social policy 9, 23–6, 34, 73, 82, 100, 383
social protection 109, 401, 404–5
Social Security Directive 372, 390, 401
sources of law 96–118
sovereign powers 9–10, 70, 138, 411
sovereign rights 70, 122, 192
sovereignty 32–4, 70, 121, 123, 126,
        129–30
    parliamentary 125, 128, 130–1, 134,
        136
Soviet Union 6, 9, 13–17, 231, 262
Spain 12–13, 20, 22, 157, 183, 185, 201
special legislative procedures 51, 87,
        90–2, 372
special powers 199–200
specialist legislative procedure 92
specialized courts 57–8, 60–1, 64–5, 169
spillover 10–11, 265
spouses 326–8, 330, 346–8, 350–2,
        361 see also family members
stability 6, 33–4
stagnation 19–21, 33, 265
standing 211, 224, 226, 231, 236–8,
        243 see also locus standi
state aids 94, 175, 236
state liability 99–100, 152–3, 166, 186,
        189–90, 216–17, 250
    extension to national courts 210–11
    extension to private sphere 210
    Francovich principle 206–11
state monopolies 122, 291
Statute of the Court of Justice 58–9, 63,
        162, 243
strict application 159, 203
students 57, 86, 225, 353–4, 359–60,
        364–5

subsequent national law 122–3, 142
subsidiarity 25, 29, 68–70, 78–82, 94–5,
        117
substantive law 99–100, 133, 135, 212,
        214
summits 12–13, 17, 20–1, 25–9, 49, 52,
        144 see also European Council
Sunday trading 298–300
supranationalism 10, 20, 143, 352, 412
supremacy 36, 120–3, 125–6, 128, 131,
        136, 141–3
    and Court of Justice 121–4
    and member state constitutional
        law 124–5
    parliamentary 131
    and reception of EU law 127–45
        Belgium 143, 146
        Denmark 144–5
        France 141–3
        Germany 138–41
        Italy 141
        Netherlands 143–4
        Sweden 145
        UK 127–38
    relationship with competence and
        transfer 69–70
    and theories of incorporation of
        international law 127
suspensory orders 181–2
Sweden 12, 14, 25, 48, 145, 291, 387
    reception of EU law 145
Switzerland 10, 14–16, 32, 107, 246

T

tachographs 104, 180, 191
tariffs 44, 107, 261–4, 266, 268, 270, 411
tax barriers 261–2, 264, 266, 268, 270,
        272, 274
taxation 47, 92, 118, 155, 158, 271–7,
        348
    discriminatory 273, 275
    indirect 51, 272–3
    internal 193, 268, 271–3
teachers 313–14, 322, 341, 359, 380,
        398
technical standards 205, 296
teleological interpretation 62, 101
Thatcher, Margaret 21, 23, 34
third countries 9, 17, 36, 72, 107, 266–7,
        351
third-country nationals (TCNs) 323, 328,
        344–6, 349–52, 361–3, 365,
        404
    association and cooperation
        agreements 349
    family members 330, 350, 362–3,
        365–6
    general rights 350–2
    workers 'posted' abroad 349–50
three-pillar structure 5, 25, 36
tide-over allowances 359–60
time limits 90–2, 159, 178–9, 196,
        213–14, 237–8, 254–5

direct actions for non-contractual
        liability 243–4
    direct actions to annul EU acts 224
tourist services 353
trade 33, 76–7, 251, 285–6, 292–3,
        300, 411
traders 229–30, 281, 283, 288, 298–300
training 316, 330, 335, 354, 360, 375,
        394
    vocational 73, 99, 316–17, 324–5,
        329–30, 353, 388
transfer
    competences 35, 69, 94
    powers 18, 30, 68–70, 94, 122,
        137–41, 144–6
    relationship with competence and
        supremacy 69–70
    sovereign powers 9–10, 70, 411
transit 53, 229–30, 252, 282, 285
transitional periods 41, 50, 331, 408
transposition 144, 176, 184, 213
transsexuals 386–7
Treaties 22–6, 28–31, 45–53, 69–83,
        97–103, 106–12, 125–9 see also
        Introductory Note; declarations;
        protocols
    Accession 15–16, 18, 31, 194
    amendments 35, 55, 58, 64, 67, 74,
        100
    Budgetary 20, 56, 65
    EEA 14, 60
    enforcement 153, 173–87, 206, 373
    founding 21, 97
    framework 102, 108
    and free movement of goods 262–3
    original 9, 11, 13, 17–18, 23–4,
        34–5, 69
    primary 18, 22–3
Treaty bases 71, 78–9, 81, 83–6, 90–1,
        104–6, 234
tribunals 65, 154–6, 161, 170, 182 see
        also specialized courts
Turkey 15–17, 32, 107, 349

U

unanimity 10, 30, 46–7, 51–2, 76, 84–5,
        90–2
Union citizenship 36, 309, 316–18, 324,
        344, 356–66
    case law 357–64
    definition 356–7
    rights 354–5, 357, 359, 364–6
    summary of law 364–5
Union competence 36, 71, 74, 76, 79, 108
Union institutions 18–21, 39–66,
        82–5, 103–6, 219–22, 239–47,
        250–3 see also Commission;
        Committee of the Regions;
        Council (of Ministers) of the
        European Union; Court of
        Auditors; European Central
        Bank; European Council;
        Economic and Social Committee

advisory bodies 40, 65
    main 40, 44, 65, 87, 99
    participation in legislative
        processes 83–6
    sundry Union bodies 66
Union law *see also Introductory Note*
    applicable 102, 132, 141
    direct effect 125, 129–30, 132–3,
        142–3, 152–4, 166, 189–207
    effective 132, 197
    effective provisions of 123, 125
    general principles of 97–8, 108–10,
        112–15, 117–18, 201–4, 243–4,
        406
    reception
        Belgium 143, 146
        Denmark 144–5
        France 141–3
        Germany 138–41
        Italy 141
        Netherlands 143–4
        Sweden 145
        UK 127–38
United Kingdom (UK) 23–7, 31–5, 54,
        179–82, 346–7, 350–1, 362–5
    applications 12, 32, 145
    courts 111, 128, 130, 132, 135–6,
        238, 298
    doctrine of parliamentary
        sovereignty 128–9
    dualist approach 128
    entry and European Communities Act
        1972 129–31
    European Union Act 2011 137–8
    judicial reception of Community and
        EU law 131–6
    reception of EU law 127–38
    relationship with EU 32–5
        to 1970s 32
        1980 to date 34–5
        accepted application 33
        rejected applications 32–3
        timing of entry 33–4
    unwritten constitution 128
United Nations 6, 10, 78, 107, 411
United States 7, 10, 90, 233, 251
universities 254, 317, 329, 335, 348,
        354, 398–9
unjustified enrichment 118, 248
unlawful discrimination 273–6,
        298–302, 309–12, 369–70,
        378–88, 402–6, 408–9
    age 405
    Art 19 TFEU 46, 113, 369, 403–5,
        407
    Art 157 TFEU 112, 368–9, 372–85,
        388, 397

direct 273, 311, 379–81, 389–90,
        394–6, 398, 406–7
equal pay 371, 374–85
    basis of comparison 379–81
    enforcement and remedies 384–5
    meaning of 'pay' 375–9
    original Directive 379
    part-time work and indirect
        discrimination 381–3
    and pensions 375–9
    scope of principle 374–85
    work of equal value 368, 372, 374,
        379–80, 383–5
equal treatment 112–13, 365–6,
        368–70, 372–3, 385–401,
        404–5, 407
    no discrimination on grounds of
        sex 386–8
    equality with regard to employment
        access, working conditions,
        dismissal and retirement
        ages 389–90
    exempt occupations 391–2
    judicial enforcement and
        remedies 399–401
    promotion of equal opportunity by
        removing existing inequalities
        affecting opportunities 397–9
    protection of women regarding
        childbirth and maternity
        392–6
    scope 388–9
expansion of EU equality law 372,
        403–9
Framework Employment Directive 404
indirect 273, 303, 311, 332–3, 381,
        383, 404
positive 372, 397–8, 409
Pregnant and Breastfeeding Workers
        Directive 401–3
prohibition of 203, 247–8, 331,
        369–70, 388, 398, 400
racial 350, 369, 404, 407–8
Racial Equality Directive 404
secondary legislation 372–3, 404–9
sex 132, 370–1, 381, 386–7, 391, 398
sexual orientation 387
Social Security Directive 372, 390, 401
Treaty Articles 372
unlawful residence 351, 362

V

validity 105, 125, 127–8, 153–4, 156,
        165, 237–8
    of national law 156, 197, 206

and preliminary rulings references
        165, 170
VAT (value added tax) 51, 101, 118,
        139, 412
vested rights 115–16
veto 12, 19, 25, 27, 35, 45–8, 84–5
vicarious liability 246
Vice-Presidents 41–2, 53
vigilance, dual 152, 190, 216
vocational training 73, 99, 316–17,
        324–5, 329–30, 353, 388
vote of censure 42–3, 56
voting 16, 19, 46–9, 51, 76 *see also*
        elections
    majority 19, 23, 46–7, 85, 137
        qualified 22–3, 26–7, 29–30, 41–2,
            46–50, 65–6, 84
        simple 47
    rights 28, 52, 185
    unanimous 10, 30, 46–7, 51–2, 76,
        84–5, 90–2

W

welfare rights 358–9, 361
wholly internal rule 345–9, 364, 366
widening 3–4, 12–18, 23, 31, 412
wine 18, 158, 230, 274–6, 284–5, 294,
        296
women 372–3, 376–8, 380–6,
        388–93, 397–9, 401–5,
        407–9 *see also* equal pay;
        equal treatment
work 44–5, 313–17, 359–60, 374,
        378–84, 393–5, 401–2
    equal 368, 372, 374, 379–80, 384
    jobseekers 315–18, 359, 361
    of equal value 368, 372, 374, 379–80,
        383–5
    of higher value 380, 384
    part-time 313, 359, 381–3
workers 306–19, 321–7, 332–4, 341–2,
        358–9, 378–81, 402–3
    breastfeeding 393, 401–2
    free movement of 71, 88, 100, 112,
        307–8, 346, 349
    frontier 326, 347
    migrant 317, 329, 350–1, 358, 360,
        362
    national 325, 346–7
    part-time 313, 373, 376, 382–3, 401
    'posted' abroad 349–50
World Wars 6–7, 9, 13–14, 32–3, 37,
        109–10, 141
WTO (World Trade Organization) 10, 44,
        76, 107, 198–9, 251, 266

Index

425